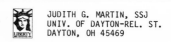

Women in American Society

Women in American Society

An Introduction to Women's Studies

SECOND EDITION

Virginia Sapiro

University of Wisconsin–Madison

MAYFIELD PUBLISHING COMPANY

Mountain View, California
London • Toronto

To my family:
William and Florence Sapiro, Graham K. Wilson,
and Adam Ross Wilson, who can now read his name here.

Library of Congress Cataloging-in-Publication Data

Sapiro, Virginia.
  Women in American society : an introduction to women's studies/
Virginia Sapiro. —2nd ed.
    p.   cm.
  Includes bibliographical references.
  ISBN 0-87484-963-2
  1. Women—United States.   2. Women's studies—United States.
I. Title.
[HQ1421.S27 1990]
305.42′0973—dc20   89-13077
                                                        CIP

MANUFACTURED IN THE UNITED STATES OF AMERICA
10 9 8 7 6 5 4 3 2 1

MAYFIELD PUBLISHING COMPANY
1240 Villa Street
Mountain View, California 94041

Sponsoring editor, Franklin C. Graham; managing editor, Linda Toy; production editor, Sondra Glider; manuscript editor, Loralee Windsor; text and cover designer, Joan Greenfield; photo researcher, Sarah Bendersky.

The text was set in 10/12 Meridien by Execustaff and printed on 50# Finch Opaque by Malloy Lithographing, Inc.

COVER: *Mary, Mary* (1987), acrylic on canvas, by Helen Frankenthaler. Private collection. Courtesy, André Emmerich Gallery.
CREDITS: Page 197: Excerpt from ''Looking at Quilts'' in *Living in the Open,* by Marge Piercy, copyright 1976 by Alfred A. Knopf, Inc., is reprinted with permission of the publisher.

Illustration credits appear on a continuation of the copyright page, p. 485.

Contents

PART ONE

Developing Frameworks for the Study of Gender and Society

Reflect Before You Read 15

v

PART TWO

Gender-defining Institutions

Reflect Before You Read 93

PART THREE

Choice and Control in Everyday Life

Reflect Before You Read   235

List of Tables

Preface

WOMEN IN AMERICAN SOCIETY is a woman-centered introduction to the study of gender. It emerged from my discontent—and that of my students—with the texts available for use in the introductory women's studies course I have taught for several years. This book offers an interdisciplinary analysis of women's situation in the United States based on current research in the social sciences. Designed to be used as the main text in courses such as Introduction to Women's Studies and Women in the United States, it assumes no prior college-level background in either women's studies or the social sciences.

Writing a book requires one to make many choices and solve many problems. For some problems there may be many "correct" solutions or choices, but for the sake of coherence one must choose. Let me emphasize some choices I have made and their significance.

Coverage

Women in American Society surveys a wide range of topics and themes that are necessary to an understanding of women's status, roles, and experiences today, including most topics usually treated in women's studies courses. The text is based on both theoretical and empirical research. Although I focus primarily on contemporary society, I have devoted considerable effort to showing the reader how an understanding of historical developments places the current situation in context and enlightens us about the nature and processes of social change, both worldwide and in America.

This book reflects the state of the field of women's studies, but it is also a unique contribution to that field. The newness of the field means that conventional wisdom, accepted methodologies, and established models do not exist to the same degree as they do in other fields. Even so, women's studies has built up a core of shared views and commonly cited works. This book, however, does not take even these for granted; many of the observations and works commonly cited in women's studies are already out of date. In some cases this means that "old friends" in the literature do not get the treatment to which they have grown accustomed, but this is inevitable as our knowledge grows. In other cases I discuss works that are not generally known inside the women's studies community.

Focus

Although I cover a wide field, no author can include all possible topics and issues and maintain rigor, coherence, and a clear focus. To make this text manageable I have chosen the following limits:

> *Women in American Society* focuses primarily on the United States. At the same time, it often views this one nation from a *comparative* perspective; that is, the book places the United States in the context of both national and international diversity.

> It is based on the social sciences. It relies especially on research and approaches used in economics, education, history, law, mass communication, political science, psychology, social work, and sociology. It emphasizes the languages and methodologies of the social sciences in a way that makes them accessible to students with no social science background. It treats social science methodology critically, but it is also shaped by social science methods.

The focus on the social sciences is further defined by emphasizing the grounding of gender in social institutions and institutionalized relationships. Cultural values and psychological character and processes are discussed within the context of social structure and specific social institutions. The social institutions approach also leads to an emphasis on the legal and policy aspects of sex/gender systems.

Women's Studies and Conventional Disciplines

The interdisciplinary nature of women's studies makes teaching and learning a great challenge. There is a difference between *inter*disciplinary and *multi*disciplinary writing. In the latter case, a book might have chapters on "the history of. . .," "the psychology of. . .," "the politics of. . .," and "the law on. . . ." In an interdisciplinary approach such as this one, the approaches, methods, and findings of different social science disciplines and subfields are interwoven to examine common themes and problems. This is not easy to accomplish; the range of difference in assumptions, focus, language, method, and interpretation is enormous. Different fields use the same terminology to discuss different ideas, and different terminology to discuss the same ideas.

It is especially difficult to achieve integration in a *rigorous* way; interdisciplinary research is not just a grab bag or pastiche of bits from various disciplines selected because they seem attractive or because they confirm one's original beliefs. Good interdisciplinary teaching requires, among other things, careful discussion of epistemology and research methods. In order to build "the findings" of diverse inquiries into knowledge it is crucial to understand how researchers arrived at their findings.

The rewards of integration are great, however. Some disciplines are often accused of focusing on individuals to the neglect of social structure; others receive the opposite criticism. Some approaches consider human thought and behavior without explicitly recognizing the power of public law and policy; others investigate law and policy without examining their relationships to human thought and behavior. An integrated interdisciplinary approach promotes a more realistic understanding of human life.

Organization

Those familiar with women's studies may find that the book's topical organization departs in certain respects from the expected, although I have divided the text into subsections to facilitate restructuring it for reading assignments. Again, many of these differences are based on carefully thought-out considerations of theory and pedagogy and the demands of working in a specifically interdisciplinary fashion. For example:

> Rather than segregating the discussion of violence against women I have integrated it with the text in subsections of relevant chapters, such as those on health, the law, and relations between women and men. The main reason for this is to show exactly how pervasive violence is in women's lives.

I begin and end the book with theory, but I end (rather than begin) with a full-fledged discussion of feminism, feminist (and antifeminist) movements, and feminist theory per se. A book like this must help the reader understand what feminist analysis is and how it differs from other kinds of study. However, my experience of teaching introductory women's studies courses has taught me that discussing the history of and need for feminism as a social movement before describing and analyzing the situation of women is putting the cart before the horse. Questions of feminism are inseparably woven throughout the pages of this book, but explicit treatment of the topic is reserved for the finale.

Diversity

My treatment of the diversity of women is also uncommon. I have taken an integrated rather than segregated approach. There is no special chapter on the unique situation of black women, older women, lesbians, or any other subgroup of women that usually receives such segregated treatment. The segregated approach tends to suggest that unless otherwise specified the text is "about" specific groups of women, such as those who are white and middle class.

Instead I have used what I consider an integrated approach involving two specific aspects:

1. I work on the assumption that all women are not in the same situation and that understanding the significance of these differences must be a part of each

theme we undertake. Where I do not name a specific group of women the reader should not assume that I am referring to any specific group. I have tried not to make generalizations about women that violate or ignore the experiences of particular groups of women. If social divisions, for example by race or age, make a difference in the gendered aspects of women's lives, the discussion of difference is integrated into the discussion of that aspect of gender.

2. In the final section of the book I focus on difference and unity among women, and one of the two concluding chapters specifically addresses difference and division among women. That chapter draws on relevant discussions throughout the book and also takes up new material. The main question in the chapter is how sex/gender systems are related to, structure, and are structured by other divisions, such as class, race, and age.

Methodology, Methodologism, and Methodophobia

This text is offered as a resource for those who want to learn about the role of gender in women's lives. It is designed to be a rigorous academic work; that is, it is based on careful analysis of research guided by feminist theory. Most of the studies I draw on employed social science methods. This said, it is important to note that these methods take many different forms, including survey, clinical, and experimental techniques; participant observation; and institutional, documentary, and content analysis.

Many students begin with at least some fear of or antagonism toward science-oriented writing, especially if it includes quantitative data analysis. (Imagine the difficulty of trying to show, in precise terms, the prevalence and gender basis of math anxiety to students with math anxiety!) Some women's studies scholars reinforce this anxiety by using the excellent literature in feminist theory on methodology and epistemology to attack any sign of "positivism" as incompatible with women's studies.

Women in American Society is based on the assumption that systematically gathered and theoretically grounded empirical research can be done in a feminist mode and in a manner that serves humane purposes. Methods of research must fit the task. Some questions are best answered by one method and some by another, and the questions we will consider are the ones social scientists happen to ask.

The text is largely devoted to discussion of the research literature and its theoretical and practical significance. I have tried to be generous with references and bibliographic comments both to document the observations I make and to provide readers with the resources they will need to learn more. Studies, bibliography, and statistics are not all there is to learning this material, of course, and at each turn it is crucial to reflect on it to decide how it fits and doesn't fit with the reader's own observations, and why. To assist this process I have provided study questions before each unit asking readers to "reflect before you read."

Feminist theory and women's studies are very diverse. At some turns I have presented alternative theories and viewpoints without reaching a definitive conclusion about which is "best." I have attempted to avoid the mind-numbing claim that knowledge and theories are all relative, while at the same time giving the student room to make theoretical and epistemological choices.

In this second edition, the basic organization, themes, and specific topics remain largely the same. Nevertheless there are important differences between this edition and the previous one. I have devoted considerable effort to cleaning and polishing the text. I hope I have removed remaining errors, stylistic awkwardness, and distracting tangents. In some cases I have reshaped and reorganized a chapter to achieve greater coherence. I have updated information and arguments whenever possible, and I have rewritten in response to important questions and comments of readers.

Acknowledgments

Many people have helped me write this book. At the top of my list are my students, the many scholars in the field with whom I have talked and whose work I have read over the years, and those who have used the book and made comments and suggestions.

The students in my various women's studies classes at the University of Wisconsin—Madison have been important in the writing of this book. They are my audience in writing: I see their faces while writing much as I do when I lecture. When I lecture, I do not see an abstract "student," but many different individuals in what some theorists like to call their "concrete situations." My students are women and men from many backgrounds with many different interests. They range from adolescence to old age. Many, of course, are full-time students, but some are working people from the community taking a single course because they are interested or because it relates to their work. Some come in as radical feminists; some are as skeptical and anxious as a student in this kind of course can be. Some are new to academic study; some are relatively advanced scholars in other fields who are investigating women's studies for the first time. This book has been written for all these people. I assume that my readers are at least as diverse as the students I have already met.

I have benefited from contact with my colleagues in Women's Studies at the University of Wisconsin—Madison, and particularly those who read portions of the manuscript and made helpful comments: Susan Friedman, Judy Leavitt, and Gerda Lerner. Although Claire Fulenwider became too busy to be a coauthor, she and I conceived the idea together. The peer reviewers chosen by Frank Graham, my editor at Mayfield, provided many helpful suggestions. These are Shirley Harkess at the University of Kansas; Geraldine Manning at Suffolk University; Sue Mansfield at Claremont McKenna College; Marilyn Myerson at the University of South Florida; Yolanda Moses at California State Polytechnic University, Pomona; Jane Prather at California State University, Northridge, who also provided suggestions for the art; and Ann Stromberg at Pitzer College. Loralee Windsor polished the prose with amazing speed and Gail Newton got the printer running at a moment's notice.

My greatest debts are to Graham Wilson and Adam Wilson—the former because, as always, he was wonderful in all the ways one could want, and the latter because his impending arrival kept me writing the first edition. The little boy who was a newborn when the first manuscript was delivered to the publisher now plays a different role. Audre Lorde (1984) said it best:

> I am thankful that one of my children is male, since that helps to keep me honest. Every line I write shrieks there are no easy solutions.

Women's Studies: An Introduction

Suppose you open a philosophy textbook that begins with the question: "What is Man?" What would you expect the book to be about? Most likely you would expect an exploration of how man differs from other animal species, or from angels, gods, and other celestial beings.

Now, suppose that you open a philosophy textbook that begins with the question, "What is Woman?" What would you expect this book to be about? You would probably not anticipate a discussion of women and animals or gods. Instead you would expect an analysis of the similarities and differences between women and men.

Why would most people's expectations of these two books be so different? One answer is that *man* is often considered a generic term, but *woman* is not; in other words, *man* can be used to refer to either one particular sex or to human beings as a species. But isn't this confusing? How do we know when *man* means males and females and when it means only males? Perhaps we can judge by the context. Unfortunately the immediate context often does little to solve the ambiguity. To avoid such ambiguity in this book, from now on *man* and *men* will be used only to refer to males.

This remedy for confusion and ambiguity is simple enough, but the important issue remains. How did it happen that one word came to refer to both the whole of humanity and one specific half of it? Why does *man* represent both males and females, while *woman* refers very narrowly to females? The question recurs as a theme throughout this book.

The answer suggested by numerous feminist theorists over the course of recent centuries is that the use of the word *man* to represent human society as a whole reflects our tendency to view men as the central actors or characters in human society and to consider what we view as male characteristics, manliness, or masculinity the central characteristics of human beings.

The word used to describe this situation is *androcentric*, which literally means "centered on men." This word was used as long ago as 1911 by sociologist and feminist theorist Charlotte Perkins Gilman (1911) in her book *The Man-Made World: Our Androcentric Culture*. *Androcentric* has parallels in three words that are more widely used and understood: *egocentric, ethnocentric,* and *anthropocentric*. *Egocentric* refers to the tendency of individuals to see themselves as the center of the world, as though everything revolves around them. *Ethnocentric* refers to the tendency of people to view their own culture as normal and to think of other cultures as deviations from their own—better—way of life. *Anthropocentric* refers to people's tendency to view the human species as the most significant entity in the universe. *Androcentric*, then, refers to the tendency to think of men as the norm against which women are compared and to the view that men are the main actors in—the center of—the social world.

An analogy using the ideas of characters and actors will illustrate the point. Consider one of the most famous plays in Western literature, William Shakespeare's *Hamlet*. Why is this play called *Hamlet*? The Danish prince is not the only person in the play; he is not even the only character who seems to have an interesting history, faces a tragedy, or dies. The title reflects the fact that the play is essentially about Hamlet and his role in the story. The events that occur in the play—even when Hamlet is absent—are significant in the eyes of the audience primarily for the ways they affect or are affected by the young prince. Although the perspectives of the other characters are significant, it is really Hamlet's perspective and problems that move the play and us.

Nearly four centuries after Shakespeare wrote *Hamlet*, another English playwright, Tom Stoppard, took the same material and twisted it inside out. His play, *Rosencrantz and Guildenstern Are Dead*, presents the same set of events and the same characters, but from the point of view of two of the most minor characters in the original play. In Stoppard's version, Rosencrantz and Guildenstern, who reflect their original minor roles by not even remembering themselves which one is which, become the central actors. The events, the characters, and the play itself suddenly become vastly different and make a very different point from the original.

Just as all the other characters in *Hamlet* revolve around, support, and gain their significance from the central character, we will see that women are seen as revolving around, supporting, and gaining their significance from men. In *Hamlet* we care that the prince is on a ship to England; it is less important to us that Rosencrantz, Guildenstern, and the ship's captain are there as well. Likewise the centrality of men in society leads observers of society and history to write, as did one eminent political scicentist, ''The analysis which this book contains is based on what might be called the storybook truth about American history: that America was settled by men who fled from the feudal and clerical oppressions of the Old World'' (Hartz 1955, 3). Some people would not notice anything odd about this sentence. Others would notice a problem: Surely American history would not have lasted this long had women not settled in America too. Acknowledging that women were also ''on the ship'' makes a great difference to our understanding of history.

A well-known study by a group of psychologists shows that this ''man-woman-human'' question is not a mere matter of playing with words (Broverman et al. 1970). These psychologists asked a number of mental health clinicians to define the characteristics of a ''healthy man,'' a ''healthy woman,'' and a ''healthy adult.'' The results showed that the clinicians defined the healthy adult and the healthy man in much the same way: rational, independent, ambitious, active, and so forth. Their healthy woman, however, had very different characteristics: She was emotional, dependent, and submissive. Thus not only in our language but also in the eyes of those who define our standards of health, the man is the real adult. To act like a healthy woman, one cannot act like a healthy adult.

Another example from a very different area of life offers another perspective on our definitions of women and men. One of the most important recent constitutional questions affecting women concerned the issue of jury service. At one time women were not allowed to serve on juries; during most of this century different states had different rules, but most of them tended to exclude women. Only in 1975 (*Taylor* v. *Louisiana*) did the Supreme Court decide that women could not be systematically excluded from juries because of their sex. In a 1946 case (*Ballard* v. *U.S.*) Justice William O. Douglas considered the question of whether women and men were simply exchangeable puzzle pieces. Many people argued that they were exchangeable in the sense that it did not matter that only men were on juries; a jury composed only of men was "as truly representative as if women were included." Douglas countered by offering the following problem for consideration:[1]

> [It] is not enough to say that women when sitting as jurors neither act nor tend to act as a class. Men likewise do not act as a class. But, if the shoe were on the other foot, who would claim that a jury was truly representative of the community if all men were intentionally and systematically excluded from the [jury]? The truth is that the two sexes are not fungible; a community made up exclusively of one is different from a community composed of both; the subtle interplay of influence one on the other is among the imponderables. To insulate the courtroom from either may not in a given case make an iota of difference. Yet a flavor, a distinct quality is lost if either sex is excluded.

Douglas's point is clear. There are two alternative arguments on which to base a claim that men can fully represent women. The first is that women and men are equal and exchangeable persons, in which case it would make no difference whether juries (or, for that matter, Congress or almost any other organization) were composed entirely of men or entirely of women. Few people seem to worry that Congress is composed mostly of males, but few people would be unconcerned if Congress were suddenly to become composed mostly of females. The other argument is that men can adequately represent women, but women cannot adequately represent men because women are narrower creatures, more parochial, less competent, or, like children, dependent on the better judgment of men. Is this the argument we want to make?

Notice what has happened in the discussion thus far. We began by talking about the meaning of words and by asking what real-life things the words *man* and *woman* represent. It became clear that words, meanings, and definitions have a great deal to do with real-life issues of power and choice, and we have gradually turned to the problem of representation: Who can represent whom in society? Can women's interests and needs be satisfied if men are invested with the task of acting and making decisions for them? If men can act for women, why can't women act for men? If men and women are not precisely the same, as Douglas argued, what are the differences? What is the significance of these differences in the way we arrange important social, economic, and governmental institutions? These are some of the questions we will probe throughout the remainder of this book.

In the course of participating in a decision of the Supreme Court, Justice Douglas had to face a series of important problems. Do men or women act as a "class"? That is, is there a set of orientations or types of behavior that are common to one sex and not to the other? If so, what difference would it make? If we compare three possible communities (or organizations), one composed only of men, one composed only of women, and one composed of both, what types of differences would there be? If there are differences, what would cause them? As Douglas suggested, differences could emerge because women and men act differently or because people's behavior varies depending on whether they are in a single-sex or mixed-sex group. But above all Douglas apparently felt we did not have enough knowledge to be able to argue that one sex or the other can be excluded from the important activities of society. He was well aware of the importance of knowledge as the basis for our endeavor to create a reasonable and just society. The creation of this knowledge is one of the major tasks of women's studies.

The passage we have been considering was written in 1946. Surely we have much more knowledge now than we had then. Education and the sciences have come a long way since World War II. The world seems more enlightened as far as women are concerned. Women can do many things now that they rarely could then. Most American universities have whole courses, if not programs and departments, devoted to the study of women.

Unfortunately our "enlightenment" has not really progressed very far. Throughout this book we will consider specific evidence of changes in the status and roles of women, and we will see that there is still quite a distance to go before women achieve full equality. But even if we consider the knowledge question alone, we find that much of what people learn in school about human society is really about the male portion of society or male views of society. There are at least three reasons for this:

1. Many aspects of women's lives are simply ignored or dismissed as unimportant compared with most aspects of men's lives. For example, basic philosophy courses pay considerable attention to what philosophers said about men and very little to what they said about women. In history we learn much more about the changes in men's activities, strategies, and equipment in battle than about changes in childbirth. If an event in history caused great suffering to men we (justly) take great interest in how and why it happened because we hope to avoid similar suffering in the future. If an event caused great suffering only or primarily to women (for example, the European witch burnings, which led to the deaths of thousands and perhaps millions of women), it does not seem quite as important to study.

2. We continue to view men as "generic." In a number of fields we are almost tricked into thinking we have studied women when we have really only studied men and simply assumed that all of us have been covered. In psychology, for example, a large proportion of "general" research involves males only but is discussed as though it applies to everyone (Holmes and Jorgensen 1971). In

sociology scores of people who study social status in fact gather and look at evidence about men only.

3. The view we often get from books and courses is a very narrow perspective on women. It usually focuses on their roles, behavior, and significance as wives, mothers, lovers, or supporting muses. These roles are important, but they are not the only aspects of women that are important. This perspective provides only a limited and distorted view of women.

In most of the social sciences women have been discussed as though they were merely a component of "the family," which is composed of an employed husband, a wife who is a homemaker, and some number of dependent children who live at home. The women who lives in such a family is probably most people's image of the "typical woman." It is a shock to find how rare this "typical woman" really is. If we eliminate women who are currently unmarried, women who are employed outside the home, and women who have no children or whose children are grown up and have left home, we are left with only 14 percent of women in the United States. If we limit our view even further to women who are homemakers and live with their husbands and at least one preschool child, only 7 percent remain. How very different is the reality from the image! (Statistics calculated from U.S. Bureau of the Census data for 1980.)

How can there be such disparity between image and reality, especially since we are talking about basic facts of women's existence? One answer is that women are seen as people want to see them: as comfortable, nurturing, always available mothers. Another answer (which does not contradict the first) is that women are seen through stereotypes, or relatively rigid preconceptions. This allows us to deal with women without really having to pay close attention to them or to any contradictory evidence in the facts of their lives.

French feminist Hélène Cixous (1976) makes a similar point in a different way. She reminds us of the Greek myth of the Medusa, the snakehaired woman who could be looked at only indirectly through a reflection. One direct look at her supposedly would turn a man to stone. Cixous argues that the myth is more dangerous than the woman herself. Looking directly at the Medusa, or at any other woman, may make us anxious at first (especially when we feel comfortable preconceptions crumbling), but it is not at all dangerous. Unfortunately, even when women have been looked at, the view has often been as distorted as the reflection in a flawed mirror. The accepted "facts" (like the appearance of the "typical woman") are often wrong. This book will introduce you to women's studies, a field that looks directly at women: at their roles in society, at their impact on society, and at the impact of social institutions and processes on them.

Women's Studies

The field of study called *women's studies* has developed since the reemergence of the women's movement in the late 1960s. At first women's studies consisted mainly of handfuls of students and instructors who came together in what were often informal, unofficial study sessions. In the early years the participants spent much of their time trying to figure out what questions they needed to ask and searching through libraries to find anything they could that would tell them something about women's history and roles in society. Those participants, who were mostly young women, seemed very radical to everyone else and, frankly, slightly obsessive and weird.

Women's studies has grown and matured considerably in the last two decades. Most universities now have some women's studies courses, and many have programs or departments devoted to the field. Thousands of instructors and students are involved, and they are a much more heterogeneous group than the early participants. Although many women's studies students are motivated by their feminist activism, increasing numbers of students take these courses not because they are involved in feminism or the women's movement (at least not at first), but simply because they wish to learn. There are as many reasons for taking a women's studies course as there are for taking a course in any other field.

What, then, is this field called *women's studies*? The answer might seem obvious at first. In economics we study economics, in political science we study politics, in women's studies we study women. In fact the definition is not as simple as that. Academic fields are defined not simply by what they study but also by how they study it. For example, the novel *1984* could be assigned reading in either a literature course or a political science course. But the reasons for reading the book, the questions asked about it, and the lessons learned from it would be somewhat different in the two fields. So students of women's studies approach their topic in different ways from other studies of women, and you must understand the differences to understand this book.

Perhaps the overriding difference between women's studies and other studies of women is the special kind of skepticism women's studies scholars bring to their studies. A good student in any field should be questioning, skeptical, and wary of easy answers. But in women's studies, skepticism plays a particularly important role because of the nature of the subject and its relationship to our day-to-day lives and even to our very senses of self (male and female). Students of women's studies are deeply skeptical of conventional wisdom about women for the reasons already mentioned. All too often what has always seemed obvious and true about women proves to be false or distorted when we actually search for evidence. For example, have labor-saving devices in the home radically altered the amount of effort women put into their housework over the course of the last century? The answer is no, as we shall see later. Thus what other people use as assumptions about women, women's studies scholars pose as questions.

Students of women's studies are even wary of their own reactions to the subject. It is the rare student in a women's studies course who never becomes angry, frustrated, anxious, or elated. The topics that are discussed, such as relations between parents and children or sexuality and violence between men and women, touch all of us very deeply. In many fields of study scholars often argue that our feelings and personal experiences should play no role in our academic efforts to discover truth. Women's studies scholars, even in the sciences and social sciences, tend to argue that our personal understandings and experiences play important roles in learning. But at the same time, if the personal nature of the subjects and themes of women's studies make it difficult to think analytically or to comprehend and use unfamiliar or uncomfortable information, the ability to learn is substantially limited. This means that in women's studies we must be critical not only of others but also of ourselves and our reactions. Only in this way can we learn from our "gut reactions."

Women's studies scholars above all pay attention to women and women's experiences more than other people (including some who study women) do. It is all too common for people to dismiss women's observations of themselves on the grounds that women are not as skilled at scientific study as men, that women are irrational, or that women are particularly likely to be biased. Once, for example, a well-known publisher purposely commissioned a man rather than a woman to write a book on feminism in the United States because it was thought a man could be an "objective outsider." Think about the assumptions that went into this decision. Does this mean that women's training in social science doesn't "stick" as well as men's? Is a man any more likely to be unbiased about issues raised by feminism (such as questions of how much power men should have over women) than a woman would be? Could a man, who would have limited access to some feminist organizations, be able to do a more comprehensive and direct study than a woman, who would probably have better access? This is not to say that a man cannot or should not study feminism and feminists. Many do and do it well. Throughout this book there will be references to research by men. The question is why the publisher assumed that a man would be a better scholar on this topic than a woman would be.

Women's studies scholars also pay more attention to women because they view women as no less central to humanity than men, as actors in their own right rather than merely as a supporting cast for men. These scholars look at the meanings that events, ideas, and social institutions have for women as well as for men. They look at experiences that only (or almost only) women have with the same care and attention that others use in examining experiences that only (or almost only) men have. They notice that even when men and women do the same sorts of things, men's activities are somehow thought of as important, but women's are considered silly, frivolous, or out of place. When men tell each other stories about another man, it is called the "old boys' network." When women do the same, it is called "gossip" or a "hen session."

Women's studies is also *interdisciplinary* in its approach. In other words, it draws on and weaves together theories, research, and insights from numerous fields throughout the humanities and social and biological sciences. This interdisciplinary nature of women's studies grows in part out of necessity. Suppose I, as a political scientist, deliver a lecture on why women are so rarely found among a country's leaders. Among the questions people usually ask me are the following: "But don't women's hormones make them less agressive, or at least less dependably stable, than men?" To answer this I need to know something about biology. I cannot guess just on the basis of common cultural views. "Didn't this system grow out of a historical division of labor that goes all the way back to hunters and gatherers, with women staying close to home and men going out to hunt and fight?" Now I am being asked to be a historian or an anthropologist. "Isn't the division of labor, with women in the home and men out in society leading and working, functional and efficient? Doesn't this system exist because it works well and not because women are any less valued?" To answer this question I need a knowledge of sociology. "Doesn't it all come down to capitalism?" Now I wear my political economy cap.

If I am going to answer all these questions intelligently, I must have wide range of knowledge. This book therefore weaves together different types of knowledge and information gained in a variety of fields, especially in the social sciences, in an effort to present a complete picture.

Having a wide range of information is not enough if we really want to understand women or anything else. Imagine a massive bag filled with all of the bits and pieces necessary to put together a Rolls Royce. The contents of the bag are useful only if you know how to put the pieces together. You need to know something about engineering and physics to make a machine that runs and something about aesthetics and human behavior and anatomy to make your machine attractive, safe, and comfortable. You also need to know the principles and methods of each of these fields and how to integrate these principles and methods. The bits of information obtained from a variety of different academic fields can be like the car pieces: a useless and confusing jumble of unlinked or incorrectly linked parts.

Academic disciplines are distinguished as much by their assumptions, theories, and methods as they are by the bits of information they provide. In order to use interdisciplinary approaches appropriately and usefully to understand the situation of women, we must learn about the methods and approaches of different kinds of research and develop the skills to integrate them coherently. For this reason we will pay attention not only to the *findings* of research on women or the bits of information such research has produced but also to the *process* by which people have arrived at these findings and the *uses* to which they have been put.

By now it should be apparent that women's studies is not just a simple matter of filling in gaps in information. It is a matter of reevaluating what we already know or think we know. We need to return to some very basic questions: What is important enough to know? To whom is it important and in what ways? Women's studies involves constant critical evaluation of our own and other people's understanding of and reactions to women. We must reevaluate (that is, place a new value on) both women and men and move beyond the narrow confines of particular disciplines to more integrated approaches and analytical skills. Both women and men find that women's studies entails much learning and questioning about themselves.

We should also be aware of the links between women's studies and feminism. Women's studies is both a result and a part of the feminist movement. As women in the late 1960s and early 1970s began to become interested and involved in groups and organizations devoted to changing the roles and status of women, they realized that they needed to know more about themselves, about the types of social forces that shaped their lives, and about the range of possibilities that might be available to them. When they thought about what they had learned about women in the past, they realized they had been taught very little. Thinking, studying, and learning became an important part of feminist political and social action. Not all students who take women's studies courses think of themselves as feminists, but the existence of these courses can be attributed to the activism of people committed to the pursuit of a nonandrocentric educational system.

Feminism shapes the practice of women's studies. Although there are many different types of feminism, they all share a central core of ideas and attitudes with women's studies. Among these are the characteristics of women's studies already discussed: skepticism about the "eternal truths" we have learned about women, a view that women are no less central to human history and society than men, a desire to understand the social world's significance to women as well as to men, and a desire to see women take control of and responsibility for their own lives and become participants and leaders in society.

Is this relationship between an academic field of study and current political and social issues unique? The answer is no—and yes. Some of the traditional academic disciplines (sociology and political science, for example) were also children of the social and political movements of their founding days. None of the social sciences is immune to the pressing problems of the world. After World War II many people began to study public opinion and the psychology of politics because they wanted to know how people came to tolerate (if not participate in) fascism and the Holocaust, and they wanted to know how to avoid a repeat performance. In the 1960s many social scientists turned their attention to questions of poverty, urban life, and race relations because these were the problems that seemed to need solving. In the 1980s awareness of AIDS spurred social as well as medical research. Contrary to the "ivory tower" cliché, universities are indeed part of the real world, and large numbers of scholars and teachers wish to use their skills to understand and improve that world.

Women's studies is unique because it responds especially to the problems and needs of women. The list of women's problems and needs is much longer than one might think. Many people think that *women's issues* refers just to women's rights, abortion and contraception, and family and child-oriented issues. But to limit ourselves to these things is to limit our understanding of what women are and what they do. As we shall see throughout this book, many social problems and policies that do not sound like uniquely women's problems actually do have different relevance to the two sexes. Women and men use energy, natural resources, time, and space differently, for example. Women are more likely to be old than men (and older women live somewhat differently from older men), and are more likely to be single at some point during their adult lives. Women are poorer than men, and they are affected differently by changes and problems in the economy. This book explores these and other examples of the different problems faced by women.

Don't men have these problems, too? Are they not affected by crises in the availability of energy and natural resources? Are they not also poor, old, or affected by economic difficulties? Yes; this cannot be denied. But because the aspects of these problems that have been most thoroughly examined in the past are those most relevant to men, the solutions that have been posed are more often geared toward solving men's problems. Indeed there have been many cases in which androcentric strategies for solving problems have actually created special problems for women. Part of the task of women's studies is to round out the picture, to see whether there are unique ways in which these problems affect women, and to try to develop solutions that will also help women. For some problems, such as sexual harassment and sexual violence, social recognition that there is a problem, has been a long time coming primarily because men are rarely the victims.[2] In such cases part of the task of women's studies is to illuminate the issue.

Women's studies offers a richer understanding of women and their relationship to the society around them. But it is impossible to learn about the female half of society without also learning something about the male half. In some cases we will *compare* the thoughts, behavior, and roles of men and women. At other times we will look at the *interactions* between men and women, including how they think about and act toward each other and how they influence each other. By examining the lives of both sexes we will gain a much wider and more profound understanding of our society as a whole. As this book will show, gender is an important part of the social structure; our society is organized partly on the basis of gender. Because of this we can possibly understand the structure and operation of our society without understanding gender.

What Lies Ahead

Although this text offers an introduction to women's studies, it makes no attempt to cover all the possible approaches and issues. It is limited to the questions and methods of the social sciences (broadly conceived). This means that the book emphasizes certain kinds of approaches to learning about society, especially systematic empirical (observational) methods, and deemphasizes others, such as those more common to literary criticism. This choice reflects the author's training, research experience, and disciplinary background. Any book needs some conscious method to limit its territory if it is to be coherent and appropriately comprehensive. The focus on social science is one of the grounds of limitation chosen here.

Even this limitation leaves a vast area to explore. So the book focuses on the United States, although we will, from time to time, consider other nations for points of comparison. The scope of the book is also defined by an institutional focus. There is minimal treatment of personality skills or social behavior in the abstract. Although these phenomena are discussed throughout the book, they are usually treated in an institutional context; that is, we study not just how women and men think and behave, but how they think and behave in the context of, for example, familial, economic, religious, or political institutions.

Beyond these limitations there are many others, both conscious and inadvertent. The subject matter and theories discussed here are very broad ranging; because this is intended as an *introduction* to women's studies the book trades depth for breadth. There is no doubt that other authors would have balanced the subjects differently.

The book is divided into four parts, corresponding to four of the most important themes in the field of women's studies.

Part One, "Developing Frameworks for the Study of Gender and Society," sets the scene for the rest of the book by providing many of the basic facts of life about women's and men's situations and experiences in contemporary America. It also shows some of the ways in which people attempt to analyze, understand, and explain these facts. Chapter 1, "Describing the Situation of Women: What Needs Explanation," presents many of the "bare facts" about women's and men's lives *as* women and men. It shows, for example, that women and men have different home lives, health problems, education, and occupations; that they commit different kinds of crimes and have different kinds of crimes committed against them; and that they take different roles in influencing both their own and other people's lives. In other words, Chapter 1 shows that gender still makes a considerable difference in the quality and characteristics of our lives.

Just knowing some of the facts is not enough, however. Simply describing women's and men's lives is not the same as explaining them. Contrary to the old cliché, facts do not speak for themselves. They need people to interpret them, and people interpret facts through particular constructions of theory. Because theory is the framework that makes an otherwise shapeless set of facts and pieces of information coherent and useful, theory construction and evaluation are among the most important tasks of students in any field. Chapters 2 and 3 discuss a variety of theories that have been offered to explain the development and significance of sex/gender systems, or the relationships between women and men in society. As we shall see, a wide variety of theories could be, and have been, used to explain sex/gender systems.

The difference between the theories presented in Chapters 2 and 3 lies in what they attempt to explain. The first type (outlined in Chapter 2, "Some Competing Explanations: How Did Society Get This Way?") includes theories that focus primarily on large-scale social, political, and economic forces to explain how sex/gender systems came to be what they are; that is, why women's and men's places in society are what they are. The theories presented in Chapter 3 ("More Competing Explanations: How Did Individuals Get This Way?") focus on individuals and explain how people fit themselves into societies, institutions, and groups.[3]

Part Two, "Gender-Defining Institutions," presents the second major theme of the book. There are many different kinds of power and control. One of the most important is normative power, or the power to define the values and standards against which we measure ourselves and others. The words *norm, normal,* and *normative* are derived from the Latin *norma,* which is a carpenter's or mason's square, a tool used for measurement and setting patterns. There are a number of social institutions with the primary purpose of setting, teaching, and enforcing values, standards, or norms. We will look at education (Chapter 4), health care (Chapter 5), religion (Chapter 6), communications media (Chapter 7), and government and politics (Chapter 8) to see how they define and enforce norms of good and bad, normal and abnormal, healthy and sick, skilled and unskilled, important and unimportant, valuable and not valuable.[4]

These chapters show, first, how interrelated these institutions and their underlying values are and, second, how they both shape and depend on gender norms. We will look at these systems as parts of a larger sex/gender system and consider how their values control women's lives and how women have influenced these values and used them to exert control over their own lives. We will also explore the development of the current norms and the potential for change within the institutions.

Part Three, "Choice and Control in Everyday Life," examines some of the types of problems, decisions, and experiences most women face constantly in their adult lives. We will look especially at how much choice women have in life decisions and how women make these choices. Chapter 9, "Gender, Communication, and Self-Expression," suggests that there are many gender-related limitations on people—

especially women—even in what they say and how they act with other people. Chapter 10, "Consenting Adults? Choice and Intimate Relationships," looks at another kind of social interaction and relationship: intimacy. We will focus on different kinds of intimacy, including sexual and nonsexual, heterosexual and homosexual, heterosocial and homosocial relationships. In this chapter we will look at one of the most widespread structures of heterosexual relationship: marriage. We will also examine some of the problems in distinguishing between sexual and nonsexual relationships and between sexuality and violence.

Chapter 11, "Reproduction, Parenthood, and Child Care," focuses on the choices and decisions women make about whether to have children, under what circumstances women have children, and what women do about children when they have them. We will also examine the effects these experiences have on women.

Chapter 12, "Work, Employment, and the Economics of Gender," includes discussions of many different types of work: paid and unpaid (housework); professional, white collar, blue collar, and agricultural; traditionally female and traditionally male. We will look at the ways in which women attempt to exert influence over their work lives and economic situation. We will also look at some sources of income other than paid labor and at questions of women's poverty, wealth, and economic resources and strategies.

Part Four, "Unity, Division, and Feminism," contains the fourth and final theme of the book. There are no special chapters in this book about black women, working-class women, older women, lesbians, or other special categories of women. This is not because these women are not important as subjects of this book; on the contrary, the lack of such special chapters is an indication of how central and important these women are. This book is not about a mythical "typical women," but about the many varieties of womanhood. Thus, although this book highlights commonalities in the situation and treatment of women, each chapter points out some important differences.[5] Each chapter raises questions about how race, class, sexual orientation, or age, for example, shape and interact with the meanings of gender in women's lives. In Chapter 13, "Commonality and Difference among American Women," we will look directly at some of the important differences among American women. This focus will lead to an important question: Given the rich variety of different experiences and life-styles among women, is it possible for organizations created by women on behalf of women to succeed? Do women share enough across the boundaries of, for example, race, ethnicity, age, class, and sexual preference for any type of "women's movement" to make sense? Finally Chapter 14, "Feminism and the Future," explores women's movements of the past and present and makes some educated guesses about what the future holds.

NOTES

1.   The full text of this Supreme Court case and most others cited in this book can be found in Goldstein (1988) and Kay (1988).

2.   And, of course, men are not only less likely to be the victims but also considerably more likely to be the perpetrators.

3.   Sometimes people argue about which explanation—the societal explanation or the individual explanation—is the better one. Even in the abstract this argument does not make much sense. These two types of theories really explain different things, which are equally important and equally partial on their own.

4.   One of the most important institutions that could be discussed in this part of the book is the family. In a sense, however, there is hardly a page of this book that does not discuss some aspect of the family. Instead of looking at the family as simply one more institution, we will look at different aspects of the family throughout this book. The family is most consistently and thoroughly discussed in Part Three.

5.   For a similar approach, in this case to lesbians, see Rich (1976).

PART ONE

Developing Frameworks for the Study of Gender and Society

WHAT is the situation of women in society and how did it get that way? Many theorists and scholars have attempted to answer this question. In the process of seeking the answers, they have developed alternative theories or frameworks that we can use to organize our analysis and interpretation of the role of gender in society. This section introduces many of these frameworks. It begins with some facts about women's lives in America today, especially how women's lives compare with men's. Chapter 1 consists mostly of bare facts with very little embellishment. As you read them, think about the significance of these facts and figures. Try to figure out how to explain them.

The section then turns successively to two sets of alternative theories that have been used to help explain women's lives. The two sets focus on different levels of analysis. The first set, found in Chapter 2, includes theories that can be used to explain how *societies* develop particular patterns of relationship between the sexes. The second set of theories, discussed in Chapter 3, includes theories that can be used to explain how *individuals* develop gender-related patterns of behavior in their individual lives. In order to understand women's situation in society it is necessary to understand *both* types of theory.

Reflect Before You Read

1. Some people say that men and women are very unequal in society today. Others say that, although there used to be inequality between the sexes, society has changed so that men and women now have equal opportunities to live the lives they choose. What position do you take? Why?

2. Women constitute a very small proportion of the people who have top positions in education, government, and business. Why? Does this matter?

1

Describing the Situation of Women: What Needs Explanation?

No ONE could reasonably argue that women's and men's lives and experiences are identical. Women and men play different roles, hold different kinds of jobs, dress differently, and even speak differently, as we shall see later. There is an obvious division of labor in the family. Even in families in which the woman is employed full-time outside the home, women and men tend to play different roles in the family. Very few women appear in the ranks of the powerful.

But to say that women and men are not the same is to say very little. They may not be identical, but how different are they now, at the end of the twentieth century? In what respects are they different? What is the significance of these differences? Why do these differences exist? Is there any possibility of change? These are the interesting and important questions; they are the ones that give meaning to the bare social facts of difference and similarity between the sexes.

This chapter offers an overview of the situation of women in American society today. We will look at comparisons of women and men to see the ways in which their lives are similar and different. From time to time we will also compare the situation in the United States with that in other countries to see the degree to which the situation of women in America is similar to that of women elsewhere. We will begin with an emphasis on demographic differences and vital statistics and then turn to psychological characteristics.

The goal here is to provide a foundation of some of the "bare facts" and to begin thinking about how to interpret the significance of these differences. In this chapter we will merely view a snapshot of society as it exists today. We will delve more deeply into gender similarities and differences and the reasons that underlie them in later chapters of this book.

Vital Statistics and Others: A Demographic Portrait

What are the basic facts of women's lives in the United States today? How long do women live and how healthy are they? What do their family and work lives look

What do you know about these two children by knowing their sex?
Are they different kinds of people?
Will they lead different kinds of lives?

like? How educated are they? How much power do they have? The following pages offer some answers to these and other questions.[1] They paint the outlines of a portrait of American women.

Life, Death, and Health

There are 95 men for every 100 women in the United States. As in every other country in which statistics are kept, more males than females are born (about 105 males for every 100 females), but males die earlier. Among people aged sixty-five and older there are only sixty-eight men for every 100 women. The median age of American males is thirty-one years; for females the figure is thirty-three. Throughout this century women have had longer life expectancies than men. A male child born in 1970 could expect to live sixty-seven years, while a female born that year could expect to live seventy-five years. A male born in 1980 could expect to live seventy years compared to seventy-seven for a female.

Gender, of course, is not the only demographic feature of our lives that makes a difference to our longevity. For example, race has some influence, but gender differences appear even when we compare the situation for Americans of different races. Among people born in 1970, white females are expected to live to about seventy-six, and white males to about sixty-eight. Nonwhite females born that year can expect to live to about sixty-nine, and nonwhite men to about sixty-one.[2]

19

Chapter 1:
Describing the Situa-
tion of Women: What
Needs Explanation?

This apparent male fragility is attributable to a number of causes. More males are born with genetically based diseases such as hemophilia, and they are more likely to die from infant diseases, heart disease, most forms of cancer, cirrhosis of the liver, AIDS, accidents, homicide, and suicide. Women, on the other hand, are more likely than men to die of cerebrovascular disease, diabetes, arteriosclerosis, breast cancer, genital cancer (except among people over 65), pregnancy and abortion, and old age. Men are more likely than women to be heavy drinkers, but only slightly more likely to smoke cigarettes. (Health is discussed in Chapter 5.)

Although men seem more fragile than women by these standards, women visit doctors and hospitals more than men do. In 1986 the average women visited a doctor 6.2 times and a dentist 2.2 times; the average man visited a doctor 4.5 times and a dentist 1.9 times. Part of the explanation for this difference is that women seek more preventive care and go to doctors regularly when they are pregnant. The female population is also older, which means that women have more of the problems that afflict the aged. Women also spend more time in hospitals: 1053 days of care for every 1000 women compared to 849 days for every 1000 men (U.S. Bureau of the Census 1987a). The difference, as one might guess, is greatest during the childbearing years; indeed women have more total days of hospital care than men only during the childbearing years. On the other hand, the average hospital stay is longer for men than for women.

In 1986 there were 65.4 births for every 1000 women age 15 to 44. Not surprisingly birthrates are the highest among women in their late twenties (109 per 1000 women), but birth is not rare among women in their early thirties (69 births per 1000 women), late thirties (24 births per 1000 women) or adolescence (51 births per 1000 women). However, most women still have their first child by their late twenties, and many have their first child before they finish adolescence.

Women who find themselves pregnant against their wishes are increasingly likely to resort to abortion. In 1985 there were 1,588,600 legal abortions in the United States. Abortion rates are highest among adolescents (especially girls younger than fifteen) and women over forty, as well as unmarried women.

Pregnancy and childbirth are much safer than they once were, but they are not as safe in the United States as they are in some countries. In 1986 there were about seven maternal deaths for every 1000 live births. The experiences of black and white women are shockingly different. In that year, five white and nineteen black women died because of pregnancy or childbirth for every 1000 live births (babies born alive). (Reproduction is discussed in Chapters 5 and 11.)

Families and Other Living Arrangements

Children are more likely to live with their mothers than with their fathers. In 1987 about 73 percent of children in the United States lived with both parents, while 21 percent lived only with their mothers, 3 percent lived only with their fathers, and 3 percent lived with neither parent. Race and ethnicity make a considerable difference in children's living situations. Whereas about 79 percent of white children live with both parents, the same is true of 66 percent of Hispanic children and 40 percent of black children.[3] While 16 percent of white children live only with their mothers, 28 percent of Hispanic children and 50 percent of black children do. Of these the majority of the Hispanic and white children live with mothers who are divorced or widowed; the majority of the black children live with mothers who were never married.

During early adulthood women are more likely than men to live with a spouse or other relative and slightly less likely to live alone. This changes dramatically later in life. Among people aged sixty-five and older, 41 percent of women and only 6 percent of men live alone; 38 percent of women live with a husband and 75 percent of men live with a wife at that time. Many more women live alone than we sometimes think. Although black women are less likely than white women to be married, they are slightly less likely to be living alone during their old age. This is because older black women are much more likely than older white women to be living with other relatives.

Men are more likely to be married than women are. In 1987, among people aged eighteen and older, 69 percent of all men and 63 percent of all women were married. Adult women and men are somewhat less likely to be married and more likely either to be divorced or never to have married at all than was true twenty years ago.

Women generally marry younger than men do. In 1985 the median age at the time of first marriage was 23 for women and 24.8 for men. The median age at first divorce was 31.9 for women and 34.4 for men. These figures represent a significant change over recent years; for both men and women age at first marriage has increased by one year since the beginning of the 1980s and two years since 1970.

Gender differences in marriage statistics increase with age. About 77 percent of all men over sixty-five are married, and only 14 percent are widowed. About 41 percent of women over sixty-five are married, while 49 percent are widowed. Men are also slightly more likely to remarry after a divorce than women are, in part because they tend to seek younger women. In 1986 6.6 percent of all men and 9.5 percent of all women aged 18 and older were divorced. (Marriage is discussed in Chapter 10.)

Being married and having children mean very different things to women and men. Surveys show that women are much more likely than men to place the blame for unachieved aspirations in education, employment, and other activities on their family obligations (Campbell, Converse, and Rodgers 1976). Men's family ties do not seem to interfere with other aspects of their lives as much as women's do. Women spend considerably more time directly serving other members of the family, shopping for them, cooking and cleaning for them, and ministering to their emotional and physical needs. This is true regardless of whether they are employed outside the home (Robinson 1980). A woman's marriage is also more likely than a man's to create additional (unpaid) work because of requirements of the spouse's job. There are more male-dominated jobs that require the spouse to make a direct contribution, including the jobs of corporate executives, the noncelibate clergy, politicians, and farmers. There are also more male-dominated jobs that require travel and relatively lengthy stays away from home, which add to the spouse's work. Researchers disagree about the distribution of power between husbands and wives, but it seems clear that husbands and wives have different degrees of power over the outcome of different types of decisions (Lips 1981). With regard to household consumption patterns, for example, men's opinions weigh more heavily in car buying, and women's weigh more heavily in the purchase of food or children's clothing.

21

Chapter 1: Describing the Situation of Women: What Needs Explanation?

Education, Work, and Wealth

Women now achieve nearly the same overall level of education as men. The median level of education for Hispanic women is 12 years compared with 12.1 for Hispanic men, 12.4 years for both black women and black men, and 12.6 years for white women compared with 12.8 for white men. In addition, women constitute a majority of people engaged in adult education. In 1987 women earned 50.8 percent of the bachelor's degrees and 50.2 percent of the master's degrees awarded. On the other hand, they earned only 35 percent of the doctoral degrees, 38.9 percent of the law degrees (LL.D. and J.D.), 31.5 percent of the medical degrees (M.D.), and 22.6 percent of the dentistry degrees (D.D.S. and D.M.D.). These figures suggest that male and female education is not as similar as it first appears. If we also consider the fields in which people earn their degrees, we find considerable segregation, as Table 1-1 shows. Although women earn the majority of master's and bachelor's

Women now earn about half the bachelor's and master's degrees.

TABLE 1-1
Proportion of Degrees Awarded to Women, 1986

Field	Bachelor's	Master's	Doctor's
Agriculture and natural resources	31.4	28.9	16.6
Anthropology	62.9	56.9	51.2
Architecture	24.0	27.5	13.3
Business and management	45.0	31.1	21.3
Communications	59.5	59.9	47.6
Computer and information sciences	35.7	29.9	13.1
Economics	34.4	26.0	19.9
Education	75.9	72.9	53.4
Engineering	13.1	11.5	6.7
English	67.1	65.8	57.6
Fine arts	68.0	63.8	70.1
Foreign languages	72.4	70.4	58.7
Geography	30.3	37.6	31.3
Health sciences	85.0	76.1	51.3
History	36.6	40.4	33.4
Home economics	93.1	87.8	74.9
Liberal studies	55.1	61.2	31.6
Library science	89.2	80.1	56.5
Life sciences	48.1	47.8	33.6
Mathematics	46.5	35.2	16.7
Music	47.2	50.0	35.9
Philosophy	32.8	29.5	22.7
Physical sciences	27.4	24.2	16.6
Political science and international relations	41.5	33.2	26.3
Psychology	69.0	64.8	51.5
Social work	85.3	79.9	64.0
Sociology	68.9	55.5	45.0
Theology	26.3	35.8	9.9

SOURCE: United States Department of Education (1988).

degrees in six fields (by generally marginal amounts), in all fields but art women have a smaller share of the doctorates than of any lower degree, generally by a fairly substantial amount. (Education is discussed in Chapter 4.)

Turning to work, we have already seen that women do more unpaid work in the home regardless of their employment status. More women than men also report doing volunteer work. This means that among married people, employed women work much longer hours than employed men, especially if there are children present. This means that women have less time for sleep, leisure, or recreation than men do. People generally think of "work" as something one is paid to do, however, which means that a higher proportion of men's labor is generally counted as work. (Work is discussed in Chapter 12.)

In 1988 76 percent of all men were in the labor force compared with 57 percent of all women.[4] Labor force participation among black and white women is very similar; 56 percent of white women and 58 percent of black women are in the labor force, as are 53 percent of Hispanic women. Labor force participation differs among men by race as it does among women: 77 percent of white men, 71 percent of black men, and 82 percent of Hispanic men are in the labor force (U.S. Department of Labor 1989). Of those who are employed, women and men are equally likely (74 percent) to be working full-time. Women constituted about 44.7 percent of the labor force in 1987. Table 1-2 compares the labor force participation of women in the United States and other countries. As that table shows, women's labor force participation in this country is relatively high.

Women's marital status and whether they have children both affect their employment rates, as Table 1-3 shows. Although women are less likely to be in the labor force if they have a husband than if they don't, and they are still less likely to be employed if they have young children, the differences are not as great as they once were. In 1988 almost 52 percent of married women with a child under one year old were in the labor force. It is simply incorrect to picture a married mother as someone who stays at home.

23

Chapter 1:
Describing the Situation of Women: What Needs Explanation?

TABLE 1-2

Proportion of Women and Men in the Labor Force,
Cross-national Comparisons, 1970–1987

	1970		1980		1987	
	Women	Men	Women	Men	Women	Men
Sweden	61	91	76	90	81	86
Norway[a]	52	88	65	90	74	89
Finland	64	88	70	83	73	81
United States	50	90	61	88	68	87
Canada	44	87	58	88	66	87
United Kingdom	54	96	62	92	65	88
Japan	55	89	55	89	58	87
Portugal[b]	52	95	55	91	58	86
Australia	46	92	53	88	57	85
France	50	87	56	83	57	78
West Germany	48	93	50	84	52	80
Italy	29	82	39	81	43	78
Netherlands[c]	30	86	36	78	41	74
Ireland[d]	34	96	36	89	37	85
Spain[a]	32	93	34	88	36	82

Note: Countries are listed in descending order of female labor force participation in 1987.
[a] First Norway and Spain figure is for 1972.
[b] First Portugal figure is for 1974.
[c] First Netherlands figure is for 1971.
[d] The Ireland figures are for 1971, 1981, and 1986.
SOURCE: Office for Economic Cooperation and Development (1988).

TABLE 1-3

Labor Force Participation of Women Sixteen Years Old and Over
by Marital Status and Presence and Age of Youngest Child, March 1987

| | | Presence and Age of Children | | |
Marital Status	Total	None under 18	Children 6–17 only	Children under 6
Never married	65.1	66.7	64.1	49.9
Married, husband present	55.8	48.4	70.6	56.8
Married, husband absent	61.4	57.9	72.6	55.1
Widowed	19.4	17.6	60.1	[a]
Divorced	75.4	71.9	84.5	70.5

[a] Insufficient data available.

SOURCE: Blau and Winkler (1989, 273) (from U.S. Bureau of Labor Statistics data).

Employment remains relatively highly sex segregated; most people work in jobs in which a clear majority of workers are people of their own sex. Women are more heavily concentrated in fewer jobs than men. About 35 percent of employed women are in clerical jobs. Adding sales clerks to these accounts for about 39 percent of employed women. Private household service workers, waitresses, and other food service workers bring the figure to 49 percent. The addition of teachers and registered nurses accounts for a majority of the female work force—almost 55 percent. This is a large proportion of people in a very small number of job categories.

Table 1-4 shows the most- and least-segregated jobs in the United States in 1988. In the first column are jobs in which more than 90 percent of the workers are women. In the third column are the jobs in which 2 percent or less of the workers are women. The middle column shows the jobs that are the most integrated: those in which 49 to 51 percent of the workers are women. The numbers show the exact proportion of women in each job. Notice that the "female" jobs are mostly clerical or personal service jobs, and the "male" jobs are mostly blue-collar jobs. Women are also underrepresented in labor unions; they constituted 35 percent of union members in 1987 (U.S. Department of Labor 1989, 225).

Jobs are segregated not only by field but also by level. Women are concentrated in jobs at lower levels with less pay, even in "female" areas. In the public schools, for example, 1986 figures showed women constituted 94 percent of the teacher aides, 98 percent of kindergarten and prekindergarten teachers, 85 percent of elementary school teachers, 55 percent of the secondary school teachers, 39 percent of faculty at two-year colleges, 31 percent of faculty at four-year colleges, and 20 percent of faculty at doctoral-level universities (U.S. Department of Labor 1989, 181–88; Fox, 1989, 228). The problem is equally apparent in the ranks of federal employees. Table 1-5 shows that, as in many other types of employment, "the higher, the fewer" is the rule that holds in governmental employment. While about 75 percent of the workers in the lowest paid federal jobs are women only about 7 percent of those in the highest paid jobs are women.

25

Chapter 1:
Describing the Situa-
tion of Women: What
Needs Explanation?

TABLE 1-4
Most- and Least-segregated Occupations, 1988

Percent of women in female-segregated occupations	Percent of women in integrated occupations	Percent of women in male-segregated occupations
Dental assistants (99)	Editors & reporters (51)	Firefighters (2)
Secretaries (99)	Painters, sculptors, & craft artists (51)	Carpenters (2)
Dental hygienists (98)	Secondary school teachers (51)	Carpet installers (2)
Prekindergarten & kindergarten teachers (99)	Underwriters (51)	Drywall installers (2)
Receptionists (97)	Accountants & auditors (50)	Tool & dye makers (2)
Private household child-care workers (97)	Buyers, wholesale & retail (50)	Heavy truck drivers (2)
Child-care workers (96)	Furniture salespeople (50)	Water transport operators (2)
Practical nurses (96)	Administrators: education & related fields (49)	Brickmasons (1)
Private household cleaners & servants (96)	Personnel & labor relations managers (49)	Electricians (1)
Teacher aides (96)	Real estate sales (49)	Excavators (1)
Registered nurses (95)	Bus drivers (49)	Heating & air conditioning mechanics (1)
Typists (95)	Advertising representatives (48)	RR transport operators (1)
Welfare service aides (94)	Bakers (48)	Roofers (1)
Bookkeepers (92)		Tile setters (1)
Bank tellers (91)		Timber cutters (1)
		Concrete finishers (<.5)
		Electrical power installers (<.5)
		Plumbers (<.5)
		Plasterers (<.5)
		Structural metal workers (<.5)

Note: Figures show the number of women as a proportion of workers in each occupation.
SOURCE: U.S. Department of Labor (1989, 181–88).

TABLE 1-5
Proportion of Women in Different Pay Grades
of White-collar Federal Employment

		Percent female	
Grade Level	Maximum pay	1987	1970
GS 1–6	$21,480	74.9	72.2
GS 7–10	$32,148	54.1	33.4
GS 11–12	$42,341	30.0	9.5
GS 13–15	$69,976	14.2	3.0
GS 16–18	$72,500	6.9	1.4
TOTAL		48.2	40.3

Note: 1987 pay levels are shown.
SOURCE: U.S. Bureau of the Census (1989, 318).

The result of differences in training and employment is that women earn much less than men do. In the mid-1980s women earned less than 70 cents for every dollar that men earned (U.S. Bureau of the Census 1987). Even in 1986 when we compared women and men of the same age with similar levels of education women earned less than men. Using twenty-five to thirty-four-year-olds as an example, Table 1-6 shows that at every level of education, from those who have less than eight years of education to those who have gone beyond four years of college, women earn less than men do. And these pay differences emerge regardless of race. There are a number of reasons. ''Women's'' jobs tend to pay less than ''men's'' jobs, and women are still paid less for doing the same job as men.

If we consider that beside commanding lower salaries women are also more likely than men to be caring for children on their own and more likely to be over 65, it should not be surprising to find that more women than men live under the poverty line. In fact in recent years women's share of poverty has been increasing. This pattern is known as the ''feminization of poverty.''

The high rate of poverty among women creates vast additional poverty among children because it is women who are primarily responsible for children. This point is best illustrated by the evidence that families maintained only by women are much more likely to live under the poverty line than families maintained by either men or a married couple. Although this is generally true regardless of race, the rates of poverty are most shocking among the families of nonwhite women, as shown by the 1986 figures on families with children under eighteen. Among whites, 8 percent of the families maintained by men or married couples were impoverished, compared with 40 percent of those maintained by women. Among blacks, 13 percent of the families maintained by men or married couples were impoverished, compared with 58 percent of those maintained by women. Among Hispanics 20 percent of the families maintained by men or married couples were impoverished, compared with 60 percent of those maintained by women (Pearce 1989, 500). (Wealth and poverty are discussed in Chapter 12.)

TABLE 1-6
Average Dollar Earnings for Twenty-five- to Thirty-four-year-olds, 1986

Years of education	Men	Women	Women's salary as percentage of men's
Less than 8 years	$12,846	$ 9,212	71.7
8 years	14,972	9,705	64.8
1–3 years high school	17,061	12,319	72.2
4 years high school	20,936	15,053	71.9
1–3 years college	24,057	17,734	73.7
4 years college	28,834	21,027	72.9
5+ years college	35,097	24,624	70.2

SOURCE: U.S. Bureau of the Census (1987).

Crime and Violence

27

Chapter 1:
Describing the Situa-
tion of Women: What
Needs Explanation?

Women and men have different experiences in the social life of the nation; they also have different experiences in its "antisocial life." In 1986 only about 17 percent of the people arrested for crimes in the United States were women and women constituted about 8 percent of the U.S. jail population and 4 percent of state prison inmates. In 1986 79 percent of the people arrested for crimes designated by the FBI as "serious" were male.

Women and men also commit different types of crimes. Men predominate much more in crimes against people (compared with against property). Table 1-7 shows the crimes in which females make up at least one quarter of the perpetrators and in which males are at least 90 percent of the perpetrators. Women constitute the majority only among prostitutes and juvenile runaways, whose offenses are often labeled "victimless crimes." The other crimes listed in the "female" column are mostly white-collar property crimes except curfew violations, also a juvenile crime.

The picture is very different when we look at the most heavily male-dominated crimes. Besides including much more violence or risk of injury to other people two of the crimes listed are largely directed specifically at women and girls: forcible rape and sex offenses. Men are more likely to kill themselves or other people than women are, although women make more suicide attempts. (Crime is discussed in Chapter 8; violence and criminal violence are also discussed in Chapters 5 and 10.)

Men are also more likely to be the victims of crimes against people, except for rape and offenses against family members. According to the Federal Bureau of Investigation (FBI), there were eighty-five reported rapes per 100,000 females aged twelve and older in the United States in 1986. Moreover, rape and wife battery are two of the most underreported crimes in the country; the FBI estimates that at best only a quarter of all rapes are actually reported to the police. Some researchers note that as many as half of all marriages involve some physical abuse of the wife.

TABLE 1-7
Proportions of Women and Men Committing
Specific Crimes, 1987

Percent committed by women	*Percent committed by men*
Prostitution and commercialized vice: 64.8	Forcible rape: 98.8
Juvenile runaways: 57.2	Weapons crimes: 92.4
Fraud: 43.5	Sex offenses: 92.2
Embezzlement: 38.1	Burglary: 92.1
Forgery, counterfeiting: 34.1	Robbery: 91.1
Larceny, theft: 31.1	Drunkenness: 90.8
Curfew, Loitering: 25.0	Motor vehicle theft: 90.3

SOURCE: U.S. Bureau of the Census (1989, 173).

Women constitute a minority of the people involved in crime prevention and control. They are 11 percent of the police officers and detectives. In 1987 they were 8 percent of the officers of the FBI and 6 percent of the Secret Service. In 1986 they were 11 percent of nonsupervisory police and detectives, but only 5 percent of police and detective supervisors (McGuinness and Donahue 1988). They were a small percentage of prison corrections officials and administrators. In 1988 they were 20 percent of the nation's lawyers and judges (U.S. Department of Labor 1989).

Authority and Leadership

We have already seen that in occupations and education, the situation of women is "the higher, the fewer," even in female-dominated fields. Women similarly constitute only a small proportion of leaders in industry and labor. In 1982 about 27 percent of wholesale and retail trade businesses were owned by women, as were 16 percent of manufacturing firms; 16 percent of finance, insurance, and real estate firms; 8 percent of transportation firms; and 5 percent of construction companies (Rix 1987). The first women was appointed to the executive council of the AFL-CIO in 1980. This pattern also held in other domains such as the mass media and other cultural institutions.

The same pattern emerges in politics. Women make up half the population, but they hold only a small minority of all political offices. They hold about 13 percent of all municipal offices, 25 percent of all county offices, and 16 percent of all state legislative offices. Following the 1988 elections less than 6 percent of the members of the House of Representatives and 2 percent of the U.S. Senators were women. There were two female governors. One of the nine Supreme Court judges was a woman, the first in history. Table 1-8, which lists in descending order the female proportion of the members of the chief national legislative body (in cases of bicameral legislatures, generally the lower house; in communist countries the central committee) in a number of countries, shows that women in the United States do not fare well compared to the women of other countries. Of course in no country have women achieved parity. (Government and politics are discussed in Chapter 8.)

Personality and Cognition: A Psychological Portrait

Thus far we have considered demographic differences between women and men; most people also seem to think they can identify at least some psychological differences between the sexes. Women are said to be nurturant, emotional, soft, weak, peaceful, and jealous; and men are said to be aggressive, competitive, strong, and particularly good at mathematics and abstract reasoning. As we have already seen, a person's emotional health is often judged by how well the individual conforms to psychological characteristics attributed to his or her sex. This section looks at both conventional wisdom and research on the relationship between gender and psychological characteristics and at the meanings of *femininity* and *masculinity*.

29

Chapter 1:
Describing the Situa-
tion of Women: What
Needs Explanation?

TABLE 1-8
Women as a Proportion of National Legislators

Country	Percent Female	Year	Country	Percent Female	Year
Norway[a]	34	1987	Switzerland	9	1987
Sweden	31	1987	Israel[a]	8	1987
Finland	30	1987	Italy	8	1984
Denmark	26	1987	Venezuela	8	1987
The Netherlands	20	1987	India[a]	7	1986
Czechoslovakia	15	1979	Panama	6	1987
Iceland[a]	15	1985	Portugal	6	1987
Luxembourg	14	1984	France	5	1987
E. Germany	13	1981	Spain	5	1982
New Zealand	13	1987	Sri Lanka[a]	5	1987
Costa Rica	12	1987	United States	5	1987
Australia	11	1987	Japan	4	1987
Austria	11	1987	U.S.S.R.	4	1981
Ghana	11	1987	United Kingdom[a]	4	1987
Mexico	11	1987	Zaire	4	1987
China (PRC)	10	1977	Algeria	3	1979
W. Germany	10	1987	South Korea	3	1987
Belgium	9	1987	Turkey	3	1984
Canada	9	1987	Greece	3	1987
Cuba	9	1979	Iran	1	1980
Ireland	9	1987			

[a] Indicates nations that have had a female chief executive.
SOURCE: Randall (1987); "Women In Government Around the World," (April 1987, 97–101).

Masculinity, Femininity, and Stereotypes

The packages of psychological characteristics people tend to associate with one sex or the other are summarized by a pair of commonly used but often unexamined concepts: masculinity and femininity. What do these words mean? *Masculine,* the *Concise Oxford Dictionary* tells us, means, "of men; manly, vigorous; (of woman) having qualities appropriate to a man." *Webster's Ninth New Collegiate Dictionary* defines *Feminine* as ". . .appropriate or peculiar to women." Notice that these definitions turn not on whether men and women actually possess masculine or feminine qualities, but on whether we think of these qualities as appropriate for one sex or the other. It is possible to say that a women is "not feminine" or that she is "masculine" and possesses "masculine characteristics." It is also possible to say that a man is "not masculine" or that he is "effeminate" and possesses "feminine characteristics." When we use these phrases, we are saying that there are certain characteristics we think women and men *should* have because we think they are more appropriate for one sex than the other.

Notice that people do not just describe people as masculine or feminine; they also describe certain personality characteristics as masculine or feminine, regardless of the sex of the person who has the characteristics. This creates confusion, as the following example shows. Suppose that we are interested in sex differences in nurturing behavior and that we think of nurturance as feminine, regardless of the sex of the person we are describing. Research on this characteristic provides conflicting evidence, but it offers little reason to believe that women and men as groups differ very much in the degree to which they have nurturing personalities, although women's roles in society involve them in more situations in which they can act out their nurturant propensities. What do we conclude? Do we say that women and men are roughly equivalent in their potential to nurture although we regard this behavior as more appropriate for women? If so, we would then have to consider strategies for making sure men don't live up to their potentials so that they won't act inappropriately. Are we arguing, as some psychologists do, that nurturant men are ''cross-sex typed'' (behave in a way appropriate to the other sex)? This too suggests that there is something wrong with nurturant men. The problem is that our definitions of masculine and feminine behavior are usually based on stereotypes.

Some people try to avoid the problem associated with the labels *masculine* and *feminine* by using the terms *androgyny* or *androgynous*. Some of these people believe an androgynous person is one whose personality is constituted of both ''masculine'' and ''feminine'' characteristics. Some go further and say an androgynous person combines the best of both sexes, meaning the ''good'' characteristics stereotypically associated with males and females. (No one seems to have devised a term for a person who combines the worst characteristics of both sexes.) Others define *androgyny* more in terms of flexibility, or the ability to call on a range of characteristics conventionally labeled masculine or feminine, depending on circumstances.

Over the years many different researchers have investigated masculinity, femininity, and androgyny. Psychologists engaged in this type of research usually measure these personality frameworks and their effects by asking people to indicate how well each of a long list of personality characteristics describes them. The researchers then tally up the score to categorize the subjects as masculine, feminine, or androgynous. One of the most important things these studies show is how many people do not conform to traditional images of gender typing. Regardless of the method used, one common finding emerges: Most people do not describe themselves in anything like uniformly ''gender-appropriate'' terms (Cook 1985). These findings cast even more doubt on the usefulness of the concepts *masculine* and *feminine*.

Many researchers have tried to discover what difference it makes if people seem to be particularly masculine, feminine, or androgynous. Some, for example, have found that ''androgynous'' people are more flexible in their ability to deal with different situations, but others (e.g., Jones, Chernovetz, and Hansson 1978) have found that ''masculinity'' is associated with greater levels of flexibility. Leanne K. Lamke (1982) and others have found that ''masculinity'' is associated with higher levels of self-esteem among both adolescent females and males and that ''androgynous'' adolescents have higher self-esteem than ''feminine'' adolescents. The literature on androgyny is too large and varied to summarize here, but many people have suggested that androgyny is a healthy alternative to rigid sex typing. However, it is important to remember that as long as we think of androgyny as the combination of "masculine" and "feminine" traits, we have not avoided the original problem. We are still implying that there are ideal male and female personality types; we are still talking about how well individuals conform to stereotypes. Psychological research certainly gives us no reason to believe that people who conform to these stereotypes are healthier, happier, or better adjusted (Cook 1985).

Stereotypes are beliefs or expectations people have about members of particular social groups. When we say that a person views women through stereotypes, we are saying that that person holds certain beliefs about the nature of women as a group (for example, that they are nurturant, passive, or emotional) and applies those beliefs to any given women, regardless of her actual characteristics. To determine what is and is not a stereotype, it is necessary to review research on the psychological and personality characteristics of women and men.

Personality and Cognitive Skills

Consistent and conclusive evidence of psychological sex differences of any type is very rare. In article after article in professional psychology journals, we find the words, "No sex differences were found." The existence of differences between men and women has been exaggerated in part because people pay more attention to the relatively few studies that find differences than to the vast number that do not.

Reviews of the literature on psychological differences almost uniformly lead to the same conclusion: Psychologists have not found significant sex differences in most personality characteristics or cognitive skills (e.g., Maccoby and Jacklin 1974; Archer and Lloyd 1982). Little girls tend to develop verbal skills more quickly, but boys catch up. Males and females seem to develop slightly more strength in different kinds of perceptual skills relating to sight, hearing, and touch (Lips 1988). Males tend to outperform females on certain kinds of visual-spatial tasks. Small but consistent differences appear in tests of mental rotation (imagining a figure from a different angle) and rod-and-frame tests (being able to make a tilted rod vertical despite a confusing context). Despite common claims, no consistent gender differences emerge in embedded-figure tests (being able to identify a figure that forms a part of a more complex figure) (Linn and Peterson 1985).

Certainly there has been considerable attention over the years to gender differences in mathematical skills. One group of researchers (Hyde, Fennema, and Lamon 1990) used a technique called "meta-analysis" to analyze the results of 100 different articles published between 1962 and 1988, representing research on three million people.

Their results would surprise many people. Overall they found females and males virtually indistinguishable in mathematical ability. No gender differences appeared during elementary or middle school in understanding of mathematical concepts or problem solving, although girls showed slight superiority in computation. In high school and college, on the other hand, males performed better than females in mathematical problem solving. The conventionally expected male edge in mathematics performance is more likely to appear in specialized and selective settings (such as among college entrance exam takers) than in more general populations (such as students in high school classrooms). Finally, gender differences have declined over the years.

31

Chapter 1:
Describing the Situation of Women: What Needs Explanation?

There is also little evidence to support the idea that the specific personality traits of women and men are basically different. There seems to be general agreement, though, that from an early age males exhibit more aggressiveness (especially physical rather than verbal aggressiveness) than females do. Certainly males seem to engage in more acts of antisocial aggression than females do (Hyde 1984). Research also suggests that females and males use somewhat different means to get their way and to influence people (Lips 1981).

Research regarding most other personality characteristics, including those that are most stereotypically masculine and feminine, shows scanty and often conflicting evidence of sex differences when females and males are given similar opportunities to display these characteristics. A review of 127 different studies of activity levels found little difference in how active girls and boys are (Eaton and Enns 1986). Likewise a review of the research on conformity and influenceability showed no consistent difference between females and males (Eagly and Carli 1981). Females report themselves to be more empathetic than males report themselves to be, but research involving observation of behavior rather than self-perception has not revealed much in the way of gender differences (Eisenberg and Lennon 1983).

Following the publication of Carol Gilligan's (1982) book, *In a Different Voice,* many researchers focused on possible differences between women and men in the way they understand and solve moral dilemmas. Gilligan suggested that men's moral reasoning is based more on principles of individualism, rights, and justice, while women's is based more on caring, obligation, and responsibility to others. This difference, she argued, is due to the different nature of women's and men's social experiences, which lead them to understand social relationships differently.

A number of other feminist scholars have made similar claims. Nancy Chodorow (1978), whose work provided some of the theoretical basis for Gilligan's analysis, concluded that women think more in terms of connectedness among people because of the continuities between themselves and their mothers. Males are more dominated by the task of separation because of the early need to distinguish themselves from their mothers in order to develop a masculine identity. The "problem" for males is that because men tend not to take a full share in nurturing children, they cannot gain the same sense of connection and continuity as girls, who are nurtured by their same-sex parent. Sara Ruddick (1982) argued that women use a form of thinking that she calls maternal thinking, which is shaped by the caring work that women do in society. None of these authors claims that these gender differences in thinking stem directly from biological differences; instead they maintain that our ways of thinking are shaped by social practices or experiences, which tend to be gender differentiated.

These arguments about women's and men's moral thinking have been very influential for a number of reasons. They are among the very few claims about psychological gender differences that appear to place women in as good or even a better light than men. This has been especially significant to many feminist scholars because a series of earlier studies had revealed similar gender differences but interpreted them as meaning that women have less sophisticated styles of moral reasoning than men's. Part of the attraction may also be that these arguments are consistent with traditional stereotypes of women without claiming that the difference is universal, biologically based, or immutable.

However, these arguments have also been the target of considerable criticism (e.g., Kerber et al. 1986). Some writers are uncomfortable with the degree to which they do resemble traditional stereotypes. Indeed evidence for these differences is very mixed and suggests that women's and men's reputation for differences outstrips their actual differences in this regard (e.g., Brabeck 1983; Ford and Lowery 1986; Lifton 1985; Walker 1984). No doubt debates about gender and modes of thinking will continue.

33

Chapter 1:
Describing the Situation of Women: What Needs Explanation?

Psychological Difference: Summary

We have only touched on research discussing differences between women and men. Throughout this book we will see other examples. But by and large research on the psychology of gender suggests that the most fruitful approach to understanding the gender basis of human characteristics and behavior is not to focus on global, abstract skills and characteristics removed from their social context, as we have been doing thus far, but to discuss these skills and characteristics in the context of social institutions and organization. When people ask whether women are happier, more anxious, more dependent, or more nurturant than men, the best answer is probably, "Under what circumstances? With regard to what situations?"

Human beings are very complex. We tend to respond in different ways to different situations. Although there may be people so thoroughly dominated by particular characteristics that they always act in the same manner, these people are a minority constituted of saints, devils, or people so out of touch with their surroundings and circumstances that they need protection from themselves. Personality characteristics depend very much on the context of behavior. Consider an example offered by Carol Tavris and Carole Offir (1977, 43):

> Suppose you were doing an observational study of timidity, following a young mother through a typical day. At 9:00 A.M. the woman's child injures herself on a jagged rock. Does the mother scream hysterically at the sight of blood? Does she faint dead away? If she is like most mothers of our acquaintance, she scoops up the child, administers first aid, and drives quickly but carefully to the nearest hospital. No fear or timidity there. But that evening the same woman is standing on a chair calling frantically to her husband because a little grey creature with a long tail has appeared. Same woman, different behaviors. Which is she—brave or timid?

What Does It All Mean?

This chapter has been presented as though understanding gender in society is a simple matter of looking at facts. Having looked at a wide range of facts, it is now time to consider one more: Even grasping the "basic information" about women's situation in society and what role gender plays in it is not as simple a matter as it first appears. The remainder of this chapter focuses on two problems that need addressing before we move on: (1) research and analysis methods and (2) interpretation of the social significance of the information.

Until now we have focused primarily on gender differences, including differences in the life situations of women and men, differences in the treatment they receive, and differences in their personal characteristics and skills. We have not yet discussed when a difference is really a difference. What do we mean when we talk about gender differences? What makes a gender difference worth talking about? A number of problems make it difficult to answer these questions.

The first problem we encounter in analyzing gender differences is the very language we use to express differences. Unfortunately the language used to describe gender difference is often imprecise, exaggerated, or otherwise misleading, thus leaving us room to read our own expectations into the situation. Suppose a test of mathematical skills was administered to forty-two men and forty two women, and the distribution of scores on this particular test was as follows:

Grade	A	B	C	D	F	Average
	(4.0)	(3.0)	(2.0)	(1.0)	(0.0)	
Number of women	5	15	16	4	2	2.4
Number of men	6	17	15	3	1	2.6

How could we put these results into words? Women demonstrate a lower level of mathematical skills than men? The average woman has a lower level of mathematical skills than the average man? Women are twice as likely to fail a particular test of mathematical skills than men? A majority of the people who got A's on a test of mathematical skill were men? If you read these words without thinking carefully, without looking at the evidence, you might conclude that women are pretty poor indeed at mathematics. You might decide that a man would be a much better bet than a woman if you needed help with a mathematical problem. Look again at the actual numbers. Do the "sex differences" in these scores really mean that you should look for a man to help you with your math problem? Wouldn't you rather have the advice of one of the five women who got A's than of one of the four men who got D's and F's?

Words like *average, most, more,* or *a majority* are summary terms for numbers, and it is impossible to understand their significance without knowing more about the numbers. Unfortunately too many people think they can understand problems of difference without any attention to precision. This much is clear: Saying that the average male and female possess certain skills or personality traits almost never means that all members of one sex are better at the skill than all members of the other sex or that all members of one sex display the trait and the others do not. In fact research usually shows much more variation *among* men and *among* women than there is *between* men and women.

A second difficulty with interpretation of sex differences stems from the problems of constructing and analyzing appropriate measures of characteristics and skills. Let us pursue the example of mathematical skills. Before we can compare the abilities of the sexes, we need to devise a specific test or set of tests that we think provides a valid measure of mathematical skills, a test that actually measures what we want it to measure and only what we want it to measure.

Many of the widely circulated reports of sex differences are faulty because the tests used in the research did not measure only what the researchers claimed to be testing. There are many different ways of measuring any given skill or personality characteristic, and differences in measures can make considerable difference in the results. Unfortunately many students find questions about research methods and statistics boring or intimidating and therefore do not pay attention to these important methodological problems.

A third difficulty in identifying gender differences even if one is attempting to be precise is the impact of bias on observation. Researchers can be prejudiced as anyone else, so two different researchers may observe the same situation or event and see different things happening depending on their own expectations and stereotypes (Lyons and Serbin 1986).[5]

A final problem in trying to identify gender differences is that we sometimes unintentionally make it more difficult to see the role gender plays in our lives because we have deemphasized other aspects of human experience. We have already seen, for example, that the family experiences of women of different races is different in some respects. In order to understand the role of gender in women's lives, therefore, it is also necessary to look at the role of race. Although being a woman or a man shapes people's lives regardless of race, it shapes their lives somewhat differently depending on race. (The relationship between gender and other forms of social differentiation is discussed further in Chapter 13.)

When and Why Are Gender Differences Interesting?

It probably doesn't seem strange to devote so much space in a women's studies book to gender differences. But why and under what circumstances are gender differences of interest to us? What types of gender differences are worth attention? Open any book on women and gender and you find a standard list of characteristics on which males and females are thought to differ and which, apparently, are worth thinking about. We have already discussed many of these characteristics.

The main reason we pay attention to certain types of differences is that they occur in what are often viewed as the characteristics that determine how a person behaves and reacts to specific situations and what a person can do and wants to do. These characteristics are often also identified as particularly masculine or feminine and therefore as characteristics that help determine why the roles and status of men and women are different.

Again consider the case of skills. If we find that men and women tend to possess different levels of a certain basic skill, we presumably have found out something about the special abilities and limitations of each sex. But deriving the social significance of these differences is not as simple as it might seem. Some people suggest that if we observe differences in mathematical skills, for example, there is no point in teaching girls mathematics because they will not be as good as boys anyway. (No one seems to have suggested that boys should not be taught much English or literature because

35

Chapter 1:
Describing the Situation of Women: What Needs Explanation?

they are, on the average, slower at developing verbal skills.) This might be an appropriate conclusion to draw if all boys were better at mathematics than all girls, if these differences were entirely the result of innate sex differences, and if girls could reach the full extent of their abilities with only a little training. However, none of these things is true.

Some people also draw conclusions about women's occupational potential from research on basic skills. They suggest, for example, that we shouldn't bother trying to get women into jobs requiring certain spatial skills or that we should not be concerned when we discover that only 4 percent of engineers are women because some studies show that men have better spatial skills than women. The logic underlying this conclusion is incorrect. The differences are marginal and there are more similarities between the sexes than there are differences.

Even if we found that there were indeed many more men than women with the particular skill needed for a certain job, we cannot rule out women from that job on the grounds that they are not as likely to be qualified. Some women will probably be as qualified and possibly even more qualified than any man. This

Why were most of the shoe salespeople in the past men?

understanding of gender differences now forms part of the basis of American law on employment. After the passage of the 1964 Civil Rights Act, which (among other things) banned discrimination in employment on the basis of sex, the Equal Employment Opportunity Commission (EEOC) ruled that employers may not refuse jobs to women because of "assumptions of the comparative employment characteristics of women in general," or because of "stereotyped characterizations of the sexes."

37

Chapter 1: Describing the Situation of Women: What Needs Explanation?

> Such stereotypes include, for example, that men are less capable of assembling intricate equipment and that women are less capable of aggressive salesmanship. The principle of nondiscrimination requires that individuals be considered on the basis of individual capacities and not on the basis of any characteristics generally attributed to the group (Goldstein 1988, 500).

Thus people must be considered on the basis of their individual merit, not on the basis of stereotypes about the social groups of which they are a part, even if the stereotype is true of a majority of the members of the group.

It is not even as simple as some people think to determine which human characteristics best enable a person to perform specific tasks or roles in society. For example, most people assume that a relatively high degree of competitiveness and aggression is required to be active in politics. They therefore assume that it is reasonable to compare women's and men's levels of competitiveness and aggression to help explain differences in male and female political participation. But is the initial assumption true, that is, *do* people need an extraordinarily high level of competitiveness and aggression to be active in politics? There is no clear indication that they do. True, a person who wishes to be elected to a political office must compete in an electoral contest, but this does not necessarily mean that that person is especially competitive or particularly cares for competition. To argue otherwise would be like suggesting that to be a doctor a person has to like taking tests, because one has to take a lot of tests to become a doctor. Thus the social significance of sex differences is rarely as obvious as it seems, and it requires careful thought and analysis.

Finally, remember that in women's studies differences between women and men is not the only area of interest. We can also be interested in women's history and situation for its own sake. If we are interested in the variety of forms women in the arts have used to express their understanding of womanhood, for example, we would probably focus on women and not on men at all. Understanding pregnancy and childbirth is not a matter of looking at gender *difference,* but rather gendered *existence.* There are many other examples that will appear throughout this book.

Above all, when looking at gender differences it is important to bear in mind what is interesting about them and what questions we are asking. We cannot simply continue to use men as a representation of the norm and ask how women differ from them. Exploring gender difference is a matter of asking how women and men are similar to and different from each other.

Difference and Inequality

It is clearer than ever that there are differences between the activities and situations of women and men. There is, as sociologists would say, a system of differentiation of women and men in the United States. But can we also say that the two sexes are so differentiated as to give them unequal value or power? That is, are they not only differentiated, but also stratified? Do women and men have not only different roles and activities, but also different statuses?

People can engage in different types of behavior without appearing unequal. For example, if I always have ice cream for dessert and you always have apple pie, or if I play piano as a hobby and you play basketball, there is no reason to believe that we are revealing a pattern of inequality. It is also possible for different people to engage in the same activities or have the same resources and be regarded unequally. If a black family and a white family with equal incomes try to buy the same house in the same neighborhood, they—and their money—may not be valued equally. Difference does not necessarily indicate inequality, just as certain kinds of sameness may not reflect equality. We want to know not just about sameness and difference but also about the values we use to measure the worth of people, activities, and resources.

We can evaluate the degree of equality between women and men by asking several questions:

1. To what degree do women and men possess similar levels of valued resources?
2. To what degree do women and men have similar ranges of life options?
3. To what degree are women and men and their major activities valued similarly?
4. To what degree do women's and men's psychological states—their mental health and degree of happiness or contentment—seem to indicate that their situations are good?

If we consider control over or possession of valued resources, we find strong indications of lower status for women. Women, as we have seen, are financially poorer than men. They hold many fewer positions of authority in society, which means considerably less control over the disposition of valuable resources, including time, labor, and deference as well as tangible goods. By this measure, we live in a very unequal society indeed.

We can also evaluate equality in terms of the degree of personal independence and choice in life options that people have. How much control over our own lives do we have? If women and men have before them an equivalent range of options from which to choose and have equal freedom to make their own choices with equivalent amounts and types of risk, we could say that they have equal status even if they choose different options.

Do women and men have the same degree of control over their lives? We already have some indication that they do not. Men have control over more valuable resources, which in turn expands the number of options they have. Men are in more positions of authority, which gives them control both over others and over themselves. Public officials, for example, make major decisions about the distribution of resources and about what people may and may not do in a community or nation, and that community or nation includes the public officials themselves. The very concept of democracy is based on the principle of self-government. As we have seen, men are vastly predominant among those who do the "self-governing." In personal life and day-to-day decision making women also seem to have—or at least to make—a much smaller range of choices. But we must go considerably beyond the mere presentation of figures to understand the relative degree of choice women and men have. We will attend to this task throughout the remainder of this book.

39

Chapter 1: Describing the Situation of Women: What Needs Explanation?

We can also consider equality by looking at the relative worth attached to people and their activities. According to one of our most tangible measures of worth, money, women and their activities are valued much less than men and their activities. "Women's" jobs have lower salaries than "men's" jobs, and women tend to be paid less even when they do equivalent jobs. Indeed many of women's acitivities are not paid at all.

Money is not the only measure of worth, of course. People still value having a male child (an heir to carry on the family name) more than having a female child. *Who's Who* lists only a few women. Many women speak of their major day-to-day activity as being "just a housewife," thus devaluing their own work. To say that a woman writes or thinks "like a man" is supposed to be a compliment, but it indicates that the way women write or speak is viewed as less good. One of the points noted by many historians is that even when women have done remarkable and valued things, they tend to be forgotten. We will see many other examples throughout the book.

Psychological states are also important to consider when we talk about equality. When confronted with the degree to which men's and women's experiences and resources differ, many people argue that there really isn't a problem because many women are happy and content with their segregated life. Although a majority of the population thinks that women are happiest when they are devoting themselves to being mothers and homemakers, some surveys have revealed that women in the traditional homemaking role are unhappier than employed women. Studies also suggest that women in traditional roles suffer more psychological problems (including "middle-aged depression") than other women. (The relationship between gender roles and mental health is discussed further in Chapter 5.)

Simone de Beauvoir (1952) suggested an even more profound criticism of the "happiness and contentment" principle for evaluating the relative status of women and men. People can learn—or be taught—to be happy in all sorts of situations, including slavery and extreme poverty; the human population is amazingly varied. If we use happiness and contentment as the sole criterion for judging whether a group has a problem, we could right every wrong merely by convincing people to be happy with their lot. Some people are happiest when they save a life; other are happiest when they kill. Are all forms of human happiness morally equivalent? Is happiness the criterion we wish to use to evaluate human activity? Some suggest it is; others say it is not. The measure that de Beauvoir uses is not contentment and happiness, but liberty.

We can conclude, even from the small amount of information we have examined thus far, that men's and women's lives and activities are not just different; they are currently unequal. Before we can probe more deeply into the ways this system of inequality works and how it can be changed, we must first find out how it came about. We turn to that question next.

1. Unless otherwise stated, all figures presented in this chapter refer to 1986 and are taken from U.S. Bureau of the Census (1987).

2. *Nonwhite* is used here only to refer to a classification used by the census bureau. It is important to remember how many different subgroups are represented by the term.

3. "Hispanic" is the census bureau classification that includes all people of Latin American extraction.

4. *Labor-force participation* refers to people who are employed or are seeking employment. *Employment* refers only to people who hold paid jobs.

5. There are many other important issues involved in understanding the process of research and learning. For a more complete introduction to social science methodology and feminist research, see Eichler (1980; 1988).

2

Some Competing Explanations:
How Did Society Get This Way?

We HAVE seen that American society is marked by both sex differentiation and sex stratification. How can we account for this situation? Is there an explanation that can tell us why women and men play such different roles in society and why and how these inequities developed historically? A number of different theories have been suggested over the centuries. Each theory is based on somewhat different kinds of evidence, looks at slightly different aspects of women's lives, and suggests different implications for the possibility of social change.

This chapter examines five different kinds of theories about sex differentiation and stratification: (1) nature theories, which offer a relatively static view based on theological or biological assumptions; (2) enlightenment theories, which emphasize progress and learning; (3) economic theories, which focus on the impact of economic needs and structures; (4) functionalist evolutionary theories, which look to a combination of biological development and social needs; and (5) sex war theories, which look most directly at antagonisms and struggles between women and men.

Each of these types of theories represents an attempt to understand the history of gender in society. Three important themes or questions can be used to compare these alternative theories:

1. What is the relationship between each theory of the structure of relations between the sexes and theories used to explain other aspects of society, such as class relations and other forms of inequality? What is the historical context of each theory? Why was each theory developed when it was?
2. How useful is each theory as a framework for understanding the roles and status of women? What, exactly, does each theory seem to explain or to ignore? What types of evidence does each theory provide, and what arguments does each make?
3. What are the political implications of each of these theories? How can each be used, and how have they been used, to justify different strategies for maintaining

or changing the status of women and men? What are the differences between feminist theories and explanations and those offered by nonfeminists or opponents of feminism?

The "Eternal Feminine": The Static World of God and Nature

There is something about the idea of the eternal or universal that human beings seem to find attractive. Despite, or probably because of, the variety of human experiences and values that extends across time and cultures, the idea of the eternal or universal offers a comfortable way of explaining the world and justifying the current order. Sometimes people describe as eternal and universal things that are quite evidently variable. This is certainly the case in some explanations of sex differences.

Theology and biology have often been called on to explain and justify the differences in the amounts and types of power held by men and women. Although theories of sex role differences that call on biology or theology do not necessarily justify inequity or pose static views of women and men, those that have done precisely this have been among the most influential and historically persistent. These frameworks are based on certain conceptions of eternal truths or principles of human existence stemming from God or nature. These principles seem to dictate that the sexes must be unequal in their earthly existence and that women must be ruled or at least led and guided by men. Although these static theories are less widely held than they once were, they have by no means been totally abandoned.

Women's Biological Nature

The first influential theorist who used biological knowledge of women and men to explain the sociopolitical differences between women and men was the Greek philosopher Aristotle (384–322 B.C.). Using the biological knowledge of his day, Aristotle claimed that the main difference between the sexes was that women are more passive. Because of their passivity and weakness, he argued, women may be regarded as a deformity, although a natural one.

Aristotle and many later theorists found evidence of women's passivity in two aspects of procreation. First they maintained that men are more active in sexual relations. Many sociobiologists writing today still see women as less active in courtship and sexual behavior and draw from this the conclusion that women are in general less active and more passive than men. (Some even suggest that the fact that men are more likely to rape than women shows the ultimate truth of the stance that women are more passive and, therefore, socially subordinate.) More importantly, Aristotle believed that the man was the active principle in procreation itself, that the male sperm created a baby out of the female material in a woman's body, much as a candlestick maker forms a candlestick out of the impassive brass. Later sociobiologists derived their conception of female passivity from different misinformation, such as the idea that sperm fight their way upstream like so many (female) salmon and then compete with each other in a mad rush to conquer the demure, stationary egg.[1] The concept of natural passivity, however derived, has generally been one of the cornerstone arguments for explaining and justifying the inequality of males and females.

43

Chapter 2:
Some Competing
Explanations:
How Did Society
Get This Way?

How do these "facts" of biological passivity become translated into theories of the development of female inferiority, dependence, and submission? Most of the theorists who have dealt with the problem argue that leadership depends on (or should depend on) strength and activity of both mind and body. These same theorists have argued that women fail on both counts. One of the most striking aspects of the history of debate over the nature of women is that although both the methods and the findings of biological science have changed drastically from Aristotle's time to ours, the conclusions that people base on biological science have remained largely the same for most of that time. Those conclusions are that women and men are not only naturally different but also naturally unequal (Bleier 1984). Many influential thinkers are undaunted when they find that they have been wrong in the past. Aristotle's understanding of the natural facts of life has long since been rejected, but his sociological and political conclusions based on those "facts" remain popular in some circles.

Theorists have searched for many biological explanations for what they regard as women's weakness, especially of mind. Menstruation has often been identified as the source. People once thought that women's periodic cycles indicated that they were unduly influenced by the moon, which causes craziness or *lunacy*, a word derived from the Latin word for moon. Later people argued that menstruation sapped the strength of women, leaving them weak. Many people now accept the "raging hormones" explanation of women's supposed instability and mental weakness. Women's wombs have also been defined as the cause of their weakness. For a long time people believed that the womb emitted vapors that caused instability. Others believed that the womb traveled around the body, sometimes causing women to faint. The word *hysteria* is derived from the Latin word for womb. The conclusion is obvious: If women are lunatic and hysterical, they are certainly not fit to take care of themselves, let alone others. (So why are women entrusted with the care of children?) These and other views of menstruation will be discussed more fully in Chapter 5.

Biological arguments about the inevitability of inequality have become somewhat more sophisticated over the centuries. By the eighteenth century, some writers were beginning to admit that the "natural differences" between the sexes did not necessarily make it impossible for women to act as men's equals. But they claimed that women's nature made it necessary for men to rule women for their own mutual good. The argument of necessary inequality began to focus much more on reproduction. Because of women's weakness, particularly during pregnancy and childbirth, women need a protector to watch over and act for them. This idea of women's natural need for protection has been used by governments to justify not only what is known as "protective labor legislation" (which we shall examine more closely in Chapter 5) but also many restrictions on women's activities. In 1873, for example, a Supreme Court justice used the following argument to explain why a woman should not be allowed to practice law, even if she was qualified to do so (*Myra Bradwell* v. *State of Illinois*): "Civil law, *as well as nature herself,* has always recognized a wide difference in the respective spheres and destinies of man and woman. Man is, or should be,

Caution. Dangerous Equipment. Do Not Use with Raging Hormones.

woman's protector and defender" (emphasis added). As we shall see in Chapter 8, until recently most of the treatment of women by the legal system was based on the idea of man as woman's natural protector and, therefore, ruler.

These are far from the only biologically based explanations of power and status differences between the sexes. We shall encounter others in Chapter 5. What we have looked at here are static theories. They share some common characteristics worth noting. Whether they argue that woman is naturally weak or passive or that she has a natural need for protection by men, they offer an unchanging view of the structure of relations between the sexes. They point to certain "eternal" and "universal" characteristics of women that do not admit the possibility of equality or the possibility that the differences between men and women can be the result of anything but biological nature. These theories are useless in any real attempts to understand either well-documented historical changes in relations between the sexes or possible future variation and change. Without arguing that biology has changed dramatically during recorded history or varies from culture to culture, these theories cannot possibly account for the fact that the structure of relations between the sexes has been variable.

It is important to note that biological theory need not be, and often is not, static in its understanding of women. We shall see one alternative posed by evolutionary theory. Biological research has also been used to underscore the malleability or flexibility of human life. But here we have begun with the tradition of biological thinking that has been predominant in intellectual history.

45

Chapter 2:
Some Competing
Explanations:
How Did Society
Get This Way?

Women's God-given Nature

Many theological interpretations of women's nature have also provided static explanations for sexual inequality. Within the Judeo-Christian tradition, the stories of creation and the expulsion from the Garden of Eden have served as the basis for ethical systems arguing for a God-given moral necessity of inequality and especially for women's submission to men. God the Father created women second, we are told, to be a helpmeet to her husband. The influential Italian theologian St. Thomas Aquinas (1225–74) argued that God had a very specific type of helper in mind. "It was necessary for women to be made, as the Scripture says, as a helper to man; not indeed as a helpmate in other works, as some say, since man can be more efficiently helped by another man in other works; but as a helper in the work of generation . . ." (1945, 880). Aquinas accepted Aristotle's idea that women were a deformity, but one that could be turned to good. He argued that women should be submissive to men because men had greater quantities of the active principle of reason. Women were created for the purpose of having babies so that men could carry on with God's work. In the order of life on earth, men are answerable to God, and women are answerable to men.

Another biblical "event" has also been used to prove the need for female submission: Eve eats fruit from the forbidden tree of knowledge. Genesis 3:16 states: "Unto the woman (God) said, I will greatly multiply thy sorrow and thy conception; in sorrow thou shall bring forth children; and thy desire shall be to thy husband, and he shall rule over thee." There have been some differences of interpretation of these words within Christianity and Judaism, but the most common interpretations include these arguments:

1. Eve's actions revealed women's moral weakness.
2. Adam's own weakness in accepting the fruit showed that women are dangerous temptresses who must be controlled if men are to be morally strong.
3. God ordained that there must be a division of labor by which women bear children (in sorrow and pain) and men produce the means of existence (by the sweat of their brow).
4. Men shall rule over women.

It is important to note that the theological explanation appears to admit of more possibility for variation in human life than the crudest of the biological theories. It is possible for human beings not to follow some aspects of the divine order, just as it is possible for humans to violate most other divine laws. But, of course, the consequences of choosing to act against God's will are dire. (In Chapter 6 we will look more closely at the role of religion in structuring women's lives.)

The traditions of biological and theological thinking described here suggest that it is very dangerous to attempt to change the relative conditions of men and women, because that would require violating the laws of God or nature. As we shall see later, these are not the only explanations that have been offered by scientists and theologians. Calling on God or nature to understand the structure and history of relations between the sexes by no means necessitates taking either a static view or one that justifies inequality. Unfortunately, however, these have been the dominant views not just of the ancients, but also of many contemporary leaders. As recently as 1972, for example, Senator Sam Ervin opposed passage of the Equal Rights Amendment on the grounds that, "when He created them, God made physiological and functional differences between men and women" (Sayers 1982, 70).

Enlightenment Theory: Inevitable Progress

The eighteenth century witnessed the formulation of a new set of theories based on liberal or Enlightenment philosophy, and these theories continue to be a widely accepted basis for understanding social relations in the West, particularly the United States. This new approach to thinking about society, which formed part of the basis for both the American and French Revolutions, began as an assault on the old order of power relations in society and government. It was quickly adopted by a number of early feminists as a means of understanding and criticizing inequalities between the sexes.

Foundations of Liberalism

The liberal argument introduced by people like John Locke (1672–1704) and Jean-Jacques Rousseau (1712–78) opposed what was identified as a patriarchal order of power and social relations. *Patriarchy* means "rule of" (*arch*) "fathers" (*patri*). The original critics of the patriarchal order were not, however, focusing on the family as such; the task of criticizing that patriarchal order was left until later. They were thinking about the basis of rule by monarchs and the privileges of the aristocratic class of men over other men in society. The logic of the patriarchal order was right, privilege, and power by birth. There were a number of different patriarchal views of society, but a good example is Jean Bodin's (1530–96) observation that

> a family is like a state: there can be but one ruler, one master, one lord. A father...is the true image of God, our sovereign Lord, the Father of all things....A father is obliged by nature to support his children while they are still weak and helpless, and to bring them up in honorable and virtuous ways. On the other hand, a child is obliged...to love, revere, serve, and support his father; to execute his commands in loyal obedience; to shield his infirmities; and never to spare his own life or property in order to save the life of him to whom he owes his own... (Jones 1963, 561).

The monarch and relations within the realm were analogous to the father and relationships within the family. Some writers went even further. Robert Filmer (1588–1653) argued in his *Patriarcha* that royal authority is not only analogous to but also derived from the power God gave to fathers over the family. Kings, he claimed, derived their power through inheritance of the power The Father gave to the first father: Adam.

The attack the liberals launched against this conception of sociopolitical order is exemplified in the lines from the Declaration of Independence that schoolchildren are still taught to memorize as a sort of secular catechism: "We hold these truths to be self-evident: that all men are created equal, that they are endowed by their Creator with certain inalienable rights, that among these are life, liberty, and the pursuit of happiness."

What was so new and revolutionary about this view? First and foremost it rejected the idea that only monarchs or certain classes of people were "endowed by their Creator" with rights and power. It argued that each individual (white) man (for at first this was not applied to women or, for that matter, to men who were not white) had an equal birthright of basic or natural rights. These rights were "inalienable"; that is, in place of the patriarchal notion that all rights stem from or are granted by the sovereign or king, Enlightenment theorists argued that individuals had certain autonomous rights that could not be taken away from them. The idea of the autonomy and independence of individuals was critical; people did not, as Bodin had claimed, owe their lives to other people because of some condition of birth.

It did not take long for some people to extend these principles to cover the situation of women. The first person to undertake this task in a comprehensive way was Mary Wollstonecraft (1759–97). In 1790 Wollstonecraft wrote *A Vindication of the Rights of Men,* an answer to Edmund Burke's conservative attack on liberal principles and the French Revolution. Two years later Wollstonecraft published her important treatise, *A Vindication of the Rights of Woman,* which applied the same principles to relations between men and women. Here she argued that autocratic and patriarchal power relations between the sexes were as unjust and indefensible as those between monarch and subject. Much of the best-known and most influential feminist ideas on women's status, particularly in the United States and Western Europe, have been based solidly on this liberal tradition.

Liberalism and Women

The liberal approach to explaining women's status is based on the notions of liberty, independence, and the natural rights of the individual, and the importance of reason in human development. Like men, women are born free and equal. They are not, and should not be, limited by conditions of birth; they have virtually limitless potential for improvement and even perfection. This possibility of perfection is available to men and women only if they are allowed to develop and use their faculties of reason. People must be free from artificial constraints on their lives in order to be able to use their reason to discover what is good for them.

How do liberals explain the difference in status and roles of women and men? One of the most complete liberal discussions of this problem was written by John Stuart Mill (1806–73) in his 1869 *Subjection of Women* (reprinted in Rossi, 1970, 1988). He argued that the system of subjection of women, like the subjection of slaves to masters or people to an autocratic king, was the result of the artificial constraints

47

Chapter 2:
Some Competing
Explanations:
How Did Society
Get This Way?

of law and social institutions that stem from people's irrational prejudices. If women appear very different from and inferior to men, it is because they have been made that way by social forces instituted by human beings who did not know any better. Such a system of inequity, the liberals claim, is harmful to both men and women, indeed to society as a whole. Women are harmed because their rights are taken from them and they are denied the opportunity to develop reason and thus improve themselves. Men are harmed because, like kings and slave masters, they have been corrupted by holding excessive power over others. Society as a whole is harmed because inequities and the lack of freedom within it makes the entire society unjust and undemocratic. Human progress as a whole is retarded by the lack of freedom of some of its members and the power some hold over others. Mill claimed that the right of men over women was the last bastion of the bygone and unenlightened days when "might was right."

To the liberal, the key to social change is the development of reason and the stripping away of blinding prejudices: the enlightenment of individuals. The immediate change that liberal feminists began to demand was education, the primary instrument of self-improvement. The next struggles involved the tearing down of barriers that kept from women the freedom to develop themselves as individuals, including laws that barred women from doing certain kinds of jobs, voting, or, if they were married, holding their own property.

In the long run, however, liberals argue that human progress depends on society as a whole becoming more enlightened, thinking more rationally, and therefore becoming more rational. Liberal feminists still regard education and the development of reason among individuals as the primary key to change. Human history is seen by the Enlightenment thinker as a progression toward increased use of reason and science as the bases of legal and social institutions. People have become more enlightened from one age to the next, which has led them to cast off old social and ideological chains, which in turn has provided the opportunity for even more improvement in understanding how people and society work and, therefore, how they can be improved.

Its emphases on creating equal rights with men within the existing social framework and on learning or socialization as both the reason for existing sex differences and the key to change are the hallmarks of the liberal tradition. Liberals sometimes dismiss the ills of the past as irrelevant by arguing that people in the past simply did not know as much as we do now; past problems were caused by human stupidity and prejudice. The situation is better today because we are more enlightened and therefore leave people freer to develop to their full potential. In political strategy liberalism focuses on identifying and adjusting the laws and policies that seem to keep people from being free. The optimistic liberal view is that the future will naturally be even better than today as we learn and progress.

Although widely accepted today, this perspective has some problems. As a theory of history it is very weak; indeed some would argue that it offers no theory of historical changes at all. Human history has not been a matter of slow and steady progress from less enlightened to more enlightened ages. The history of women and women's status offers many examples of this. Historians and anthropologists alike note that political and economic development, both in the United States and elsewhere, has often been marked by increased gaps between women's and men's status, at least at the early stages of change. In the United States, women became increasingly restricted at the beginning of the nineteenth century. (Some examples of this growing gap can be found in Chapters 11 and 12.) A similar phenomenon is noted immediately following World War II, when the idea of women's "proper" role at home was reestablished with renewed vigor. Students of African society and history have found that in many places the sexes became more unequal and the power of women was decreased by the impact of "enlightened" Western law and custom (e.g., Hafkin and Bay 1976).

49

Chapter 2:
Some Competing
Explanations:
How Did Society
Get This Way?

Liberal theory gives us little idea of what conditions cause changes in the roles and status of women. It gives no hints of what creates movements for change other than a vague notion that some enlightened (or unenlightened) people become active and push for change. It suggests no reasons why cultures differ in the arrangements of relations between the sexes, except for a vague notion that people in different cultures somehow have different ideas about what is right and proper. It suggests that all we have to do to achieve changes in the status of women is change people's minds, or "resocialize" them. As we shall see, the matter is not as simple as that.

Finally, although the optimism of liberalism has spurred many people to action, it can also breed a kind of complacency. If we expect human beings to progress merely because we become "smarter" about ourselves as we gain experience in the world, we have little reason to do anything about the status of women other than go about the business of improving ourselves as individuals. It is interesting to see how often just this argument has been launched against feminism over the past century. It seems that each generation feels that the battles for equality have been won and that the only thing that holds women back is women's own lack of initiative. Unfortunately good works by single individuals have rarely enabled any subordinate social group to achieve changes toward equality and liberty.[2]

Economic and Historical Materialist Theories

By the middle of the nineteenth century numerous observers of social life were beginning to question the liberal understanding of social relations, history, and change. This critique of liberalism was not a conservative one (although conservative critiques also existed); these critics argued that liberalism did not offer an adequate understanding of how history and society worked and therefore could not offer a workable solution to the ills that plague society. The most famous of these critics and theorists were Karl Marx (1818–83) and Friedrich Engels (1820–95).

Foundations of Marxism

The differences between the Marxist, or historical-materialist, analysis of society and the liberal, or Enlightenment, analysis can be approached through Marx and Engels's well-known assertion in *The German Ideology* (1845–46) that "the first premise of all human history is, of course, the existence of living human individuals" (Marx and Engels 1947, 7). This sentence may not appear terribly remarkable at first, but the conclusions Marx and Engels drew from it make all the difference in the analytical world. The two theorists suggested that people may well argue that human beings "can be distinguished from animals by consciousness, by religion or anything else you like" (7), but the first fact of human life is their physical existence and sustenance. "Life involves before everything else eating and drinking, a habitation, clothing and many other things" (16). The key to seeing the impact of these ideas is to understand that "before everything else" refers not just to the historical fact that human beings learned to feed and clothe themselves before they learned to read and write, but also to the idea that the maintenance of life is more primary in human life than the aspects of consciousness we generally identify as distinguishing human beings from other animals.

Marxists argue that consciousness, thought, language, religion, law, and other such manifestations of the human mind flow from and are shaped by material needs and the social and institutional arrangements, the economic production, through which people satisfy these needs. Language and the ideas it expresses are developed to help fulfill these needs and experiences of day-to-day life. Thus those who control the means of production to a large degree also control ideas and language. Dominant thought systems (religion, theory, and so forth) are ideological; that is, they reflect the interests of those in power and justify the economic, social, and political arrangements by which that power is maintained.

To the Marxist, the history of the world is "the history of class struggle." Divisions of labor within the economy do not simply mean that different people do different jobs. Within the divisions of labor that have developed under feudalism and later under capitalism, those in control of the means of production also control the products and the labor of those who actually make them.

The labor power and therefore the laborer are exploited by the capitalist in the sense that it is in the capitalist's interest to get as much production out of the worker for as little money as possible. It is in the worker's interest as well to get as much money for as little work as possible, but the struggle between the two is far from an even match since the capitalists control the material means of living and production and the ideology of society.

The only way the struggle will be ended and the people will retrieve control over their own labor, life situations, and consciousness, is by destroying the capitalist system and putting in its place a system in which no single individual or class can own the means of production: communism, or common ownership. Only by substantially rearranging economic institutions can political and social values and structures be truly altered. Any other action may change the group that has control but will not alter the fact that one group has control over others.

Marxism and Women

How is this theory related to understanding the condition of women? Let us begin with the classical Marxist formulation and then move to some conclusions that have been more widely accepted. The earliest exposition of a Marxist analysis can be found in Friedrich Engels' *Origins of the Family, Private Property, and the State* ([1884] 1972) and somewhat later, in August Bebel's *Women and Socialism* ([1910]

1970). Marx and Engels suggest that in subsistence economies, in which all individuals participate in the production process and provide for themselves with no significant amount of surplus, men and women are fairly equal because they have equal control over their labor and over the products of their labor. The subservience of women began with the development of private property. As people began to find more efficient ways of producing, they were able to produce more than they needed for immediate consumption; they created a surplus, which had value in that it could be exchanged for other products. Because men were the producers of goods with exchange value (a situation not fully explained by Marxist theorists), men controlled and owned both the means of production and the surplus products themselves, which is, according to Marxist analysis, the key to power in exchange economies. Marx and Engels argued, therefore, that the division of labor between men and women in the family paralleled the division in the larger society into capitalist and proletariat classes.

With the invention of private property, men came to feel that they needed to pass their property on to their own children (again, for reasons not entirely explained). Because of the nature of reproduction, the only way for men to ensure this was to control women in monogamous (at least for the woman) marriages. Women then became subservient to men, and their labor power and the products of their labor were now at their husbands' disposal. The primary locus of the exploitative division

51

Chapter 2:
Some Competing
Explanations:
How Did Society
Get This Way?

Patriarchy begins at home.

of labor between the sexes is found in the family and is caused by, or at least related to, the structure of economic and other power relations outside the family. In other words, the institution of private property and the means by which it is created is the cause of gender stratification.

Although more recent historical and anthropological research contradicts the details presented by Engels, several points that flow from this and other Marxist analyses are widely accepted by Marxist and non-Marxist historians and anthropologists alike.

1. The divisions of labor and power between men and women, especially the relative value placed on men's and women's work, does seem to depend at least in part on the structure of the economy as a whole. As noted earlier the development of industrialization and the shift to a fully capitalist economy seem to be marked by an increasing gap between the power and value of men and women. It makes sense to talk about being ''just a housewife''—a phrase of relatively recent vintage—only if the labor that occurs in the home is not seen as central and valuable to the economy. Although there are still many arguments about the exact relationship between the general economic structure and the structure of relationships between the sexes, this is one of the important elements in women's studies research.

2. The structure of power within one social institution is not independent of the structure of power in other social institutions. Although this observation is also raised by other types of theories, the materialist analysis focuses our attention on economic questions, especially division of labor and control over production and value. One of the most important ways in which this observation has been used in women's studies research is to focus on the relationship between the division of labor inside and outside the family and to point to divisions of labor within the family as the source of inequities outside the family. The jobs that are viewed as particularly appropriate for women to hold are those that seem most to resemble the tasks that women are supposed to undertake in the family. Even people who claim to desire equality for women in the marketplace tend to feel that women can seek employment only if their children are already taken care of. We do not ask the same of men. The underlying assumption, of course, is that children and the care of the home is the woman's, not the man's, responsibility. Above all, however, it appears that legal changes, such as nondiscrimination laws, are helpful but have little effect on some of the more primary inequities in the family, which are important bases of women's opportunities and roles outside the family. The best that laws seem to do is give women the opportunity to take on a double burden of labor inside and outside the home.

3. *Division of labor* can mean much more than simply different people doing different types of work. It can also mean division of power and control. Consider the division of labor in marriage. In the traditional arrangement (reinforced by law), men are supposed to seek employment to support the family, while women are supposed to do most of the labor required for family upkeep. At one level this may appear to be merely a functional and efficient system, not to mention (as some people would) a particularly nice one for women because they get to devote their time to caring for the people they love while men are out working in

competitive, alienating jobs. If we look at it another way, however, this is by no means a system of cooperation between equals. The man is designated the "head of the household." Can there be equality among a group of people when only one is designated as the "head" of the group? In effect the husband is the woman's employer. She is entitled to support from her husband not because of anything having to do with love but because she does the work at home that he might otherwise have to do, or pay for.

53

Chapter 2:
Some Competing
Explanations:
How Did Society
Get This Way?

Compare the following situations: In one case a married couple is living together, but no longer particularly love each other. The woman, however, continues to cook the meals, wash the clothes, and so forth. In the other case a married couple love each other, but when the man comes home from work he finds that none of the household jobs have ever been done, and he has to do them himself. Which wife would seem to be more entitled to support from her husband?

4. Ideological definitions of women and women's roles more often than not flow from institutional arrangements of divisions of power and labor and from the concrete, material aspects of life. If we look at some of the changes in ideology that have occurred during American history, we can see how this works. Historians have noted that the belief in the joys of pregnancy and the cult of young motherhood developed in the United States only after the facts of reproductive life had improved considerably. In the colonial era, for example, when one out of five reproductively active women died as a result of childbirth and many babies did not survive past one year, what women were taught about pregnancy and motherhood had a lot more to do with resignation to possible death than with the joys of motherhood.

People are sometimes startled to realize how recent are our supposedly traditional ideologies of womanhood. In the early nineteenth century "productive labor" (and with it, men) moved increasingly out of the home and an ideological framework developed that historian Barbara Welter (1966) has called the "cult of true womanhood." Women began to be viewed as delicate, frail, asexual, and the keepers of the home fires to which men could return after a harrowing day in the world. Such an ideology would not make sense if it was necessary for women to toil together with men. In fact this ideology was applied only to specific classes of women. Slaveholders in the South had no such view about the black women they owned, for example, and Boston Brahmins hardly worried about the femininity and delicacy of their Irish maids.

More recent examples underscore the point that ideology often flows from institutional and social arrangements rather than the reverse. Freudian psychoanalysis became very popular in the 1950s as an explanation of why a population of women who were increasingly educated and had experienced employment should feel happy staying at home making babies. During World War II, the figure of "Rosie the Riveter" had been used to convince women that working in armaments factories was important and appropriate (feminine) for women. After the war a new construction of ideas was necessary to convince women to repopulate the country and give the jobs back to men. Ideas about women's roles began to change again later, as the structure of the economy changed and masses of new auxiliary jobs (such as clerical work) opened up, education expanded dramatically, and more workers were needed in the "helping professions" such as nursing and social work.

Marxism, Women, and Change

How can we use the Marxist perspective to understand social change? A wide variety of conclusions can be drawn from Marxist theory and from theories that have been influenced by Marxist analysis. The most orthodox Marxist position may be found in works like Bebel's *Women and Socialism* ([1910], 1970), which argues that the condition of women, like other inequities and forms of oppression within society, has its source in the class system—the structure of property ownership, particularly of the means of production—found in capitalist societies. Many orthodox Marxists argue that women are oppressed in this system because they make possible men's labor from one day to the next by feeding, clothing, and caring for them and they constitute a marginal labor force that can be brought into the labor market and thrown out according to the needs of the system. The situation during and after World War II is an example of this.

Thus the orthodox Marxist position holds that the liberation of women can come only when working-class women participate with men in the overthrow of the capitalist economic structure that causes their oppression. Any separate feminist movement is seen as a diversion from the true course to liberation. Most feminist writers, including those who employ Marxist analysis, now reject this argument primarily because they see aspects of women's condition that cannot be explained solely by the existence of personal property and a capitalist class structure.

What many feminists have found particularly useful in Marxist analyses of change are the concepts of consciousness and ideology.[3] Materialists argue that our social relationships and ideas about ourselves reflect and justify the social arrangements and institutions that exist, and especially the power relations within them. In short, ideologies support the power of the powerful. Dominant ideas of what is natural for women and what women "want" change over time, but they support existing arrangements and shape our perceptions of people and events. For example, when we look at experimental research on perceptions of women in Chapter 9, we will see that many people, including women, view a woman as less qualified than a man for a "masculine" job even when they are equally qualified (Deaux 1976). Psychological research shows that these ideological constructions of men and women affect not just how men perceive and treat women but also how women perceive and treat themselves, both as a group and as individuals.

How can change occur? Here is where consciousness becomes important. At certain times in history some portion of a subordinate group (in this case women) becomes conscious of their situation; in a sense, they begin not only to live according to the ideology but also to see the workings of the ideology itself and the contradictions in their situation. For example, in the current wave of feminism women see through the claim that men and women are equal in society to the fact that women are not treated equally with men. An important part of this consciousness is women's understanding that they are affected as a group rather than as individuals; that is, they notice that some problems are not individually unique but seem to stem from the fact that they are women and that women share certain problems. This type of group consciousness makes a considerable difference in how we formulate strategies for change.

Consider the masses of women across the country in recent decades who never thought they would have to earn a living but found, because of widowhood, divorce, or the recession, that they had to seek employment to support themselves and their families. We can imagine millions of women who blame themselves for their inadequate abilities to earn money and say, ''I don't have sufficient skills,'' ''I didn't get enough training,'' or ''I dropped out of school to support my husband and to have children.'' On the other hand group consciousness could lead such women to see that the fault is not theirs alone but is common to women because education and training are not considered to be as important for women as for men and because women are encouraged to get married and have babies at a young age and drop out of school if necessary. Women without a group consciousness simply regret their ''fault'' and do whatever they can as individuals to better themselves. When the system is rigged against them, such solutions are doomed to failure. Women with a group consciousness work to change the situation of women as a group.

55

Chapter 2:
Some Competing
Explanations:
How Did Society
Get This Way?

Functionalist and Evolutionary Theories

The nineteenth century saw the development of a second influential set of explanations for the development of societal sex differentiation and stratification: functionalist/evolutionary theories. These explanations, which grew out of the work of people like Charles Darwin (1809–82) and Herbert Spencer (1820–1903), used the new approaches of evolutionary biology to understand both the physiological and the social history of human life. Most, although by no means all, of the theorists who have used evolutionary perspectives to explain the situation of women have concluded that both differentiation and stratification are inevitable, or at least desirable, if human life is to progress. This type of functionalist/evolutionary theory is often called social Darwinism, although Darwin himself did not subscribe to it.

Foundations of Functionalist/Evolutionary Thought

Herbert Spencer believed that human society evolves through physiological adaptation to its surroundings and that any change that occurs through evolution is good: Nature is always progressive. The mechanism by which this progress is achieved is based on the principle of ''survival of the fittest'': Those who are best adapted to the needs of human life will survive and reproduce their characteristics, and those who are not will not survive. As human beings discover the social arrangements that are most functional, that is, that contribute most to their ability to survive, they will also develop the characteristics best fitted to these arrangements.

Human beings are under constant pressure to produce enough to feed themselves and take care of their other physical needs. Following the thought of Robert Malthus (1766–1834), Spencer argued that as we become more successful at taking care of our subsistence needs, our population will increase at a faster rate. This will cause us to perfect our means of production even more, and so on. At each stage the unfit will drop out of the picture. Along with many economists Spencer believed that the hallmark of progress in human life is the division of labor into specialized functions. Just as division of labor in industry makes production more efficient, so division of labor between the sexes makes human society as a whole more efficient.

The most important division of labor of all in human life is that between men and women. According to the early versions of evolutionary theory, as human life progresses, women become increasingly relieved of the burden of breadwinning and increasingly fitted to the exclusive tasks of childbearing and taking care of the home. The higher the level of society, the more differentiated women and men are. Evolutionary theorists thought they could see these biological principles working even within societies. Some noted that there was less differentiation between the sexes in the lower orders of society, by which they meant the working class, immigrants, and the poor. This only went to show, they said, that the more evolved people are, the more distinct men and women are. Of course to accept this argument we also have to accept the idea that people in different classes or societies are on different rungs of the evolutionary ladder, that they are biologically different. Many people did just that, and social Darwinism became an important justification of racism, class exploitation, and imperialism.

Spencer argued that the sexes are not merely different but also necessarily unequal. Women have become increasingly well fitted to domestic duties, but have had no need to become fit for anything else. Only men have evolved the characteristics necessary for other aspects of social, economic, and political life. Since it appears that men continue to evolve while women do not, men must dominate women and reinforce their inequalities if society is to continue to progress.

A century ago many people used evolutionary/functionalist theory to argue that women should not be allowed to vote. Many people continue to use the same argument to show why women and men should not be allowed equality in other areas. Although many evolutionary theorists have claimed to trust evolution to move society in the direction of progress, they also seem to feel that only men know what that direction is.

Early Feminist Critiques

Evolutionary theory was called to action by some observers of the division of labor between the sexes who came to very different and more feminist conclusions. Antoinette Brown Blackwell (1825–1921) was an American feminist who began her career as a theologian and whose best-known work was a response to the writing of Darwin and Spencer. Her book, *The Sexes Throughout Nature*, written in 1875, is a fascinating early discussion of bias in scientific research (for extensive excerpts from the text, see Rossi 1988). She did not question the idea of evolution as the basis of human development, nor did she question the conclusion that the division of labor between the sexes was caused by evolution or that men's and women's personalities and abilities had evolved to be very different. In this way she stands apart from most contemporary critics of evolutionary theories of sex differences. What she did

Spencer's biological arguments did not appear to apply to pioneer women.

object to were the conclusions the social Darwinists had drawn from those arguments. In a sense she took the arguments of evolution and functionalism more seriously with regard to men and women than many of the more conservative writers did.

Blackwell agreed that the sexes had developed different characteristics over time, but she argued that this did not mean that the sexes were unequal but that they were complementary; men and women constituted two balanced halves of the whole of humanity. Far from concluding that sex differentiation should mean that men should restrict women or that women were unfit to do anything but take care of children and the home, she felt that it would be dysfunctional—contrary to the proper functioning of society—to exclude women from public life. Whereas men could contribute necessary force and rationality to society, women could contribute necessary gentleness and spirituality. This view agreed with that of other evolutionists that evolution is a natural movement toward improvement of the human race as a whole. Using the principles of evolution, therefore, Blackwell reached exactly the opposite conclusion from Spencer's. Women, she said, must be freed as much as possible to make their own special contribution to human society.

A similar argument was made by many proponents of women's suffrage, such as Jane Addams (see, e.g., the selection in Rossi 1988), who thought that if women took a full role in politics, the addition of their propensity for nurturance and their skills as housekeepers would upgrade the quality of politics and political decisions. Many people now make the same point when they suggest that having more women in positions of authority will improve society.

The sociologist Charlotte Perkins Gilman (1868–1935) offered quite a different feminist interpretation of functional/evolutionary theory. She also thought that divisions of labor between the sexes had developed through the struggle of human beings to survive. At one time, when human life required both grueling labor for production and nearly constant attempts to reproduce simply to replace the current population, a relatively strict division of labor made sense. But, she argued, the changes that had taken place in society now meant that divisions of labor as they had existed were no longer functional. In industrialized societies, work depended decreasingly on physical force and increasingly on intellectual and technical skills. Women did not need to become pregnant as often as they once did to ensure survival of the race. In her view, human beings had become "oversexed," by which she meant that they were exaggerating and overemphasizing differences between the sexes in a way that was becoming dangerous to the preservation and improvement of the human race.

Gilman thought that by their attempts to hold women back men could only hold themselves back as well. Human society was wasting half its brain power and turning the female half of society into useless parasites living off the work of others. Better, Gilman said, to advance useful divisions of labor based on skill, training, and efficiency and to do away with harmful ones such as those based on sex. She thought that rather than having all women do cooking, cleaning, and child care in their individual homes whether they were good at these things or not, such tasks should be done cooperatively by trained specialists outside the home whenever possible.

The Debate Today

59

Chapter 2:
Some Competing
Explanations:
How Did Society
Get This Way?

Debates over the role of evolution in the development of sexual differentiation and stratification continue today. One of the most influential themes among anthropologists and sociologists is "man the hunter." Although there are variations on this theme, the basic idea is that in primitive times social arrangements between the sexes developed into a functional division of labor between men the hunters and women the gatherers and nurturers, and that our social arrangements since that time have continued to diverge from that original division. Encumbered by pregnancies and children women could not travel far and in any case did not have the strength to engage in the hunt. Although women contributed considerably more than men to daily subsistence—some estimates suggest that at least 80 percent of the food consumed was the result of women's labor—men gained dominance and control in society as their hunting bands were transformed into warring bands and, ultimately, into governments. Sociobiologists such as E. O. Wilson (1975) claim that male dominance and divisions of labor have been reinforced by genetic differences through the evolution process. Sociobiologists disagree about how much equality is possible in the future, but almost all are deeply skeptical about the possibility of full equality.

Criticisms of sociobiological theories based on evolution stand on a number of points:

1. Recent research calls into question some of the assumptions often made about hunting and gathering societies. Female gatherers apparently traveled long distances to accomplish their tasks. Moreover, the division of labor was not always as rigid as many theories suggest; in some hunter-gatherer societies men participated in what we now think of as domestic tasks.
2. Sociobiologists tend to select examples to suit their arguments, examples ranging from the most primitive times to modern, postindustrial societies, without any careful historical analysis.
3. Sociobiologists often seem to confuse human evolution (changes in the physiological structure of the species) with human history (changes in culture, social structure, and human events). Some sociobiologists even seem to accept the Lamarckian position that characteristics acquired during a person's life are passed on to that person's children through biological mechanisms.[4] Although social structures and culture have changed during recorded history and even during living memory, there is little, if any, evidence that relevant physiological and genetic characteristics have changed in significant ways during that time.
4. Even if sexual divisions of labor and dominance were once functional, we must still ask Charlotte Perkins Gilman's question whether these divisions are still functional or should be erased for better adaptation to our needs at this point in history.

Current biological research offers little support for the thesis that men and women have evolved into creatures that are well suited for the divisions of labor and dominance we see in society. Although all known societies are marked by some division of labor between the sexes, the exact content of that division varies from one culture to another. On almost any personality or psychological test devised, most men and women reveal the same range of traits or characteristics. Biological science has failed to establish direct links between physiological characteristics and social roles and arrangements. If these divisions are natural, it is difficult to understand why people have had to work so hard to enforce and maintain them. It is more likely that if women and men were left truly free to develop their abilities, their roles would look different from the destiny mapped out for them by most evolutionary functionalists.

Sex War: The Struggle for Dominance

Generally when one nation or class or people dominates another, we can reasonably assume that this situation was brought about and is maintained through competition and force. At first glance men and women seem to pose the major exception to this rule. The very idea of a battle between the sexes is greeted either by laughter (perhaps nervous) or anger and anxiety by most people. It is unthinkable that men and women have opposing interests that lead them to struggle for power and dominance. After all, if men and women were at war, they certainly wouldn't choose to live with each other, would they?

The idea of a primeval struggle through which men have asserted their dominance over women is more deeply embedded in our ideas than we might at first think. Recall the story of the Medusa, discussed earlier, in which man must struggle to overcome woman or women's evil. A similar theme occurs in numerous myths and stories, such as the Greek myth of the Sirens, in which dangerous women drive sailors to self-destruction; the story of Eve, in which Eve seduces Adam from grace; and the Mozart opera, *The Magic Flute,* in which the deceptive Queen of the Night is overcome by male rationality.[5] Many cultures have myths of an originally powerful goddess—the Mother Goddess—who was overthrown by men or a male god, who thereby put the world in proper order. Marx and Engels and numerous later theorists argued that there must have been a struggle for men to win control over women and property.

In fact many theorists have suggested that the current power relations between the sexes are the result of a war between the sexes that women so far have lost. Some theorists see a struggle that is derived from conflicts of interest in the roles and personalities of women and men, and some point directly to sexuality as the battleground. It is important to note that these views have been held in different forms by both feminists and antifeminists. We shall look briefly at both versions.

Freud and the War between the Sexes

It is no coincidence that the founder of modern psychoanalysis, Sigmund Freud (1856–1939), was one of the first writers to make mutual antagonism an important element of a theory of relations between the sexes. Whatever else may be said about

Freud, he did not shrink from speaking about what was, at least at that time, unspeakable. Sigmund Freud is most often thought of with respect to his theories of individual development, and psychoanalysis in general is used primarily to talk about individuals. (In Chapter 3 we will look at psychoanalytic theories of individual gender development.) But Freud's work, and psychoanalysis more generally, has also been used to examine social change and historical development. In this chapter we consider Freud's story of the battle between the sexes, which may be found in its most complete form in his essay, "Femininity" ([1933] 1965) and in *Civilization and Its Discontents* ([1930] 1961).[6]

61

Chapter 2:
Some Competing
Explanations:
How Did Society
Get This Way?

According to Freud, the trauma of a girl's life is the discovery that she is not male, that she has no penis. (Some recent feminists accept the outline of this argument but interpret the discovery symbolically. To them the penis, or phallus, is simply the symbol of male power, which women lack.) This causes her to grow hostile to her mother, who made her deficient like the mother herself, and to attach herself first to her father and later to potential fathers. She also develops the need to acquire the missing penis, at least symbolically, by giving birth, particularly to a boy. She is thus set on the track toward heterosexuality; her choice of a love object is conditioned by her struggle for restitution of the penis. Love, to Freud, is based not on spiritual purity but on the need for self-gratification and, for women, on envy.

But even getting married and having a son does not end a woman's struggle. First she tries to live through her son; that is, she places on her son all the ambitions she as a woman cannot or is not allowed to fulfill. This causes a struggle for autonomy between mother and son and is part of a larger battle between men in general and the mother in women. Moreover, although in one sense a woman plays the relatively passive female role in relation to her husband, because of her continuing need to acquire the instrument of power (having a son does not really give her a penis or the power it represents), she tries to achieve her ambitions not just through her son but also through her husband. Freud concluded, therefore, that a marriage is not secure until the wife has succeeded in making her husband her child as well and in acting as a mother to him.

Finally, according to Freud, the battle between men and women is carried to a broader field. Women's energies are focused on the home and family; men's energies are devoted to the larger society. As men increasingly turn their energies outward and away from the family and home, a struggle develops between men and women. Women resent men's lack of attention to them and battle against it, and they come to resent civilization itself, which stole men's attentions from them. Men are destined to win this battle, however, because, after all, they have what women want.

Some feminist writers have argued that Freud may have been right in some sense, but that womb envy is much more important than penis envy. Men, they argue, resent the fact that only women can produce life from within their bodies and have spent most of their history trying both to control this powerful force and to make up for their own deficiencies (e.g., Horney 1967). It is important to remember that the role of fathers in procreation is not readily apparent; women's power in reproduction is considerably more obvious.

Writers from a wide spectrum of viewpoints suggest that even if we don't know how male dominance began, it is maintained through struggle and violence. As early as the end of the eighteenth century, Mary Wollstonecraft argued that the division of power and labor between the sexes created a constant war between them. Although the balance of power is on men's side, human nature leads women to pursue their own interests by using whatever power they might have over men. If men force women to be mere sex objects or objects of beauty, women will use their sexuality and beauty against men. If women are not allowed to be forceful and direct, they will be cunning, manipulative, and sly. The only way to end this battle, Wollstonecraft argued, was to grant both men and women the human dignity that comes through independence and equality.

Modern feminists have further developed the theme of sex war. One idea that runs throughout feminist literature is the possibility—to many the certainty—that one social group does not take and maintain power over another without a struggle. Feminists point to different types of evidence to show the signs of struggle and antagonism. Although not all feminists are women, and not all antifeminists are men, the history of feminist movements is in part a struggle to gain rights and increased powers for women from governments, employers, and other male-dominated organizations. Women gained their new rights slowly through considerable effort and sometimes bloodshed.

Many feminists point not just to legal battles but also to what Kate Millett (1970) called the *sexual politics* of everyday life. Some, following an argument similar to that offered by Friedrich Engels over a century ago, claim that men dominate women to be sure their lineage is maintained through legitimate children and to retain access to the free personal services and labor women provide. Marxists do not have a monopoly on this argument. Many contemporary feminists also agree with the liberal democratic theorist John Stuart Mill, who argued that men do everything in their power to make women "willing slaves" (for the text, see Rossi 1970). Other feminists point specifically to sexual control, the signs of which one can see in double standards of sexual morality and in the "privileges" women receive when they are associated with men, especially through marriage.[7] Whether the sex war is fought on the battlegrounds of sexual politics or sexual control, many argue that men have numerous privileges they derive merely from being men and will not give up without a struggle.

What tactics do feminists see in the war between the sexes? Men certainly have the law, politics, and economic resources on their side. As we shall see in Chapter 9, Mary Wollstonecraft was right when she suggested that inequality leads to a constant power struggle between men and women in their everyday lives. Social psychologists and linguists have documented numerous ways in which men take control from women even in normal conversation (Colwill 1982). Feminists point out that the battle is often violent and that rape and wife battery can be seen as means of physical control of women.

Feminists are not the only observers of gender systems who see the condition of women as the result of a sex war. The conservative sociobiological theory of the "selfish gene" suggests that men seek to dominate women to be sure they reproduce themselves by passing on their genes to a new generation. Along similar lines, many sociobiologists argue that men have an instinct to control women sexually (and even have a natural tendency to rape) because they are driven to impregnate as many women as possible. Nor is the battle ended when pregnancy occurs. The man, having accomplished what he wanted, has little interest in the child he helped create, but the woman, who has made a significant investment in the child through her pregnancy, focuses her attention on the child.

63

Chapter 2:
Some Competing
Explanations:
How Did Society
Get This Way?

Some sociobiologists see relations between the sexes as a continual battle in which each sex seeks to outwit and control the other; they argue that these relations are essentially mutually exploitative. Others argue that men dominate women because they are biologically capable of doing so; men are stronger and more aggressive. The conclusion these sociobiologists reach is that a battle between men and women is inevitable, and it is also inevitable that women must lose. These theories are currently very influential.

One of the most interesting antifeminist approaches to the sex war theory is found in Helen Andelin's best-seller, *Fascinating Womanhood* (1974). Andelin bases her book on her antifeminist, fundamentalist Christian beliefs. The book is intended to help women improve their marriages and their relationships with their husbands. Women, Andelin argues, must be childlike and submissive to their husbands. The reason she offers is not that women are inferior or naturally submissive, but that men have such weak egos and such difficult, insensitive, and crude personalities that women must learn to manipulate them through coquettishness and apparent passivity. Andelin says that men and women have very different and basically antagonistic characters. Women are gentle, sensitive, religious, and nurturant, and men are insensitive, aggressive, and temperamental. Much of her advice to women is of the kind generations of mothers have passed on to their daughters: Never appear threatening. Never nag if your man is being bad (as he is wont to be, because men are like that). Never show that you are your man's equal, and certainly never take an obvious lead in sex or appear smarter or more skilled at anything than he is. Andelin also takes matters a step further. If a woman's husband beats or physically abuses her, Andelin says, the woman should pout, stamp her foot, shake her curls, perhaps pound weakly on his chest and say, "How can such a big strong man hurt such a poor little girl?"

There are several important points to be drawn from the sex war theories of male dominance.

1. These theories are not the sole property of feminists, as some people might expect. The view that dominance grows out of sexual antagonism goes back in antifeminist thought at least to the time of Charles Darwin.
2. Different theories regarding the sex war have different implications for the future. Generally antifeminist sex war theories suggest that both antagonism and male dominance are inevitable. Most feminist theories argue that equality is possible and, therefore, more harmonious relations between the sexes are also possible.
3. Acceptance of sex war theories does not necessarily mean that one believes this war is a conscious conspiracy of nasty people. Sociobiological approaches generally assume that sex war is fostered by unconscious biological instincts and capabilities.

Feminist theorists usually suggest that war is a natural outcome of inequity and therefore can be ended if inequity is defeated. As long as inequity exists, at least some members of the group with less power will fight for increased control over themselves, and at least some members of the group with power will try to justify their strength and will not willingly relinquish it.

Toward Understanding Social Change and Women's History

The five types of theories discussed here attempt to explain how societies develop particular structures of power and relations between women and men. They suggest somewhat different routes societies may have followed to get where they are now, and they also suggest different possible futures. Although most of these theories have both positive and negative points, none is perfect, and all must be evaluated carefully in light of the evidence.

Consider the treatment of social change in each of these theories. The static nature approach, whether based on theology or biology, does not offer a clue about why and how change has taken place or might take place. It tells us only that difference and inequality now exist and always will, at least to some degree. The Enlightenment theories do very little to help us understand the historical processes and causes of change, but they do suggest some strategies for change. At least some of the variations on the economic, functionalist, and sex war theories suggest why change has taken place and also how further changes might be instigated.

With the exception of the static theories, none is necessarily and exclusively feminist or antifeminist. People with a variety of political viewpoints have found something appealing in most of the theories outlined here. Sex war theories, for example, are found in different forms in the writings of some of the most radical feminists, such as Mary Daly (1978), and the most radical antifeminists. The difference lies in how the theories are formulated and applied and in how evidence is brought to bear on them.

Feminist theorists agree that it is essential to understand how the structure of power and relations between the sexes changes within a society over time. This does not simply mean that we should know the major events of women's history but also that we should identify important historical patterns and forces suggested by the theories discussed in this chapter. Theoretical analysis of this sort helps us make sense of the specific facts of women's experiences and social change. Feminist scholars also agree that attention to theories of change at the societal level is an important corrective to the widespread view that to improve their lot women need only do the best they can in their individual lives. As Chapters 13 and 14 discuss in more detail, feminists disagree about what aspects of these theories best explain the world around them. Evaluation of the theories and evidence, however, is one of the most exciting tasks of feminist scholarship.

NOTES

1. This widely held view of conception has been revealed to be mistaken by recent scientific research showing that sperm are not entirely self-propelling but are carried along by the actions of the woman's body and the fluids within it.

2. For further discussion of liberal theory, see Jaggar (1983) and Eisenstein (1981).

3. For recent feminist critiques and elaborations of Marxist theory, see Sargent (1981), Barrett (1980), and Jaggar (1983).

4. The most famous example of the Lamarckian principle is the suggestion that if the tail of a rat is cut off during its lifetime, its offspring will be tailless.

5. For Mozart fans (of which the author is one) it is important to remember that both Pamina and Tamino (the heroine and hero) are allowed to enter a condition of enlightenment.

6. Freud's observations on society and history are found primarily in his later works, written especially in response to the rise of fascism.

7. By *privileges*, feminists mean the higher status and social respect women have when they are married or are at least associated with a man, and such benefits as the relatively greater degree of safety women have in traveling or even walking around their own communities when they are accompanied by a male ''protector.'' (See e.g., Rich 1980).

3

More Competing Explanations: How Did Individuals Get This Way?

IN CHAPTER 2 we looked at several theories of how a system of differentiation and stratification of women and men evolved; that is, how differences, especially in power and dominance, developed between women and men as groups. Those theories focused our attention on historical change.

In this chapter we will examine a set of theories that attempt to explain differences between women and men as individuals. For example, why is an individual woman more likely to enter certain occupations than a man is, and vice versa? One might respond, "Ah, because of history or culture." But the question remains: How do you and I, as individuals, come to take our places in history or culture? The theories discussed in this chapter focus on biographical change.

Individual differences require different explanations from group or societal differences. A theory that explains how the structure of relations between women and men developed over time does not necessarily explain why, in a given society, individual women and men behave as they do. Marxist theories of social differences, for example, suggest that the relative status of women and men depends on historical changes in the structure of the economy. But how is it that individual people come to "fit into" this system? How do we acquire the beliefs, ideology, personality characteristics, or patterns of behavior that are appropriate to a given social or cultural system? How do each of us, as individuals, come to understand that we are female or male, and what that means? To answer these questions, we will draw upon the fields of physiology, psychology, and social psychology.

This chapter discusses five different types of theories that can be used to help explain how individuals come to be the kinds of people they are and especially how they come to adopt particular variations of gender norms. The first type rests on pure biological explanation; that is, males become "masculine" and females "feminine" because it is their biological nature by virtue, for example, of their brains or hormonal structures. The second theory we will consider is psychoanalytic theory, especially that proposed by Sigmund Freud, who understood the development of gender and sexuality as a conflictual process involving psychological adaptation to the demands placed on the psyche by both biology and the environment.

67

Chapter 3:
More Competing
Explanations:
How Did Individuals
Get This Way?

The third theory, cognitive development, also defines gender as involving an interaction between biology and environment (although leaning toward the former), but sees the development of gender as a process of trying to maintain identity and a sense of competence in understanding the self and the world around it. The fourth theory, social-learning, emphasizes individual learning as a process of interaction with the environment, especially learning from experience in the world that involves the teaching mechanisms of incentives, rewards, and punishments.

After pausing to consider some general comments on learning and development, and some attempts to synthesize the different theories, we will conclude with a very different approach to understanding how individuals become "gendered": discrimination theory. This approach suggests that the whole story of living a gendered life is not told when we have taken account of how individuals learn or internalize gender norms. The discrimination model reminds us of the possibility that individuals can be forced into gendered behavior against their will.

"Natural Differences": What Is the Role of Biology?

To what degree does nature bestow on each of us limits or capabilities that depend on whether we happen to be male or female? To what degree are our individual lives shaped by our sex? These are two of the most controversial questions among those who study women.

Sex and Gender

Let us look first at a pair of related concepts that are very important in women's studies: sex and gender. To state the point simply (although it will not remain simple as we proceed), sex is a physiological phenomenon, and gender is a social or cultural one. We shall see that figuring out which is which is not an easy task.

Sex is determined by one of the twenty-three pairs of chromosomes that are in the fertilized human egg cell. The ovum, or egg, contributed by the mother contains only X chromosomes. These thus appear in every human being, and they contain genetic information that affects a wide range of physiological functions. The father, through the sperm, may contribute either another X or a Y chromosome to the egg. If the father contributes an X chromosome to the sex-determining pair, the baby will have an XX pair and be a girl. If the father contributes a Y chromosome, which is much smaller and therefore more limited in the amount of genetic information it carries, the baby will have an XY pair and be a boy.

Sometime during the first trimester of a pregnancy, the genetic information on the sex-linked chromosomes begins to send out information about what mixture of hormones the glands are supposed to produce. The same hormones are produced in both males and females, but the mixture of them, along with the other sex-linked information in the genes, tells the body whether to develop a male or female structure.

Male and female bodies are analogues of each other; they are shaped from the same basic form. Depending on the genetic instructions that are released, one set of glands will become either ovaries or testes, another part of the body will become either a clitoris or a penis, the breasts will grow and eventually develop functioning mammary glands or remain small and functionless. When we ask about the effect of sex on an individual, we are asking about effects caused by the presence or absence of the Y chromosome and the genetic information it carries and the mix of hormones it stimulates.[1]

Gender involves these phenomena and much more. At the simplest level, we know that sex determines whether we can menstruate, bear children, and lactate, but it doesn't tell us whether people would be startled if a teacher wore a nice skirt and a small touch of lipstick into the classroom. If the teacher were male they certainly would be startled. Sex doesn't tell us whether it is more appropriate for us to train as nurses or doctors, or whether we should aspire to be lawyers or legal secretaries. It doesn't even give us complete guidelines about how we should act when we are menstruating or how we should relate to the children we or our mate bear. Gender can be viewed as the interpretation of the significance of sex. Gender roles are organized patterns of behavior we follow that are based on our interpretation of the significance of sex. They structure our choices and guide our behavior in ways that are viewed as gender appropriate.

It is often difficult to tell what is a function of sex and what is a function of gender, partly because our views are colored by our own ideological preferences. Antifeminists, for instance, are often eager to label differences as biologically based and to view them as the major cause of the inequities we observe in society. On the other hand, some feminists are loathe to see any influence of biology (unless it "favors women") and are even suspicious of anyone who studies biology. Believing in sex differences that do not exist can have real effects on human beings; rejecting the possibility of sex differences doesn't make these differences any less real. In neither case is the cause of learning advanced.

Another reason it is difficult to distinguish between the roles of sex and of gender is that one of the most powerful functions of gender is to tell us what is natural and inevitable about people. Anthropologists and historians have noted repeatedly that different cultures do not simply define what is appropriate behavior for women and men but also consider this behavior to be natural and inevitable. In some cultures, for example, there is a belief that if a man has sexual intercourse with a menstruating woman, he will become impotent. And sure enough, many men who accept this belief do become at least temporarily impotent when they find that the woman with whom they wanted to have sexual relations has "the curse." Cultures also vary in how they view childbirth, and research shows that the physical experience of childbirth differs from culture to culture depending on that view. If a society believes that women have no natural ability to be great artists and thus doesn't waste valuable resources training them, showing their work, or writing about it, it will be easy to "prove" that women aren't capable of being great artists.

It is also difficult to disentangle sex and gender because of the difficulty of determining causation: Which causes a person to act in a certain way—biology or society? In order to be absolutely sure whether an individual's personality is caused by nature or nurture, we would have to be capable of examining an individual totally removed from the context of society and any prior social training. Indeed important contemporary currents of scientific thinking suggest that the very idea of assuming causation by biology or society, as compared with the interactive impact of both, reflects a primitive understanding of human nature and society (see, e.g., Bleier 1984).

69

Chapter 3:
More Competing
Explanations:
How Did Individuals
Get This Way?

Thus far we have referred to the "structure of relations between the sexes" and to "systems of differentiation and stratification." These concepts are encompassed by the term *sex/gender system* (Rubin 1974), which refers to the system or structure of roles, power, and activities predominant within a society that are based on the biological distinctions between males and females and further elaborated and interpreted through culturally defined gender norms.

What types of behavior are matters of sex, and which are matters of gender? The question has yet to be answered entirely, but nevertheless, the conceptual and linguistic distinction is useful to maintain. What follows is a brief overview of some of the conclusions reached by scientists who study human biology.

The Role of Genes

Let us return to the question of sex and its role in the differential structuring of men and women's lives. First, contrary to common belief, human beings are not neatly divided into two sexes, female (XX) and male (XY). Out of 2500 females 1 is born with only one X chromosome, a condition known as Turner's syndrome. Females with Turner's syndrome differ from other females in that they are relatively short and their ovaries don't function. Out of 700 males 1 is born with two X chromosomes and one Y, and the same proportion of males has two Y chromosomes and one X. Actually "normal" people can have quite a variety of combinations of X and Y chromosomes. Hormonal mistakes also cause some individuals to be born half male and half female, with one ovary and one testicle (hermaphrodites), with extremely ambiguous external genitals, or with external genitals that conflict with their internal organs. People with each of these different characteristics have been studied to determine the effects of naturally occurring variations in sex-determining chromosomes and hormones.

One of the most-studied populations in the United States—other than students in introductory psychology classes—is the population of people confined in prisons and mental institutions. Researchers discovered that a surprising proportion of male inmates were XYY's. They concluded that the Y chromosome has aggression instructions written on it, so men are more aggressive than women and XYY men are more aggressive than XY men. Later research called this conclusion into question. For one thing, there are many XYY men in the general population who have not committed aggressive, antisocial actions. Perhaps more critically men with extra X's (for example, an XXY male) appear in institutionalized and noninstitutionalized populations in roughly the same proportions as men with extra Y's. Some researchers have concluded that strong aggression may be a problem of people with abnormal chromosomal arrangements, not just of people with extra Y's. This suggestion does not rule out the possibility that a tendency toward aggression is sex based; it simply points out that this type of research doesn't tell us about sex differences.

There is more conclusive evidence that sex (as opposed to gender) makes a difference in certain other areas, but the implications of these differences are often shaped by gender. The female body, of course, has no facility for producing sperm, and the male body has no facility for bearing children or producing milk. Other than these differences in reproductive abilities and functions, though, there is no conclusive evidence from studies of biology that there are any other sex-based differences in motivations and abilities related to reproduction and child raising.

Males are prone to many more genetically transmitted diseases and handicaps such as hemophilia and color blindness. The male body develops stronger muscular structure and more red blood cells on average than the female body (although the female body is more agile in certain ways). As we shall see in Chapter 5, however, sex differences in strength have been vastly exaggerated by the different types of training and experiences males and females receive. As girls and women have been trained more vigorously in sports, the gap between male and female athletes has diminished considerably. (Interestingly, some of the difference in potential agility

Women's athletic ability has increased dramatically as they receive
better athletic training.

is not apparent to people. One reason may be that because of differences in training, men fulfill more of their potential than women do.)

Although we will probably never see men and women competing directly against each other in sports that depend solely on strength, the larger social significance of strength differentials depends on the social construction of human tasks. Technological advances, for example, have decreased the importance of strength in many types of jobs. Moreover, it has been very difficult in the past to identify in a way that is not gender biased what the actual physical requirements of different jobs are and what potential different people have for meeting these requirements. For example, protective labor legislation used to keep women out of jobs that required carrying loads ''too heavy for women.'' Many of these limits were lower than the weights of the small children, grocery packages, and laundry baskets that women commonly carry.

71

Chapter 3:
More Competing
Explanations:
How Did Individuals
Get This Way?

The Structure of the Brain

Much research has focused on sex differences in the brain. In the nineteenth century one popular notion was that female brains were smaller than male brains, and that therefore women's capacities were more limited than men's. These observations led theorist and politician John Stuart Mill to remark that by the same logic we should conclude that elephants are much smarter than people because of the relative sizes of elephant and human brains.

Current research focuses more on the organization of the brain and the functions of its component parts. One of the most interesting and controversial arguments concerns brain lateralization (that is, which hemisphere, or side, is dominant in what functions) and its effects, especially on verbal and spatial abilities. Many researchers now argue that male and female brains process information in different parts of the brain. In right-handed men, only one side of the brain (the left hemisphere) processes language. In many left-handed men and, many argue, in women both sides of the brain process language. This, researchers suggest, accounts for somewhat poorer spatial abilities of both women and left-handed men because, since spatial information is processed in the right brain hemisphere, their brains are processing language and spatial information on the same side, causing interference with spatial abilities. Some people have suggested that this difference in lateralization means that women (and presumably left-handed men) can never achieve as (right-handed) men do in fields like engineering or architecture.

These conclusions are far from universally accepted. Observed differences between males and females in spatial abilities are not nearly wide enough to account for the occupational differences between men and women. Further, research scientists still do not agree that these studies of brain lateralization really distinguish between *innate* brain capacity and *developed* brain capacity. Training and environmental factors not only enhance or limit capacity but also affect what part of the brain does what. It is possible that even some of the differences observed in young children are the result of the different types of games and activities undertaken with male and female children, just as some of the differences between left- and right-handed people could be caused by the common attempt to force left-handed children to become right-handed. Some people speculate, therefore, that differences in training help determine differences between males and females not only in acquired skills (that is, how much of their potential they actually fulfill) but also in apparent biological potential. Moreover, some researchers find no evidence of sex differences in brain lateralization (Shepherd 1982).

The Role of Hormones

A considerable amount of research on sex differences focuses on the effects of hormones. For ethical reasons much of this research has been performed on animals rather than on humans. Our discussion will be restricted to conclusions based on observations of human beings. This is not to say that research on other animal species is irrelevant to understanding human physiology. But contradictory findings make the topic confusing enough to the introductory reader without the added problem of discussing findings that have not been validated by research on human beings.

Females develop more quickly than males do. This difference appears before birth and continues until adulthood. Some research suggests that testosterone, a hormone produced in greater amounts in males than in females, is responsible for slowing down the process of physiological development, which causes males to grow more slowly, develop coordination and perhaps verbal skills at a later stage, and reach puberty at an older age. How these differences affect the process of learning and eventual adult roles and behavior is unclear.

Perhaps the greatest amount of research on the role of hormones in sex differences focuses on menstrual cycles and the onset of menopause. The balance of hormones in women shifts throughout the menstrual cycle. Many scientists have hypothesized that this shift causes mood and behavioral changes, some of which may have a great impact on women's capabilities and social activities. Many nonscientists, of course, suspect the same thing because of conventional wisdom. How many times have we heard people worry about menstruating pilots crashing airplanes or menstruating presidents blowing up the world?

As usual, early consensus has dissolved in the face of contradictory evidence and interpretation. Many of the symptoms conventionally associated with menstruation in our society do not appear at all in other societies (Paige and Paige 1981). Although most researchers in the area agree that women tend to experience mood changes in association with their menstrual cycles, the symptoms identified vary considerably. Changes that appear to be associated with the menstrual cycle may not actually be caused by the hormonal changes themselves. In her research comparing women using birth control pills (which affect hormone levels) and those not using them, Karen Paige found that negative psychological symptoms were related to how heavy the menstrual flow was. She also found that the degree of acceptance of traditional menstrual taboos and gender ideology was related to menstrual distress. Furthermore,

73

Chapter 3:
More Competing
Explanations:
How Did Individuals
Get This Way?

A nineteenth-century engraving of a Native American menstrual lodge.

as most women have found at one time or another, stress—which often causes mood changes—can affect a woman's normal cycle. And finally many critics have pointed out that most of the research that finds a correlation between menstrual cycles and mood changes is not designed to rule out the possibility that negative reactions to menstruation might be caused by a socially constructed negative attitude toward menstruation and menstruating women.

These criticisms point to a problem that plagues the study of women and social science in general: Correlation does not necessarily indicate causation. In other words, just because two events happen at the same time, we cannot be sure, without further investigation, that one causes the other. Hormonal changes can affect moods, but moods can also induce hormonal changes. Hormonal changes bring on menstruation, and mood changes may be associated with the menstrual cycle, but something else—for example, a feeling that menstruation is embarrassing or that one's lover can't abide sexual relations with a menstruating woman—may actually cause the mood changes. If we constructed a study to look at the relationship between thunderstorms and ice cream consumption in New England, we would find that the months with relatively high incidence of thunderstorms are also the months with relatively high levels of ice cream consumption. Do thunderstorms cause people to eat ice cream?

Recent research has added a new twist to the study of hormonal fluctuations and cycles: Men have them too (Doering et al. 1974). Men appear to have cycles in a variety of physiological and psychological respects. Whether these are related to fluctuations in sex hormones is still open to question. We do not yet know whether we should ground male pilots at "that time of the month."

Perhaps the most certain conclusion we can reach regarding our current knowledge of the effects of biology on the development of distinct male and female personalities, roles, and activities is that our understanding is incomplete and contradictory; there are innumerable avenues open for further investigation. Biological research alone has not yet been able to point clearly to a reason for the degree of gender differentiation and stratification in our society, and it certainly has not accounted for the varying levels of differentiation and stratification across societies.

Human life and activity are products of an intriguing relationship between biology and society, nature and invention. We will refer repeatedly to the questions and points raised by biological research and models when we examine the specific activities and roles of women.

Psychoanalytic Theory

As we have seen, biological research has not been very successful in explaining how individuals in society come to be (or not be) part of the prevailing sex/gender system. Let us now turn to approaches arguing that although becoming a "masculine" male or a "feminine" female is in many respects a matter of biology (they differ in what role they assign to biology), the human mind as it encounters its environment after birth is the predominant determinant of masculinity and femininity. In trying to understand how individuals come to be the kind of people they are, these theorists emphasize the degree of change that occurs in individuals' lives over time. They emphasize the different phases or stages that occur during the course of individuals' development.

We will begin with one of the most influential psychological theorists of the twentieth century, Sigmund Freud. In Chapter 2 we looked at the role of conflict between women and men in Freud's psychoanalytic theory. Now we will review his theories of psychosexual development.

Sex Similarity

Freud argued that, for all intents and purposes, human personalities are not sex differentiated at birth, and the development of females and males is very similar for the first few years. At this time any observed "sexual differences are not. . .of great consequence: they can be outweighed by individual variations" ([1933] 1965, 118). Freud defined the psyche in the same terms for both males and females. The bulk of the psyche is composed of human instincts or drives. Freud called this part of the psyche the *id* ("it" in Latin). These drives and instincts are defined as psychic energy. Like other types of energy, they have no particular form or object other than self-gratification and can be channeled to have any of several forms, objects, or effects.

This is why a single feeling (for example, hatred of another person) can take on either a destructive form ("I'll kill him") or a constructive form ("I'll show him—I'll get this done faster and better than it's ever been done before").

75

Chapter 3:
More Competing
Explanations:
How Did Individuals
Get This Way?

The nature of the id and human drives meant to Freud that females and males are born essentially undifferentiated and—very importantly—bisexual. If the human drive for pleasure is unshaped or unchanneled, as is the case in infants, it cannot care how that pleasure is achieved. A human infant will try sucking on almost anything, it is happy to have almost any part of its anatomy stroked, and it feels no shock if a person of one sex or the other strokes it. The *libido,* or pleasure-seeking drive, knows nothing of sex or gender, even if it is the source of sexuality and eroticism. For a human being to become heterosexual, which to Freud is central to appropriate sexual maturity and gender roles, this part of the human psyche has to be repressed and rechanneled.

How do these relatively undifferentiated masses of gurgles, cries, and burps turn into males and females? How do they acquire masculinity and femininity and develop particular psychosexual orientations? In Freudian theory, the process is posed as a series of stages through which people must pass to achieve maturity. It is important to note, however, that progress through these stages is by no means automatic; it might best be described as a hazardous struggle both within individuals and between individuals and the social world around them. The process can go wrong at any stage owing to events that occur in the child's environment or to the relationship between the child and others.

The first stages of psychosexual development are similar for boys and girls. The first stage, the oral phase, is marked by the importance of the mouth in receiving pleasure. Sucking and feeding is the primary business of life for infants. This changes when children face the first demand that they become self-conscious and exert control over themselves during the anal phase, which is triggered by the experience of toilet training. This is a very complex transition. The infant finds that he or she can please another person, but only under certain circumstances. The child can give a gift of properly deposited feces, but this act requires a certain amount of self-denial. Because of the role of self-denial (the first of many instances of self-denial to be learned), this stage is achieved only with resistance. The assault on the id by the *ego* (the "I," or potentially conscious or self-conscious self) has begun. The third phase, the phallic phase, is the time during which the child begins to learn about genital pleasure. Now the trouble begins.

Development of Difference

The Freudian picture as we have described it thus far still presents girls and boys as relatively undifferentiated and unrestrained pleasure seekers. The pleasure drives have yet to be regulated; in other words, both the ego and the *superego* (literally "over I") have yet to be developed. The superego has often been described as the conscience. It is the (relatively small) part of our consciousness that flows from the world around us. It contains the moral rules and personal sense of right and wrong derived in large part from social and cultural dictates. The superego joins or pushes the ego in battle against the dark, unruly drives of the id. It is the ego and superego that have to learn what masculinity, femininity, and sexuality are about. (The id will never learn and remains in conflict with the ego and superego.) Freud thought that this task is more difficult for females than for males because it takes females two extra steps to achieve the final goal of maturity.

Both boys and girls originally derive their pleasure from a woman, the mother. This poses a special problem for girls. In finding his mother his primary erotic object a boy is on the way to mature masculinity. He will have to give up his mother as a consciously sexual object, but to become heterosexual he will merely have to turn to other women. This involves a struggle, but it is not as difficult as the task girls have before them. Girls have to turn from the mother much more completely if they are to become mature heterosexual women. They must shift their focus of eroticism (or pleasure seeking) from women to men.

What could wrench girls' affections so completely from women that in place of the original pleasurable feelings the majority eventually think of physical relations with women only with horror or, at least, anxiety? For Freud, the answer lies in the female version of the castration complex. "After all, the anatomical distinction between the sexes must express itself in psychical consequences. It was, however, a surprise to learn from analyses that girls hold their mother responsible for their lack of a penis and do not forgive her for being thus put at a disadvantage" (Freud [1933] 1965, 124).

Like many people Freud could not imagine that a woman's body might be regarded as complete, even by a female. His standard for a "complete" human body is the male anatomy. According to Freud, one sight of a male's "superior equipment" ([1933] 1965, 126) and a girl is overcome with mortification for her own body, envy of the male's, and a need to place blame for her mutilated condition. She becomes hostile to her mother, who she finds is deformed like herself and apparently has purposely castrated her, or at least managed to create her without the essential organ. By generalizing her view of herself and her mother, women become "debased in value for girls just as they are for boys" ([1933] 1965, 127). The girl is now on the road to maturity. She rejects women and turns to her father who, after all, possesses a penis. She also begins to suppress her former feelings for her clitoris, or deficient penis, to pave the way for vaginal eroticism, which prepares her for heterosexuality and motherhood. This transfer of erotic feeling from one organ to another is the other major developmental step that girls, and not boys, must take.

From the time she discovers her castration, the girl has a very difficult journey ahead. According to Freud she may take any of three roads:

1. She might develop "sexual inhibitions or neurosis," especially frigidity. This happens if the girl is so traumatized by her discoveries that she suppresses not only her "infantile" sexuality, but also all sexuality.
2. She might develop a "masculinity complex." In this case, she rebels against femininity and retains her more "infantile" form of sexuality, which means, among other things, homosexuality.
3. She may "renounce" infantile sexuality, which includes both women as love objects and her own clitoris as the focus of erotic pleasure, to achieve "normal femininity."

77

Chapter 3:
More Competing
Explanations:
How Did Individuals
Get This Way?

Some people point out that the switch to vaginal eroticism—difficult to achieve because of the relative lack of nerve endings in the vagina compared to the clitoris—is particularly convenient to male-centered sexuality. What about the penis envy? This becomes transformed into a desire for a child, and, if at all possible, a child with a penis.

What differences between males and females develop as a result of this process? Freud believed that women become oriented toward home, husband, and child, and men turn their interests outward. Men also develop a stronger superego, or conscience, than women do. To explain this, Freud turned to the castration complex and the child's feelings toward the mother and father. Boys continue to be sexually oriented toward their mothers (and women in general). What force imposes itself against the id to keep boys from becoming literally incestuous? Boys compete with their fathers for the mother's attention, but they also fear the power of their father and, especially, the punishment of castration. (This psychic relationship with the father is called the Oedipus complex.) This fear keeps males in line and strengthens their abilities to integrate societal rules into their psyches.

Women do not have to fear castration because it has already happened, and thus they have less reason to develop this social orientation. Rather than learning to be governed by societal rules, they become passively oriented toward men's will to achieve their goal of having a child. Notice that unlike other theorists who put women in "their place," Freud argued that women are not passive by nature but "give preference to passive aims" ([1933] 1965, 115) because of the process of psychosexual development. The difference is subtle but important.

Women's development has other effects that distinguish women from men. Their repression of their "masculinity" (especially their aggressiveness) makes them masochistic. Drives like aggressiveness do not disappear when they are repressed but remain alive in the id. The woman who achieves "normal femininity," therefore, turns her aggressive energy inward. Women also remain dominated by the envy sparked by their discovery of their castration. They therefore have less sense of social justice than men because social justice is incompatible with envy. They become more rigid than men and age more quickly, primarily because of the more arduous path they have taken. Freud thought that women appear tired out, spent, and aged by the time they reached 30 years of age in comparison with men, who at this age were just reaching their peaks.

Evaluating the Psychoanalytic Perspective

The psychoanalytic perspective on the development of males and females certainly offers a rich body of theories and observations. In its variety of interpretations and applications, it has been both celebrated and rejected from every point of view, from the radically antifeminist to the radically feminist. What are the sources of these reactions?

First there is the question of methodology. Numerous observers have pointed out that the subjects of Freud's study were his own patients and those of his colleagues; in other words, women who appeared in a psychoanalyst's office for one reason or another at the beginning of this century. To accept Freud's arguments, we must accept the idea that his conclusions about psychosexual development can justifiably be generalized from these women to the general population.

The nature of both the clinical method (in-depth discussion with and observation and interpretation of one person by another) and psychoanalytic theory itself creates a problem for substantiation of the theory. The psychoanalyst seeks the meaning and motivation of a person's perceptions and actions. As we have seen (in the earlier example of how hatred of another person can lead to destructive or constructive activity), very different acts can have the same meaning or motivation. How do we know that the observer, Freud, is not unconsciously biasing his own observations toward a conclusion he has already reached?

The methods used by psychoanalysts are particularly open to the charge that one can see whatever one *wants* to see. Consider the case of penis envy. From the Freudian viewpoint if a girl asks her mother why she can't have a penis like her brother, she is displaying penis envy. If she suggests that it must be neat to be able to urinate standing up (or tries it), or if she playacts at having a penis, she is also expressing penis envy. But what if she, as many girls do, expresses the feeling that having a penis must be strange or uncomfortable or that it must get in the way when one is riding a bicycle? The psychoanalyst argues that this too is a sign of penis envy, expressed through her hostility to the male body. Many psychoanalysts go even further and regard almost any attempt by a woman to enter a traditionally masculine domain as a sign of penis envy. In fact, attempts to validate Freud's conclusions by using other methods, such as experimental evidence and even projective techniques, have found little confirmation for important cornerstones of Freud's theory such as the universal existence of penis envy.

Another question raised by Freudian theory concerns the relative roles of biology and society in shaping individuals. Contrary to the interpretations of some of his followers and some of his greatest critics, Freud did not neglect the role of society and culture in his examination of female and male development. The superego is shaped by the individual's interaction with the social world, and thus the sense of self, the ego, is in part a product of interaction with the environment. Because it regards human beings as shaped not exclusively by nature or society but by the struggles between the two, Freudian theory can encompass the effects of tangible reality, biology, social relationships, myths and symbols, the rational, and the irrational.

Freud argued that human suffering and unhappiness, both male and female, comes from three sources: "the superior power of nature, the feebleness of our own bodies and the inadequacy of the regulations which adjust the mutual relationships of human beings in the family, the state and society" ([1930] 1961, 33). A large part of the human struggle, therefore, is to civilize humanity and remove the sources of suffering as much as possible. This observation has opened the way for feminist theorists such as Juliet Mitchell (1974) and Nancy Chodorow (1978) to suggest that Freudian theory can be used to explain the particular nature of suffering under patriarchal conditions and to point out how the restructuring of social institutions can have profound and positive effects on psychosexual development. Freudian theory thus can be used to criticize the powerful effects of patriarchy on human society.

Freud's notion of the human drive toward "civilization" raises another point of contention. Many feminists consider Freud a patriarchal, oppressive "Victorian" (a word many people use to mean prudish). We will review the evidence of his patriarchal views shortly and find this accusation just. As for his oppressive outlook in general, we must have some qualms. Civilization, he argued, is necessary to help us divert our self-destructive tendencies. Civilization can help share the struggle between the id and the superego and channel violent acts of power and domination into creative social projects. But "at the same time we have been careful not to fall in with the prejudice that civilization is synonymous with perfecting, that it is the road to perfection preordained for men [sic]" (Freud [1930] 1961, 43). Civilization, Freud believed, is no friend of liberty, and civilization has rarely been based on justice.

Freud remarked repeatedly on his dismay at the degree of sexual repression he saw in society. "The requirement . . . that there shall be a single kind of sexual life for everyone, disregards the dissimilarities, whether innate or acquired, in the sexual constitution of human beings; it cuts off a fair number of them from sexual enjoyment, and so becomes the source of serious injustice" (51). As we have seen, Freud thought that homosexuality was an infantile form of sexuality, but he would have been among the last to favor social or legal penalties for the homosexual. The man who pointed to the nature of the unconscious and the id, and who declared that human beings are naturally bisexual, not to mention incestuous, found little favor with the public, most of the medical establishment, and certainly the moral establishment of his day.

It would be hard to deny that Freud and a great many of his influential followers were patriarchal and, in some cases misogynistic. The great majority of Freudian psychoanalysts accept the notion that the penis is superior equipment, and that women who achieve normal femininity are uncreative, jealous, unjust, and masochistic creatures. Psychoanalysis has been used to try to make women view any frustration they feel as based on penis envy and the wish for a child. Psychoanalysis is one of the many modes of thought that view women's own perceptions as unreliable. In one of Freud's most famous cases, a woman traced her problems to a childhood experience of being raped by her father. Freud reinterpreted the woman's story as a fiction that revealed an extreme case of normal childhood penis envy and father love. His "evidence" that the child only wished to have sex with her father was the father's claim that he had not raped his daughter.

Freudian orthodoxy has been extremely harmful to women in many respects. Many feminists, however, have begun to return to psychoanalysis and the theories of Freud and others such as Karen Horney (1885–1952), a contemporary of Freud's. Some argue that men both fear women and, in a sense, "envy" the womb (Horney 1967).[2] This, they argue, accounts for the male need to dominate women, in contrast to the Freudian idea that penis envy leads women to seek domination by men. Some argue that the general outline of Freudian theory is correct, although the substantive conclusions often reached have been shaped by androcentric ideology. They suggest that Freud's writing on women should not be taken as a theory of what *must* happen but as a description of what *does* happen in a patriarchal or androcentric society. One

79

Chapter 3: More Competing Explanations: How Did Individuals Get This Way?

could argue that Freud's conclusions about "normal femininity" are right on target and serve as an excellent guide to the pernicious nature of "normal femininity" as an ideal woman should seek to attain.

Some feminists have concluded that Freud's view of penis envy is also correct, but only within the context of a culture that perceives the phallus as a symbol of power, dominance, and liberty. If our cultural conceptions of sex and gender were not "phallocentric," if the phallus were not a symbol of power, there would be little reason to be jealous of those who possess a penis. This interpretation has bolstered the argument that no change in society can occur until our social construction of sexuality is changed and the penis is regarded as merely an anatomical organ.

Cognitive Developmental Theories

Psychoanalytic theory is not the only approach to understanding the differentiation of individual males and females that uses the concept of stages of development. Developmentalists, who focus on cognitive processes do also, but in a way that is very different from that of the psychoanalyst.

Unlike psychoanalysts, developmentalists are particularly concerned with styles of thought and reasoning, the conscious part of the mind. They are interested in the development of the frameworks people use to understand, analyze, and cope with questions of self-identity, social and physical relationships, and principles such as morality. Many (although not all) developmentalists have a more rigid notion than psychoanalysts of the succession or hierarchy of stages through which an individual passes. Most developmentalists claim that once an individual has passed from one stage to the next, she or he will not return to a previous stage. Psychoanalysts make no such claims; in fact, the ideas of regression to previous stages and of constant tensions between earlier and later impulses figure very importantly in their views. For the developmentalist, different modes of thought are skills; a person would no more return to an earlier mode than he or she would forget how to ride a bicycle.

We will briefly examine the basic aspects of the developmental view of gender differentiation here and then focus on some of the controversies that exist within the developmental literature. Further details will be filled in later when we discuss social learning.

Becoming Boys and Girls

Most developmentalists see growth as a matter of both biology and interaction with the environment. During the earliest stage of life infants develop both basic physical capabilities, such as seeing and hearing, and the ability to manipulate physical objects purposefully. At this time, for example, a baby learns the wonderful game of throwing things on the floor during feeding time. During the next stage, babies become capable of some awareness of objects that are not physically present; they begin to show signs of imagination and memory. Until this stage, when we take an object away from a baby, it ceases to exist for the child. In the next stage it is not so easy to take candy from a baby, for the baby knows the candy still exists.

More sophisticated cognitive abilities develop in the third stage, especially the ability to classify and name objects and to put different ideas together. At the simplest level, for example, a child learns that not all fruits are apples, that apples and oranges are both fruits, and that although both an apple and an ice cream cone are edible, they are not both fruits. The child has begun to learn about the relationship among different objects. Finally children reach an even more sophisticated stage when they learn to solve more complex problems that require the ability to manipulate symbols and abstract ideas.

81

Chapter 3:
More Competing
Explanations:
How Did Individuals
Get This Way?

Developmentalists use this focus on how people learn to think to help explain how children develop gender identification and learn to "be" girls and boys. As Lawrence Kohlberg, one of the most important developers of cognitive-developmental theory wrote, "[Basic] sexual attitudes are not patterned directly by either biological instincts or arbitrary cultural norms, but by the child's cognitive organization of his social world along sex role dimensions." Developing gender is a process of making sense of the world. "It is not the child's biological instincts, but rather his cognitive organization of social role concepts around universal physical dimensions, which accounts for the existence of universals in sex role attitudes" (Kohlberg 1966, 82).

According to Kohlberg, the process of gender development begins in the first years of life when little girls figure out that they are girls, and little boys figure out that they are boys; that is, they engage in cognitive self-categorization. They acquire gender identity. It normally takes up to three years for this to happen. Next children learn that everyone has gender; everyone is a boy or a girl. Only after this, around the age of six, do children begin to learn that gender does not change (if you are a girl, you are going to be a girl forever) and that gender has meaning. At this stage children begin to recognize that girls and boys do different things, like different things, and have different amounts of power. They begin to learn about masculinity and femininity.

Learning about gender is one thing, learning to follow gender norms is another. How does this happen and why? Learning has both a cognitive dimension, involving thought and analytical skills, and an affective dimension, involving feelings or emotions. Children do not just learn about themselves; they also learn to value themselves and, through generalization, people like themselves. As children learn about gender, they begin to value their gender and the meanings that surround it. Boys want to do "boy" things and girls want to do "girl" things. Once a child develops a framework for understanding the world, ambiguities are painful until she or he acquires considerably more sophisticated analytical abilities. They are thus careful to uphold gender standards.

Kohlberg (1966) argued that as a boy becomes acquainted with the power and prestige of males, the desire to act like a male increases. The boy identifies with his father and wants to act just like him. Boys reach the stage of wanting to be only with other males and to avoid anything that seems girlish. This process is not exactly the same for girls. Research indicates that girls do not become as rigid in their gender stereotypes as boys do, and they are not as adamant about doing only "girl" things (witness the tomboy) or about playing only with other girls.

Kohlberg said that boys want to be boys in part because to identify with maleness is to identify with power and prestige. Girls also know that males have more power and prestige, which is presumably why they are not as reluctant to be masculine as

Developmentalists argue boys want to be like their fathers and girls like
their mothers.

boys are to be feminine. Kohlberg also believed that both boys and girls define the
male body as the "basic" body and the female body as the negative of the masculine
rather than as a positive entity. Nevertheless, he argued, girls also want to identify
with and act like their same-sex parent. Why? Part of the answer, Kohlberg said,
is that boys may value the masculine attributes of power and prestige, but girls value
the feminine attributes of niceness and nurturance.

More important, however, is the developmentalist's argument that people are
very egocentric, with a strong motive to value themselves and people like themselves.
The higher prestige of males means that boys are more adamant in their preferential
valuation of their own sex (the prestige lends reinforcement to their egocentrism),
but children of both sexes tend to think their own sex is better. Kohlberg also argued
that children tend to view physical and social regularities in moral terms. He reminded
us of Piaget's conclusions that there is a "tendency for the young child to view any
deviation from the social order as bad or wrong, even if such a deviation would not
be considered bad by adults. The child does not distinguish between conventional

social expectations and moral laws and duties." Thus, he argued, "The physical constancies underlying the child's concepts of gender identity tend to be identified with divine or moral law, and the need to adapt to the physical realities of one's identity are viewed as moral obligations" (Kohlberg 1966, 122).

Developmental theory, therefore, offers a handle on the growth of gender identity, its associated meanings, and the importance it plays in the individual's life. The developmental approach regards the individual as struggling to adapt to or cope with the social and physical world (sometimes labeled *competence strivings*) and to develop and preserve a positive and stable self-image. This struggle leads children to develop gender identity, gender stereotypes, and a motive to become gender typed early in their lives.[3]

83

Chapter 3:
More Competing
Explanations:
How Did Individuals
Get This Way?

Childhood Socialization and Social Learning

The most widely used approach to understanding how gender differentiation at the individual level occurs is based on the process of social learning. Those who study socialization generally assume that most gender differentiation is caused by an individual's experiences after birth. People learn to become women and men as society defines them because other people reward them or give them incentives for behaving in gender appropriate ways and punish them for acting otherwise. The result of socialization is the development of individuals who fit into society because they have been shaped to do so. The social learning approach to socialization leads researchers to investigate the ways in which agents of socialization, such as parents, peers, schools, and the mass media, encourage and discourage different types of behavior in males and females.

Development of Difference

It is easy to see that the important people with whom children have contact design the world to produce gender-appropriate behavior in girls and boys. From the moment of birth, girls and boys are treated differently, even by their parents. Parents differ in the way they interact with their male and female babies—how they respond to their crying, how much they handle and talk to them, and what tone of voice they use toward them. Parents treat baby girls as though they are more fragile than boys, and they treat baby boys as though they are more independent than baby girls.

It is possible that parents treat baby girls and boys differently because they are different. Boys start exhibiting more physical aggression than girls at a fairly young age, and in most other respects girls mature faster than boys. Mothers and fathers certainly think that baby girls and boys act differently (Rubin, Provenzano, and Luria 1974). There is reason to believe, however, that parents are creating differences between girls and boys more than they are reacting to real differences. If girls mature faster than boys, why are boys treated as more mature and independent? Some research shows that if a person is told that a baby is a girl or boy, regardless of what the sex of the child really is, that person is likely to describe the child in terms "appropriate" to the supposed gender and to treat the child accordingly. Parents give female and male children different kinds of clothes, games, and books. As the children grow and are given more responsibility within the home, parents begin to teach them ''gender-appropriate'' tasks.

It is sometimes difficult to see the degree to which the environment of the child is designed to give stereotypic messages. Parents and other agents of socialization may give the child very explicit gender messages: ''Go and help your mother in the kitchen so when you grow up you'll be a good mommy too.'' ''You don't want that toy—that's for girls!'' ''Don't sit like that—it's not ladylike!'' ''No, you may not phone Sam. A girl should wait for the boy to phone.'' More often, the teaching is not explicit or even conscious. For example, gender-stereotyped toys often appear without any direct explanation. A study of mothers reading stories to their children found evidence that they unconsciously taught their children to think of the male as the norm. In 95 percent of the cases in which the sex of the character was indeterminant, the mothers referred to the character as a male (DeLoache, Cassidy, and Carpenter 1987). Parents and other teachers set a constant example. If mommy and daddy are equally capable of driving, but mommy never drives if daddy is in the car, children learn who is ''supposed'' to drive the car.

Parents are not the only teachers of gender norms. Despite efforts to change gender stereotyping on television, the message offered has changed very little. Female characters are remarkably absent in the mass media. A study done in 1974 showed that 72 percent of the characters on prime-time television were male. When women did appear, they were primarily gender typed. In another study done in the mid-1970s, 38 percent of all females in television advertisements were shown inside the home as compared with 14 percent of all males. In addition, 75 percent of all advertisements using females were for products used in the kitchen or bathroom (Tuchman 1978). A content analysis of 1480 television commercials shows that although by the late 1980s women were shown more frequently outside the home and in a wider range of occupations, little else had changed (Ferrante, Haynes, and Kingsley 1988). (For further discussion of the mass media, see Chapter 7.)

Schools teach not only the three R's but also gender roles. We will discuss schools and education more completely in Chapter 4, but we can summarize the findings of research as follows. School textbooks and lessons focus more on males and male activities than on females and female activities. Teachers act differently toward girls and boys and encourage somewhat different types of behavior. Guidance counsellors help children pursue gender-appropriate aims.

Adults are not the only agents of socialization; children's peers also help out. Boys still beat up other boys for being ''sissies'' or for being too studious. Girls still make fun of other girls who act too smart, don't wear the right clothes, or are not interested enough in boys. This type of peer pressure is by no means limited to interaction between children of the same sex. A boy quickly finds out that it is easier to get dates if he is the captain of the football team rather than the president of the physics club. Even in the latter case, however, he will have an easier time than a girl who is head of the physics club, especially if he is at least good looking. A girl who is the ''class brain'' will often have trouble finding dates, even if she is physically attractive. Being athletic is no longer the problem it once was for girls who want dates (depending on the sport), but it is still unacceptable for a girl to be able to match or beat a boy at ''his'' own game.

85

Chapter 3:
More Competing
Explanations:
How Did Individuals
Get This Way?

This process of socialization does not stop at the end of childhood. University and occupational training continues the task of gender role teaching, as do family members and peers. Perhaps even more than during childhood people expect different things from adult women and men, and they give rewards to people who act as expected and punish those who do not. Women who pursue nontraditional careers or activities often find that the only way they can succeed without tremendous opposition or disapproval is to make sure they also play their more "feminine" roles to the hilt.

The Complexity of Learning

The social-learning model of socialization is very powerful and has proven quite useful in providing insights about how gender differentiation and stratification are maintained from one generation to the next. It is not, however, without its problems.

Girls and boys and women and men are not given only one message about how they are supposed to think, feel, and act. The social environment is complex and varied, offering many different values and patterns from which to choose. As parents know only too well, even carefully structuring a child's life to enforce certain values doesn't always work. Moreover, the world itself changes during the course of an individual's lifetime. The fact that no one in the 1930s or 1940s was encouraged to be an astronaut didn't mean that no one was available in the late 1950s to fly in space rockets. In fact we can argue that one of the norms that children learn in modern life is not only to expect change but also to participate in it. Young people expect that they will be different from their parents' generation in many ways, and they learn to be able to be different.

This point leads to another criticism that can be made regarding some uses of social-learning theories. In contrast to the cognitive-developmental approach to socialization, social-learning theory is sometimes used to buttress the idea that the mind is a passive piece of clay ready to be stamped by anyone who wants to make an impression on it. People excuse their behaviors by saying, "Well, I was socialized in this way," as though socialization precludes active, independent thought.

Perhaps the best caution against using socialization theory as an excuse to maintain the status quo is to review the findings regarding gender differences presented in Chapter 1. If social learning had produced unidimensionally "feminine" girls and "masculine" boys, we should be seeing many more differences between males and females in abilities, attitudes, personality characteristics, and behavior. Doubtless the pressure to conform to gender stereotypes is quite strong, but there is still considerable room for variation. We must be careful to avoid painting a portrait of oversocialized, passive, conforming people (Weitzman 1979).

More on the Learning Theories

Adult Life and Learning

The developmental and social-learning approaches to understanding individual gender roles emphasize the processes by which people develop values, attitudes, abilities, and patterns of behavior as they grow up. These theories suggest that by the time people reach adulthood, they are prepared to perform their adult roles. Socialization theorists use the concept of anticipatory socialization to label the process by which children acquire the attitudes and behavior patterns that are not yet appropriate because of their age but will be when they grow up. A good example of this activity is the game, "playing house."

Many sociologists have pointed out that anticipatory socialization is not all it is cracked up to be. Jessie Bernard (1972) and Helena Lopata (1971), for example, point out that adjustment to adult roles, including the roles of wife and husband, mother and father, is a much more difficult task than most romantic young people expect. Books, television, homemaking classes in school, playing house, and even the experience of growing up in a family leave women and men only vaguely prepared for the lives that lie ahead. The amount of attention paid to socialization and learning during childhood and adolescence sometimes obscures the fact that females and males become increasingly differentiated after adolescence and that people continue to learn their gender roles as they go through adulthood. This is particularly important because many young people now believe that their adult lives will be very different from those of the current older generation.

Many researchers argue that although some of the groundwork for gender differentiation is laid during childhood, only when people actually live in the adult world do they begin to conform to gender stereotypes. They do this because of the demands that are placed on them by the specific situations they encounter. As the situations in which people find themselves channel their behavior and options, they establish patterns of appropriate gender-role behavior.

In 1980 Joanna Bunker Rohrbaugh reported on a pair of studies that suggest the effects of situational factors on adult women. The first, done by Alice Rossi (1965), found that among women in their twenties, those who chose marriage and child-rearing as full-time occupations seemed happier, had higher senses of self-esteem, and were less anxious than women who chose careers. Young career women worried about whether they had made the right choices and whether they were good enough to do well in their jobs. Rossi suspected that at some point the homemakers would begin to feel less satisfied and complete, especially as their children went off to school and needed them less, or at least less constantly. The career women, she believed, would eventually find more satisfaction in their jobs and would feel more challenged and competent to handle the challenges.

The second study, done by Judith Birnbaum (1975), confirmed Rossi's suspicions. Birnbaum compared full-time homemakers who had been top students in college fifteen years before with both married and single professional women. Compared to all the professional women, the homemakers had low senses of self-esteem and personal competence, felt lonely and unattractive, and missed a sense of challenge and creative involvement. They were also much more likely than the married professional women to think that marriage was restricting, demanding, and burdensome.

One study of young adults shows very clearly how the pressure of adult life continues to shape the enactment of gender roles. Foster, Wallston, and Berger (1980) found that even though large numbers of young women (and men) now think that they will follow less traditional, more egalitarian paths than earlier generations did, the pressure of day-to-day life in adulthood still tends to shape their career decisions to reflect the older patterns in which the man's career takes precedence.

87

Chapter 3:
More Competing
Explanations:
How Did Individuals
Get This Way?

Many women find that their adult family lives, their jobs, and their household commitments shape them in ways they did not expect. Many women who take a few years off to have children find they never quite get back on track. They especially find themselves out of touch with the activities and interests in which they were once involved. Since the job market is still segregated, men and women spend their work lives in very different kinds of jobs. Thus the socialization effects of employment can continue to create increased differentiation by gender. The obligations of child and household care continue to push women away from doing things they might otherwise do.

Adulthood can also be a time in which people who have learned traditional gender and sexual orientations can experience a process of resocialization toward very new and different roles and identities. The feminist movement has been an important agent of socialization to new gender orientations (Sapiro 1989). In their introduction to a collection of life stories of women in the arts and sciences, for example, Sara Ruddick and Pamela Daniels described the experience of a group of women "educated in the 1950s, at the height of the feminine mystique." This is a group of women who "encountered the women's movement late, usually in [their] thirties" (Ruddick and Daniels 1977, xxviii). As a result of contact with the women's movement,

> All of us have had to relearn our pasts. We have had to reevaluate our purposes in working and re-view our commitments to our work and to those we love. Raised consciousness, whatever its ultimate value, has brought vulnerability and has invited risk. It has insisted on change. Our stories are the evidence that significant changes can and do occur in adult lives—after we are supposed to be "grown up" and "settled down." (Ruddick and Daniels 1977, xxix)

Synthesis of Learning Theories: Gender-schema Theory and Doing Gender

In recent years some scholars have attempted to combine the insights of cognitive-developmental and social-learning theories by developing what they call gender schema theory. Sandra Bem, a leading theorist in this field, defines *schema* as a "network of associations that organizes and guides an individual's perception" (1983, 603); a gender schema, therefore, is a network of associations with the concepts of male and female (or masculinity and femininity) that organizes and guides an individual's perception. Bem notes that these gender-related networks encompass

> not only those features directly related to female and male persons—such as anatomy, reproductive function, division of labor, and personality attributes—but also features more remotely or metaphorically related to sex, such as the angularity or roundedness of an abstract shape and the periodicity of the moon. (1983, 603)

As social-learning theorists would argue, the content of the gender schema (the ideas found within it) is learned in large part from interaction with the social environment and the gender-linked practices of the social world. The gender schema is then used by the individual to process information by structuring and organizing perception and by helping the individual to evaluate incoming information (including information about the self) with regard to gender norms. The emphasis on cognitive frameworks and the active role of the mind in learning and processing information reflects cognitive-developmental theory.

The most important insight of gender schema theory is that people follow gender schemas to different degrees and in different ways. Some people, for example, organize many of their thoughts, perceptions, and evaluations around concepts of male and female, masculine and feminine. These people, whom we might describe as highly sex typed, rely heavily on gender stereotypes and symbols to understand the social world. They see a wide variety of human characteristics, behavior, roles, and jobs as decidedly masculine or feminine and evaluate themselves and others according to how well they conform to gender norms and stereotypes.

Other people follow gender schemas less closely or not at all. This does not necessarily mean that they lack what the highly sex-typed person might regard as appropriate masculine and feminine characteristics. Gender may simply not be the central means by which they organize their perceptions of themselves and the social world. Whereas the highly sex-typed person might immediately understand words such as *pink, nurturant, blushing, librarian,* and *curved* as "feminine," these words might not have any immediate gender connotation to the person with no gender schema.

Gender-schema theory predicts (and some research shows) that individuals who tend to operate on the basis of gender schemas are particularly likely to accept for themselves culturally defined gender-appropriate attributes. Such individuals use their gender schemas not only to guide their behavior but also to structure their further learning. Individuals with less rigid gender schemas do not limit their perceptions or learning in the same way; they are more open to new information, regardless of whether it conforms to cultural stereotypes.

The interesting question from the point of view of gender schema theory is not just what people learn about gender, but how they learn it and why different people living in the same culture learn to use concepts with culturally based gender connotations in different ways. Research on learning has not yet found a complete answer to this question.

Discussion of gender schemas focuses our attention on the way we think about gender. But it is clear that gender is more than ideas and symbols. It involves action and interaction, behavior that displays and even asserts femininity, masculinity, or the rejection of these concepts.

Recognition of the importance of action, interaction, and display has led Candace West and Don H. Zimmerman (1987) to write about "doing gender." They argue that "a person's gender is not simply an aspect of what one is, but, more fundamentally, it is something that one *does,* and does recurrently, in interaction with others" (140). Gender, they contend, is not just a matter of roles that have been learned and are repeated automatically; it involves continual work to reproduce in one's everyday behavior. Because gender is an important basis for social organization, doing gender, even while we are engaged in other activities, helps define our place and keep social relations orderly.

89

Chapter 3:
More Competing
Explanations:
How Did Individuals
Get This Way?

Women may be especially aware of doing gender while they are deciding how to dress for specific situations each day. How "feminine" should one appear at a job interview? At work? It depends on the job and special circumstances. The same woman may well highlight her gender much more forcefully when dressing to go to a party than when she goes to work. Sometimes deciding how much to do gender takes very careful thought.

Gender-schema theory can be used to understand the meanings (and variability of meanings) of gender, while Zimmerman and West's notion of doing gender reminds us of the effort and activity it takes to learn and display (or refuse to display) our gender. The insights of cognitive-development theory can contribute to understanding the relationship between identity and gender meanings. It emphasizes the active nature of learning and the participation of individuals in their own socialization. Social-learning theory, on the other hand, focuses our attention on the social order and the means by which social interaction imposes rules and meaning.

Discrimination: Being Forced to Be Different

This final explanation for differences between male and female activities suggests that men and women often do not learn to be different or choose to be different but are forced to be different. According to this view women are forced out of certain roles and activities because their passage has been barred through discrimination. This point is important: If we argue that most differences between the lives women and men lead develop because they have learned to choose different paths, we arrive at one set of solutions to the problem of gender differentiation and stratification; if we find that, regardless of what people have learned, they take different roles because they are forced to do so through discrimination, the solutions will be different.

The verb *discriminate* is derived from the Latin *discernere,* meaning "to distinguish between." Not all forms of discrimination are bad. In art and music, for example, we talk about the discriminating eye or ear. We discriminate between children and adults in meting out punishment. The type of discrimination with which we are concerned here, however, is not so commendable. Our use of the word refers to the act of singling out a person for special treatment not on the basis of individual merit, but on the basis of prejudices about the group to which that person belongs. When a woman is barred from a job or receives relatively low pay not because of her lack of ability but because she happens to be a woman, we say that she has been discriminated against on the basis of sex.

At one time many graduate and professional schools explicitly required higher entrance qualifications from women than from men. Many employers explicitly prefer not to hire women. As we have seen, a substantial minority of the population cannot say they would vote for a woman for president even if she were qualified. Some employers would prefer not to hire women because they assume from the start that most women are not qualified for the job. These people might claim that they are not discriminating, they are only looking for qualified people. As long as these employers automatically rule out women and do not consider them on the basis of individual merit, however, they are discriminating, and according to the 1964 Civil Rights Act they are engaging in an illegal activity.

A person does not have to be conscious of what he or she is doing to discriminate, but unconscious discrimination is more difficult to identify. None of us always sees people objectively; our expectations of people affect how we see them. Claudia Cohen (1981) did an experiment to find out what people see and remember about other people. She first developed a list of stereotypes her subjects had about particular occupations. After showing them a short movie that identified the occupation of the main character and included some details that conformed to the stereotypes and some that did not, she asked the subjects in her experiment to tell her what they remembered about the movie. She found that her subjects "were selectively more accurate in remembering those characteristics that fit their prototype than those features that were inconsistent with the target person's occupation" (1981, 447).

Marianne Carlsson and Pia Jaderquist (1983) tested the memories and perception of first graders by reading them stories, some of which had gender-appropriate girls and boys as main characters and some of which had gender-inappropriate characters. The children tended to reconstruct the gender-inappropriate stories to conform more closely to gender stereotypes. This tendency was even stronger when children were questioned about the stories seven days later. Dana Christensen and Robert Rosenthal (1982) found that men's expectations bias their perceptions of other people more than women's do. These studies support the notion of gender schemas discussed earlier.

Other research suggests that people often use labels meaning very different things to describe a characteristic or activity that is similar in women and men. Mayer and Bell (1975), for example, found that a sociable man is often described as friendly and cooperative, and a sociable woman is often described as unreliable and talkative.

Numerous studies have investigated the possibility that people see women and men and their qualifications differently even when they are objectively the same. One of the most widely used research designs follows a model first used by Philip Goldberg in 1968: The subjects are asked to evaluate an essay, speech, job application, piece of artwork, or musical composition. All subjects are given the same work to evaluate, but some are told that a man created the work, and some are told that a woman did.

Many of these experiments (not including Goldberg's) found evidence of prejudice against women. A meta-analysis of 123 such studies concludes that we do not have the evidence to say simply that women are evaluated more negatively than men because of the great differences in the results of these studies. That study concluded that, "Gender-biased evaluations indeed occur, but the complexity of the conditions under which such evaluations occur and the flexibility of social perceivers' thinking must be taken into consideration" (Swim et al. 1989, 424).

These experiments suggest that people are more likely to be prejudiced in their evaluations if the situation or activity is stereotypically masculine. The more information people are given about an individual the less they rely on stereotypes (Swim et al. 1989). Discrimination is particularly likely to emerge in evaluations involved in hiring decisions (Glick, Zion, and Nelson 1988). Some research finds men more likely to be prejudiced against women than women are (e.g., Sapiro 1982b).

These types of research suggest first that people who discriminate may not know they are doing so and second that it may be very difficult to identify cases in which discrimination has occurred. There is considerable evidence of sex discrimination in job and education counseling, letters of recommendation, and evaluations of individuals that affect hiring, salary, and promotion. How much discrimination is there? As long as discrimination can occur unconsciously and most of the important decisions about us are made confidentially, we cannot know.

91

Chapter 3:
More Competing
Explanations:
How Did Individuals
Get This Way?

Individual Development and Social Change

We have looked at six different approaches people use to explain the existence of differences between women and men at the individual level. Each is based on a different type of research and evidence, employs different assumptions, and comes to different conclusions.

Which of these theories is "correct"? The answer is that no single theory completely explains the process of gender role development and differentiation. Each has drawbacks, and each focuses our attention on a slightly different aspect of the problem. These different approaches are by no means mutually exclusive; one can argue, for example, that psychoanalytic theories explain some aspects of gender development, cognitive-development theories others, and discrimination theories still others. These different theories can provide complementary insights that fill in the whole picture. The task for the student of gender development is to learn to evaluate and use these theories skillfully and appropriately.

These theories of individual differences also need to be integrated with the theories of social differentiation and stratification reviewed in Chapter 2. We began this chapter by observing that theories used to explain how a given sex/gender system evolves and is maintained in a given society do not necessarily tell us how individuals in a given society come to fit or not fit into that system. By the same token, theories that explain how individual gender development occurs do not tell us how the society as a whole comes to be structured in a particular way. The theories offered in this chapter may help us understand why so many young women today will become secretaries rather than business executives. They do not tell us why in this century secretaries are usually women, although in the nineteenth century they were usually men, or why, since secretarial positions have come to be primarily female jobs, they have fewer promotion prospects than the lower-level business jobs held predominantly by men. Societal theories can help explain how and why the institution of marriage came to be based on patriarchal norms (and why those norms seem to be threatened now), and how the institution of marriage is linked to other social, political, and economic structures of society. Individual theories suggest some of the reasons why most women continue to participate in those arrangements, and why some do not. (For further explanation, see Chapter 10.)

Women's studies scholars are interested, therefore, in the insights offered by both the societal theories outlined in Chapter 2 and the individual theories outlined in this chapter because they investigate both the historical development of sex/gender systems and the development of individuals within given societies. For this reason each of the following chapters of this book includes discussion of both levels of analysis.

NOTES

1. A good basic text on female biology is Sloane (1980).
2. This book is a compilation of papers Horney wrote between 1922 and 1936.
3. Kohlberg was also responsible for initiating the study of moral development. Some of his conclusions about the relationship between gender and moral development have become the subject of considerable controversy, especially since the publication of Carol Gilligan's *In a Different Voice* (1982). See Chapter 2 for more discussion.

PART TWO

Gender-defining Institutions

IN THIS SECTION we will take a closer look at some social institutions and organizations whose primary function is defining cultural norms: the values through which we understand ourselves, other people, and the world in which we live. We will focus on educational and health-care institutions, organized religion, the mass and cultural media of communications, and government.

Each chapter will examine the ways in which these institutions define, maintain, and change gender norms and sex/gender systems. The chapter on education, for example, shows how gender norms are taught in educational institutions, and the chapter on health care shows how definitions of health and health-care practices shape and are shaped by definitions of gender. We will look especially at how these institutions shape women's lives and at the influence women have had on these institutions. In looking at women's influence we will focus not only on women's leadership positions within these institutions but also on the kinds of influence women have had as community and family members. We will see that although women's power has been limited by androcentric sex/gender systems, women have also had much more scope for shaping their own and others' lives than is often realized.

Although it is the most important norm-defining institution, the family does not have its own chapter in this section. Instead, because of the importance of understanding families as social institutions when studying gender and women, each chapter will devote considerable attention to the family. Part Three will also focus directly and intensively on women and the family.

Reflect Before You Read

1. Think about the education you have had up to this point, including, if applicable, your religious training. What did you learn about women? About men? Did your education give you any hints or guidelines about what it should mean

to you that you were born male or female? If you had been born of the other sex, how might your education have been different?

2. Enjoy yourself this week. Watch television, go to the movies or a play, listen to music on the radio, or watch a sporting event. What do you see women and men doing? What are their characteristics? What do these entertainments teach you about women and men, femininity and masculinity?

3. The vast majority of state and federal legislators are men. Why is this? What would it take for more women to get elected? What difference would it make if most of the members of these institutions were women? Why do so many people think that politics is ''men's business''?

4

Education: For Whom? By Whom? For What?

EDUCATION has been a central focus of women seeking to improve their condition and raise their status for well over two centuries. The issues of women as teachers and learners were topics of profound dispute during the early American colonial period and have been almost constant subjects of debate ever since. Some of the reasons should be obvious. Education imparts skills that create options for individuals, not just in economic life but also in social and political life. Education is an instrument for attaining positions of high prestige and power, and in and of itself it grants prestige and respect to the individual. The high school dropout and the person with a Ph.D. do not have the same social status or respect from others. Education provides contacts and experiences that alter people's lives; it also affects the way people think and act. The education system is one of the most important definers of gender norms and one of the most important components of a sex/gender system. No wonder so many women have fought for education when it was denied to them.

This chapter examines the roles education and educational institutions play in shaping women's lives and the roles women have played in shaping education.

Historical Perspectives on Women's Education

We begin with two premises.

1. To think of education only as what happens in school buildings on weekdays from early autumn to late spring is to ignore much of what has constituted education, especially women's education, during most of history.
2. Observers and theorists of education have long recognized that the substance and process of education imparts far more than the three R's or even what we generally think of as school subjects.

95

Education has generally been regarded as the imparting of ways of thinking and living as much as anything else. The process and goals of education are linked to societal views of what types of people and characteristics are needed in society, and what place specific groups and individuals should have in society. The notions that everyone should get as much education as possible and that the government should guarantee this by paying for most of it is very recent indeed. It is an idea that is fitted to a very specific conception of the goals and characteristics of society and its members.

Early Efforts

Until the nineteenth century, relatively few people had formal education of any sort. Most people learned what they needed to know either by trial and error or from someone more experienced. Trades and other work were learned by apprenticeship or from parents or other relatives. Mothers and fathers passed their skills and knowledge on to their daughters and sons. For the most part, women taught women what they ''needed'' to know, and men taught men what they ''needed'' to know. For those who attained literacy the only textbook was frequently the Bible, for that was the only book people ''needed'' to read.

Formal education was largely restricted to the wealthy and well connected, generally the men of the upper class. Formal education was considered irrelevant for most free citizens, and dangerous and even illegal for black people held as slaves. Although there are numerous examples of well-educated women, education for upper-class women was generally confined to a bit of literature, a bit of music, and perhaps a bit of foreign language, all taught at home. The purpose of this education was to train the woman for her station. She should be pretty, witty, and, above all, a good complement to her husband.

The first real American battle over women's education revolved not around schooling per se but around whether women should write and speak and what they should write and say. An early focus of this controversy was women's speaking and teaching on religion. Early on women were active as religious teachers, but limits were imposed on them. As Lyle Koehler has reported (1982, 41), in 1637 ''a synod of elders resolved that women might meet 'to pray and edify one another,' but when one woman 'in a prophetical way' resolved questions of doctrine and expounded Scripture, then the meeting was 'disorderly.' '' Women could preach, but only to other women, and then they could teach only thoughts that were derivative of their husband's or minister's thoughts. Women who went too far in their learning or teaching posed a danger to social order and even to their own sanity. In 1645 Governor John Winthrop of Massachusetts wrote that Anne Hopkins, the wife of Connecticut's governor, had gone insane because she spent too much time writing and reading. Her sanity might have been saved had she ''attended her household affairs, and such things as belong to a woman'' (Koehler 1982, 37). Winthrop's view bears a remarkable resemblance to advice offered to many women in the twentieth century.

Perhaps the most famous battle over women's education during the colonial period was waged between Anne Hutchinson and the religious authorities of the Massachusetts Bay Colony. Although the strict Massachusetts colony dealt harshly

97

Chapter 4:
Education:
For Whom?
By Whom?
For What?

with all cases of suspected heresy, part of the reason offered by the authorities for excommunicating and banishing Hutchinson was that her teaching activities stepped beyond the bounds of women's proper role.

Debates of the late eighteenth and nineteenth centuries show very clearly how the design of education is linked both to broader social goals and to ideological conceptions of the places of different groups within society. As we showed in Chapter 2, the Enlightenment theorists placed great emphasis on the development of rationality and knowledge as the keys to a better and more democratic future. If people were going to create a new kind of society based on reason, individual merit, independence, competition, and achievement, individuals had to be created who would fit into that society.

Some theorists, such as Jean-Jacques Rousseau (1712–78), turned their minds to the question of education and how to fit men and women to their positions in this new world. They came to different conclusions about men and women: All thought that men should be given an education that would fit the liberal values because it was their job to carry on the major work of society. But some said that women didn't need this education. In fact they thought that such education would be counterproductive because women's tasks were to get married, be submissive and ornamental to their husbands, raise their children, and do or supervise the necessary domestic work. Other theorists, like Mary Wollstonecraft in England and the Marquis de Condorcet (1743–94) in France, argued that the values of a liberal society must also extend, at least in some degree, to women. They agreed that most women's primary occupations would be those of wife and mother, but they couldn't imagine how women could be fitting companions to these "new men," or instill in their children the right kinds of minds and behaviors if they themselves had not learned reason and independence of mind.

The debate raged in the new American republic from its inception through the nineteenth century: What kinds of men and women are needed in this new country? How should they be trained? Liberal European ideas on education had great influence in America. Some included and some excluded women. Some theorists went only as far as Benjamin Rush (1745–1813), who argued, "The equal share that every citizen has in the liberty and the possible share he may have in the government of our country make it necessary that our ladies should be qualified to a certain degree by a peculiar and suitable education, to concur in instructing their sons in the principles of liberty and government" (Kerber 1982, 91). This is hardly a radical view to twentieth-century eyes, but in the 1780s it was a significant move forward.

That women should be educated to be good mothers was not a new view, but the conception of what type of education would accomplish this was beginning to change. In fact Rush delivered his speech to the Young Ladies Academy, established in Philadelphia in 1786 as the first school for girls in the United States. Above all Rush and others recognized that education and educational institutions are not merely independent institutions for the pursuit of learning but also important arms of society designed to give people the kinds of skills and characteristics currently deemed desirable. An intellectual leader like Rush probably knew that the verb *educate* is derived from a word meaning "to rear." Most of all he and others realized that all mothers are teachers and are involved in education regardless of their own schooling.

Other people went even further in their views on women's education. Many observers criticized the typical "ladies education," which consisted of bits of this and that combined with studious attention to fashion and manners (as opposed to morals). Charles Brockden Brown (1771–1810), generally recalled as the first American novelist, agreed with Mary Wollstonecraft (whose work he read) that education for dependence could only make women fall prey to unscrupulous men.[1] Judith Sargent Murray (1751–1820), writing as "Constantia," was one of a number of women who argued that as long as women's education was aimed at producing wives and mothers, it would create dependent people rather than the independent people required by a republic.[2]

Murray was also one of the first feminists to argue that females and males do not naturally have different characteristics but are shaped to be different. In one of her most famous passages she asked her readers,

> Will it be said that the judgement of a male of two years old is more sage than that of a female's of the same age? I believe the reverse is generally observed to be true. But from that period on what partiality! how is the one exalted and the other depressed, by the contrary modes of education which are adopted! the one is taught to aspire, the other is early confined and limited! (Rossi 1988, 19.)

Other women also pointed a finger quite directly. In her 1793 graduation speech at the Young Ladies Academy, Pamela Mason charged, "Our high and mighty Lords . . . have denied us the means of knowledge, and then reproached us for the want of it" (Kerber 1982, 87). The charge is remarkably similar to one Wollstonecraft had voiced the previous year in her *Vindication of the Rights of Woman*.

Despite these arguments, women gained little in the way of formal education in those early days. They continued to teach each other, and to learn informally in the home and in the churches. That many women learned despite the lack of formal opportunities is evidenced by the number of women writers. Even during colonial days some women joined their husbands in publishing newspapers and took over when their husbands died. Many women also submitted their writings to newspapers, often under assumed names (a practice also employed by men). We can still read the poems of women such as Anne Bradstreet (1612–72) and Phyllis Wheatly (1753–84), one of the first black American poets. Mercy Otis Warren (1728–1814) was the first historian of the American Revolution, and the letters of her friend Abigail Adams, the wife of President John Adams, remain as examples of the prolific writings of many early American women. (For examples of these letters, see Rossi 1988). Finally, women continued to learn trades and skills such as millinery, midwifery, and, as we can see from the number of widows who took over their deceased husbands' businesses, business and accounting.

Expanding Access

More formal educational opportunities for women opened up in the 1830s and 1840s. As free public schools began to open, especially in the Northeast, girls joined boys in elementary school. Public education at higher levels was available almost

99

Chapter 4:
Education:
For Whom?
By Whom?
For What?

exclusively to boys until after the Civil War. Although the first American colleges opened their doors in the seventeenth century (Harvard in 1636, William and Mary in 1693), none were open to women. In 1821, however, Emma Willard (1787–1870) opened the Troy Female Seminary, which offered a curriculum similar to that offered by men's colleges. Willard expanded opportunities for women (and many later schools were modeled after hers), but she expanded the idea of the purpose of women's education only a little. She wished her students to be good American mothers or teachers. Her school, which still exists as the Emma Willard School, fared better than one of the first schools for black girls opened in 1833 by Prudence Crandall in Connecticut. Crandall was jailed on false charges, and her school was burned down.

The 1830s saw the beginnings of college education for women. Oberlin College in Ohio opened its doors to men and women, whites and blacks in 1832 and was followed by the second coeducational college, Lawrence College in Wisconsin, in 1847. Wheaton College was opened as the first real women's college in 1834, followed by Mount Holyoke in 1837. The New England Female Medical College was started in 1848, followed closely by the Philadelphia Women's Medical College in 1851.

Although only a tiny proportion of women went to these schools, which remained largely dedicated to producing fit mothers and teachers, they had a major influence on American life. Within the list of the earliest female college graduates we find the names of some of the leaders of the post–Civil War feminist movement, as well as the first formally trained female doctors, clergy, and other professionals.

These formal schools were not the only places women taught and learned. Women continued to read and write in an effort to educate themselves and others. Women also organized their own groups or seminars in order to read and discuss a variety of subjects. Anne Hutchinson had done this back in the seventeenth century; in the mid-nineteenth century women not only met together to learn but also began to develop self-conscious feminist theories of women's education. Margaret Fuller (1810–50), a member of the American Transcendentalist group (along with Emerson, Thoreau, and Bronson Alcott) and editor of their journal, *The Dial,* held "Conversations," or seminars, at which only women were allowed. She believed, as many feminists do today, that there must be at least some separate time and space in which women can learn among themselves, unimpeded by the hierarchical relations between the sexes. (For some of her writings, see Rossi 1988.)

While Fuller discussed philosophy, the classics, and other topics in the rarified atmosphere of Boston, thousands of women across the country traded information and knowledge among themselves at quilting bees and other such gatherings. And women by no means restricted themselves to such safe, though revolutionary, activities. Despite the fact that it was illegal to teach black slaves to read, women were known to do so; after the Civil War women organized missionary societies that sent women throughout the South to teach newly freed blacks. Others, organized by Catherine Beecher (sister of Harriet Beecher Stowe) in the late 1840s, went west to teach on the frontiers.

By 1873 sixty percent of all American secondary schools had mixed-sex classes. By 1867 the number of coeducational colleges had increased to twenty-two, and by 1872 the number was ninety-seven (Leach 1980, 72). Although opportunities for formal education increased during this period, women's education lagged behind men's in two respects:

1. Women received less education than men.
2. Even if they went beyond the elementary level, women's programs were different and to a large degree continued to be oriented toward producing good wives and mothers.

It is important to note that what constituted an appropriate program to produce wives and mothers had changed, but relatively few people thought education for females and males should be the same.

Increasing Leadership Roles

Women also gained some ground as teachers, administrators, and other shapers of education. Throughout the middle decades of the nineteenth century, the proportion of teachers who were women increased; in the first part of the century the vast majority were men, but by the late 1880s the majority (up to 90 percent in some cities) were women (Sklar 1982, 146). Some estimates suggest that by the mid-nineteenth century, up to one-fifth of all New England women served as teachers at some point in their lives (Jones 1980, 48). Was this growth a sign of progressive enlightenment on the part of school administrators? Kathryn Kish Sklar (1982) argues that it was more a matter of practical finances. Women were paid considerably less than men as teachers for three reasons:

1. It was argued that women did not have to support families as men did.
2. It was assumed that women taught only temporarily, until they married, and therefore deserved less pay for what they did.
3. People argued that low salaries for women were merely determined by the mechanisms of the free market; women would accept lower salaries, and so they got them.

Hiring women was a practical way of allowing mass education to grow cheaply. For women, the expansion of teaching jobs, even if they were poorly paid, meant the opening of a sector of jobs appropriate for a decent lady.

Women made less progress in entering administrative and policy-making roles, although these expanded somewhat as well. We have already noted that women began to open their own schools. These efforts increased at the end of the nineteenth century and the beginning of the twentieth century. Most of what became the "Seven Sisters" colleges (Mt. Holyoke, 1837; Vassar, 1861; Wellesley, 1870; Smith, 1871; Radcliffe, 1879; Bryn Mawr, 1880; and Barnard, 1889) were opened by women late in the last three decades of the nineteenth century. In 1904 Mary McLeod Bethune (1875–1955), a daughter of slaves, opened a small school for blacks in Daytona Beach, Florida. She herself had been educated by missionary teachers. She began her school using charred splinters of wood as pencils and elderberry juice as ink; she eventually turned the school into what is now Bethune-Cookman College (Bethune [1941] 1982).

101

Chapter 4:
Education:
For Whom?
By Whom?
For What?

Mary McLeod Bethune, educator and political activist, turned a small school
into what is now Bethune-Cookman College.

Even in women's schools, however, women remained constrained by restrictive
views of women's place. Emily James Putnam (1865–1944), a scholar and dean of
Barnard College in New York, was threatened with the loss of her job when she
married. Although she survived that round, when she became pregnant she was forced
to leave: Employment and marriage didn't mix well, and employment and
motherhood was even worse. Presumably a pregnant educator was also a bad influence

on young girls, who would then know that their female teachers had "done it." Until World War II most school boards demanded that women resign when they married; some wouldn't even wait until the end of the school year. The last of these laws disappeared as recently as the mid-1950s. Such laws, if they applied only to women, would now be illegal under the 1964 Civil Rights Act.

Women's roles in shaping education also grew in less direct ways. Qualifications for voting are determined primarily at the state and local level, and in 1837 the first state began to allow some women to vote under certain circumstances. Property-owning (white) widows in Kentucky with children in school were allowed to vote in school board elections. Kentucky allowed only property owners to vote in school board elections because schools were paid for out of property taxes, and women with husbands were not allowed to vote because they were represented by their husbands in politics. It seemed fair, however, that a widow with children in school should have some say in school-related matters. As time passed, increasing numbers of states and localities extended the school board vote to women because education came to be viewed as an appropriate arena for women's action. Soon the right to vote in school board elections was followed by the right to run for school board offices (first in Illinois in 1872). By the end of the nineteenth century a number of women served on school boards, some even as school superintendents, across the country.

As the number of educated women rose at the end of the nineteenth century, women became increasingly active in trying to shape education. The number of women's clubs and organizations directed at improving education mushroomed. The 1870s saw the rise of "moral education" or "moral science" societies, groups of women who began to discuss among themselves a range of topics including sexuality, marriage, and birth control (Leach 1980). Suffrage groups and others interested in women's roles in society held lectures, seminars, and other such meetings to educate women for citizenship.

The rise of social science in America, especially the view that the knowledge gained from the study of social science could help make a better society, created another avenue for women's involvement in education. Women were not only active in the American Social Science Association (ASSA) but also formed their own social science associations and clubs beginning in the 1870s. As early as 1874 Franklin Sanborn, a leader in the ASSA, was arguing, "The work of social science is literally women's work, and it is getting done by them more and more; but there is room for all sexes and ages in the field of social science" (Leach 1980, 316). These women's groups, which later took leading roles in the politics of the Progressive era, all lobbied for educational reforms.

Many women also began to take on quite radical issues, as demonstrated by the address of Dr. Alice Stockham to the Illinois Social Science Association in 1878. She argued that it should be obligatory "that every child should get special instruction in procreation and reproduction. Let us see to it that no girl should go to the altar of marriage without being instructed in the physiological function of maternity" (Leach 1980, 321). Margaret Sanger (1883–1960), the birth control campaigner, brought education about reproductive issues to working-class women in the immigrant ghettos. Feminists were just as concerned as others about the quality of women's lives as wives and mothers, but their approach was then, as it is now, quite different from that of nonfeminists.

103

Chapter 4:
Education:
For Whom?
By Whom?
For What?

By the end of the nineteenth century a new group of women had to be considered in the design of education: immigrants and the children of immigrants. Once again, the debate about educational programs for immigrants in general and immigrant women in particular demonstrates the degree to which education reflects people's views about the needs and characteristics of society and the social groups within it. School administrators, other government officials, and a variety of women's groups, including the newly formed groups of social workers, applied themselves to figuring out what kind of education immigrants needed and what kind of women America needed or wanted to create.

Their conclusions were the usual ones: Education should help immigrant women be good American wives and mothers. Immigrant women needed to know English so they could run their households properly and teach their children. They needed courses in household arts or home economics so they could make proper American homes and budget properly to ward off the discontent of poverty. They needed to be Americanized to be able to control their children and ward off juvenile delinquency. And they needed to be taught trades (appropriate for females) so they could avoid being drawn into the "white slave trade" (prostitution) until they got married.

Special efforts devoted to the education of immigrant women had only mixed success. Much more effort was devoted to educating immigrant men. Even in public schools, overcrowding meant school officials were more willing to let girls drop out to create places for boys. The norm in the majority of immigrant families was that girls should leave school early to help support their families and put their brothers through school.

Maxine Seller (1982) suggests that many of the most popular and successful programs were run by ethnic and cultural groups and churches, such as the Polish Women's Alliance of America, the Union of Czech Women, the National Council of Jewish Women; by trade unions, such as the Ladies Waist Makers Union or the International Ladies Garment Workers Union (ILGWU); or by socialist groups.

Achieving Higher Education

Education for women grew and continued to grow in the twentieth century despite resistance and occasional slowdowns. Resisters worked very hard to keep women back, sometimes calling on the assistance of supposedly "scientific" theories, such as those of Edward Clarke. In the 1880s Clarke argued that if women got too much education, the energy that should be going to their wombs would go to their brains instead and leave them too feeble to produce good children. By the middle of the twentieth century, the question whether women should be educated up to the secondary level had been resolved, and the battle focused more on facilitating women's access to university education, advanced degrees, and training programs in traditionally male fields such as business and industry.

As we near the twenty-first century, women and men have now reached parity in the number of B.A. and M.A. degrees they earn (see Table 4-1). It is clear from these figures that progress has not been slow and steady. The proportion of women earning B.A.s increased until World War II, fell, and then increased again. Some of the drop, especially in the 1950s, can be accounted for by the fact that colleges

While these Smith College students studied chemistry in 1889 some theorists
argued that too much education was bad for women's health.

were filled by male veterans of World War II assisted by the G.I. Bill. The year 1930
marked a high point for women earning M.A.s that was not surpassed until the 1970s.
Likewise women's share of Ph.D.s rose until 1920, then dropped until an impressive
upward shift during the 1970s. The decline in the proportion of higher degrees gained
by women occurred not because the absolute number of women fell, but because
the number of men seeking these degrees rose so steeply in a time of massive
discrimination against women. Progress in the traditionally male fields of medicine,
dentistry, and law began in the 1970s and has been impressive since then. (For more
introduction to women's education today see Chapter 1.)

Women's Education Today

Except for state laws requiring both males and females to remain in school until a
specific age, there has been no public policy to promote equal education for males
and females until recently. Women waited until 1972 to see a clear statement from
the U.S. government supporting equal education and forbidding discrimination. Title
IX of the Education Amendments Act of 1972 reads, ''No person in the United
States shall, on the basis of sex, be excluded from participation in, be denied the

105

Chapter 4:
Education:
For Whom?
By Whom?
For What?

TABLE 4-1
Proportion of All Degrees Awarded to Women, 1890–1987

Year	B.A.	M.A.	Ph.D.	Medicine (M.D.)	Dentistry (D.D.S.)	Law (L.L.D. & J.D.)
1890	17	19	1			
1900	19	19	6			
1910	23	26	10			
1920	34	30	15			
1930	40	40	15			
1940	41	38	13			
1950	24	29	10	10	1	
1960	35	35	11	6	1	2
1970	42	40	13	8	1	5
1980	47	49	28	23	13	30
1987	51	50	35	32	23	39

SOURCE: Deckard 1979, 316; U.S. Bureau of the Census 1982; U.S. Department of Education 1988, 215.

benefits of, or be subjected to discrimination under any education program or activity receiving federal financial assistance." This act covers all public schools and many private ones. In the late 1970s, however, most observers, including the American Association of University Women and the U.S. Commission on Civil Rights, thought that the act actually had done little to increase educational opportunities for women.

How Much Education?

Two questions need to be asked about the quantity of women's education:

1. Do women and men get the same amount of education?
2. Do women get the amount of education they need?

These are not merely different wordings of the same question. Even if levels of education are similar for men and women, we cannot necessarily assume that women are getting the amount of education they need. Some people would say, for example, that if men and women get the same amount of education, either women are overeducated, or men are undereducated. For certain purposes, like earning the same amount of money as men, women may need more education than men. The law now requires that all children, male and female, go to school from the age of five or six to sixteen. The law poses no requirements before that age or after, so it is in those periods that we will look for differences.

Education before first grade has become increasingly popular since World War II. Kindergartens and nursery schools are seen as important settings for the transition to "real school." The popularity of these programs was bolstered by the increased value placed on education in general; the growth in the number of employed mothers; and the growth of programs such as ''Project Head Start'' in the 1960s, which were seen as means of helping children from poverty-stricken families ''catch up.'' In 1967 government figures showed that about 32 percent of all children aged three to five, and a slightly higher proportion of white children, were enrolled in preprimary education programs; by 1986 about 55 percent of all children were enrolled in such programs. The figures for boys and girls are nearly the same.

As Table 4-1 shows, the proportion of males and females going beyond high school has also evened out, at least to the M.A. level. Colleges and universities are not the only types of postsecondary education available; adults may also enroll in technical, vocational, business, and other kinds of training programs. Women are a majority of those enrolled in adult-education programs (U.S. Bureau of the Census 1989, 161).

Women also get their adult education from different sources than men. They are more likely to take courses from local schools and two-year colleges, private tutors and instructors, or private community organizations. The courses men take are more likely to be provided by business and industry, labor unions or professional associations, or their own employers.

Women are also continuing their long tradition of educating themselves outside the school. Women's church groups, professional and labor organizations, and political and social clubs continue to hold lectures, meetings, courses, and training institutes for women to learn a wide range of subjects and skills. One of the most important functions of the new women's movement has been education. It has spawned innumerable lectures, seminars, and small informal discussion groups, as well as books, articles, newspapers, magazines, and publishing houses.

Overall women have about as much education as men, but their education is not equivalent. As we noted in Chapter 1, women's higher degrees are concentrated in different fields from those of men, most of them in fields more traditionally considered ''women's fields''; in particular they are not concentrated in the most prestigious fields and those likely to lead to the most lucrative jobs, though even equivalent levels of education do not offer women and men the same results in terms of jobs and pay, as we saw in Chapter 1 (Table 1-6). At every level of education, women earn less than men do.

Even when girls and boys are in the same classrooms, there is evidence that they receive different amounts of education. Teachers tend to react differently to girls and boys, and they have different amounts of contact with them. Numerous studies show that boys get more negative treatment or criticism from teachers, although there is contradictory evidence as well (Bank, Biddle, and Good 1980). Criticism in the classroom, however, is not necessarily harmful to education. One study (Dweck et al. 1978) found that boys get more criticism from teachers, but it is very different from the criticism that girls receive. Boys were more likely to be criticized for not trying hard enough to do well, which seems to assume that they could do better if they wanted to. Girls were more likely to be criticized for their academic performance itself, which may be a less-encouraging evaluation. Another study finds that girls, and particularly black girls, get less feedback than boys (Irvine 1986).

107

Chapter 4:
Education:
For Whom?
By Whom?
For What?

Even the amount of contact teachers have with students is different for the two sexes. One study of second graders shows that teachers made more contacts with girls during reading classes and with boys during mathematics classes (Leinhardt, Seewald, and Engel 1979). Another study suggests that girls and boys have to act differently to get the same amount of attention from their teachers (Serbin et al. 1973). In that study girls who were physically close to their teachers received more attention than boys who were physically close; boys who were aggressive received more attention than girls who were aggressive. Perhaps that is why boys initiate more interactions with teachers than girls do (Irvine 1986). These findings support the assertion that schools provide a hidden curriculum of gender role training.

There is, of course, a fine line between quantitative differences in education and qualitative differences; that is, it is possible that a person might receive a lot of education of the wrong or counterproductive kind. The next aspect of education we will explore, therefore, is the type of education males and females receive.

What Did You Learn in School Today?

We have already proposed that males and females sitting in the same classrooms may not be getting the same education. Educators talk about two different types of content in teaching: the overt curriculum, or what people claim to be teaching, and the hidden curriculum, or things that may be taught consciously or unconsciously but are not part of the apparent lesson plan. Critics of American education argue that within the hidden curriculum there is still strong support for traditional gender roles and, more specifically, discouragement for girls who might otherwise stretch themselves beyond traditional gender boundaries in intellectual skills and interests.

Consider the content of school lessons and the textbooks used to complement them. In the book's Introduction, we briefly discussed the content of school curricula and showed what a very small place women have in what we learn in school. Even in the nineteenth century some educational reformers realized it was necessary to give girls examples of women who had achieved notability in a variety of fields in order to expand their ambitions and horizons (Leach 1980). In the 1970s a group of women published a study of 2760 children's stories to demonstrate the lessons girls and boys learn about women's potential (Women on Words and Images 1972). They found females notably absent from the world presented to children. There were five boy-centered stories for every two girl-centered stories, three adult male characters for every adult female character, and six biographies of males for every biography of a female. Although males were considerably more present than females, the word *mother* appeared more often than the word *father,* and the word *wife* appeared three times as often as the word *husband*. Similar findings have emerged from studies of textbooks at the primary and secondary levels (Weitzman 1979).

Bias in school books is by no means limited to the primary and secondary levels. Reviews of college- and graduate-level textbooks show the same pattern. A review of medical textbooks, including those used in obstetrics and gynecology classes, shows that women are often presented in thoroughly negative terms and used gratuitously as sex objects in illustrations and examples (Scully and Bart 1973). Little changed in later years (Elder, Humphreys, and Laskowski 1988). Perhaps even more shocking if we are concerned with possibilities for change in education is Sadker and Sadker's (1980) content analysis of the most widely used education textbooks, which found the same pattern of bias. Despite all research on gender and sexism in education done in recent decades, only one book the Sadkers looked at devoted even .5 percent of its space (1 page out of 200, for example) to issues of sexism. Another book discussed guidelines for nonsexist language but did not itself follow the guidelines. A review of introductory sociology textbooks published between 1982 and 1988 also found little material on women (Hall 1988).

Does this bias in textbooks make a difference? Many psychologists emphasize the importance of role models in developing children's senses of identity and in giving them examples to follow. These books not only support traditional and relatively restrictive roles for women but also present an unrealistic view of contemporary social life. They offer children and young adults fiction in the guise of fact. In the textbook world women are wives and mothers; in the real world many are wives and mothers, but they are many other things as well. Two pieces of research show how textbooks affect what children learn and think. In one study Ashby and Wittmaier (1978) read to fourth-grade girls either a story presenting women only in their traditional family roles or a story showing women in nontraditional activities. The girls were then asked to rate a series of jobs and characteristics according to how appropriate they were for women. The girls who had heard the stories with the nontraditional themes rated traditionally male jobs and characteristics as appropriate for females more frequently than the other girls.

In another study (Schneider and Hacker 1973), researchers gave college students titles for chapters in a forthcoming general sociology textbook and asked them to select appropriate photographs for each of the chapters. Some of the students were given the chapter titles "Social Man," "Industrial Man," and "Political Man." The others were given the chapter titles "Society," "Industrial Life," and "Political Behavior." The latter chose pictures with a greater number of women in them. Apparently the first set of titles created (or supported) images of the world as predominantly male in the minds of the students given those titles to illustrate.

The history of education, and women's education in particular, shows very clearly that education is designed not merely to transmit information to new generations but also to fit these generations as far as possible to the roles they will play in the adult world. After the U.S.S.R. launched the satellite Sputnik in the late 1950s, U.S. schools began to place special educational emphasis on mathematics and the natural sciences. The schools blunted the message to a considerable degree, however, by offering a conflicting message to girls. The second message was that the most important role for a girl was still that of wife and mother (even if she also studied physics) and that a girl should not "sacrifice her femininity" to pursue education or a career.

The message to girls continues to be contradictory. As we saw in the discussion of the history of women's education, even training for motherhood does not remain static from one generation to the next. Earlier in this century, home economics and domestic science courses were introduced into secondary school and college curricula to teach women (and generally only women because domestic care is *their* job) how to be modern housewives. The modern housewife, experts claimed, needed more

109

Chapter 4:
Education:
For Whom?
By Whom?
For What?

than her mother's recipes to be successful; she needed firm knowledge of nutrition, psychology, sociology, and even biology and organic chemistry to run her household scientifically. If a mother was going to be nurturant and helpful to her children, she needed some advanced mathematics and even physics to help them with their homework. However, if a woman wanted a career, it should be one that would fit in with her "inevitable" family commitments and could be dropped for a few years when her children needed her most. (For further discussion of this topic, see Chapter 12.) Much of this restrictive philosophy still exists today.

Children learn very young that some subjects are "masculine" and some are "feminine." We have already discussed some of the problems surrounding mathematics. One study (reported in Tobias and Weissbrod 1980) found that adolescent girls refrain from studying mathematics because they think boys don't like girls who study mathematics. Julia Sherman (1980) found that the degree to which high school girls considered mathematics a male domain affected their performance in the subject, and among eleventh-grade girls it affected how much confidence they had in their abilities to learn math. Thus a girl who thinks that mathematics is a masculine subject will not have much confidence in her ability to learn mathematics or may feel it is better to avoid the subject for social reasons. Neither of these attitudes will help her peformance.

The gender messages in education are not restrictive only to girls. In the United States (although not in all countries) girls tend to be better than boys at reading in the younger grades. Carol Dwyer (1974) studied the problem and found that boys who did poorly in reading were more likely to consider reading to be a "feminine" occupation.

Gender definitions are learned very early and are very central to our senses of self. Labeling different kinds of subjects masculine or feminine can only restrict education. As Florence Christoplos and JoAnn Borden (1978) found in their study of school children, both boys and girls do well on school problems that are directly related to what they view as appropriate gender norms and poorly on those at odds with these norms. It is, of course, quite possible for young people to assert themselves against these norms, but, as Michelle Stanworth has written, "It takes considerably more determination (and support) for [boys and girls] to choose a subject or career which is not considered appropriate to their gender" (1983, 17). Unfortunately we have little evidence that many teachers, even at the university level, are willing to help young people assert themselves in this way, partly because they are unaware that there is a problem.

Young people's interest and confidence in their abilities seem to be linked to how gender appropriate they find a particular subject or activity. The reasons people use to explain men and women's experiences, especially their successes and failures, also differ according to gender expectations. Experimental research shows that people tend to express male success and female failure in terms of possession or lack of skills and to explain male failure and female success in terms of other factors, often things out of their control. (For a review of this research, see Deaux 1976.) In one study, for example, people were told about males or females who did well or poorly in school. They were then asked to make up stories to explain these successes and failures. The same pattern found in other studies emerged: In the stories the subjects composed, males did well because they were smart and poorly because they were unlucky. Females did well because the test was easy, because they tried harder, or even because they cheated; they did poorly because they were not smart. This pattern holds particularly for gender-inappropriate tasks.

Perhaps the most disturbing aspect of this body of research is that males and females apply these different perceptions to their own experiences. Girls learn not to expect much from their own abilities, which leads many to underrate themselves. By the same token, males show a tendency to overrate their own work. Two studies provide examples. Marcia S. Halperin and Doris L. Abrams (1978) did a study of students in an undergraduate economics course. The students were asked to complete questionnaires indicating, among other things, how much they thought their performance in the course depended on luck, skill, the difficulty of the course, and so forth. Among the most successful students, both men and women explained their performance on a midterm exam with reference to their own ability. Among students who did less well, however, the men more than the women tended to blame their relative lack of success on a lack of effort, as though they could have done better if they had tried (which may well have been true). The women blamed a lack of luck, which again suggests that they might have done better, but many more women than men blamed a lack of ability. The same pattern held true for the students' evaluations of their performance on the final examination.

Michelle Stanworth (1983) investigated self-evaluations of adolescents in British schools and found related evidence for girls' lack of confidence and boys' over-confidence. She asked both students and teachers to rank students in their classes according to how well they were doing academically. Nineteen of the twenty-four students ranked themselves differently from the way the teacher ranked them. All the girls who differed from the teacher's evaluation underestimated their own ranking. All but one of the boys who differed from the teacher overestimated their own ranking. In most of these cases, the girls incorrectly ranked themselves lower than a boy, and the boys incorrectly ranked themselves higher than a girl.

Parents also assess their children's school work and abilities on the basis of gender. A study of seventh-grade mathematics students found that among students of average ability fathers (but not mothers) held lower achievement standards for daughters than for sons. Parents (especially mothers) attributed their daughters' math successes more to effort than they did for sons, and attributed their sons' successes more to talent than they did for daughters (Yee and Eccles 1988).

Gender norms do have direct effects on school performance. We have already seen that girls may be discouraged from pursuing ''male'' subjects because they are afraid of being unpopular with boys. Many girls have been advised that if they are too competitive, boys will not like them. One study shows what wide effects these attitudes have throughout American culture. Carol C. Weisfeld, Glenn E. Weisfeld, and John W. Callaghan (1982) studied groups of adolescent Hopi and black girls who were highly skilled at playing dodgeball. They found that the girls reduced their level of competitiveness—actually held back their own performances—when they played with boys, especially when they played with boys who were relatively unskilled. Further investigation showed that the girls were unaware of what they were doing. Similar behavior in boys playing girls, would be regarded as chivalrous, but because the girls' behavior is unacknowledged, the implication is different. It simply offers further, although mistaken, evidence to all involved that boys are better than girls.

111

Chapter 4:
Education:
For Whom?
By Whom?
For What?

Segregation and Schooling

One of the oldest debates over women and education concerns the benefits and drawbacks of mixed- versus single-sex education. For a long time, education was quite rigidly segregated because it was thought improper for the sexes to be mixed too much. Moreover, regardless of whether the sexes were educated separately or together, many fields of study were segregated, or available only to one sex or another. Girls in particular were barred from subjects thought too indelicate for them. For example, women had particular trouble training as artists because they were not allowed into classes with (nude) life models. Medical training also posed problems because of the parts of the body that must be discussed and viewed. The very idea of women working on cadavers was considered indecent.

Many reformers of the nineteenth century advocated mixed schools. As William Leach (1980, 78) notes, "At the heart of the coeducational rationale lay the conviction that everything 'one-sided' and dangerous happens in a segregated sexual world where everything is hidden." In her *Vindication of the Rights of Woman* Mary Wollstonecraft argued strongly for mixed-sex schools for these reasons. She was particularly adamant about the "immodesty" and impropriety of behavior in single-sex boarding schools; no doubt one of the things she feared was exploration of homosexuality among the young. To many, mixed-sex schools seemed more open and enlightened for other reasons, as Elizabeth Cady Stanton noted in 1870: "In opening all high schools and colleges to girls we are giving young men and women better opportunities of studying each others' tastes, sentiments, capacities, and characters in the normal condition" (Leach 1980, 80). Nearly a century earlier Wollstonecraft had wondered how men and women could be good companions for each other if they had never had a chance to get to know each other as ordinary human beings.

By the twentieth century, most public schools were mixed, and as the century continued, an increasing proportion of colleges and universities were also mixed, including most of the long-segregated "Seven Sisters" and "Ivy League" schools of the Northeast. The number of women's colleges declined from 228 in 1969 to 94 in 1989 (Fiske 1989). A considerable degree of sex segregation remained, however. Even a coeducational school can remain segregated in some respects. Physical education classes were (and are) rarely mixed, even in sports that could easily be played by mixed groups. Many schools segregated the sexes into special "gender appropriate" classes: Girls learned cooking and sewing, and boys learned metal- or woodworking or mechanical drawing. In sex-education classes, boys and girls are often segregated, giving boys, for example, no opportunity to learn about menstruation.

By the time students are offered more options in secondary school and college, males and females still "choose" different subjects, resulting in further segregation. Any male or female who is interested in a "gender-inappropriate" field knows how daunting it can be just to enter the classroom. Gender segregation in some academic fields has decreased dramatically in recent decades but certainly not across the board.

The degree of gender segregation depends on the social context. Table 4-2 shows that the amount of gender imbalance in professional degrees awarded varies by race and ethnicity. Dentistry is a much more male-dominated field among whites than among students of other ethnic groups. The majority of law and veterinary medicine degrees awarded to black students in 1985 went to women. In contrast women predominated among Hispanic and Asian-American recipients of professional degrees in pharmacy. In general the amount of gender parity in professional degrees is greatest among blacks.

To say that there is or is not segregation is not to say whether segregation is good or bad. There is evidence on both sides. When segregation limits opportunities to learn, there is a problem. There is no reason to believe it is good for a male to be ignorant of how women's bodies work or to be unable to make dinner or sew a button on his shirt. Likewise it is not beneficial for a woman to be unable to build shelves, change a tire, or learn skills that might open up interesting jobs for her. It is not conducive to learning to be the odd woman (or man) out in a classroom filled with people of the other sex. One of the things people learn in school is how to understand, work with, respect, and get along with others. There is much justification in Elizabeth Cady Stanton and Mary Wollstonecraft's belief that it is detrimental for women and men to grow up regarding each other as mysterious and foreign creatures.

In 1904 most women art students still learned from clothed models.

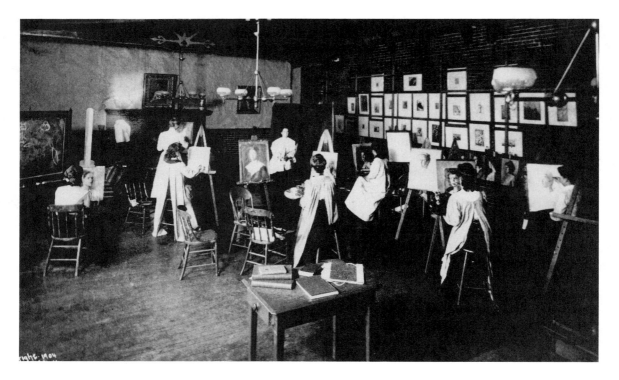

TABLE 4-2

113

Chapter 4:
Education:
For Whom?
By Whom?
For What?

Proportion of First Professional Degrees Awarded to Women,
by Race and Ethnicity, 1985

Field	White Non-Hispanic	Black Non-Hispanic	Hispanic	Asian/Pacific American	American Indian
Dentistry	19 (87)	43	39	31	29
Law	38 (91)	53	39	45	30
Medicine	30 (87)	45	32	33	28
Pharmacy	47 (77)	47	58	64	*
Theology	20 (90)	23	13	7	*
Veterinary Medicine	48 (96)	61	41	40	*

Notes: Numbers not in parentheses indicate the proportion of degree recipients within each ethnic group who were female. Numbers in parentheses indicate the proportion of degree recipients who were white.
* Less than 10 degree recipients who were American Indian.
SOURCE: U.S. Department of Education 1988, 228.

But segregation has benefits in certain circumstances. Advocates of women's colleges point out that when women at these schools take physics or chemistry classes, they cannot be discouraged by being in the minority; there is no peer pressure from male classmates not to be smart. Likewise women at women's colleges don't face the usual hassles from male friends when they take women's studies courses; men are not there to make fun of them. Women at these schools are not distracted by heterosexual courtship rituals in the classroom and have no reason to hide their assertiveness or brains. A study by Elizabeth Tidball (1980) shows that twice as many of the women who appear in *Who's Who of American Women* went to women's colleges as to coeducational colleges.

Many educators in former women's colleges that have since become mixed or merged with men's colleges regret the change. In many cases men have become dominant in the traditionally male fields. In some cases, such as that of Harvard and Radcliffe, the schools have not merely merged; the women's college has, for all intents and purposes, been swallowed by the men's school.

Some feminists look back at intellectual forebears such as Margaret Fuller, who felt that women needed to meet among themselves to learn from each other, and Virginia Woolf, who talked about a woman needing a "room of her own." Although most of these feminists do not suggest that all education should be segregated, they do argue that there are certain circumstances under which it should be. One example is segregating classes in traditionally male fields to help women gain confidence in themselves. Another area in which segregation might be useful is courses on topics directly relating to questions of gender and sexuality. Men often regard women's discussion of these topics as hostile and become antagonistic and defensive when women talk honestly about their perceptions and questions. Many women worry about hurting men's feelings if they discuss some of the issues raised in gender relations in front of men. Further, feminists point out that women have long been expected to learn about themselves through the opinions of male "experts." As we shall see in Chapter 9, the gender composition of a group affects who talks and how they talk; men tend to dominate discussions even if they are a minority. If women are to learn to think and talk independently and honestly, especially about gender and sexuality and the areas of life they affect, there may be some times during which they must withdraw to work among themselves. Some male feminists make the same point, arguing that before men can deal honestly with women about questions of sexuality and parenthood, for example, they must be able to talk honestly among themselves.

Women as Educators

We are told education is a woman's field but is it? What proportion of the people responsible for shaping and dispensing education are women? Table 4-3 shows the proportion of women who are educators or are preparing to be educators. It is clear that there are some levels at which women appear in large numbers, but at the higher levels, men predominate by a large margin. Women receive the majority of the B.A.s and M.A.s in education but a minority of the Ed.D.s and Ph.D.s. They are a majority of the elementary school teachers, about half of the secondary school and postsecondary, noncollegiate teachers. When we look higher up in postsecondary education, however, we find a smaller and smaller proportion of women among the teachers. At the elementary and secondary levels there is a higher proportion of female teacher aides than teachers and a much higher proportion of female teachers than school administrators. In every type of college or university, the higher the rank, the fewer the women. School boards are supposed to constitute the most "female" arena of politics, but women actually are only about 15 percent of school board members.

What holds women back in the field of education? We will look more closely at women and employment in Chapter 12, but for now we can say that many of the same problems exist in education as in other jobs. Although certain parts of the field of education are considered particularly appropriate for women, the more the job departs from traditional stereotypes of women's nature and interests, the more obstacles women face. Many people argue that women are naturally suited to be educators, but few seem to believe that women's natures fit them to control the education process or to work at the higher educational levels. They see women as nurturers fit for kindergartens, not scholars fit for universities. In the nineteenth century women were not encouraged to teach in secondary schools because it was felt they could not discipline older children as well as men could; they were not encouraged to be administrators because management was believed to be a man's job (Strober and Tyack 1980). Some of these attitudes linger.

Are women held back because they possess lower academic qualifications than men? Government figures show that in 1986 about 60 percent of male classroom teachers and about 46 percent of female classroom teachers had degrees beyond the B.A., a fact that is reflected in the greater numbers of men at the secondary level.

115

Chapter 4:
Education:
For Whom?
By Whom?
For What?

TABLE 4-3
Women As a Proportion of Educators

Education degrees: proportion granted to women, 1986

	B.A.	M.A.	Ph.D./Ed.D.
Pre-elementary	98.0	97.3	*
Elementary	92.6	90.6	76.4
Secondary	61.0	62.1	52.9
Education administration	*	52.2	47.7
All education fields	75.9	72.9	53.4

Elementary and secondary educators, 1988

Teacher aides	95.9
Prekindergarten and kindergarten	98.2
Elementary teachers	84.8
Secondary teachers	51.2

Full-time faculty, higher educators, 1986

Institutional type

Two-year colleges	38.5
Four-year colleges	31.2
Universities	20.4

Rank, all institutions

Lecturer	49.5
Instructor	53.3
Assistant professor	38.4
Associate professor	24.6
Professor	12.3

* Fewer than 100 degrees total.
SOURCE: Fox 1989; U.S. Department of Education 1988; U.S. Department of Labor 1989.

While this could suggest one reason why males are more likely than females to be promoted into school administration, it does not account for the size of the difference in male and female administrators. Differences in experience and length of service do not account for the great discrepancy either. In 1986 the median number of years served by male public school teachers was seventeen; the median number of years served by females was fourteen (U.S. Bureau of the Census 1989). Even in the mid-1970s a review of research on women as leaders in public education pointed out that about equal numbers of male and female teachers had the credentials needed to become administrators; however, women put in an average of fifteen years and men put in an average of only five years in the classroom before they became elementary school principals (Estler 1975). An analysis of one case study of a parent-teacher organization suggests that there is a similar pattern of discrimination in favor of males in PTA's as well (Sapiro 1979). In that study men who became presidents of the PTA had less experience in the organization than women.

Research shows similar patterns at the college and university levels. The amount a professor publishes is a better predictor of men's rank and salary than of women's; women's publications apparently do not guarantee women's promotion the same way that men's do (Unger 1979, 439). Even student evaluations of teachers are gender biased, although males' evaluations show more evidence of bias than females' (Basow and Silberg 1987; Martin 1984). Women are evaluated less highly on traditionally male characteristics.

What difference would it make if more women entered the higher ranks of education? It would make considerable difference to women who wish to pursue careers in education. Whether it would make a difference in the type of education people receive is a more complex question. It is not clear that women would run their schools or school districts very differently from men. But one study (Gross and Trask 1976) of 91 female and 98 male principals and 1303 teachers in forty-one cities found a higher level of professional performance among teachers and a higher level of student learning on average in schools run by women. At least the presence of more women at higher levels would provide more heterogeneous models for students to follow. In colleges and universities women have certainly led the efforts to bring women into the curriculum, remove bias from evaluation procedures, and end sexual harassment on campus.

What difference does the gender of a teacher make in the classroom? Some research suggests that students benefit from contact with teachers of their own sex. One study found that children perform better on intelligence tests with an examiner of their own sex (Pedersen, Shinedling, and Johnson 1968). Another concluded that students in science classes are more likely to consider science as a career for themselves if their teacher is of their own sex (Stake and Granger 1978). There can be few female college and university professors who have not had small hordes of female students beating paths to their doors because they are women. (On the other hand, too many female college professors find an unusual number of both male and female students wanting to hand in papers late because they thought ''a woman might be nicer than a man.'')

Unfortunately it is clear that female teachers participate in the hidden curriculum we have been discussing. This should not be surprising. They grow up in the same sexist society, sit in the same classrooms, and read the same biased textbooks that men do. Many women become teachers because it is an occupation that is regarded as particularly appropriate for women. It will take considerably more than simply putting more women into positions of responsibility to eliminate the sexist bias of schools. Educators are becoming increasingly aware of the problem, however, and are beginning to seek solutions to it.

Education and the Future

It should be clear by now that we need to attack certain problems if women and men are to be better served by education. Let us review some of them.

Do girls and boys and women and men have the fullest possible opportunity to get the education they choose? Research suggests they do not. Subtle and not so subtle messages still track students according to gender and limit girls' attainment in particular. Among other things schools teach girls to devalue themselves. Females and males may technically be free to choose their educational goals, but this freedom resembles the freedom to run a race in which one person faces a somewhat hilly track and the other faces a small mountain.

Some questions affecting choice in education are particularly difficult to tackle. Much of the sexism of people's attitudes and behavior is not conscious; teachers, for example, are often not aware of what they are doing when they treat female and male students differently. When female and male students make their choices in education, they are certainly not always aware of the pressures that have led them to their decisions. Much of the evaluation that goes on in schools and universities—test results, letters of recommendation, promotions, and committee meetings—is confidential, which means it occurs in a secret way that does not permit comparison of individuals and often does not allow even the subjects to know why they were evaluated as they were.

Some of the clearest examples of unconscious or subtle sex discrimination in education is the process by which colleges and universities handle promotions among faculty. When considering an individual for tenure or promotion, these institutions usually look for a complex combination of scholarship (generally, publication of original research), teaching (both how much and how well), and service to the institution (participation on committees and other decision-making bodies in the institution). Measuring these qualities and determining how well the individual will do in the future is immensely difficult.

How do we know when a teacher is really good? A teacher may be relatively unpopular with students but prove in the long run to have given them a fine education. Another may be very popular but may be dispensing something like educational cotton candy: fun and even interesting at the time but insubstantial over the long run. Some people may produce a great deal of research that is forgotten before the ink is dry on the paper; others may write very little, but what they write may continue to teach people for years. Or they may do research in areas that are unpopular with or considered unimportant by their colleagues—areas like women's studies. Because these judgments are in large part necessarily subjective, considerable room is left for conscious or unconscious discrimination. Moreover, these judgments are supposed to be collective and confidential; that is, *individuals'* decisions and the rationales for them are not supposed to be revealed. It should be no surprise that in recent years there have been court battles over the process and substance of decision making in educational institutions.

Unfortunately the appearance of choice is too often an illusion. How can the degree of choice be increased? Two common answers, "We must change people's minds or resocialize them to be less sexist," and "We should make laws against discrimination," are inadequate. The first is too vague, and the second is too narrow, primarily because for the most part it has already been done and hasn't worked as well as we hoped.

Education for What?

Until recently, the schooling of women was designed almost exclusively to prepare them to be good mothers and wives. This is still largely the case because women are still tracked into areas that are supposed to be compatible with the roles of wife and mother. Schools also play a role in tracking women into lower status jobs than men. A study of 300 high school guidance counsellors in Michigan in the 1970s found that guidance counsellors tended to direct young women to occupations that were lower paying and more highly supervised and required less education than those to which they directed men (Donahue and Costar 1977).

Schools and school boards are often unwilling to handle the problem of gender stereotyping directly within school curricula. Most have done little to correct gender biases in teaching methods and school curricula. Many conservative schools and school board administrators are concerned that the impact of feminism in the schools has already been too strong and that new textbooks and teachers belittle women's traditional roles. Many school officials who want their female students to grow up to be responsible wives and mothers balk at the idea that schools should teach students about sexuality and reproduction. As a result many American children still think babies come from cabbages, storks, and supernatural acts or from parts of the body not connected to the reproductive system, while children in countries such as Sweden, where sex education is introduced in the first grade, understand the basic facts of life at an early age (Parsons 1983). By the time American schools get around to teaching sex education—late in high school if at all—up to one-half of the students have already begun having sex, and many have accidentally found out where babies come from (Zellman and Goodchilds 1983).

Research shows repeatedly that education does not "pay off" for women in the same way it does for men. Men get better jobs, more pay, and higher social status for the same amount of education. It is no wonder that many women become discouraged and curtail their studies even when they are fully qualified to continue them. Helen F. Durio and Cheryl A. Kildow (1980) found that of the 273 women and 1953 men enrolled in an engineering program at the University of Texas during the mid- and late 1970s the women who left the program (unlike the men who left) did not leave because of academic failure and in fact tended to be better qualified academically than the men.

Education for and about Women

Some progress has been made in including women in the world about which students learn. The most progress has been made in relatively ghettoized women's studies courses and programs in colleges and universities and, to a lesser extent, in high schools. For the most part, "women" are still a special topic, and women have to work hard to make their own space in existing schools. In the late 1980s supporters of women's studies grew concerned about a nationwide "back to basics" movement among some educators. Their worry was that for many critics of recent changes in education, women's studies would emphatically not be included in the "necessary basics." Many advocates of traditional education have directly criticized women's studies as being harmfully ideological and nonacademic. Female students have to work particularly hard to learn about themselves and to do what Adrienne Rich (1979) calls "claiming an education."

119

Chapter 4: Education: For Whom? By Whom? For What?

It is daunting to consider the vast web of institutions involved in education when we consider how to find the keys to change. Of one thing we can be sure: The battle must be fought on several fronts. Students themselves can take an active part in creating their own education by being watchful and demanding changes in their educational institutions when they see evidence of bias or closed opportunities. Most colleges and universities have women's groups or caucuses, and many high schools do as well. Parents also have a role to play, either as individuals or through groups such as the PTA.

Teachers and school administrators can also work to achieve change. There are women's groups within most professional societies and unions, and there are professional journals devoted in whole or in part to discussing the problem of sexism in schools. These professional and labor organizations, as well as feminist groups such as the National Organization for Women, increasingly have special reports, programs, and training sessions designed to help teachers and administrators fight sexism in schools.

One point that must not be forgotten is that most educational institutions in the United States are run by the government; they are paid for and regulated by a complex web of local, county, and state school boards and superintendents of schools; local, county, and state legislators; and Congress and the U.S. Department of Education. Politics thus play a major role in education.

A case in point is the battle over implementation of Title IX of the 1972 Education Amendments, which bars discrimination in educational programs. One of the areas of university education in which discriminatory treatment is most obvious is in sports, particularly in schools with big money-making male sports, as Table 4-4 shows. Much less money is spent on women's sports than on men's, and institutions spend more on each individual man than on each individual woman. Consequently one of the most heated struggles over Title IX was between women's groups and the National College Athletic Association (NCAA), both of which lobbied heavily with members of Congress. The NCAA called on legislators, many of whom had played NCAA sports and had some loyalty to the "old boys club," to exempt sports from Title IX.

TABLE 4-4

Per Capita Sports Budget for University Women
as a Percentage of the
per Capita Sports Budget for Men

NCAA Division 1	41%
NCAA Division 2	60%
NCAA Division 3	69%
All NCAA	45%

SOURCE: Adapted from Gelb and Palley 1982.

Thus far they have not won their case. Title IX is still in place, and lawsuits may be launched against schools either by the Office of Civil Rights in the U.S. Department of Education or by private individuals.

In addition to Title IX numerous other laws and policies have been put in place to equalize educational opportunities for women and men, although most observers argue that they are either not sufficient or not enforced rigorously enough. Programs such as those under the 1974 Women's Educational Equity Act (WEEA) have been developed to provide funds for new programs or research projects designed to promote women's education. Sex discrimination in employment, including employment in education, remains illegal under Title VII of the 1964 Civil Rights Act, and sex discrimination in pay is illegal under the Equal Pay Act of 1960. Experts, however, cite two particular problems in using legal means to redress sexism: (1) The laws are vague (Vladeck 1981), and (2) the courts generally approach each case on the basis of its individual merit, thus making it difficult to focus the battle on the real issue, which is discrimination against a group of people (Abel 1981).

Women have formed interest groups to combat sexism in education. Joyce Gelb and Marian Palley (1987) report that at least sixty different women's groups have been involved in Title IX battles. Some, such as the Women's Educational Action League (WEAL), the National Organization for Women (NOW), and the National Women's Political Caucus (NWPC), are quite clearly associated with the feminist movement. Others, such as the League of Women Voters, the American Association of University Women (AAUW), and the Girl Scouts, are more traditional women's organizations. Issues concerning education have often united women from diverse backgrounds and political perspectives, however, and these groups have joined to form the National Coalition for Women and Girls in Education.

Many people feel strongly that education must continue to change; the dilemma is how to create change and where to start. There probably cannot be major changes in the status and roles of women in society in general until education changes, but it is doubtful that education can undergo major changes until other social institutions change as well.

NOTES

1. See Brown's delightful feminist utopia, *Alcuin*. This book was originally published in two parts, the first half in 1798 and the second in 1815.
2. For some excerpts from Murray's writing, see Rossi (1988).

5

The Problems of Being Healthy and Normal

A PREGNANT woman is chatting with a friend during their lunch break at work. "Are you hoping for a boy or a girl?" her friend asks. "Oh, I don't care what sex it is—as long as it's a healthy, normal baby I'll be happy!" A student wakes up the first day of final exams and refuses the breakfast offered by her roommate. "I feel really ill," she explains, and both of them believe it but make no move to get her to a doctor because they know there is nothing physically wrong with her. A 95-year-old woman dies in her sleep, and her children comfort themselves by expressing happiness that she was "healthy and in good shape up to the end." A man is seen walking down the street in high heels, skintight leather trousers, and heavy eye makeup. "That's really sick!" someone comments. In 1982 John Hinckley, who shot President Ronald Reagan, was judged not guilty of a crime "by reason of insanity," causing people to argue that the high crime rate in the United States is evidence of a "sick society." In 1973 the American Psychological Association changed its collective mind and declared that it no longer considered homosexuality a sickness.

Words connoting health and sickness, normality and abnormality are among the most common and important we use to describe and evaluate people as individuals and as groups, but they are also among the most confusing and difficult to define. What constitutes health or normality differs from culture to culture and over time. What doesn't change is the *evaluative* content of these concepts: the ideas that health is good and its absence bad and that the absence of health (or the presence of sickness) should be corrected if at all possible.

David Mechanic, an influential medical sociologist, argues that "the concept of disease usually refers to some deviation from normal functioning which has undesirable consequences because it produces personal discomfort or adversely affects the individual's future health status" (1978, 25). Notice the importance of the concept of *normal* in this definition. Mechanic points out that we (including health professionals and lay people) compare the way we feel or act to some standard of normality to determine whether we are healthy or not. I declare myself "unwell"

121

and possibly seek consultation with my doctor when I notice a deviation from my normal state of mind or body that interferes or may interfere with my normal activities. My doctor compares my symptoms to various standards of normality to determine whether I am not healthy and to find out what the "problem" is so we can restore me to health.

How are our standards of health or normality set? Mechanic argues that they depend on the state of health institutions and health science as well as the "social and cultural context within which human problems are defined" (1978, 26). Even with the simplest health problems, we can see how definitions of health shift and leave considerable leeway for subjective interpretation. The average temperature of the human body is 98.6 degrees Fahrenheit. If my temperature is 99 degrees, is this a problem? Possibly not; some people's normal temperature is higher or lower than average. So at what point do we declare that my temperature has deviated enough from the norm to say that I am not healthy? Defining health is much more difficult when we talk about more complex physiological problems, not to mention those involving human psychology, mental health, and social behavior.

Observers generally agree that cultural and social values play large roles in the determination of health and that this aspect of health science and care can be very dangerous. If health is understood in terms of normality, health care can become extremely repressive. Above all there is the plaguing question: If healthy people are those who fall within "normal" ranges, or are like most people, isn't it too easy to define as "unhealthy" people who are different or unique or violate social custom? What can we do to guard against this tendency?

One aspect of cultural context that is related to definitions of health is the definition of normal gender roles, including notions of femininity and masculinity. In the book's Introduction we briefly discussed a study (Broverman et al 1970) that found that many health professionals do not define health for males and females in the same way. What this means is that in the process of teaching us how to be healthy, health professionals are also teaching us how to conform to gender norms; in the process of restoring us to health when we show signs of abnormality, they may also be restoring us to "normal" masculinity and femininity.

We have already reviewed some evidence that perceptions of the social world are androcentric. Because society is androcentric, and males are regarded as the norm, we should (and will) find that females are regarded as unhealthy to the degree that they differ from the (male) norm. The aspects of women's bodies that differ most from men's (especially the reproductive organs) should be seen as particular sources of ill health. Female functions and activities that would be abnormal in men—even those like pregnancy, childbirth, and lactation that are normal in women—should be viewed as a deviation from the norm and, therefore, unhealthy.

Like the family and schools, health institutions impart values and knowledge, define what constitutes personal and social problems, and then seek to prevent or correct these problems. In this chapter we shall look at the relationship between gender and standards of health and health care. We shall show the ways in which institutions and people charged with managing our health also manage gender. *Health* is used very broadly here and includes physical, mental, and social health. A wide range of interrelated institutions fall into our view, including those most obviously concerned with health, such as hospitals and clinics, and other less obvious institutions, such as families, schools, social welfare agencies, and even the criminal justice system.

Like most other fields of human science, medicine is an imperfect science in a number of ways. Even when a health problem has been well researched and is one with which doctors have considerable practical experience, it is never certain that any particular case will fit the general pattern precisely. Even when the state of knowledge about a given medical problem is limited, doctors still try to help, relying if necessary on educated guesses. In contemplating any given procedure, doctors analyze its possible risks, benefits, and costs in comparison to other possible courses, including inaction. These risks, costs, and benefits are rarely, if ever, perfectly known.

The imperfect state of medical knowledge has caused several problems:

1. The fact that some portion of the practice of medicine is subjective (although educated) guesswork leaves considerable room for the influence of ideology, including gender ideology.
2. The history of medicine is marked by the attempt to use procedures that are based on the best guesses and the values of a given era, but which sometimes appear wrongheaded and even disgraceful at a later period.
3. The best of intentions can lead to disaster.

Let us look at how these problems are manifest in the health care of women.[1]

Definitions of Women's Health and Treatment

We have already seen that definitions of health are to some degree subjective, and they are certainly different across time and culture. This section discusses the questions: How are sex, gender, and women's gender roles related to definitions of health and illness? How have health practitioners viewed and treated women? We begin with medical views of women's anatomy and reproductive systems. We then turn to the relationship between women's health and their roles in the family and at work. Finally we look at the relationship between women's health and conceptions of female beauty and fitness.

Anatomy and Health

In 1870 a doctor addressing a medical society noted that it seemed ''as if the Almighty, in creating the female sex, had taken the uterus and built up a woman around it'' (quoted in Ehrenreich and English 1979, 108). Although the Bible tells us that God began with a rib rather than the uterus, writers and practitioners of health care have tended to view women largely in terms of their reproductive organs and capacities. Women's reproductive organs have not merely been seen as different from men's; they have been regarded as the defining characteristics of women and their potential for health. In fact, they have generally been treated as particular health hazards.

We will look briefly at the history of medical strategies of removal of women's unique organs as a means of health care to see how health has been defined for women, beginning with surgical removal of the ovaries and clitoris. These procedures have now been discredited and discarded as inappropriate strategies. We will then discuss removal of the uterus and breast when cancer is present; these procedures have undoubtedly saved countless lives but are now thought to be overdone for reasons related to gender norms.

In the late nineteenth century, women's ovaries came to be regarded as sources of trouble and particularly dangerous to mental health. Because of their link to women's periodicity and thus presumably to women's apparent emotional instability, the ovaries were assumed to control women's personalities to a large degree. This "psychology of the ovary," as Ehrenreich and English (1979) have called it, had disastrous effects on women when doctors put their minds to the task of figuring out how to care for women. Experimental use of the ovariotomy, or surgical removal of the ovaries, appeared to cure women of a variety of "problems," so many doctors adopted the technique. It is estimated that about 150,000 women underwent the operation in 1906 alone. The specific reasons for these operations were numerous; they were used to "help" women who ate too much, masturbated or had "erotic tendencies," attempted suicide, or suffered from persecution manias (and no wonder!). In some cases husbands brought their wives to the doctor for this surgery hoping to cure them of unruly behavior (Ehrenreich and English 1979, 111–12). Although we know now that the procedure could not have "cured" these problems for physiological reasons, the underlying gender ideology supported use of the ovariotomy long after it should have been abandoned.

Women's potential for sexuality has often been seen as particularly dangerous and unhealthy. Despite Victorian notions of women's sexual repression and the belief

An early chastity belt.

that women are supposed only to tolerate not to enjoy sex, it was long believed that women are insatiable, "raging volcanos of desire" (Shorter 1982, 12). To control women's sexuality and its "dangerous" effects men have used various means, including chastity belts and segregation, the latter especially by religious law and authority.

In the mid-nineteenth century American doctors found a new cure for such problems as "nymphomania," masturbation, and other sorts of unruly feminine behavior: clitoridectomy, or surgical removal of the clitoris. Once again, some husbands at a loss to control unmanageable wives presented them to doctors for "female circumcision," as it is often mistakenly called. This gruesome practice has disappeared among Western doctors, although it remains part of some cultures' female initiation rites, particularly in parts of Africa. Feminists and such organizations as the World Health Organization, have mounted a worldwide campaign in recent years to eliminate this dangerous practice (see Hoskin 1980).

The end to clitoridectomy in the West does not mean that the clitoris has otherwise been regarded as a healthful organ. Remember that Sigmund Freud argued that to become healthy and mature adults, women had to be able to transfer their erotic feelings from the clitoris to the vagina; a woman should become capable of "vaginal," as opposed to "clitoral," orgasm. Physiological research shows that no such transfer is possible, because even when orgasm results from penetration by the penis, orgasm is caused by indirect stimulation of the clitoris (Gersh and Gersh 1981; Hyde 1986). Despite this evidence, Freudian psychotherapists still try to help women become more "sexually mature" according to these unfortunate notions.

In Chapter 2 we discussed some of the history of the womb, which has long been regarded as the cause of both physical and emotional problems, or "hysteria." For a long time people thought that the uterus was alive, or at least that it travelled around the body in a dangerous fashion (Shorter 1982). As recently as the nineteenth century most of women's diseases were attributed to the presence of a womb (Ehrenreich and English 1979). The uterus is still regarded as more dangerous and unhealthful than it actually is.

Hysterectomy—the removal of the womb—has been one of the most important life-saving procedures in the history of women's health. The medical profession might have been as wrong in pursuing this procedure as it was in the cases of the clitoridectomy and the ovariotomy, but it was not; hysterectomies regularly save the lives of women with uterine cancer. However, numerous observers argue that there is considerable abuse of the technique based on androcentric views of women and their health. According to these critics, hysterectomies are among the most overdone surgical operations in the medical repertoire. In the calculation of risks, costs, and benefits, doctors seem particularly inclined to perform hysterectomies on older women because "they don't need their wombs anymore." In this case age stereotypes combine with gender stereotypes to create problems for women.

Like cancer of the uterus, breast cancer is a danger that has always plagued women. In the 1880s radical mastectomy—the removal of the breast plus underlying muscles and lymph nodes—was introduced to treat women with breast cancer. Although this procedure greatly reduced the possibility of recurrence of cancer, in recent years observers have concluded that the radical mastectomy, like the hysterectomy, is overdone; too much surgery is done too often. Again this surgical technique seems particularly likely to be overused on older women partly because there is a cultural view that older women don't "need" their breasts.

Thus the organs of women's bodies that are most different from men's—those that compose the reproductive system—have long been identified as sources of peculiar mental and physical health problems. Part of the willingness to excise women's reproductive organs seems based on the perception that they are extraneous in any case, particularly in women who are considered past the age at which they are likely to bear children or appear sexually attractive to men. There seems to have been no analogous tendency to remove men's unique reproductive organs (except, at some times in history, as a cure or punishment for rapists)—but of course men's reproductive organs are regarded as normal and necessary to the healthy male.

Most observers who call attention to this situation do not argue that doctors wield their knives against women with the intention of hurting them (although some seem to suggest this); instead they argue that an underlying androcentric view of women's bodies, combined with imperfect knowledge, causes the harm. This suggests two solutions, neither of which is sufficient by itself: (1) continued research to improve our understanding of both male and female bodies, and (2) continued efforts to destroy androcentric conceptions of human health.

Reproduction and Health

Like the organs themselves, the normal functions of women's reproductive organs have been seen as health problems. Let us look briefly at two examples: menstruation, and pregnancy and childbirth.

Menstruation

Menstruation has generally been seen as a health problem not just for women but also for other people. Most cultures have some menstrual taboos: beliefs that menstrual blood can make crops fail, wine go sour, infants die, men become impotent, and so on. In our own culture many men find the idea of having sexual relations with a menstruating woman appalling, and many women find the idea embarrassing. Some religions, including Orthodox Judaism, ban sexual relations during menstrual periods and require women to undergo cleansing rituals after their periods are over.

There is little doubt that menstrual periods were once considerably more unpleasant for most women than they are now. Edward Shorter (1982) reminds us that modern ideas of hygiene, such as the importance of regular bathing, are quite recent. Even a century ago bathing was considered unhealthful for anyone, and as recently as the middle of the twentieth century many people still believed that bathing or showering was dangerous for menstruating women. Fresh menstrual blood is no more unhealthful than blood tapped from any other part of the body; but left to sit in warm dark places it is no doubt both unappealing and a good breeding ground for germs.

Even with the present availability of sanitary pads, tampons (invented in 1933), and sponges, the old menstrual ideology persists today. The current variation is enunciated most clearly in advertisements for "feminine hygiene" products (Toth 1980), which imply that even a menstruating woman can be normal and feminine—if she is careful to cover all signs of her condition. Recent developments in the "feminine hygiene" industry have even created some real health dangers for menstruating women. The search for bigger and better tampons led to the distribution of tampons that increase the risks of toxic shock syndrome, a potentially fatal illness.

We briefly discussed the controversy over physical and psychological menstrual distress in Chapter 3. There is no doubt that many women suffer from problems associated with menstruation and menstrual cycles. There is also no doubt that for some women these difficulties are caused by the physical functioning of their reproductive or hormonal systems. Some women experience physical and emotional difficulties at puberty and menopause. Excessive amounts of bleeding and the lack of bleeding in a woman of reproductive age can be symptoms of other health problems. Uncomfortable amounts of weight gain or cramps are not just products of the mind. Medical researchers disagree about the existence and causes of the premenstrual syndrome (PMS), a range of emotional and behavioral problems associated with the time preceding the menstrual period. Researchers are not agreed about which of the psychological and physical correlates of menstruation are more generally caused by the physiological aspects of the menstrual cycle and which are caused by people's expectations about menstruation or the way menstruation and menstruating women are treated.

Research by Jeanne Brooks-Gunn and Diane Ruble (1982) offers important evidence that at least some menstrual difficulty is social in origin. They found that girls have quite clear ideas about the symptoms of menstruation as early as the fifth grade. Interestingly, girls who had begun to menstruate reported experiencing less severe menstrual distress than those who hadn't yet begun expected to have. They further found that the level of distress young girls expected was related to the level they felt when they actually reached menarche. And girls who had learned more about menstruation "from male sources rated menstruation as more debilitating and negative than those who learned less from male sources" (1576). Thus biology alone is not responsible for whether a woman who is menstruating feels good. Even this basic physiological event is partly shaped by culture and society (Buckley and Gottlieb 1988; Delaney, Lupton, and Toth 1988; Lander 1988).

Pregnancy and Childbirth

Most people believe that it is normal for women to want to have children, and that women are happiest when they do. However, those same people often regard pregnancy and childbirth as major health problems. Part of the reason for this of course is that for much of women's history childbirth *was* tremendously dangerous to women's health (see, e.g., Ehrenreich and English 1979; Shorter 1982).

Until the past century health in general was problematic. Even if we consider only nutrition and hygiene, it is not surprising that masses of women died from reproduction-related problems. Edward Shorter (1982) observes, for example, that the widespread problem of rickets posed a special difficulty for pregnant women because rickets causes deformities of the pelvis that make labor and delivery difficult and dangerous. Other types of malnutrition also affect women's muscular structure or energy level, and status rankings in the family used to mean that women received considerably less (and often less nourishing) food than their husbands. This increased women's risk of malnutrition. Lack of good hygiene results in infestations and diseases of various kinds.

Women's bodies were also subject to other stresses that increased the health risks of pregnancy. Women of the laboring classes generally had to stay on the job up to the end of pregnancy and begin again soon after delivery. For women of the wealthier classes, clothing caused problems during the middle and end of the nineteenth century. Corsets could exert 28 pounds of pressure (in extreme cases, considerably more) on internal organs. Over time this constant pressure had disastrous effects on body structure. Women's clothing was also very heavy; street clothing averaged thirty-seven pounds in the winter, nineteen of which were suspended from the waist (Ehrenreich and English 1979, 98).

By far the most consistent focus of attention on the relationship of health to reproduction in recent years has been the role of health practitioners and the treatment and advice they have given women. The process of childbirth has changed quite radically over the last two centuries. Let us look at the ways in which these changes contribute, or do not contribute, to health.[2]

Few people seem to realize that the widespread practice of having doctors deliver babies in hospitals, with the mother on her back and her feet in stirrups, is very recent. Most babies were born at home until World War II; the proportion of births in hospitals rose from 37 percent in 1935 to 79 percent in 1945 and 99 percent by the end of the 1970s (Shorter 1982, 157). Midwives delivered about half the children born in the United States at the turn of the century; after 1910 the majority of women were assisted by male doctors. The use of the lithotomy position for birthing (back down, feet up; named after the operation used to remove gallstones) accompanied the anesthetized deliveries that became prevalent after the middle of the nineteenth century. Before that women gave birth lying on their sides, squatting, standing, or sitting. Let us analyze these and other changes in the history of childbirth.

At one time delivery of babies was thought to be beneath the dignity of doctors. In the late seventeenth and eighteenth centuries, however, doctors began to compete with midwives, especially in cities, where people had the money to pay. (Doctors were apparently happy to leave births to midwives in rural areas and among the poor and immigrants, at least until the early twentieth century.) The doctors charged that midwives were incompetent and did more harm than good to both mothers and babies. Most research shows something quite different; midwives were at least as competent as doctors, and trained urban midwives were even more competent. (When we talk of medical incompetence we are referring not just to whether practitioners help solve health problems but also to whether they create health problems. We shall see that in trying to do the former a practitioner sometimes inadvertently does the latter.)

The innovations doctors brought to childbirth included new technology and surgical skills. The forceps were invented by Peter Chamberlin, a barber-surgeon, in the early seventeenth century and remained a family secret for many years. Eventually other doctors began to use them. Forceps are appropriately used only in problem deliveries and only under certain circumstances. The use of forceps can be painful and, if misused, dangerous to mother or child. Unfortunately forceps were too often used incompetently, and after the 1920s doctors began to use forceps with increasing frequency. The use of forceps has recently declined partly because so many doctors have turned instead to birth by surgery (caesarean section), a much safer procedure.

Doctors have increasingly used their surgical skills during childbirth for two procedures. The first is the episiotomy, which is designed to enlarge the opening to the vagina by cutting the tissue at its base. If an episiotomy is not done, this tissue may be torn (perhaps dangerously) by the emerging infant's head. Over the years, however, the episiotomy has become increasingly routine, especially in hospitals. One study showed nine times as many episiotomies in hospital births as in home births, but also nine times as many severe tears (supposedly prevented by episiotomies) in hospital births (see Rothman 1982, 44). One reason for the high frequency of tears could be that the favored hospital birth position, the lithotomy, increases the risk of tearing. In any case, research suggests that episiotomy actually causes some of the problems it is designed to prevent (Rothman 1982, 58).

The other surgical procedure that has become increasingly popular among doctors is the caesarean section, or surgical delivery of the baby through the abdomen. Caesareans were used in emergencies (generally unsuccessfully) as early as the sixteenth century. They became considerably safer at the end of the nineteenth century, although they were rarely used in the United States until very recently. The rate of caesareans increased dramatically from an average of 4.5 percent of births in 1965 to 24 percent in 1986 (Taffel, Placek, and Less 1987; U.S. Bureau of the Census 1989, 65). The increase has been particularly great among patients in private hospitals, which suggests that finances may have as much to do with the rate of surgery as health. Some observers suggest that the high rate of caesarean sections is due in part to the scheduling preferences of hospital staff. Further, because caesarean births are now extremely safe, doctors may prefer this strategy to riskier procedures (including a lengthy and difficult labor), partly because of the widespread incidence of malpractice suits.

Debates also rage over other aspects of current birthing practices. Hospitals claim the lithotomy position for birth is superior because it makes it easier for doctors to monitor the fetus and deliver the baby. On the other hand, the lithotomy position makes it harder for women to give birth. It increases the risk of tearing, works against gravity, and makes it more difficult for women to push because their feet are elevated. When proper hospital decorum dictates that the patient stay immobile in bed rather than walking around, labor lengthens. To compensate for these problems, some doctors do episiotomies, use more drugs to decrease the pain that is increased by these other procedures, and induce births or perform caesarean sections to shorten labor.

The invention of anesthesia in 1847 made it possible to relieve considerable pain, including the pain of childbirth, and increased the feasibility of such medical interventions as the surgical procedures discussed in the preceding paragraphs. Far from being restricted to cases of extraordinary pain or emergency, however, the use of a wide variety of tranquilizers and anesthetics has become routine. One negative result is that many women cannot use their voluntary muscles, which makes it difficult for them to participate actively in childbirth and makes the need for surgery more likely. Women who have had otherwise uncomplicated pregnancies and labor may be too drugged and incompetent even to hold their newborn infants, and if the mother is drugged, so is the fetus. Despite these problems, the use of drugs continues to be widespread. One study of women who had "normal vaginal deliveries" found that the average woman is exposed to eleven different drugs during pregnancy and seven different drug administrations during childbirth. Further, women are given very little information about what drugs they are receiving and why (McManus et al. 1982).

What conclusions can we draw about women and health from this very brief survey of the relationship between health professionals and birth? The history of childbirth in the West, especially the United States, is marked by the growing influence of what is called the medical model of pregnancy and childbirth. As Barbara Rothman describes it,

> (Within) the medical model the body is seen as a machine, and the male body is taken as the norm. Pregnancy and birth are at best complications, stresses on the system. At worst, they are diseaselike states. In either case, in that model, they need treatment, medical management (1982, 24).

In many births today, women are transformed into patients and are treated, and expected to act, as though they are sick people. Many medical definitions of what is normal during pregnancy are based on norms for nonpregnant women (a more "normal" state), which means doctors end up attempting to cure women of "abnormalities" that are actually normal in pregnant women (Rothman, 1982, 141–57). Sometimes it seems as though the doctor and not the woman births the baby.

Women have learned to accept the medical model, including the notion that something in their bodies is likely to go wrong. They have also learned to think of pain as the most salient feature of childbirth. The medical model has turned pregnancy and childbirth into one set of precautions after another. Some of these precautions are overused or of dubious utility for most pregnant women.

Most doctors and women still prefer hospital births "just in case," that is, because medical technology, drugs, and specialists are available in hospitals. But in the hospital "just in case" procedures may be routine. Further, as Judith Leavitt (1983) points out, when birthing women began to use hospitals rather than delivering at home, they lost control over the process. We will discuss this point more later in this chapter.

For a variety of reasons, most of them having to do with advances in medicine, pregnancy and childbirth have become safer for women and babies in recent history. On the other hand, infant and maternal mortality rates are not as low in the United States as they are in much of Western Europe, where there is generally less medical intervention. And mortality rates alone do not tell the whole story. Many of the changes in birthing practices and health care for pregnant women that have taken place over the last century have not only saved the lives of mothers and babies but also made women and children considerably healthier. Not all of the changes, however, are unmitigated blessings. Current birthing practices often make the experience less healthful and satisfactory than it might be, partly because normal women are treated as though they are unhealthy. Many women and health-care practitioners are beginning to seek more healthful alternatives.

Families, Family Roles, and Health

In 1963 Betty Friedan published *The Feminine Mystique,* a book that became very influential in the rise of the new women's movement. Friedan took a second look at the presumably happy, hopeful world of post-World War II suburbia, and she found a problem among homemakers that was widespread but had no name. In her book she offered some doctors' views of the problem:

> [One] found, surprisingly, that his patients suffering from "housewife's fatigue," slept more than an adult needed to sleep—as much as ten hours a day—and that the actual energy they spent on housework did not tax their capacity. The real problem must be something else, he decided—perhaps boredom. Some doctors told their women patients they must get out of the house for a day, treat themselves to a movie in town. Others prescribed tranquilizers. Many suburban housewives were taking tranquilizers like cough drops. "You wake up in the morning, and you feel as if there's no point in going on another day like this. So you take a tranquilizer because it makes you not care so much that it's pointless."

This type of observation and others we shall discuss made increasing numbers of people wonder: Was it possible that family life was not as healthy for women as people had thought?

In 1972, Walter Gove published an article that showed different relationships between marital status and mental health among men and women. He found that married women had higher rates of mental disorder than married men, but single, divorced, and widowed women had lower rates of mental disorder than similarly situated men. What could be the cause of these differences? Many observers point to the burdens and stresses that individuals assume or relinquish when they marry or when their marriages break up. Jessie Bernard (1972) argues that when men and women marry, they do not really enter into the same situation; they are in what she calls "his" and "hers" marriages.

Marriage means something very different to most men than it does to most women. Married men usually have little responsibility for their day-to-day maintenance. They do little cooking, cleaning, or shopping for themselves, let alone anyone else, and someone else takes care of most of the other daily tasks and errands. Men who find themselves on their own must manage these things themselves. Given the nature of gender socialization and training, this can be very difficult indeed, because vast numbers of men never learned how to do any of these things. Some studies show that after a divorce involving children men find interacting with their children particularly stressful because women normally manage the children, so men seldom develop child-care skills.

The situation for women is different. If the woman is the manager of a household, the husband is, among other things, another person within the family to be managed. Besides doing domestic labor, a "good" wife is supposed to provide emotional support to the husband. The husband's job is generally regarded as more important than the wife's, and his job-related problems take precedence over hers. If a woman is a full-time homemaker, she is supposed to be understanding and helpful when her husband comes home from work regardless of what her day was like. Although a woman faces tremendous burdens when her marriage breaks up, particularly if she is left with the responsibility for children, she is also left with one less person to manage.

Of course, there are many problems that men and women are likely to share. Both may experience conflict among their various commitments, and the majority of them have jobs and financial responsibilities that may cause stress. Neither sex has a monopoly on insecurity and loneliness. But the conditions under which these problems arise and the way women and men cope with them may be different. Women suffer more than men from a loss of autonomy in the early years of marriage (Lopata 1971). Sometimes the reaction is particularly destructive, causing *agoraphobia* (fear of open spaces), which is most commonly found among women in the early stages of marriage (Unger 1979). This affliction makes women fearful of venturing outside the home and, sometimes, even of answering the door or telephone or leaving the curtains open. What this means is that the agoraphobic woman cannot even carry out the normal routine of a homemaker.

Many social scientists have pointed to the construction of gender divisions of labor in the family as potential health hazards for women. Consider the effect on a woman's life of having small children. Women with small children are less likely to have employment outside the home than women without small children. Women with small children, therefore, are more likely than men not only to be socially isolated but also to spend much more of their day in exclusive contact with children rather than adults. Research suggests that such isolation is related to both depression and loneliness. An interesting perspective on this problem is provided by Ann Seiden (1976), who discussed research among day-care workers showing that six hours is the maximum contact with children that day-care workers can tolerate before their abilities to function are diminished. Watching television—an activity many women may use to pass the time and to give themselves "contact" with people other than children—is not without its dangers. One study (Shaver and Freedman 1976) found that the more hours women spent alone with children, the more lonely they felt, and the more television they watched, the more worthless they felt.

In recent years, increasing attention has been paid to another family health hazard: violence within the family. Estimates are that about 3.8 percent of American children aged three to seventeen—two million children—are abused each year and that in 1979 some violence between spouses occurred in approximately 16 percent of two-parent families (Gelles 1980).

Child abuse is very difficult to define, especially as a health problem, because some level of violence against children by parents is still considered a normal, even necessary part of child rearing. Using a national sample, Ursula Dibble and Murray Straus (1980) found that 63 percent of Americans admitted to having pushed, shoved, slapped, or thrown something at their children. Further, evidence from this study shows that parents do not consider these abnormal—that is, unhealthy—acts. Almost 82 percent thought that slapping a twelve-year-old child is necessary, normal, or good, and 65 percent thought that slapping a twelve-year-old child is necessary, normal, *and* good. Whether a low level of violence against children or wives is considered a health problem, then, depends in part on whether one considers some violence a normal part of family life. Nevertheless, the records of hospitals, shelters, and social workers show that numerous children and women suffer both physical and psychological injuries within the family.

What causes violence within the family? Wini Breines and Linda Gordon (1983) point out that there are two apparently contradictory images of the family: the "peaceful haven" and the "cradle of violence." It may be precisely some of the aspects of the family that make it a peaceful haven that transform it into a cradle of violence. Breines and Gordon say, "Intimate and family relationships are filled with contradiction, with longing and expectations so ambiguous and ambivalent that they may not be conscious" (493). As we have seen, Sigmund Freud would certainly agree and so would many present-day psychologists and sociologists.

In his review of recent research on family violence, Richard J. Gelles (1980) identified four different, but not mutually exclusive, theories about family violence. The first is that violence is more common in families with lower socioeconomic status. It is important to note that this does not mean that family violence is limited to working-class or poor families, but merely that it is somewhat more common among these groups. Socioeconomic status and intrafamily violence are most likely linked partly because of a second source of violence noted by Gelles: stress. Stress may stem from a variety of sources, including financial problems, employment problems, feelings of inadequacy, single parenthood, or even pregnancy. None of these sources of stress, of course, is limited to a single class. Carlton A. Hornung, Claire McCullough, and Taichi Sugimoto (1981) found, for example, that the risk of violence between spouses is particularly high when there is a great status difference between husband and wife, especially when the wife's occupation is of higher status than the husband's. Thus the sex/gender system can feed the problem of violence; it may be particularly stressful for a man to have a wife with a higher-status occupation only because of a general belief that husbands are supposed to be superior to their wives.

A third theory identified by Gelles is that family violence is related to social isolation. The general view is that a family is supposed to be a self-contained, self-sufficient entity that can solve its own problems. This also means that the members of a family are relatively isolated in the family roles they play as individuals. When we talk about the "role of the family," most often we are really talking about the roles played by specific individuals, such as the mother, wife, father, husband, or child. Suzanne Salzinger, Sandra Kaplan, and Connie Artemyeff (1983) studied a group of women at a clinic for mothers who had abused their children and a control group of mothers who hadn't done so. The main difference between the two groups was that the abusive mothers were under more stress and were more socially isolated. They were pressed for time, often because besides taking care of small children they were employed or in school, and they had smaller social networks, especially fewer adult friends. Clearly violence is not simply a result of stress; individual coping strategies and the support groups available have a significant impact on how stress is manifested.

The fourth theory of violence Gelles discusses is the "cycle of violence," or the idea that those who grow up in a violent family are especially likely to engage in family violence as adults. This idea has been the object of some criticism over the years partly because it suggests that family violence is not related to the particular situations and stresses people confront as adults and that it is unavoidable among some groups of people. In fact the "cycle of violence" theory need not (and, based on empirical evidence, cannot) imply that only adults who experienced violence as children will be violent as adults; that all, or even most, adults with this experience will be violent; or that violence is in any way inevitable among these people. The theory suggests only one of the many sources of violence, and it argues for a propensity, not an inevitability.

Patricia Ulbrich and Joan Huber (1981) analyzed a national sample survey and found some interesting evidence regarding cycles of intraspousal violence. They were interested in the degree to which childhood observation of intraspousal violence is related to the development of belief systems that accept violence against women, even when the individuals do not engage in violence against women themselves. They found that men who had seen their fathers hit their mothers were more likely to think that violence against women can be justified than those who hadn't. In contrast women who had seen their fathers hit their mothers were less likely to think violence against women can be justified. Both men and women were more likely to find justification for violence against women if they saw their mothers hit their fathers. There is no inevitable cycle of violence, especially given new health, counseling, and relief agencies designed to help both the perpetrators and victims of family violence, but Ulbrich and Huber's work shows that even observing family violence as a child can help give the future adult particular attitudes toward violence against women.

In recent years there has been increasing public and professional awareness that the family can be both source and location of tremendous health problems. Family therapy has developed as a special field of psychology to help family members cope with their problems together as related individuals. Many women in families have found feminist consciousness-raising and other support groups valuable as places to share problems and explore solutions. Some headway has been made in the area of family violence as well. By 1967 all fifty states had passed laws requiring anyone with knowledge of a case of child abuse to report the case to the police, and in 1974 the federal government established the Center for the Identification and Prevention of Child Abuse (Breines and Gordon 1983). Women across the country have established shelters for battered wives, and there are increasing numbers of support networks for parents in distress. Because many family problems bring people into contact with law enforcement officers, police are now receiving more training and guidance in dealing with family violence. It is clear that families are not as healthy for women as they might be partly because of their role in the sex/gender system. The recognition of family health problems is growing, however, and this is a first step toward recovery.[3]

Work and Health

In the late nineteenth century many psychologists and medical practitioners were disturbed by women's tendency to seek more education and employment. As

Ehrenreich and English (1979, 114) argue, "Medical men saw the body as a miniature economic system, with the various parts—like classes or interest groups—competing for a limited supply of resources." It was argued that if women used either their brains or their brawn to study or work, they were depleting the energies that would eventually be needed to bear and raise children. Some found evidence in the tendency (which still exists) for female college graduates to be less likely to marry and to have fewer children than females who are not college graduates (Ehrenreich and English 1979, 115). Although this particular theory has long since lost its original popularity, the trade-offs between employment and women's health, especially women's reproductive health, is an important theme in women's economic history. We will look at some of the issues beginning with the effects of combining employment and family roles, then turning more directly to health and the workplace.

Many social scientists have investigated the relationship between health and the employment status of women. The results are mixed. Some studies find employed women healthier than full-time homemakers (e.g., Welch and Booth, 1977) while others do not (e.g., Newberry, Weissman, and Myers 1979). A survey of black women found no difference between homemakers and employed women in their levels of depressive symptoms, but did find more depression among unemployed women (Brown and Gray 1988). Another study that observed no difference in the psychiatric status of employed women and homemakers found that homemakers liked their work less, found it less interesting, and felt less adequate in their jobs (Newberry, Weissman, and Myers 1979).

Because men tend not to share many household tasks an employed woman really has two jobs: the one for which she is paid and her housework. A woman who has young children has a particular burden and longer hours than other women or men. What is the impact of this combination of roles?

Not surprisingly, women's health depends on the combination of burdens they have. A national study of mental health found that among married women who were not employed the presence of children was associated with increased depression, while among married women who were employed depression was not affected by children per se, but by the level of difficulty they had in arranging child care and whether or not their husbands participated in child care. Employed mothers who had sole responsibility for children and difficulty in arranging child care showed the highest levels of depression. Neither the presence of children nor the availability of child care affected husbands' levels of depression (Ross and Mirowsky 1988).

Women's experience of combining roles also depends on their attitudes toward them. A study of first-time mothers of babies five to nine months old compared women who had been very involved in their work before the birth with those who hadn't. Among the new mothers who were not employed at the time of the study, those who had previously been very involved in their work showed greater irritability, decreased marital intimacy, greater depression, and lower self-esteem and perceived higher costs of motherhood than mothers who had not been so involved in work (Pistrang 1984).

Until recently most observers assumed that women faced tremendous stresses of role conflict simply by combining motherhood and employment. We now know the relationship between women's family and work roles and health is more complex than that. The impact of employment depends on the combination of responsibilities, burdens, and supports women have and their own attitudes and motivations. At minimum we have to consider the mother's access to child care and the role played by the father or other people in the household in either creating more stress or alleviating it.

Another issue in work and health is occupation health. One strategy used to guard women from health dangers at work is protective labor legislation, laws that bar women from jobs requiring them to engage in activities regarded as dangerous to their health. Before discussing the specific types of restrictions and their effects, it is necessary first to explore the underlying assumptions of special protective legislation for women. The first assumption is that certain jobs involve tasks or situations that are dangerous to women but not to men, or at least not to the same degree. The second assumption is that if the law did not bar women from these jobs, women would seek them against the interests of their own health and welfare; women therefore need to be protected against themselves or against employers who might require them to work under dangerous conditions. Labor unions at the turn of the twentieth century were particularly favorable toward protective labor legislation for women, partly because they thought such policies would protect male wages and partly because they thought such policies for women would lead to more universal protection for workers. It appears that both notions were correct. (For more discussion of protective legislation, see Chapter 12.)

Until 1908 the Supreme Court remained antagonistic to the idea of protective labor legislation, not because they were worried about sex discrimination but because, as they said in *Lochner* v. *New York* (1905), any type of protective legislation for workers (regardless of sex) constituted interference with the right to enter freely into a contract. In 1908 the Court changed its mind in the case of *Muller* v. *Oregon,* which concerned a maximum hours law applying only to women. The justification offered by the Court for allowing such legislation contains the classic argument for restricting women's employment:

> That women's physical structure and the performance of maternal functions place her at a disadvantage in the struggle for subsistance is obvious. This is especially true when the burdens of motherhood are upon her. Even when they are not, by abundant testimony of the medical fraternity continuance for a long time on her feet at work, repeating this from day to day, tends to injurious effects upon the body, *and as healthy mothers are essential to vigorous offspring, the physical well-being of woman becomes an object of public interest and care* in order to preserve the strength and vigor of the race. (Emphasis added)

Notice the Court's implication that whether or not an individual woman is pregnant or a mother, she should be treated as though she were. The law has an interest in protecting not women's health as such, but women's health as reproducers and mothers. All women should be treated as though they are mothers because women are potential mothers. As the Court further said, "Her physical structure and a proper discharge of her maternal functions—having in view not merely her own health, but the well-being of the race—justify legislation to protect her from the greed as well as the passion of man." The restrictions "are not imposed solely for her benefit, but also largely for the benefit of all."

Most of the original pieces of protective labor legislation have disappeared because they are in conflict with employment policies that ban sex discrimination in employment. Maximum hours legislation now covers female and male labor equally, as do minimum wage laws. Prohibitions against women's doing night work have been dropped, as have prohibitions against women's working in underground mines in most states. Gender-specific weight-lifting restrictions are now illegal because they run counter to Title VII of the 1964 Civil Rights Act, which bars discrimination in employment on the basis of race and sex. The Supreme Court has interpreted this law to mean that employers may not make personnel decisions on the basis of their assumptions about the capabilities of members of a sex or race but must consider the merit of the individuals who apply for a job.

Protection of women's reproductive systems and their capability as mothers continues to be an important question in employment law and policy. One focus of debate and attention is in the area of occupational safety and health concerned especially with exposure to toxic substances in the course of work. The federal Occupational Safety and Health Administration (OSHA) was established by the 1970 Occupational Safety and Health Act to develop and enforce guidelines to protect workers from health and safety hazards at work. Jeanne Mager Stellmen (1977) argues that relatively little attention has been paid to women's special occupational health problems, although some are quite widespread and serious. For example, she points out that the hospital jobs generally held by women have the greatest risk of skin diseases. Other jobs that place workers at special risk of skin diseases are cleaning, hairdressing, food service, and homemaking—heavily female sectors of the economy.

Many employers have made efforts to protect women, and especially pregnant women, from substances thought to be hazardous to reproductive health. This is usually accomplished through segregation, which often involves women's being prohibited from doing certain jobs. Such segregation has included both pregnant and potentially pregnant women—those of child-bearing age. One of the most serious criticisms of this kind of policy is that it is discriminatory. Many of the hazards to reproductive health are hazardous to *both* sexes but only women are barred from jobs involving these substances; men's health is left at risk. Moreover, as Vibiana M. Andrade (1981) has observed, protective labor practices of this type are generally applied less rigorously in jobs that are traditionally female than in those that are traditionally male. In other words, there seems to be greater effort to protect women from hazardous "male" jobs than from hazardous "female" jobs. The debate continues over how the government and employers can ensure safety and health at work, nondiscrimination, and efficient and productive work practices all at the same time.[4]

Other controversies on protection in employment center on pregnancy itself. For a long time many employers refused to hire pregnant women and fired employees who became pregnant. As late as 1964, 40 percent of all U.S. employers fired women for pregnancy. Although some offered unpaid pregnancy leave, over 50 percent of these required a woman to leave before the seventh month of pregnancy. Only about 6 percent permitted the use of sick leave for pregnancy-related illnesses or disability

(Gelb and Palley 1987, 164). Airlines required stewardesses to take unpaid leave as soon as they knew they were pregnant. Some companies that would not otherwise fire pregnant women would do so if a woman was unmarried. Some employers would not hire women who were mothers. It is quite clear that in many of these cases restrictions were not designed to protect anyone's health but were based on moral considerations or on stereotypes of mothers at work.

The first step forward came in 1971 when the Supreme Court decided in *Phillips* v. *Martin Marietta* that an employer could not refuse to hire a woman because she was a mother. Pregnancy discrimination took longer to defeat. In 1974 the Supreme Court declared in *Cleveland Board of Education* v. *La Fleur* that compulsory maternity leave (in this case at the end of the fifth month) violated women's privacy with regard to childbearing. Employers could consider only whether a woman was capable of fulfilling her duties. In 1977 the Court ruled in *Nashville Gas Co.* v. *Satty* that the practice of denying women accrual of seniority (in this case removing their seniority) while they were on leave to give birth is illegal under Title VII of the 1964 Civil Rights Act.

There have been other forms of discrimination against pregnant women. For example, the General Electric Company used to provide its workers with a medical benefits package that did not cover pregnancy, although it did cover such things as prostatectomies, vasectomies, and circumcisions. In *General Electric Co.* v. *Gilbert* (1976) the Supreme Court argued that this benefits plan discriminated between pregnant and nonpregnant workers not between women and men, and it therefore found this kind of discrimination acceptable under the law.

As a result of political agitation following this and other decisions, Congress passed the 1978 Pregnancy Discrimination Act, which amended Title VII of the 1964 Civil Rights Act to make it illegal for employers to discriminate against pregnant women. It is interesting to note that the coalition that fought for an end to pregnancy discrimination included such diverse groups as feminists, church groups, unions, and antiabortion groups. The coalition against the measure included chambers of commerce, the National Association of Manufacturers, the National Retail Merchants Association, and insurance companies.

Many of the rules and laws that ''protected'' women's health at work have come to be viewed as roadblocks selectively placed in the path of women's advancement. These mechanisms usually reduced women's means to earning a livelihood and improving their employment status rather than protecting women at work.

Women now have more choices, but as Andrade says, such choices also give women the opportunity to pay with their own flesh (1981, 78). Women face a range of health hazards at work that we are only beginning to understand. Among these are stress, which has important psychological and physical effects. Not only are women entering more stressful jobs, but also they are doing so without the same sort of help at home that men receive. Women are also entering fields in which they are likely to encounter discrimination and sexist attitudes and behavior, which will put even more pressure on them. Although old-style protective labor legislation is not the answer, some means must be found to protect the health of the nation's work force.

In recent years there has been increasing attention to physical fitness for both men and women. Health professionals and the public alike have become more aware, for example, of the relationship between weight, body tone, and health. Definitions of health have become intricately linked to conceptions of beauty and appearance. Looking good and feeling good seem to go hand in hand. Consider the trends in advertisements for cosmetics, clothes, and other "beauty aids." Shampoos, nail polishes, and skin creams are now guaranteed not just to make our hair and skin beautiful but also to make them "healthy looking." Women athletes and dancers are increasingly used as models and promoters in television commercials.

At the same time people are becoming aware that females in general have been discouraged from athletics and other activities that might promote health but were thought to make women unattractive and unfeminine. Throughout women's history we can see that standards of femininity and feminine beauty have sometimes been remarkably detrimental to women's health and that at times a lack of health has been considered attractive in women.

Standards of health and beauty change over time but they are always related. Until surprisingly recently—perhaps the beginning of this century—bathing was considered unhealthful by Europeans, in contrast to the Chinese and Japanese, who have understood the benefits of bathing for centuries. Europeans often went most of the winter without bathing at all. We can only assume that body filth was not as unattractive as it is now, when we generally regard someone who does not bathe as both unhealthy and unattractive. What we consider a healthful and attractive amount of weight has also changed; compare the robust chorus girls in the movies of the late 1920s and early 1930s with the svelte models of today. Doctors too have changed their ideas about what constitutes optimal weight for health.

Shifting standards of health and attractiveness have adversely affected both sexes, but women have endured more than men in the pursuit of beauty, particularly in the last two centuries. In the late nineteenth century, white, non-working-class women—not men—adopted the "consumptive" look as an ideal of beauty. For most of recent history, white women avoided showing any sign that the sun and fresh air had touched them. Such behavior may have contributed to the relatively high rates of tuberculosis (also known as "consumption") among women compared with men. Similar women today bake themselves mercilessly in the sun or use chemicals to simulate a tan, thus encouraging the growth of skin cancers. Black women meanwhile have been urged to try to bleach their skin. In the nineteenth century swooning—when not caused by corsets that were too tight—was faked to show feminine delicacy. The ideal of the delicate, swooning woman could be pursued only by relatively few women. In the nineteenth century working-class and black women were considered naturally stronger and hardier than other women. They were fit to be workhorses, not ideals of femininity.

Women with the means and time to do so have resculpted, recolored, and otherwise altered their bodies, sometimes dangerously, in the pursuit of current standards of beauty. Many of these alterations have been encouraged, or at least aided and abetted, by both the medical profession and the fashion industry. Only rarely has

How to achieve the "classic" hourglass figure: with a
stiff corset.

the natural shape, color, or smell of the female body been promoted as attractive.
We have already mentioned the fantastic weight of female clothes in some eras and
the pressure exerted by the corsets of wealthy women. Extended use of the nineteenth-
century corset could literally change the shape of the body, cramping and moving
vital internal organs in the process. Even after the middle of the twentieth century
women were encouraged to push themselves into girdles rather than to achieve natural
muscle tone through exercise. At various times in the past century women's breasts
have been bound to make them look small, raised by stiff brassieres to make them
look large, exaggerated with padding, and left virtually undressed.

In the post–World War II era, surgery was increasingly used to alter bodies,
sometimes with disastrous results. Women have had face-lifts and "nose jobs,"

implants to enlarge breasts, and operations to remove layers of fat. For a time it was common for female models to have their back teeth removed to give them hollow cheeks and the appearance of high cheekbones. One wonders why Americans have tended to view the old Chinese practice of foot binding with such horror.

Other adornments used by women and not (or at least rarely) by men emphasize the degree to which the female body has been at odds with the standards of beauty. Hair coloring, especially coloring to hide the normal signs of aging, is more common among women than men. Countless forms of coloring have been used on women's faces. Rarely has the color of women's lips been regarded as appropriate, and even when it has, lipsticks have been created to look "natural." Even the length of women's eyelashes and fingernails have required augmentation, and artificial lashes and nails have been created to help out.

Feminists raise three criticisms about these "beauty" practices. The first is that it should not require so much ornamentation and alteration to make women attractive. They also note that these practices require a considerable investment of women's time and money. The second criticism concerns choice and control. Standards of beauty are established and guided in large part by the fashion industry, especially through advertising, and by the commercial entertainment media such as television and motion pictures. Although these industries may not be able to manipulate women as though they were lifeless puppets, their powers of direction are considerable. To what degree do women look they way they want to look, and to what degree do they look the way other people want them to look?

The third criticism of these fashion and style practices directly concerns the question of health. No doubt many of the surgical and medical alterations to women's appearance put women at risk. It is also clear that the chemical composition of some women's toiletries is harmful. Women's clothes have generally not been designed with comfort in mind and can be restrictive to women who are or might otherwise be active. Women's shoes are a good case in point. Who would ever guess from the high spindly heels, pointed cramped toes, or high platforms of some women's shoe styles that the primary function of feet is transportation? It is no wonder that dress reform has been a major goal of feminist movements since the 1840s.

The contemporary women's movement has also included within its agenda these questions of dress, cosmetics, and alteration of the female body. In the 1970s its attention also began to turn to weight and fitness. What gave rise to this attention was the increasing awareness of two related illnesses or "eating disorders" found principally among women: anorexia nervosa, or self-starvation, and bulimia, or binge eating alternated with self-induced vomiting and fasting. Both are serious illnesses, not just cases of "going too far" in attempts to lose weight. They involve compulsive and dangerous behaviors, often hidden from family and friends until they are well advanced, and they result in emaciation, a variety of other physical symptoms, and in some severe cases death. The anorexic continues to regard herself as fat and ugly even after she has lost a dangerous amount of weight.

From 85 to 95 percent of all anorexics are women (Rohrbaugh 1980, 411). The majority of these women are in their late teens and early twenties and are somewhat overweight, although not necessarily extraordinarily so. They tend to be "good girls" from affluent homes, who have well-educated parents and are under pressure to succeed. Anorexia seems to strike at the time when major changes are occurring in a young woman's life—as she prepares to go to college or get married.

A number of different theories have been advanced to explain these illnesses. They agree about the profile of the anorexic and what happens to her; they also agree that anorexia and related eating disorders are linked to gender roles and sexual pressures on young women. They disagree, however, about the precise cause and meaning of these problems. Some argue that anorexia is a flight from femininity. Others consider it an attempt to fulfill norms of femininity and feminine beauty run amok. Others argue that anorexia is based on feelings of dependency and unworthiness.

Concern for beauty is not just a health problem for women who are chronically ill. From a very young age girls are taught to be more aware of their appearance than boys are, and girls tend to be more dissatisfied with their appearance, especially their weight, than boys are. One study of adolescents (Musa and Roach 1973) found that girls are more likely than boys to rate their own appearance as worse than that of their peers, while boys are more likely than girls to rate their appearance as better. Girls' self-evaluation of appearance is more closely related than boys' to other measures of adjustment. The relationship between weight and self-adjustment is particularly important for women because of the normal fluctuations of weight with the menstrual cycle. At the same time it is important to remember that the standards women use to evaluate their own weight differs for different ethnic groups (Dawson 1988).

One study of pregnant women and maternity clothes reveals an interesting aspect of women's reactions to weight gain, especially how their self-evaluations are mediated by external forces. Dianne Horgan (1983) surveyed both expensive and less expensive department stores and found that where the maternity clothes were located was related to the "class" of the store. In the more expensive stores, maternity clothes were near the lingerie department. In the stores aimed at working-class women, maternity clothes were located near the clothes for large women and the uniforms. In surveying pregnant women, Horgan found that the wealthier pregnant women felt sexier and more attractive than other women, and the less wealthy and working-class pregnant women felt fatter and unattractive.

All other things being equal, body weight and tone depend on both diet and exercise. One problem that has received increasing attention is that females tend to diet to control their weight and males are more likely to exercise (Dwyer and Mayer 1968). Part of the reason for this is that girls have been discouraged from sports and most forms of exercise that would strengthen and tone their bodies. Muscles were considered unflattering in women, and engaging in most sports was thought to be either unfeminine or dangerous. Since menstruating and pregnant women were considered disabled, until the last few years exercise was considered especially bad for them. Attitudes are changing, however, and now even pregnant women are encouraged to exercise.

The issues and debate surrounding Title IX and sports in schools (see Chapter 4) point to the degree to which sports have been institutionalized as a male domain. Philosopher Jane English (1982) argues that our very concept of sports has been androcentric. She writes that "the few athletic activities permitted to women—mostly forms of dance—were not thought to fall under the concept of sport, and are still classified as arts or entertainment instead. Speed, size, and strength seem to be the essence of sports. Women are naturally inferior at 'sports' so conceived" (266). Women's bodies, their "small size, flexibility, and low center of gravity combine to give women the kind of natural hegemony in some sports activities such as the balance beam that men enjoy in football" (265). English suggests that if women rather than men dominated the sports world, "competitions emphasizing flexibility, balance, strength, timing, and small size might dominate Sunday afternoon television and offer salaries in six figures" (266).

It is also important to realize that because more opportunities are now open to women, and especially because girls are now receiving better training, the gap between women and men in such abilities as speed and strength has been considerably reduced. Indeed, even though men and women still perform differently in many sports requiring these abilities, women athletes now match or break records set by men a few decades ago—a feat that seemed biologically impossible then.

Which sports are most lucrative and whether top female athletes can compete against top male athletes are questions of only tangential interest to most of us. Our activities are not chosen on the basis of whether we can beat everyone else. Regular exercise is important for physical health, and women who try to control the way they look through dress, cosmetic alterations, diet, or surgery are often unsuccessful unless they also include exercise in their lives. Research suggests that sports activity is also good for mental health. One study of high school and college students, for example, found that young women who were athletes rated their bodies more positively, and female high school athletes also felt more feminine than their less active peers.

Women and the Practice of Health Care

Thus far we have looked at particular aspects of women's health. Let us now draw together some of the disparate information on women and health care to reach some conclusions about how women are viewed and treated in health-care institutions. To what degree do we find evidence of androcentrism or sexism in health-care systems? Does the fact of being male or female affect the type of treatment a person receives?

There is some impressive evidence that health-care professionals view and treat males and females differently. As was mentioned earlier, in 1970 Inge Broverman and her colleagues found that mental health clinicians described a "healthy male" and a "healthy adult" in roughly the same way, and used other terms to characterize a "healthy female." A few years later Alice Aslin (1977) administered the same test not just to male and female therapists, but also to members of the feminist Association for Women in Psychology. She got the same results as Broverman and her colleagues, but only among men.

Diane Kravetz and Linda E. Jones (1981) also studied mental health professionals' ideas of what constitutes a healthy man, woman, and adult by having them respond to items on the Bem Sex-Role Inventory Scale (BSRI) and then scoring these responses to see whether the professionals described healthy men, women, and adults in masculine, feminine, or androgynous terms. Table 5-1 shows their findings. Very few mental health professionals described any healthy person in feminine terms. About

TABLE 5-1

Proportion of Mental Health Professionals
Describing a Healthy Man, Woman, or Adult
in Masculine, Feminine, or Androgynous Terms

	Man	*Woman*	*Adult*
Masculine	51%	40%	28%
Feminine	2%	2%	0%
Androgynous	47%	58%	72%
Total	100%	100%	100%

Note: N (size of the sample) = 183.
SOURCE: Kravetz and Jones (1981).

half (51 percent) described healthy men in stereotypically masculine terms, and about half (47 percent) used androgynous terms. Healthy women were somewhat more likely (58 percent) and adults were much more likely (72 percent) to be described in androgynous terms (See also O'Malley and Richardson 1985).

Other studies show that mental and physical health specialists also react differently to males and females partly because of their attitudes toward gender roles, masculinity, and femininity. Peter B. Zeldow (1976) found that when hypothetical female patients expressed attitudes or preferences conventionally associated with males, evaluators judged them as more disturbed than when they expressed attitudes or preferences conventionally considered neutral or feminine. The same statements did not affect evaluators' views when they were made by males. In another study comparing reactions to males and females who act the same way, counselors who listened to tapes of either a man or a woman expressing the same concerns about work rated the woman as more masculine than they rated the man, possibly because these concerns, which seem normal in a man, seem abnormal in a woman (Hayes and Wolleat 1978). In another study (cited in Unger 1979) evaluators were presented with a psychotherapeutic vignette featuring a patient who was either male or female and either aggressive or dependent. The evaluators responded more negatively to the dependent male and judged him to have more serious problems than the dependent female. The reverse was true if the patient was presented as aggressive.

Other aspects of health practitioners' ideology also appear to affect their judgments of patients. One study in which professional counselors were presented with bogus client profiles found that examiners who were politically conservative perceived greater psychological maladjustment in women who leaned left politically than in men with a similar political bias (Abramowitz et al. 1973). Some research suggests that health practitioners assume women are more difficult patients or clients than men are, although a study of 800 clinical psychologists suggests that this depends on the class background of patients. Joan M. Settin and Dana Bramel (1981) found that the higher the social class of a male patient, the more favorably the therapist viewed him, but the higher the social class of a female patient, the less favorably the therapist viewed her. If we assume that patients of higher social class are more articulate (which does not mean smarter), less deferential, and apparently less dependent, we can see how class and gender interact to produce this result. The males of higher social class would be acting in ways therapists find preferable in males, and females of the lower social class would be acting in ways therapists find preferable in females.

Another study claims that clinicians' attitudes have changed over time so that the problem is less that they see women and men differently per se and more that they define the situations in which they expect to find women and men differently. These clinicians defined mental health characteristics differently for people in the home and at work. Appropriate characteristics for people in the home were the ones traditionally regarded as feminine while appropriate characteristics for people at work were those traditionally regarded as masculine (Poole and Tapley, 1988). Of course the result will continue to be differential evaluation of women and men if they think of women at home and men at work.

Thus far we have considered differences in practitioners' attitudes toward and perceptions of men and women. Research also suggests that male and female patients are *treated* differently. When Barbara Bernstein and Robert Kane (1981) interviewed 253 physicians, they found doctors are more likely to consider emotional factors important in diagnosing a woman's problems and that they are more likely to expect a psychosomatic diagnosis of a woman's problem. These differences are especially true if the patient does not mention any personal problems during the course of the medical interview.

In their study of mental illness William Tudor, Jeanette F. Tudor, and Walter R. Gove (1977) noted that both psychotic and neurotic males are kept in mental hospitals longer than females with similar disorders are, and that psychotic males are channeled into psychiatric treatment more quickly than females. After reviewing their own and other people's research they concluded, "Standards of normality for females are reported to be lower than standards for males, and females are apparently less stigmatized for symptoms of mental incompetence" (101). Here is more evidence that from the medical point of view a normal female is not quite as healthy as a normal male, or that an unhealthy female is more normal than an unhealthy male.

The most consistent difference found in the treatment of males and females is the higher prescription rate of psychotropic drugs such as sedatives and tranquilizers for women. Research repeatedly shows that women are more likely than men to use prescribed psychoactive drugs, while men are more likely to use self-prescribed (for example, over-the-counter drugs and alcohol) or illegal drugs (Cooperstock 1971). This pattern exists even in specialized populations. Even if we hold levels of anxiety constant, elderly women are given more major tranquilizers than elderly men are (Milliren 1977), and women in prisons are given more psychotropic drugs than men in prisons are (Shaw 1982).

Why are women more likely than men to be drugged by doctors? Interviews with physicians reveal a variety of reasons, including beliefs that women are more vulnerable and need drugs more, that men are reluctant to use drugs, and that women have the kinds of stress that can be alleviated by these drugs. Both women and doctors are likely to understand women's problems in psychological rather than purely physical terms (Cooperstock 1971). Some doctors believe that the side effects of psychotropic drugs are less troublesome to women because women don't have to be as alert as men do (Prather and Fidell 1975).

Drug advertisements play an important role in helping doctors to match drugs with patients and symptoms. Content analysis of drug ads shows that they tend to associate psychoactive drugs with women and nonpsychoactive drugs with men. Men in these advertisements have more specific or work-related problems, and women have more diffuse anxieties and tensions and are shown as difficult patients (Prather and Fidell 1975). Robert Seidenberg (1971) found that drug advertisements tended to suggest that a woman's reluctance or inability to do housework was a sign of mental illness, recalling Betty Friedan's picture of tranquilizer-popping housewives in the 1950s. (For more discussion of commercials and advertisements, see Chapter 7.)

Several factors combine to create problems for women in the health-care system. If a culture is sexist or androcentric, health-care practitioners and patients alike assimilate these attitudes and perceptions. Any patient is to some degree dependent on the medical expert and relatively vulnerable to him or her. For women, however, there is the additional problem of gender-linked dependency. If patient and doctor are unequal in status, a female patient and a male doctor are even more so. Although consumer movements in health care have grown recently, "doctor's orders" are still commanding, particularly for women who, because of gender ideology, feel incompetent to question males in what is regarded as a male field.

These problems are exacerbated by the training of health-care professionals and the organizations in which they work. Textbooks used in medical schools reinforce sexist views of women, as does much of the biological, medical, and psychological research on which health-care training is based. Sometimes the lack of regard for women on the part of medical research is shocking. Elizabeth Anne Mills (1982), for example, reviewed the literature on rape in medical journals from 1880 to 1960 and found consistent support for the belief that there is no such thing as rape, or at least that a "real" rape is extremely rare. There was a recurring view that women (and even children) make false charges out of revenge or hallucination, to force marriage, or to punish men. Doctors were counseled to interrogate women carefully because women sometimes get so hysterical that they show false physical signs of struggle or hurt themselves to lend evidence to their lies.

Medical definitions of femininity are changing, however. In many communities medical personnel and hospitals are becoming more tolerant of, and even favorable toward, women who want to be more in control of birth. Doctors increasingly expect women to take birth preparation courses such as Lamaze classes, and they are giving women and their partners more opportunities to make more choices in the birthing room. Pregnancy is decreasingly viewed as a disability that necessitates withdrawal from work, sports, and other activities. Fitness among women is emphasized as it never was before. Women who do not conform to traditional female roles appear less likely to be suspected of being psychologically unhealthy.

Altering health-care institutions and procedures requires changes in the training health-care practitioners receive. Moreover, change often appears risky, and neither the public nor health-care professionals are likely to take risks that might threaten health. All patients are faced with harassed and overworked doctors and nurses, often in settings such as hospitals and clinics that must closely watch their schedules, finances, and paperwork. As much as many of us would like to shape our own health care, few of us are likely to feel the confidence to question the training and experience of the professional. Patients may feel they have increased their power by using the threat of medical malpractice suits, but this threat both increases the cost of health care dramatically and tends to make doctors even more resistant to using anything but their own medical judgment and high-technology safeguards.

Health care is expensive, particularly in the United States. Unlike most other industrialized nations the United States has a health-care system based on the principle that except under certain circumstances, the person receiving health care should be responsible for paying the bill. Although there are programs such as Medicare and Medicaid, which share the cost of health care for the aged and poor, it is not sufficient, particularly in cases of severe illness. The facts that women are poorer than men, care for more children, and live longer make the economics of health care particularly relevant to them.

A growing consumer movement and the women's movement have argued that the public must be more active in shaping their health care. We will therefore turn directly to the question of women's influence in health-care systems.

Women's Roles in Shaping Health Care

Women are now, and generally have been, the people who have provided most of the world's health care. However, the study of women in society repeatedly shows that a group that constitutes a numerical majority is by no means necessarily a group that has the most power and control. Even when a group does have some power over itself, it will not necessarily use that power in its own interest. Health care is such a situation.

Throughout this chapter thus far we have looked at how women are treated and viewed by the institutions charged with shaping health norms. We will now look more closely at the people who shape health care and values. What have been the roles of women? What contributions have women made to health care? We will begin by looking at the people whose primary job it is to provide health care: health professionals and other workers. We will then turn to health activists and to social movements and organizations that attempt to influence health-care institutions and practices. Next we will consider one of the largest groups of health-care providers: mothers. Finally, we will look at the largest group of all: patients and health-care consumers.

Healers, Doctors, and
Other Health-Care Professionals

Most health care is not now, and certainly was not in the past, provided by professional physicians. As we have seen, until recently midwives performed most gynecological and obstetrical care. Many women—often these same midwives—also served as healers, employing herbal remedies and other means to manage the health of people who sought help from them. Although many of their remedies were at best useless and at worst harmful (as were the strategies of male doctors of the same eras), current medical research shows that many of them may have been very helpful.

It is important to remember that professional medical training is a very recent phenomenon. Until the modern era doctors trained in academies concentrated their study primarily on philosophy, theology, and perhaps astrology. Under such circumstances the women's herbs were at least as good as the men's stars and prayers. Even in the nineteenth century much of the male doctor's training, especially with regard to gynecology and obstetrics, was theoretical in nature, so doctors were ill-prepared when they began their practice on real women (Leavitt 1983). Part of the reason for this questionable training was the constraints placed on men because of gender ideology: A man should not offend the delicacy of a woman who is not his wife by looking at her naked body. Surgery was a relatively low-status occupation performed by men who doubled as barbers; the red and white barber pole, symbolizing a bloody rag, is a reminder of the dual role barbers once played. Most medical knowledge, including that of the healers and midwives, was learned on the job from those who were more experienced.

As late as the 1840s about 70 percent of all male physicians in the United States had no formal training. In a sense, this information casts a slightly different light on the fact that the first female to finish formal medical training in the United States didn't do so until 1849. As Mary Roth Walsh has written, Elizabeth Blackwell (sister-in-law of Antoinette Brown Blackwell, discussed in Chapter 2) ''was recognized as the first woman medical doctor because she was the first woman who earned a degree from a medical college, a criterion which, if applied to her male colleagues, would have sharply reduced their numbers'' (Walsh 1979, 448).

Competition and antagonism between female healers and male doctors (and other male-dominated institutions) developed as early as the fourteenth century and was well established by the fifteenth and sixteenth centuries. This growing antagonism was manifested in the witchhunts of the late medieval period, when, it is estimated, thousands of people were executed as witches, about 85 percent of whom were women (Ehrenreich and English 1979, 31). Among the charges leveled against the women were the crimes of healing, using drugs to ease pain, and assisting with contraception and abortion.

Although in early American history women continued to serve as healers and midwives, their activities became increasingly restricted during the nineteenth and twentieth centuries. Medicine came under increasingly strict licensing requirements and eventually required training that at first only men could receive. Women's medical colleges began to open in the 1840s, and other medical schools began to admit women in the 1870s. By 1900 there were about 5000 trained women doctors, but at about that time the mixed medical colleges that admitted women began to impose quotas restricting the number of women. Those women who did gain admission were often harassed by their male colleagues. The powerful professional organization and interest group, the American Medical Association (AMA) admitted women to full membership only in 1951, 104 years after it was founded. Medical schools explicitly imposed tougher entry standards on women than men until the 1970s, when such actions

Nursing was always a "women's occupation," but different from its stereotype.
In this photo, a nurse crosses New York rooftops to visit her patient.

became illegal. As soon as women were required to be only as good as men rather than better to get into medical school, the proportion of women in medical schools rose dramatically.

The late nineteenth and early twentieth centuries saw the rise of a number of health-care fields such as nursing, social work, and mental health, some of which became predominantly female. Nursing poses a particularly interesting case in the study of women. At first nurses were generally trained on the job, as ward workers in hospitals and clinics, for example. The first training school for nurses was established at Bellevue Hospital in New York City in 1873. Nursing education expanded and was gradually professionalized, although it was not regulated and licensed until after World War II. Since that time nursing organizations and new nursing labor unions have worked to foster a view of nurses as highly trained health-care professionals rather than the old "Nurse Nancy" view of nurses as cocktail waitresses (or maids) in white. In the twentieth century, especially in the recent era of rapid technological and scientific development in medicine and health care, the number of female technicians and laboratory workers has also grown.

However, men continue to hold higher proportions of the high-status roles in health-care organizations. In 1988 only about 20 percent of the nation's physicians and 9 percent of the dentists were women. Among the female dominated health jobs women constituted 99 percent of the dental assistants, 98 percent of the dental hygienists, 96 percent of the practical nurses, 95 percent of the registered nurses, 86 percent of the dietitians, and 90 percent of the health and nursing aides. Just 31 percent of the pharmacists were women. Women doctors have tended to go into fields with high patient interaction and, often, relatively low pay and status, such as general practice, psychiatry, and pediatrics, although these patterns are now changing.

Some evidence shows that patients and clients tend to prefer male health-care practitioners in some fields, although not in others (Tanney and Birk 1976). Dorothy Rosenthal Mandelbaum (1978) reports that research shows that across class lines patients prefer male doctors. Phyllis Chesler (1971) found that patients tended to prefer a male psychotherapist. This is particularly intriguing because most people come into much more contact with female than with male practitioners in mental health clinics. Rohrbaugh (1980), for example, cites a 1977 study showing that in community mental health clinics, psychiatrists, one-tenth of whom were female, provided 15 percent of the therapy hours; psychologists, one-third of whom were female, provided 8 percent of the therapy hours, and psychiatric social workers and general clinicians, two-thirds of whom were female, provided the other 77 percent of the therapy hours. Many women, on the other hand, prefer women as health-care practitioners, particularly, one might suspect, as gynecologists and obstetricians and, as Tanney and Birk (1976) show, as therapists for personal and social problems.

Little research has been done to see whether women and men perform differently as health-care practitioners. Alice Aslin (1977), who conducted a survey among male and female therapists and members of the feminist Association for Women in Psychology, found that only males still described "healthy women" and "healthy adults" as different. Another study of clinicians (Sherman, Koufacos, and Kenworthy 1978) found women more informed about issues relating to the psychology of women. One study shows that female doctors are more likely than male doctors to let their patients talk (West 1984). Another study shows that in hospitals staffed by women doctors, there are fewer operative deliveries of babies and lower maternal mortality rates. It is certainly true that women do most of the feminist research in health-care fields. Women are also particularly involved in trying to restructure health-care practice and organization to make it more suitable to the needs of women.

Health-care Activists

No discussion of the people involved in shaping health care can be restricted to people actually employed as health-care workers. One of the most striking aspects of the history of women's organizations and feminist movements is the degree to which these groups were active very early in trying to improve the quality and quantity of health care in America. Women were active in the health-care reform movements of the 1820s, 1830s, and later periods. Amelia Bloomer, a feminist, editor of the *Lily,* and proponent of more healthful and functional dress for women, was only one of the many women who organized the dress reform movement of the 1840s and 1850s. William Leach (1980) points out that throughout the nineteenth century feminists were committed to and involved in ideas of "preventive hygiene," which included not just medical treatment, but what we now call environmental health, fitness, mental health, and social health. It is no coincidence that numerous suffragists and other feminists were active in the temperance movement. Their motivation was, by and large, protection of the health of women and children who suffered at the hands of drunken husbands.

These "health activists" were particularly likely to see individual health as related to morality, equality, justice, and the "health of society." Elizabeth Cady Stanton, for example, declared that "Sickness is a crime since it is an evidence of violation of some physical law" (Leach 1980, 20). These reformers believed that such crimes were partly based on the structure of society and social relations. Jane Addams and others involved in the settlement house movement, which emphasized the needs of immigrants; Margaret Sanger, Emma Goldman, and others in the birth control movement, which focused on working-class women; and Ellen Richards and others who developed the field of home economics (endorsed in 1899 by the AMA) were motivated in part by a concern for the health of individuals and of society as a whole.

As the nineteenth century came to a close, women became particularly active in the push to have government directly involved in assuring the health of society through regulation and improvement of sanitation facilities, hospitals, parks, and prisons. In these endeavors they found special allies in the Progressive Movement, an early twentieth-century movement dedicated to social and political reforms. As William Leach (1980) points out, by the end of the century, women, including many feminists, were actively involved in state and city politics and government and the agencies that managed sanitation, health, and health education in schools. Today these same concerns remain prominent in the feminist movement and in women's social and political activity more generally.

Mothers as Health-care Providers

One relatively unchanged aspect of the role of wife and mother is caring for the family's health, both by creating a healthful home and dispensing most of the immediate health care and by making sure that members of the family who need treatment from professionals receive it. As Eugenia S. Carpenter notes, "Women are the principal brokers or arrangers of health services for their children and spouses" (1980, 1214). This responsibility of women for family health care entails certain problems.

David Spiegel (1982) argues that this responsibility is in many ways a burden. "Because we have been willing to believe that mothers do something special for their children—something that cannot be replaced by anyone other than the mother—mothers have been given an inequitable share of the responsibility for childcare and undue blame for the mental illness of their children" (105). This burden becomes greater when a woman is employed for much of the day outside the home without any major change in the division of labor at home. "Both the monetary and non-monetary costs women incur in fulfilling their family responsibilities for health care of other family members are increasing" (Carpenter 1980, 1215).

It is important to see how much the view of parents as health providers is shaped by gender ideology. Mothers do have more responsibility and take more blame than fathers in family health matters because they are given more responsibility in general for family care. But even beyond this, people tend to blame parents for gender-linked problems in their children (Kellermen 1974). For example, a child's problems may be blamed on a "domineering mother" or a "henpecked father," both pejorative judgments of women.

Gender ideology can have very tangible effects on people. Until recently, for example, in child custody disputes courts almost always awarded children to their mothers on the assumption that a mother can provide a better home for a child. (This imbalance in decisions is beginning to change; for more discussion see Chapter 11.) If the mother was a lesbian, however, a child was not usually awarded to her on the grounds that she could not provide a healthful environment for the child, even though research finds no greater likelihood of emotional problems among children in single-lesbian-parent households than in single-heterosexual-parent households (Kirkpatrick, Smith, and Roy 1981). In fact research reveals virtually no differences in gender identification or gender-linked toy preferences among children in these two groups (Hoeffer 1981; Kirkpatrick, Smith, and Roy 1981). Courts are beginning to take the view that a parent's homosexuality should not play a role in determining custody arrangements.

The Influence of Women as Health-care Consumers

It is all too easy to think of health-care consumers as passive patients whose only real source of power in health care is to pick a doctor wisely. Much of the writing about women and health emphasizes women's role as passive victims of health care institutions. Current movements to strengthen the role of the consumer as well as new research into the history of health and medicine point out that health-care consumers do not have to be totally passive recipients and that they never have been devoid of power as a group.

We have already seen some examples of the ways in which women have exerted some control over their own health care. In addition to being primarily responsible for ministering to the health-care, nutritional, and sanitation needs of their families, they are also responsible for their own health needs. Women have provided much of their own training, often disparagingly referred to as "old wives' tales" or "household hints" they pass on to each other.

Women have also organized to influence other health-care providers. Recent writings remind us that women have not just been passive victims, but have often taken a strong hand in determining what treatment they received (Leavitt 1980, 1983; Smith-Rosenberg 1975; Leavitt and Walton 1982). As many people have pointed out, women controlled the process of birth before the widespread use of physicians or hospitals for birthing. Birth was a cooperative effort among women, including the mother, midwife, and female relations and friends. That control did not disappear in a single blow; medical science did not simply appear at the door and force unwilling women to accept new models and practices and ship women off to hospitals. Women continued to exert considerable control as long as birth occurred in "their" territory: the home. A doctor could be thrown out of the birthing room by a woman if she disapproved of the doctor's methods. Doctors found themselves without patients if they were known to engage in practices women didn't like. Judith Walzer Leavitt cites the advice one doctor gave to others about attempting to shave a woman's pubic area before birthing:

> In about three seconds after the doctor has made the first rake with his safety [razor], he will find himself on his back out in the yard with the imprint of a woman's bare foot emblazoned on his manly chest, the window sash round his neck. . . .Tell him not to try to shave'em (1983, 294).

Taking control was no easy task for the doctor.

Women have often staunchly searched for and demanded the best treatment they thought they could obtain, including trained doctors in preference to midwives and state-of-the-art procedures and drugs. "Old-fashioned" practitioners who refused to use the new procedures (many of which are discussed earlier in this chapter) found themselves rejected in favor of those who were more "modern." Eventually women began to seek hospital rather than home care for childbirth. Once they left "their" territory, however, they also lost their control of birth. Increasing numbers are now trying to regain that control.

Toward a New Understanding of Women's Health

Health and the pursuit of normal states of mind and body, plays a central role in our lives. As we have seen, standards of normal health cover a wide range of our characteristics and activities and are intimately tied to definitions of gender and gender roles. Incomplete medical knowledge means that in the pursuit of high standards of health, gender ideology is likely to play a role in the development and application of health-care values and procedures.

The study of women and health is highly charged and controversial. Some writers, such as Mary Daly (1978) and Barbara Ehrenreich and Dierdre English (1979), suggest that women have been passive victims of medical professionals' purposeful attempts to destroy them; others, such as Edward Shorter (1982), suggest that medical science has singlemindedly saved women from their self-destructing bodies. The truth seems to be somewhere else. The practice of medicine and, more broadly, health care has saved women's lives and improved the quality of their lives in very gender-specific ways. It has also hurt women at times and not lived up to its potential for improving the quality of women's lives in other gender-specific ways. Women have been victims, sometimes passive victims. They have also often taken active charge of themselves and their health care and struggled to increase their control, sometimes for better and sometimes for worse.

The health care system in the United States has changed in recent decades with respect to women's health care. There is considerably more organization on behalf of women. The National Women's Health Network, which includes a membership of over 20,000 individuals and organizations, focuses on women's health issues. There is also an increasing number of feminist health centers, which are run by women who explicitly identify with feminism. More and more hospitals and Health Maintenance Organizations (HMO's) include designated women's centers or women's programs. The question is whether these centers are providing something fundamentally new or are simply repackaging and marketing something old.[5] Perhaps most important of all, even where these special organizations do not exist, women are beginning to take their health and fitness more seriously.

NOTES

1. For more discussion of the history of women and health in America, see Leavitt (1984).

2. There is considerable controversy on this subject. Compare, for example, the very different interpretations of the history of women's health and health care offered by Ehrenreich and English (1979), Rothman (1982), and Shorter (1982). For further discussion of the history of childbirth, see especially Leavitt (1986).

3. For further discussion of violence against women, see Chapters 8 and 10.

4. For more discussion of women and occupational safety and health, see Chavkin (1984).

5. For more discussion of women's health centers and the women's health movement, see Worcester and Whatley (1988).

6

Women and Religion

IN 1780 Judith Sargent Murray, an American writer and the daughter of a minister, argued against the interpretation of Scripture that presented women as inferior and dangerous people. In 1837 the English social observer Harriet Martineau argued that American women's morals were crushed by the repressive teachings of religion. In 1848 the participants at the Seneca Falls convention, a meeting often described as the beginning of the American feminist movement, decried the treatment of women in churches. In the 1880s Elizabeth Cady Stanton, Matilda Joslyn Gage, and many other feminists published attacks on church teachings about women. Emma Goldman declared organized religion one of the most vile oppressors of both men and women. Feminist attacks on organized, male-dominated religion continued through the 1970s, when Mary Daly, a professor of theology at a Roman Catholic college, argued that male religious authorities are guilty of gynocide—murder of women—physically, psychologically, and morally.[1]

These events reveal only one aspect of the relationship between feminism and religion. The history of American feminism also includes uncountable numbers of women, such as Sarah and Angelina Grimké, Lucretia Mott, and Elizabeth Cady Stanton, who derived their principles of justice, freedom, and equality; their strength and bravery; and their skills as speakers and organizers from their religions. Many women have fought from the inside to transform their religions and have demanded to be allowed to become religious leaders and authorities. Others have sought alternative forms of religion more suited to their principles of equality and freedom.

Organized religion is one of the most powerful institutions involved in shaping people's beliefs, attitudes, values, and behavior. Vast numbers of people see religion, or at least their own religions, as among the most valuable social institutions we have. Others, like Freud and Marx, have argued that religion is an "illusion" or an "opiate" that is used to pacify and limit people. Almost everyone, however, acknowledges the power of religion to shape society.

155

Because the theology, cultural precepts, ceremonies, and rituals of most religions contain messages and dictates about gender and sexuality, it is difficult to understand the institutional roots of sex/gender systems without analyzing the role of religion. To do this we will look at the teachings about women, gender, and sexuality found in the major American religions. We will then turn to the role of women in shaping religion and the ways in which women have influenced society through their religious activities. Before we examine these issues, however, we must first consider some of the difficulties involved in any discussion of religion. "Organized religion" cannot be discussed as though it is a single, homogeneous entity. Although religions share certain characteristics, they differ so markedly that it is all too easy to overgeneralize. Even within a single family of religions such as Christianity, we find substantial differences among denominations. Quakers and Roman Catholics are both Christians, both believe in a single deity that sent a son to earth, and both use the Old and New Testaments of the Bible as their chief texts, but beyond this they diverge widely, especially on issues of gender.

Nevertheless we cannot consider all American religions in detail here. The U.S. Bureau of the Census (1989) lists 86 different religious bodies with memberships of 50,000 or more, ranging from the Bulgarian Eastern Orthodox Church with 13 churches to the United Methodist Church with more than 38,000 churches and 9.5 million members. In addition, the Census Bureau reports nearly 14,000 churches belonging to religious bodies with fewer than 50,000 members. Because of these vast numbers, we will limit our discussion to the religions that have had the most widespread influence on American society and values either because of the size of their membership or because of the distinctive roles their adherents have played.

The study of religion in American society poses some unique problems and questions. Unlike many other countries the United States does not have an established or national religion. Even more importantly the principles of American law and ideology call for a "wall of separation" between religion and such aspects of public life as law and politics. Despite this wall, foreign observers are often amazed, amused, and confused by the central role religion plays not only in American personal life but also in public life.

Surveys in the mid-1970s showed that 58 percent of all Americans considered their religious beliefs very important compared, for example, with 36 percent each of Italians and Canadians, 23 percent of Britons, 22 percent of French, and 17 percent of Germans. Moreover, 94 percent of Americans claimed to believe in God, compared with 89 percent of Canadians, 88 percent of Italians, 76 percent of Britons, and 72 percent each of French and Germans. And 40 percent of all Americans claim to go to church regularly. As for the wall of separation, 34 percent of all Americans say they favor a Constitutional amendment making Christianity the official religion of the United States. This attitude is particularly widespread among Protestants, people with less than a high school education, and blacks (Benson 1981). The wall of separation staunchly maintained in law is in fact quite porous and flexible in practice. One need only look at the number of times that Supreme Court decisions have referred to the Creator's attitudes toward women to see how porous this wall has been.

Although the long history of each religion is important for understanding that religion's contemporary ideas and practices, we will look primarily at the American religious experience. We will not ask what Jesus and Paul really said or meant when they talked about women but what American Christians have thought they said and meant, and how these interpretations affect American life. We will not ask about the forms patriarchal principles took among the ancient Israelites, but we will explore the norms of American Jews.

Religious Teachings about Women

The major world religions and denominations offer very different teachings to their adherents, but there are some remarkable similarities among their traditional views on women. Women and men have different missions to perform and different standards of behavior. Women are to some degree subordinated to men, although most religions declare women equal to men in the eyes of the deity. This section looks at religious definitions of women and women's roles, as well as at some of the changes now taking place. We begin with a discussion of images of God and then turn to religious prescriptions for everyday life and morality for women. The section ends with a look at some new and alternative views of women.

God Talk: Is It Male?

God the Father. God the King and Lord. The Father, the Son, and the Holy Ghost. If we are to believe the words used in Judaism, Christianity, or Islam to describe God, the deity is male. Some people argue that the use of *He* to refer to God is a generic term, but it is difficult to say the same of *Father, Lord,* and *King.* To see the importance of "he" words in religion, try taking a religious text or prayer and substituting female-gender words. Think about your reactions as you hear yourself refer to God as *She, the Queen,* or *my Lady* or to the *Daughter of God.* Sophisticated religious adherents are supposed to understand that God is not a human being; they are not supposed to make the "childish" error of anthropomorphism. Even theological sophistication, however, is not a sufficiently powerful force to eliminate what we might call "andromorphism." God may not be human like us, but "he" is still male.

The gender images attached to Jesus in Christian theology and tradition are particularly interesting. As many commentators have pointed out, whereas the character attributed to God has generally been unambiguously masculine, the character of Jesus is considerably more androgynous. Whereas God's compassion can be described as *fatherly,* the word does not seem appropriate when describing the compassion of Jesus. Although Jesus was male, his unfailing gentleness, humility, simplicity, and nonviolence; his healing qualities and immediately forgiving nature; and his suffering for others were very close to what Western culture considers femininity. On the other hand, the fact that Jesus and the disciples were male has often been used to argue that God did not intend for women to take positions of highest religious authority. Many leaders in the Anglican and Episcopal Churches used this view to argue against the installation of the first female bishop in the Episcopal Church in 1989.

The obvious "he" words used to describe and identify God are only a small part of the problem of androcentrism in religion. The language we use is not a matter merely of labels but also of the expression we give to our conception of God, authority, goodness, and holiness. Religions define for their adherents the purpose of life and rules for proper conduct, social organization, and even thought. If God is a Father but not a Mother, that says something not just about our conception of God but also about our conceptions of fathers and mothers and, by extension, men and women.

Religion played a crucial role in the formation of American ideology during the colonial and early post-Revolution eras. Although the Anglican colonials of the South had a somewhat less stern outlook than the Puritans of the North, a literal reading of the Bible and a patriarchal view of God and society were important bases of thought in either case. When people learned to read, their text was the Bible; even if they could not read, they learned their lessons in church each Sunday or, if they were farther from civilization, from the traveling preacher.

The Puritans especially based their views of women on the Old Testament and their interpretation of the patriarchal ancient Hebrew values. Woman's purpose was to be a helpmeet for her husband, to be fruitful and to multiply. Man and woman alike must fear God and Satan (although in different ways), but woman's life was also marked by her submission to her husband, the moral authority of the household, and to her work, especially the pain of childbirth, which is viewed by Christians as a punishment for Eve's insubordination: "I will increase your labor and your pain, and in labor you shall bear children. You shall be eager for your husband, and he shall be your master" (Gen. 3:16).[2] For the rest of woman's work and virtues, one could turn to Proverbs (31:10–32), which lists at least twenty-five characteristics of a good wife, most of which revolve around diligence. The book of Leviticus taught about women's periodic impurity.

In the New Testament Puritans and others found more warnings for women to submit themselves to their husbands: "for man did not originally spring from woman, but woman was made out of man; and man was not created for woman's sake, but woman for the sake of man" (1 Cor. 11:8–10). Women should be silent in church, and learn from their husbands (1 Cor. 14:34–35, 1 Tim. 2:9–15). "Wives, be subject to your husbands as to the Lord; for the man is the head of the woman, just as Christ also is the head of the Church. Christ is, indeed, the Savior of the body; but just as the church is subject to Christ, so must women be to their husbands in everything" (Eph. 5:22–24). Although more egalitarian than other denominations in matters concerning public speaking, even the gentle Friends, or Quakers, accepted the patriarchal view that man is to woman what Christ is to humans (Frost 1973).

Religion and the Bible provided examples of the female character, particularly in the persons of Eve and Mary, that served as lessons for all. Not only did the religious find proof in Genesis that woman was created as an auxiliary of man, but they also learned that woman is likely to sin if left to her own devices and that she is a temptress to man. The main lesson of this story has been that if women are not controlled, they will reenact the fall. Rather than being a maternal image of the mother of us all, Eve has come to represent woman's treachery. Although Jews interpret the story of the Garden of Eden somewhat differently from Christians (neither the Fall nor

Original Sin are part of Jewish theology), women and men are customarily separated in Orthodox synagogues because women are by nature temptresses to men and must be set apart so that men's thoughts will be free to turn to higher things. In Islam this separation is achieved through veiling and *purdah*.

Within the Christian tradition (especially among Roman Catholics) the primary female image posed as a contrast to Eve is Mary, the mother of Jesus, who some Catholic traditions believe was conceived without sin (that is, without recourse to sexual relations) and who most Christians believe conceived Jesus without sin. She is the ideal woman and, most important for understanding religious norms of womanhood, an unattainable ideal. Although the cult of the Virgin has perhaps never taken hold in the United States to the same degree that it has elsewhere, Mary is a powerful model in Christian life.[3]

Biblical stories are interpreted differently by different people and traditions. Many Jewish and Christian feminists have reinterpreted the story of Eve; they see her as the person responsible for making humans capable of knowledge of good and evil. Jewish feminists have rehabilitated Vashti in the book of Esther in the Apocrypha. Vashti was rejected as a wife by King Ahasuerus in favor of Esther because Vashti refused to dance before her husband and his drunken friends at a party. Here the

In Islam, the separation of women and men is achieved through veiling.

feminist intention is not to diminish the accomplishments of Esther but to reject the teaching that a woman is bad if she does not accept the role of unquestioning submission to her husband. Other commentators point to additional female religious models such as Deborah, the judge, or Ruth and Naomi.

Despite these alternative stories and interpretations, the predominant message of most religions is that women and men have very different roles and characters, that religious authority speaks mostly in a male voice, and that woman's primary role is to accept that authority and to bear and raise children.

It is important to understand how religions presumably dedicated to holiness and justice support such a system of inequality and submission. Many religious authorities of different denominations have argued that the enforcement of these differences does not create or enforce inequality. They say that by fulfilling their different duties men and women are equal in the eyes of God, or, in religions with a concept of heaven, earn equal places in heaven. Others argue quite simply that God designed women as inferior beings. Apparently decreasing numbers of people, including theologians, accept these arguments. Some people oppose them vehemently.

Morality for Everyday Life

Religion does not simply teach by providing general models for people to follow; it also offers guidelines for proper behavior and thought. In some cases these are considerably more than simple guidelines; they are rules that must be followed for fear of punishment. In other cases religious authorities do not threaten individuals with punishment but work hard to instill self-regulating senses of right and wrong, or conscience. In this way religious institutions are like many others: They provide both explicit rules and regulations and more generalized norms that people internalize and enforce on themselves.

The Bible has been a common and important source of moral guidelines and regulations for both Christians and Jews. It is important to remember that the same text is used as a source of authority by different denominations with different rules and values. Mormons, for example, referred to the biblical patriarchs to support the institution of polygamy until polygamy was made illegal by an act of Congress directed at Mormons in Utah. Other Christians and Jews, revering the same patriarchs in the same Bible, have always regarded polygamy as uncivilized and sinful or contrary to God's law. Orthodox and, to a lesser degree, Conservative Jews continue to follow the biblical laws on female pollution found in Leviticus, which defines a woman's natural bodily functions as unclean and prescribes purification rituals. Other denominations, including many that claim to accept literal biblical dictates, do not enforce these biblical laws. However, the traditional definition of women as unclean and even dangerous at times of menstruation has not yet disappeared.

Sexual morality is carefully regulated by religious authority, and this regulation affects much of women's—and men's—lives. Regardless of how different religions view sexuality and sexual practices, most agree that sexual relations may appropriately and rightfully take place only within marriage and that the primary, if not the sole, purpose of sexual relations is reproduction. Two of the ten commandments serve as authority in this regard; one forbids adultery, and one forbids a man to covet his neighbor's wife, house, slaves, or other possessions. Notice that the latter not only defines proper sexual relations but also reinforces the idea that women are men's (sexual) property.

Marriage is the cornerstone of the sexual, moral, and social order. If people may have sexual relations only within marriage, and if religious authorities have the power to allow or deny marriages, those authorities can determine the types of relationships that people may have with others, and they can define categories of people who may engage in different types of relationships. They can also define the types of sexual activities that may properly take place within the contract of marriage they have established.

If sexual relations are acceptable primarily for the purpose of reproduction, and if they may take place only in marriage, homosexuality is necessarily wrong. Christians and Jews alike have used religious authority to forbid homosexuality (Lev. 18:22, 1 Cor. 6:9–11), although church authorities were particularly vigilant in their suppression of homosexuality only in the twelfth and thirteenth centuries and again in the nineteenth century (Weeks 1977). Early American laws against sodomy were based directly on religious teaching and sometimes used the language of the Bible. Some homosexual acts were punishable by death, and the penalty has been invoked in American history. The Bible has also been used to declare masturbation (Gen 38:3–10) and transvestism (Deut. 22:5) sinful and wrong.

Religions further regulate sexuality and social relations by dictating who may and may not get married. The Bible enumerates forbidden marriages, such as those considered incestuous. Many authorities do not allow interfaith marriage within their communities unless the "outsider" agrees to convert. Some rabbis and Roman Catholic priests perform interfaith marriages, but generally in these cases they require that any children be raised as Jews or Catholics, respectively. The recognition that the family is the primary social institution that inculcates religious values in children is perhaps the most important reason for requiring sexual separation of people of different religions.

God's law has also been used to bar sexual relations and marriage between people of different races (miscegenation), as this quotation from a Virginia court case in the 1960s shows: "Almighty God created the races white, black, yellow, malay, and red, and he placed them on separate continents. And but for the interference with his arrangement there would be no cause for such marriages. The fact that he separated the races shows that he did not intend for the races to mix."[4]

Although no denomination expresses pleasure at the possibility of a continued rise in divorce rates, many have long supported the idea of personal choice, at least to some degree, although the Eastern Orthodox, Episcopal, Mormon, and Roman Catholic Churches have generally held that marriages are indissoluble. Many denominations do not permit divorce except on strict grounds of adultery or desertion; many religious authorities will not remarry a divorced person unless that person was the "innocent" party in the divorce or the ex-spouse is dead. Some denominations, such as Congregationalists, Christian Scientists, Jews, and Unitarians, have left the question of divorce to the conscience of the individuals involved; others, such as Baptists and Disciples of Christ, have left it to the conscience of the minister.

We should not overestimate the impact of sexually repressive religious teachings on people's behavior. Historians, for example, have offered ample evidence of "prematurely conceived" (as opposed to birthed) babies back to the beginnings of the nation. It is also true that attitudes toward sexuality even among the sterner of American clergy were not necessarily as repressive as they are sometimes painted. Some of the Puritan ministers were careful to point out that they were different from Roman Catholics in that they did not extoll the virtues of virginity to the same degree, although they did condemn sex outside of marriage. In his research Edmund Morgan found that ([1944] 1978, 364), "The Puritans were not ascetics; they never wished to prevent the enjoyment of earthly delights. They merely demanded that the pleasures of the flesh be subordinated to the greater glory of God: husband and wife must not become 'so transported with affection, that they look at no higher end than marriage itself.'" Morgan even found evidence that a church expelled one of its male members for denying "Congiugall fellowship unto his wife for the space of 2 years."

Nevertheless, the conflict between being holy and experiencing sexual feelings is an important theme throughout the history of sexuality and religion. Witness, for example, the sentiments expressed in a love letter the feminist Quaker Angelina Grimké wrote to her husband-to-be in 1838:

Ought God to be all in all to us on earth? I tho't so, and am frightened to find that He is not, that is, I feel something else is necessary to my happiness. I laid awake thinking why it was that my heart longed and panted and reached after you as it does. Why my Savior and my God is not enough to satisfy me. Am I sinning, am I ungrateful, am I an IDOLATOR? (Rossi 1988, 289)

The Roman Catholic Church has gone even further in posing a contradiction between sexuality and holiness: A person who dedicates his or her life to God by becoming a priest or nun must remain celibate. The interpretation of this celibacy is slightly different for females and males. Nuns wear wedding rings to symbolize their marriage to Christ. Priests, of course, are not married to Christ because such a relationship, even though spiritual, would imply the sin of homosexuality. It is interesting to note the importance of sexuality and marriage in images of women; while nuns are married to Christ, women designated as witches are said to be married to or have sexual relations with the Devil. Thus, even in images of profound goodness or profound evil, women are defined by their relations to male authority.

Although there is wide variation in the way in which different denominations view the "earthly pleasures" of sexuality, there has been widespread agreement that the primary (in some cases the only) reason for engaging in sexual relations is reproduction. This view has two important implications. The first is that if only sexual acts that could result in conception are natural and good, sexual acts that could not result in offspring are unnatural and bad. The biblical view of masturbation is that it is a waste of semen and, therefore, wrong. Homosexual behavior is likewise unnatural. Sexual activity between women and men that cannot result in conception (that is, sodomy) is also wrong.

The second implication of this view of sexuality is that the practice of birth control is wrong. Roman Catholic authorities remain adamant that any form of artificial birth control is sinful. Most Protestant denominations and Jews, however, officially leave the decision about whether to conceive to individual choice, although many religious authorities informally discourage the use of contraception. Unitarian churches, on the other hand, have often taken very strong stands in favor of birth control.

Abortion is an even thornier issue than birth control because it involves terminating a life that has already begun. Historically theologians and the common law generally viewed abortion as murder only after quickening of the fetus took place, and abortion was generally tolerated within the first forty days after conception. In 1869 Pope Pius IX changed the position of the Catholic Church, declaring almost all abortions murder and therefore sinful. According to Catholic doctrine it is not acceptable to terminate a life purposely, even to save another life. The Church has remained firm on its stands on both birth control and abortion, although there is widespread controversy within the Church, and some Catholics have felt particularly alienated from their religion because of its stands on these matters. Catholics can even be found in the highest ranks of the National Abortion Rights League, an interest group dedicated to reproductive choice for women.

Contemporary sociological studies show that people's religious attitudes and behaviors do shape their sexual views and behaviors. In their study of American couples (which included married and unmarried heterosexual and homosexual couples), Philip Blumstein and Pepper Schwartz (1983) found that regular church attenders were more conservative about sexual matters than those who were not as overtly religious. Religious heterosexuals are more opposed to civil rights for homosexuals, for example, than are less religious people. Another study (Hare-Mustin, Bennett, and Broderick 1983) found that Catholics have a more conservative reproductive ideology than do members of other religions. James Robbins's (1980) study of black women who had had abortions found that the more involved these women were with religion, the less happy they were with their own decisions to have abortions. Blumstein and Schwartz found that, although there may be differences in attitudes,

> . . . there is very little difference between religious and nonreligious people when it comes to how they act. They have the same amount of sex. They are just as satisfied. They have no more and no less conflict about sex. And they are just as traditional about the woman's right to initiate it. But perhaps the most startling finding is that religious people are as nonmonogamous as anyone else. However attached people may be to religious institutions, they do not seem to be insulated from the temptations of the flesh (1983, 285).

It is not entirely clear whether religious messages about morality have more impact in shaping people's attitudes, behavior, or simply feelings of guilt about doing the same things other people do.

Religious morality does not regulate gender norms solely through its views on sexuality. Theologians have elaborated on the theme of separate spheres and characters for women and men and have equated preservation of women's place with preservation of morality and of a civilized (and American) way of life. A sermon delivered in 1837 by Jonathan F. Stearns, a Presbyterian minister, demonstrates the degree to which regulation of women's sphere, Christian morality, and civilization were intricately intertwined. The preservation of the moral order, he argued, depended on the preservation of distinct spheres for men and women. Women were responsible for determining whether civilization would rise or fall:

> Yours it is to decide, under God, whether we shall be a nation of refined and high-minded Christians, or whether, rejecting the civilities of life, and throwing off the restraints of morality and purity, we should become a fierce race of semi-barbarians, before whom neither order, nor honor, nor chastity can stand (Kraditor 1968, 50).

The morality of separate spheres for the sexes, with women's spheres subordinate to men's, has remained an important religious theme; there are numerous examples of God being called on to reinforce limitations placed on women. In 1887 Senator George Vest of Missouri argued against women's suffrage on the floor of the Senate by saying, "I do not believe that the Great Intelligence ever intended (women) to invade the sphere of work given to men, tearing down and destroying all the best influences for which God has intended them" (quoted in Kraditor 1968, 195). Making a similar point at the turn of the century, President Grover Cleveland argued, "I believe that trust in Divine Wisdom, and ungrudging submission to divine purposes, will enable dutiful men and women to know the places assigned to them, and will incite them to act well in their parts in the sight of God" (200). And as we have already seen, Senator Sam Ervin called God into battle against the Equal Rights Amendment.

The predominant message of most religious denominations has been that women and men are both to be carefully restricted to their distinct spheres, and that women's roles on earth are to be good wives and mothers and to preserve the traditional moral values, especially the modesty and domesticity of women. The punishments of religious women who transgressed the boundaries of these spheres have been enormous, including death (during colonial times for witchcraft and homosexuality), damnation to hell, separation from the religious community, and charges of responsibility for the downfall of a religion or of civilization as a whole.

Because of these views organized religions have often played leading roles in political debates over the status of women and other issues specifically concerning women. Ministers and other church officials have participated by voicing their views in sermons, writings, and other teachings. But churches have also participated by organizing political activists and providing some of the tangible resources they need for political action.

In the nineteenth century, for example, many church leaders were particularly concerned about women becoming public speakers for reform movements inappropriate for ladies. Citing the biblical injunction, "suffer women not to speak," the clergy reacted angrily to activist women: "We cannot . . . but regret the mistaken conduct of those who encourage females to bear an obtrusive and ostentatious part in measures of reform, and countenance any of that sex who so forget themselves as to itinerate in the character of public lecturers and teachers" (quoted in Rossi 1988, 305–306). A woman's duty was to exert moral influence in her role as wife and mother and perhaps as a teacher in Sunday school. That was all.

Such attitudes carried over to the issue of female suffrage, which was opposed by many clergy and laypeople on religious grounds. In 1869 Orestes A. Brownson, an American Transcendentalist leader, said, "The conclusive objection to the political enfranchisement is, that it would weaken and finally break up and destroy the Christian family" (quoted in Kraditor 1968, 192). "Let the hand which rocks the cradle teach the coming young men and women of America the Lord's Prayer and the Ten Commandments," said a New York politician in 1894, "and you will do more for your emancipation . . . than you can do with both hands full of white ballots" (198).

Religious organizations have been leading opponents of divorce reform, liberalization of birth control and abortion, educational policies that would reform gender messages in textbooks and make sex education part of the curriculum, legislation supporting civil rights for homosexuals, and the Equal Rights Amendment. In the first decades of the twentieth century, some religious organizations opposed the reforms urged by feminist and progressive groups on the grounds that they were socialist and therefore antireligious. Contemporary studies of antifeminist activist groups show that participants in those groups share the characteristics of being particularly attached to religion and particularly antagonistic to communism (Conover and Gray 1983; Burris 1983; Mueller and Dimieri 1982).

Numerous politically and socially active women have been punished or reprimanded by their churches. We have already discussed the case of Anne Hutchison. Lucy Stone (1818–93) was expelled from the Congregational Church for her abolitionist activity, and other women were strongly rebuked. In the 1980s the Mormon Church excommunicated Sonia Johnson for her support of the Equal Rights Amendment. In 1983 the Catholic Church gave Agnes Mary Mansour the choice of resigning her post as director of social services in Michigan or dismissal from her order of nuns for tolerating the use of federal funds for abortions. She left the order (Briggs 1983). In many cases these women were rebuked precisely because they claimed to derive their "deviant" views from their religious values; in these cases they were punished for coming to their own conclusions about spirituality and religiosity.

By no means all of women's religiously based reform and political activity has been suppressed by religious institutions. There have been women's reform associations connected with churches and religion since the early nineteenth century. These women's organizations were instrumental in the social purity movements of that century, which encompassed temperance, opposition to pornography, and a range of other issues tied to desires to improve women's lot. Indeed many suffragists were involved in these issues and organizations. But the power of these women to define their own terms, goals, and activities was limited; if their message provided too clear an alternative to traditional religious teachings, they found themselves opposed by the higher, male authorities.

Alternative Teachings

A few examples show the types of alternatives many feminists have posed to the more orthodox views of their religious bodies.

Sonia Johnson, feminist activist and political candidate,
was excommunicated by the Mormon Church for her
support of the Equal Rights Amendment.

Two of the best-known feminist religious thinkers of the nineteenth century were the Quaker sisters Sarah (1792–1873) and Angelina (1805–76) Grimké. Angelina Grimké's most famous work is her "Appeal to the Christian Women of the South," written in 1836.[5] She argued that women had to be instrumental in ending slavery, even if their actions brought great suffering to themselves, because they had to follow what they knew to be God's will rather than sinful and oppressive laws created by men. Drawing on the New Testament statement that "there is neither male nor female," the Grimké sisters argued that enforcing separate spheres for women and men and withholding religious and political rights for women were unchristian acts. Their work, like the work of many other feminist religious activists, shows that the same texts and basic ideas can be interpreted in a variety of ways with very different effects.

Elizabeth Cady Stanton and a committee of other feminists went a step further than the Grimkés and wrote *The Woman's Bible* ([1895] 1974), an exegesis and criticism of the Bible, which they regarded as a man-made, error-filled document. Much more recently Mary Daly has written a series of critiques and "re-visions," arguing that our understanding of God and religion must be exorcised to blast away the androcentrism of religion, much as the evil influence of Satan was exorcised by traditional Catholic ritual. A wide range of Christians and Jews have offered similar criticisms of the teachings of their own religions (Reuther 1974; Heschel 1983; Christ and Plascow 1979).

Efforts to provide alternatives to conventional religious ideas go far beyond criticism of past traditions. Some women have followed Stanton's lead and are revising the texts and traditions of their religions, partly by rediscovering ideas, rituals, and female figures that have been forgotten and partly by creating new ones.

Some people have attempted to "degenderize" their religions, often by developing nonsexist liturgies and rituals. At one time the important Jewish initiation rite of Bar Mitzvah (Son of the Commandments) was available only to boys, but for several decades Reform Jews have celebrated the same ritual for girls, called the Bat Mitzvah (Daughter of the Commandments). In 1983 the National Council of Churches began to publish translations of Bible passages under the title of *Inclusive Language Lectionary* amidst considerable controversy. The lectionary refers to God as "the Father and Mother" or "Sovereign" rather than as "Father" or "Lord," and it refers to Jesus as the "Child" rather than as the "Son" of God to reduce the emphasis on male religious imagery. Some churches gave the lectionary a warm reception, and others attacked it as "tampering with the word of God."

Some people, notably those in the women's spirituality movement, emphasize the development of a specifically female religious and spiritual experience. They desire religious values and practices that speak directly to women. Many of these women are now developing a view of religion based on the symbol of the Goddess, a female conceptualization of deity. Others consider witchcraft to be the appropriate women's religion, because the word *witch* (which comes from the word *wicce,* meaning "wise ones") has been the general name for female priestesses, healers, and sages throughout the ages. If women have rejected the long tradition of the *wicce,* they argue, it is not because the tradition is itself bad, but because men have feared and therefore punished it, generally by execution. Sometimes in our eagerness to reject the violence of these men's actions we have forgotten that many women have practiced witchcraft, although that practice bears little resemblance to the descriptions in the more orthodox religious texts.

These movements for change involve religious authorities, clergy, and members of traditional religious organizations, as well as people outside these organizations who are attempting to create their own. Although all these people have different points of view, they are linked by the convictions (1) that religious organizations are among the most forceful institutions that shape and define sex/gender systems; (2) that women have had very little control over these powers; and (3) that religion should free the human spirit rather than keep it in bondage.

Women's Religious Activities and Influences

Thus far we have looked at some of the teachings of religion and the ways in which they can shape women's lives. We will now turn the question around and look at the influence of women on religions, and the roles women have played through religious organizations and activities in shaping their own and other people's lives.

Everyday Life as Religious Activity

In her article "The Cult of True Womanhood," historian Barbara Welter identifies the central role women were supposed to play in American religious life:

> The nineteenth-century American man was a busy builder of bridges and railroads, at work long hours in a materialist society. The religious values of his forbears were neglected in practice if not in intent, and he occasionally felt some guilt that he had turned this new land, this temple of the chosen people, into one vast countinghouse. But he could salve his conscience by reflecting that he had left behind a hostage, not only to fortune, but to all the values which he held so dear and treated so lightly (1966, 21).

That hostage was woman. Although a good woman was supposed to be submissive to her husband and her Lord, she was also supposed to create a religious home. She was responsible for guarding the spiritual life of her family, which sometimes meant acting outside the home and becoming, in effect, the backbone of church organizations.

Women are more diligent church attenders than men. This diligence was particularly important during the period of frontier expansion. In her study of women's roles in the frontier West, for example, Julie Roy Jeffrey found that many of the newly gathered congregations of the mid-nineteenth century were composed primarily of women. "Women not only swelled membership rolls but were quickly recognized as recruiters and forcibly reminded of their responsibilities [by ministers]" (1979, 96). Jeffrey also found evidence that women often gave solace and encouragement to the struggling missionary ministers who were depressed and frustrated by their apparent failures to bring God's word to the frontier. What role might religion play in American life today were it not for the women who populated churches and supported their ministers a century ago?

When we look at traditional views of women's roles it is nearly impossible to separate specifically religious activities from women's other activities. Woman's role in the family can be seen as an expression and enforcement of her religious values. Consider, for example, the argument made by Catherine Beecher in her 1841 manual for the homemaker, *A Treatise on Domestic Economy* ([1841] 1977). She set her advice on topics as diverse as nutrition, clothing, charity, exercise, and flower cultivation in a deeper philosophical and religious context. She began by arguing that "the democratic institutions of this country are in reality no other than the principles of Christianity carried into operation. . ." (10). She then argued that "the success of democratic institutions (and therefore, by logical extension, Christian institutions). . .depends upon the intellectual and moral character of the mass of the people" (13). According to Beecher the responsibility for securing this character depends on the woman. "The mother writes the character of the future man; the sister beds the fibers that after are the forest tree; the wife sways the heart, whose energies may turn for good or for evil the destinies of a nation" (13). Because every detail of a household must be arranged according to important basic principles, and "These general principles are to be based on Christianity" (145), the activities of household management are expressions of religious duty and participation.

The same beliefs are held in other religions. A central tenet of Jewish life is that the wife and mother is responsible for creating a Jewish home; she is thereby responsible for maintaining Jewish life and Judaism itself. Every meal that is eaten in the home of an Orthodox Jewish family is a reminder of religion and woman's role in it. The woman must carefully follow the laws of *kashrut* in buying, preparing, and serving food, thereby enforcing Jewish law and custom within her family. The religious aspect of women's domestic activity is particularly apparent in Judaism because so many of the most important rituals and celebrations take place in the home rather than in the synagogue. The Sabbath meal is itself a religious service and includes traditional foods and the lighting of the Sabbath candles by the woman. Passover, one of the most important Jewish festivals, is celebrated entirely in the home. Much of the woman's work during Passover week is regulated by the fact that it is Passover; her very domestic labor is a ritual act.

For women who are the wives of clergy and missionaries, wifehood is itself a religious occupation. The ministry is one of the many male-dominated jobs in which the wife has special tasks that are unpaid extensions of the husband's job; in fact the husband's job creates nearly a full-time job for his untrained, unsalaried wife.

The job of a minister's wife varies from denomination to denomination and from congregation to congregation. Generally, however, she is expected to attend most religious functions (or at least those that allow women), regardless of her own interests. She is expected to serve on committees, especially those that revolve around "women's concerns" such as education and entertainment. When the minister entertains congregants, visiting ministers, and others in his line of duty, she does the work. Above all the minister's wife is the highly visible representative of her husband and his religious values. Minister's wives, like the wives of other highly visible authorities, are subject to constant criticism and gossip if their homes, children, clothes, and smiles aren't perfect or appropriate for the values of the congregation. The importance of this job is evidenced by the controversy surrounding ministers' wives who pursue independent careers, and therefore do not have the time or the inclination to serve their husbands' congregations full-time.

Ministers' wives played prominent roles in nineteenth-century missionary life. The missionaries that churches sent to the frontier West to "civilize" (meaning to Christianize) the new communities were urged to bring wives for help and support. Julie Jeffrey found that most of the wives thought of themselves as missionaries (as well they might have, given the work they did), even if their husbands and churches regarded them only as helpmates. But, as Jeffrey points out, "Few anticipated the potential conflict between [the roles of wife and missionary]. Nor did their religious enthusiasm and lofty idealism prepare them for the reality of missionary work" (1979, 100).

These women performed the hard duties of a frontier woman, plus many of the difficult duties of missionary work. They recruited women, taught, organized social events, and were responsible for fund-raising—often through their own labor rather than through collections—so that their husbands could tend to more spiritual needs. They were shuffled from one place to another as their husbands were called to new missions. The toll on these women and their families was often great. It is unfortunate that these hard-working women are often forgotten or remembered only as the wives of the men who tamed the West.

Making a home is regarded as a religious activity of central importance; for many people this is proof enough that women are highly regarded by their religions and are free to pursue a full life within their religious communities and to be influential in them. For many women—including, of course, those who are not wives and mothers, as well as those who simply see wider horizons and want more choice and control of their own activities—this is not enough.

Women's Service Outside the Home

The most prominent women's religious activities are service and charity. Women have always constituted a substantial portion of the people who have practiced their religious values in the service of others. For many women bound by the most traditional domestic values these service activities and the religious organizations that undertake them have often provided the primary or even sole channel for extrafamilial public action and personal development. Religious organizations have provided ways for women to have an impact on their communities and society that they could not achieve in the male-dominated worlds of politics and the professions.

Women's activities in charity and service have not only been tolerated but also been considered by many to be a necessary part of a homemaker's life. As Catherine Beecher observed, "It is also one of the plainest requirements of Christianity, that we devote some of our time and efforts to the comfort and improvement of others" ([1841] 1977, 145–46). Such activities were especially appropriate because the focus of women's lives within their families was the comfort and improvement of others. Beecher included service work in her advice to women on how to schedule their time wisely: "The leisure of two afternoons and evenings could be devoted to religious and benevolent objects, such as religious meetings, charitable associations, Sunday school visiting, and attention to the sick and poor" (147).

Just as the work of ministers' wives is often obscured or forgotten, so is the charitable and reform work of the women associated with religious organizations. Even today these women are sometimes dismissed as "volunteer ladies" or merely overlooked.

The impact of women who express the social implications of their religious concerns through organized activities is immeasurable. The number of people who have been fed, clothed, housed, educated, and otherwise comforted by religious organizations of women is uncountable. Through these organizations women have pressed social and political concerns at all ends of the political spectrum and all levels of politics. Throughout the twentieth century representatives of women's religious organizations have testified frequently before local and state legislatures and congressional committees. The social issues and concerns of churches are often manifest largely in the work of women.

Women as Religious Authorities and Leaders

We have already seen that with some exceptions, most Judeo-Christian religions explicitly reserve leadership and positions of authority for men. Nevertheless women have assumed a variety of leadership roles, and they are pressing for more.

Women have been the founders of a number of American Christian denominations. Among the most important and well known are Ellen White, who founded the Seventh Day Adventist Church and led it for fifty years; Aimee Semple McPherson, a charismatic evangelist who founded the Church of the Foursquare Gospel; and Mary Baker Eddy (1821–1910), who founded the Church of Christ, Scientist, best known for the beliefs that the spirit and mind are the central facts of life and that illness, disease, and death are mere illusions that can be overcome by spirituality.

Another church founder was Ann Lee (1736–84), an immigrant from England who, as a young woman, belonged to a religious group known as the "Shaking Quakers" (because of members' behavior while praying). While imprisoned in England for heresy and accusations of witchcraft, she experienced revelations. After she was freed, she led a small group of followers to New York, where she established the first Shaker community. The Shakers lived according to the principle that only through celibacy could a person achieve the highest spirituality; the growth of the community thus depended on new converts. The Shaker community was based on sharing and hard work, and it is noted for its well-crafted furniture. By the middle of the twentieth century only a handful of old women were left in the community. These women decided to let the Shaker community die a natural death and sought no more converts.

Much attention has been focused on the issue of ordination of women. Antoinette Brown Blackwell (1825–1921) was the first American woman to be ordained as a minister and to have her own congregation. At least three Protestant denominations have ordained women for a century or more, including the United Church of Christ, the American Baptist Churches, and the Disciples of Christ. Change has come much more recently in most denominations, however. The first woman Reform rabbi was ordained in 1972, and the first female Episcopal bishop was installed in 1989. Orthodox Jews still do not ordain women, and women still may not become Roman Catholic priests.

Despite the relatively long-standing ordination of women in some denominations, the proportion of women ministers remains quite low. Table 6-1 shows the date when selected Protestant denominations first ordained women, the proportion of ministers who were women in 1981, and the proportion of divinity students who were women in 1980. Although women are still a small fraction of all ministers, these numbers are likely to change as more women train for the ministry. In 1989 the National Council of Churches found that of 172 denominations for which information was available, 84 ordained women, 82 did not, and 6 didn't ordain clergy. It also reported that women constituted about 8 percent of the clergy in denominations that ordained women ("Women in Full Ministry Doubles" 1989).

Carroll, Hargrove, and Lummis found in their survey (1981) that the early experiences and motivations of male and female Protestant clergy differed as did men and women's experiences as members of the clergy. Women were more likely to have upper-middle-class backgrounds, to have highly educated parents, and to have mothers who were employed. Men were more likely to have attended denominational colleges, partly reflecting the fact that women made their decisions to enter the ministry later than men. Men were more likely to feel that their families and pastors supported their decisions to enter the ministry in the first place. Women entering

TABLE 6-1
Female Clergy in Selected Protestant Denominations

Denomination	First ordination	Percent female ministers 1981	Percent female divinity students, 1980
United Church of Christ	1853	7.8	45
American Baptist Churches	100+ yrs	1.8[a]	24
Disciples of Christ	1888	4.8	26
United Presbyterian	1956	4.5	32
United Methodist	1956	3.6	29
Presbyterian, U.S.A.	1964	3.3	21
Lutheran Church in America	1970	2.6	24
American Lutheran Church	1970	1.3	NA
Episcopal Church	1977	3.4	27

[a]This is a 1977 figure.
SOURCE: Carroll, Hargrove, and Lummis 1981, 6, 7, 102.

the ministry tended to have better academic records than the men. More women than men said their motivation in seeking clerical training was personal spiritual growth or service to Christ; more men than women said they pursued religious studies to become parish ministers.

The researchers also uncovered other differences. Men were more likely than women to feel that the ordained ministry carried with it particularly high "prestige and dignity." More women than men felt it was very important to "change the sexist nature of the church." A majority of the female ministers also revealed strongly feminist attitudes toward women in the church, compared with only 24 percent of the men. Clerical attitudes toward women's roles in the church vary from denomination to denomination. While 39 percent of the United Church of Christ ministers expressed strongly feminist attitudes, only 15 percent of the Episcopal clergy did so.

Women in the ministry face some segregation and discrimination just as women do in other jobs. Men find it easier to become ordained after attending the seminary, although this varies by denomination. Ordained women tend to be placed in smaller churches with older members, and their salaries are lower than men's. As we might expect, the congregants in women's churches tend to be less conservative than those in men's, although surveys show that in most denominations, lay leaders tend to be more conservative on gender issues than the clergy themselves.

As with other jobs, the fact that some women are now working in this male-dominated profession does not mean that their day-to-day experiences are the same as men's. Women and men feel themselves to be especially competent at different aspects of the job. Carroll, Hargrove, and Lummis (1981) found that women felt more confident about their abilities to preach, lead worship, and teach children, and men felt more confident about their abilities to manage the church budget. Women and men both felt they got on well with different age and gender groups within their congregations. Most of the female ministers thought that the fact that they were women played a role in conflicts or difficulties they encountered in their jobs; 27 percent thought their sex was a very important factor.

Studies suggest that the entry of women into the ministry is forcing change. Women change the ministry and its imagery merely by pursuing their vocations. They have somewhat different attitudes than their male colleagues; they could not believe that church authority is necessarily masculine and remain in the career they have chosen. Women in the ministry have become increasingly aware of the problems of women partly through their own experiences. Carroll, Hargrove, and Lummis (1981) found that clergywomen are somewhat more likely than clergymen to think that their congregations should get involved in social and political issues, including the rights of women and minorities.

There is growing evidence that women have a different effect on their congregants than men have. Rabbi Laura Geller (1983, 210) for example, reported the following reaction of two of her congregants:

> Rabbi, I can't tell you how different I felt about services because you are a woman. I found myself feeling that if you can be a rabbi, then maybe I could be a rabbi too. For the first time in my life I felt as though I could learn those prayers, I could study Torah, I could lead this service, I could do anything you could do. Knowing that made me feel much more involved in the service—much more involved with Judaism. Also, it made me think about God in a different way. I'm not sure why. (a middle-aged woman)
>
> Rabbi, I realized that if you could be a rabbi, then certainly I could be a rabbi. Knowing that made the service somehow more accessible to me. I didn't need you to "do it" for me. I could "do it," be involved with Jewish tradition, without depending on you. (a young man)

It seems to be an almost universal religious theme that negative aspects of the world can be lessons for the good. Geller's experience might be an object lesson of exactly this sort.

The relatively low status of the female rabbi, at least in these cases, brought people closer to their own spirituality. These two people were reacting in part to women's lower status, to the jarring image of a female leader in a masculine world, to their stereotypes of women. But as Geller noted, "The lessening of social distance and the reduction of the attribution of power and status leads to the breakdown of hierarchy within a religious institution." In this case the breakdown of gender hierarchies did indeed seem to lead to a breakdown of religious institutional hierarchy because the two are interdependent; they mutually reinforce each other. This is, of course, precisely what conservative leaders fear will be the result of the entrance of women into traditionally male leadership roles. But as these quotations also suggest many people find a new spirituality and a renewed sense of religious affiliation and purpose when the hierarchy of religious institutions is weakened. Geller noted that a female friend of hers who was an Episcopal minister had a similar experience. "When she offers the Eucharist people take it from her differently from the way they would take it from a male priest, even though she follows the identical ritual.

Episcopal Bishop Barbara Harris became the first female
bishop in the worldwide Anglican church in 1989.

People experience her as less foreign, and so the experience is more natural, less mysterious'' (211).

Women take many other leadership roles in religious organizations. Many denominations have long allowed women to be deaconesses, and the Roman Catholic, Eastern Orthodox, and Episcopal churches have orders of nuns. In some cases these women have been instrumental in changing the status of women. Many Roman Catholic sisters have worked for changes within the Church; other women have worked to change the larger community through their service, teaching, and community leadership, and even through secular feminist organizations.

Most denominations also allow women to fulfill other organizational leadership roles, such as committee work and leadership in religious education, some of which are designed only for women and some of which are open to both women and men. We should not underestimate the impact women have had in these various roles; however, many of these roles are limited by very specific boundaries, which also limit women's potential impact on religious life. Women who want to reach further within their religious organizations are still forced, for the most part, to ask permission from male authorities, curb their own spiritual needs, or leave.

Religion and Society

Few subjects stir up as much controversy and passion as the relationship between religion and gender norms. Often those on opposing sides of the debate do agree about one point: Organized religion has been one of the most powerful human institutions for defining and controlling gender, sexuality, and "woman's place." There is strong disagreement, however, about what can and should be done about this power. The solutions offered are wide ranging.

Like the other institutions discussed in this book, religious institutions are not isolated enclaves; they are integrally linked to the wider society and its values. They both influence and are influenced by it. They are powerful producers and enforcers of gender norms, but they are also affected by changes in these norms in other social institutions. Many aspects of religious teachings and structures depend on specific conceptions of women and their roles; when these begin to change outside of religious institutions, the institutions are also affected.

Religions have promoted inequality between women and men and have supported great violence against women—and men—who stepped out of their assigned gender and sexual roles. Because women have been assigned the subordinate place—as exemplified in the idea that Christ is the Lord of woman and man and the husband is the lord of the wife—they have been particularly prone to punishments for gender-specific reasons. For example, the crime of the thousands of women accused of witchcraft was not only that they were heretics but also that they had engaged in activities such as healing, that were part of the province of men. In modern times many religious organizations have formally and officially resisted changes in the status of women, even outside the institutions themselves.

The story of religious institutions is not a simple history of victimization of women. Denominations differ in their treatment of women, and most have changed to some degree in recent years. Millions of women have found strength and inspiration in their religions, which has sometimes allowed them to battle their own religious institutions and to transform themselves and women's roles in sometimes subtle ways. A delicate balancing act is required to recognize both the religious power and influence of women (especially when it is often so subtle) and the very real gender-specific limits that have been placed on women in almost all their religious activities.

One of the most striking aspects of the study of women and religion is the degree to which given rituals and texts can offer different messages to different people. The same Bible has proven to some people that women and men are equal and that women should take full leadership roles in religions and society and to others that women are inferior, periodically unclean, dangerous, and subordinate to men. Some people take religious prescriptions for women's domestic roles as a sign of the high esteem in which women are held; others find them the primary indications of women's subordination and even enslavement. These variations are sources both of the stability and resilience of religious institutions and of their potential for change.

NOTES

1.   To read some of these women's writings, see Rossi (1988), which includes essays by Murray, Martineau, Stanton, and Goldman; Stanton ([1895] 1974); Gage ([1900] 1972); and Daly (1973, 1975, 1978).

2.   All Biblical quotations are from the *New English Bible with the Apocrypha* (New York: Oxford University Press, 1970).

3.   For a history of Mariology, see Warner (1976).

4.   This is a quotation from the 1967 Supreme Court case *Loving* v. *Virginia,* which invalidated the Virginia law against miscegenation.

5.   This is reprinted in Rossi (1988).

7

The Institutional Media of Communication

Females constitute 27.7% of the U.S. population. Half of them are teenagers or in their 20's. They wear revealing outfits, jiggle a lot, but don't do much else. More than a third are unemployed or without any identifiable pursuit or purpose. Most others are students, secretaries, homemakers, household workers, or nurses.

Portrait of American women as presented on television.[1]

MOST of the information we receive about the world around us and our relationship to that world does not come from direct experience or contact. Our knowledge about human life and how people think and act is not based only on the people we have met; a considerable amount of it is gained secondhand from the mass media of communication—radio, television, newspapers, and magazines—or from the artistic media of communication—the performing, graphic, and literary arts. For this reason the collective normative power of the people and organizations who manage these media is enormous.

As the description that opens this chapter suggests, the tremendous normative power of the media has often distorted the image of women in society. The questions we will pursue in this chapter are: What images of women are presented in the institutional media of communication and why? What impact do the media have on the construction of gender? What roles have the media played in social change? What impact do women have on the media? We will begin by looking at the mass media, including radio, television, newspapers, and magazines. We will then turn to advertising and commercial media and to cultural and artistic media.

The Mass Media

The mass media of communication both reflect the values of the society around them and help to create and alter those values. Although it has become common for social observers (often speaking through the medium of television, radio, or the newspapers) to blame many of the problems of modern society on the media, the media are not monolithic and do not present us with a single message. Indeed the mass media offer one of the most important channels for achieving social change. This complexity makes the mass media very important objects of study for anyone interested in the social meanings of gender and the position of women. Our discussion of this topic will look first at women's roles in the print (newspapers and magazines) and electronic (radio and television) media. We will then look more closely at the gender-related content of the media by considering the messages sent by the media and the impact of these messages.

Women in the Print Media

In looking back to a time before the existence of truly mass media, we find that women are no newcomers to the media. In her book, *Up from the Footnote: A History of Women Journalists* (1977), Marion Marzolf points out that women were influential in the print media from its beginning in America; in fact the first printing press was brought to America and installed by a woman in 1638. There were at least fourteen female printers by the Revolution, and four women published weekly newspapers. Elizabeth Timothy became the first female editor-publisher in 1738 with the publication of the *South Carolina Gazette*. Political pamphlets, broadsides, and propaganda pieces, perhaps more important than newspapers in the early days of this country, were often written or published by women. It was a woman who first printed the Declaration of Independence complete with the names of all signers (Marzolf 1977, 6).

In some cases we have not heard of these early female printers because history books tend to focus on the male members of a printing family. A good example is the Franklin family, which included Deborah, who ran the print shop when her husband Benjamin was away; Ann Smith Franklin, Benjamin's sister-in-law, the state printer of Rhode Island in 1736, and a newspaper publisher in her own right; and Margaret H. Bache, also a newspaper publisher, who was the wife of Benjamin's grandson (de Pauw 1975, 35). The Franklins were not unusual in this regard; a print shop was often a family business, and women were included.

The public press became increasingly important in the nineteenth century, and women continued to exert an important although restricted influence. By 1831 there were at least 1297 printers, of whom about 30 percent were women and about 17 percent boys. Women and boys received about one-third the average wages of men (Marzolf 1977, 9). By 1850 women were about 16 percent of all newspaper compositors. Although the tasks they were allowed to do were limited and their pay less than that of similarly occupied men, women earned more as printers than they could doing "women's" work (DuBois 1978, 129). The print unions did not accept women as full members until 1873, thus helping to restrict the number of women involved in the trade and forcing women to organize their own union for a time (DuBois 1978).

The interesting questions about women's involvement in the press concern not just how many were active but also what they did and their special impact. Ann Douglas (1977) argues that women writers, especially those who wrote for the periodical press when it began to approach what we now call a mass medium, helped shape important aspects of nineteenth-century American culture. Douglas believes that the upsurge in women involved in these media and their success in attracting mass readership indicated a "drive of nineteenth century American women to gain power through the exploitation of their feminine identity as their society defined it" (7). If the "cult of true womanhood" was oppressive, some women found a way to bend it to their needs. By the mid-nineteenth century women's influence in all aspects of periodical production was sufficient to provoke resistance by men.

Women submitted numerous stories, poems, and religious pieces to newspapers and magazines. Some women were also regular contributors to periodicals, and some were editors, including Margaret Fuller, who edited the Transcendentalist magazine, *The Dial*. Most remarkable, however, was the rise of the women's periodicals, or magazines oriented toward female readership. Among the most famous of these were the *Ladies' Magazine* (1828–36) and *Godey's Lady's Book* (1837–97), edited by Sara Josepha Hale (1788–1879), perhaps the first truly popular mass-circulation magazines. Now remembered chiefly for its color fashion plates, which are expensive collectors' items, *Godey's* was an arbiter of taste voraciously devoured by women across the country. This magazine was one of many designed for women, but its circulation outstripped most of the others. Although many of these magazines were not explicitly feminist, they did favor expansion of women's rights and influence.

The ladies' magazines were not the only ones written for women. Others more explicitly feminist in their content were edited by feminist activists and organizations. Among these were the *Free Enquirer*, established in 1828 by Frances Wright as the first reform periodical published solely by women; Amelia Bloomer's *Lily* (1849–59); Pauline Wright Davis's *Una* (1854–56); Elizabeth Cady Stanton and Susan B. Anthony's *The Revolution* (1868–71); Lucy Stone's *Women's Journal* (1870–1917); and *The Woman's Era*, designed for black women. These publications varied considerably in radicalism, but none was content to tell women only about the latest fashions and recipes. They served as important links in the nineteenth century women's movements.

The popularity of women's magazines did not go unnoticed by the rest of the press. Women wrote for many newspapers and magazines, and now these periodicals also began to pay special attention to women as an audience. In 1859 Jane Croly (1829–1901) began the first women's page—actually a newspaper column—in a mass circulation newspaper. After a time most other newspapers followed suit, institutionalizing a segregated portion of newspapers designed especially to appeal to women, or at least to a stereotyped view of them. As newspapers and magazines began to use advertising to support themselves, they also began to appeal to women through fashion advertisements.

The last half of the nineteenth century and the beginning of the twentieth century witnessed the rise of the female reporter. Marzolf (1977) found two well-known types of female reporters promoted by the press to its readers: "stunt girls" and "sob sisters." The stunt girls were just that: They performed great, or at least curious, feats and wrote about them. A good example was Elizabeth Cochrane, who drew on Jules Verne's popular book and beat Phileas Fogg's fictional record by circling the globe in 72 days, 6 hours, and 11 minutes. This rather trivial example, however, masks the fact that many of these stunts were important contributions to the growth of serious investigative journalism. For example, when Cochrane was twenty-two years old, she feigned insanity to investigate conditions in insane asylums. Some investigative journalists did not do stunts but nevertheless performed dangerous acts. Ida B. Wells (1862–1931), a black woman who was editor and part owner of the *Memphis Free Speech* in the early 1890s, compiled a list of lynchings that was published by abolitionist Frederick Douglass. Ida M. Tarbell (1857–1944), who exposed the monopolistic practices of Standard Oil for *McClure's Magazine,* followed in this tradition.

The sob sisters focused on crime, often painting the details in lurid colors. Many of the sob sisters later went into other types of journalism. Both sob sisters and stunt girls spurred the sales of newspapers and magazines.

Women's roles in journalism expanded in the late nineteenth and the twentieth centuries. In 1890 women constituted 14 percent of the people involved in printing and publishing; in 1905 they constituted 20 percent. They held 24 percent of the editing and reporting jobs in the early 1920s, 32 percent in 1950, and 37 percent in 1960. But they remained restricted in many ways.

Women had to fight for what they gained. We have already discussed the resistance to female printers on the part of male printers' unions, as well as women's relatively low pay. Similar problems were encountered by female journalists. When women became eligible for membership in the Capitol Press Gallery, their numbers in the gallery rose from 4 in 1870 to 20 in 1879, but then women were virtually eliminated from membership by a new rule barring part-time reporters and limiting news organizations to one reporter each. In 1919 only 10 of the 110 reporters accredited to cover Congress were women. During World War II the number of accredited women rose to 98, but it fell to 30 right after the war.

Women in many fields complain that their profession seems like a "men's club"; in journalism it was almost literally true. When it was founded in the nineteenth century, the National Press Club barred women, which prompted Jane Croly to found Sorosis, one of the first major women's clubs. Women also founded the Women's National Press Association in 1885 and the Women's National Press Club in 1919. The National Press Club did not admit women to membership until 1971, and about the same time the Women's National Press Club admitted men and changed its name to the Washington Press Club. The prestigious Gridiron Club did not admit women until 1974, and Sigma Delta Chi, a professional journalism society, did not admit women until 1971. Although women journalists had earned Pulitzer Prizes, no women were admitted as jurors for the prize until 1972. Women often used only their initials or pen names for their articles to avoid the stigma of being identified as females.

Many women became prominent journalists in the years between the two world wars. Sylvia Porter began her financial reporting in the *New York Post.* Anne O'Hare McCormick became a foreign affairs commentator for the *New York Times* in the early 1930s and won a Pulitzer Prize in 1937. Dorothy Kilgallen began her career in 1931. Freda Kirchwey, whose specialty was foreign affairs, worked for the *Nation* from 1918 until 1955, serving as editor from 1932 and also as publisher from 1937. Martha Gelhorn, a journalist for *Collier's,* was a war correspondent during the bombing of Helsinki, the Spanish Civil War, and the German occupation of Czechoslovakia. Dorothy Thompson, a foreign affairs correspondent who worked

for the *New York Herald Tribune,* the *New York Post,* and the *Ladies' Home Journal,*
had the honor of being thrown out of Germany by Hitler himself. Mary Heaton
Vorse was a magazine writer known primarily for her coverage of labor issues. Eleanor
Roosevelt helped promote women journalists by allowing only women at her morning
press conferences, thus giving good opportunities to such women as Lorena Hickock
of the Associated Press and May Craig, who later became a regular interviewer on
the television program *Meet the Press.*

These women differed in their views of women and gender. McCormick was relatively traditional in her views as was Thompson until she was "converted" to feminism
by reading the work of Simone de Beauvoir. Kirchwey was a feminist activist, as was
Vorse, and both wrote on the subject of feminism (Sochen 1973, 1981; Marzolf 1977).

As in other male fields women's influence and involvement rose during World
War II and then stalled after the war. The absolute numbers of women and their
proportion in journalism did not decline from their prewar levels, but women's roles
became more limited. Many complained that they were relegated to reporting
traditional women's issues, and young women seeking training and first jobs in
journalism were encouraged to stick to these issues. The difference between men
and women's pay and status remained considerable. Press organizations restricted
women's assignments, using the old canard that some stories were just too dangerous
for women to handle and ignoring the track record of the women who had been
war correspondents and had risked themselves for decades in the course of their
investigative reporting.

Nearly forty years later women are still fighting both to enter the field of
journalism and to be given due respect in it. In the late 1970s women began to take
the print media to task, and complaints and lawsuits charging sex discrimination
were filed against such major press organizations as the *New York Times,* the
Washington Post, Newsweek, and *Time.* In 1970, for example, female employees charged
Newsweek with violating Title VII of the 1964 Civil Rights Act by its practice of
designating news writing as almost exclusively a male domain and news researching
(which was at the time given no byline) as almost exclusively a female domain. In
1974 the Equal Employment Opportunity Commission found that the *Washington
Post* engaged in illegal employment practices.

In 1978 women won back pay, among other things, from the *New York Times*
after filing 90 charges of discrimination against that paper. Grace Glueck, an art news
reporter, explained how the complaint developed:

> In the beginning, even as a group, we had on our white gloves and party manners.
> How we got started was that in 1972 Grace Lichtenstein was kvetching about
> the fact that the *Times* would not permit the use of the title "Ms." in the paper.
> Several of us, including Grace, got to thinking that this style rigidity was symp-
> tomatic of more basic problems. And so we began what you might call a group
> grope, meeting several times before drawing up a petition to the publisher and
> his board members. We pointed out the inequities of male-female salaries, the
> total absence of women in management jobs, and the stringent patterns of our
> nonpromotion. The managing editor then took it upon himself to call us
> troublemakers into his office and complain that our action was divisive.[2]

When the women did not receive satisfaction they filed a lawsuit against the paper. Some things did change at the *New York Times,* including acceptance of the term *Ms.* in 1986.

Efforts to achieve equality in the journalism field continue, aided by women's press organizations and women's own publications, such as the *Media Report to Women*. But although some changes have taken place, much is left to be done.

Women in the Electronic Media

Women's involvement in radio and television broadcasting parallels in many ways their involvement in print media in the twentieth century. The electronic media are managed by gender-segregated, male-dominated organizations in which men hold the visible, high-status positions, and women hold jobs that are primarily auxiliary and of lower status.

The first female radio news commentator was Kathryn Cravens, who in 1934 launched her program "News through a Woman's Eye" in St. Louis. Pauline Frederick joined the American Broadcasting Company (ABC) radio network in 1948 and for twelve years was the only woman hard news commentator on radio and television (Marzolf 1977). One of the justifications used by mass-media organizations for the small number of women commentators was that people didn't like the sound of women's voices: They were too soft and shrill (that is, high pitched), and they lacked authority.

There have, of course, been many highly visible women in television and radio in recent decades. Women like Lucille Ball, Mary Tyler Moore, and others made their mark in situation comedies. Television journalist Barbara Walters and radio journalist Susan Stamberg are only two of many women who have held important posts in electronic journalism. Overall, however, women's involvement in radio and television has been restricted. One of the best-known histories of the Columbia Broadcasting System (CBS), for example, lists 593 people in its index, only eighty-seven, or 15 percent, of whom are women (Metz 1975). A closer look reveals that twenty-one of these women (22 percent) are listed because they were wives, sisters, aunts, mothers, daughters, or girlfriends of people associated with CBS. Thirty-seven women were included in their capacity as performers (sixteen associated with comedy shows), and many of these were not regularly associated with a particular program. Four journalists, two gossip columnists, and five other writers, only one of whom wrote regularly for radio or television, were also mentioned. Four women administrators were included. One of these was a librarian who the author said had no influence, and the other was an administrator who he claimed had much less power than she probably would today. Most of the other women were "personalities" or subjects of news; a secretary, a drama coach, and a philanthropist were also among the women listed.

These data may be regarded as subjective, but studies show they are by no means off the mark. In 1972, although 42 percent of the CBS work force was female, the company had no female directors. There were two female correspondents then and five in 1974. One out of ninety-two crew members was female, as were 21 out of

126 producers, three out of sixty-four film editors, and six out of twenty-five news writers. By 1979 a government report showed that the figures had improved, but only to a limited degree (U.S. Commission on Civil Rights 1979). Indeed, after a period of improvement the representation of women dropped in the late 1970s.

Women began to use legal means to improve their status in television and radio in the late 1970s. Although many of their lawsuits were settled out of court, many women who have faced discrimination have been compensated by media organizations.

By the beginning of the 1980s some improvements were evident, as a 1982 survey by the Radio and Television News Directors Association found.[3] The proportion of women on camera in news broadcasts was 16 percent at NBC-TV, 24 percent at CBS-TV, and 14 percent at ABC-TV. The figures are somewhat higher at local affiliate channels and on cable news channels. It is clear that women are far from having achieved equality, at least in television news. One study shows that in 1987 there were 36 women among the 239 network news correspondents. Even worse, in counting the amount of air time the correspondents had, the top six men were on camera more than all the women put together. About 12 percent of the stories that appeared on the three networks in 1986 were reported by women. A very high proportion of stories reported by women were aired on weekends, a lower-status and less visible slot for reporters (Sanders and Rock 1988, 113).

One of the jobs in which women's gains have been greatest is that of anchoring news broadcasts. Marlene Sanders, who has been involved in television broadcasting since its earliest years, illustrates the reaction to women in newscasting by quoting from an article by a *New York Times* television critic the day after Sanders served as temporary replacement for a news anchor who was ill that day:

> The masculine evening news line up received a temporary female replacement last night . . .when Marlene Sanders stepped in at 6:45 p.m. . . . People who should know report that never before has a distaff reporter conducted on her very own a news broadcast in prime time. For the record, then, the courageous young woman with a Vassar smile was crisp and businesslike and obviously the sort who wouldn't put up with any nonsense, from anyone. Her 15 minute show was not spell-binding, but that could have been because her delivery was terribly straightforward and her copy somewhat dull.

Sanders' reaction at the time was to wonder how one could deliver news other than in a straightforward manner. She was not aware that news anchors were usually "spell-binding." (Sanders and Rock 1988, 49–50)

By 1982 36 percent of news anchors were women, and 92 percent of television stations had at least one woman serving as an anchor. The fact that this is the area in which women have made considerable progress should be understood in the context of the nature of the position of anchor as opposed to other news broadcasting positions. The anchor of a local news program generally does not research or write the news stories; anchors are not reporters. They are performers, and they are selected largely for their public appeal as television performers, even though many of them have been reporters in the past.

News anchor Christine Craft was labelled "unattractive,
too old, and not deferential to men" by her employer.

The implications of this position became clearer in 1983 when Christine Craft, a former reporter serving as anchor for a local television station, sued that station because she was demoted on the grounds, she claimed, that she was "unattractive, too old, and not deferential to men."[4] The station involved claimed that news anchors must be attractive to their audiences if the station is going to keep its audience, and market research showed that audiences regarded Craft as lacking warmth, too casual in her dress, and too opinionated. Craft's lawyers later claimed that the method used to solicit audience reaction to Craft was discriminatory because it encouraged people to respond in a stereotypic way. Two juries found in favor of Craft, but she lost her case on appeal. When she appealed to the Supreme Court, only Justice Sandra Day O'Connor voted to hear the case.

Many female news anchors and journalists contended at the time that higher standards for appearance were set for women on camera than for men, and that they were judged in part on how well they conformed to gender stereotypes. Is the problem sexist audiences or sexist media organizations? It is hard to tell, but as early as 1976 one study (Whittaker and Whittaker 1976) found that audiences judged male and female news broadcasters equally acceptable, believable, and effective.

What image of women and norms about gender do people receive from the mass media? Gayle Tuchman, Arlene Kaplan Daniels, and James Benet (1978) argue that the media portrayal of women, and the lack of it, amounts to symbolic annihilation of women. Women appear much less frequently than they do in real life. When they do appear they are denigrated, presented as victims, or trivialized. George Gerbner (1978) argues that the media are major instruments of cultural resistance to changes in the roles and status of women. He says this happens in three ways:

1. Women and the women's movement are discredited by the media, which focus on the bizarre and the threatening.
2. Women are isolated or segregated and ghettoized. They are shown in special places (for example, the kitchen) and on special shows.
3. Exploitation and victimization of women is shown on television shows as common, routine, and entertaining.

Let us look at the evidence.

Empirical studies of the image of women on television agree: Women appear considerably less than men on most programs, and when they do appear they are not only portrayed unrealistically, but also denigrated and undercut by the roles they play. A study in the late 1970s showed that 45 percent of the people shown on television were women (Tuchman 1979). A study in the mid-seventies revealed that 85 percent of the characters on public television in one week were men (Cantor 1978). The U.S. Commission on Civil Rights reported in 1979 that 28 percent of all prime-time dramatic characters were women, but only 7 percent of all newsmakers shown on news broadcasts were white females, and less than 1 percent were minority women. We have already seen that newscasting is dominated by men. Only in soap operas are there as many females as males (Downing 1974). In prime-time television women are particularly concentrated in situation comedies (Tuchman 1979). Otherwise, in all types of programming men outnumber women in proportions that would spell demographic disaster in real life.[5]

Research also shows that the image of women who do appear on television is highly stereotypical. Rickel and Grant (1979) found that in soap operas, family television shows, and cartoon and other children's shows fewer than 30 percent of the women appear to work outside the home. The U.S. Commission on Civil Rights found in the late 1970s that 46 percent of the minority women and 40 percent of the white women on television had no identifiable job.[6] When women do hold jobs, they generally hold stereotypically feminine, low-status jobs. When they hold professional positions, they are rarely shown actually doing their jobs (Rickel and Grant 1979).

Research shows other differences in the portrayal of men and women on television. Rickel and Grant (1979) reported that nearly all the victims in cartoons are female, that men in television programs are presented as both more aggressive and more constructive than women, and that although 1 percent of all male soap opera characters are presented as emotionally or psychologically unstable, 14 percent of all women soap opera characters are. Judith Lemon (1978) found that male characters generally dominate female characters by occupational differences (for example, male doctors versus female nurses) and by verbal and other kinds of interaction (for similar findings, see Turow 1974).

Many people have commented on the gender messages aimed at women in newspapers and magazines. Magazines have come under considerable scrutiny because most are aimed at gender-segregated markets. Magazines aimed at women include such publications as *Family Circle, Ladies' Home Journal,* and *Redbook,* which are targeted at women in general and emphasize women's roles as homemakers, and magazines with special themes such as fashion, weddings, and so forth. Since the early 1970s, there has been a significant increase in magazines aimed at employed women, such as *Working Woman,* and feminist magazines such as *Ms.* In 1988 Frances Lear, who had been disturbed by the way the mass media treated older women especially, founded *Lear's;* a magazine, she claimed, ''for women who weren't born yesterday.''

Betty Friedan's analysis in *The Feminine Mystique* (1963) is perhaps most responsible for alerting people to the image of women in women's magazines. Friedan, who wrote for women's magazines in the 1950s, documented a postwar change in the portrayal of women in fiction and nonfiction. Good fiction, she claimed, left the pages of women's magazines, as did nonfiction that was not concerned with women's stereotypic roles. By the end of the 1950s she found women portrayed almost exclusively as mindless but attentive homemakers. ''In 1958, and again in 1959, I went through issue after issue of the major women's magazines...without finding a single heroine who had a career, a commitment to any work, art, profession, or mission in the world, other than 'Occupation: housewife''' (38). This change in content was paralleled by a change in format: ''The very size of (the women's magazines') print is raised until it looks like a first-grade primer'' (58).

This situation did not begin to change in a serious way until the 1970s. In 1970 feminists entered the offices of the *Ladies' Home Journal* and confronted the editors over issues of sexism. The women's magazines began to change their editorial policies, supplementing their articles on domestic concerns with articles on other aspects of women's lives.

One of the most dramatic events was the publication of *Ms.,* first as a supplement of *New York* magazine in 1971, and then, as an independent magazine in 1972. *Ms.,* of course, was not the first feminist periodical, and it is only one of hundreds that exist today, but this magazine, originally edited by Gloria Steinem, is the best known, the most popular, and certainly the slickest. E. Barbara Phillips (1978) did a content analysis comparing the image of women in *Ms.* with that presented in a more traditional women's magazine, *Family Circle.* Phillips found significant differences between the two magazines. She found 120 women discussed in eight issues of *Ms.* in contrast to 18 women discussed in sixteen issues of *Family Circle.* The majority of the women spotlighted by *Family Circle* were homemakers, including women who gave up professional careers to be homemakers; none were in politics or public service. *Family Circle* tended to emphasize how employment interferes with women's home lives. Almost half of the women *Ms.* focused on were in politics and public service, and none were presented as homemakers. The people portrayed in *Family Circle* were white; the people portrayed in *Ms.* were from a variety of racial backgrounds. The two magazines were different in another way as well: *Family Circle* (circulation: about 8 million) was read by many more people than *Ms.* (circulation: about 380,000).

As noted earlier mass-circulation newspapers have for many years had segregated sections for "women's news." The content of these "women's pages" has undergone changes that parallel those in the content of women's magazines. During and just before World War II, women were presented as relatively heterogeneous creatures. In the 1950s, however, they were viewed almost exclusively as homemakers. Gaye Tuchman (1978) points out that most news about women has generally been put on the women's page rather than elsewhere, thus casting stories about women as "soft" (peripheral) rather than "hard" (important) news. Tuchman shows how this approach can trivialize significant events:

> In 1965 [the *New York Times* women's page] ran a brief story in which Betty Friedan announced the formation of N.O.W. Placed between a recipe for turkey stuffing and an article announcing that Pierre Henri was returning to Saks Fifth Avenue, the article clearly indicated that Friedan had been interviewed at least several days before. The founding of N.O.W. was treated as soft news (201–2).

Although women's pages can be used to trivialize and segregate women and women's news, Tuchman notes that many journalists argue that these pages can be revolutionary. Content analysis shows that newspaper coverage of the women's movement and women's politics in general has been minimal, often trivializing and, as Gerbner (1978) claims, undercutting these important topics. Women's news is pushed aside for news that editors regard as more important or of more general interest. A women's page can take women's issues seriously and give them space. Often if news involving women did not appear on the women's page it would not appear at all.

In the 1970s newspapers began to indicate, at least symbolically, that items appearing on women's pages were of general interest by calling these pages "Style," "Living Today," or some similar title. The type of articles that appear on these pages, however, has changed little; the segregation of women's news continues.

Even when news about women is not segregated, it is treated differently from news about men. Karen G. Foreit and her colleagues (1980), for example, found that coverage of women was more likely to mention personal appearance ("the petite blonde lawyer"), marital status, spouses, and children. Coverage of women is also more likely to mention the person's sex explicitly. Few if any newspapers feel compelled to write about the "male lawyer."

Overall research on the gender messages transmitted through the electronic and print media agree with Tuchman and Gerbner's conclusions. Women are treated as though they are relatively few in number and of little importance. When they appear they are usually either isolated as though they are a parochial special-interest group or are pictured stereotypically. Despite growing attention to these problems, the mass media resist change. In fact many observers argue that coverage of the women's movement itself has been particularly biased. The mass media were quick to pick up on the image of feminists as "bra-burning libbers" and have often given less than serious, thorough coverage to the women's movement and women's political activities.

A good example of this negative and minimal treatment was found in a survey of how the Equal Rights Amendment (ERA) was reported in the *Los Angeles Times,* one of the country's most prestigious newspapers. During 1977, an important year in the history of the ERA, there were thirty-six news stories on the ERA. Not one quoted the whole amendment; only two quoted the first section of it, which consists of only twenty-six words. None told the status of the amendment in California, and fewer than one-third reported the national status of the amendment. Some of the articles told about successful actions in state legislatures to rescind ratification; none told of unsuccessful attempts to rescind it.[7] This type of reporting of the women's movement is not unusual. A review of how the 1978 National Women's Conference in Houston was reported showed that coverage trivialized the event by, for example, emphasizing bickering and sensationalism.[8] Such data is one reason that so many periodicals produced by the women's movement have sprung up in recent decades.

The Impact of the Mass Media

Demonstrating that the mass media present an androcentric or distorted view of women is not the same thing as demonstrating that the mass media have an impact on the way people think about women. Millions of people watch the same television shows, but they do not think alike. What impact do the media have on people's views of women? How is this impact achieved?

Mass communication experts discuss a number of ways that the mass media influence people. Perhaps most importantly the media serve as gatekeepers. There are limitless bits of information that could be funneled to us at any moment, but the media can present to us only a tiny fraction of that information and limited perspectives on it. As anyone who has ever used a camera knows, a photograph can capture only certain aspects of an object, and even the best effort to offer a balanced or realistic picture fails in some respects. On the other hand, the best effort to offer a particular and limited view often cannot completely mask details that point to the broader picture.

The individual does not receive the images and information transmitted through the media as a piece of clay receives a thumbprint. Psychologists have long been aware of the processes of selective exposure and selective perception. *Selective exposure* refers to our tendency to focus on only certain types of messages; if we are not interested in women's politics, we will not read articles on this topic even if they are in the paper. (How much of a newspaper do we really need? Why do we choose to read one paper rather than another?) *Selective perception* refers to a less conscious process whereby we notice only certain details out of everything that is presented to us. Our minds highlight, blank out, or exaggerate portions of images. For example, if we expect women to be more emotional than men, we may see emotionality in women more readily than we see it in men. Communications researchers also find that our reception of information depends on our cognitive abilities, the setting in which we use the media, and our interaction with other people during or after using the media.

Much of the research on media impact has involved children. By the time children enter school they have already spent more hours watching television than they will later spend in college classrooms. Most children spend more hours per week in front of the television than in school (Rickel and Grant 1979).

Children prefer to watch programs that contain characters of their own sex. And they watch more carefully and pay more attention when these characters act in gender-typed ways, almost as though they know what they are supposed to be learning (Sprafkin and Liebert 1978). Children who watch a lot of television reflect more stereotypes in their gender views than those who watch little, and stereotyped views, especially those held by males, increase with age among heavy viewers (McGhee and Frueh 1980). A study of both college-aged and elderly people also shows that those who watch more television are more stereotyped in their views and that they view themselves in more stereotyped terms (Ross, Anderson, and Wisocki 1982).

These studies do not reveal whether people who watch a lot of television become more gender biased or gender-biased people watch more television and pay closer attention to gender stereotypes. This question is not answered even by a study indicating that feminist women watch less television than nonfeminist women, especially among the more educated (Lull, Mulack, and Rosen 1983). Some experimental research, however, has been more enlightening.

In one study children were shown a television program and then asked questions. Some children saw a show in which women appeared only in gender-typed roles, and others saw a show in which a woman was a police officer. The children who saw the latter show were more likely to think later that women really could be police officers. Similar studies yield similar results (Tuchman 1978; Sprafkin and Liebert 1978). In another study children watched television advertisements that portrayed various toys as appropriate for one sex or the other. Afterward the children were allowed to choose from a number of toys. Both girls and boys were more likely to pick toys that had been presented as gender appropriate than those that had been presented as gender inappropriate (Cobb, Stevens-Long, and Goldstein 1982).

There is relatively little similar research on adults or other media, but the little that has been done reveals that the media have an impact on gender views. Signe Dayhoff (1983) looked at how sexist language and style in newspapers affected people's perception of female candidates for office. She found that sexist language and style in newspaper articles had a negative impact on readers' evaluations of female candidates for ''masculine'' (for example, sheriff) or relatively ''neutral'' positions but a positive effect on evaluations of female candidates for ''feminine'' offices (for example, president of the League of Women Voters). In other words, linguistic sexism highlights and exaggerates stereotypically feminine details, thus making the woman being described appear less appropriate for ''masculine'' or even ''neutral'' positions and more appropriate for ''feminine'' positions. (We will discuss language and gender more extensively in Chapter 9.)

It is harder to design research that clearly and rigorously shows the impact of media messages than to design research that describes the messages. We can conclude that the media do shape the way people think about gender and gender issues, but that the process by which this occurs is very complex. Media messages are not monolithic, and they come from many different sources. Individuals have choices about what they watch, listen to, and read.

The process by which people learn from the media is generally well accounted for by the cognitive developmental approach to learning. Children and adults play an active role in learning, and they do so both consciously and unconsciously. Children do not necessarily choose to pay more attention to gender-typed characteristics; they are influenced by previous knowledge and attitudes toward themselves and others. People also differ in the degree to which they can recognize stereotypes; one study of college students, for example, showed that women are more sensitive than men to gender-stereotyped depictions (Lull, Hanson, and Marx 1977). Although media messages are powerful and can help maintain or change sex/gender systems, they are by no means all-powerful. They do, however, constitute an important link in sex/gender systems.

The Commercial Media

It is nearly impossible to avoid seeing or hearing communications intended to sell us something. Radio and television programs, newspapers, and magazines are filled with advertisements attempting to sell us products and ideas. Public broadcasting is no exception; sponsors are mentioned not just to thank them for their support but also to show us they are nice companies to buy from. Media organizations run advertisements for their own products: their shows. Everywhere we see billboards, bumper stickers, and even T-shirts trying to sell us something. Our mailboxes are stuffed with advertisements and sometimes trial products. Advertisements fill the programs for concerts and plays. The packaging of food and other items in stores is designed to advertise the contents. Newsletters or surveys from our representatives in Congress or our state legislatures are also advertisements.

Women and gender have played important roles in the history of commercial communication, or advertising. Advertising began to develop as serious business with the rise of industrialism in the nineteenth century. By the 1920s it had become professionalized; throughout the following decades it became increasingly technical and scientific in its approach.

In his history of advertising in the United States Stuart Ewen argues that "the advertising which attempted to create the dependable mass of consumers required by modern industry often did so by playing upon the fears and frustrations evoked by mass society—offering mass produced visions of individualism by which people could extricate themselves from the mass" (1976, 45). The goal of advertising is to make people feel that they need or want a specific product. An advertisement for a special brand of vaginal douche or cornflakes has to convince people both that they need the product and that they want this brand rather than others. The advertiser therefore transmits the message that without this product potential customers will be less healthy, attractive, happy, secure, or caring than if they purchase the product. Advertisements are aimed at specific audiences; they play on or even create the fears, needs, or desires of specific groups of people. Because of this they can have a powerful influence on creating, or at least maintaining, specific gender norms.

A study of 167 magazine advertisements for menstruation-related products published between 1976 and 1986 provides a good example. Menstruation was consistently presented as a hygienic crisis in which women greatly need the security and peace of mind provided by the product. Women who used the advertised products were always depicted functioning at optimum levels (Havens and Swenson 1988).

Some of the first important efforts at directing advertising at women occurred in the late nineteenth century. One of women's most important economic functions is to be consumers, and women played an important role in the growth of the consumerism in industrialized American society. The health of American business depends not just on a dependable mass of consumers, but also on a dependable mass of female consumers. We have already seen that women's magazines began to be filled with fashion plates showing women what they should wear. In such advertisements the sales pitch merges with social information; women read the advertisements as well as the articles in *Vogue* and other such publications to learn what the current styles are, and adolescents pore over the pages of *Seventeen* and similar magazines to gain knowledge from people who are trying to sell their wares.

There is a long tradition of presenting advertising under the guise of helpful and necessary advice. Clothing manufacturers had to create markets in the late nineteenth century for their new products: ready-to-wear clothes. Department stores—sometimes called fashion palaces—were developed at that time. They were designed to convince women that they could be elegant and fashionable, and they sometimes had "experts" available to help women make the "right" choices.

Observers sometimes exaggerate the power of advertising. For advertising to sell, it must reflect the social values of the time; it cannot create needs out of thin air. At the turn of the century, for example, when *science* and *progress* were the catchwords of the day, advertising directed at women began to play on these principles, especially on the new views of scientific home management, or home economics. From then on advertising presented itself as a source of expert information about how women could keep their families healthy, their homes germ free, and their households efficiently managed. Personal-hygiene product promotion keeps up this tradition today, alerting women to germs and health hazards they never knew existed or that do not exist.

In the 1920s advertising used feminism and the image of the emancipated woman for its own purposes, just as advertising now uses the image of the liberated woman. The 1970s Virginia Slims campaign, "You've come a long way, baby," hearkens back to a 1929 campaign by the American Tobacco Company that attempted to convince women to smoke.

The twentieth century has also been marked by the promotion of "labor-saving devices" to women. These promotion campaigns promise a more healthful and efficient household, as well as release from the drudgery of housework to spend more time in family or social activities or even other occupations. The promise was unfulfilled, as many studies of time use and technology have shown (see, e.g., Vanek 1980; Robinson 1980). Homemakers today spend at least as much time on housework as housewives did in the 1920s. In his study in the mid-1970s John Robinson (1980) found that so-called labor-saving devices make remarkably little difference in the time women spend on housework. Despite the claims of advertisers, a microwave oven reduces the average workday by only 10 minutes, a clothes dryer by only 5 minutes, and a vacuum cleaner by only 1 minute. A freezer adds 6 minutes to the working day, a washing machine adds 4 minutes, and a dishwasher and sewing machine each add 1 minute.

An early "labor-saving" vacuum cleaner.

If these figures seem implausible, consider the effects of these goods on a household. A woman with a washer and dryer does not wash the same amount of clothes in less time, she washes clothes more often in about the same time. Special new kitchen appliances such as food processors lead people to do different kinds of cooking from the type they did without them. Although Stuart Ewen is right in suggesting that, "rather than viewing the transformations in household work as labor-saving, it is perhaps more useful to view them as labor-changing" (1976, 163), the voice of the expert in advertisements convinces women otherwise.[9]

During the two world wars business responded to, and helped develop, the theme that women's efforts could help win the wars. The promotional voice of the expert urged women to participate in programs to save resources needed for the war efforts. Advertisements showed women how to rearrange their household management to do their part and, incidentally, how this could be accomplished only by using Product X. Particularly during World War II advertisements promoted the virtues of women working in nontraditional jobs for the sake of the war and, naturally, how these good women used the right products; even Rosie the Riveter could keep her hands lovely and feminine. After the war advertisements showed how happy women were to be back in the household caring for their families.

Commercial media continue to send out gender messages. Images remain gender typed, as they do in the mass media more generally. Television commercials directed at children include many more boys than girls, and girls play passive and gender-typed roles (Feldstein and Feldstein 1982, Macklin and Kolbe 1984). Mamay and Simpson (1981) show that women in television commercials generally play one of three roles: mother, housekeeper, or "aesthetic" interest. Women are generally pictured inside the house, usually in the kitchen or bathroom. Women are also used as sex objects in advertisements directed at men; they are draped over cars in revealing outfits, for example, as though for an extra price they could be purchased as optional equipment along with the air-conditioning.

Particularly interesting is the portrayal of expertise and authority in contemporary advertising. The "expert" in television commercials is usually a man, even in commercials aimed at women (Mamay and Simpson 1981). The voice of the expert in television commercials is generally the unseen "voice-over," and most of these are male voices even when the commercial shows only women.

The portrayal of expertise took an interesting twist in the 1970s with the rise of the women's movement and objections to commercial sexism. Many advertisements emphasized women's expertise, but this expertise was demonstrated in vignettes showing male incompetence at household work. In these portrayals men rather than women were the objects of the jokes, but the underlying message was the same: Housework is for women. Many of the gender messages observers criticized in earlier years remain on television (Ferrante, Haynes, and Kingsley 1988).

As with other media, advertisements have undergone some changes. Women are portrayed in a wider range of occupations and outside the home more often than before (Ferrante, Haynes, and Kingsley 1988). Classified advertisements were changed by law; it is no longer legal for "help wanted" columns in newspapers to categorize jobs as "male" or "female" because this constitutes employment discrimination. Women's organizations have exerted pressure on companies with sexist advertisements by, for example, writing letters and urging boycotts. The underlying problem, however, is that companies would not use gender-typed techniques if they did not sell products. But they do, so they do.

The Cultural and Artistic Media

It might seem odd at first to discuss the mass and artistic media in the same context. There are, however, many reasons for considering the role of gender in these different media together. At the simplest level, cultural and artistic media are often presented *through* the mass media. In addition to situation comedies, game and crime shows, news broadcasts, and self-help shows, television and radio also present theater, films, music, poetry readings, and art history. In addition to soap operas, television also may present another kind of opera, such as Wagner's magnum opus *Der Ring des Nibelungen*.[10] The recent spread of cable television has made this overlap even greater.

There are other ways in which the mass and artistic media are similar that are important in looking at their relationship to gender norms. The artistic and mass media are, after all, media of communication. They are channels through which some people express themselves and their perceptions of events, people, ideas, and feelings and to which a much larger number of people turn to share, learn about, and possibly evaluate these perceptions. Most of the people on the receiving end of these messages know very little about the processes behind the media. We tend to learn about the media as we learn about so many other things: from the media themselves.[11]

None of the media has a monopoly on specific types of messages. Each has been used at some time to inform, convince, threaten, entertain, or expose. Each is a part of the cultural traffic of society, its appeal or utility based in part on the relationship of both form and content to surrounding cultural symbols, ideology, and social events. Each has a central role in the process of defining culture and social values.

There are also organizational and procedural similarities among the different media. Most of us know the mass media are often managed by large, bureaucratic organizations with a wide range of goals besides merely "getting the message across." Journalists must conform to some degree to the values of their editors, coworkers, producers, other administrative personnel, and the organization as a whole. Their product must sell, even if selling mitigates against some of their journalistic standards. Some ideas are too controversial, risky, or unfamiliar to be accepted by the media organization for transmission; there is not always complete agreement among the public or coprofessionals on what is most desirable in form and content. Censorship can occur in a variety of ways.

The same is true of artistic media. Publishing and movie houses, museums, theaters, and concert halls all share these same problems, although in different forms. It has often been necessary for people in all fields of communication to establish alternative channels, because of the barriers set up by the values and goals of the established organizations.

Many of the problems and issues raised about the mass and commercial media, therefore, can also be raised about the full range of artistic and cultural media. The art world has been gender segregated, and women have been valued less than men. The images reflected through the arts, especially the high-status arts, are often gender typed. This link between the arts on the one hand and questions of power, politics, and status on the other has often been ignored. Sociologists and political scientists, for example, have paid less attention to the arts than they have to the mass media.

People in the mainstream of the art world have also generally ignored these issues, particularly as they pertain to women and gender. Speaking of literary criticism, Catherine Stimpson argues that "this has not happened because [critics and artists] are vicious, but because, as they work, they tend to believe themselves to be too decent to be guilty of such crude errors." Stimpson offers some reasons for the neglect of gender power structures in literature, and these also apply well to other arts. "The study of literature is remote enough from centers of political and economic power to permit people to think that it can be relatively uncorrupt." Artists, she argues, believe in the "ennobling nature of the free exercise of consciousness," and often believe that the artistic will can be free of the constraint of political ideology (1979, 55).

Too many people both inside and outside the art world forget, or refuse to believe, that artists and art critics are very much a part of the social world. As with the other communication media, indeed with most of the other institutions we have discussed, the values and norms generated by the artistic media reflect, maintain, and help change the values found in the wider society. As with the other media, these messages are not monolithic but reflect the diversity of human nature.

It is impossible to do more here than touch on some art and cultural forms or to take more than a brief look at special issues raised by the arts. We will explore some of the parallels among the cultural and artistic media, the commercial media, and the mass media by looking at examples of some of the issues raised by different forms. We will look first at women's roles in the arts and then at some of the gender messages transmitted through the arts.

Women as Artists

It is impossible to bar people totally from participating in the arts. People can sing, compose, paint, write, or otherwise create beauty for their own pleasure if not for someone else's. Groups of people can, however, be permitted or denied access to the art community, and they certainly can be denied influence, professional status, and recognition.

For a person to be recognized as a great artist requires ability, access to the field, and the favorable judgment of others. Historians of women in the arts suggest that access and the judgment of others have been the major stumbling blocks for women. As Linda Nochlin (1971) suggests, the often-asked question "Why are there no great women artists?" can be answered in several ways: There have been, but they were not recognized. There have been, but they have been forgotten. There have been, but not many because women were not allowed to be artists. There have been, but not many because women are not able enough.

There is considerable evidence that women who might have developed their artistic talents were blocked in their efforts to seek the necessary education. For a long time women were not admitted to the great academies for the graphic arts, so they could not obtain the same training as men. They were also barred from one of the most important aspects of art training, life drawing from a nude model. Aspiring female musicians were not allowed into many of the major music academies and courses. Schools of architecture were reluctant to admit women until recently, and from 1915 to 1942 American women who wanted to be architects could train only at the all-female Cambridge School of Architecture and Landscape Architecture (Berlo 1976). Although we know of many great women writers, many of them found it easier to be accepted if they used a male pen name.[12]

Art institutions continue to practice discrimination, and it is still very difficult for women to gain access to them. Although about 50 percent of all graphic artists are women, one can find relatively few reviews of women's work in art magazines

Chapter 7:
The Institutional
Media of
Communication

and newspapers. Women are underrepresented among teachers at professional art schools, museum administrators, and the artists shown.

The situation in music also shows a long history of discrimination with some recent changes. Until the twentieth century orchestras generally refused to play music composed by women, to admit women instrumentalists, and, until very recently, to play under female conductors (Levy 1983; Jepson 1975–76). Even by the early 1970s none of the 159 orchestras of the Symphony Orchestra League had a woman music director or conductor. Sarah Caldwell and Margaret Hillis became regularly appointed conductors only by founding their own orchestras (Jepson, 1975–76). The New York Philharmonic Orchestra did not include a female instrumentalist until 1966. The lack of orchestra seats for women changed when orchestras introduced blind auditions in which the judges could not see the player. By 1985 women were 28 percent of the instrumentalists in major U.S. orchestras and 47 percent in metropolitan orchestras (Rix 1988, 222). As in other fields, "the higher the fewer" is still the case. In the 1980s about three-quarters of the members of the Music Teachers National Association were female while the same was true of only 22 percent of full-time college-level music faculty members (Rix 1988, 221).

There are art fields in which talented women have achieved considerable recognition. This includes fields, such as acting and singing, that specifically call for women artists. American dance is another field in which women, including such key figures as Isadora Duncan and Martha Graham, have excelled; in fact only in recent decades have men become as important as women in dance. Although classical music composition has been dominated by men, women have been particularly important in the blues, jazz, and folk genres, where artists such as Bessie Smith, Billie Holliday, Ella Fitzgerald, and Joan Baez are prominent. Even in the traditionally male-dominated fields women are now achieving recognition; in 1983, for example, Ellen Taafe Zwillich became the first woman composer to win the Pulitzer Prize in music. We can single out names of successful women in most fields of art, but we cannot escape the conclusion that in many of the important fields, women have not been treated as seriously as men.

This leads us to the question of how people judge women as artists. In many fields opinion leaders have argued that women are incapable of greatness by nature. In music it has been thought that women lack the physical strength to be great pianists, the strength of character to be conductors, and the imagination to be composers (Levy 1983). Could a woman lead a performance of such masculine works as Beethoven's Fifth Symphony (Jepson 1975–76)? Many music professionals have thought that women do not have the mental capacity to teach music theory because it is so technical and mathematical.

Critics of architecture have worried about women's inferior spatial perception, as have critics of painting and sculpture. Literary critics have worried about women's "personalism," their lack of strength, and their inability to "write like a man." Criticism of women in various fields of the arts focuses especially on the influence of their personal lives and characteristics on their art much more than is the case for men. Critics are particularly prone to interpret women's work through stereotypes of women: They notice its interior dimensions, its intuitiveness and sensitivity, and any links with other artists that might mark it as derivative. If the artist is a feminist, critics either notice the "shrillness" of the art, or compliment it for not being shrill, as though in the normal course of events it must be.

There is some question whether the works of male and female artists differ. Because men's and women's experiences and training are often different, it would make sense for their artistic expressions to be different. Portions of the art community go beyond this, however, and argue that differences exist and are rooted in the different sexual natures of men and women. Even people in the mainstream of the arts have used this as an argument for women's inferiority. Many radical feminists, especially those who argue for a special "women's aesthetic," also see differences springing from nature, but they place a positive value on "feminine art."

Investigating women and the arts raises some of the most fundamental questions about the nature and role of the arts in society that we can ask. What is the distinction among arts, crafts, and other forms of expression? What is a "high" form of art? What function do the arts play in society?

In recent years many feminist artists and art critics have called for the art world to give more serious attention to the forms that have been the special domain of women, including, for example, quilts, embroidery, weaving, and certain kinds of pottery. These forms have been virtually excluded from art history courses, books, and museums, not because they have been designed and made by women but because they have been considered crafts rather than fine arts. Crafts, and therefore much of women's artistic work, have a lower status in the art world than the fine arts. The distinction turns on purpose and function: Crafts spring from the practical purposes of feeding, clothing, and sheltering, for example, and arts are "divorced from use, are 'useless' in any practical sense" (Hedges and Wendt 1980, 2). In music there is also a distinction between serious, high forms of music, and lower forms such as folk, blues, rock, and pop.

Poet Marge Piercy (1974, 86–87) has used her artistry to ask why there is a distinction between arts and crafts:

> Who decided what is useful in its beauty
> means less than what has no function beside beauty
> (except its weight in money)?
> Art without frames: it held parched corn,
> it covered the table where soup misted savor,
> it covered the bed where the body knit
> to self and other and the
> dark wool of dreams.

Anyone who has seen the intricate and beautiful work of quilters or reads about a pieced quilt that contains 30,000 pieces, each one-half inch by three-quarters inch in size[13] wonders why quilts have so often languished in attics and trunks while Mondrian's painted squares hang proudly in the world's great museums. Such skill, taught by ordinary women in their homes rather than by famous people in academies, also makes one wonder how women could ever have been considered technically and cognitively incapable of mastering "higher" forms of art. Women's crafts, like the other arts, have shared symbols, forms, and traditions and are manifest in unique displays of individual creativity and artistry.

Contemporary analysis casts into doubt the appropriateness of making such distinctions between art that is utilitarian and art that is for aesthetic pleasure alone. A review of the history of the arts, the social roles the arts perform, and the social roles the artists perform, suggests that these dichotomies were false, or very suspect, all along.

The fine arts are of utilitarian as well as aesthetic value in many senses. Humans need food, shelter, and so forth, but they also need sensory stimulation. Studies of the effects on people of deprivation of stimulation to the five senses show that people need sensory stimulation to survive perhaps as much as they need food and water. Environmental research is making us increasingly aware of the effects of design, color, noise, and the use of space on people. Is there such a thing as thoroughly useless art?

There are other links between the "higher" and "lower" arts. Some of the greatest "fine" music in the West originated as church music designed to create a mood and help people praise, glorify, mourn, and celebrate. Do these utilitarian purposes diminish the value of Bach's cantatas, Beethoven's Mass in B Minor, or Verdi's Requiem? If not, we cannot argue that women's lullabies and native American women's healing songs are necessarily lower forms of music simply because they were composed for specific purposes (Jaskoski 1981).

The history of the sampler provides a fascinating study of utility versus aesthetics, status and art, and gender norms. Toni Fratto (1976–77) writes that samplers, or small works in which girls and young female adolescents demonstrated their skill at embroidery, were made primarily during the sixteenth through the nineteenth centuries and reached their greatest popularity in the late eighteenth century. The skill and beauty of these samplers is amazing to the contemporary eye, particularly considering the age of the artists.

Samplers were useless in that they were meant for display. A closer look, however, reveals purpose. Beside the ABC's that might be stitched into the sampler are poems and prayers praising the home and feminine virtues as well as pictorial symbols of the same messages. Fratto writes, "The sampler was to be the outward sign of a girl-child's willingness and readiness to enter into her place" (13). Indeed Fratto found "another and perhaps even more powerful function. . . . Like the painting on glass, theorem work on velvet, and watercolor painting of the time, the sampler was meant to serve as the sign of gentility, to establish the girl's credentials as 'a lady'" (13).

Fratto argues that because the samplers became increasingly bound by conventions of status and design, their quality declined in the early nineteenth century. "What they gained by not being Art they lost by being a symbol of genteel culture" (Fratto 1976–77, 15). They provided training for both gender and class norms, and they now fetch enormous sums of money in antique shops.

Women play crucial roles in the life of the arts. They decorate their houses, sing lullabies, and tell stories to their children. In some fields, such as singing, dancing, acting, and poetry and novel writing, there have been many great and famous women. In other fields it does not take long to uncover the names of women who should be remembered along with the others. It cannot be argued that the value of all arts and artists is the same; we probably do not want to rank the flower arrangement a woman puts on her dining room table with the sculpture of Barbara Hepworth. But in their segregation of men and women into different artistic fields, treatment of women artists and women's arts, and denigration of the functions women's arts perform the artistic and cultural media of communication are important parts of sex/gender systems.

Gender as a Subject of Art

The treatment of gender in the arts is related to the values, frustrations, and goals of the times. The sexual tensions, role reversals, bawdy jokes, and portrayals of dominant women in Restoration comedies reflect that period of uncertainty and changing roles. These popular plays were banned from the late eighteenth century through the nineteenth century because they were considered too lewd and unsuitable for decent people. Whereas cuckolding was a favorite theme of the Restoration period, and everything generally worked out well in the end, during the nineteenth and early twentieth centuries the philandering woman became the fallen woman; a fictional female who committed adultery generally died (often by her own hand) for her sins, or at least went mad.

The history of the cinema has also been marked by changes in the treatment of women's roles. In the earliest days of film moving pictures were particularly popular among urban immigrants. As Elizabeth Ewen (1980) points out, the central figures in movies were common people, and working-class immigrants flocked to neighborhood movie houses to see people acting out their own tensions and problems. Movies presented themes of gender and sexuality from both feminist and antifeminist perspectives. After World War I the film industry became more reflective of established, middle-class Americans. In fact movies were sometimes thought to be potentially powerful tools of assimilation, capable of teaching immigrant women how to be good American housewives.

One of the most interesting shifts in film images of women occurred between the late 1930s and the 1950s. In the late 1930s and early 1940s there were many significant female parts, often showing women as strong, independent, employed, and even professional. After World War II this began to change. In the late 1940s came the introduction of the *film noir,* in which strong women were often dangerous temptresses leading men astray. Then in the 1950s the strong women went home, became bird-brained sex objects, or both.

Parallel historical shifts can also be seen in other art forms, as Kathlyn Fritz and Natalie Hevener (1979) show in their study of twentieth-century detective novels. They found that the image of the female detective changed quite dramatically from the 1920s to the 1970s. Before the 1960s women detectives in these novels were often not really detectives; they were amateurs who solved crimes. They also tended to be unattractive or elderly. In the 1920s and 1930s 44 percent of the female detectives did not have a career; the same was true of 40 percent of the female detectives in novels of the 1940s and 1950s. In recent decades, however, only 10 percent of the female detectives had no careers, and these characters were often portrayed as attractive women.

Katharine Hepburn, actress and daughter of a suffragist,
portrayed many strong female characters. Here she and
Morris Carnovsky rehearse a scene between Portia and
Shylock in *The Merchant of Venice*.

Jennifer Waelti-Walters (1979) reminds us of how early in life androcentric norms are taught to us through art forms, in this case, the fairy tale. After reviewing the lives of fairy tale princesses she concludes, "Nobody in her right mind could possibly want to be a fairy tale princess" (180). Most fairy tale princesses are passive victims or merely decorative or must die in order to be loved. If they resist these roles, they are generally portrayed as evil or mad.

At times the sexual and gender politics of art has erupted into major battles. One of the best known of these controversies involved a massive work by Judy Chicago called *The Dinner Party*. *The Dinner Party* consists of a large, three-sided dinner table decorated with place settings constructed of various women's arts and crafts representing thirty-nine different well-known women. The names of 999 other women are embedded in the tablecloth and table base. Many viewers and critics have been disturbed by the distinctly vaginal form of much of the design. Whereas critics seem relatively undisturbed by phallic iconography and symbolism, the graphic themes of Chicago's work repulsed and even angered them. Established art critics are less likely to ask "Is it art?" of androcentric art, because androcentric art is "normal." They ask "Is it art?" of gynocentric art, because gynocentric art is interpreted as political and therefore not artistic.

Sexuality is one of the most profound and ubiquitous themes in art; it plays a major role in art criticism and discussion of gender and the arts. Many critics have argued, for example, that no matter how or how much sexuality is expressed in the arts, only heterosexuality is treated as potentially normal and desirable. However, the issues they are concerned with are not simply whether artists discriminate against homosexuals in their work, or whether there is discrimination against homosexuals and lesbians in the art world. Feminist critics also raise the issue of how we define the erotic, especially considering its relationship to pornography and expressions of violence against women.

Feminist observers have become increasingly concerned about how often images intended to be erotic involve some form of violence against women. For example, advertisements for films very often present an "erotic" image of a terrified woman. In films during incidents of terror against women, such as rape, the camera usually takes the assailant's viewpoint rather than the victim's; we watch the victim being terrified rather than the assailant being terrifying. The presentation of violence against women as erotic and entertaining reached a new level in the late 1970s with the popularity of "snuff" films—films of women literally being tortured to death.

These and other examples raise many important questions. What is the difference between erotic art and pornography? One study investigated a random sample of "adult" movies available in family video rental stores in southern California. Over half the explicit sexual scenes were predominantly concerned with domination and exploitation (Cowen et al. 1988).

Why do so many images variously defined as erotic or pornographic involve violence against women? Why do so many people find this violence entertaining, arousing, or otherwise worth seeing? What impact do these images of violence have on audiences? Many researchers have investigated the relationship between viewing violent pornography and engaging in violence against women such as rape. Although relatively few find conclusive evidence that such pornographic images cause violence, many argue that it can be a contributing factor. Research on long-term exposure to video violence against women found that as male viewers saw more over time their anxious and other negative reactions to it diminished and they even perceived less violence in the videos than they had at first. The researchers concluded that exposure to violent pornographic images desensitizes men to violence against women over the long haul (Linz, Donnerstein, and Penrod 1988).

How can a society stop identifying violence against women as sexy and entertaining without infringing on freedom of expression? Where do we draw the line?[14] Scholars and activists alike disagree about the answers.

Media of Change?

We have looked at three overlapping types of media of communication: mass media, commercial media (advertising), and artistic media. In each of these we find evidence of segregation of women, often into lower-status positions. In each we find that the mainstream of the media often project androcentric views of society and a lower status for women. At the same time we can find women who have had a powerful impact on society through these media. We also find that women working in these fields have organized to look at women's roles in different ways and have worked to provide alternative visions and alternative forms.

Our observations of the relationship between gender and the media leave us with problems and questions that need to be solved. Growing numbers of people work in the media as writers, performers, publishers, market analysts, artists, journalists, and technical personnel. Those of us in these fields have a responsibility to understand how our work reflects or shapes gender roles and ideology. Mere understanding is not enough, however, and individual action is difficult. Individuals are constrained in their ability to bring about change by the organizations in which they work, by the demands and preferences of their audiences, and by the need to earn a living. Few people can afford to sacrifice their incomes for the principle of gender equality in media messages, particularly if lack of compromise means losing the ability to speak through the media. On the other hand, few people aware of the problems of gender messages in the media can ignore these problems entirely in their work. What action can feminists who work in the media take?

Although only some of us work in the media, all of us are consumers. We also face important problems and questions as media consumers. We have a responsibility—to ourselves and, if we have them, our children—to understand how the media reflect and shape gender roles and ideology. It takes effort and expense to identify and use the media that promote less androcentric views of the world, and it certainly takes effort to attempt to influence those who offer us an androcentric view. This, however, is what needs to be done.

NOTES

1. U.S. Commission on Civil Rights, *Window Dressing on the Set: An Update,* 1979, quoted in *Media Report to Women,* February 1, 1979, p. 1.
2. "Grace Glueck Tribute to Attorney Harriet Rabb Recalls Beginning of Suit at 'Times,'" *Media Report to Women,* December 31, 1978, 2.
3. *New York Times,* August 6, 1983.
4. *New York Times,* August 6, 1983.
5. See Franzwa (1978) for an annotated bibliography.
6. "TV Has Made Virtually No Progress for Women and Minorities in Two Years: CCR," *Media Report to Women,* March 1, 1979.
7. "LA Times' News Stories Did Not Give Basic Factual Information on E.R.A.," *Media Report to Women,* September 1, 1978.
8. "Media Version of Houston Conference: Lindsy van Gelder Covers the Coverage for *Ms,*" *Media Report to Women,* March 1, 1978.
9. For further discussion of the history and impact of changes in domestic technology, see Cowan (1983).

10. One might argue that Wagner's story of everyday life among the gods is a massive soap opera with music. It has love, hate, incest, illegitimacy, murder, identity and family crises, repetition, and everything else that makes a soap opera work.

11. Think about how much we "know" about how television works because we watched "The Mary Tyler Moore Show" or the movie *Network* or *Broadcast News;* how much we "know" about newspapers because we watched "Lou Grant" or the movie *All the President's Men.*

12. On the other hand, male writers of romances have often used female pen names.

13. This quilt is mentioned in Hedges (1980).

14. For further discussion of issues relating to sexual violence see Chapters 8 and 10.

8

Law and Policy, Government, and the State

OF ALL THE institutions that exert control over people's lives by teaching and enforcing values, those associated with government are the most powerful and authoritative. Government has the power to regulate, at least to some degree, all other institutions of society. Even the decision that a government may not regulate a certain aspect of life is generally made and enforced by an arm of the government such as the courts.

Despite the common complaint that government has grown too big, many people do not realize just how much government touches their lives and how tied to the sex/gender system it is. Government policy influences most aspects of our lives in one way or another, including even our most intimate relationships and personal choices involving sexuality, family relationships, and reproduction.

Many political scientists describe the workings of government as the "authoritative allocation of values." By values they mean questions about right and wrong, good and bad, and the distribution of goods and services such as health care, education, jobs, wealth, and so on. One important difference between the institutions of government and the other social institutions discussed in this book is that when government supports or "teaches" particular values, including those related to gender, it does so with the power of coercion.

One of the questions to pursue in looking at women and government is the role of gender in the distribution of these values. Are equal values accorded to women and men? If the values government attempts to distribute include, for example, freedom or a decent standard of living, do law and policy actually work to grant these values to women and men equally? A second question concerns the impact of women and men on government. Do they have the same opportunity to shape government policy? Do they play equal roles in government and politics? If not, can we call the political system democratic? In this chapter we will seek answers to some of these questions.

Governmental Views of Women

205

Chapter 8:
Law and Policy,
Government, and
the State

Protection of Rights

In 1776 a group of people (all of them men) meeting in Philadelphia wrote a document that read, "We hold these truths to be self-evident; that all men are created equal, that they are endowed by their creator with certain inalienable rights, that among these are life, liberty, and the pursuit of happiness." They further argued that the purpose of government is to ensure these rights, and that if government does not do so, the people have a right to "alter or abolish" the government.

Seventy-two years later a group of people (most of them women) meeting in Seneca Falls, New York, rebuked the government by rewriting that same document to show how men withheld from women the rights to which they were entitled. Their document, which was called the Declaration of Sentiments and Resolutions rather than the Declaration of Independence, included the passage, "We hold these truths to be self-evident: that all men and women are created equal. . . ."

In 1868 the Fourteenth Amendment to the U.S. Constitution was ratified. From then on the Constitution included the statement that no state shall "make or enforce any law which shall abridge the privileges or immunities of citizens of the United States, nor. . .deprive any person of life, liberty, or property without due process of law, nor deny to any person within its jurisdiction the equal protection of the laws."

Since 1923 thousands, perhaps millions, of people have worked hard to insert words such as the following into the Constitution as well: "Equality of rights under the law shall not be denied or abridged by the United States or by any state on account of sex." They have wanted this amendment to the Constitution because they do not believe that the Fourteenth Amendment has been used rigorously enough to give women and men equal protection of the law. Indeed until 1971 the Constitution was never used to stop discrimination against women. That was the first year in which the Supreme Court declared unconstitutional a law that discriminated against women. For well over a century now, feminists have been arguing that the government has not extended the same protection of the law to women as to men. Most go one step further and argue that law and policy have been based on androcentric and patriarchal norms and therefore maintain and enforce these norms.

When we explored the topic of health, one of the key questions we asked was whether health-care practitioners regard women as normally healthy. When we looked at religion, one of our central questions was whether religious authorities regarded women as normally moral and righteous. In looking at politics, we ask a parallel question: How do government authorities regard the quality of women's citizenship? To what degree have women been treated as equal and responsible members of the political community? To what degree are they included as part of a democratic system of political decision making?

Chapter 2 pointed out that political revolutions (notably in France and America) were fed by the antipatriarchal ideas of Enlightenment political thinkers. Feminist thinkers in this tradition, from Mary Wollstonecraft on, argued that the transformation from a patriarchal to a democratic system was taking place for men only, or at least that it was happening considerably more quickly for men than for women. At least some men were becoming citizens rather than subjects, but all women retained their subject status.

The law is not a random package of legislation and court decisions. There are different systems and traditions of law, each with its own sets of underlying views of rights, obligations, and relations among people and proper procedures for settling how laws should be interpreted or applied in any given case. Law and policy are expressions of a political community's underlying set of values or ideology, and they are also instruments used to enforce those values. Our task, then, is to look into legal and policy decisions to see the ways in which the ideology expressed through law is linked to the ideology of the prevailing sex/gender system.

What did the Founding Fathers have in mind for women when they began designing the American republic? The evidence we have from the stray words of Thomas Jefferson, John Adams, Benjamin Franklin, and others is that citizenship was not going to mean the same thing for women as for men. Jefferson, for example, wrote, "Were the state a pure democracy there would still be excluded from our deliberation women, who, to prevent deprivation of morals and ambiguity of issues, should not mix promiscuously in gatherings of men" (quoted in Kay 1988, 1). From the beginning, government and politics were regarded as a male domain.

In general, free women in the early republic could not vote or hold political office.[1] Married women especially could not sue, be sued, or serve on juries. They could not make contracts and therefore could not seek employment without their husbands' permission. They could not own property, and they had no direct legal control over their children. Husbands had nearly undisputed rights of control and custody over their children. What rationale was used to deny women these rights in a self-proclaimed democratic republic?

The major justification can be found in the common law views of women, especially of married women. The common law is an English legal tradition that was the basis for much of the structure of the law in the United States as it affected women. As William Blackstone wrote in 1765 in the *Commentaries on the Law of England,* "By marriage, the husband and wife are one person in law: that is, the very being or legal existence of the woman is suspended during the marriage, or at least is incorporated and consolidated into that of the husband; under whose wing, protection, and cover she performs every thing...." (quoted in Kay 1988, 163).

Blackstone pointed out repeatedly that the law cannot treat a woman as having an existence separate from that of her husband. Upon marriage they become one person, and the husband is her "baron, or lord," Blackstone pointed out, that "there are some instances in which she is separately considered; as inferior to him, and acting by his compulsion." These instances are primarily in cases of crime. For the most part, however, a married woman was considered "civilly dead"; she had no legal existence apart from her husband.

Women's lack of rights, then, rested in part on the principle that legally women did not exist apart from their husbands. Women could not represent themselves politically by voting because their husbands were assumed to vote for the interests of the family; a woman could not have an interest that was different from her husband's because she was a part of her husband. Further, women were considered not fully competent, rational, or responsible for themselves, particularly in politics, which was thought to be a man's world. A basic principle of politics was that women needed protection, and men should be women's protectors. Women needed protecting especially because of their roles as mothers. We will look more closely at the implications of this protection later.

A new twist was added to these justifications in the nineteenth century as democratic reforms spread and it became even more difficult to justify the exclusion of women from democratic norms. The public and private worlds, epitomized by government and economy on the one hand and the family on the other, came to be seen more and more as separate, distinct, and even antagonistic arenas of human life. The public domain was a man's world of competition, aggression, and rationality, but the private domain—the family—was a woman's world of compassion, tenderness, and loyalty. Woman's role, it was argued, was of equal importance to man's, even if women were excluded from public leadership and decision making, because women were responsible for preserving the more human side of life. Therefore, while more people acknowledged that it was *possible* for women to be active in the public world, they argued that it would be destructive to human life and values—and femininity—if women actually did so. Women's even more important political role was to raise their sons to be good American citizens, a notion Linda Kerber (1986) calls "republican motherhood."

The official legal ideology regarding women and women's citizenship can be deciphered from the text of Supreme Court decisions. It is the job of the courts to interpret the law when there are cases of dispute over what, in practical terms, the intent of the law is. The Supreme Court also has the additional and critically important power of *judicial review,* which means that it can nullify a law if it appears to contradict the spirit of the Constitution. This is what is known as "declaring a law unconstitutional." How did the Supreme Court view laws that discriminated between the sexes? Very few cases of sex discrimination reached the Court until the last thirty years, but when they did the message was clear. Granting women fewer rights than men was viewed as consistent both with the Constitution and with the principles of democracy. Following are some examples of this judicial logic.

In *Bradwell* v. *Illinois* (1873) the Court accepted the State of Illinois' argument that women could be prohibited from admission to the bar because the decision over who may be a lawyer was a state right and not something with which the federal government could interfere. One judge offered a different justification for the same decision, but one that is deeply embedded in American political culture. He said that women and men have separate spheres and different personalities and that women's naturally disqualify them from many jobs. Further, "man is, or should be, woman's protector and defender," which presumably means he has the right to protect her from unfeminine jobs. Finally, "the harmony, not to say identity, of interests and views which belong, or should belong, to the family institution is repugnant to the idea of a woman adopting a distinct and independent career from that of her husband." What about unmarried women? "The paramount destiny and mission of women are to fulfil the noble and benign offices of wife and mother. This is the law of the Creator. And the rules of society must be adapted to the general constitution of things, and cannot be based upon exceptional cases." In other words,

A march for women's suffrage in New York City, 1912.

women should be treated as though they are all wives and mothers because that is their natural role.

The next sex-discrimination case was *Minor* v. *Happersett* (1874). Virginia Minor was one of many women who tried to vote in the 1872 election, claiming that state laws forbidding women to vote were unconstitutional according to the Fourteenth Amendment because they denied women the rights of U.S. citizenship. The Supreme Court dismissed her argument quickly, saying that people (for example, women and children) could be citizens of the United States without being able to vote because states and not the federal government have the power to say who can vote. If the people (meaning men) want women to vote, they will say that through their elected representatives, who will pass appropriate laws.

Another early Supreme Court case shows an important new development in gender-related policies, but one that also had the effect of continuing different treatment of women and men. In *Muller* v. *Oregon* (1908) the issue was whether women could be prohibited from jobs requiring more than ten hours of work per day. The Court agreed that this law was acceptable; indeed it was a good thing because it was an instance in which women were being protected in their delicate positions as mothers. If a woman was not a mother, the Court seemed to assume that she would be someday and therefore must be protected as a mother at all times. (For further discussion of protective legislation, see Chapter 5.)

The Supreme Court had little else to say about women for the next six decades. Indeed few courts in the United States did anything about women's roles and status until the 1960s and 1970s other than to protect women in their roles as wives and mothers, usually by restricting their abilities to participate in activities outside the home.

The history of legislation in the nineteenth and twentieth centuries has not been marked by slow and steady progress toward democracy and full citizenship for women, but by struggles that moved women sometimes forward and sometimes backward. In the 1840s most states passed "Married Women's Property Acts," which gave (free) married women the right to own and manage property. This change, which has often gone unnoticed, was one of the great democratizing reforms of the last few centuries and probably resulted in more redistribution of wealth than any other single policy. It also opened the way for numerous other rights that are based in some way on property rights.

In the late nineteenth century many states began to grant women the right to vote and hold public office, which despite the 1874 argument of the Supreme Court had already become one of the key symbols of full citizenship in a democratic community. The Nineteenth Amendment to the Constitution, ratified in 1920, brought the rest of the states into line.

There were movements in the opposite direction as well. Toward the end of the nineteenth century, laws on abortion and contraception became stricter, and by the turn of the century abortion had become illegal across the country for the first time (Petchesky 1984). The main reasons for this legislation included protection of women from unsafe operations and protection of their morals. (Why would women be engaging in sexual activity if not to procreate?) Only in the twentieth century was the "protection of the fetus" argument accepted more widely as the primary justification for banning abortion. (For further discussion of laws on contraception and abortion, see Chapter 11.) The turn of the century also witnessed the beginning of protective labor legislation, which primarily excluded women from certain jobs.

Beginning in the 1880s Congress began to take away the tenuous grasp women had on citizenship by making women's citizenship totally dependent on that of their husbands. A succession of laws dictated that a woman's citizenship would now automatically follow that of her husband on the principle that a husband and wife are one and the husband is the pair's representative. This meant that if a foreign woman married an American citizen, she automatically became an American, and if an American woman married a foreign man, she automatically lost her citizenship and became an alien, even if no other country in the world claimed her as a citizen. Some members of Congress argued that this loss of American citizenship would be no great loss to American women, because they couldn't vote anyway.

Some of the more disastrous implications of these laws became clear during World War I, when American women who had previously married Germans found that they were regarded by the American government not just as aliens but as enemy aliens. Once the Nineteenth Amendment was ratified, such women found themselves stripped of their right to vote merely because their husbands were not U.S. citizens. Congress began to give women back their citizenship in the 1920s, but problems remained. By the mid-1920s a woman could keep her citizenship even if she married an alien, but only men could pass their citizenship on to their children. Congress finally gave women equal citizenship in this respect in 1934 (Sapiro 1984).

As increasing numbers of women sought more rights to seek education and jobs, the degree to which law and policy rest on different values for women and men became ever clearer. At every step they found that legislators and judges tolerated, approved of, and even reinforced restrictions on women, in most cases because they thought the restrictions protected women, women's roles as mothers and wives, and women's femininity.

Change has occurred, however, especially in the last two to three decades. Congress has passed many laws that place women and men on a more equal footing. Some of these focus specifically on employment and will be discussed more completely in Chapter 12. These include the 1963 Equal Pay Act, which demanded equal pay for women and men doing the same job; Title VII of the 1964 Civil Rights Act, which barred sex discrimination in hiring, firing, promotions, and working conditions; and the 1978 Pregnancy Discrimination Act, which declared that employers could not discriminate against pregnant women. Other important laws include the 1974 Educational Amendments Act, which barred discrimination in education, and the 1974 Equal Credit Opportunity Act, which increased women's opportunities to get financial credit. In 1972 Congress finally passed the Equal Rights Amendment after 50 years of consideration. The amendment did not become part of the Constitution, however, because it was not ratified by the required number of states.

The force of these laws depends on both the interpretation of courts when there are disputes and the degree to which agencies in the executive branch of government actually enforce the law. Title VII of the 1964 Civil Rights Act serves as a good example. Dozens of Supreme Court cases have refined the meaning of that statute. What exactly is sex discrimination? Under what circumstances is it illegal? Does discrimination have to be intentional to be illegal? Is the burden of proof on employers to prove they did not discriminate or on employees and job candidates to prove the employer did discriminate? Following 1971 when the Supreme Court first decided a case involving Title VII (*Phillips* v. *Martin Marietta*) it gave increasing force and breadth to the law. As President Ronald Reagan took the opportunity to add more conservative judges to the Court, however, it began issuing more restrictive interpretations in the late 1980s.

The executive branch of the government (bureaucracy) also became involved through the Equal Employment Opportunity Commission (EEOC), which was designed to help enforce the 1964 Civil Rights Act. At first the EEOC was given little real power, and therefore the act itself had little effect. Only in the 1970s, when the EEOC was given the power to sue on behalf of people who face discrimination, could Title VII be regarded as having any teeth. The executive branch became further involved when Presidents Lyndon Johnson and Richard Nixon issued executive orders outlining the affirmative action employers must pursue to comply with Title VII properly. The force of law changed with the administration in office. Ronald Reagan expressed opposition to affirmative action programs and most other policies designed to create more equality between men and women and did not vigorously enforce the laws that exist.

The Supreme Court has shifted its position on the toleration of sex discrimination. As we have seen, up through the 1960s the Court generally saw no contradiction between democratic and constitutional principles and discrimination against women, even in the face of the Fourteenth Amendment guarantees of equal protection under the law. It took until 1971 (*Reed* v. *Reed*) for the Supreme Court to declare unconstitutional a state law that discriminated on the basis of sex. From then through the end of the 1980s the Supreme Court took a very dim view of most forms of discrimination against women. The change came late in our history, but the change was substantial. For the most part, when a policy is defined in terms of *rights,* the authoritative view is now that it should apply to women and men equally.[2]

Fulfillment of Obligations

Citizenship offers both rights, which governments guarantee, and obligations, which citizens owe to their political communities. Until recently women have not had the same rights as men. Some people have argued that women also have not had the same obligations as men, and that if women want equal rights they must accept equal obligations. The three primary obligations citizens owe to the state are taxes, jury service, and military service. Have women had the same obligations as men? If not, why not? Can women share the same rights as men without sharing the same obligations?

Of the three forms of obligation individuals are said to owe the state, taxation is the one that women have historically shared with men. Indeed women can be said to have given more than their due. The obligation to pay taxes can be seen as a fair exchange for receiving rights, protection, and services, and women have received less of these than men have, although they have been subject to the same taxes. Feminists might well take the Revolutionary cry, "Taxation without representation is tyranny!" as an appropriate slogan for their own social movement.

The situation is different when we turn to jury duty. To ensure the constitutional right to a trial by a jury of peers, people are drafted to serve on juries; moreover, the Supreme Court holds the view that "the requirement of a jury's being chosen from a fair cross section of the community is fundamental to the American system of justice" (*Taylor* v. *Louisiana*). Until this century, however, women were generally barred from serving on juries. In this century many states continued to bar women outright, and others said women could serve if they wanted to (unlike men, who were drafted). The Supreme Court heard three important cases in recent decades on the question of women as jurors. In *Ballard* v. *U.S.* (1946) the Court decided that the fact that women were systematically excluded from serving on *federal* juries in California "deprives the jury system of the broad base it was designed . . . to have in our democratic society."

In 1961 case of *Hoyt* v. *Florida* reflects much more clearly the historic governmental view of women as jurors. In this case the Court considered the Florida practice of affirmative registration, or the exclusion of women from juries unless they specifically asked to serve. Few women, however, volunteered for jury duty. The Supreme Court decided that this practice was constitutional for the following reason:

> Despite the enlightened emancipation of women from the restrictions and protections of bygone years, and their entry into many parts of community life formerly considered to be reserved to men, woman is still regarded as the center of home and family life. We cannot say that it is constitutionally impermissible for a State, acting in pursuit of the general welfare, to conclude that a woman

should be relieved from the civic duty of jury service unless she herself determines that such service is consistent with her own special responsibilities.

In other words, women are exempted from this obligation to the state because they have others—motherhood and homemaking—that come first; only when those obligations are fulfilled need a woman participate in other acts of citizenship. It was not until 1975 that the Supreme Court changed its opinion. In *Taylor* v. *Louisiana* (1975) the Court said that the motherhood argument was not strong enough to relieve women of their civic responsibilities. It is essential for juries to be representative of the community, and the community includes women.

Military service is the third form of obligation citizens are supposed to owe the state on the ground that the defense of citizens cannot be provided unless citizens join in that defense. As in the case of jury duty the government assumes the right to draft people into service. Throughout most of Americn history, women have been barred from military service except in auxiliary capacities. With the exception of a few famous women, such as the Revolutionary fighter "Molly Pitcher," women participated in military action only in the gender-appropriate duties of nursing, cooking, cleaning, and so forth. Although by World War I the military included an auxiliary corps of nurses, women who served in this corps were not at first given formal military status. In World War II a few women served as bomber pilots, but they were not given formal military status and privileges.

In 1948 Congress formalized and integrated women's position in the military more thoroughly, but at the same time it put a ceiling of 2 percent on women in the military. After the end of the draft in the 1970s, defense experts were afraid there were not enough people to fill the armed services, so the ceiling was raised and women were allowed into the military academies. When Congress reinstituted registration for the draft in 1980, the original intent was to include women, but this provision was dropped in the face of substantial resistance. Recruitment into the military is now similar to recruitment into jury service in previous years: Men are subject to conscription, and women may serve if they wish. Although women may participate in most military tasks, they are still barred from combat.

The issue of women and military defense raises a multitude of questions, but discussion here will be limited to women's citizenship and obligation to the state and how this compares with men's. Three court cases illuminate this issue, including two Supreme Court cases and one case heard before a federal district court.

In 1929 the Supreme Court heard the case of *U.S.* v. *Schwimmer*.[3] Rosika Schwimmer came to the United States from Hungary in 1921. Schwimmer, a lecturer, writer, and pacifist, petitioned to become a U.S. citizen in 1926. During the course of her citizenship interview, she was asked the usual question, "If necessary, are you willing to take up arms in defense of this country?" She replied that she could not because of her pacifism, and that she would be ineligible anyway because she was a woman and she was too old. "I cannot see that a woman's refusal to take up arms is a contradiction to the oath of allegiance," she said.

Schwimmer's petition for naturalization was turned down because, the Court said, "That it is the duty of citizens by force of arms to defend our Government against all enemies whenever necessity arises, is a fundamental principle of the constitution." The Court concluded that "the fact that, by reason of sex, age, or other cause, they may be unfit to serve does not lessen their purposes or power to influence others." A willingness to serve in the armed forces was thus held to be an important condition of citizenship, even for people barred from actually doing so.

The point is even more stark in another naturalization case, from the same year, in which Martha Jane Graber, a pacifist, said she could go to the front in her profession as a nurse, but she could not bear arms. She said, "I could not bear arms; I could not kill; but I am willing to be sacrificed for this country." That was not enough for the officials; they would not grant her naturalization. In both cases women were barred from citizenship because they were pacifists even though both, as women, would be barred from military action.

If military service is an important condition of citizenship, why are women not required to serve when men are? This was a question asked by James St. Clair when he refused to serve when drafted during the war in Vietnam. He charged the government with sex discrimination because it did not draft women, and his case, *U.S. v. St. Clair*, was heard in a U.S. district court in 1968. The court rebutted St. Clair's argument by saying:

> Congress made a legislative judgment that men should be subject to involuntary induction but that women, presumably because they are "still regarded as the center of home and family life (*Hoyt* v. *State of Florida*...)" should not. In providing for involuntary service for men and voluntary service for women, Congress followed the teaching of history that if a nation is to survive, men must provide the first line of defense while women keep the home fires burning.

Once again, women's role as citizens was held to turn on women's roles as mothers and wives.

The case of *Rotsker* v. *Goldberg*, decided by the Supreme Court in 1981, evolved from the controversial reintroduction of the military draft in 1980. Both the Carter administration and Congress were divided over whether the sex discrimination in the male-only draft was constitutional. The arguments against including women in draft registration rested on two issues: the physical differences between the sexes, and the effects of military service on women's family roles. A Congressional subcommittee report states that:

> drafting women would place unprecendented strains on family life, whether in peacetime or in time of emergency. If such a draft occurred at a time of emergency, unpredictable reactions to the fact of female conscription would result. A decision which would result in a young mother being drafted and a young father remaining home with the family...cannot be taken lightly, nor its broader implications ignored (quoted in Kay 1988, 21).

How did the Supreme Court view mandatory registration of men but not women? It argued that because women are not allowed to engage in combat and because the purpose of draft registration is to provide a pool of people who can be moved quickly into combat, women need not be registered. The Court did not consider the combat restriction itself. Justices Thurgood Marshall and William Brennan dissented from this decision, arguing that it is "inconsistent with the Constitution's gurantee of equal protection of the laws."

This brief review of rights and obligation shows that women's and men's citizenship has not been treated the same way by government and that the exclusion of women from many of the activities, rights, and obligations expected of men has long been held to be consistent with the democratic principles in the Constitution. The reasons offered almost always mention women's unique roles as mothers and wives. Women have not had full citizenship in the "normal" sense; that is, in the male sense. The question that must be resolved is whether citizenship should mean different rights and obligations for men and women.

Law and Policy Concerning Women: Current Questions

In recent years there has been much discussion of "women's issues" and the degree to which policy makers address these issues. But what are women's issues? If we are going to explore the ways in which government can be used to support or change existing gender roles and norms, what specific areas of public policy and law must be considered? Why are some issues called "women's issues," while others are not?

When people talk about women's issues, they are generally referring to policies that most obviously affect women's roles and activities, or those that affect the

Leaders of the National Women's Political Caucus present their goal:
Women should be fifty percent of the delegates to the 1972 Democratic
Convention. They were. *Front row:* Gloria Steinem, Shirley Chisholm,
and Betty Friedan. *Back:* Bella Abzug.

structure and workings of the family. The policy issues that have received most attention in recent decades are discrimination in employment, education, marital property laws, taxation, social security laws, and the granting of credit, as well as abortion and birth control, family welfare programs, violence against women, and child care and support.

These are most decidedly women's issues because they have profound implications for the quality of women's lives and the amount of control they have over their lives. There is, however, a problem with the use of the term *women's issues*. It is far too restrictive and can limit our understanding of the relationship between women and government. Let us look more closely at this problem.

A moment's thought should make it seem curious that issues concerning the structure and workings of the family are designated specifically as women's issues. Don't policies affecting the family have an impact on men as well? The main reason that family policy is often discussed as a women's issue is that our dominant ideology states that women are more central to families, and families are more central to women than to men.

As many family policies are implemented they affect men as little as possible. Consider the case of child care. In a family headed by a two-career married couple, child care is still usually the primary responsibility of the woman, so it is the woman, not the man, whose job may conflict with child care. To solve this conflict, child-care centers and baby-sitters may be used to change the structure of the woman's time, without any real change in the father's time or responsibility. Moreover, because most child-care workers are still women, even widespread use of day care for children may alter the current structure of gender roles less than we might think. Women continue to have the main responsibility for child care, although more are paid for their work than in the past. Little has changed from men's point of view, except perhaps the need to pay for the child care.

One aspect of women's issues suggests why male-dominated political systems are so slow to develop policies that would be of specific benefit to women. Many of the conditions that limit or hurt women benefit men in some important way. If a medical school has only a limited number of places, men have an easier time obtaining medical training if the school discriminates against women than if it does not. The same is true of the job market. If family- and employment-related policies charge women with primary responsibility for child care, men have more freedom to engage in activities outside the home and make their own independent decisions than if policies supported a more egalitarian division of family labor. If women had more control over marital property, men would have less. If the state were more vigorous in its attempts to eradicate wife battery, men would have less power in their personal lives.

Many areas of public policy not generally specified as women's issues do affect men and women in different ways and, therefore, are as related to gender as are those more often considered women's issues. Feminist experts on public policy are increasingly researching the gender-specific implications of all government issues. Particular employment policies, for example, may cover certain sectors of the economy, such as heavy industry, but not others, such as clerical work. The fact that the labor market remains extremely segregated could make apparently gender-neutral policies discriminatory in reality.

Many other policies that appear gender neutral actually affect women and men differently. Social welfare policies affect women and men differently because women and men use different kinds of social services and benefits and because many benefits are aimed at children, who are usually the primary responsibility of women, or at older people, who are often cared for by women family members. In fact social services often involve labor that is otherwise done by women for their familes; therefore, there is often a direct tradeoff between the availability of social services and the amount of unpaid labor women do.

General fiscal policy (policy on taxes) and monetary policy (policy on the money supply) affect how much money is available to individuals and families and therefore affect consumption patterns. There is a tradeoff between certain kinds of consumption and women's labor: Below a certain threshold women will mend clothes rather than buy new ones, do more labor-intensive cooking rather than buy more expensive convenience foods and restaurant meals, or spend more time directly caring for children and other dependents rather than hire other people to do it.

The purpose of law and policy is to put into practice the values and goals of the government. As we have seen, throughout most of American history one of the government's stated purposes was to protect what was regarded as the traditional family and traditional family values.[4] This resulted in the implementation of government policies that confined women to being wives and mothers or performing other functions that were consistent with those roles. In the past two decades there has been a growing tendency to see women not just as wives and mothers but also as citizens whose rights need protecting the same as men's do; traditional family ideology is no longer as widely accepted as sufficient reason to deny equal protection to women. Although family ideology is changing, feminists argue that many women's issues still need to be addressed by government as the authoritative voice of the people.

Women, Crime, and Justice

One function of government is to help keep people secure in person and property and, in cases of crime, to dispense justice fairly and equitably. In recent years certain issues have been raised that point to a link between gender and crime and criminal justice; among these are the treatment of prostitution, rape, and wife battery and the apparent rise in crimes committed by women. The criminal justice system is an arm of government that plays an important role in establishing and enforcing values. Is the criminal justice system neutral? We will look at the evidence relating first to women as criminals and second to women as victims. (For an introduction to the issues, see Chapter 1, p. 27.)

Women as Criminals

Women constitute a very small proportion of the people arrested for crimes and an even smaller proportion of the prison population. They commit a particularly small proportion of the most serious and violent crimes and those involving use of a weapon. Although the number of crimes committed by women in the last two decades has increased, this is largely attributable to increases in property crimes rather than crimes against people.

Like men, women commit the majority of crimes against others of their own sex. Nicolette Parisi found that between 1973 and 1976 the victims of male criminals were male 72 percent of the time, and the victims of female criminals were female 85 percent of the time (1982, 120). The picture looks different for murder: About 80 percent of both male and female murderers kill men (Wilbanks 1982, 169). The more serious the crime, the more likely a female criminal's victim is to be male. This is true to only a weak degree for male criminals (Parisi 1982, 120).

When women use weapons they tend to be kitchen knives and other household implements related to female roles (Parisi 1982, 118–19). Despite the general view that women tend either to be men's accomplices or that they get men to commit crimes for them, research shows that, for the most part, they tend to work alone. If they work with someone else, they tend to work with women (Parisi 1982, 113). So the crime world, like other domains of social life, is segregated by sex.

Why have women's crimes against property recently increased at a faster rate than men's? Three general answers have been offered. One popular answer in the public press is that the women's movement has helped eliminate differences between the sexes in many areas, including criminal activity (see, e.g., Freda Adler 1975). This view is androcentric in that it assumes that if men and women become more similar, women will be more like men, and men will stay the same. Research that tests the hypothesis does not support it (Parisi 1982, 123).

A second reason offered for the increase in women's property crimes is that changes in employment give women more opportunity to commit property crimes (see, e.g., Rita Simon 1975). The evidence for this hypothesis is mixed. Among single women, labor force participation rates are related to property crime (Parisi 1982, 123). On the other hand, the segregation of the labor force did not decrease much during the years in which the crime rate changed. Moreover, we need evidence not just that more women are employed, but that they are moving into positions that increase opportunities for crime, and that the women entering these new positions are the new criminals.

Some authors suggest that women's crime has not changed in type substantially but that arrest rates have risen for traditional female crimes such as shoplifting (see e.g., Steffensmeier 1981; for further review of this theory, see Rafter and Stanko 1982). Because there is no way of knowing how many female criminals weren't arrested in the past, this hypothesis is particularly hard to test. Research indicates, however, that the increase in property-related crimes among women may be accounted for by women's committing more of the same types of crimes they committed in the past, which suggest that some change can be accounted for by changes in arrest rates.

Like other women, female criminals can be viewed through the prism of gender ideology. In their review of research on female criminality, Nicole Hahn Rafter and Elizabeth Anne Stanko note

> Nearly all traditional commentaries on female offenders, whether focused on the serious or the minor criminal, have been overwhelmingly concerned with violations of gender prescriptions. . . . [Theorists] have attributed . . . low arrest

rates to the inherently law-abiding nature of women. Accordingly, they have assessed the female criminal by the fit of her crime to men's crime and the extent to which she violated her naturally law-abiding nature. Since crime was assumed to be a masculine phenomenon, women who committed crime were thought to do so either because they were too masculine (the evil women theory) or because they had been led astray (the bad little girl theory) (1982, 6–7).

To what degree is treatment of the female offender shaped by gender? There is considerable debate over whether female criminals are given different sentences than men for the same crimes. Some states discriminate by law; some have statutes that require indeterminate (and therefore maximum) sentences for women but not for men. One of the arguments that has been posed for longer sentences for women is that they are more likely than men to benefit from rehabilitation, so it is worthwhile to incarcerate them longer. In this light it is interesting to learn that from the time of the first separate women's prison established in Indiana in 1869, women's prisons were generally called reformatories. Another view is that women receive longer sentences when their crimes seem particularly unfeminine because they are breaking not only the law but also gender norms.

Other observers have argued that judges and prosecutors act chivalrously toward women by giving them lighter sentences. Some suggest that people find it difficult to believe that women can be as dangerous as men and therefore don't lock them away for as long. Just as the rehabilitation argument can bolster stricter sentencing, it can also support more lenient sentencing. Finally some argue that because women are more likely than men to have responsibility for child care, the presence of children may be taken into account because incarceration usually means lengthy separation of mother from child.

After controlling for the type of crime and other factors it appears that there is a tendency for women to receive more lenient treatment than men in certain sentencing and parole situations and harsher treatment in others. For example, Parisi notes that "although it is fair to conclude that the direction of differential disposition is most often advantageous, it occasionally appears that negative (punitive) treatment is accorded females for 'manly' crimes" (1982, 215). In any case it appears that women are now given longer prison sentences than used to be true (Rix 1988, 304).

There are some differences between the prison experiences of men and women. Because so few women are incarcerated compared to men, women's prisons and prison programs are much neglected. They are underfunded and poorly equipped, even in comparison to men's prisons. On the other hand, the old reformatory model persists. Nicole Rafter points out that this model is apparent in "its characteristically low security; its tendency to provide living quarters that (to the outsider, at least) resemble college dormitory rooms rather than cells; and in its paternalistic aspects, such as its tendency to treat female inmates as errant children" (1982, 256).

Prisons reinforce gender norms through their rehabilitation programs. Occupational training in women's facilities, for example, typically includes hairdressing and cosmetology. This "little house" environment is supposed to turn female convicts into proper women. The staff at some women's prisons is reported to be concerned that the women not use "unladylike" language.

Male and female life in prison is different in other ways that need to be taken into account in designing prison programs. Nancy Stoller Shaw (1982) has outlined some important health problems of incarcerated women. Women experience abnormal weight gain in the early months of their sentences as a result of "required meal attendance, poor diet, boredom, distress, and lack of exercise" (264). They also suffer high rates of gynecological problems. The use of prescribed psychotropic drugs is up to ten times higher for female than male prisoners. Although prisoners of both sexes may suffer from isolation from their families, mothers in particular suffer from separation from their children. In most prisons women are segregated from their infants, including those born while they are in prison.

One of the notable differences between men's and women's prisons is that women's prisons are less violent. One of the most common dangers for young men in prison is brutal rape, but such attacks are relatively more rare among imprisoned women. Many observers claim that while male social life in prison is violent and hierarchical, women tend to develop closer relationships and networks resembling families as a way of coping with life inside.

Thus far we have talked about "crime" in general without focusing on specific forms of crime. Let us now look briefly at two different types of crime to probe further into the relationship between criminal justice and gender. One is the primarily female crime of prostitution and the other is the apparently gender neutral crime of murder.

Between 100,000 and 500,000 American women are working prostitutes. One of the main facts about prostitution is that it is a "women's" crime only because most of the people arrested for it are women. The male participants in prostitution, including the pimps and especially the clients, are relatively untouched by the law. Prostitutes are the subject of legal attack as though it is only they and not the men who pay for their services who are the wrongdoers.

The state has long had an ambivalent attitude toward prostitution. Officials and other interested parties cannot seem to decide whether prostitution is a crime with victims that must be eradicated, a victimless crime or social ill that should be contained and eliminated if possible, an unfortunate aspect of life that should be kept out of sight as much as possible, or a useful enterprise in certain circumstances.

Does prostitution have victims? Those who are forced to take part in prostitution, prostitute and client alike, surely are. Those who become diseased or subject to other crimes because of it are also victims; these include prostitutes, clients, and, in the case of disease, the families of either. The question of disease has become even more serious since the spread of AIDS in the 1980s. After analyzing the findings of a study by the Harvard Center for Criminal Justice Barbara Milman concluded (1980, 62):

> Looking at all the data, one cannot say that prostitution is a victimless crime. On the other hand, the data . . . suggest that prostitution victimizes society only in specific and limited ways. On the basis of the data, it does not appear that prostitution presents the far-reaching dangers to society that may once have been imagined.

One specific conclusion was that the prostitutes themselves are as victimized as anyone else.

Milman argues that if prostitution is more a moral and health problem than a crime problem, criminal sanctions are inappropriate. Many people now recommend alternative treatments of prostitution that do not put the full burden of punishment on the prostitute. Even if rehabilitative programs are more widely used for prostitutes, however, will the public also support programs to rehabilitate the men who buy sex? Would most people even think that men who buy sex are in need of rehabilitation?

It is important to note that the state has accepted and, in some cases, supported prostitution. Police have often turned a blind eye to prostitution, only occasionally hauling in women to beef up a lagging arrest rate. Some people claim that the system of charging and fining prostitutes from time to time constitutes a quasi-official license to practice. (This is not to say that prostitutes are not sent to jail. They are.) Police find prostitutes useful informers because they know what is happening on the streets. It has also been noted that the areas around state capitals and party nominating conventions are sometimes known for a high concentration of prostitutes, who apparently find good business there. Prostitution has sometimes gained acceptance at the highest levels. In the early 1970s President Nixon allowed prostitutes onto U.S. military bases in Vietnam to "help morale" among the troops. Even though these women were, in a sense, employees of the U.S. government, they were refused free medical treatment for the resulting venereal diseases and pregnancies.[5]

At first glance murder seems to be a straightforward gender-neutral crime. However, it also poses some interesting questions for the study of gender and law enforcement.

Homicides perpetrated by women are particularly likely to involve family members and to take place at home (Wilbanks 1982). Further, as indicated earlier, most women who murder kill men. Female murderers are more often first offenders than male murderers, and they tend to use as weapons any implements that are handy rather than firearms. These points suggest that a large proportion of the murders committed by women are done in self-defense.

Violent crimes against women, including rape and wife battery, are rampant. Until 1977 women who killed in self-defense against rape or battery almost always lost their cases in court. The reasons are based on the legal definition of the self-defense plea, the characteristics of murder by females, and stereotyped views of women.

Two criteria must be met to claim justifiable homicide on the grounds of self-defense:

1. The killer must have had a reasonable apprehension of danger and a reasonable perception of the immanence of that danger. In other words, the danger does not have to have been real as determined by later investigation, but it must have appeared to be real to a reasonable person (traditionally, a "reasonable man"). And killing has to have appeared to be the only viable course of action.
2. Deadly force cannot be used against nondeadly force.

The problem for women who kill in self-defense is whether women can be considered reasonable and what constitutes deadly force. Women have often been labeled hysterical and overemotional, and their testimony has therefore been regarded with great suspicion. It is difficult for a woman who has been raped, for example, to convince the court that a rape actually occurred and that she did not "ask for it" or enjoy it. It is even more difficult for a woman to convince a court that there was a reasonable probability of being killed as well. The courts have often held that a person may not use a deadly weapon against someone using "only" naked hands. This ignores the fact that if a relatively small woman is victimized—especially one who, like most women, has not been trained in the use of physical force against others—an unarmed man may easily exert deadly force with no weapon but his body.

The case of *State* v. *Wanrow*, heard by the supreme court of Washington State in 1977, marked the beginning of change in cases in which women claim self-defense to justify a killing. The court argued that the law and judicial proceedings tend to view women from an androcentric perspective and do not consider the perceptions and physical conditions of women. The court further argued that the standards of self-defense presented to the jury "through the persistent use of the masculine gender leaves the jury with the impression the objective standard to be applied is that applicable to an altercation between two men." In other words, *he* is not a gender-neutral term. Since that case courts have moved toward a fairer consideration of women who kill in self-defense. This case represents a dramatic event in the history of criminal justice: a court's recognition that the legal system has been androcentric.

Cases involving sexuality—or apparent sexuality, as when a woman kills her attacker while defending herself against rape—raise other problems as well. Courts and the public have generally not been able to understand why a woman would kill in self-defense during a rape. As one person said during the 1977 trial of Inez Garcia, a rape victim who killed her attacker, "you can't kill someone for trying to give you a good time." This stands in marked contrast to men's situation. The courts have generally acquitted men who use deadly force to protect themselves from rape by another man. And these are not the only situations in which men have had more rights to violence against what they perceived to be misplaced sexuality. The old "paramour" laws, which permitted murder in reaction to uncovering adultery, were based on similar norms. Men who found their wives in bed with another man could get away with murder; women who found husbands in bed with another woman could not.

Women as Victims

Wife battery and rape are two forms of criminal violence against women that have received considerable attention in recent years. They share many characteristics that demonstrate the role of gender ideology in law enforcement and the special problems women face. We will look at some of the similarities between these two crimes first and then turn to some issues specific to each type of crime. (For discussion of violence against women as a health problem, see Chapter 5; for discussion of the relationship between violence and sexuality, see Chapter 10.)

Both rape and wife battery are among the most underreported crimes. Perhaps one in four rapes is reported to the police, and one in ten cases of serious wife battery is reported. Only a very tiny proportion of rape and wife battery cases end in conviction and punishment of the offender. In both cases women fear reprisals if they do anything about these crimes; in both cases offenders are unlikely to be jailed, thus leaving them free to mete out reprisals.

Both rape and wife battery have been tolerated under the law and in public opinion to some degree. Under common law husbands were allowed to "chastise" their wives physically, as Blackstone wrote, "in the same moderation that a man is allowed to correct his apprentices or children; for whom the master or parent is also liable in some cases to answer" (quoted in Kay 1988, 192). This law, enlightened in that it stressed moderation, used the "rule of thumb": A man should not hit his wife with a stick any thicker than his thumb. Even in the early 1970s only a small number of states actually allowed a woman to sue her husband for intentional physical attacks (Rohrbaugh 1980, 359). The lawmakers were afraid that such suits would destroy the "peace and harmony" of the home.

Many people still think it is necessary for men to hit their wives from time to time, and many men certainly act as though they have the right to do so. In one experiment (cited in Rohrbaugh 1980, 351) psychologists staged fights in public to see how people would respond. Male passersby came to the aid of a man being attacked by another man or a woman and a woman being attacked by a woman. They did not try to assist a woman being attacked by a man. Why? Presumably because a man attacking a woman may be the woman's husband and therefore have proprietary rights over her. In this case violence is regarded as a private matter with which individuals, and the law, do not like to interfere.

The husband's proprietary rights are also apparent in rape laws. Most states define rape as a situation in which a woman is coerced into having sexual relations by a man who is not her husband. Men within these states who force their wives to have sexual relations against their wills are acting within the law. Once again, neither the law nor the public generally has wanted to interfere in what is viewed as a private matter between husband and wife. In addition, it has long been held that consent to sexual relations is given by entering into marriage and cannot be revoked during the course of marriage. A number of states no longer accept the "marital exclusion" in rape, or at least not as automatically as they did in the past.

The public and legal treatment of rape and wife battery also involves the issue of "victim precipitation," the idea that the victim has in some way provoked the attack against herself. Courts have long accepted this idea with regard to rape. In a notorious case in the late 1970s a Wisconsin judge argued that women are raped because they wear halter tops and because there is general promiscuity in society. The judge was removed from office by an irate public but many police, prosecutors, and attorneys continue to hold this view, as reflected by the fact that many attorneys spend as much time interrogating the rape victim (to find out what she did wrong) as they do the rapist himself, and police sometimes ask rape victims whether they enjoyed the rape or whether they had an orgasm.

Because of this belief in victim precipitation, women have often needed physical evidence that they fought "to within an inch of their lives" in order to prove their cases. In other words, if they show they suffered considerable brutality other than rape, they may be able to get rape convictions. If a woman managed to kill her attacker in her efforts, however, she could be in even worse trouble. Similarly, victims of wife battery are often thought to get neurotic pleasure out of their maltreatment: Otherwise why would they not leave their husbands? The insensitive treatment of female victims at the hands of the criminal justice system has often been labeled the second or double victimization of women; they are victimized first by the criminal and then by the criminal justice system. Another effect of these legal and public views is that many victimized women actually feel guilty for what was done to them.

Elizabeth Anne Stanko (1982) found that prosecutors are wary about pursuing cases involving these crimes against women because they tend to believe either that women will not be credible witnesses or that women will drop their cases and leave the prosecutors with unsuccessful cases on their records. Prosecutors consider how the witness will be viewed by the jury, and whether the victim will be convincing enough to yield a conviction. Stanko argues that they assess victims through stereotypes of women accusing men of rape or battery.

Police and courts have been particularly loathe to involve themselves in cases of wife battery. Assault within the family is not labeled "assault" but "domestic disturbance." The word *disturbance* masks and trivializes a multitude of problems, some of them recognized at least implicitly by police. Police give low priority to domestic-disturbance calls partly because such calls are dangerous to the police officers involved. (More police are injured or killed when answering these calls than when answering any others.) A 1971 study in Kansas City showed that in 50 percent of the intraspousal homicides the police had earlier been called at least five times because of domestic disturbances; in 85 percent of the cases they had been called at least once. About half of all police calls are for family disputes (Klein 1982). In 1985 FBI figures revealed that 30 percent of all female homicide victims were killed by their husbands or boyfriends (Rix 1988, 297).

In the 1960s it was explicit police policy in most areas to try to mediate domestic problems and avoid arresting anyone (Klein 1982). It soon became clear that these policies were pushed to their limits. Police and courts sometimes refused to arrest violent husbands even when their wives requested it, and they refused to enforce restraining orders against violent husbands.

By the late 1970s women began to respond by suing police officers and court employees. They argued that they were being denied equal protection in comparison to people assaulted in places other than the home and that the "arrest avoidance policy was based on the broad and archaic sex-based assumptions that a man is privileged to punish his wife" (Woods 1981, 43).

As a result of such suits, many cities have changed their policies. Police and courts have also begun to cooperate with such agencies as shelters for battered women, which now exist in many towns and cities. These shelters, which offer refuge to victimized women and their children have often received partial government funding in response to efforts by the feminist groups that established them. Unfortunately many lost their funding as a result of social program cutbacks in the early 1980s. The withdrawal of funds was urged particularly by conservatives who wished to "protect the family" and believed that these "homes for runaway wives" interfere with family life.

Some changes have occurred in rape law and policy in recent years. Although old attitudes die hard, many police forces have begun to work more closely with community-based rape crisis centers, and they employ specially trained police officers, often women, to deal with rape victims. Changes in the law have also helped. Until recently a victim's prior sexual history could be used in court to "prove" that she probably "asked for it," but this is now illegal in most jurisdictions. However, it is still extremely difficult for a woman to get her rapist convicted unless the offender is a stranger, which is the case in only a minority of rapes.

Some states have followed the example of Michigan, which in 1974 enacted a rape-reform law that classified sexual offenses by degree in categories ranging from sexual contact to penetration by force with a weapon involved. Women's organizations have worked hard to educate people about the remaining problems and offer assistance to women who need it. Change remains slow, however, and the criminal justice system is still at least partially based on a gender ideology that defines protection differently for women and men.

Women in the Criminal Justice System

There is now considerably more awareness of issues relating to women and criminal justice than was true only a few years ago. Much of the impetus for change has come from the women's movement and from women who have become victims of crime and were politicized by the experiences they had, both during the crime itself and in the course of trying to seek help from the criminal justice system.

Until recently women have had little hand in the formal enforcement and administration of justice. As late as 1987 no major city had a female police chief, although eleven smaller cities did. Women were only 5 percent of police and detective supervisors and only 11 percent of nonsupervisory police officers and detectives. Like women in other traditionally male fields, women in law enforcement have begun to organize themselves in groups such as the Committee on Women in Federal Law Enforcement and the International Association of Women Police. It will be interesting to see if further changes are instigated by women inside the law enforcement and criminal justice system.

Women's Political Participation and Influence

It is commonly argued that women have been kept out of politics almost entirely, and that for a variety of reasons women do not participate in politics. In fact women have never been as fully absent from American political life as many people believe. There is no question, however, that women still have considerably less political power than men, and only a small fraction of governmental decision makers are women. To what extent do women participate in politics? How much influence do they have? Does it matter whether more women become active in politics or even obtain positions of political power? (For an introduction to some of these issues, see Chapter 1, p. 28.)

Mass Participation

After the long hard battle for women's suffrage was won, many activists were disappointed to find that women were not as likely to use their right to vote as men were. Although the gap narrowed somewhat, this remained true until recently. For about the last decade, however, there has been very little difference between women's and men's voting rates. Indeed in some elections, among people who are young, highly educated, or black more women have voted than men. Since turnout rates for both men and women fluctuate from election to election, the size of the difference between them depends on the election. Women and men are also about evenly matched in participation in such campaign activities as displaying buttons and bumper stickers, going to meetings and rallies, and doing campaign work. Women give less money to political campaigns than men do, because women have less money than men do.

It should not be surprising that women are so involved in electoral campaigns. Women have long been known as the backbone of the political parties—making phone calls, ringing doorbells, stuffing envelopes, compiling lists, and watching polls, as well as cooking and cleaning up for party and campaign picnics and other functions. Women became involved in this kind of work even before they had the right to vote.

It has taken a long time for women to reach near parity with men in electoral participation. Research suggests a number of reasons for this:

1. Voting is a habit that most newly enfranchised groups, including immigrants and young people, take time to develop.
2. Education and related socioeconomic factors determine how politically active people are; in general, the greater the gap in education, the greater the gap in electoral participation.
3. Gender ideology and gender roles have had an impact. In the 1920s many women didn't vote because they didn't think it was appropriate. Women with an egalitarian gender ideology are still more likely to be active in elections than those who are more androcentric in their views of social and political roles (Sapiro 1983). Women, especially single women, who are responsible for children also are less politically active than women without children.

Electoral participation is only one category of political participation. Women have long been noted for engaging in politics and community action through churches, clubs, and numerous other organizations, and government figures showing that women constitute a majority of the people involved in volunteer work (U.S. Bureau of the Census 1989, 371) support this view. One of the largest nonpartisan political organizations, the League of Women Voters, is predominantly female. Research shows that among women and men active in community political organizations, women probably give many more hours of work (Lee 1977).

The importance of community and organization work in politics is underestimated because of the usual emphasis on elections. It is important to remember that a large part of our public problem solving is done by people who are not government officials but are motivated to become involved. This is especially true at the local level, where issues about education, land use, and the availability of other services are most focused.

The image of the "volunteer lady" is an old and familiar one in American history. This image goes back to the nineteenth century "Club Movement." At the end of the nineteenth century women organized and became increasingly active in formal and informal organizations that served many different purposes. Some were organized for cultural activities and self-improvement, and others were organized for social philanthropy, or volunteer work and community service. Historians point out that even groups not organized explicitly for the purpose of participating in politics nevertheless often engaged women in politics or political discussion. Many women's clubs, for example, served as audiences for suffragists as they traveled across the country lecturing on women and the vote.

In 1890 many of these clubs joined together to form the General Federation of Women's Clubs (GFWC), which had over a million members by 1910. Many GFWC affiliates were instrumental in establishing the early framework for public social welfare programs through their work in health, education, poverty relief, and municipal reform. Club women were among the chief lobbyists for local and state government responsibility for social welfare. Interestingly, although these women thought it was crucial for women to be involved in "social housekeeping" and public affairs, the GFWC did not endorse the women's suffrage amendment to the Constitution until 1914 because many of its members thought that their own successes proved that women already had enough power in government, and they did not want women to become involved in "dirty" partisan politics. On the other hand, these same successes may have made it necessary for them to change their minds. As government increasingly took up their concerns with public policy and management, women found their continued involvement limited in those states that barred women from voting or holding office.

There is an unfortunate stereotype that women's organizational and grass-roots political activity involved only middle-class white women. This is far from the truth. Although middle-class women historically had more time to devote to these efforts (at least until the 1930s, because until then they were unlikely to be employed and likely to have domestic servants), women of different classes and many ethnic and racial groups organized for community action and problem solving. For example, as early as the 1820s to 1840s black women organized literary societies that also helped needy black women and gave financial assistance to black newspapers (Giddings 1984, 49). There was a large black women's club movement. White ethnic immigrant women also formed many organizations around the turn of the century.

Women have tended to be less active than men in protests and demonstrations, partly because demonstrations are regarded as particularly unfeminine political activities. Women with a more egalitarian gender ideology are more likely to participate in such activities than other women. This is not to say that women with more traditional or antifeminist gender ideologies do not engage in protest, as the recent antiabortion demonstrations show. Another reason for women's relatively low levels of participation in demonstrations is that many, such as labor strikes and pickets, depend on organizational membership, which is related to gender. Although this is changing, women's jobs have been much less likely than men's to be organized, and women constitute only about a quarter of the members of labor unions.

Even if women have been less likely than men to participate in protest activities and demonstrations it is important to recognize that women have organized and engaged in these activities when they felt there was no alternative. Women's independent labor activity goes back at least to the 1820s (Foner 1982; Kessler-Harris 1982). There are many instances in U.S. history of women organizing boycotts and other consumer-related political actions. A good example is the 1917 boycott that resulted in massive demonstrations among Jewish immigrant women living in New York's Lower East Side (Frank 1985). The women's suffrage movement itself, of course, provides numerous examples of women's protest activity. This tradition continues to the present day with women's "Take Back the Night" marches protesting violence against women and women's peace marches and camps.

There have been few major social movements in American history in which women were not involved in large numbers; among the more notable are the movements for abolition, temperance, health reform, peace, progressivism and municipal reform, civil rights, and, of course, women's liberation and suffrage.[6]

Women are now nearly as active as men in mass-level politics. Thanks in part to education and changing gender role ideology, more people than ever now think that political activity is appropriate for women. But unfortunately it appears that girls are still socialized to express less interest in politics than boys (Owen and Dennis 1988).

Women's gender-related roles help shape the degree to which women become politically active as well as the ways in which this activism is manifest. Motherhood has a greater impact on political activity than fatherhood; child-care responsibility can inhibit women's participation in some aspects of politics (especially for single mothers), but it can also push women, especially homemakers, into political activity in local and school affairs (McGlen 1980; Jennings 1979; Sapiro 1983). The mere fact that a woman is either employed or a housewife does not have as strong a relationship with political participation as some people think (McDonough 1982; Sapiro 1983). Employment can expand the number of contacts a woman has, and her occupation may help shape the kinds of interests she has. More important, however, may be the way a woman interprets her own roles and how compatible she thinks her roles are with political activism. It is important to remember that for a long time Sojourner Truth's occupation was slave and Elizabeth Cady Stanton's was homemaker; neither of them shied away from political activity.

Women as Political Leaders

At higher levels of politics, men's and women's involvement differs more markedly. The more powerful or authoritative, the better paid, or the more visible a political position is, the less likely it is that a woman holds it. Despite women's yeoman work in political parties, until recently they have been a small minority of the delegates selected to participate in decision making at the national nominating conventions. Only a small number of women are among the major party decision makers. Until recently women were not given many top decision-making roles in electoral campaigns, although this is changing. In 1988, for example, women were very prominent among the top levels of campaign management. But women still constitute only a small percentage of local, state, and national elected and appointed officials, not yet more than about 15 percent.

Why is this the case? If women are so active in politics at the mass level, why are so few influential and professional political actors and governmental administrators women? Different people cite different reasons, including: (1) Women aren't motivated, (2) women's roles and femininity are incompatible with professional politics, and (3) discrimination and sexism have hindered women. We will review the evidence for each.

It has often been said that women don't become political leaders because they are not interested in politics or don't want to be leaders. We can rule out the question of political interest immediately. Studies show that women are about as interested in politics as men are. We have already seen that at the mass level women are almost as active as men, and in some cases more so. The few percentage points difference between women's and men's political interest and mass-level activity couldn't possibly account for the fact that men outnumber women nearly six to one in state and local offices (the most favorable ratio) and forty-nine to one (as long as there are two women there) in the Senate.

Studies of men and women who are already very active in politics—community activists and national nominating convention delegates, for example—show that women are less likely to want to hold a political office, although the difference is not large enough to explain the substantial gap in the proportion of male and female officeholders (Lee 1977; Sapiro and Farah 1980; Jennings and Farah 1981).

Several reasons have been offered to explain the gender differences in political ambition. One is that women are naturally less competitive and aggressive, which causes women not to want to hold positions of political power and authority. We have already discussed this hypothesis in Chapter 1. There is no evidence that sex differences, even in aggression, exist to the degree this hypothesis suggests. It is difficult to understand why an underlying propensity to attack people physically or psychologically would qualify a person to become a member of a local school board or the House of Representatives. An ability to engage in competition may be helpful in gaining many types of governmental positions, but that is true of a wide range of activities in which women participate (such as ballet).

Lack of self-confidence may contribute to women's limited political ambitions, although this has yet to be tested directly. It is true that politically active women expect to attain lower offices than men do (Farah and Hoag 1976). A very large proportion of politically active women also expect to encounter discouragement and discrimination in politics, especially from their male colleagues (Lee 1977).

Another reason for ambition differences between women and men rests on the second major explanation often offered for the low number of women in positions of political leadership: Politics is incompatible with women's roles and femininity. It has often been argued that conflict between women's family roles and political ambitions leads them to reject, or at least delay, the commitments to politics that holding a political office entails. Research shows that women and men both feel that family and political roles can conflict, but that women tend to resolve these conflicts in favor of the family and men make the opposite choice. This is why comparisons of male and female officeholders show that the women are less likely to be married or to have young children than the men are (Sapiro 1982a).

It is important to note that the role incompatibility problem can offer only a limited explanation for women's absence from governmental offices. We have already seen that, at least in community politics, women activists may actually give more time than male activists. A wide range of government positions are actually part- or full-time occupations. A majority of American women show their willingness to seek employment by having chosen to do so. Why should women view political and governmental jobs any differently from other jobs? Do these jobs simply constitute another male-dominated sector in a segregated labor market?

If we examine the channels through which people enter political and governmental positions, it is clear that segregation takes place early in the process. An extremely large proportion of legislators and most judges are lawyers, and the law remains a male-dominated field. Business and engineering are two other male-dominated professions that supply many political and governmental leaders. One study, however, suggests that gender differences in education and occupation do not account for the large differences in the numbers of male and female officeholders (Welch 1978).

These observations suggest a third reason for the low numbers of women in positions of political leadership and authority: discrimination. There is adequate evidence that women are kept back by discrimination. Women in politics often testify about the discrimination they face in the political parties and other mixed or male-dominated political organizations. The same sort of discrimination appears to exist in local, state, and federal jobs as in other jobs. (Recall the discussion of school administrators in Chapter 4.) A study of congressional races from 1916 to 1978 shows that women are put forward more often than men as candidates for seats their party is unlikely to win (Gertzog and Simard 1980). Women already in political office report that they are subject to various forms of discrimination, and they are often left out by men who prefer to work and talk among themselves.

As in other cases, not all of this discrimination is conscious. One researcher did an experiment in which she gave university students a speech to read that was supposedly given by a candidate for the House of Representatives (Sapiro 1982b). Half the students were told the speech was by Joan Leeds, the other half were told the speech was by John Leeds. Comparing the responses of the two groups showed that John's policy proposals were regarded as better than Joan's and that John was considered more likely to win. Men, but not women, judged John to be more competent than Joan at dealing with military, business, farm, and crime issues.

Attitudes toward women in politics are changing. For example, the Gallup Poll sometimes asks "If your party nominated a woman for president, would you vote for her if she were qualified for the job?" In 1971 29 percent said no, while in 1984 17 percent said no (Toner 1987). In a 1986 national sample of the high school class of 1980 91 percent of the men and 96 percent of the women agreed that "Women should be considered as seriously as men for jobs as executives or politicians" (U.S. Department of Education 1988, 334).

Even if the majority of Americans indicate they would seriously consider female candidates, and increasing numbers of women win elections, most people think women and men have different qualifications for public office. Table 8-1 shows women's and men's responses to a public opinion poll asking them to say whether they thought a male or female candidate would be more likely to have certain characteristics. These data reveal a number of interesting patterns. Women and men did not differ very much in their responses. A minority of the people responding to the poll thought a male and female candidate would be similar in most characteristics.

At the same time they are less agreed than one might think about which sex is more marked by which characteristic. They were more likely to give women the edge in honesty, compassion, standing up for their beliefs, and liberalism and more likely to think men would be tougher and back arms control. Women's and men's

TABLE 8-1

Perceived Differences between Women and Men
as Candidates for Public Office, 1987

Characteristic		Male candidate	Female candidate	No difference
		Candidate who would do a better job		
Speaks honestly about issues	Women	10	36	45
	Men	13	28	50
Hard working	Women	16	23	53
	Men	23	17	52
Handles a crisis	Women	27	22	42
	Men	39	10	42
Compassionate	Women	6	53	34
	Men	7	52	35
Stands up for beliefs regardless of political consequences	Women	12	31	48
	Men	17	26	48
Backs arms control	Women	43	16	22
	Men	37	20	36
Favors women's rights	Women	5	58	29
	Men	6	54	33
Tough	Women	31	15	44
	Men	35	12	33
More liberal	Women	19	28	41
	Men	16	31	42
More conservative	Women	26	26	39
	Men	31	20	39
Able to handle family responsibilities while serving in office	Women	19	34	39
	Men	26	25	40

Notes: The table is based on responses by 1502 registered voters to a survey conducted by Hickman-Maslin Research.

SOURCE: *New York Times,* 13 August 1987, 8.

perceptions differ in only a couple of respects. Men are more likely than women to think men are better at handling crises. Both sexes are more likely to think someone of their own sex is more hard working and better able to handle family responsibilities while serving in office.

There is one last explanation for the small numbers of women in public office, one that many scholars are convinced is the major roadblock women now face (Darcy, Welch, and Clark 1987; Carroll 1985). Even if women's ambitions are high, they get the right training, they can manage their public and private roles, and discrimination continues to decrease, the increase in women's numbers in public office depends on certain structural opportunities. Let us take the House of Representatives as an example. Incumbents (current officeholders) are rarely defeated for reelection. A woman's best chance of getting elected to the House and increasing the number of women is to run for an open seat in a district dominated by her party. This fortunate confluence of events rarely occurs. At least one calculation taking into account such structural factors predicts that at best women may constitute about one-third of the House members the decade after the turn of the century. Parity is much further off (Darcy, Welch, and Clark 1987).

The Impact of Women in Politics

What difference does it make whether women participate in politics? One way of answering this question is to see whether males and females think about politics differently. There is some evidence that some of their attitudes differ, and that this may have a significant effect on government.

The conventional wisdom has been that women are more conservative and moralistic and more passive and trusting than men in their political thinking and that they tend to oppose the use of force and violence and support social welfare programs. Let us consider what public opinion surveys reveal about this characterization. Some of this conventional wisdom was supported and some contradicted by the appearance in the 1980s of the "gender gap," some clear differences in public opinion.

In the 1950s women were somewhat more likely than men to support the Republican Party. In recent years women have identified more with the Democratic Party than men. Although they have been about equally likely to identify with the Republican Party, they are less likely to call themselves Independents.

Women and men have reacted differently to presidential candidates a number of times. Women were more supportive of the Republican candidate in 1952 and 1956 (Eisenhower), 1960 (Nixon), and 1976 (Ford). They cast a higher proportion of their votes for the Democrat in 1964 (Johnson), 1968 (Humphrey), 1972 (McGovern), 1980 (Carter), 1984 (Mondale), and 1988 (Dukakis). Women and men gave a majority of their votes (usually by small margins) to different people in 1960, 1968, and 1976.

More women than men oppose policies relying on or encouraging violence and tend to see violence as a last resort. Women are less hawkish on military and defense issues, more opposed to capital punishment, and more supportive of gun control than men (Sapiro 1983). A survey of the foreign policy opinions of American leaders shows similar results: Female leaders tended to oppose militarism and the use of the CIA to undermine governments and to support the use of international organizations like the United Nations (Holsti and Rosenau 1981).

Recent figures show that women are more supportive than men of legislation strengthening protection of the environment. Women have shown themselves to be more supportive of government policies to help the poor and guarantee full employment. Women's support of feminism and so-called women's issues is uneven. Women are more moralistic in the traditional sense of many issues, which may account for some of their ambivalence about feminist issues; more women than men support prayer in public schools, for example.

In contrast to the view that women are more passive and more trusting of government, by the late 1970s and early 1980s there was evidence that in some ways women had become more cynical than men. Women were less confident about the economic future of the United States and more likely to feel that this country would get into a war.

Women's and men's political attitudes are quite similar in most respects, but they do differ in important ways. There is certainly reason to believe that these differences stem not from innate predispositions but from the differences in the kinds of lives they lead. Even so it is hard to make generalizations about gender differences in political orientation and their sources and implications. Many of the gender differences that appear in U.S. public opinion polls, for example, do not show up in the public opinion polls of other countries.

Would it make any difference if more women held positions of authority? Thus far there is little evidence, partly because the women currently in government work within a predominantly male system. Experimental evidence shows that women who are identified as feminists may have difficulty gaining office (Perkins and Fowlkes 1980). Other evidence shows that even when males and females claim to support similar policies, it is the women in public office who generally do most of the work to put more egalitarian gender principles into practice. In most other ways, however, research suggests there is little difference between the behavior of women and men in political and governmental office. Studies of state legislators show women and men voting in similar ways and sponsoring the same number of pieces of legislation. Research on judges shows that, by and large, male and female judges make the same kinds of decisions (Gruhl, Spohn, and Welch 1981).

Even though we cannot yet know whether policies would be very different in a more sexually balanced government, some things would surely change. Government would be more representative of society as a whole. Women would have more of a role in governing their own lives as citizens. And, to the degree that government is a model of society's values, that model would show women as leaders and full participants.

Women, Feminism, and Democracy

The people of the United States have long thought of their government as close to ideal in the principles and practice of democracy. American schoolchildren still learn that theirs is a government "of the people, by the people, and for the people." There is no question that this government is indeed one of the most democratic in the world. But has it been as democratic as Americans have claimed?

Throughout the history of this nation feminists have argued that we have a long way to go before our democratic claims are truly fulfilled. Our standards for democracy have become tougher over the years; not so long ago we described ourselves as democratic even though at least half the adult population was barred by law from voting. Even now many people find no contradiction between democratic principles and the low degree of governmental power that women share. Most people are unaware of how unequally law and policy affect women and men. Some don't even think women should participate in governance except as voters and taxpayers.

The central theme of democratic theory is the distribution of power in a political community: the degree to which people are free to share in making decisions about the community and, ultimately, themselves. The central theme of feminist theory is the distribution of power between women and men, especially the amount of power women have over themselves. Feminism, therefore, seeks to raise our standard of democracy.

It is true that women are now very active in mass-level politics and that they are more visible at higher levels. We have seen a number of political "firsts" and other records in recent years. In 1984 Geraldine Ferraro became the first woman to be a major party candidate for vice president. Ella Grasso (Connecticut) became the first female Democratic governor in 1975 and Kay Orr (Nebraska) became the first Republican governor in 1986. In 1977 Patricia Harris became the first black female member of the cabinet. In 1981 Sandra Day O'Connor became the first female Supreme Court judge. In 1987 Wilma Mankiller was elected the first female chief of the Cherokees. Numerous women's political groups have sprung up since the growth of the women's movement, including organizations of women in Congress, women judges, women in state government and so on. But this is still only part of the beginning.

NOTES

1.   Unless otherwise stated, the discussion of legal rights refers to the rights of free women (most of whom were white) under the law. Women held in slavery (most of whom were black) did not have legal rights.
2.   This does not mean that there are no more problems. There is still the issue of defining exactly what "equal" means. Further, some policies cannot easily be translated into issues of "equal rights," particularly those that concern conditions that affect only one sex or primarily one sex.
3.   The House of Representatives held hearings on this and related cases. The report makes very interesting reading. (See U.S. Congress 1930.)
4.   For more discussion of women, the family, and the development of U.S. social policy, see Sapiro (1986). In this book other social policies are further discussed in other chapters,

including education policy (Chapter 4), family law and policy (Chapter 10), reproductive policy (Chapter 11), and employment and welfare policy (Chapter 12).

5.   For further discussion of the military and prostitution, see Enloe (1983).

6.   Women's social movements will be discussed more extensively in Chapter 14.

Choice and Control in Everyday Life

ONE OF THE important themes in this book is the relationship between gender and power, control, and choice. Throughout Part Two we looked at the ways in which values defining individuals and their life choices are shaped by the gender norms embedded in the structures of social institutions. We also looked at some of the ways in which women have influenced these institutions and attempted to expand their options.

In Part Three we turn to the choices women face and the experiences they have in everyday adult life. We will look at the areas in life in which people are said to express and act on their own feelings, abilities, and desires as individuals, including the ways they act and interact with others and the ways in which they pursue satisfying personal and work lives. The question that unites these chapters is: To what extent does gender limit the control women have over their choices and experiences?

Reflect Before You Read

1. Imagine that tomorrow morning you wake up to find you have become the other sex. Describe in detail what tomorrow will be like. How will you feel? What will you do? How will people treat you? What will you miss about your old sex? What will you like about your new one?

2. You have been restored to your current sex. Describe your adult life as it has been and as you imagine it will be. How much of it—which of your choices, important experiences, major dilemmas, and turning points—is determined in any way by your gender? What would be different if you were of the other gender?

3. Think about the five people who are closest and most important to you. Imagine they all suddenly changed their sex. Can you imagine them being just as they are now in all other respects? If not, what would be different? Would you feel differently about each of these people? Would you act differently? How? Why?

9

Gender, Communication, and Self-expression

SOCIAL LIFE and social structure depend on communication. Without communication we are not a society but atomistic, unconnected individuals. It is impossible to understand power and control—and therefore sex/gender systems—without examining communication behavior and interpersonal relations. Power is not a lump of something that people possess; it is a characteristic of a relationship among people. It depends in large part on communication among people.

The word *communication* does not refer solely to acts of writing and speaking but also to many kinds of nonverbal behavior. I might express myself or attempt to exert control over a situation by smiling, shaking my head, raising my hand, walking away, or hitting someone. Both verbal and nonverbal communication have vocabulary and grammar. They employ words or gestures that symbolize or encode meaning understood by people within a specific language group ("speakers").

One of the most important tasks individuals have in the course of their development is the learning of language and communication skills. Language provides the basis on which we become social beings able to act and interact with others. It is, as Marx and Engels suggested, "practical consciousness"; that is, the means by which we categorize, recognize, or name tangible and intangible objects. When people cannot attach a word to an object they call it "indescribable," something that cannot be identified, defined, or communicated to others. Objects or feelings we consider particularly dangerous or frightening we call "unmentionable" or "unspeakable," as though we could wipe them out of existence by excluding them from social discourse.

Language also provides the basis on which we become independent, autonomous beings; it is critical in the development of the self. As Claus Mueller wrote in *The Politics of Communication,* "Language has a crucial function in the socialization process. During primary socialization the child can potentially learn to develop and represent his [*sic*] self through the medium of language. . . . This self-presentation allows the child to develop autonomy" (1973, 61). In examining language and communication, therefore, we are looking at the means by which individuals develop and express

237

themselves as both social beings and independent, autonomous beings. Studying patterns of communication helps us understand the delicate balance between the two.

The task of analyzing language and communication is complicated by the fact that there are many variations within any given natural language (such as English, French, or Hindi). Most of us are familiar with regional dialects and language variations that result from particular cultural factors, such as ethnicity, race, and religion. Language and language use also vary by age, class, occupation, and gender. Sometimes the differences are so great that people from one group unwittingly misinterpret or have difficulty understanding those from another group. Individuals also vary the way they communicate from one situation to another. Most people use different language with a stranger and a friend, a parent and a child, a superior and a subordinate, and a woman and a man. This is partly due to subcultural variations among these groups and the effects of status and hierarchy rankings on communication behavior.

The remainder of this chapter will explore the relationship of gender to language and communication behavior. We will begin by examining the language we use. We will focus in particular on the ways in which sex/gender systems are defined, maintained, and changed through the language we use to discuss gender and ourselves as men and women. We will then turn to gender differences in the way people express themselves and the impact of gender on social interaction. If we have been correct in identifying the existence of a hierarchical sex/gender system, people's communication behavior should reflect gender differences in status and relationships of dominance and subordination. Finally we will consider the problem of communication and social change.

Referring to Women, Men, and People

Most of us have had the experience of saying to someone, "don't put words into my mouth," usually when the words we have used are interpreted in a way that conflicts with our intended meaning. Sometimes this happens because specific words and phrases have connotations we do not immediately recognize but which, nevertheless, are understood by the listener as part of the message.

Women's studies scholars in linguistics, psychology, and philosophy have devoted considerable attention to analyzing the connotations of words used to refer to males and females. They have found that, even when we do not intend them to, these words have connotations that reflect the current nature of sex/gender systems and hierarchical social relationships.

Gender-Specific Terms

Let us first consider the words that most obviously refer to gender: *male* and *female*, *man* and *woman*, *girl* and *boy*, *feminine* and *masculine*. Each of these pairs consists of two words that are generally regarded as antonyms, or terms of opposite or contrary meaning. In everyday language we reinforce this idea by talking about "the opposite sex." This turn of phrase should lead one to ask: In what sense are *male* and *female* antonyms?

This question might at first seem trivial or obvious. Among human beings, those who are not female are male, and those who are not male are female. On the other hand, to say that these pairs of gender words are opposites may imply more than this. The designation *opposites* does not refer to the words themselves, which are merely strings of symbols we call letters, but to the things to which these symbols refer. Our question may thus be rephrased: What is it about the things to which these words refer that are opposites?

Male and *female* are antonyms in part because they are culturally linked to other pairs of antonyms generally regarded as traits associated with males and females—the stereotypes we have already discussed in Chapter 2. Recall the study (Broverman et al. 1970) in which researchers found that mental-health clinicians used words identified with stereotypical gender traits to characterize healthy males and females. Table 9-1 shows some of the words the clinicians used to describe healthy males and females, but which we have seen are considerably more shared by men and women than they are distinct attributes of one sex or the other. Notice that the lists consist of antonyms referring to psychological and behavioral traits.

These are not simply words people use to describe men and women; they also reflect the deeper meanings people associate with these terms. This sense of the deeper meaning of ''male'' and ''female'' words points out an important issue in the relationship between choice and control on the one hand and language on the other. Even if we carefully choose the words we use to express ourselves, will other people understand what we mean?

All the words we use, including the words we commonly use to refer to females and males have a range of connotations, or associated or implied meanings. People use *male* and *female* in a generic sense to refer to all persons of one or the other sex, and we also use many other words to limit our meaning further to males or females

TABLE 9-1
Stereotyped Characteristics of Men and Women

Men	Women
aggressive	unaggressive
unemotional	emotional
logical	illogical
rough	gentle
blunt	tactful
direct	sneaky
ambitious	unambitious
active	passive
independent	dependent
sloppy	neat

SOURCE: Adapted from Broverman et al. (1970); Rosencrantz et al. (1968).

of particular ages, marital status, or characteristics. Some terms connote respect, some are informal, and some are derogatory. How and when these different words are used depends on what we mean and the situation.

Table 9-2 lists some of the words most commonly used to refer to males and females. A review of this list reveals the connotations of these words and how asymmetrical many of these male and female terms are. In some cases, male and female terms are loose equivalents; in other cases there is no obvious equivalent for one or the other sex. Thus, although we have just argued that *male* and *female* are often viewed as opposites, there is an important sense in which they are not really treated as opposites in language or otherwise. Opposition in the sense of antonyms implies balance and symmetry. We shall shortly see that this does not necessarily exist in the definition of male and female.[1] These differences often suggest that certain statuses and situations are more important to define for one sex than for the other, females and males in the same situations are regarded differently, and the language we use to discuss gender reflects and helps maintain differences in social status and power. Some examples follow.

Although most of the words in Table 9-2 imply at least some age characteristic, there are four sets in which age is a particularly important part of the meaning: *woman-man, girl-boy, spinster-bachelor, matron-?*. If the first two sets are considered as analogues, then *woman* is to *man* as *girl* is to *boy*, because the first pair constitutes the female and male adult analogues of the second pair, the terms for a female and male child. Or we could say that *woman* is to *girl* as *man* is to *boy*, because the first pair is composed of the terms for a female adult and child, and the second is composed of the terms for a male adult and child.

A more careful look indicates that in common usage the male and female terms are not precise analogues, partly because they carry additional meanings. *Girl* is widely used to describe females of all ages, including adults. The question that needs to be asked is not only why people often refer to adult women as girls, but also why they do not often refer to adult men as boys, particularly in polite settings.

It is sometimes claimed that calling an adult woman a girl is a compliment because it suggests the woman is young. This argument and the asymmetrical use of *girl* and *boy* are based on particular views of both gender and aging. *Girl* refers not to youth but to childhood; is it a compliment to call an adult woman a child? Calling a man a boy belittles his experience, competence, and manly attributes. The asymmetrical use of *girl* and *boy* coincides with the social view that aging in early and especially middle adulthood detracts more from women's attractiveness than from men's. It has also been argued that the use of *girl* for adult women is a sign of affection. Once again, we must ask why *boy* is not an equivalent term of affection for men, and also, why *girl* is used in settings where terms of affection are inappropriate, such as business offices.

The use of childhood referents for adults in large part reflects status. Thus the one use of *boy* to refer to an adult male until recently was a derogatory term applied to black men by whites. To call a black man *boy* indicated his subordinate, servile status or ''stripped him of his manhood.'' (Notice, at least in this case, the close ties between the politics of race and gender.) Abolishing the term *boy* was an important symbolic issue during the civil rights movement of the 1960s. Within a generation

TABLE 9-2
Gender Referents: Nouns and Titles

241

Chapter 9:
Gender,
Communication,
and Self-expression

Female referents	Male referents	Additional connotations
Female	Male	Generic.
Woman	Man	Generic. Also implies age. *Man* is also used to mean "human."
Girl, Gal	Guy, Boy	Informal. *Girl* also connotes age. *Boy* is (singular) rarely used for adult male.
Dame, Broad, Chick, Skirt	?	Derogatory generic. This is a small selection; some are obscene.
Ms.	Mr.	Generic title. *Ms.* is used much less often than *Miss* or *Mrs.*
Girl	Boy	Age. *Girl* is also used to refer to adult females, especially those in a subordinate status. Until recently boy was also used to refer to adult black males by whites.
Lady	Gentleman	Age and class; polite form.
Madam	Sir	Age and class; respectful address. *Madam* also a title for a woman who runs a bordello.
Spinster	Bachelor	Age and marital status.
Wife	Husband	Marital status.
Bride	Groom	Marital status and length of marriage. *Bride* is also used for a young married woman; *groom* is generally used only on the wedding day. *Bride* is often used as the object of a possessive noun ("John's bride"); *groom* is not ("Jane's groom").
Housewife, Homemaker	Breadwinner. (Househusband)	Marital and occupational status.
Divorcée	? (Divorcé)	Marital status.
Matron	? (Patron)	Marital status, age, social status.
Widow	Widower	Marital status. *Widow* is often used as the object of a possessive noun ("John's widow"); *widower* is not ("Jane's widower").

TABLE 9-2 (cont.)
Gender Referents: Nouns and Titles

Female referents	Male referents	Additional connotations
Miss, Mrs.	?	Title connoting marital status.
Mistress	? (Master)	Marital status and heterosexual relationship.
?	Cuckold	Extramarital sexual relationship of spouse.
Prostitute, Whore, Tramp, Slut, Hooker, Nymphomaniac	Lecher, Stud	Heterosexual behavior.
Lesbian, Dyke, Homo, Queer, Gay	Queer, Fairy, Pansy, Fag, Molly, Homo, Gay	Homosexual behavior or personality attributed to homosexuals.
?	Sissy, Pansy, Weak sister, Mamma's boy, Swish, Poof, Wimp	A "feminine" person.
Tomboy, Amazon, Dyke, Butch	Stud, He-man, Macho man	A "masculine" person.

Note: Words within parentheses are apparent equivalents that are rarely used or are completely different in meaning.

the usage has virtually disappeared. The connotation of subordinate and servant status remains, however, in the use of *girl,* for example, when people use the term to refer to their female domestic help ("My girl is wonderful; she's absolutely devoted to the children") or to their female secretaries ("I'll have my girl phone your girl to make the arrangements").

Spinster-bachelor is another word pair with interesting age connotations, this time combined with an indication of marital status. *Spinster* and *bachelor* both refer to unmarried adults, but the words do not have precisely the same meaning. Consider the sentence, "They were always careful to have at least one attractive _____ at their parties." One could well imagine *bachelor* as the appropriate word to fill in the blank, whereas *spinster* does not seem to fit, partly because the word *attractive* does not seem to go with it. We talk about a "confirmed bachelor"; that is, a man who chooses to be unmarried, but not a "confirmed spinster." Why is there no positive term to refer to an adult unmarried female?

Many feminists have pointed out the asymmetry in the titles assigned to women and men. The standard title used for adult men regardless of their marital status is

Mr. Although the generic female title *Ms.* is now available, most people continue to prefer a title for women that also indicates marital status: *Miss* or *Mrs.*[2] This reflects the fact that marital status is a much more important determinant of a woman's role and status than of a man's.

Marital status is so important in the definition of women that most married women still change not only their title but also their personal identity tag: their name. The practice of women's giving up their surnames of birth and taking their husband's was long enforced by law on the grounds that a married woman had no legal identity apart from her husband and was legally incorporated into him. Most state laws no longer make it difficult for women to retain their birth names, but once a woman gives up her birth name, it can be difficult and expensive to recover it legally. As Table 9-3 shows, a married woman's name is a very variable thing.

Some people argue that it is confusing for husband and wife (or, as the traditional marriage service has it, man and wife) to have different surnames. It is confusing only because people *expect* a husband and wife to share a surname. Parents and married daughters generally do not share a surname, but they know they are related and so do other people who know the family. Sharing a surname does not make life much less confusing if the name is a common one. The confusions and problems faced by couples with different surnames does not compare with the problems any of us might have in trying to find an old friend or business acquaintance who has since married and changed her name. A woman may make life even more confusing by giving up both her first and last names and becoming ''Mrs. John Smith.'' The very language both she and other people use to describe her tells us that it is more important to know her husband's name than to know hers.

Many people have pointed out that there is a whole range of derogatory, or at least disrespectful, generic terms for women, but there are few, if any, for men. What

TABLE 9-3
What's in a Name?

Lucy Stone marries Henry Blackwell

While married, she might be addressed as	*While married, he might be addressed as*
Lucy Stone	Henry Blackwell
Ms. Lucy Stone	Mr. Henry Blackwell
Mrs. Lucy Stone	
Lucy Stone Blackwell	
Lucy Blackwell	
Mrs. Lucy Blackwell[a]	
Ms. Lucy Blackwell	
Mrs. Henry Blackwell	
Miss Lucy Stone *and* Mrs. Henry Blackwell[b]	

---

[a]Many people feel this is a correct address only for a widow or divorcée.
[b]Used by women who keep both a professional and a married name.

is the male equivalent of *broads* or *chicks? Guys* is informal, but it is not belittling or derogatory. What social conditions create the need for so many derogatory terms to describe a particular social group?

It is also interesting to note the difference between the terms used to describe a heterosexually active male or female. Whereas *lecher* or *stud* can be used in an admiring sense, the female equivalents are clearly derogatory terms. A woman who likes sexual activity "too much" is a nymphomaniac. What is the name for a man who likes sexual activity "too much"? Is there such a thing? The English language is considerably richer in the number of terms it offers to label a sexually permissive woman than in terms for a sexually permissive man. Julia P. Stanley found 220 terms to refer to the former, and only 22 to refer to the latter (cited in Eakins and Eakins 1978).

The admiration-derogation distinction vanishes when we look at the terms referring to homosexually active people. In this case the words used for both men and women are derogatory, and there are more derogatory terms for the homosexual male than for the homosexual female. Likewise, there are more derogatory terms for an "effeminate" male than for a "masculine" female. Our language seems to suggest that if a woman acts "too masculine" (or unfeminine) she is deviant, but at least she is emulating the superior sex; if a man acts "too feminine" (or unmasculine) there is something profoundly wrong with him.

Gender-based modes of address and naming make a difference, but one that women notice more than men. For example, a survey of New Jersey attorneys (New Jersey Supreme Court Task Force 1986) showed that although 61 percent of women claimed to have heard a judge speak to a female lawyer using her first name or a term of endearment while men were addressed by surname or title, 76 percent of men thought they had not heard this happen. While 85 percent of the women had heard a male attorney use inappropriate forms of address to a woman attorney, only 45 percent of the men had. Many female attorneys experience courts as gender-biased because of their perception of persistent patterns of linguistic discrimination. This is only one example of how language use can become part of an institutionalized system of inequity.

Social movements are very aware of the politics of language and the impact on people of derogatory terminology. In the 1960s, for example, the black power movement declared, "Black is beautiful" because up to that time *black* had always had culturally negative connotations. The gay movement used the slogan, "Gay and Proud" because homosexuality was supposed to be shameful. Lesbians took a term that had traditionally been extremely derogatory (*dyke*) and used it publicly as a symbol of pride.

There are many words that are not initially "about" gender but are often transformed to indicate gender information. This pattern is clearest in terms for occupations, especially gender-typed occupations. There is nothing in the construction of the words *lawyer, poet, nurse, sculptor,* or *journalist* that indicates the gender of the person being described, but many people seem to think it is important to modify these words to indicate gender if the person being discussed is a woman (lady lawyer, poetess, male nurse, sculptress, lady journalist), even when gender information is irrelevant or even redundant (Mary Jones, a lady lawyer . . .).

"Black is beautiful" was an important slogan in a culture
in which a famous TV commercial declared, "If I have
one life to live, let me live it as a blonde!"

The use of suffixes such as *-ess, -ette,* or *-ix* to denote female gender in these types of words is particularly interesting and has actually changed people's understanding of the English language. Feminist linguists have argued against the use of feminine suffixes for three reasons:

1. The suffixes *-ess, -ette,* and *-ix* indicate feminine gender.
2. These suffixes modify the standard forms of the words, indicating in a sense that women are modifications of the standard or normal occupants of these positions; the "male" forms are the ones used to refer to these positions generically.
3. Most of the original forms do not linguistically indicate gender in the first place. If *-er* or *-or* indicated male gender, we would have to say not just waitress or

sculptress but also workress, professorix, and stock brokerette. We would hear of people introducing "Madeline Kunin, the governess of Vermont," or "Kathy Whitmire, the mayoress of Houston." Members of the U.S. Congress might say, "I defer to my colleague from Kansas, Senatrix Nancy Kassenbaum." All of these would sound silly to the American ear, although "mayoress" is considered proper usage in Great Britain.

There are other occupational terms in which gender has been an integral part of the occupational or positional term, including, *businessman, chairman, Congressman,* and *fireman,* in which *man* is part of the word. For these terms, the standard practice used to be to use the *-man* form as a generic form or to refer to men, and to use either the *-man* form (as in "Madam Chairman") or the *-woman* form to refer to women. Increasing numbers of people are attempting to remove irrelevant gender connotations by substituting either *person* (as in *businessperson*) or a neutral alternative form, such as *chair* (for *chairman*), *firefighter, representative,* or *member* of Congress, for the gender-specific term.

Gender-Neutral Terms

Few controversies over the use of language have aroused as much hostility as that over the use of generic, non-gender-bound terms. The dispute over the use of *man* alone has created considerable debate and innumerable snide jokes about "personhole covers" and the like.

This book began with a consideration of the supposed generic uses of *man* and *he*. At the most practical level, such usage is ambiguous and confusing. It is clear that in many cases when *man* and *he* are supposedly being used generically, people actually receive a gender-bound meaning (Sniezek and Jazwinski 1986). For example, Joseph W. Schneider and Sally L. Hacker (1973), found that using *man* rather than gender-neutral terms in chapter titles made students think of males more often.

Another study (Cole, Hill, and Daly 1983) found that *man* was especially likely to bring males to mind when paired with the supposedly generic *he*. These researchers asked students to write a story flowing from the statement: (1) "In a large coeducational institution the average student will feel isolated in his introductory course," or (2) "In a large coeducational institution the average student will feel isolated in his or her introductory course." In the former case 84 percent of the men and 52 percent of the women wrote about a male. In the latter case 77 percent of the men and 22 percent of the women wrote about a male. The change in pronouns had very little effect on the men. It is significant, however, that only with gender-neutral terminology did women focus on their own sex as often as men focused on theirs. Some people label gender-neutral language "inclusive" language. This study suggests that the label is appropriate, especially for women who may feel the world being described to them actually includes them for the first time. It should not be surprising that males both use more gender-biased pronouns and regard sexism as less relevant to language use than females. Research also shows that people who use gender-biased pronouns more hold stronger gender stereotypes about occupations and have less positive attitudes toward nontraditional women (Matheson and Kristensen 1987). (See Chapter 6 for additional discussion of gender-inclusive language.)

The apparent gender neutrality of a word does not necessarily mean that the word provokes a nonsexist image or has a nonsexist meaning. Claus Mueller argues that the language we use encodes shared understandings of the surrounding social environment and reflects the structure of that environment. He writes,

> Language, . . .or more precisely, the code a group shares, is context specific. The possibility of transcending the content of one's code is contingent upon accepting and learning other codes. Change from one code to another implies, therefore, not only a change of the language spoken but also a change of the social context (1973, 14–15).

If the social context is one in which gender structures roles and hierarchies, can even the most apparently gender-neutral terms still have gender-based meanings for people? There is considerable evidence that they can.

Consider terms such as *engineer, kindergarten teacher, army officer,* and *telephone operator.* Each of these is technically a gender-neutral term, but two of these would probably conjure up specifically male images in the mind of the reader, and two would probably conjure up specifically female images. The reason is not that any of the words is gender specific, but that the social reality to which they refer is, by and large, gender specific. Most engineers and army officers are male, and most kindergarten teachers and telephone operators are female. The social reality, especially the social reality of the past, structures our mental image when we hear these words. Our understanding of these words in turn structures our perception of the social reality.

Even if increasing proportions of engineers and army officers are female and increasing numbers of kindergarten teachers and telephone operators are male, we may continue to connect gender-specific images to these supposedly gender-neutral terms. And people who do not conform to this image will seem odd or out of place. Some sociolinguists argue that in this way language can help forestall social change. Although language may change rapidly in certain ways, in other ways it is very resistant to change.

Research by Erica Wise and Janet Rafferty (1982) demonstrates the extent to which apparently gender-neutral terms can evoke gender bias. They were primarily interested in finding whether people still used the same stereotypes to evaluate men, women, and adults as Broverman and her colleagues had found a decade earlier. Wise and Rafferty asked students to define the characteristics of a healthy man, woman, and adult and a healthy boy, girl, and child. Their results were very similar to those obtained in the earlier study. Then they asked the students to write about a healthy adult or child. Most of the students described the adult or child as a male. In other words, the "gender-neutral" terms *healthy adult* and *healthy child* provoked male images on the parts of both men and women.

Many apparently gender-neutral words take on different meanings when they are applied to women and men. Consider the words *selfish-generous* and *loving-unloving,* for example. A woman who pitches in only once in a while to cook or clean for her family would probably be regarded as an unloving selfish person, whereas a man who cooks full meals for his family or cleans the house once in a while is regarded as very loving and generous indeed. A stereotypical loving wife and mother bends her schedule around her family's needs, is proud to carry her husband's name, and is willing to uproot herself if her husband's job demands it. These things are generally not expected of a loving husband. Most people would not call a man unloving or selfish if his job usually takes priority in his household or if he refuses to take his wife's name as his own.

As these few observations and the exercise in Figure 9-1 suggest, words may actually have different definitions depending on whether we are talking about a man or a woman. Many other words also have gender-bound meanings. *Aggression* and *success,* for example, also mean different things depending on whether we are talking about men or women.

FIGURE 9-1
Is *selfish* a Gender-neutral Word?

The *Oxford English Dictionary* defines *selfish* as "devoted to or concerned with one's own advantage or welfare to the exclusion of regard for others." Imagine a scale like the following on which we might measure the amount of selfishness an individual displays in different situations:

Using this scale we might rate people who always go out of their ways to help other people as point 1, least selfish, and people who always expect other people to drop what they are doing so as to serve them as point 7, most selfish.

For each of the following situations, where on the selfishness scale do you think most people would place the individuals involved? Where would you place these individuals?

Most People's Rating	*My Rating*	
————	————	A woman who does not want to entertain her husband's business associates because she finds them boring
————	————	A man who does not want to entertain his wife's business associates because he finds them boring
————	————	A woman who does not want to move to a new town where her husband has found a better job because her own job prospects would be diminished
————	————	A man who does not want to move to a new town where his wife has found a better job because his own job prospects would be diminished
————	————	A woman who refuses to bake cupcakes for her child's school party because she is preparing for an exam
————	————	A man who refuses to bake cupcakes for his child's school party because he is preparing for an exam
————	————	A woman who does most of the cooking and cleaning at home

FIGURE 9-1 (cont.)

249

Chapter 9:
Gender,
Communication,
and Self-expression

Is *selfish* a Gender-neutral Word?

Most People's Rating	*My Rating*	
_____	_____	A man who does most of the cooking and cleaning at home
_____	_____	A woman who does not spend much time caring for her children because she is busy with her job
_____	_____	A man who does not spend much time caring for his children because he is busy with his job

How language maintains or changes gender norms is a complex issue. Looking at the face values or dictionary meanings of words is not enough. It is also necessary to look at the underlying meanings, associations, and uses of words, and these cannot be divorced from the social context in which the words are used or the social phenomena and situations to which they refer. We shall discuss social change and communication at the end of this chapter, but it should be clear by now that sexism in language is not a trivial matter and that sufficient change will not be effected simply by substituting *person* for *man*.

Autonomy and Control in Communication

Research on gender and communication does not focus only on the gender content of words; it is also concerned with the ways women and men speak and interact. Scholars in this field agree that women's and men's communication patterns are different and that the way we communicate depends on the sex of our audience. Scholars also agree that these patterns reflect and help maintain gender differences in status and power. We display these patterns of behavior every day of our adult lives, and we are usually not conscious of what we are doing. This section examines some of these important, but often unconscious, aspects of our lives.

Male and Female Language

Most observers of gender and communication agree that there are differences in the ways women and men communicate. Some go as far as Robin Lakoff (1975) to argue that there are fairly distinct female and male dialects within the English language. Let us look at some of the differences people have observed.

Women and men use slightly different vocabularies.[3] Because of their different experiences and training they use different specialized vocabularies. Women make finer distinctions in naming colors and, on the average, know and use more technical and precise words connected with clothing (especially words connected with sewing), food and cooking, and so on. Men use numbers more often and more precisely in ordinary conversation than women do. They also swear more and use more language generally regarded as obscene or aggressive. Many people also note differences in women's and men's descriptive vocabularies, especially in adjectives. For example, American men are less likely than American women to describe someone or something as adorable, darling, marvelous, or teeny-weeny.

Child development experts generally agree that girls learn verbal language more quickly than boys. Research on adult speech also suggests that women are more likely than men to use standard English (the type our English teachers wanted us to learn). Many observers have argued that this is the result not of men's lack of ability or knowledge, but of an effort to show toughness and independence. Some theorists explain women's use of standard English as a means of obtaining higher status or respect (Adams and Ware 1989, 476).[4]

In light of controversies over the use and teaching of black English it is interesting to note that these gender differences in the use of standard English appear among both blacks and whites. Patricia C. Nichols (1978) studied this pattern and came up with some results that have important implications for understanding the relationship of gender to language use among both blacks and whites. She investigated gender differences in the use of a local black dialect in a rural southern area. In one locality women were more likely than men to use this dialect rather than standard English; in a second locality the reverse was true. In probing more deeply Nichols found that the use of the more prestigious form was linked to economic differences between the two localities. In the second locality women had more opportunity to have higher-status jobs that required standard language skills; in the other men had greater opportunities. It is likely that the same underlying principle may explain gender differences in the use of prestigious language forms regardless of race. For people from working-class or poor families, women's job opportunities (for example, service work involving much social interaction or clerical work) are more likely to depend on language skills, and men's are more likely to depend on physical labor.

Another common observation of women's language style is that it is self-deprecating. In other words, in the way women speak they appear to be more hesitant and doubt their own credibility more than men do. Some, although not all, research suggests that women are more likely to use the self-qualifying tag question, as in "That was a good movie, wasn't it?" Some research also indicates that women are more likely to blunt or hedge their statements by adding personalizers ("In my opinion...") or "Personally, I think...") or disclaimers ("I may be wrong, but...") rather than simply stating opinions and observations straight out.

Women are also more likely to hedge their demands by phrasing them as requests or using long, complex sentences that blunt the request. To caricature the difference, the hedging form of the polite demand, "Please close the door," might be, "I hope you wouldn't mind terribly, but I would be ever so grateful if you would please close the door." Women also blunt their communication by using rising intonation as though asking questions or permission when they are making statements. For example, when Bob asks his wife Sally when dinner will be ready, Sally, who knows exactly when it will be ready, answers, "In ten minutes?" as though asking permission or confirmation.

There are other gender differences in language use. Men use more words, for example, when describing objects (Eakins and Eakins 1978, 25–29). Marion Wood (1966) found that whereas men tend to describe things in more objective terms ("he is about 6 feet, 1 inch tall"), women use more interpretive language ("he looks very worried about something"). Women often use a higher pitch and more breathy voice than is physiologically required, and they use more variation in intonation than men do (Eakins and Eakins 1978).

It is important not to exaggerate the differences between female and male speech and to remember that there is considerably more similarity than difference. No single speech attribute consistently or dramatically distinguishes women from men. Nevertheless we can argue that female and male styles differ, as research by Mulac and Lundell (1986) shows. They taped forty people describing the same photographs. They first asked a group of observers to read the transcripts of the descriptions and guess the sex of the speakers. They were not able to do this very well.

Mulac and Lundell then had the transcripts coded for the presence of the types of characteristics we have been discussing. They found these characteristics did distinguish between female and male speakers in the ways we might expect. "On the basis of the formula determined by [statistical analysis], 85 percent of the male transcripts could be accurately determined on the basis of the relative presence or absence of the 17 language features" (90). Further analysis showed the characteristics associated with male speech were viewed as more dynamic and those associated with female speech were viewed as more aesthetic. Even if the observer could not name the gender of the speaker, gender made a difference in the impact of the speech.

Communication is an interactive process, depending on social context and the people with whom one is communicating. If I speak in a hesitant manner, it may be because I always do this, because I am unsure of the particular topic I am discussing, or because the person to whom I am speaking makes me feel uncomfortable. Most investigators argue that many of the most important differences between female and male communication behavior are the result of the structure of power and authority relations between them.

The Right-of-way: Gender and Status

We all follow many rules, generally unconsciously, when we communicate or interact with others. Some of these are the rules of grammar that allow us to put together strings of words in a way that will transmit meaning clearly to others. (Would difficult understand be to if my message not were it correct grammatically through sentences transmitted.) Others are the rules of style that set the tone and indicate, for example, whether we are speaking formally or informally, as intimates or strangers, or as superior and subordinate (I mean, like, it would be *really* distracting and might screw up your studies really badly—and I wouldn't want to do that!—if I wrote this whole book in the style I'm using in this sentence. Y'know what I mean?). Some of these rules may be regarded as the traffic rules we use to facilitate communication. They include norms of politeness, which facilitate comfort and ease of communication and have the practical advantage, for example, of requiring people to take turns in conversations.

The communication rules we use depend in large part on the status rankings of the people involved. Status and hierarchy rankings are largely reflected through the communication behavior of individuals. People who break the traffic rules of interpersonal relations, for example, by not taking proper turns in speaking, are not regarded as conversational bad drivers but as impolite or, if the infractions are major enough, crazy. Violations of communication traffic rules by a subordinate in relation to a superior are not just impolite; a subordinate's demand for equality in the traffic rules by taking even an equal speaking turn without the superior's permission may be viewed as insubordination. Although politeness is the act of granting some amount of respect to other individuals, it is also a matter of giving the appropriate amount of respect given the relative status of the individuals involved.

Gender differences in communication and social interaction reflect the existence of a hierarchical sex/gender system. More particularly, they are governed in part by traffic rules calling for males to have the right-of-way in both the use of social space and in conversation. Other hierarchical gender-related communication patterns also exist.

RIGHT-OF-WAY IN SPACE.   Men take up more space than women do. This is not just because men are generally larger than women, but also because they occupy, use, and move through space differently from women. Social psychologists and others have noticed that people of relatively high status act as though they have a right to more space or territory than people of relatively low status. This pattern is reflected by men and women.[5]

Men sit and stand more expansively than women do, much more often spreading their arms and legs outward or sideways or sitting with their heads and trunks leaning backward and their legs spread out in front of them. American men tend to cross their legs in the ankle-over-knee position. Women position themselves as though to shrink themselves, with arms and legs closer to the body. No matter how women sit, including when they cross their legs, their knees are closer together, and when they sit "properly" their knees touch, a position many find uncomfortable. These leg positions have sometimes been explained on grounds other than status. For example, some people suggest that women keep their legs close together when they wear skirts so their underwear will not show, or that men cannot sit with their legs together (for example, with legs crossed at the knee) because their genitals get in the way. However, women are likely to sit with their legs close together whether they are wearing short or long skirts or slacks; and there are cultural variations in the ways men cross their legs. French men, for example, cross their legs at the knees.

It is true that male and female clothing differences help maintain some of these differences in demeanor and use of space. It is difficult, for example, for women to walk with long, free strides when they are wearing high heels. Skirts and some types of women's blouses also inhibit movement and rule out certain postures if women want to avoid displaying their underwear. Many popular "dress for success" guides of the early 1980s urged businesswomen to wear a female variety of the male business suit precisely because such attire hides the body underneath. Even such outfits, however, which include a skirt and high-heeled shoes, did not eliminate the need to sit and walk in a circumspect, modesty-conscious way.

Men have more personal space than women do, which is another characteristic of people with high status. Like other animals we need a certain amount of territory. We become uncomfortable or even angry if the wrong people invade that space. Most of us are uncomfortable if someone stands too close to us when conversing. Two people who meet under these circumstances can move in a way that resembles an odd dance, with one person progressively moving backward to create more distance and the other moving forward to diminish that space.

People have different boundaries for others, depending on their relationship, and they assume different rights with regard to others' personal space. The more intimate and friendly a person is, the closer that person is allowed to approach. High-status people assume a right to invade the personal space of lower-status people, whereas lower-status people must respect the personal space of superiors.

Studies of gender behavior show considerable evidence that the behavior of women and men reflects these differences. Observers often remark on the relative absence of private places for women as compared with men. It is common in households that can afford it for a man to have his own room or other place that no one else in the family may enter without permission. Even when the household cannot afford such a luxury, it is more common for a man to be allowed to hide behind his newspaper, surrounded by a symbolic "do not disturb" atmosphere, which is often enforced by his wife.

Women are much less likely to have any such private territory. "Their" room, the kitchen, is one of the most public in a home. Likewise, secretaries are usually placed out in the open with their tools and desks available to any passerby. Not even lower-status businessmen are so exposed. Not only do women in these positions lack territory of their own, they also lack privacy, which means that their work or leisure is regarded as less important than men's and subject to interruption. One might argue that it is characteristic of much of women's work that they are supposed to be available, so their space is designed to facilitate interruption.

Women's lack of totally private space does not mean that they lack all control over their surroundings. In the home, for example, women have a relatively large amount of control over the design of the physical environment through their responsibilities for decoration and cleaning. Bedrooms and bathrooms, for example, which are shared spaces, are generally decorated and furnished in what is regarded as conventionally feminine taste. The decoration and furnishing of a man's study or workroom often stand in stark contrast to that of the rest of the house. (For a parallel point, see the discussion in Chapter 5 of women's control of the at-home birthing room.)

People respect men's personal space and give them more of it in other ways as well. Studies of behavior patterns on sidewalks, for example, show that people give men a wider berth than they give women. This type of behavior can easily be observed in any library with relatively narrow stacks. When a man or woman is sitting or standing in the middle of an aisle that is open at both ends, and another person wants to look at books at the other end of the aisle, women and men respond differently. Women tend to walk through the next aisle, especially if the alternative is to brush close to a man. Men are more likely to walk straight through, especially if it is a woman who is blocking the aisle.

As the library example shows, touching behavior is also regulated by status relations. Higher status people assume a right to touch and sometimes do not even notice what they are doing. Lower-status people, however, will arouse a reaction if they touch higher-status people. A male boss may greet a subordinate in the morning by slapping him on the back and saying, "How are you doing there, Sam?" Even if boss and subordinate are on a first name basis, Sam would not be wise to greet his boss in the same way. Research shows that both men and women respond positively to being touched by someone of higher status than themselves. Research also shows that "when the toucher and the recipient are of equal or ambiguous relative status. . .women generally respond postively to being touched whereas men generally react neutrally or negatively, particularly if the toucher is female" (Major 1981, 28).

In the occupational world women such as secretaries or nurses are usually subordinate to men and are therefore touched regularly by people they themselves cannot touch, at least not without the contact being misinterpreted. (We will discuss this further shortly.) This touching behavior is by no means limited to occupational situations or those in which the male toucher is clearly of higher occupational status than the female being touched. Men in blue-collar jobs touch women who are white-collar secretaries as freely as men who are business executives. When receiving change men of all statuses often prolong touching the hands of female sales clerks.

The differences in touching behavior are also clearly observable in nonoccupational settings. A favorite game for men of all ages is grazing against women's breasts or bottoms "accidentally." Even when men are not playing this type of sexual game, they are much more likely to touch women than women are to touch men. Women sometimes find strange men holding them by the back or shoulders as they move past in bus aisles, for example. Many women find themselves pushed into small segments of bus seats and benches because the men next to them are using their right-of-way to spread themselves out. Men, much more than women, drape their arms across the backs of the chairs of the people sitting next to them.

One of the best-known observers of gender and nonverbal behavior, Nancy Henley, writes of an encounter she had with two high-status administrators at a university where she was working (1977, 95):

> After a large meeting one spring, the Vice Chancellor came over to me and took my upper arms in his two hands, saying he wanted to tell me something; he continued holding me in this restrictive fashion as he proceeded to talk with me. After he finished, and he had finally let go, I grabbed him back, then remarked that I would have to tell him sometime about my thesis which is [about gender and touching behavior]. He expressed interest, so I began telling him about it, and he found it plausible; at this moment the Chancellor approached, the only man on campus with higher authority, laid his hand on the arm of the Vice Chancellor, and urged him to accompany him to the next meeting. The V.C. and I were both struck by the aptness of this action and I think I made my point.

This story also illustrates the point that higher-status people are relatively free to interrupt lower-status people.

Research shows that dominance-deference relations are displayed even in touching behavior between male and female intimates. Among couples it is still expected that sexual contact will be initiated by the male. One study (Borden and Homlied 1978) of heterosexual couples walking together holding hands found that if one member of the couple is left-handed and the other is right-handed, they walk with their dominant hands clasped together. If they are both either left- or right-handed, however, the man tends to hold the woman's weaker hand with his dominant hand.

Gender norms and status also influence eye contact. We sometimes call initiation of contact with another person "catching the person's eye." Initiation of eye contact, especially staring, is the prerogative of higher status people, and once again research and common experience suggest that it is also the prerogative of men. When a woman and man who do not know each other pass on a street and catch each others' eyes, the woman ordinarily drops her gaze first. If the woman holds her gaze, it may be interpreted as an invitation to sexual pursuit.[6] Men are supposed to approach women or initiate relationships, not the reverse. Susan Green and Philip Sanders (1983) found in a study of undergraduates that people still react more positively to a male who initiates a relationship.

What happens when women violate the traffic rules of space? Think of a woman who sits with her arms and legs spread out, who stares at, touches, and drapes herself on strange men. What message will a man receive from such a woman? Most women are fully aware that if they sit with their arms spread back rather than in front of them, men are likely to become distracted and stare at their chests. (It is difficult to have a serious conversation with someone who is staring at your chest.) Thus, when a woman behaves the same way men do in their use of space, she communicates a very different message.

Some research has examined gender differences in the relationship between the use of public space and status. It seems natural to us, for example, that in groups the leader or person of highest status should sit at the head of the table or alone in the front of the room. When husband and wife sit at opposite ends of the family dinner table, the man's place is generally called the "head" of the table, and the woman's the "foot." This arrangement helps the higher status person control the situation and be the focal point of communication.

Natalie Porter and Florence Geis (1981) did some interesting research showing that the differentiated status rankings of women and men are strong enough to overcome the convention that the person of highest status occupies the authoritative position. They showed subjects pictures of a group of people sitting around a table. Some of the groups were all male or all female, and some were mixed. Each showed one person at the short end of the table and three people down each side. Whenever a man was shown sitting at the head of the table, most observers perceived him to be the leader of the group. In all-female groups the woman at the head of the table was also perceived to be the leader of the group. In mixed groups, however, when a woman occupied the head of the table, many people chose one of the men at the sides of the table as the leader. Thus space use and positioning is an important indicator of status, but gender may be even more important.

This study is similar in implication to one done earlier by Dale Lott and Robert Sommer (1967). Students were given diagrams of a rectangular table and told they were going to meet either Professor Susan Smith or Professor Henry Smith there. When asked where they would seat themselves, most placed the professor at the head of the table. This was not true in all cases, however. The students were more likely to choose the head of the table for themselves when meeting Professor Susan Smith than when meeting Professor Henry Smith.

RIGHT-OF-WAY IN CONVERSATION. One of the most common stereotypes of women is that they talk too much, so much that men "can't get a word in edgewise." If this were true, it seems that women must have the right-of-way in conversation. Research shows, however, that in mixed-group discussions not only do men both talk more and take stronger leads in discussions, but also they employ techniques, often unconsciously, that silence women and diminish their abilities to influence the group. Where, then, do people get the idea that women talk too much? Perhaps the notion is based in a status-related pattern that linguists have found: Higher-status people often think that people of lower status talk and interrupt more than they do, even though research shows that it is higher-status people who talk and interrupt more.

Men employ a number of techniques that curb and limit women's speech. The most important is that they interrupt women considerably more often than they interrupt other men or than women interrupt anyone else. One study found that over 90 percent of all interruptions in conversation were instigated by men (Zimmerman and West 1975. See also Smith-Lovin and Brody 1989). Men are more likely to overlap women's speech or to begin talking after women have begun and continue to talk at the same time. These speech challenges may be sustained either by one person forcibly holding his or her ground and continuing to speak or even by saying something such as, "I'm not finished yet." Men are more likely to sustain challenges than women are (Smith-Lovin and Brody 1989).

Despite the assumed right to interrupt and overlap that higher-status people (men) have, there are some variations in the pattern. Kathrynn A. Adams (1980), for example, studied sex and race differences in this kind of behavior and found that white males and black females were particularly likely to sustain verbal challenges. This research suggests that white females are especially susceptible to being silenced by men's challenges.

One of the intriguing aspects of studying communication behavior is its complexity and subtlety. A person's speech may be stopped by a verbal challenge, but it may also be stopped by silence. To continue talking we tend to require some indication that the other person is paying attention. Listeners demonstrate attentiveness by verbal conventions, such as adding the occasional *mm-hmm, uh-huh, oh,* or *yeah* or laughing appropriately. If the listener does not use these conventions during a telephone conversation, the speaker is likely to elicit a response purposely, or even to ask, "Are you still there?" In face-to-face conversations, listeners also signal their participation by nonverbal behavior: nodding or some facial response. Showing no response tends to distract the speaker and eventually kill the conversation. Men tend to do this to women more often than women do it to men.

Other patterns emerge in discussions among women and men. Men initiate new topics more than women do, but this is partly because a man is especially likely to introduce a topic other than the one a woman is discussing. A higher proportion of men's sentences are statements, a higher proportion of women's are questions. Some observers even suggest that in a discussion in which a woman has made a valuable point, it is often attributed by others to a male in the group.[7]

These differences in verbal behavior are reinforced in day-to-day life by the different positions males and females who interact are likely to hold. In cases involving a male boss and a female secretary or other subordinate or a male doctor and a female patient, part of the man's right-of-way is derived from the higher status of his position. Males, however, tend to take a right-of-way reflecting higher status regardless of their occupational positions. Even when women hold high-status positions they do not gain, or do not use, the same privileges in communication traffic. Female doctors, for example, are much less likely than male doctors to use their positions to dominate verbal interactions with patients. Patients, moreover, interrupt female doctors more than they interrupt male doctors (West 1984).[8]

THE RIGHT-OF-WAY: CONCLUSION.   Thus far we have seen that the traffic rules of communication and interaction are governed in part by a hierarchical relationship between women and men, by patterns of dominance and deference and a male right-of-way. Victor A. Thompson's work (1961) on communication and hierarchy offers an instructive way of looking at this relationship and its impact on communication behavior. Although he was specifically considering the relationship between manager and subordinate in a bureaucratic organization, Thompson's analysis is appropriate for other kinds of hierarchies as well, including the one that exists between women and men.

Thompson argues that status and hierarchy rankings are reflected in the rights and duties individuals have with regard to transmitting and accepting information and directives. Superiors generally have communication rights, and subordinates have communication duties or obligations. Many of these rights and duties are left unstated, even in formal organizations, because the rules are obvious to everyone.

Thompson (1961, 60–66) listed the communication rights of the superior in a hierarchical relationship:

1. The right to veto or affirm the goals or proposals of subordinates.
2. The right to expect obedience and loyalty.
3. The right to monopolize communication both within the organizational unit and between the unit and the outside world (especially the latter).
4. The right to expect deference from subordinates.
5. The right to be "somewhat insensitive as to subordinates' personal needs."

Thompson further argues that there is a "halo effect of status" that "requires high-status persons to speak out on all sort of matters from a position of almost complete ignorance" (1961, 67).

Subordinates in a hierarchical relationship have a series of obligations that are the inverse of the superior's rights. Subordinates are expected to leave the final word to superiors, to defer to superiors, to be obedient and loyal, and to be aware of and responsive to superiors' needs and desires.

These descriptions characterize the communication behavior between women and men quite well, in part because in most occupations and organizations women remain segregated in the lower-status subordinate positions. Even within the institution of the family women are traditionally supposed to be obedient, loyal, and deferential. The double standard of loyalty is illustrated by the double standard of sexual morality. Although women do take a considerable role in communication within the family (particularly in the absence of the husband/father) and between the family and outsiders, many of the most important communications between the family and other institutions are expected to be carried out by the husband or under his supervision. The trite (and not always true) image of the unequal degree of sensitivity husbands and wives show toward each others' needs and feelings at the end of a hard day of work illustrates the different responses women and men evince toward each others' needs.

Does the interaction between women and men follow hierarchical patterns of communication only because women and men occupy different formal positions in organizations, or do these hierarchical patterns exist between women and men as such? Is gender in and of itself a status marker that leads to hierarchical patterns of interaction? We have much of the answer already: Evidence of the male right-of-way is exhibited in many day-to-day informal interactions. Gender-based communication patterns conform remarkably well to Thompson's analysis of organizations. The male right-of-way allows men to monopolize communication, to veto or affirm subordinates' goals or proposals, to gain deference, and to be insensitive to subordinates' personal needs. When women use patterns of interaction that show hesitation and self-deprecation, they become parties to this dominance-deference system.

Women appear to be better equipped than men to respond to the needs of others. In reviewing seventy-five studies on the subject, Judith Hall (1978) found that women are better able than men to decode other people's nonverbal cues. The ability to read people's behavior is often interpreted as a defensive skill developed by low-status people; blacks have been found to be particularly skillful at behavior decoding. For both women and blacks these skills are especially strong in detecting negative feelings and reactions. Women also look at people with whom they interact more than men do, which can be interpreted as part of this ''reading'' behavior. Consider these findings in relation to two characteristics often attributed to women: intuition and ''oversensitivity.''

The one observation by Thompson that we have not yet discussed is that high status ''requires'' a person to ''speak out on all sorts of matters from a standpoint of almost complete ignorance.'' Men do speak more than women, but are there gender differences in the amount of knowledge people need before they are willing to offer their views? Women speak somewhat more hesitantly than men, and they also have a tendency to undervalue their own abilities and skills (for a review, see Deaux 1976). As a result they may require more knowledge than men do before voicing their views.

At least one study suggests that men may indeed be more willing to speak on the basis of little knowledge. Ronald Rapoport (1981) studies people who voiced political opinions in public opinion surveys. He divided his sample into three groups—those who seemed to be very knowledgeable, those who seemed moderately knowledgeable, and those who seemed unknowledgeable about politics—and he then compared the first and last groups. Rapoport found that knowledgeable men and women were equally willing or able to offer opinions on political issues to the interviewer. Men who knew very little about politics continued to voice opinions, however, while unknowledgeable women tended either to acknowledge their ignorance or to offer no opinion. Rapoport's work suggests that, at least in the male-dominated field of politics, men may be more willing to discuss things about which they know very little, perhaps because of gender-role pressure not to appear ignorant.

One of the most important features of the relationship between gender and communication is that people expect women to exhibit the communication and interaction patterns characteristic of subordinates. Consider some of the stereotypical traits found in the list provided by Sandra Bem (1975) in her study of masculinity, femininity, and androgyny. Yielding, loyal, sympathetic, sensitive to the needs of others, understanding, and soft-spoken were all characteristics attributed to women. In contrast, stereotypic male traits included defends own beliefs, is willing to take a stand, and acts as a leader. As we have seen many times, if people expect women and men to conform to gender-stereotyped norms, they will perceive and treat women and men as though they are actually doing so.

The principle "ladies before gentlemen" seems to contradict the argument about the male right-of-way. The social custom of "ladies first" appears to suggest that it is women who are accorded the right-of-way. Men are supposed to open doors for them and allow them to enter rooms first, to help them put on and remove their coats, to pull out chairs for them, to rise when they enter rooms, and to remove hats in their presence. Men are also supposed to refrain from swearing in women's presence and, in the past, to save their talk about aggressive topics such as sports, business, and politics until the ladies have left the room. Many a woman has voiced her objection to feminism by saying, "I believe in equal pay for equal work, but I still like a man to open doors for me."

As early as two centuries ago Mary Wollstonecraft argued that male chivalry was a ruse, albeit an unconscious one. Since that time feminists have continued to ask *which* doors men open for women and why they do so. As with other behaviors and interactions, to understand these acts we must examine the circumstances under which they are done, why they are done, and how they relate to other acts. Most feminists argue that men who take the right-of-way when it really counts but continue to open doors for women or help them put on their coats are showing paternalistic power, noblesse oblige that shows that men are stronger and in control. These acts symbolically reinforce the ideal of feminine delicacy and dependence. This kind of chivalry sometimes makes it difficult for a businesswoman to pick up the luncheon check for a client. What would be wrong with a system of politeness in which people hold doors for each other? After all, the woman who can manage to carry the laundry without male help can surely manage a door.

Strategies of Influence and Control

Thus far we have been discussing research that reconfirms the existence of a hierarchical sex/gender system not just in the structures of social institutions but also in people's everyday behavior. Over the years people interested in gender-based

Is chivalry respect, helpfulness, or a ruse?

patterns of interaction have also asked a slightly different question: When women and men are trying to influence others or achieve their own goals in a social setting, do they behave differently? As we shall see, it is considerably easier to find evidence that people think gender differences do and should exist than it is to find solid evidence that women and men actually act differently in similar circumstances. Studies of women and men who hold formal positions of power in business, for example, generally show that women and men exercise authority in very similar ways (Colwill 1982).

Numerous theorists have argued that men and women do use different styles of influence, although surprisingly few have attempted to provide convincing and systematic empirical evidence. One line of thinking suggests that women's and men's communication goals, and therefore behavior, are different. The sociologist Talcott Parsons (1951) led his field for a long time in arguing that men emphasize instrumental values (getting things done), while women emphasize expressive values (creating group harmony and good feelings). Many others have offered variations on this theme, including those who suggest that men emphasize agentic values (concern for the impact of the individual on decisions and activities) and women emphasize communal values (concern for the group, group values, and group activities).

There is some evidence for these theories, but it is not strong and consistent. David Buss (1981) found, for example, that when people were asked about the desirability of 100 different acts of dominance, the ones found less desirable by women than by men were acts of "unmitigated agency" (variations of selfishness). The ones found more desirable by women were more mixed and communal acts. Likewise the acts Buss's subjects thought were less desirable when performed by women than by men were the highly agentic acts. (One of these was "She/he refused to cook or clean the house."). Overall, however, when the subjects were asked which acts they themselves had ever performed, the men claimed to have performed more acts of dominance of almost all sorts.

Other theorists leave aside overall goals and look specifically at strategies of influence. Paula Johnson (1976), for example, argues that the style a person uses to exert influence may fall along three different continua: direct-indirect, personal-concrete, and helplessness-competence. Johnson claims that women's and men's attempts to exert influence can be distinguished along all three lines. Women display a more indirect, and even manipulative style than men, rely on personal appeals, and use a style that rests on helplessness rather than on arguments or displays of competence. What causes these differences? For a long time feminist theorists have argued that women use whatever strategies of influence are open to them. If they are not allowed to be direct and forthright, they will find devious means to obtain their objectives. If this is true, it is easy to see how women might be trapped into fulfilling the stereotype of the sneaky, manipulative woman.

Johnson and others have found evidence that people consider these different styles particularly masculine or feminine and that they react more positively to someone who uses the "gender-appropriate" style. One study, for example, asked subjects to react to speeches by a man and a woman who used either the "male" power base of expertise or the "female" power base of helplessness. The subjects responded more positively to the male speaker than to the female when both used the power base of expertise, and they responded more positively to the female speaker than to the male when they both used the power base of helplessness. When the investigators compared the subjects' attitudes toward speakers of a single sex according to the style of speech used, they found that the subjects preferred the speakers who used "gender-appropriate" speech, regardless of sex (Falbo, Hazen, and Linimon 1982).

Evidence of actual behavioral differences between men and women are not as easy to find. Certainly men are more likely than women to employ physical violence to get their way, as crime statistics show, but what of more peaceful means? Toni Falbo (1977) found that both men and women differ among themselves in how they exert social influence according to whether, in general, they have "feminine," "masculine," or "androgynous" personalities. In responding to an exercise called "How I Get My Way," males and females with "feminine" personalities were more likely to report using tears, subtlety, and mood changes, and those with "masculine" personalities were more likely to report using assertion. "Masculine" types used a smaller range of influence strategies than "feminine" and "androgynous" types. The only clear gender difference that Falbo found was that women claimed to use reason to influence people more often than men did.

Another study (Instone, Major, and Bunker 1983) supported the finding that men make more attempts to influence others than women do in similar situations. This same study also revealed that men use a wider variety of types of influence. On the other hand, these investigators found that the small gender differences in the types of influence strategies all but disappeared when they took the subjects' levels of self-confidence into account; in other words, women used different strategies of influence because they had less self-confidence than men. In the same study both women and men had lower expectations of success when trying to influence the opposite sex than when they were trying to influence members of their own sex. Low expectations of success in exerting influence are generally related to the use of coercion (when people assume that nothing else will work); men and women trying to influence people of the other sex used more coercive strategies than those trying to influence people of their own sex.

Researchers have detected gender differences in interaction relatively early in childhood. Miller, Danaher, and Forbes (1986) observed children's interactions on a playground and found girls and boys both used a range of strategies to deal with conflict, but there were some differences. Boys were more likely than girls to start with "heavy-handed" behavior (aggression) whether they were interacting with girls or boys. Girls were also heavy handed at times, but only with boys and not so quickly. The strategies girls used more often included acknowledging the feelings of others, changing the topic, and indirect displays of anger.

Overall there is considerable evidence that women and men are expected to use different types of influence and are viewed more favorably when they do. We also have some evidence that there are gender differences in strategies for exerting social influence. The interesting question is why these differences occur. Here are three possible answers:

1. Women and men occupy different positions in social institutions, and they use the forms appropriate to their positions.
2. Strategies for exerting social influence depend in part on self-confidence and expectations of success, and women and men do not experience similar levels of self-confidence or anticipation of success in similar situations.
3. Social pressure is exerted on individuals to make their behavior conform to appropriate gender norms. People are not liked or accepted as much when they deviate from the norm.

This discussion has emphasized observation of gender differences in communication strategies. It is important to restate how complex the structure and process of communication is and how difficult it is to study. Perhaps the most difficult aspect to study is not what people communicate and how they communicate it, but what people do not communicate. Many feminist scholars have become aware that women have often been considerably more in control of their own behavior than they have been pictured. However this control is often a matter of self-protection in the face of the dangers presented by the subordination of women. Women have learned to mask their abilities in "masculine" areas to avoid the possibility of punishment. Women have variously hid their sexuality or faked orgasms to avoid the dangers of offending men's sexual sensibilities. They often expend considerable effort in controlling their reactions to sexual harassment. It is more important for women than for men to keep smiling no matter how they are feeling (Deutsch, LeBaron, and Fryer 1987).

If gender subordination creates a special need to be strategic about self-presentation, women who face additional problems of social subordination need to be even more careful. For example, in a homophobic society lesbian women cannot avoid issues of whether to mask their sexuality. Darlene Clark Hine has written very powerfully about the culture of dissemblance among black women, or "the behavior and attitudes of Black women that created the appearance of openness and disclosure but actually shielded the truth of their inner lives and selves from their oppressors" (1989, 912).

Hine argues that the effort to appear open while hiding one's persona was an imperative of the conditions of oppression and sexual violence:

> A secret, undisclosed persona allowed the individual Black woman to function, to work effectively as a domestic in white households, to bear and rear children, to endure the frustration-born violence of frequently under- or unemployed mates, to support churches, to found institutions, and to engage in social service activities, all while living within a clearly hostile white, patriarchal, middle-class America. (1989, 916)

Exactly what one reveals and fears revealing differs from one context of social subordination to another, but close inspection reveals similar elements within all subordinate groups. Hine recognizes the trap of dissemblance: It is an important strategy of self-protection but at the same time buttresses the system that provoked the dissemblance. It is not a trap of the victim's making, but if one plays dumb, one looks dumb.

Future Options

The structure of communication has been the subject of heated controversy in recent decades. On one side are feminist activists and scholars who claim that the ways that people express themselves and behave in social situations are determined and restricted by a gender ideology that grants men higher status and more power to control their own and others' lives than it grants to women. Moreover, feminists argue, the language we use to refer to men and women captures this androcentric and sexist ideology, thereby limiting the ways women can speak about and express themselves.

These foreclosures on women's options are particularly powerful for three reasons:

1. How to communicate and interact with others are among the first skills we learn in infancy. Learning how to express ourselves to other people and how to understand and react to others are in many ways the central tasks of learning to be

human. If the structure of communication is determined by gender, the process of learning to be human is at the same time a process of learning how to be male or female, "masculine" or "feminine."

2. Many of the patterns discussed in this chapter become unconscious and automatic once they are learned. Many of the male behaviors described earlier that render women silent or ineffective are done unconsciously; men are unaware of what they are doing. Although we may speak of "choosing our words carefully," anyone who considered all the implications of every word, gesture, facial expression, posture, and reaction would quickly be immobilized.

3. Limiting language and communication patterns is so powerful because it is so ubiquitous, and its effects can be felt in so many ways. This chapter has emphasized everyday communication, but if we return to earlier discussions of the structure and impact of important social institutions it is possible to see numerous practical applications of these patterns. Consider the languages of health, theology, or politics and the gender-based patterns of interaction within health, religious, and political institutions. Any single instance of sexist communication—for example, a married woman's difficulty in getting people to address letters to her under her name rather than her husband's—may seem trivial. But together such instances form a comprehensive and enveloping system with enormous impact.

On the other side of the debate are people who attack any effort to analyze and change the style and structure of communication. Most of these efforts focus on attempts to eliminate sexist language. Let us look at some of the arguments against such efforts.

Some people argue that the movement to use gender-neutral or inclusive language necessarily strips our language of its richness and renders it awkward, ungrammatical, and odd sounding. In most cases this is simply because people are unaccustomed to nonsexist forms. Unfamiliar forms often sound awkward, and it feels awkward to have to think about terms that were previously used automatically. Many people express great concern about the ugliness and difficulty of pronouncing *Ms.,* for example, when they have done perfectly well with the rhyming words *fizz, 'tis,* and, certainly, *his.* When used fluently, nonsexist language is no more likely to be ungrammatical than sexist language: people certainly make grammatical mistakes in both forms.[9] It is not clear why language that excludes women is richer and more vivid than language that includes them. Some opponents of language change claim to find language that includes women less authoritative and weaker than traditional male forms. (See, for example, the discussion of male God language in Chapter 6.) This is precisely the point: Our language reflects and supports the values of the surrounding society.

Some people object to language change on the grounds that language is a valuable cultural possession with which we must not tamper. They remind us of the horrors of "Newspeak," the language used in the fictional world created by George Orwell in his novel *1984.* In that frightening world the government dictated that language conform to politically correct principles laid down by its Ministry of Truth. Language is indeed a valuable cultural possession, and Orwell was no doubt correct that language can be used to control the thoughts and lives of individuals and groups in society. This is precisely the point at hand. Who possesses language? Whom shall it serve? Who determines the uses to which it is put? Can a serious argument be made that we should continue to use a language that denigrates the majority of humanity? Can women and men choose to speak in a way that connotes respect for themselves?

Language changes over time as human experience changes. The language we use changes dramatically from one generation to the next because it is the means we use to categorize and refer to human experience. Just as those who view women in ways that are defined by androcentric gender ideology find nonsexist language awkward and irritating, those who view women as complete beings and full members of society find androcentric language awkward and irritating. It is perhaps true that at times feminists and antifeminists do not understand each other; they speak different languages. The difference is that most feminists now alive have been, at least at some point in their lives, bilingual. They grew up with the old androcentric language and have learned the new inclusive language.

Changing the language we speak is not as easy as it might appear. It is easy enough to eliminate the most obvious signs of androcentrism with a little thought, and there are numerous guides available that offer assistance. Some examples of the types of changes people might make can be found in the list in Figure 9-2, compiled by Barbara and Gene Eakins. Nonsexist language cannot flow naturally, however, if we do not experience the world in a nonsexist way. As discussed earlier, sexist language is not simply a matter of how one uses the word *man* or whether one retains *man and wife* and the asymmetrical *obey* in a marriage ceremony. If apparently gender-neutral words such as *love, selfishness, strength,* and *consent* are applied in different ways to men and women, language remains gender laden.[10] To concern ourselves with language requires that we consider not only the words we utter but also the way we think and see.

FIGURE 9-2
Nonsexist Treatment of Women and Men

1. Avoid typecasting in careers and activities.
   a. Avoid typecasting women in traditional roles.
   b. Avoid showing men as subject to the "masculine mystique" in interests, attitudes, and careers.
   c. Attempt to break job stereotypes for women and men.
   d. Show married women who work outside the home and emphasize the point that women have choices about their marital status.
   e. Address course materials to students of both sexes.
   f. Portray women and girls as active participants the same as men and boys, and not only in connection with cooking, sewing, shopping.

2. Represent members of both sexes as whole human beings.
   a. Represent women and men with human (not just feminine or masculine) strengths and weaknesses. Characteristics praised in males should also be praised in females.
   b. As in portraying men and boys, show women and girls also as active, logical, accomplishing.

266

Part Three:
Choice and Control
in Everyday Life

FIGURE 9-2 (cont.)
Nonsexist Treatment of Women and Men

   c.   Sometimes show men as quiet and passive, fearful and indecisive, just as women are sometimes portrayed.

3.   Accord women and men the same respect and avoid either trivializing women or describing them by physical attributes when men are described by mental attributes.
   a.   Avoid: (1) girl-watching tone and sexual innuendoes; (2) focusing on physical appearance; (3) using female-gender word forms, such as "poetess"; (4) treating women as sex objects or as weak and helpless; (5) making women figures of fun or scorn (not "the weaker sex" but "women"; not "libber" but "feminist").
   b.   Avoid references to general ineptness of males in the home or dependence on women for meals.
   c.   Treat women as part of the rule, not the exception (not "woman doctor," but "doctor"). Avoid gee-whiz attitude toward women who perform competently.
   d.   Represent women as participants in the action, not as possessions of men. (Not, "Pioneers moved West, taking their wives and children," but "Pioneer women and men moved West, taking their children.")
   e.   Avoid portraying women as needing male permission to act.

4.   Recognize women for their own achievements.

5.   In references to humanity at large, use inclusive language.
   a.   Avoid the generic word *man,* since it is often not interpreted broadly. (Not "mankind" but "humanity"; not "manmade" but "artificial"; not "primitive man" but "primitive peoples.")
   b.   Avoid the generic pronouns *he, him, his* in reference to a hypothetical person or humanity in general.
      (1)   Reword sentence. (Not "The average American drinks his coffee black," but "The average American drinks black coffee.")
      (2)   Recast into plural. ("Most Americans drink their coffee black.")
      (3)   Replace the pronoun with "one," "you," "he or she," and so forth.
      (4)   Alternate male and female expressions and examples: "I've often heard supervisors say, 'She's not the right person for the job,' or 'He lacks the qualifications.'"
      (5)   If the generic he is used, explain in the preface and in the text that the reference is to both females and males.
   c.   Replace occupational terms ending in *-man* by inclusive terms. (Not "businessman," but "business manager"; not "fireman," but "firefighter."
   d.   Avoid language that assumes all readers are male. (Not "you and your wife," but "you and your spouse.")

6.   Use language that designates and describes the sexes equally.
   a.   Use parallel language for women and men. (Not "man and wife," but "husband and wife" or "man and woman." Not "Billie Jean and Riggs," but "King and Riggs" or "Billie Jean and Bobby.")
   b.   Identify women by their own names, not in terms of their roles as wife, mother, and so forth. (Not "Nehru's daughter," but "Indira Gandhi.") Avoid unnecessary reference to marital status.
   c.   Use terms that include both sexes; avoid unnecessary references to gender.

FIGURE 9-2 (cont.)
Nonsexist Treatment of Women and Men

267

Chapter 9:
Gender,
Communication,
and Self-expression

d.   Use nonsexist job titles. (Not "maid" and "house boy" but "house" or "office cleaner.")
e.   Avoid linking certain pronouns with certain work or occupations. Pluralize or else use "he or she" or "she and he." (Not "the shopper. . .she," but "shoppers. . .they"; not "the breadwinner. . .his earnings," but "the breadwinner. . .her or his earnings."
f.   Do not always mention males first. Alternate the order: "women and men," "gentlemen and ladies," "she or he."

SOURCE: Eakins and Eakins (1978, 186–97).

Changing the patterns of social interaction is even more difficult and requires even more self-consciousness and will. Men and women who try to break free of the gender-based structure of interaction encounter resistance, frustration, and even pain. Some tasks are relatively easy, including extending common courtesies to both sexes rather than maintaining them as acts of male chivalry toward delicate females. But research on communication and interaction behavior suggests that women find acceptance or respect difficult to obtain and may be seen as loud, harsh, demanding, and overly masculine if they do not automatically yield the right-of-way to men or carry and present themselves with confidence. Men may be regarded as weak if they choose to share ground with women more equally and treat them as more equal partners. Many feminists claim that the primary reason they seem to lack a sense of humor is that they don't find demeaning treatment amusing.

Individuals' choices in self-expression are also limited by the perceptions others have of them. The last two decades have witnessed the organization of numerous seminars, courses, and training groups designed to help people interact with others in a more egalitarian and respectful manner. Assertiveness training sessions, for example, are aimed at helping women express themselves clearly and confidently; other groups work on the parallel task of helping men become more aware of what their patterns of behavior have done to women and learn how to change.

Aware of the power that is gained by those who steal the floor and the power that is lost through lack of confidence in self-expression feminist organizations have experimented with different types of group interaction to try to achieve more open and participatory styles and to encourage the shy to assert themselves. Some feminist groups, for example, used to pass out chips or markers at the beginning of meetings. Each time a woman spoke she gave up a marker and could speak no more when she ran out. This seems a very artificial way of managing interpersonal relations, but it can provide a lasting lesson about the nature of power, self-expression, and interaction. Feminist therapists have tied the issue of styles of communication to the question of mental health. Feminist therapists not only work on clients' communication skills and abilities but also try to restructure the process of therapy to reflect a less hierarchical structure in the therapeutic relationship itself. Their argument is that therapists cannot meet the needs of clients if therapy takes place within a hierarchical environment.

Male-only clubs have excluded women not just from their facilities, but from important social networks. This activist won a court injunction in her favor on March 6, 1972.

One of the issues to which feminists have paid increasing attention in recent years is the degree to which networks of communication have been used by women. Women and men have always had networks within their separate spheres through which they sought and gave support, information, and exerted social control. The system of "old boy" networks has long been recognized as important to men's lives. Unfortunately, although women's networks have been equally important to their lives, the value of these channels of communication has not been recognized until recently and in the past have been dismissed as "kaffeeklatches," "hen sessions," and "ladies clubs."[11] Women are now taking their communication networks more seriously, partly because they find themselves excluded and isolated as they enter male-dominated occupations. Throughout this book are references to the communication networks that women have established in almost all domains of life. Women are beginning literally to give voice to their needs and experiences.

NOTES

1. Simone de Beauvoir makes a similar argument in *The Second Sex* (1952).

2. It is interesting that some people and institutions seem to think that the only people who use *Ms.* are single women, and perhaps those who are somewhat embarrassed about being single. Some businesses have instituted the practice of including only the following options in checkoff boxes on application forms: Ms., Mrs., Mr.

3. Good reviews of this research can be found in Eakins and Eakins (1978) and Key (1975).

4. Research also shows, however, that males are more likely than females to have speech impediments and defects (Eakins and Eakins 1978, 92–94).

5. A very good review of the research offering evidence for the points raised in the following discussion can be found in Henley (1977).

6. Try this as an experiment: Next time you are walking in a crowded area, pick a stranger out of the crowd and try to hold that person's eye. Use only your eyes. Observe what happens, how you feel, and how you think the other person feels.

7. This is related to the tendency for people to see women's work in the arts as derivative of men's (See Chapter 7).

8. For an excellent bibliography on women, language, and health care, see Treichler (1984).

9. Sounding awkward and speaking incorrectly do not always go together. Most Americans seem to feel more comfortable with the split infinitive ("we need to carefully explore the gender implications of language") than they do with proper construction ("we need to explore carefully the gender implications of language."). Similarly, many people find it less awkward to say that "many surgeon generals have warned us against smoking" (which is incorrect) than "many surgeons general have warned us against smoking" (which is correct).

10. An excellent discussion of what "consent" means—and doesn't mean—when applied to women can be found in Pateman (1980).

11. For an influential historical view of women's networks, see Smith-Rosenberg (1975).

10

Consenting Adults? Choice and Intimate Relationships

THE MOST abiding concern of the historical debate over women's roles and status is the relationship between men and women. Although personal relationships have been a persistent theme in feminist debate and scholarship, the specific themes have changed over time. In the eighteenth and early nineteenth centuries the relevant debates were phrased almost entirely in terms of marital rights and obligations, but public attention shifted increasingly to issues concerning regulation of people's personal and sexual relations, male violence against women, and the role of the institution of marriage in society. In recent years discussion has encompassed not just personal relationships between women and men but also those between women and between men.

This chapter looks at women's personal and sexual relationships. First we will look at the role gender plays in defining personal relationships. Then, we will examine sexuality and sexual relationships and how these are related to gender ideology and sex/gender systems. Finally we will turn to a very specific form of human relationship, marriage, and ask how it is defined by the state. Above all this chapter is concerned with the degree to which women and men have been able to be ''consenting adults'' in their own lives, that is, to make their own choices about their relationships with other people.

Friendship and Other Relationships

Human beings are social animals; few of us can live secluded from human contact. People need friends and lovers, care givers and supporters on whom to take out frustrations or with whom to share life's delights.

There is considerable evidence that the roles people take in social relationships and the functions these relationships play in their lives depend to a great extent on gender. We have seen hints of some of the differences in previous chapters. Mothers and fathers do not interact with their children in the same way, and girls and boys do not interact with their parents in the same way (see Chapter 3). Women and men act toward others in different ways (see Chapter 9).

271

Chapter 10:
Consenting Adults?
Choice and Intimate
Relationships

Conventional wisdom and stereotypes suggest that there are many differences between men's and women's personal lives and relationships. We often hear that women cannot get along with each other because they are jealous creatures, a point for which Sigmund Freud offered elaborate explanations. Most people believe that men need sex more than women do. Women are supposedly fickle, although they are also said to be less promiscuous and to need marriage more than men. Conventional wisdom, however, is untrustworthy and in some cases simply false. Moreover, it often ignores some very important aspects of women's and men's lives.

Women have historically depended on personal relations, especially with other women, to cope with their daily tasks, fears, and frustrations. Since the industrial era men have been apt to spend their day in formal organizations with explicit lines of communication and procedures for dealing with problems. Women have relied on informal but close networks of female relatives, friends, and neighbors. We shall see that men face tremendous social pressure to avoid showing dependence, emotions, or weakness, which in turn prevents them from using friendships the way women do.

Contemporary emphasis on gender integration (the increasing tendency for women and men to share interests, activities, and roles) sometimes makes us forget how rich women's social networks can be. Modern ideas of personal networks often scorn the old-fashioned ideas of segregated social life, and sometimes dismiss women's traditional relationships and activities as impoverished and limited compared with men's. In contrast, Carroll Smith-Rosenberg's research on relationships among women in the nineteenth century led her to conclude that "women . . .did not form an isolated and oppressed subcategory in male society. . . .Women's sphere had an essential integrity and dignity that grew out of women's shared experiences and mutual affection" (1975, 9–10). As Smith-Rosenberg points out, it is no wonder: In a world that is highly sex segregated, to whom would women turn? Women turned to each other for solace and aid. They were each others' teachers; they helped each other give birth; and they helped each other die. Many historians are now investigating the importance of female friendships in women's lives (Freedman 1979; Ryan 1979; Leavitt 1983).

Despite anthropologist Lionel Tiger's (1969) argument that men are leaders in society because they, and not women, have "bonding instincts," Smith-Rosenberg and others find in women's letters and other reports of their lives considerable evidence that women have long depended throughout their lives on the constancy and intimacy of their female friendships. These historians are now correcting the problems Smith-Rosenberg identified in the early 1970s: "The female friendship of the nineteenth century, the long-lived, intimate, loving friendship between two women, is an excellent example of the type of phenomena [sic] which most historians know something about, which few have thought much about, and which virtually no one has written about" (1975, 1).

Research on contemporary women's lives has captured some of the same sense of closeness and interdependence among women including, for example, Carol Stack's (1974) work on black women in urban ghettos. We see hints of it in Mirra Komarovsky's

Women value friendship for sharing confidences.

(1967) study of married working-class women. Circumstances make it likely that female friendships have changed over time; for instance, male and female domains are more integrated than they once were and sexual mores have changed. Women can socialize with men more freely today without their relationships being regarded as sexual. Ironically the intimacy of some female friendships of the nineteenth century would today be interpreted as explicitly sexual and therefore might be inhibited.

Social scientists have observed some important differences between the types of relationships men and women have. Men generally report having more same-sex friends than women, but their friendships are not as emotionally close or intimate as women's. Men often view their special male friends as people with whom they go in groups to drink or play sports; women are more likely to define their special friends as the people with whom they can share confidences and to whom they can turn when they feel vulnerable. Robert Lewis (1978) speculates that the relative distance between male friends is the result both of men's fears of appearing vulnerable and of *homophobia* (the fear of homosexuality). He points out that men often discover their most intimate and close male relationships in two special activities: sports and war.

Lewis suggests that American men are especially likely to avoid touching each other ''unless it is roughly done as in a game of football or other contact sport''

(1978, 112). To this we might add ritual greetings such as slaps on the back or handshakes. The link between social and sexual norms is related to people's cultural backgrounds. For example, heterosexual American men generally do not kiss each other or dance with each other, but men in some other countries are more physically expressive; many, for example, have dances that only men do with other men.

Women tend to rely on friendships and personal relationships to cope with stress more than men do. Ladd Wheeler and John Nezlek (1977), for example, studied the social interaction of male and female students during their first year of college in the 1970s. In the first semester women had much more social interaction than men did. Wheeler and Nezlek suggest that this is further evidence of women's style of coping. By the second semester, when the women had become integrated into their new lives and felt more comfortable, they began to be more selective in their social interactions and to do more things on their own. At that point women also expanded their friendships with men.

Sexual and Intimate Relationships

It is difficult to discuss personal relationships without discussing sexuality. As we have seen, even friendships are sometimes viewed as having sexual undercurrents. Therefore we must understand the role of sex in relationships of all kinds.

What Is a Sexual Relationship?

It might seem odd to ask how sexual relationships can be distinguished from other relationships. Don't we generally know whether a relationship is sexual? The answer is no, partly because of the links between gender and sexual ideology. It is often difficult to distinguish between sexual and other types of intimacy, and it can also be difficult to distinguish between sexuality and violence. This confusion is of great significance to the way people interact with others as men and women.

Sigmund Freud was the theorist most responsible for alerting us to the difficulties of distinguishing between sexual and other relationships and feelings. Freud's views on the matter were more radical than most people would accept, but it is worth reviewing them to see some of the most important questions and controversies. (For further discussion of Freud's views and writings, see Chapters 2 and 3.)

Freud argued that unconscious drives or instincts resemble undifferentiated formless energy. He said that the libido is similar in men and women, and that it does not care what its object is or how it is satisfied. Only through training, coercion, and the mechanisms of repression (excluding these drives from consciousness) and sublimation (transforming basic erotic drives into less threatening or more acceptable forms) do people channel their pleasure seeking into acceptable forms and make conscious distinctions among feelings and actions we would describe as sexual and nonsexual, aggressive and nonaggressive, good and bad. Shame, guilt, and morality are alien to the infant and remain alien to the adult unconscious. Unconscious drives

273

Chapter 10:
Consenting Adults?
Choice and Intimate
Relationships

threaten our conscious senses of self and morality, so the psyche works to reduce the resulting tension by transforming or reinterpreting the meaning of these drives. What is often called the "Freudian slip" might be viewed as a momentary leakage in the system.

For Freud, then, there is no fundamental instinctual difference between seeking one or another kind of pleasure or attachment to another person. The unconscious aim of all these interactions is erotic pleasure; the conscious mind makes moral distinctions only as a result of the strength of the superego and ego. Freud, in fact, labeled platonic love and attachment "aim-inhibited eroticism"; in other words, an erotic or pleasure-seeking relationship in which the sexuality is repressed.

Even if one does not fully accept the psychoanalytic viewpoint, it does illuminate questions that need asking: What is the essential difference between a sexual and a nonsexual caress? What is the fundamental difference between platonic and nonplatonic love and affection? Is the difference merely where and how people touch one another, or whether people consciously initiate genital contact for the purpose of giving or receiving pleasure? Why does there seem to be such a strong link between sexuality and aggression or dominance behavior? As Susan Brownmiller (1975) points out, rape has often been used as an instrument of war and domination. One fast walk through an adult bookstore reveals how much of what people consider erotic involves aggression, violence, and domination. It can, at times, be difficult to distinguish between physical struggle and sexual passion.

Hot flashes. Tingles. Shakes. Dizziness. A need to cling to someone. What are we describing? Fear? A fever? Or sexual arousal? It could be any of these.

The early phases of sexual arousal greatly resemble other emotional states. How then do we distinguish between sexual arousal and other emotions? Research on sexual arousal indicates that people take their cues at least as much from the situation as from the feelings they are experiencing (Rook and Hammer 1977). Something must make an individual label his or her emotion sexual arousal rather than something else. This means that if our upbringing tells us that we should not be sexually aroused in a given situation, we are likely to label our emotion in that situation something other than arousal; if we are supposed to be sexually aroused, that is how we interpret the feeling. And it is possible for a person to mislabel an emotional reaction, as experimental research has demonstrated (White, Fishbein, and Rutstein 1981). Most of us have probably heard someone say, for example, "I thought I felt like it—but then I realized I really didn't. It was all a mistake." The implication here is not that the speaker has changed his or her mind, but that the original feeling was misunderstood.

If people have difficulty interpreting their own feelings, they are certainly going to have difficulty interpreting those of others. This is a particularly acute problem for men and women in two additional respects:

1. Males and females communicate differently (see Chapter 9) and therefore can misunderstand each other. This misunderstanding may be especially great on the part of men, who tend to be less able to read nonverbal signals than women.
2. Sexual norms tend to define women as sexual objects and men as sexual pursuers with a right-of-way in sexuality and communication.

What are the practical effects? As Antonia Abbey notes,

275

Chapter 10:
Consenting Adults?
Choice and Intimate
Relationships

> Available literature on date and acquaintance rape suggests that males are unable
> to distinguish females' friendly behavior from their seductive behavior because
> of the differential meaning that the relevant cues have for the two sexes. Men
> may have been socialized to view any form of friendly behavior from a woman
> as an indicator of sexual interest. (1982, 831)

Abbey's own experimental research provides additional evidence that men read sexual messages into women's behavior that neither the women themselves nor other female observers see. Indeed men perceive greater sexuality than women in the behavior of both women and men (Shotland and Craig 1988). There are also circumstances in which women read sexual cues into other women's behavior that men claim not to see.

These studies might merely help explain the small dramas of crossed signals between men and women were it not for two points:

1. The situations that involve conflicting definitions are not simply random and occasional events; they form a widespread pattern that reflects a gender-based and androcentric sexual ideology. Women find they have to be on guard constantly to avoid being misinterpreted by men.
2. Conflicts in the definition of sexuality play an important role in two serious problems that confront most women at least indirectly: sexual harassment and rape.

Sex and Aggression

In the dominant sexual ideology in the United States, male and female sexuality and sexual roles are very different. The double standard has not disappeared. Men are still supposed to be the "takers." Young men are pressured to conform to this role and to exploit women sexually. The ideology supporting male sexual dominance makes it difficult for men to cope with more independent and self-assured women, and the pressure to conform to the standard of the conquering sexual hero creates strains of its own for men (Komarovsky 1976; Harrison 1978).

Although the double standard creates problems for men, in the final analysis men still hold the more powerful position, and the penalties women suffer under the system are greater. Comparative research indicates that the sexual double standard tends to be more apparent in cultures in which women lack power relative to men. As Naomi McCormick and Clinton Jesser write,

> Male-dominated societies seem to permit men to use power to have sex while
> women are allowed to exercise power only to avoid sex with unsuitable partners.
> In such a society, a woman who uses power to seduce a man openly is regarded
> as "bad" and possibly dangerous. A man who uses power to avoid sex with
> a "turned on" woman is regarded as "religious" at best, and inept, stupid,
> and unmanly at worst. (1983, 68–69)

Just as the research discussed in Chapter 9 provided evidence of a male right-of-way in communication, investigation of sexual ideology and behavior reveals the existence of a male right-of-way in sexuality. That right-of-way is an everyday problem for women. It is one of the most important buttresses of male power over women in most domains.

SEXUAL HARASSMENT.   A common female experience that stems from men's sexual dominance is sexual harassment, the explicit use of sexuality as a tool of power or dominance. Hardly a woman who has passed an American construction site has not been bombarded with catcalls, hoots, whistles, and sexual innuendos. The purpose of this behavior is, at minimum, to make a woman feel embarrassed and self-conscious; that is, to exert psychological power over her. She is not allowed to be anything but a submissive recipient. If she were to say politely that she didn't like the situation, the laughter and remarks would probably only increase. If she were to react angrily, the remarks would probably become more aggressive and abusive, often making the undercurrent of sexual dominance and violence more explicit. ("Why don't you go home and make babies. . .," or "What you need is a good. . ."). Women are subject to these kinds of psychological sexual attacks almost anywhere they go unless they are accompanied by a male protector, although such assaults appear more subtly in many social settings.

Sexual harassment has taken on a more specific meaning as people have become aware of the use of sexuality as an instrument of domination and control in the workplace and in educational institutions. Such harassment may take a number of forms, ranging from verbal or physical sexual innuendos, which women are expected to receive cheerfully or passively, to superiors' expectations of sexual favors in return for career or educational advancement.

Study after study shows that most employed women experience sexual harassment at some point in their working lives (Backhouse and Cohen 1981). Most women do not complain about this harassment, either because they don't think anything (or anything serious) would be done to the perpetrator, or because they think they would be penalized for complaining. Because in most cases these expectations are met, sexual harassment is a successful tool of domination, and it doesn't cost the man anything. (Law and policy regarding sexual harassment and employment discrimination is discussed in Chapter 12.)

Men and women interpret sexual harassment differently. Men often argue that harassment is not a serious problem and that women who claim to be harassed are actually misinterpreting men's friendly behaviors. The women, they say, should feel complimented that men pay such attention to them. These people fail to note that if a woman engaged in the same "friendly" behavior, it would be considered a sexual advance and inappropriate in the workplace. Men also argue that charges of harassment are phony, and that what is really occurring is normal sexual interplay between men and women.

The link between traditional sexual and gender ideology and attitudes toward sexual harassment is underscored by the evidence provided by Inger Jensen and Barbara Gutek (1982). In their study of over 1200 people Jensen and Gutek found that men were more likely than women to blame women for being sexually harassed, and that the degree to which women blame themselves and other victims of harassment depends on their gender ideology. The more strongly women believe in traditional divisions of labor and power between men and women, the more likely they are to believe it is a woman's own fault if she is the victim of sexual harassment. A traditional gender ideology thus supports the perception of victim precipitation.

277

Chapter 10:
Consenting Adults?
Choice and Intimate
Relationships

Those who accept the argument of victim precipitation ignore women's feelings, reactions, and experiences. Women who have been victims of sexual harassment overwhelmingly report that they feel embarrassed, demeaned, intimidated, angry, or upset. Many are frightened or suffer physiological symptoms, such as headaches, tiredness, and nervousness, brought on by stress (Backhouse and Cohen 1981). To return to an earlier question, if sexuality can be used in this fashion, what is the difference between sexuality and aggression?

RAPE.   The line between sexuality and aggression becomes even less distinct, and the relationship between gender and sexual ideology even clearer, in the case of rape. (For discussion of law and policy relating to rape, see Chapter 8.) Feminists argue that rape is a logical outcome of an androcentric sex/gender system and its supporting ideology, which grants men sexual right-of-way. Because of men's right-of-way and a sexual ideology that assumes men to be sexually demanding by nature and women to be submissive, there is no strong barrier to rape other than men's mutual agreement not to rape because this protects ''their own'' women from other men. Our sexual ideology says rape is wrong, but it gives men who do rape an excuse. For this reason at least one author has called the laws about rape a ''male protection racket'' (Peterson 1977).

The way rape laws have been enforced has provided considerable evidence of such a racket. Penalties assessed against a rapist have been higher when the rape victim was married than when the victim was unmarried, and it was often the husband of the married victim rather than the married victim herself who could sue for damages—of his property. Susan Brownmiller (1975) has provided ample evidence that rape has been used as a tool of war and domination by men of one society against men of another. Rape can be a weapon of war because the ability of the men of one nation to rape the women who belong to the men of another is an important symbol of domination and humiliation. Conquerors rape for much the same reason that they confiscate or damage other property of the vanquished.

The traditional wisdom on rape is that men are at the mercy of their sexual drives and therefore rape when they are overly frustrated or when the opportunity arises. (See, for example, the discussion of sex-war theories in Chapter 2.) Contemporary sociobiologists often use this argument to show why sex equality will never occur. Social science research, on the other hand, shows that the proclivity to rape and attitudes toward rape depend considerably on culture and ideology. Peggy Sanday's analysis of societies around the world (1981) indicates that rape is by no means universal. In some societies rape is virtually unknown; in others it is a normal, ritualized part of men's and women's lives. American society falls somewhere in between (see also Gordon and Riger 1989). FBI statistics based on police reports show that in 1987 about 73 out of every 100,000 females and 88 out of every 100,000 females over the age of twelve were victims of rape or attempted rape. That amounts to

91,110 reports of rape or attempted rape in one year. These figures seriously under-estimate the actual number because only a minority of rapes and rape attempts are reported to the police and none of these figures take marital rape into account (U.S. Bureau of the Census 1989, 169).

Stephanie Gordon and Margaret Riger (1989) argue that although annual rates seem to mean women have less than a 1-percent chance of being raped in any given year, a more significant figure in terms of consequences for women is the likelihood that a woman will be raped during her lifetime. Calculated this way, an American woman has about a one in twelve chance of being raped in a twenty-five-year period and a higher chance if she lives in an urban area. Gordon and Riger's survey of women show that women's fear of rape is based more on lifetime than on annual chances.

Gordon and Riger's survey also shows that women and men define rape differently. Almost all the women and men they surveyed thought that "unwanted sexual intercourse with someone when physically forced or overpowered" is rape. About 95 percent also thought that "sexual intercourse with someone without their consent" was rape. However, the examples of gender differences in definitions of rape are important. About 91 percent of women and 83 percent of men defined "a relative having sexual intercourse with a child" as rape. About 80 percent of women and 64 percent of men defined "a relative having sexual intercourse with a teenager under age 18" as rape. About 63 percent of women and 44 percent of men defined "unwanted sexual intercourse between a husband and wife" as rape. Finally, 23 percent of women and 10 percent of men defined "a stranger pinching or grabbing in a sexually suggestive way" as rape (Gordon and Riger 1989, 61).

Martha Burt (1980) did an important empirical study of the role of gender and sexual stereotypes in people's beliefs about rape. She points out that widely accepted cultural rape myths maintain that women are at least in part responsible for their own victimization, that rape is not as common as women believe, and that rapists are in large part not responsible for their own actions. Research on rape shows that these beliefs are false. Burt found that people who accept traditional gender role stereotypes or who believe that heterosexual relationships are adversarial are more likely to accept rape myths. And the more people accept interpersonal violence in general, the more they accept rape myths. In other words, acceptance of the predominant rape myths is part of a package of ideas that include belief in men's social and sexual superiority and acceptance of the inevitability of male power and violence. An adaptation of Burt's survey is shown in Figure 10-1.

Neil M. Malamuth (1981) has pursued this line of inquiry further by investigating the links between rape and people's beliefs and attitudes. Like most other investigators of rape he notes that research consistently fails to reveal many psychological differences between men who have raped and men who have not. In other words, rapists are psychologically similar to normal (nonraping) men.

Malamuth discusses several studies asking samples of normal men whether they would rape if they thought they could get away with it. In a typical study 35 percent said there was at least some chance they would, and 20 percent said it was fairly likely they would. In a study of nearly 4000 college students, 23 percent of the men said that they had been in a situation in which they had been so aroused that they "couldn't" stop, even though they knew that the woman didn't want to continue.

FIGURE 10-1

279

Chapter 10:
Consenting Adults?
Choice and Intimate
Relationships

Sexual Ideology: Adversarial Sexual Beliefs, Sexual Conservatism,
and Rape-Myth Acceptance

Following are three lists of statements that indicate three different but related aspects of sexual ideology. Do you agree or disagree with each of these statements? Do you think most of your friends would agree or disagree? The police? Most people? What difference does it make?

Adversarial sexual beliefs

Greater *agreement* with these statements indicated greater belief that heterosexual relationships are adversarial relationships.

> A woman will only respect a man who will lay down the law to her.
> Many women are so demanding sexually that men just can't satisfy them.
> A man's got to show the woman who's boss right from the start or he'll end up henpecked.
> A woman is usually sweet until she's caught a man; then she lets her true self show.
> A lot of men talk big, but when it comes down to it, they can't perform well sexually.
> In dating relationships women take advantage of men.
> Men only want one thing.
> Most women are sly and manipulative when they want to attract men.
> Many women seem to get pleasure in putting men down.

Sexual conservatism

Greater *agreement* with these statements indicates greater sexual conservatism.

> A woman who initiates a sexual encounter will probably have sex with anybody.
> A woman shouldn't give in sexually to a man too easily or he'll think she's loose.
> Men have a biologically stronger sex drive than women.
> A nice woman will be offended or embarrassed by dirty jokes.
> Masturbation is not a normal form of sexual activity.
> People should not have oral sex.
> I have no respect for a woman who engages in sexual relationships without any emotional involvement.
> Having sex during the menstrual period is embarrassing.
> The primary goal of sexual intercourse should be to have children.

Rape myth acceptance

Greater *agreement* with *unstarred* statements and greater *disagreement* with *starred* statements indicate greater acceptance of rape myths.

> A woman who goes to the home or apartment of a man on their first date implies that she is willing to have sex.
> *Any female can get raped.
> One reason that women falsely report a rape is that they frequently have a need to call attention to themselves.
> Any healthy woman can successfully resist a rapist if she wants to.
> Women who go braless or wear short skirts and tight tops are asking for trouble.
> In most rapes the victim is promiscuous or has a bad reputation.
> If a girl engages in necking or petting and she lets things get out of hand, it is her own fault if her partner forces sex on her.
> Women who get raped while hitchhiking get what they deserve.

FIGURE 10-1 (cont.)

Sexual Ideology: Adversarial Sexual Beliefs, Sexual Conservatism,
and Rape-Myth Acceptance

A woman who is stuck-up and thinks she is too good to talk to men on the street deserve to be taught a lesson.

Many women have an unconscious wish to be raped and may unconsciously set up a situation in which they are likely to be attacked.

If a woman gets drunk at a party and has intercourse with a man she's just met there, she should be considered fair game to other males at the party who want to have sex with her too, whether she wants to or not.

Many women who report rapes are lying because they are angry and want to get back at the man they accuse.

SOURCE: Adapted from Burt, 1980.

But only 3 percent of the men in the sample reported that they had actually used physical force. (At the same time, 8 percent of the women in the study said a man had used physical force against them.) A proclivity toward rape appears to be widespread.

What psychological differences distinguish rapists from other men? Malamuth (1981, 139) says there are two that show up in the literature on rape: the tendencies ''to hold callous attitudes about rape and to believe in rape myths'' and ''to show relatively high levels of sexual arousal to depictions of rape.'' Malamuth further investigated these observations in his own research. He found that compared to other men those who said they were likely to rape if they could get away with it were more accepting of rape myths, more tolerant of interpersonal violence against women, and more readily aroused by depictions of rape.

But are the men's statements about their own proclivity to rape any indication of their real tendency to be violent toward women? Malamuth investigated this question by conducting an experiment in which men were told they could choose to punish another person for incorrect responses in solving a problem. The problem solver was a female confederate. Malamuth arranged for the woman to mildly insult or reject each man before the experiment. In the course of the experiment, the men who had reported that they had a higher likelihood of raping were angrier and more aggressive toward the woman and reported a greater desire to hurt her than the other men.

These results are consistent with studies of men who have been convicted of rape. Rapists often report not on their feelings of sexual arousal or attraction to their victims, but on their desire to hurt or dominate them. When rapists admit what they have done, they often feel their actions were justified under the circumstances (Wolfe and Baker 1980). For this reason there has been a tendency in the last few years toward classifying rape as a crime of aggression or violence rather than a sexual crime. Sexual organs are involved (in part as weapons), and the act of rape resembles other sexual acts in some outward respects. But the main point of the encounter is not fulfillment of sexual or erotic desires unless one accepts violence as an erotic act.

The thesis maintained by feminists is that the tie between sexuality and aggression, and especially the definition of aggression against women as erotic and sexual, is a logical result of an androcentric and even misogynist gender ideology. The research reviewed here shows that (1) an inegalitarian and androcentric gender ideology is associated with an androcentric sexual ideology; (2) these are associated with a belief that aggression against women is justifiable and necessary, at least in some circumstances; and (3) these values help support the existence of actual violence against women.

Men who accept traditional sexual and gender ideologies may find it difficult to understand, at least in the abstract, what is so horrifying about rape. They may wonder why women don't just "lie back and enjoy it." Frances Cherry reports on how she sees this problem and how she tackles it in her teaching (1983, 247):

> When I have introduced the topic of rape in my classes, students often snicker when I raise the possibility that a man can be raped by a woman. Some of the men have sat back in their desks, opened their arms, and sighed, "rape me." When I further suggest we consider that men are raped by men, the men's chortles and sighs abruptly turn to nervous laughter, downward turning of the head and closing of the legs and arms.

It is reasonable to guess this reaction is not just because of the men's fear of homosexuality, although that undoubtedly plays a part. Through this example the men are probably realizing that rape can be violent, aggressive, and truly against one's will, and that there may be no recourse if the rapist is at least the victim's physical match in size and strength. It is important to note, however, that men are taught to fight off attackers but women are often counseled to avoid further harm by submitting.

Rape myths do not just support men's proclivity to rape; they are also important mechanisms for controlling and limiting women's activities and movements and decreasing their abilities to defend themselves and make appropriate responses to rape. Conventional wisdom is that potential victims, women, can help decrease the incidence of rape by limiting their activities. This is a logical outcome of the view that women are in large part responsible when rape occurs. Such social control over women is made effective by women's fear of rape and their knowledge that there is a very small likelihood that a rapist will be caught, let alone convicted.

Women's lives are indeed limited by a fear of rape; one study of three major cities showed that while 18 percent of the male residents expressed some fear about being out in their own neighborhoods at night, 40 percent of the female residents had such fears. Those who felt most vulnerable were the old, low-income people, blacks, and Hispanics (Gordon and Riger 1989).

The idea that women are responsible for their own victimization is accepted by many women, so much so that women who have been raped commonly report feeling guilty for their own victimization. This response is probably encouraged by an important difference between the myth and reality of rape. The myth says that rapes occur on dark deserted streets between strangers, but in reality a majority of victims and perpetrators know each other (not counting rapes of wives by their husbands)

281

Chapter 10:
Consenting Adults?
Choice and Intimate
Relationships

and rapes often occur in the home. One of the most painful issues related to rape concerns "date rape" or "acquaintance rape." On college campuses women are becoming aware how common it is for women to be raped by a "friend" or date. In these cases self-doubt is a particular problem. The fact that women often blame themselves and that they can be sure others will be suspicious of their testimony minimizes the number of victims who report these rapes to the police.

Women who accept the traditional adversarial ideology of sexuality, which states that normal heterosexual sex involves an active pursuing male and a reluctant female, may not even understand their own experiences of rapes and near rapes as what they are. Women who enter shelters for battered wives often report that situations in which their husbands forced them, sometimes violently, to have sexual relations had not occurred to them as incidents of rape for a long time. As in other forms of wife battery, a woman who is dependent on her husband is relatively unlikely to leave home until the situation becomes intolerable.

Traditional gender and sexual norms leave women relatively defenseless against rape. The traditional advice to women who found themselves victimized (advice often offered by police) was "Lie back and enjoy it"; in other words, submit passively. Any women who did so thereby gave up the possibility of legal recourse because she would have no proof to offer to show she had not consented. Women who have learned to reject aggressive reactions as unfeminine and have not developed physical agility and strength have few options.

Women as a group are no longer the passive victims they might once have been. Public awareness is rising, and hundreds of organizations are involved in educating people about the facts of rape and giving psychological and legal assistance to those who have or might become victims. Research by Pauline Bart and Patricia O'Brien (1984) indicates that those who successfully avoid rape attempts have a larger range of preventive actions at their disposal than other women. Among other things, they are able to respond aggressively to their attackers. If nothing else, women who defend themselves successfully know how to kick off their heeled shoes if necessary and run. In many towns women have organized to establish women's transit systems to help women avoid rape without having to lock themselves away.

The law and criminal justice system is changing its treatment of rape. Rapists are now less likely to go unpunished, partly because more women are willing to report rapes. The law is moving away from the man's point of view and toward an understanding of what rape means to women. (This is discussed more fully in Chapter 8.) Law and policy are beginning to acknowledge the incidence of intrafamilial rape. Some states now recognize the possibility of rape within marriage, and incestuous rape, particularly of children, has become the subject of more vigilant policy.

Above all, however, the fight against rape involves a struggle against sexual and gender norms, the ideology that increases the likelihood of rape and that justifies the crime. Women have given the symbolic message that they intend to do something in "Take Back the Night" demonstrations, in which large numbers of people march through often notoriously dangerous parts of towns at night in a show of strength.

PORNOGRAPHY.   Feminists have found some specific targets of action in so-called adult book stores and movie houses and pornography in general. These specialize not simply in presenting women as sexual objects but also in incorporating a high level of violence against women under the label of erotica. The point feminists make is twofold:

283

Chapter 10:
Consenting Adults?
Choice and Intimate
Relationships

1. Because sexual values and behavior are in large part learned, pornographic materials that repeatedly associate violence against women with sexual pleasure for men reinforce the idea that violence against women is sexy. The story line of pornography usually depicts at least some of the myths and beliefs listed in Figure 10-1.
2. Research shows that although men and women are sexually aroused by similar nonviolent erotica, men also have a tendency to be aroused by depictions of violence against women. Men are certainly more likely to be exposed to these materials; a study in San Francisco found that men constituted 97 percent of the people who go to adult book stores and the same proportion of those who frequent adult movie houses.[1] Although researchers are far from agreed on whether pornography encourages rape, research does show that depictions of rape, especially when shown to a man whose anger has been aroused against a woman, encourages violence against women (Fisher 1983).

There have been vigorous efforts in recent years to make a clearer distinction between acceptable sexuality and eroticism on the one hand and aggression and violence on the other. The task is not easy given traditional definitions of male and female sexuality. Definitions of acceptable sexuality depend very much on more general definitions of masculinity and femininity. There have also been efforts in many cities and states to enact legislation that would ban the sale of pornography. These efforts have been controversial even within the feminist movements because of questions about the additional consequences of such censorship. Many people argue that much as they do not like pornographic material and even find it dangerous, banning the sale of pornography would infringe First Amendment rights of freedom of speech. They worry especially about the precedent that would be set by such legislation.

Sexual Orientation

We have already seen that people's beliefs about sexuality and gender are related. Analysis of sexual orientation—heterosexual, bisexual, or homosexual—shows very clearly that people's ideas about sexuality and gender are not just related but also interdependent; people's views of gender depend on their views of sexuality, and people's views of sexuality depend on their views of gender.

Letitia Anne Peplau and Steven Gordon (1983) argue that people often confuse three different components of individuals' identities: (1) gender identity, or a person's understanding of being male or female; (2) gender role behavior, or a person's repertoire of "masculine" and "feminine" behaviors, and (3) sexual orientation or preference. "Masculinity" and "femininity" are both judged according to how well people conform not just to traditionally prescribed gender divisions of labor but also to traditionally prescribed heterosexual behavior. Indeed, "masculinity" and "femininity" depend not just on appropriate sexual behavior but also on whether a person possesses the characteristics that are sexually attractive to members of the "opposite" sex.

Sociobiologists and much of the public suggest that gender differences in personality and division of labor are actually caused by a particular construction of heterosexual behavior: Men are the pursuers, and women are the pursued and possessed. Many sociobiologists believe that the construction of gender and gender roles inevitably follows from this fact of sexual life. Feminist theorists who analyze sex/gender systems argue that although gender and gender roles have been so constructed as to serve and maintain this sexual system, neither is inevitable.

The logic of the confusion that Peplau and Gordon describe is that to be masculine a person must possess the characteristics appropriate to male sexual roles and to be feminine a person must possess the characteristics appropriate to female sexual roles. A woman who is sexually oriented toward women or a man who is sexually oriented toward men is not appropriately feminine or masculine. According to this view homosexuals must experience confusion in their identities.

The widespread belief that heterosexuality is both the most natural sexual orientation and that it is the primary determinant of people's personalities and behaviors is illustrated by some common myths and stereotypes about homosexuals. Most people think it is easy to distinguish between heterosexuals and homosexuals. Men who appear to have too many "feminine" characteristics and women who appear to have too many "masculine" characteristics are generally suspected of being homosexual. People tend to express great shock when they find out that a woman who seems very feminine or a man who seems very masculine is actually a homosexual. Homosexuals are expected to act like they belong to the other sex.

Stereotypes of lesbians in particular reveal important aspects of the links between sexual and gender ideology and the way people understand the relationship between gender and sexuality. One commonplace idea is that lesbians do not really prefer women as sexual partners but that some trauma in their relationships with men made them hate and reject men and turn to women by default. It is often said of homosexuals that if they could just experience the proper kind of heterosexual relationship, they would be able to change their sexual orientation. People often have difficulty believing that homosexuals could be as happy with themselves as heterosexuals are. They also assume that the stereotypical masculine-feminine, dominance-submission heterosexual pattern is the natural form sexuality must take. This is why the stereotype of lesbian relationships involves the "butch" and "femme" partners; that is, one woman who plays male, and one who plays female.

In fact there is no evidence that homosexuals experience more confusion about their gender identities than anyone else. It is not even clear how much homosexuals and heterosexuals differ from each other in the degree to which they have "masculine" and "feminine" traits. One study of women from the ages of twenty to fifty-four, for example, compared lesbians and heterosexual women using the Bem Sex Role Inventory (BSRI). The result was that lesbians scored no less "feminine" than other women did. They were, however, more androgynous, because they scored higher on "masculine" characteristics than the heterosexual women (Oldham, Farmill, and Ball 1982). No one is exactly sure why people adopt the sexual orientation they do, but homosexuality does not necessarily involve trauma and rejection, and homosexuals do not necessarily imitate stereotypical heterosexual roles.

285

Chapter 10:
Consenting Adults?
Choice and Intimate
Relationships

It is not surprising that people are confused and ignorant about sexual orientation. Until recently homosexuality was seldom discussed except as a sort of illness. In the 1970s a survey of 3000 people who had had a sex education course revealed that more than 60 percent had been taught nothing about homosexuality, and two-thirds of those who had been taught something were simply taught that homosexuality was wrong (Levitt and Klassen 1974).

Before we look more closely at attitudes toward different types of sexual orientation, let us first define *heterosexual*, *bisexual*, and *homosexual* orientations. This is not an easy task, and there are many methods from which to choose.

Some people seem to think that a person who has had any desire for sexual contact with someone of the same sex is really a homosexual, despite any behavioral proof to the contrary. Philip Blumstein and Pepper Schwartz argue that the reason for this view is ideological (1977, 39): "Our cultural logic holds that it is almost impossible to have only some homosexual feelings. The idea is seldom questioned that a single homosexual act or strong homosexual feelings reveal the 'true person.'" By this definition there can be no such thing as a bisexual; a person is either heterosexual or homosexual. There is no parallel view that if someone who normally prefers homosexual sex has a heterosexual fantasy or encounter, that person is really a heterosexual.

Other people take their cues more specifically from people's sexual behaviors. It is common, however, for individuals to engage in homosexual relationships, even quite regularly, and still think of themselves as heterosexuals (Blumstein and Schwartz 1977). Some people who live as heterosexuals and are even married understand their own preferences to be homosexual. How much sexual activity of a given type is required to make one or another label appropriate? In their work on bisexuality, Blumstein and Schwartz write. (1977, 32)

> The inescapable—but often escaped—conclusions from Kinsey, et al.'s findings are that a mix of homosexual and heterosexual behaviors in a persons' erotic biography is a common occurrence, and that it is entirely possible to engage in anywhere from a little to a great deal of homosexual behavior without adopting a homosexual life-style.

People's sexual orientations often vary quite considerably over a lifetime.

Sexual orientation may also be defined by the way people identify themselves. In a four-city survey Blumstein and Schwartz found that just as people with extensive homosexual experience may still identify themselves as heterosexuals, many people adopt homosexual or bisexual identities without having had any homosexual experiences. Sexual self-definition does not require any sexual experience at all. People, of course, face tremendous pressure to reject any idea that they might be homosexual. The social sanctions have been so severe that people are often afraid to admit their feelings even to themselves. Research on sexuality and moral reasoning find that guilt plays an important role in the way people think about sexuality (D'Augelli and D'Augelli 1977). The power of guilt feelings can only be increased when people find themselves with sexual preferences so often described as sick and sinful.

Carmen de Monteflores and Stephen Schultz (1978) have studied the process of "coming out," or acquiring a homosexual social identity, among women and men. They note that coming out is not a single event but a psychological process that takes place over time. They found that the process is generally not the same for women and men. The men they talked to often had their first homosexual experiences before they really understood the meaning of homosexuality or thought of themselves as having any preference for men. In explaining their earlier encounters they tended to emphasize sexual gratification and to deny responsibility for their choices (to say, for example, "I was drunk"). The women tended to act on their preferences only after they had recognized them and to emphasize the emotional bonds they had with their first female partners before having sexual relations with them. The men focused on the special circumstances of their first homosexual encounters, and the women emphasized their special partners. Men also report more difficulty in identifying themselves as homosexual, for reasons we will discuss later (Blumstein and Schwartz 1977).

The process of coming out involves a number of stages. Individuals first grapple with their own sense of identity and personal choice. Next they reveal this new identity to others, generally people in the gay community. Because of the likely negative repercussions, it continues to be difficult for gays and lesbians to express their sexual identity to people in the "straight" world, including family, friends, and employers. Since the issue of sexual orientation has become increasingly politicized, and since gay communities are much more active and cohesive than they once were, for many people coming out also involves becoming a member of an identifiable social and political community.

The process of developing self-identity is not necessarily easy for heterosexual people either. Freud, for example, thought the process of becoming heterosexual particularly difficult for females, and young heterosexual men devote considerable time and effort to proving themselves healthy, masculine, heterosexuals. But the problems are by no means equivalent to those of people with different sexual orientations. It is precisely the fear of not being heterosexual enough and the fear of homosexuality that motivates some of the stuggles of heterosexuals. Homosexuals and bisexuals certainly need not worry about not being strong enough in their orientations to satisfy societal values; any amount is too much. Bisexuals have a unique problem as well because they are often not trusted by either the homosexual or the heterosexual communities. Most people do not believe a person can really be bisexual; they believe a person must be one thing or the other (Blumstein and Schwartz 1977).

These definitional problems suggest that the attempt to label a person heterosexual, bisexual, or homosexual is a misguided effort. Historians note that although people have varied in their sexual orientations since the beginning of recorded history, the designation of a "homosexual role" or of specific individuals as homosexuals is of recent vintage, going back only to the nineteenth century (Weeks 1977). When we consider both the variability among individuals and within each individual's lifetime, trying to classify people can seem futile. Shere Hite, for example argues that "the terms *heterosexual* and *homosexual* should be used not as nouns but as adjectives, and . . . should be used to describe activities, not people. Other than that, these words have no meaning. And even used as adjectives referring to activities, the words are vague. . . ." (1981, 809). On the other hand, if these words are used not just as descriptions of sexual relations but also in the more political and sociological senses to refer to communities and life-styles, Hite's suggestion may not be adequate.

287

Chapter 10:
Consenting Adults?
Choice and Intimate
Relationships

One thing is certain: A large number of people are homosexual. Alfred Kinsey and his associates found in the 1940s that 28 percent of their sample of almost 8000 women had had some homosexual experience (Kinsey, Pomeroy, and Martin 1948). In Shere Hite's (1981) study of over 7000 men, 11 percent said that they preferred to have sex with another man. In her earlier study of women (1976) 8 percent said they preferred sex with another woman, and 4 percent said they were bisexual.

Much research has been done on attitudes toward homosexuality, especially on homophobia, the fear or hatred of homosexuality. Homophobia is a form of prejudice, like sexism or racism. When research uncovers gender differences in attitudes, the difference is usually that men are more hostile to and threatened by homosexuality than women. Morin and Garfinkle (1978) were interested in finding out what factors explain male homophobia. After looking at a range of possible factors, including age, education, religion, and various attitudes, they found that the single best predictor of homophobia was whether a person accepted traditional family ideology. The more strongly the men believed that a family should consist of a dominant father, submissive mother, and obedient children, the more likely they were to show signs of homophobia. The second best predictor of homophobia was gender ideology. The more strongly the men believed in traditional women's roles and characters, the more homophobic they were likely to be.

Several experimental studies show how homophobia and stereotypes affect the way people think. In one study psychologists provided subjects with a vignette of an individual. Later they gave the subjects information indicating that the individual in the vignette was either a homosexual or a heterosexual and then asked the subjects what they remembered about the individual. As the researchers expected, the subjects mentally reconstructed the facts of the story to fit their stereotypes of the sexual orientation assigned to the individual (Snyder and Uranowitz 1978). It is interesting to compare these findings with those of Carmen de Monteflores and Stephen Schultz (1978), who found the same process of reconstruction in the process of coming out among gays and lesbians. As newly self-identified homosexuals go through the process of labeling themselves, they also tend to reconstruct their past by remembering events and feelings they had forgotten, or reinterpreting the meanings of different events and relationships in their lives.

David Shaffer and Thomas Case (1982) looked at the effects of knowledge about a person's sexual orientation on jury decisions. They first administered a psychological test to their subjects to find out how high they scored on a dogmatism scale. They then presented the subjects with testimony by a fictional suspect. In some cases the testimony included the information that the suspect was homosexual. The dogmatic jurors judged the homosexual defendant more likely to be guilty than the heterosexual defendant. Surprisingly the nondogmatic jurors judged the homosexual less likely to be guilty than the heterosexual defendant. The authors speculated that this latter group may have been compensating for the possibility that the homosexual was an object of discrimination.

With the exception of some psychoanalysts psychologists long held that homosexuality was a sign of illness. In contrast, Sigmund Freud argued that human beings are essentially bisexual and that only through a process of developmental struggle do people forsake their homosexual tendencies to become exclusively heterosexual. Although Freud did not consider homosexuality an illness in need of a cure, he did consider it a sign of psychosexual immaturity.

Despite the declaration of the American Psychological Association in 1973 that homosexuality is not necessarily a sign of psychological illness, many psychotherapists continue to regard homosexuals as less healthy than other people. In a study of 400 California psychologists Ellen Garfinkle and Stephen Morin (1978) presented therapists with a profile of a client, whom they described as either male or female and either heterosexual or homosexual. When the client was presented as a male homosexual, they found male therapists particularly likely to view the client negatively and see him as less healthy, less masculine, and more feminine than heterosexual clients.

Homosexuality has always been suppressed in the United States. Leadership in suppression of homosexuality has come especially from organized religion and government. Homosexuality has been defined by religious authority as sinful. Governments have adopted the religious view and labeled homosexual acts, especially by males, as criminal activities (punishable by death in certain circumstances in the past). As late as 1986 the Supreme Court case *Bowers* v. *Hardwick* declared that private intimate acts between consenting adults are not protected under the constitutional right to privacy, which means that state laws on sodomy, used primarily against homosexuals, are perfectly legal.

Why is sexual orientation, especially homosexuality, a key issue in feminist research and activism? The primary explanation is so obvious that it is often neglected: Lesbians are women who defy in an important way the stereotypes of womanhood and femininity. At the same time the fact that a woman is a lesbian increases the likelihood that she will experience the effects of androcentric values and women's lack of freedom. For example, gender discrimination in employment affects women regardless of their sexual orientation, but lesbians are less likely than others to have a higher-paid male's salary to share. Moreover, lesbians are subject to employment discrimination as both women and homosexuals (Levine and Leonard 1984). Lesbians with children also have the problems of single motherhood, with the additional problem that much of society is antagonistic to the idea that lesbians should raise children. All women are justified in fearing the violence of rape, but lesbians cannot rely on male protectors as they go about their business.

If women in general suffer from constricting stereotypes of femininity, so do lesbians. But because they deviate from the stereotypes in an obvious respect, lesbians face the further problem of being defined as unhealthy and not ''real'' women. Women are subtly and not so subtly directed to make their lives revolve around a man's. For this reason some feminists, such as Adrienne Rich, argue that one of the most rebellious things a woman can do is to defy the norm of ''compulsory heterosexuality'' (1980).

Many feminists have argued that homophobia and heterosexism oppress women regardless of their sexual orientations. Charlotte Bunch (1979; 1981) has made this point very well. Her argument is that heterosexism (prejudice against homosexuality) and sexism assume that "each woman exists for a man—her body, her children, and her services are his property. If a woman does not accept that definition of heterosexuality and of herself, she is queer—no matter who she sleeps with" (Bunch 1979, 554). Women are given marginal status in the work force and education partly because of the assumption that they will ultimately depend on men. Women also gain much of their social status and privileges through their relationship with men. "One of the things that keeps heterosexual domination going is heterosexual privilege; those actual or promised benefits for a woman who stays in line: legitimacy, economic security, social acceptance, legal and physical protection" (Bunch 1979, 554).

289

Chapter 10:
Consenting Adults?
Choice and Intimate
Relationships

If a heterosexual woman does not recognize heterosexism and heterosexist privilege, Bunch argues, she cannot see how very dependent she is for her rights and privileges on men, and how easily she can lose them if she does not conform to the standards set by men. In at least one respect radical feminists and right-wing antifeminists are in substantial agreement. Both see increasing equality for women as threatening to traditional sexual mores, and both see the breakdown of traditional sexual mores as threatening to the life of the patriarchal family.

Feminists like Charlotte Bunch and Adrienne Rich also argue that heterosexism is a powerful force limiting the ability of women to respect themselves and organize socially and politically. Homophobia certainly decreases personal intimacy among men (Lewis 1978). Although there appears to be somewhat more intimacy among women, heterosexism defines women as incomplete without a man, and it defines women as incomplete without a man, and it defines relationships with men as more important than relationships with women. (For example, a woman often reneges without hesitation on a commitment to go out with another woman if a man later asks her for a date at the same time.) Turning away from heterosexism implies the ability to imagine limitless love and respect for women as independent and complete people.

The issue here is not necessarily whom one chooses as a sexual partner, but the degree to which one accepts or rejects androcentric sexual and gender ideologies at the most personal level. This is the reason that Adrienne Rich (1979) chooses to define *lesbianism* not by people's habits of sexual behavior but by the way people understand and identify with women. Antifeminists may be right that the women's movement has encouraged more women to choose to be lesbian, but it can also be argued that the women's movement has meant that more women could choose to be heterosexual without having to devalue themselves.

Couples

Thus far we have discussed sexuality, intimacy, and personal relationships in a fairly abstract manner. Much research has been devoted to studying the actual behavior and relationships of males and females in both heterosexual and homosexual relationships. Let us look at some of the conclusions.

LOVE, SHARING, AND SEXUALITY.   As much as it might surprise most people, especially the devotees of conventional wisdom, men seem to fall in love more quickly than women do (Hill, Rubin, and Peplau 1976; Kanin, Davidson, and Scheck 1970). But love and the beginning of a relationship mean different things to women and men. Sex appears to be more central and important to men in a relationship than it is to women, and men describe their love in slightly more passionate terms than women do (Peplau, Rubin, and Hill, 1977; Hatfield 1983). Women are slightly more likely to feel a companionate love for their partners, or a love that emphasizes friendship and sharing. Some research suggests that a woman more carefully considers whether to live with a man because deciding to do so commits her to undertaking domestic labor and responsibility for the two of them. A man living with a woman generally expects her to take on most of the cooking and cleaning.

Philip Blumstein and Pepper Schwartz' (1983) study of American couples reveals some interesting characteristics of attachment in relationships. Their study (which will be discussed often here) focused on married couples, heterosexual cohabiting couples, and gay and lesbian cohabiting couples.[2] The researchers found widespread division of emotional labor within the relationships, which generally included one partner who was more oriented toward the relationship than the other was. "The majority of couples, heterosexual and homosexual, have at least one partner who is relationship-centered. Couples without a relationship-centered partner are less satisfied and less committed" (170). The traditional division of labor assigns women this role, although women by no means constitute all of the relationship-centered partners. Of course, among same-sex partners such a division of labor could not be gender based.

Blumstein and Schwartz found some interesting differences in how people managed and felt about their relationships. "Among heterosexual couples, young men have less desire for their partner's companionship than do young women, but the tables are turned as the couple ages" (176). This observation is consistent with earlier studies of marital relationships (see, e.g., Lopata 1971). The early stages of marriage can be difficult for women who expected constant sharing and companionship with their new husbands only to find that the husbands turned much of their attention to their jobs and other interests.

With the birth of children wives often withdraw some of their attention from their husbands as they devote themselves to care of the children. This is one reason why the early stages of parenthood can be so stressful for husbands in particular. For traditional employed husband–homemaker-wife couples, the man's retirement can again pose a problem. The men may now be ready for companionship with their wives, but the women's well-established lives and routines may not fit their husbands' new needs.

Same-sex couples appear to share more of their leisure activities and their time than heterosexual couples do (Blumstein and Schwartz 1983, 180). Part of the reason is that just as the economic world is segregated by sex, so are many leisure and social activities. This barrier does not divide homosexual couples.

Private time away from one's partner is also important to a relationship. Of the types of couples that Blumstein and Schwartz studied, "Cohabitors feel most strongly about having time away from their partners" (1983, 186), a characteristic consistent with the generally higher levels of independence that mark these couples. Perhaps a more surprising finding given women's desire for companionship in relationships is that women express a stronger wish than men for more time to themselves. The need for private time does not necessarily indicate a lack of love for one's partner.

291

Chapter 10:
Consenting Adults?
Choice and Intimate
Relationships

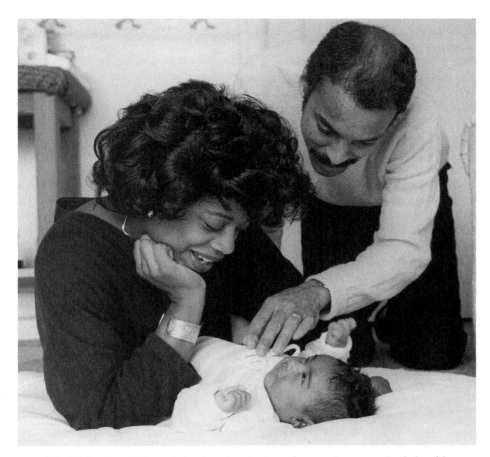

The birth of a child can bring joy, but it also refocuses the parents' relationship.

As we have already seen, women have less control over their time and space than men do (see Chapter 9), and women with young children can feel especially hemmed in by their families (see Chapter 5).

Blumstein and Schwartz also looked at the role of possessiveness in relationships and found women to be slightly more possessive than men. Further analysis revealed the reason: Men tend to have more power and control within their relationships, and women's possessiveness is in part a reaction to insecurity. Only among wives in the study did possessiveness seem to be related to the degree of commitment to a relationship; the more they wanted the relationship to last, the more possessive they were. Men's degree of commitment did not affect how possessive they were of their wives.

The issue of possessiveness raises a related topic: sexual fidelity and monogamy. Public opinion polls generally show that women are more conservative than men in their attitudes toward extramarital sex and divorce. One possible reason is that women actually gain protection by safeguarding a traditional sexual morality because they are generally in a weaker position. Gender differences in couples, especially married couples, are consistent with these often-noted observations as Table 10-1 shows. Women are somewhat more likely to value monogamy more than men do, and married men and women value monogamy more than unmarried men and women do. It is interesting to note that cohabiting and lesbian women resemble each other very closely in their values, whereas gay men place a very low value on maintaining monogamous relationships. (It is important to note that this study was done before the AIDS epidemic.) The gender differences suggest that commitment to monogamy among women is not entirely a matter of weakness within a relationship but is part of women's definition of a stable relationship. It is also consistent with findings that for women personal commitment and affection more often precede the initiation of sexual relations. Another study of couples in the 1970s also concluded that lesbian and heterosexual women are very similar in their desires for close, permanent, and loving relationships (Peplau et al. 1978; Peplau and Gordon 1983).

Shere Hite's study (1981) of male sexuality provides more insight into men's views of extramarital sex. About two-thirds of the married men in her sample claimed to have had at least one extramarital affair. Most did not view this activity as having anything to do with their marital relationships, and most did not think that it detracted from their love for their wives. What they were searching for in their affairs

TABLE 10-1
Monogamous Attitudes and Behavior of American Couples

	Married couples		Heterosexual cohabitors		Gay couples	
	Men	Women	Men	Women	Men	Women
It is important to be monogamous	75	84	62	70	30	71
I have been nonmonogamous in this relationship	26	21	33	30	82	28
I have been nonmonogamous in this relationship (couples who have been together 10+ years).	30	22	[a]	[a]	94	43
My partner is not aware of my nonmonogamy.	27	28	24	20	7	16

Note: Numbers represent the proportion of people in each category who gave this answer.
[a]There are very few cohabiting couples who have been together for at least 10 years.
SOURCE: Adapted from Blumstein and Schwartz (1983, 270–73).

293

Chapter 10:
Consenting Adults?
Choice and Intimate
Relationships

was sex, often because they thought they didn't have enough with their wives. Most thought that sex within marriage eventually becomes boring. However, most of the men strongly disliked the idea of their wives' having affairs.

What do we know about patterns of sexual intimacy within relationships? The frequency of sexual intercourse decreases over the life of a relationship. Table 10-2 shows Blumstein and Schwartz' findings about the frequency of sex in different kinds of relationships. Over time the different types of couples converge in their behavior, with the exception of lesbians, whose level of sexual activity remains lower than others'. Another study, however, finds that lesbians have sex with about the same frequency as heterosexuals of the same age (Peplau and Gordon 1983). It is difficult to determine how much of the decrease is the result of habituation and how much the result of aging. Sexual activity does tend to decrease after midlife because of physiological aging, but not nearly to the degree that young people generally suspect. Men's physiological capacities for sex begin decreasing at an earlier age and to a greater extent than women's. But as A. R. Allgeier concludes in his discussion of aging and sexuality, "The North American stereotype of the sexless older person is inaccurate. Sexy young people mature into sexy middle-aged and elderly people. The sexually disinterested elderly person was probably not very enthusiastic about sex in youth" (1983, 144).

Blumstein and Schwartz's couples study also shows that the traditional sexual division of labor is alive and well among heterosexual couples. The majority of people—53 percent according to female cohabitors and 67 percent according to husbands—thought that one partner in the couple tended to initiate sex, and in heterosexual couples this partner tended to be the male. A calculation of the difference between the proportion of people who claim that the man is the usual initiator and the proportion who claim that the woman is the usual initiator shows that the balance goes to the man by 35 percentage points according to husbands, 36 percentage points according to wives, 20 percentage points according to male cohabitors, and 25 percentage points according to female cohabitors.[3] Married people, in other words, are most likely to follow the traditional gender division of labor in sexuality.

TABLE 10-2

Proportion of Couples Who Have Sex Three or More Times per Week

No. years couple has lived together	Married	Heterosexual cohabiting	Gay men	Lesbians
0–2	45	61	67	33
2–10	27	38	32	7
10+	18	a	11	1

[a]Very few cohabiting couples have been together 10 years.
SOURCE: Blumstein and Schwartz (1983, 196).

Shere Hite's work is particularly notable for what it reveals about couples' sexual relationships. Above all it shows how little heterosexual couples understand each other's sexuality, especially how little men understand and pay attention to women's sexuality. Such widespread ignorance is hardly surprising: Research on sex education and sexual knowledge shows that American children are retarded in their understanding of sexuality and reproduction compared with those in other countries. By the age of nine, for example, only 10 percent of American children know that a woman must have sexual intercourse to have a baby. By the same age 25 percent of Australian children, 35 percent of English children, and 60 percent of Swedish children know the basic facts of life (Goldman and Goldman 1982).

Hite's respondents sometimes displayed an amazing ignorance about women's bodies and how they work. Many men could not tell whether their partners had orgasms, and many thought the question not particularly important anyway. Many did not know about the clitoris or its role in women's sexuality. Numerous men equated sexual intimacy with genital penetration and considered that women's orgasms should happen during penetration if they happened at all.

Although many men also responded differently to Hite's questions, these responses illuminate why the average man seems more eager for sex in relationships than women. Men have greater control, and sexual encounters are structured more by their desires and needs. This pattern also explains the finding that women in lesbian relationships experience more orgasms than those in heterosexual relationships, even though lesbians have sex less often: Women understand how their own bodies work. Americans, male and female, begin adult life with inadequate knowledge about sexual intimacy and the needs of the other sex, and many are unable to ask for or to give the information needed to make their relationships more fulfilling. The phenomenon is largely attributable to traditional sexual and gender ideology.

POWER AND DEPENDENCY. One of the major findings in Blumstein and Schwartz's research on couples (1983, 53) is that ''Money established the balance of power in relationships, except among lesbians.'' The balance of power is more even in households with employed wives than in those of other married women, perhaps because these women earn money of their own.

Feminists have long maintained that married homemakers' lack of financial resources puts them in a dependent situation and gives them little leverage in a marriage. They also argue that such wives do not get the respect they deserve from their husbands because the wives are dependents who can easily (and wrongly) be accused of not earning their keep. The couples study shows that a woman gains additional respect from her husband if she is employed. On the other hand, employment of wives can introduce strains in marriages, especially given the lingering ideology of the patriarchal family with traditional gender roles. Married women continue to do most of the housework regardless of their employment status, which means their days are particularly burdened. Blumstein and Schwartz found that although cohabiting couples are somewhat more egalitarian about the division of domestic labor, even in those couples the woman does most of the domestic labor.

Both heterosexual and homosexual men feel that a successful partner should not have to do housework, unless that partner is female (Blumstein and Schwartz

1983, 151). Men in general do not demonstrate that they are ready to share domestic labor; the more housework a husband does, the more conflict the couple has (146). We will look more closely at the relationship of work and marriage in Chapter 12.

295

Chapter 10:
Consenting Adults?
Choice and Intimate
Relationships

In addition to financial dependency it is also important to consider the role of psychological dependency, a situation in which an individual's sense of self-esteem, purpose, and ability to get along revolves around another person. Traditional gender ideology encourages psychological dependency in women by defining women's purpose as hinging on others, and by defining women as incapable of autonomy and independence. By the same token it is possible to argue that traditional gender ideology also encourages a form of psychological dependency in men. If to feel ''masculine'' and have a strong sense of self-esteem a man needs to have the woman he cares most about be weak and economically dependent, we can argue that he is psychologically dependent on her weakness relative to him.

Women's dependency in marriage has been empirically demonstrated to have other effects as well. Blumstein and Schwartz discovered that in a heterosexual relationship, the more the power balance tips toward the man, the more the couple's sexual activity will be limited to intercourse with the man in the top position. This means that the balance of sexual satisfaction is also tilted toward the male. Power relations thus can shape almost all aspects of a couple's life together.

Both economic and psychological dependency are related to wife abuse, although in different ways. Women's subjective or psychological dependency seems to be related to relatively minor acts of abuse, while economic dependency seems to provide a breeding ground for more major acts of abuse (Kalmuss and Straus 1982). The role of economic dependency in giving men the power to abuse women is also suggested by a study of women who were subject to wife abuse. It showed that among abused wives, women who were not employed were less likely than employed women to leave the relationship (Strube and Barbour 1983). Inequality and male dominance in marriage are clearly not healthy for women. (For further discussion of the relationship of health and inequality in marriage, see Chapter 5.)

A Sexual Revolution?

In the late 1960s mass circulation magazines announced that a new revolution was under way: the sexual revolution. Americans were told that more people were having more different kinds of sexual relations with more people than ever before and that these changes were due in part to the emergence of the new, liberated woman. Public opinion figures and statistics provide evidence that Americans' sexual thinking and behavior have undergone considerable change during the second half of the twentieth century. People have become more tolerant of variation in sexual life. They appear to be more knowledgeable about their bodies and sexuality. By the 1970s only a minority of people were virgins on their wedding day, and in some areas of the country the number of babies each year born to single women now outnumbers those born to married women.

These are significant changes. But have people's views of women's sexuality really changed? Has the balance of sexual power between men and women been altered by this ''revolution''?

One new development is that women's sexuality has become the subject of public, political, and scholarly debate. In the late 1940s Alfred Kinsey and his associates announced to the world that women were not engaging in sexual relations solely for the purpose of procreation or even simply to satisfy the needs of men (Kinsey, Pomeroy, and Martin 1948; Kinsey et al. 1953); women had sexual feelings and needs too. Once this was realized, the nature of women's sexuality and sexual potential became an open question. We shall look at two such questions in particular: women's orgasms, and the double standard.

THE VAGINAL, CLITORAL, NONE, ONE, MANY DEBATE. Considerable attention has been paid to women's orgasms, at least in the scholarly literature on sexuality. This attention has focused on two questions:

1. How many orgasms can and should a woman have?
2. What kinds of orgasms can and should a woman have?

There was once general agreement that women's orgasms were secondary to men's; men had a greater need for relief of sexual tension, and many women were "frigid," or anorgasmic, anyway. As Shere Hite's subjects indicate many women are not given any alternative possibility by their husbands. Women who know better but are afraid to speak up for themselves have probably found sex a very frustrating experience. Indeed most women have probably always known better, as research on masturbation shows. But the label "frigid" is applied to women who do not or cannot have an orgasm from the thrusting of a penis inside the vagina. Why should a woman bother getting excited and being responsive when her own sexual tensions will not be relieved?

Public attention now has shifted from the question whether women can have orgasms to how many they can have at a time. Many women felt bad enough that they could not have even one orgasm during sexual intercourse when they were hit with the report that with proper stimulation many women could reach climax many times in succession. The flood of clinical reports has often left women and men no more enlightened but more anxious than ever. Women worry about frigidity, while men worry about their performance and whether it is good enough to tap and satisfy women's apparently insatiable sexuality. Women fake orgasms to protect their own and their partner's self-esteem. These worries are hardly conducive to sexual enjoyment. The facts seem to be that (1) with proper stimulation, which in most cases is not achieved merely by penile penetration, most women can reach a climax, and many can do so more than once; (2) the physiological phases of sexual excitement and resolution are roughly similar in men and women; and (3) sex can be enjoyable to many people even if orgasm is not achieved.

The second issue about orgasms centers on what area people define as the locus of sexual stimulation that can lead to orgasm in women. Following Sigmund Freud's theory of psychosexual development (see Chapter 3), conventional and scientific opinion argued that there are two kinds of female orgasms: the clitoral orgasm, reached by direct stimulation of the clitoris; and the vaginal orgasm, the more "mature" orgasm achieved during penetration. Despite the clinical evidence that most orgasms are physiologically caused by stimulation of the clitoris, many people continue to think that a woman should be able to climax during sexual intercourse, which does not always offer the clitoral stimulation women need to have an orgasm.

297

Chapter 10:
Consenting Adults?
Choice and Intimate
Relationships

The "vaginal imperative" helps preserve the male's place as the dominant and more central character in sexual activity. What people do before a man enters a woman—even if it includes orgasm for the woman—is still usually called foreplay, the overture to the main act. The vaginal imperative helps reinforce the idea that women have less sexual drive than men, because only a minority of women are stimulated enough by sexual intercourse alone to have orgasms. If sexual activity between women and men is to be more responsive to women's needs, men must place more value on sexual activities that cannot directly result in their own orgasms. Both women and men have to stop worrying about their performance and what they are "supposed" to do and feel.

THE DOUBLE STANDARD, POWER, AND DOMINANCE.   Successful revolutions usually result in a redistribution of power or resources. In the past women had relatively little power over their own sexuality. Has the sexual revolution resulted in a reallocation of power? The answer seems to be yes, within limits.

Women certainly appear to have more opportunity to think, learn, and talk about their sexual needs and experiences than they had in the past, although formal sex education (for both sexes) remains limited. It also appears that people are freer to make choices in their sexual lives. Indeed many people are upset by the degree to which traditional sexual morality has changed.

The double standard, which essentially validates different rules and degrees of power for men than for women, has been weakened and widely questioned, but it has by no means disappeared. A study of dating couples in college revealed that although the students were fairly egalitarian in their views of whether males and females should have sex without being married if the partners loved each other, the double standard persisted when they talked about casual sex; they considered casual sex less acceptable for females (Peplau, Rubin, and Hill 1977). Men are still more likely to initiate sexual relationships. Women retain their power to say "no," although they are pressured to use that power less often than they once were because of misguided interpretations of what constitutes a "liberated woman." This has become even more dangerous since the spread of AIDS.

The persistence of the double standard means that women remain more likely to be criticized for engaging in "inappropriate" heterosexual relations. The persistence of a gender division of labor means that women are held more responsible if conception occurs. One fact of life will never change: It is the woman who becomes pregnant.

Sexual liberation and women's liberation are linked and interdependent. Both involve increasing the power of women to express themselves and make responsible choices about themselves; both raise serious questions about women's power and freedom. Research shows that men with high needs for power tend to hold relatively exploitative views of women and limit their wives' choices (Lips 1981, 28–33). Gender equality and sexual equality must be attained in tandem. It appears that a revolution has begun, but it is not over yet.

Marriage: Family, Property, and State

At the center of our sex/gender system lies a relationship institutionalized by acts of government and religion: marriage. Adult women's status, roles, rights, and obligations historically have been governed by marriage and the norms that underlie it. Female children have been taught to think of marriage as the single most important goal in their lives. Experimental research shows that women who have never married are evaluated more negatively than other women and more negatively than either single or married men (Etaugh and Foresman 1983). Hardly a woman who has reached age thirty without marrying has avoided being barraged with, "So when are you getting married?" or the whispered, "Don't worry, your time will come." After age thirty these comments come less frequently; indeed a woman who has not married by then is often viewed with pity. In the end most people marry at least once in their lives.

Marriage is an institution that is created and defined by government. In the United States the level of government responsible for ruling marriage is the state; only a representative of the state can marry people. Even if two people are married by a member of the clergy, it is the state that grants the cleric the right to officiate. The only terms of a marriage that are enforceable are those that are established by governmental law and policy. The state decides who may marry, at what age they may marry, and under what circumstances they may marry. Only the state may declare a marriage ended. Sexual relations outside of marriage are illegal in many places. Children born outside of marriage are designated illegitimate, or outside the bounds of law.

The Marriage Contract

When two people marry they agree to live under the terms of a marriage contract. This contract is much like others in one respect: it defines the rights and duties of the contracting parties. Beyond this, the marriage contract is very different from most others in three ways:

1. Most contracts are written, and the terms of the contract are spelled out clearly to the parties involved. People are generally advised to "read the fine print" carefully and possibly consult a lawyer before they sign on the dotted line. They may even negotiate amendments or alterations to the contract. In contrast the terms of the marriage contract are not written in any single place, and they are not made available for review. Instead the terms are scattered throughout the laws and court decisions that have been handed down over time. Most people have very little idea about what is in the marriage contract, and very few even

consider consulting an attorney to find out what their rights and obligations are before they marry; it just doesn't seem very romantic.

2. The terms of most contracts cannot be changed while they are in force without the knowledge and consent of the signing parties. In contrast, because the terms of the marriage contract are defined by legislators, judges, and other policymakers, the only way to find out what changes have been made is to read newspapers and law reports very carefully. When marriage laws change they affect all married people, and no one sends couples notification that the rules governing their marriages have changed. Moreover, the most important marriage laws are state laws, and they cover only residents of a particular state. If a couple marries in one state and settles there, they are covered by that state's law. If the same couple moves to another state, they are covered by the laws of the new state as soon as they become residents there. The contractual terms for marriage in that state may be very different from the terms they originally "agreed to."

3. The fact that marriage contracts are defined by state law means that generally no private agreement by husband and wife can alter the terms set out in those laws. When a man and woman say "I do," they are agreeing to accept these definitions, rights, and obligations. Joan Krauskopf provides an example of how one state words this provision: "Husband and wife cannot, by any contract with each other, alter their legal relations except that they may agree to an immediate separation and make provisions for the support of either of them and their children during the separation" (1977, 191). Decisions about marital duties are deemed too important to leave to the choice of individuals.

What values do states attempt to support through the regulation of marriage? We have already discussed some of these principles in Chapter 8 as they relate to the common law. Marriage law has been designed to maintain the patriarchal division of roles and power between men and women because that division has been regarded as the moral basis of a stable society. To what degree does the law continue to define a wife's identity as incorporated and consolidated into that of the husband? To answer this question we must look at the legal definition of marriage, or the content of the marriage contract.[4]

NAMES AND PLACES. The most obvious and immediate results of marriage used to be that a man and woman would begin to live together, and the woman would assume the man's surname. Even though couples now often live together before marriage, only marriage actually gives them the legal right to do so. The law also grants the husband the right to choose his place of residence, and it imposes on the wife what is almost an obligation to be domiciled in her husband's choice of residence. Even if a couple actually have different residences, in most states they are assumed to be domiciled at the husband's residence. If a wife refuses to move with her husband to another city, she is assumed by law to have abandoned him; if a husband refuses to move with his wife to another city, she is still assumed to have abandoned him. In many states a woman may now establish a separate domicile for a specific purpose

299

Chapter 10:
Consenting Adults?
Choice and Intimate
Relationships

TABLE 10-3
Whither Thou Goest...

"Suppose both a husband and wife work at good and interesting jobs and the husband is offered a very good job in another city. Assuming they have no children, which one of these solutions do you think they should seriously consider?"

	Women	*Men*
Husband should turn down the job	10%	19%
Wife should quit and relocate with husband	72	62
Husband should take new job and move/wife should keep her job and stay	6	5
No opinion/DK	12	14

"If the wife is offered a very good job in another city?"

Wife should turn down the job	55%	58%
Husband should quit and relocate with wife	20	22
Wife should take new job and move/husband should keep his job and stay	8	6
No opinion/DK	17	14

Note: Data are from a Roper survey of approximately 3000 women and 1000 men conducted in 1985.
SOURCE: Simon and Landis (1989, 272).

but the assumption remains that the head of the household—the husband, whenever he is present—determines where a family lives.

The traditional norms about domicile embedded in law are not just remnants of the past; they remain part of our cultural values. As Table 10-3 shows, most people still think wives should follow their husbands. It will be some time yet before husbands and wives are considered equal partners.

The surnames that a couple or family use are also part of the marriage contract. Contrary to what most people believe, the practice of a woman taking her husband's name is derived from custom, and the legal requirement that a woman use her husband's name is of relatively recent vintage. Most states now give women full rights to retain their birth names, although some still require them to use the husband's surname for specific legal purposes such as obtaining a driver's license. Federal courts have declared that such laws do not violate a woman's constitutional rights. (For further discussion of this issue, see Chapter 9.)

The law has also generally assumed that children take the name of the parent who is the head of the household, usually the husband, unless the child is illegitimate, in which case he or she is given the surname of the mother. This rule has become more flexible recently, and many states now recognize the right of parents to give their child a name different from the father's. Some unmarried couples are now seeking the right to give their children the father's surname.

301

Chapter 10:
Consenting Adults?
Choice and Intimate
Relationships

RIGHTS AND OBLIGATIONS. If the heart of marital law is the relative rights and obligations of husband and wife, the marriage contract bears a striking resemblance to a (nonnegotiable) labor contract. According to law the marital relationship is simply this: The wife owes the husband household, domestic, and companionship services, and the husband, in return, has the duty to support the wife. To what degree and in what ways are these principles enforceable by law?

The husband's right to his wife's services is largely unenforceable by law in any direct sense. There are, however, some extremely important consequences of this aspect of the marriage contract. Because of the notion of "conjugal rights," until recently a wife in most states could not charge her husband with rape. The rationale was that by getting married individuals consent to sexual relations with their spouse, and that consent could not be withdrawn during the duration of the marriage. In recent years many states have been changing this policy, recognizing the possibility that coerced sex is illegal even in marriage.

Because the wife is obliged to perform domestic labor and therefore is not entitled to any direct compensation for it, until recently a wife's contribution to the family's economic welfare through her labor was not considered in adjudication of property division, for example, during divorce proceedings. This labor is now sometimes taken into account. Because the wife's obligations are unspecified and can cover any work she does in her home or any assistance she gives her husband as a "helpmeet," if a third party injures her, her husband may sue for the value of the household service he has lost, even though he has no legal obligation to pay his wife, and if he owns a farm or business and the wife performs duties associated with these ventures, she is not entitled to compensation. Joan M. Krauskopf (1977) cites a case that shows that it is possible that the income earned by a wife in the home, perhaps for baby-sitting, may actually belong to the husband because the definition of domestic services is so vague.

The wife's rights to support by her husband are also largely unenforceable. Court cases concerning the husband's duty point to a single conclusion: As long as a husband and wife live together, whatever support he chooses to give her is sufficient. A woman who feels her husband is not providing for her has virtually no legal recourse.

PROPERTY. If this book had been written before the middle of the nineteenth century, this section would be very short. Following the common law tradition accepted in most states at the time, wives could not own property (with a few exceptions). All property a woman owned when she married, all income earned by her labor, and all property acquired by other means during the marriage belonged to her husband and could be managed by him without her knowledge or consent. If he wished he could use her income to fulfill his obligation of support and provide her with necessaries.

By 1989 forty-one states had marital property systems based in the common law that call for separation of assets. The basic rule for determining who owns what is "property follows title." In common-law property states, as states following this rule are called, the husband and wife are treated as individuals with independent rights to own and manage property. Whoever has proof of title to specific assets owns them. If no one has specific proof of title, however, most courts assume that the husband is the owner, particularly if the wife has remained at home as a homemaker; she has no claim to these assets because she is viewed as having had no income with which to acquire them. There have been cases in which joint bank accounts have been viewed as the husband's property if the wife did not earn income; the wife simply had been allowed to draw on the husband's account.

Assuming that most husbands earn more than their wives, and that in a substantial minority of marriages women earn virtually nothing, common-law property states give considerable leverage to husbands. Even if the husband and wife are both income earners, they have to pay attention to how they divide payment of expenses. If a couple divides its expenses equally, but the husband pays for investment and the wife for immediate consumption expenses, the husband ends up with the property and the wife does not.

A second type of marital property regime—community property—is found in nine states, primarily in the Southwest and West plus Louisiana and Wisconsin. In community property states assets acquired during a marriage, with certain exceptions, are assumed by law to be jointly and equally owned by husband and wife. This system does not presume that the husband is the economic head of the family, even when the wife is a full-time homemaker. It does make it difficult for either husband or wife to maintain independent and separate assets.

Property laws affect people most directly when divorce or the death of one partner occurs. Common-law property states compensate widows to some extent for what could be the cruelty of the situation by following the principle of the "widow's share," which grants a minimum proportion of the husband's property to the widow. Because of the law's view that such a widow inherited property that belonged to someone else, however, inheritance taxes levied against the property can prove so burdensome that she must sell the property.

In recent years the distinctions between these different kinds of marital property laws have begun to blur, partly in response to claims that women's economic contributions to marriage should be taken into account and partly because of a desire to protect the economic situation of children of divorced and widowed parents. Some of these changes are discussed in Chapter 11.

THE STATE'S VIEW OF MARRIAGE.   What does marital law and policy tell us about the state's definition of marriage? Marriage is viewed in part as a couple's commitment to carry on their lineage by conceiving and raising children. As the Minnesota Supreme Court argued in 1971 (to explain why homosexuals could not be legally married). "The institution of marriage as a union of man and woman, uniquely involving the procreation and rearing of children within a family, is as old as the book of Genesis" (*Baker* v. *Nelson*). The institution of marriage is also the primary means the state has to regulate the distribution of property within and across generations. Moreover, it provides free labor and services that might otherwise have to be provided by the government. Political debate in the 1980s made the connection clear. Conservatives, including the president of the United States, argued that one of the main reasons that so much public money had to be spent on social welfare was that women were not doing their jobs properly. If women would stay at home and take care of children and old people, less money would have to be spent to replace their labor.

Although there have been many changes in marital and family property laws over the years, the laws continue to maintain women in a dependent position. If a husband and wife continue to love each other and are kind and generous with each other, the law will have little effect on them, particularly if they die at the same moment. However, the law continues to define women as subordinates dependent on their husband's good will.

303

Chapter 10:
Consenting Adults?
Choice and Intimate
Relationships

Many people have pointed to a cruel irony in marital law and policy. The women who fulfill their designated roles most completely are most hurt by these laws and policies. The full-time homemaker has few assets of her own and is most vulnerable during and after a marriage. Despite years of labor and service the "displaced homemaker" has few marketable skills that can earn her a living. At the turn of the century Charlotte Perkins Gilman ([1898] 1966) pointed out the inequity of the familial services-support relationship. The woman from a poor family has the hardest labor as a homemaker and is supported at only the most meager levels by even the most generous husband; the woman from a wealthy family does relatively little strenuous labor but is handsomely supported.

Changes in marital law and related policies have been substantial. There are more choices available to people, and especially women, then there ever have been before. Young women changed their expectations about marriage over recent decades, but especially in the 1960s and 1970s (Weeks and Botkin 1987).

Divorce

In 1985 well over one million marriages ended in divorce. Ending a marriage was not always so easy; the marriage contract had few escape clauses, and divorce was rarely granted. Throughout most of American history there have been very few grounds on which an individual could sue for divorce. To sue for divorce one partner had to prove that the other partner had provided the grounds, that is violated the marriage contract by, for example, committing adultery. Only the innocent party could file for divorce; the person at fault could not.

Divorce procedures were not designed to try to achieve the most amicable agreement; to the contrary, if the partners were amicable there couldn't be much reason for divorce. Could the partners who wanted a divorce simply cooperate and agree to say that one or the other had committed adultery? Unlikely. A divorce suit could be turned down if it appeared there was collusion between the divorcing partners, and property division depended in part on the assignment of fault or innocence. Because the guilty party had committed a crime against state law in violating the marriage contract, he or she could not profit by divorce.

Since the 1970s most states have moved toward no-fault divorce. In a no-fault divorce, one partner does not have to charge the other with a crime; instead the couple can seek a divorce on grounds of "irretrievable breakdown." Although this has made divorces easier to obtain, these procedures are not without pitfalls. Consider the homemaker who has been the victim of cruelty or finds that her husband has been having affairs. In earlier days she could charge her husband with the fault and seek a divorce. As the innocent party she would likely be rewarded a considerable proportion of the couple's property. Under the current system if that same woman and her husband divorce on no-fault grounds there is no reason for the court to award her more than is legally hers anyway. Most states are trying to relieve this problem by giving courts the power to redistribute property, particularly where children are involved.[5]

A major source of contention and controversy in recent years has been the awarding of alimony. Herma Hill Kay (1988) points out that the practice of forcing a husband to pay alimony dates from the time when divorce was not possible except under conditions of fault. Under early laws, which followed church rules, a divorced person could not remarry. In effect a divorce meant that a husband and wife were not allowed to live together any more, but they were still husband and wife and could not remarry. In its inception alimony was "a judicial order entered during the existence of marriage fixing a husband's duty to support his wife while they were living apart due to his fault." Kay calls this a "functional substitute for the duty of the husband to support his wife." (272).

By the middle of the twentieth century alimony was granted to wives in only a minority of cases, and in many of these the wives never actually received payments. In the 1960s and 1970s many states declared that either the husband or the wife could be awarded alimony, depending on the circumstances of the case. In 1979 the Supreme Court reinforced this principle be declaring unconstitutional an Alabama law restricting alimony to payments by husbands to wives (*Orr* v. *Orr*). The court argued that alimony is awarded on the basis of need, and "there is no reason . . . to use sex as a proxy for need."

New issues that have important consequences for women and men continue to be raised in the context of financial settlements accompanying divorces. In recent years courts have been working out new arrangements for the division of marital property, particularly in common-law property states. By 1983 only three states still treated marital property during divorce so that ownership follows title: Florida, Mississippi, and West Virginia. As in the states instituting no-fault divorce, state legislators began to order courts to divide property equally between divorcing partners. This system has been rejected by most states, however, because it created problems in divorces involving children. We shall look at these problems in more detail in Chapter 11.

Most states now allow courts discretion in apportioning marital property equitably as opposed to equally; in other words, according to the merits of the case. As attorney Martha Davis points out, this change results from changes in the views of gender roles in marriage: "This modification of the common law system reflects changed ideas of economic fairness which dictate that the homemaker's nonmonetary contributions to the marriage be recognized and acknowledges that title is an inaccurate indicator of participation in marriage" (1983, 1092–93). It also allows courts the flexibility to decide what is best for each case individually.

There are other new developments in treatments of divorce that reflect more generally on how people think about marital relationships. Some people now argue that a wife who quits school or training to support her husband through an educational or training program that enhances his earning power has a right to the benefits of the training she bought; and some courts regard it to be unfair for a husband to receive continuing financial benefit from an action that may have diminished his wife's own earning power. Other changes in divorce laws and policies call into question the definition of marriage and the marriage relationship itself. Divorces involving children raise some especially difficult issues, which we shall review in Chapter 11.

305

Chapter 10:
Consenting Adults?
Choice and Intimate
Relationships

The Law on "Living in Sin"

Most states had done away with common-law marriage by the 1920s. A common-law marriage was one in which two people were declared married after seven years of living together; that is, after the statute of limitations had run out on the crime of having fornicated outside of marriage. Such a definition makes it clear that common-law marriages were merely tolerated; they were not favored practice.

Increasing numbers of couples are now choosing to live together and run households without getting married. In some cases this choice reflects a conscious rejection of the problems raised by marital law and policy. But if marriages are not always made in heaven, neither are the relationships of unmarried couples. Can the agreements they make be enforced? As we have seen, divisions of labor do not tend to be any more equitable among cohabiting couples than among married couples. If a relationship breaks up, does the women get adequate compensation for her unpaid domestic labor? What happens to accumulated property?

The law remains in a state of confusion. Unmarried individuals are in a better position than married people to have their private contracts enforced, although there are limitations. If it seems that the couple is exchanging sex for support, the contract is not enforceable because it is in effect a criminal agreement for prostitution. Moreover, when people simply move in together, their agreements are generally oral or even simply implied.

The most famous court case on cohabitation is *Marvin* v. *Marvin,* which was decided in the California Supreme Court in 1976. Lee Marvin and Michelle Triola (who used Marvin's surname) lived together for seven years. After breaking up, Triola claimed that they had had an agreement that she would provide household services, he would support her, and they would share their property, which, because Marvin was a successful actor, was considerable. Triola charged that Marvin reneged when they broke up, and she demanded that the court order him to make an equitable property division. The court declared that such an agreement had to be honored. In the past, it said, such an arrangement would have been regarded as prostitution and therefore not enforceable, but times had changed. "To equate the nonmarital relationship of today to such a subject matter is to do violence to an accepted and wholly different practice." At the same time the court made its view of marriage clear:

> We take this occasion to point out that the structure of society itself largely depends on the institution of marriage; and nothing we have said in this opinion should be taken to derogate that institution. The joining of the man and woman in marriage is at once the most socially productive and individually fulfilling relationship that one can enjoy in the course of a lifetime.

In the end Triola received very little.

This precedent has not held firm in courts throughout the United States, partly because of fears that it would weaken the institution of marriage. The Illinois Supreme Court, for example, came to the opposite conclusion in 1979 in *Hewitt* v. *Hewitt,* a case involving a couple who lived in an "outwardly appearing conventional family relationship" complete with children. The court argued that treating an unmarried couple as though they were married would contravene the state "policy strengthening and preserving the integrity of marriage." To do otherwise would be to recreate the common-law marriage, which the court did not want to do.

Some people might argue that enlightened and progressive law should respect people's choices and treat the unmarried as though they are married. But would this eliminate the problems we have discussed? Or would it just allow more people to share the same old problems, plus create some new ones? Consider the problems with marital law itself. What fundamental principles governing people's personal relationships do we want enforced? The question cannot be dismissed by saying simply that people should make their own choices. These personal choices affect the community as a whole and are sometimes mere reflections of the larger, androcentric sex/gender system.

The Politics of Personal Life

One of the reasons feminism is so threatening to many people and creates so much contention is that it makes us think of our personal lives—our friendships, intimacies, and sexual relationships—in unaccustomed ways. The structure of sex/gender systems shapes us in the most private aspects of our lives, not just because our private relationships are in part governed by law, but also because the gender ideologies we have learned affect the way we interact with others and because most social institutions are based to some degree on expectations about the nature of relationships among people. Most of us don't want to think about our personal lives in political terms as matters involving struggles over power, but research supports feminist arguments that our personal lives, particularly our sexual lives, constitute a key arena for the oppression and eventual liberation of women.

This analysis suggests why change in sex/gender systems is both difficult and frightening. Sexuality is central to our sense of identity, and, at least in American culture, it is also a source of tremendous anxiety. To question our sexuality and the patterns it takes is to question our very sense of self. Men who have learned that masculinity requires them to be the successful pursuer and to dominate women in sexual and other intimate relations are threatened by women who either demand equality in their personal relationships or do not see their relationships with men as sexual.

Increasing numbers of women and men are thinking carefully about the significance of their intimate behavior and the choices they make in their private lives. As this chapter has suggested, even when one is aware of the problems, making choices is not easy because of social constraints and personal feelings. People can be hurt in the process. But feminists argue that the reward for facing these challenges is great: a chance for friendship, love, and intimacy that are not based on domination and coercion.

Over a century ago the feminist Margaret Fuller summed up her ideal of a personal relationship between a husband and wife, not as a couple in which two were merged into one and thus lost individual autonomy or equality, but as the progress of "two pilgrims toward a common shrine" ([1845] 1971, 80–81). As Fuller's words show, the application of feminist theory and the pursuit of autonomy for women does not mean we must abandon all sense of mystery and romance in our lives.

307

Chapter 10:
Consenting Adults?
Choice and Intimate
Relationships

NOTES

1.   Why are the institutions in which men obtain vicarious pleasure from watching other people having sex and men hurting women labeled "adult"?

2.   This study surveyed over 12,000 people, including 4314 heterosexual couples, 969 gay male couples, and 788 lesbian couples.

3.   This "balance figure" was created as follows. Individuals were asked whether they or their partner usually initiated sexual relations, or whether they both did equally. The balance was calculated by subtracting the proportion who said one partner usually initiates from the proportion who said that the other partner usually initiates sexual relations.

4.   It is impossible to discuss marital law in detail because it differs from state to state.

5.   For an influential discussion of the faults of no-fault divorce, see Weitzman (1985).

11

Reproduction, Parenthood, and Child Care

MOTHERHOOD has generally been seen as the destiny and the special mission of women. Through the ages when anyone discussed women's roles, status, and activities, one of the first questions anybody was likely to ask concerns the possible effects of changes in women's lives on their roles as mothers. Law, theology, and medicine each have their special perspectives on the matter, but for the most part when authorities in these areas think about women, they are thinking about women as mothers and potential mothers.

In the last century motherhood and reproduction have become questions for analysis and debate for at least three reasons:

1. Childhood was a historical "invention." Through his influential book, *Centuries of Childhood,* the historian Philippe Aries (1962) showed that the idea of childhood as a special time of life when people are supposed to be nurtured and protected from adult concerns is a new notion that evolved in Western culture only in recent centuries. A walk through an art museum shows how people's perception of children has changed. Up to the eighteenth century children in paintings look like miniature adults; only later do they begin to look like children as we know them today.

    Although Aries had little if anything to say about mothers, it is reasonable to expect that only when the child became a special category of person did the mother also become a special category of person. Julie A. Matthaei (1982) argues, for example, that in colonial America even the suckling of infants was not necessarily the biological mother's work. If families could afford it, they hired wet nurses. Child raising meant introducing children to their adult work as soon as possible, and because women and men had different work to do child raising was done by mothers, fathers, and other family and nonfamily members. Matthaei shows that much of the work of parenting—especially the parts considered most important—was done by fathers.

2. The growth of industrialization separated production from the home. As a distinct sphere of "family life" emerged, so did distinct roles within that sphere. As Matthaei writes, "Family relationships—between husband and wife, between parents and children—began to gain a content of their own" (1982, 110). Homemaking, including motherhood, became a vocation.
3. Motherhood was transformed into an activity regarded as having great social importance. Part of the reason for this change was the growing realization that people could actually control and make choices about whether and when to reproduce and the ways to raise children. As more people realized that choices could be made, they began to evaluate and weigh alternatives. One of the questions they considered was which choices would be beneficial and which detrimental to society as a whole.

In the nineteenth century numerous debates began to flow from this new consciousness. Should control be exerted over the number of people born? What was the best way to raise children? How much control should individual men and women have over reproduction? What type of mother would produce the best children? What responsibilities did society as a whole (especially through the force of government and law) have for the production and care of children? The debate over these questions continues today. Let us look more closely at these issues.

To Be or Not to Be a Parent

"If the right of privacy means anything, it is the right of the individual, married or single, to be free of unwarranted governmental intrusion into matters so fundamentally affecting a person as the decision whether to bear or beget a child." This was the view taken by the U.S. Supreme Court in 1972, when it declared unconstitutional laws barring single people from purchasing contraceptives (*Eisenstadt* v. *Baird*). The major breakthrough in giving individuals more control over their own decisions had come in 1965, when in *Griswold* v. *Connecticut,* the Supreme Court first declared that there is a constitutional right to privacy, and indicated that this right meant that married people could not be barred from purchasing contraceptives. The Court restated and further developed its point in 1977 in *Carey* v. *Population Services International* when it declared that an unmarried minor should be able to obtain contraceptives: "The Constitution protects individual decisions in matters of childbearing from unjustified intrusion by the State." How well protected is this constitutional right? How free are people, especially women, to make their own decisions over whether and when to become a parent?

Reproduction and Choice

Birth patterns have changed over the course of this century. Women are about as likely to have children as they ever were, but they have fewer children now than they did at the beginning of the century. Women's reproductive behavior is influenced by historical conditions; during the Depression women had fewer children than they do now, but they had more right after World War II.

Socialization and social pressure play important roles in people's thinking about reproduction and parenthood. Not only do most people expect to bear children; not having children is generally viewed negatively, especially in women. Consider the words we use to describe an adult who has no children: There are mothers, fathers, parents, and childless people. Lucia Valeska (1975) asks what would be people's reaction if more women without children described themselves as ''child free.'' The term seems jarring to most people because it suggests that one might be happy about being without children. It suggests that there might be more than one correct choice for a person with respect to childbearing. At this time, however, women without children are often viewed and treated as not quite adult themselves.

Joanna Ross and James Kahan (1983) did an interesting study to investigate reactions to married couples' decisions about having children. They read to college students one of three versions of a story about a married couple. One version included the information that the couple did not want children, another said that the couple had two children already, and the third said nothing at all about children. The students were then asked to imagine what the couple's life would be like in one year and in twenty-five years. Of those who heard the story about the couple who did not want children, 50 percent thought the couple would have children anyway. Only 37 percent thought the couple would remain child free. Among the thirty-eight

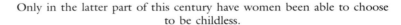

Only in the latter part of this century have women been able to choose
to be childless.

people who received no information about the couple's parental status and wishes, twenty-six specifically mentioned that the couple were parents in their projections. In the twenty-five-year projections the child-free couples were much more likely than the other couples to be described as divorced. An interesting gender difference emerged in the reactions of the students. Women regarded the couple with children as most satisfied, and men regarded the couple without children as most satisfied.

Children are somewhat more central to a woman's sense of self than they are to a man's. In a Canadian survey nearly 800 people were asked to list up to twenty items in response to the question, "Who am I?" Women were significantly more likely than men to mention their parental status (94 percent versus 85 percent), and they put parental status higher up on their lists of self-descriptions. Note that although motherhood seems more central to women than fatherhood is to men, the vast majority of both sexes included parenthood in their lists (Mackie 1983). Even by adolescence, however, females feel more pressure than males to have children (Thompson 1980).

Eleanor Macklin (1980) points out that about 10 percent of all women who are married at some point in their lives never have children, about half of these by choice. Her review of research indicates that child-free women are more likely to have college educations and high-status jobs than other women, and they tend to be older than average at the age of their first marriage. They are also more likely than average to believe that having children has some negative effects on parents' lives. Psychological studies show that they are more likely to be androgynous, and they appear to have above-average mental health. Harold Feldman's (1981) study of married couples found no differences in family background or in marital happiness between those with children and those without. The main difference he found was that the child-free couples had less traditional attitudes toward women and tended to interact with each other more than couples with children.

Although to most people it does not seem odd to ask why a person does not want children, few seem to wonder why people do want children. People choose not to have children for many reasons. Those who are single face particular burdens if they want children or find themselves confronted with an unwanted or unplanned pregnancy. People who are married may reject parenthood because child raising does not fit their goals and interests, they do not have the financial resources to care for children adequately, they feel they would not be good parents, or they worry about overpopulation. People choose to have children for many different reasons as well, although few parents ever have to think of their reasons. For many people, of course, reproduction is not seen as a choice; it is simply what adults do.

At one time having children was an important economic resource. Children were needed to work in the family, and parents hoped that children would provide old-age insurance. Those who make a conscious choice to have children now may do so because they like the idea of having children, they think they would be good parents, they view having children as fulfilling in their marital relationship, they believe having children will provide personal fulfillment, or they believe having children is a way to leave a mark on the world. Some minority and religious groups urge their members to have children to preserve or expand the group itself.

One decision that increasing numbers of people seem to be considering more carefully is the timing of births. In the late 1960s and early 1970s the press began to sound the alarm that women were giving up having babies. After a while it became clear that the primary change was not in whether women were having children, but in when they did so. In 1970 the majority of mothers had had their first child by the time they were twenty-five years old: about 36 percent before they were twenty and 46 percent between twenty and twenty-four years old. In 1987 about 23 percent had had their first child under the age of twenty and 33 percent between twenty and twenty-four. The trend toward older first births is also marked in the increased proportion of women who have their first birth when they are thirty and older. In 1970 this included 4 percent of births, while in 1987 the figure was 16 percent.[1]

There are several reasons for the change toward later births:

1. Wider availability of contraception and abortion make such choices possible.
2. Changing health-care technology and medical views have raised the age at which pregnancy is considered relatively dangerous.
3. Women's education levels have increased and women are starting careers in unprecedented numbers, thus making childbearing at a later age desirable.
4. Attitudes have changed, leading many women to make a new kind of choice. Women once believed that motherhood necessarily came first and perhaps could be followed by a career. But now more women, especially those entering professional careers, are establishing themselves in their careers first and then having children. Doctors also now understand that having children in the late thirties is not as dangerous as they used to assume.[2] We will look more at the implications of the decision in Chapter 12.

Another new development that has been greeted with alarm is that a higher proportion of single women than ever before are having children. In 1950 4 percent of all births involved single women; in 1970 the figure was almost 11 percent; in 1980 it was 18 percent; and in 1985 it was 22 percent. There are large differences between black and white women; in 1986 about 16 percent of all births to white women involved single women, and about 61 percent of all births to black women involved single women. A very large proportion of these births involve very young women, many in their teens. Indeed about a third of births to single females involve young women who have not yet reached their twentieth birthday. Although the proportion of births to single women has increased in all age categories since 1950, the increase is greatest among those between the ages of fifteen and twenty-five. Young motherhood is especially prevalent in communities in which young women do not stay in school much longer than they have to and have no careers for which they are likely to be making long-term plans.

It is clear that many, perhaps most, of these births are not the result of considered decisions, especially among those who have barely passed childhood themselves. For the young and the poor, lack of adequate knowledge about contraception hurts an increasingly sexually active population. People of lower socioeconomic status tend to begin their sexual activity younger than other people, which means they begin with less information (Weinberg and Williams 1980). Governmental decisions allowing states to refuse public funding for abortions also mean that poor women do not have the options wealthier women have.

On the other hand, many single women are having children by choice. About one quarter of pregnant teenagers say they intended to become pregnant (Resnick 1984). For many of these young women, however, the "choice" is based on misunderstanding. Large numbers of teens who have children by choice believe that having children will make them more adult, make others treat them more like adults, or at least give them a way to leave home and their family problems.

Many relatively wealthy professional women who have the financial means to provide a home for a child are choosing to have children regardless of their marriage prospects. For some of these women the reason for their choice is age. As they move into and through their thirties they worry that their biological aging will take away the choice to have a child they may want. These women face important moral dilemmas: Is it right to marry a man just because one wants a child? Is this fair to the man? Because having a husband tends to increase the amount of work women have to do at home, is it fair to the woman? Some people argue that it is fairer to children to provide them with two parents, but if the marriage was really only an expedient, how long will it last?

The theme of choice in reproduction has been persistent in the last century of feminism. Choice, however, means more than simply the availability of birth control and abortion. Many nineteenth-century feminists who fought for voluntary motherhood were not arguing for birth control but for ways to manage reproduction to bolster the dignity of mothers and their abilities to carry out their important social functions (Gordon 1982). The anarchist Emma Goldman argued forcefully for wider availability of contraception but she, like Margaret Sanger, saw this as only one of the ways to give women the chance to be the best mothers they could be. Some feminists, including some of the best-known suffragists, even supported the idea of eugenics, the "science" of determining which people should be allowed to reproduce. The goal of eugenics is to produce a better race of people, and its proponents generally support racist, conservative points of view.

In her utopian novel *Herland* ([1915] 1979), progressive feminist Charlotte Perkins Gilman envisioned a society of women who had decided that only women with the right temperament and skills for motherhood would conceive. Only babies that were wanted would be born; in Herland the idea of abortion was considered utterly appalling. In the real world, however, if we are to consider control over reproduction, we must investigate the questions of both contraception and abortion.

Contraception

There have been many changes in the technology of contraception over the last century and a half. Changes in the process of manufacturing rubber in the nineteenth century produced more effective and comfortable condoms and led in the latter part of the century to the development of the diaphragm as we know it. The design of intrauterine devices (IUDs) has changed radically in recent years. Spermicidal agents and douches differ in content from those that were used for centuries. Methods of sterilization have changed since the 1960s. Even the rhythm method has changed

Margaret Sanger, a birth control activist.

in technique with the use of basal temperature charting, although the principle and the results are the same. Of course abstinence is now, as it always has been, the safest, most effective method of preventing conception.

Despite the changes that have occurred, however, there is only one form of contraception used now that was completely unknown in any form before the nineteenth century: the Pill. The approval of the birth control pill by the Food and Drug Administration (FDA) in 1960 was regarded as the harbinger of a new revolution. As we shall see, there are now questions about how successful that revolution was.[3]

There is clear evidence that various means of contraception were widely used in the nineteenth century (Degler 1980; Gordon 1977; Petchesky 1984). Birthrates declined among some groups of women. Historians have uncovered the words of many women relating their birth control experiences. The fact that there was a massive political and governmental onslaught against contraception in the 1870s demonstrates how widespread the growing use of birth control techniques was.

The governmental response came in the form of the Comstock Laws, inspired and promoted by a self-proclaimed emissary of God, Anthony Comstock. These laws were intended to control pornography. The following quotation from one such law reveals the definition of pornography:

> Whoever (within the United States) shall sell . . .or shall offer to sell, or to lend, or to give away, or in any manner to exhibit, or shall otherwise publish or offer to publish in any manner, or shall have in his possession, for any such purpose or purposes, any obscene book, pamphlet, paper, writing, advertisement, circular, print, picture, drawing or other representation, figure, or image on or of paper or other material, or any cast, instrument, or other article or any drug or medicine, or any article whatever, for the *prevention of conception,* or for causing unlawful *abortion,* or shall advertise the same for sale, or shall write or print, or cause to be written or printed, any card, circular, book, pamphlet, advertisement, or notice of any kind, stating when, where, how, or of whom, or by what means any of the articles . . .can be purchased or obtained, or shall manufacture, draw, or print, or in any wise make any of such articles, shall be deemed guilty of a misdemeanor. . . (quoted in Kerber and Mathews 1982, 438).

The means to control reproduction was defined as pornographic. The punishment was between six months and five years imprisonment at hard labor, or a fine of between $100 and $2000.

Women's first battle in birth control was for access to information about their reproductive systems and the techniques available to control them. Techniques have long been available even when they were not widely used. The people who have been most affected by the repression of information are the poor and those with little education. Middle-class women uninhibited by theology have been limiting their number of pregnancies quite effectively for a considerable time. Those who can least afford to have numerous pregnancies and births are the same people who are most affected by the anticontraception laws. As early as the turn of the century women like Margaret Sanger and Emma Goldman understood this and worked to help poor, working-class, and immigrant women find the solution they needed and wanted. Sanger and Goldman were arrested under the Comstock laws for their efforts.

A cruel irony of history is that although poor women have often in effect been denied access to contraception, at other times sterilization has been forced on these women. In the 1960s and 1970s a new issue arose when it became known that many poor women, especially poor black women, were being forced to undergo sterilization without their consent or under considerable pressure to consent. Coerced sterilization has been performed most often on women on the welfare rolls by doctors or hospitals who argue that women who have too many children and cannot afford the medical treatment should be stopped from having more children. Earlier in the century sterilization of prisoners and the ''feeble-minded'' was a respected practice. Although the government now has issued guidelines to eliminate abuse of this kind, it has apparently not been stopped completely. There remain legal loopholes. In *Walker* v. *Pierce* (1977), for example, a U.S. Court of Appeals decided in favor of a doctor who refused to treat pregnant patients who already had two children if they could not pay their own medical bills (for example, if they were on Medicaid) unless they underwent sterilization.

Coerced or involuntary sterilization is an important issue. In *Skinner* v. *Oklahoma* (1942) the Supreme Court showed a realization of what sterilization could mean if it was guided by the wrong rules and practices:

> We are dealing here with legislation which involves one of the basic civil rights of man. Marriage and procreation are fundamental to the very existence and survival of the race. The power to sterilize. . . may have subtle, far-reaching and devastating effects. In evil or reckless hands it can cause races or types which are inimical to the dominant group to wither and disappear. There is no redemption for the individual whom the law touches.

It is no wonder that many black feminists do not define the right to contraception or abortion as a central issue for them. Control over reproduction is a question not simply of whether the means to avoid pregnancy or childbirth is available but also of whether the means to choose parenthood is available.

Comstock-style contraception policy was not attacked effectively until 1965. Many different groups had been fighting for legalization of birth control, but it was a Supreme Court decision that made the difference. In *Griswold* v. *Connecticut,* one of the most important Supreme Court cases of recent decades, the court declared it unconstitutional for a state to make a law prohibiting the use of contraceptives by married people. The significance of this decision goes beyond this relatively narrow statement about contraception. The reasoning behind this decision had a profound impact on later decisions about contraception, abortion, and other issues. The court argued for the first time in American history that the Bill of Rights grants Americans a constitutional right to privacy. In this case it concluded that the law could not invade the privacy of the marriage bed.

The Supreme Court expanded its application of the right to privacy in the 1972 case, *Eisenstadt* v. *Baird*. (See earlier discussion on page 309.) This case involved the distribution of contraception to single people, and the court concluded that the decision whether to have a child was a private decision protected by the Constitution regardless of the marital status of the individuals involved. The Supreme Court recognized the fact that many people would regard this decision as contradictory to the idea that single people should not be engaging in sexual relations. It noted, however, that barring single people from obtaining contraceptives does not keep them from fornicating, and in any case it would be unreasonable to make "the birth of an unwanted child [a] punishment for fornication." The Supreme Court reinforced its view once again in 1977 in *Carey* v. *Population Services International* by protecting the right of a minor to gain access to contraception.

Legalization of contraception does not mean that people have the knowledge and information necessary to make decisions about birth control. Adolescents in particular often lack a clear understanding of reproduction and of the likelihood that they will become pregnant (Zellman and Goodchilds 1983; Resnick 1984). Young men are certainly under no great pressure to understand reproduction.

Traditional sexual ideology and guilt also play their roles in guiding people's behavior. Even people who know about contraception may not use it. Joanna Rohrbaugh's (1980) review of the research shows that women who have learned to feel guilty about having sexual relations are less likely to understand and use contraception than people who do not feel guilty. This is true in part because a woman who takes care to use birth control must admit to herself that she is choosing to do something she thinks is wrong. Instead she can say to herself, ''I couldn't have *meant* to do this because after all I wasn't prepared.'' Traditional ideology, which holds men to be the pursuers, may lead women to assume that men will take care of contraception (an assumption that shows more trust than wisdom) and make men believe it is women's business to avoid getting pregnant.

Traditional sexual ideology and guilt about sex may hinder partners from discussing contraception and may make the actual process of donning a condom or inserting a diaphragm more distasteful and sexually inhibiting than it is for people who are more comfortable with themselves and each other. Traditional sexual ideology and guilt lead many people to abstinence or unwanted pregnancy. One study of women aged eighteen to thirty-four found that those who used contraception regularly differed from women who took more risks when they had sex. They were more likely to initiate sex and reported having more orgasms. They were more likely to be living with their partners and for a longer time. They were also more likely to be from non-Catholic backgrounds (Harvey and Scrimshaw 1988).

Even for people who seek contraception, good means and complete knowledge are difficult to obtain. Each available method has drawbacks, some of them serious. The rhythm method, douches, withdrawal, and spermicides used with no other contraceptive device have high failure rates. Douches and spermicides can cause irritation, and some intrauterine devices and the birth control pill can cause major medical problems. Many forms of birth control are psychologically difficult for people to use, either because they require considerable attention or distraction from the sexual activity or because they are messy or uncomfortable. Scientists and doctors are unsure about the risks of some methods, such as birth control pills.

After it became widely available in the 1960s, the birth control pill quickly became the most popular means of contraception used in the United States, particularly among young people. Doubts about the safety of the Pill, especially for cigarette smokers and women over thirty-five, led to greater caution on the part of many women. Many doctors had special worries about young women's reactions to information about side effects, because for them going off the Pill often meant not using any birth control method. The Pill is the easiest method of birth control to use, and a young woman is especially likely to neglect more interventionist alternatives because she might still be more concerned with not ''putting off'' her boyfriend than she is with protecting herself.

Nevertheless the popularity of the Pill increased from the beginning to the end of the 1980s, when 76 percent of women had positive attitudes toward it. The condom had not been a very popular form of birth control among women until the 1980s, when women's attitudes became increasingly positive, partly because of the fear of AIDS. On the other hand intrauterine devices (IUDs) became less popular because of safety issues and failure rates (Forrest and Fordyce 1988). Each method has different benefits and risks. Women and their medical advisers face a dilemma that can be resolved properly only by careful thought and careful assessment of each individual situation.

One point is clear: In the sexual division of labor, contraception is still women's responsibility. There are only two relatively effective means of contraception available to heterosexually active men: condoms and vasectomies. Condoms are not as reliable as some other methods (although more reliable than some), and many men object to them on aesthetic grounds. Many women support men's objection to condoms because they don't want their partners' pleasure diminished, but others consider men's mild discomfort a small price to pay compared to the discomfort and side effects of the means available to women, even though these means are more effective. On the other hand, although condoms have drawbacks as contraceptive devices, they do have an advantage not shared by other methods: They help prevent transmission of disease, especially the killer AIDS.

Vasectomies, or male sterilization, is reversible in most cases, although doctors are reluctant to perform this operation on very young men or men who have not yet had children. Many men find the idea of sterilization distasteful because of mistaken notions that their masculinity or sex drive will be decreased; however, many men opt for sterilization, especially if they have had children.

Work on effective male forms of contraception has progressed very slowly. Scientists argue that because the male reproductive system is more complex intervention is more difficult. Moreover, the safety standards now observed in developing a male birth control pill appear to be higher than those used in the development of the female birth control pill, partly because safety standards in general have become more stringent over the last quarter of a century. In any case contraception will probably remain primarily women's responsibility for the foreseeable future. Even if most people agreed that greater sharing of responsibility is desirable, many women wonder whether they want to entrust contraception to men, who cannot get pregnant.

Abortion

When the United States adopted the English common law it accepted the view that abortion could not be considered a crime until quickening; that is, the time at which the fetus's movements can be felt. The first law in the United States that explicitly discussed abortion was an 1821 Connecticut statute that reinforced the common law. The first statute dealing with an unquickened fetus was New York's 1828 statute that made abortion of an unquickened fetus a misdemeanor and abortion of a quickened fetus second-degree manslaughter unless the abortion was necessary to preserve the life of the mother. The number of abortions rose considerably in the 1840s. Soon more states began to pass restrictive legislation that abolished distinctions among abortions and increased penalties. In the late 1860s, the Roman Catholic Church condemned most abortions. By the beginning of the twentieth century abortion was illegal throughout the United States. The option of a legal abortion was all but foreclosed until the 1960s unless a woman could afford to go to a country that allowed them, such as Sweden.

Why did abortion law become more restrictive? The Supreme Court asked itself precisely this question in 1973 when it was trying to decide what to do about the question in the case of *Roe* v. *Wade*. Justice Harry Blackmun, who wrote the court's opinion, found three reasons:

1. The new abortion laws helped to support the morality of the time, which, as we have seen, defined control over reproduction, including abortion, as pornographic and obscene.
2. Abortion was hazardous when not performed properly, and the medical field was filled with quacks. The restrictive laws, therefore, were sometimes forwarded in an effort to protect women.
3. These laws were viewed (relatively rarely) as ways to protect the life of the unborn from the time of conception. This became much more important to the prevailing public view in the twentieth century than it had been previously.

The 1960s saw a rise in the agitation for abortion, and some states began to reform their laws. Once again, however, the real change was instigated by the Supreme Court, which in January 1973 tore down much of the edifice of antiabortion laws in its decisions on two cases, *Roe* v. *Wade* and *Doe* v. *Bolton*. The court again used the right to privacy enunciated in *Griswold* v. *Connecticut* in 1965. The justices argued that abortion must be included in the right of individuals to decide whether to have a child. But they also said, "a State may properly assert important interests in safeguarding health, in maintaining medical standards, and in protecting potential life. At some point in pregnancy, these respective interests become sufficiently compelling to sustain regulation of the factors that govern the abortion decision." At what point? The court decided that it was in no position to argue that theological or philosophical question of when life begins, although it did agree that under the law a fetus is not treated as a legal person with civil rights. It therefore divided pregnancy into three stages, distinguished by the relative claims a state could make in intervening in a woman's decision.

In the first stage, covering roughly the first trimester, the claims of the woman are strongest when weighed against other factors, and therefore the state may not interfere with her right to choose abortion by making restrictive policies. At this stage, the court reasoned, the state does not have sufficiently strong grounds to restrict a woman's constitutional right to privacy.

Whereas in the first trimester, "mortality in abortion may be less than mortality in normal childbirth," during the second trimester abortion becomes riskier for women. In the second trimester, therefore, "the state, in promoting its interest in the health of the mother, may, if it chooses, regulate the abortion procedure in ways that are reasonably related to maternal health."

Finally, "For the stage subsequent to viability, the state in promoting its interest in the potentiality of human life may, if it chooses, regulate, and even proscribe, abortion except where it is necessary, in appropriate medical judgment, for the preservation of the life or health of the mother." In the final stages of pregnancy states have almost full latitude to ban abortion.

This decision effected a compromise between those who speak unilaterally about the rights of the fetus, and those who speak unilaterally about the rights of the woman. Many people regard this case as having attained a delicate balance among conflicting and essentially irresolvable claims. Instead of settling the question, however, the decision increased public debate over abortion.

Many court battles have been fought over abortion since 1973 for two reasons:

1. As is generally true when a court makes a major new decision *Roe* v. *Wade* left many finer points of interpretation unarticulated.
2. The foes of abortion strengthened their political forces considerably and began to do everything in their power to use the law to chip away at and confine the 1973 decision.

One example of a later Supreme Court case that for the most part reinforced the expansion of abortion right is *Planned Parenthood* v. *Danforth* (1976). This case dealt with the constitutionality of several provisions of a Missouri law limiting abortion. The results of this case point to some of the ways states have attempted to narrow the impact of earlier abortion decisions, and it raises some interesting questions about the nature of choice and justice in abortion decisions. Among the court's conclusions were the following:

1. States may use a flexible definition of *viability* in deciding when abortion should be forbidden; they do not have to adhere to a strict trimester rule. Given advances in medicine, this enables states to expand the time during which they may ban abortion.
2. A woman may be required to give consent in writing before undergoing first-trimester abortion. Some states have used this provision to require that women review graphic descriptions of even minutely possible risks before having an abortion, as well as pictures of aborted fetuses and fetal development. The purpose of this kind of "informed consent" is to deter women from having abortions.
3. It is unconstitutional to require a spouse's consent for a first-trimester abortion on the grounds that this would constitute granting the spouse a veto over the women's decision. In effect she would have the right to choose an abortion only if her husband wanted her to have one. As the Court said,

   > Ideally, the decision to [abort] should be one concurred in by both the wife and her husband. . . . But it is difficult to believe that the goal of fostering mutuality and trust in a marriage and of strengthening the marital relationship and the marriage institution will be achieved by giving the husband (an unlimited) veto power.

4. It is unconstitutional to require parents' consent for a first-trimester abortion for an unmarried minor. "Minors, as well as adults, are protected by the Constitution." The Court further argued, "It is difficult . . . to conclude that providing a parent with absolute (veto power) will serve to strengthen the family

unit. Neither is it likely that such veto power will enhance parental authority or control. . . .''

5. It is unconstitutional to make saline amniocentesis illegal. Some states had attempted to do this on the grounds that the primary purpose of amniocentesis was to screen the fetus for certain defects which, if found, might end in the woman's choosing to abort.

6. States may require that hospitals keep records of every abortion performed in a state.

7. It is unconstitutional to require doctors to make every effort to save the life of the fetus without specifying the stage of fetal development at which this must take place. In an effort to dissuade doctors and hospitals from performing abortions, Missouri's law had made a blanket statement that doctors were required to try to save the aborted fetus.

The Supreme Court reached a legal turning point in *Webster* v. *Missouri* (1989). For the first time since *Roe* and *Doe* a majority of the judges signalled their intention to restrict the legal right to have abortions, although they did not make clear how far they would go. *Webster* reemphasized the court's identification of viability rather than trimesters as the key to whether abortion is a woman's constitutionally protected right. The decision made it clear that if women have a constitutionally protected right to abortion as *Roe* and *Doe* stated, this right exists only while there is no chance the fetus could be viable. Four of the judges indicated that they disagreed with the earlier decision that abortion is part of a constitutional right to privacy. They believed instead that it is a political issue that should be decided by legislatures. Above all the *Webster* decision signalled states to formulate new more restrictive policies if they wished. The court gave strong hints that it would reconsider the issue of constitutionality in a future case.

There have been a number of unanticipated consequences of the Supreme Court decision that first legalized abortion. The method of analysis the court used was to say that at the early stages of pregnancy states could not interfere with the private abortion choice in part because the mother had the deciding claim against any notion of fetal rights. At the same time, the decision opened the way not just for closing off the possibility for abortion later in the pregnancy, but also for asserting other rights of the fetus in the later stages. In fact, *Roe* paved the way for court-ordered caesarean sections and other interventions on behalf of the child in the womb (see e.g., Gallagher 1985).

FEDERAL FUNDING.   One of the most successful strategies used by those opposed to individual choice in abortion falls particularly heavily on the poor: the curtailing of federal and other public funds for abortions.

As part of the ''Great Society'' legislation of the 1960s Congress added an amendment to the Social Security Act (Title XIX) establishing the Medicaid program. Medicaid provides federal funding to states for medical services rendered to the poor. Participation in the program by any given state is voluntary, but all states that choose to participate must accept certain federal regulations. One of these is that Medicaid cannot be denied to anyone if the services rendered are medically necessary. All states have chosen to participate in the Medicaid program.

The first case decided by the Supreme Court that concerned abortion and Medicaid was *Beal* v. *Doe* in 1977. Pennsylvania had refused to use Medicaid funds to pay for abortions that were not deemed medically necessary. The Supreme Court saw no problem with this law. At the same time the Court decided that cities may refuse to allow nontherapeutic abortions to be performed in public hospitals on the grounds that public money is necessarily involved, and the public cannot be forced to pay for medical services that are not necessary.

The case with the greatest repercussions for individual choice in abortion was *Harris* v. *McRae,* decided in 1980. The law under consideration was again Title XIX of the Social Security Act, this time a portion of it known as the Hyde Amendment.

Since 1976 Henry Hyde and a small group of other conservative members of Congress had led Congress to pass legislation forbidding the use of federal funds for abortions of certain specified types. The specifications have varied over the years; in some years, for example, federal funds have been available for abortion of pregnancies caused by rape, and in some years they have not. The Hyde Amendment made the funding of medically necessary abortions optional. In other words, states could refuse to pay for medically necessary abortions through Medicaid funds.

Harris v. *McRae* upheld this law. The Supreme Court argued that the amendment does not violate the statutory intent of the Medicaid program to provide financial assistance to the poor who require medically necessary services. The "Hyde Amendment . . . is rationally related to the legitimate governmental objective of protecting potential life." Although Medicaid funds are used to fund medical costs incurred during pregnancy and childbirth, the Court also ruled that it is not discriminatory to treat the medical needs of one class of pregnant women (those who need to have abortions) differently from those of another (those who carry the fetus to term). The Court argued that the government had a right to offer incentives to make childbirth more attractive than abortion, ignoring the plight of women whose health is threatened by pregnancy and childbirth.

The pattern of denying public funds for the use of abortions continued in the late 1980s. In *Webster* v. *Missouri* (1989) the Supreme Court upheld Missouri's right to bar medical personnel from performing abortions in public hospitals. Other planned legislation would deny public funding to any private organization that performed abortions.

These court cases, of course, do not affect all women equally; all decrease the likelihood that a poor woman can obtain a safe abortion. As dissenting Justice Thurgood Marshall pointed out in the *Harris* case, the sponsors of these pieces of legislation specifically and openly wished to interfere with women's choices to have abortions, and such intention was specifically declared unconstitutional in the *Roe* and *Doe* cases. Moreover, the legislation places special burdens on the poor, an act which, he argued, is unconstitutional discrimination. The majority of the Court, however, claimed that they were not creating discriminatory burdens, but were simply not going out of their way to remove barriers that were not of the government's making.

One argument in favor of Hyde-type legislation is that the public cannot afford and should not be required to pay for abortions. However, those who need public funds for abortions also need them for prenatal, delivery, and postnatal care; and additional children pose financial burdens on poor women, a burden that will fall on the public treasury and that will make it more difficult for women to seek employment or additional training to improve their financial situations. One study calculates that the cost to the public of an unwanted birth averages 100 times the cost to the public of the abortion it turned down (Sommers and Thomas 1983). Of course these arguments carry no weight with people who define abortion as murder.

CURRENT ATTITUDES.   Attitudes toward abortion have fluctuated in recent years. A study that tracked national public opinion throughout the 1970s shows that from before the *Roe* and *Doe* cases until five years later most people favored allowing abortions in cases where a woman's health was endangered by pregnancy and childbirth, in cases of rape, and in cases in which the baby would be born with severe defects. The public was more divided over whether abortion should be allowed when a married or unmarried woman feels she cannot afford or does not want another child. Opinion had become slightly less favorable toward abortion by the end of the 1970s, when only about 40 percent of the population supported abortion for married or unmarried women who do not want a child (Ebaugh, Fuchs, and Haney 1980).

At the end of the 1980s the abortion debate heated up as the Supreme Court showed its intention to change its policy.

Opponents of abortion have become increasingly active in recent years.

A public opinion poll from early 1989 shows that a majority of Americans believed abortion should be legal under at least some circumstances. In that poll 87 percent said they thought a woman should be able to get a legal abortion if her health was seriously endangered by the pregnancy and 69 percent believed in abortion if there was a strong chance of a serious defect in the baby. A minority agreed abortion should be legal if a family had a very low income and could not afford any more children (43 percent), or if the pregnancy interfered with the woman's work or education (26 percent). Only 9 percent thought that abortion should not be permitted at all.[4]

Table 11-1 shows that different groups in society react differently to questions about abortion. These data agree with most earlier studies: Women and men do not differ much in their attitudes toward the legal standing of abortion, although women may be slightly more favorable toward some restriction.

The lack of gender differences in public opinion polls does not mean that men and women think about abortion in precisely the same way. The question of abortion can touch men very deeply, and many feel hurt when their partner makes a unilateral decision to have an abortion. But even when stated abstractly the question of abortion has a personal significance and complexity for a woman that it cannot have for a man. Barbara Finlay's (1981) study of college students shows that although overall attitudes toward abortion are not very different between women and men, men's attitudes are structured more simply than women's. Whereas men's attitudes toward abortion are related to their degree of conventionality in sexuality and social matters,

TABLE 11-1
How Groups Differ on Abortion Attitudes, 1989

Percent saying	Abortion should be legal as it is now	Abortion should be legal only in certain cases	Abortion should not be permitted at all	They know someone who had an abortion
TOTAL ADULTS	49	39	9	51
SEX AND MARITAL STATUS				
All women	47	40	11	54
Unmarried	54	37	7	60
Married	42	42	14	50
All men	51	38	8	48
Unmarried	60	31	7	55
Married	46	41	8	45
AGE				
18–29 years	56	35	8	66
30–34 years	49	40	9	64
45–65 years	45	39	12	36
65 and over	39	45	9	26
EDUCATION				
Less than high school	37	41	16	39
High school graduate	47	41	9	47
Some college	56	35	7	60
College graduate	58	35	5	67
RACE				
White	49	39	9	51
Black	45	42	13	54
RELIGION				
All Protestants	44	44	9	51
Religion very important	34	49	13	46
Not so important	61	36	1	59
All Catholics	48	36	13	45
Religion very important	28	49	22	41
Not so important	72	22	4	50
POLITICAL PHILOSOPHY				
Liberal	65	28	5	61
Moderate	54	38	6	54
Conservative	38	46	13	46

TABLE 11-1 (cont.)
How Groups Differ on Abortion Attitudes, 1989

Percent saying	Abortion should be legal as it is now	Abortion should be legal only in certain cases	Abortion should not be permitted at all	They know someone who had an abortion
EXPOSURE				
Women saying they had an abortion	79	12	9	95
People who know:				
Someone who had an abortion	58	34	7	100
No one who had an abortion	39	44	12	0

Notes: Data are from a *New York Times*/CBS NEWS Poll of 1412 adults conducted 13–16 April 1989.
SOURCE: *New York Times*, April 26, 1989, p. 13.

women's are also tied to questions of the value of children in their own life plans and to their views of life and the right to life.

Table 11-1 also shows married people more favorable toward legal restrictions. Young people supported a relatively nonrestrictive law, and they were also more likely to know someone who had had an abortion. The more educated people were, the more they favored choice and the more likely they were to know someone who had had an abortion. Race made little difference in abortion attitudes.

Religion predictably made a lot of difference. More religious people were more in favor of restrictions, especially among Catholics. Religious Catholics were more opposed to abortion than religious Protestants, but among those who were not very religious Catholics were more prochoice than Protestants. Research consistently shows that the more devout (especially the more fundamentalist) people are, the more they oppose abortion (Baker, Epstein, and Forth 1981). Moreover, the more they attend church, the more opposed to abortions they are (Granberg and Granberg 1981).

The 1989 poll data also showed that liberals were more prochoice than conservatives. Other research shows attitudes that distinguish prochoice and antiabortion groups. Those who oppose abortion have more traditional gender ideology than those who favor choice, and they tend to believe in larger families. Those who favor choice are more committed to protection of a range of civil liberties (Baker, Epstein, and Forth 1981; Granberg and Granberg 1981). Overall, however, antiabortion advocates are not very different from prochoice advocates in their attitudes toward capital punishment, gun control, government spending on health, a national health service, or military spending, although antiabortionists do tend to oppose right-to-die practices and condemn suicide more strongly than prochoice advocates.

We should not be surprised to find that women who have had abortions are more prochoice than other women, but people who have known someone who had an abortion also favor fewer legal restrictions. For women, the abortion question involves personal decisions about their own bodies and their obligations to others and to the life that might be inside them. Whatever their personal decision about abortion, they must also question whether they can or should impose this decision on other people.

Parenthood

Most people become parents at some point in their lives. What choices and decisions do people have to make as parents? How does parenthood change people's lives? What are some of the differences between mothering and fathering? What are some of the questions about parenting raised by changes in gender roles and sexuality?

Motherhood and Fatherhood

When young people contemplate growing up, getting married, and having babies, few understand just how much having children will affect their lives and marriages. Married couples may know well enough that they have to prepare the baby's space at home and that they will not be as free as they were to come and go as they please without making arrangements for the child. But the new baby will bring additional shocks to family life, some of which are related to gender roles and ideology.

Conventional wisdom says that having a child brings a couple together and fulfills and cements a marriage. Of course this can be true, and the joy of new parents who wanted children can be immense, but at the same time the appearance of a first child changes the marriage relationship. The husband and wife have less time and energy for themselves as a couple and as individuals. This is particularly true for women, who experience a large reduction in their free time because of the persistence of traditional divisions of labor. Men often feel that they are being cared for less than they were before their wives became mothers. If women leave employment to become full-time mothers, husbands and wives may find that their lives become increasingly dissimilar. Despite any plans they had before parenthood, the most egalitarian marriage may quickly begin to conform to traditional norms once children arrive.

Parenthood can create considerable marital tensions. Studies of the effects of parenthood on marital satisfaction and happiness show that the effects are generally negative (Glenn and McLanahan 1982), partly because people are not prepared for what will happen to them when children arrive. Jacqueline Ventura and Pauline Boss (1983) note that although most people are aware of the need to find ways of coping with the shock of losing a family member, few are aware that they may need to learn how to cope with the addition of one. They found that parents use many different strategies to cope with their lives. Overall, women use a wider range of strategies than men. Some seek outside social support, others turn inward to the family itself, and some work on their attitudes toward life as a parent. They found only one strategy that fathers found more useful than mothers did: engaging in outside social activities, in other words, leaving family problems behind.

Some of the effects of motherhood on women have already been discussed in Chapter 5. The degree and type of change a woman experiences seem to depend on whether motherhood is structured as an exclusive and isolating relationship, that is, whether it becomes her sole occupation. The effects of motherhood on women are most negative when it cuts them off from the outside world. Studies of child abuse show that solitary confinement of mother and child is not healthy for the child either.

It is more difficult for a woman to be a full-time mother than it once was. Earlier in this century women were more likely to be able to count on their mothers, grand-mothers, and other female family members as well as the women with whom they had grown up to share their experiences, provide a support group, and ease the transition to and through motherhood. The geographic mobility of Americans has changed this. Young people move to seek education and job opportunities, and their parents move to seek pleasant locales for retirement. Most women have at least part-time outside employment, even when children are small, which leaves few people in the neighborhood for full-time mothers to talk to during the day. There is also increasing social pressure for women to seek employment, especially among more educated people.

Life has changed for women, regardless of whether they are employed or are full-time homemakers. The post–World War II development of suburbs increased the isolation of homemakers. Suburbs were designed to give space and privacy and to make clearer distinctions than ever between private and public space, residence and commerce. On the whole they are also designed with the private automobile in mind. As more women seek employment, the remaining suburban housewives face more loneliness than ever, certainly more than their mothers or grandmothers faced.

The last generation in which full-time mothering was the predominant style was also the first generation to enter motherhood in the post–World War II era. In 1950 about 28 percent of all women with school-aged children were in the labor force. A decade later the figure was almost 40 percent, by 1970 it was nearly 50 percent, and by 1980 it was 60 percent. In 1988 almost 73 percent of married mothers of school-aged children and 57 percent of married mothers of children under six years old were in the work force (U.S. Bureau of the Census 1989, 386). Women are continuing to choose motherhood, but that choice no longer forecloses other choices as it once did.

The increased employment rate of mothers has not been an unmitigated blessing for them, because the trend toward greater sharing of familial roles has moved much more slowly. In other words, women have changed their behavior more than men have changed theirs. The result is that women's energies are more divided and their lives more frantic. Men often claim that they would take on greater responsibilities at home but cannot because of their job commitments and exhaustion at the end of the day. Women who are employed, however, have to manage both.

Stress is particularly intense for women competing in traditionally male jobs in which employers feel that they are the most important claimants of their employee's time and command it at will. However, not just women but also increasing numbers of men may be beginning to reject this assumption. To discuss this possibility we need to explore what people do when they ''mother'' or ''father'' a child.

The issues raised by parenthood were already complicated enough when the question of what constitutes motherhood was thrown open in the late 1980s as more people chose to enter parenthood through "surrogate" arrangements, in which a woman carries and gives birth to a baby for a couple in which the woman cannot do so herself. In these arrangements the biological mother contracts out the use of her womb, not to mention her genes, and is called a surrogate mother.

Public discussion became heated during the trial about Baby M, in which the biological/surrogate mother sued for custody of her child and lost. The contract she had made to have a baby and then give it up was viewed as unbreakable. This type of case raises many crucial questions: Should women be able to make an unbreakable contract to conceive, carry, and give birth to a child and then relinquish the child to the father and his partner? If it is illegal for women to rent their bodies for sex, why is it legal to rent them for baby making? Above all, what is a mother? (For more discussion, see Field 1988.)

Mothering and Fathering

He fathered that child. She mothered that child. The connotations of these two sentences are different. *Fathering* a child generally refers to the act of conceiving a child, and *mothering* a child refers not only to conception but also to birthing and caring for a child and to the style of care given. The commonsense differences between mothering and fathering is also illustrated in these two sentences: Don't mother me! Don't father me! The first means don't treat me as though I can't stand up for myself; the second doesn't make any sense at all.

The mother is at the same time one of the most revered and one of the most denigrated of our cultural figures. One could hardly begin to describe the feelings of love, tenderness, and reverence that people have for their own mothers and that are expressed through the cultural media. The relationship is an ambivalent one, however, as psychologists are quick to point out. The child, young or otherwise, wants to be nurtured but also wants to be autonomous. The mother who wants to nurture and care for her children also needs that care herself; a mother is also a daughter. The tremendous responsibility accorded to motherhood is double edged. The ties that bind can be interpreted as both supportive and restrictive.

This unequal responsibility for parenting also means that mothers rather than fathers receive the blame for their children's problems. Numerous popular books and studies explore the ill effects of mothers on society. Philip Wylie's book, *A Generation of Vipers* (1942), for example, told people how stultifying to young people, especially young men, mothers and "momism" are. Wylie blamed many of society's problems on the selfish overprotectiveness of women.

In a controversial and provocative article Nancy Chodorow and Susan Contratto (1982) discuss the problem of blame and idealization of mothers as a central theme in our cultural ideology. They argue that it is especially difficult for us to analyze motherhood because of our emotional ties to a particular version of reality: the child's-eye view of our own mothers.

[The ideology of blame and idealization of mothers] gains meaning from and is partially produced by infantile fantasies that are themselves the outcome of being mothered exclusively by one woman. If mothers have exclusive responsibility for infants who are totally dependent then to the infant they are the sources of all good and evil. Times of closeness, oneness and joy are the quintessence of perfect understanding; times of distress, frustration, discomfort, and too great separation are entirely the mother's fault. For the infant, the mother is not someone with her own life, wants, needs, history, other social relationships, work. She is known only in her capacity as mother. (651)

In the process of growing up we are likely to discover that our mothers are indeed human; thus the rage of disillusionment—and blame.

Chodorow and Contratto argue that some feminist writers have also been subject to these "infantile fantasies." They point out that some feminist writing seems to suggest that the only problem with women's mothering is the oppression of women themselves. If liberated, these writers suggest, all mothers would be like the mothers in Charlotte Perkins Gilman's *Herland:* eternally rich, warm, loving, and not only all-giving to their children but also active and fulfilled by their rewarding outside lives. Indeed many women (and men) may be trying to live up to this ideal in their own lives, with the frequent result of guilt over their own human limitations and emotional and physical stress. This view also helps keep men out of the picture by deemphasizing their potential impact as fathers.

Like motherhood, fatherhood has changed over time. When parenting meant introducing children to their adult roles as soon as possible men with sons had a very important parental role to perform because of the gender division of adult labor. Men also used to be regarded as the moral heads of the family, responsible for safeguarding the morals of wife and children. With the separation of production from the home and the extention of schooling and childhood, however, men became more separate from their children than ever before.

Men also lost some of their parental authority through the course of the nineteenth century. Until that time all legal rights over children rested with the father. Under the common law (although to a lesser degree in the United States than in England) a man had an unquestioned right to the custody of his children in cases of separation or divorce, and he could even turn custody over to someone other than the mother after his own death. Today some vestiges of patriarchal authority over children remain even though the power of mothers over their children has become greater. "Wait until your father gets home" is a token of this authority.

Fatherhood lost some of its clear definition. The father seemed to become an absentee landlord who crammed his fathering into weekends and holidays. This image is probably as misshapen a portrait as the one of the mother. In a sense it is a complement to the image of the mother as the all-powerful parent who deserves all praise and all blame. It is certainly not consistent with psychological research, which continues to show that fathers play a central role in child development.

Many people share an unfortunate assumption that there is a perfect correlation between time spent with children and the quality of parenting. This argument has been used both to discourage women who want to have careers and commitments outside the family and to underestimate the role of fathers in families. Research shows that more parenting does not necessarily mean better parenting; in comparisons of employed mothers with full-time homemakers, for example, women who have less time to spend in direct contact with their children actually devote more direct attention to the children and interact with them more when they are with them. As many employed women argue when they are asked about conflicts in their commitments, quality, not quantity, is what counts (Johnson and Johnson 1977).

The tasks of child rearing are divided very unevenly. The dominant gender ideology still assumes that those who are naturally fitted to bear children are also naturally fitted to raise them, even if both mother and father are employed outside the home. Women are responsible for more child care, and women and men continue to believe that most child-care activities are better or more appropriately done by women. One study of thirty-one middle-class parents showed that of eighty-one different child-oriented tasks, a large proportion were described by the majority as tasks that mothers should do, a somewhat smaller number were seen as tasks that should be shared, and a very small number were seen as tasks that fathers should do. Fathers' jobs included developing children's skill at sports, self-defense, and mechanical tasks (Kellerman and Katz 1978).

Couples face many difficulties when they attempt to share parenthood. Just as people have been taught that women are naturally better at child care and other domestic tasks, they have been taught that men do not have the appropriate natural talents for child rearing. Men may lack the confidence to assume roles that have previously been women's, and many women may be reluctant to give up control or trust fathers to be competent. Sharing would require that men and women reorganize their time and commitments. Women who are employed have learned to manage both work and family life because they have had to do so, but fathers are not under the same kind of pressure.

The norm of self-sacrifice is so central to cultural definitions of motherhood that women have to fight strong guilt feelings to change themselves. Even when women know their children are being well cared for by someone else, even when the caretaker is the father, many still have the nagging feeling they have forsaken a responsibility. In the end the traditional division of roles is often followed simply because it is the path of least resistance. Sharing requires discussion and negotiation, which can take more effort and energy than simply doing what needs to be done. Such discussions would often take place within earshot of the child. How might children react to hearing negotiations over who should take care of their needs? Role sharing may be healthier and more just, but it isn't necessarily easier.

One of the abiding issues in discussions of mothering and fathering is the way gender structures parent-child relations. Although most people accept the idea that children need the nurturance of a female parent, people also tend to believe that proper child development, especially for sons, requires a male parent. The reason most often given for this need is the preservation of gender roles and the suspicion that a boy will not be able to develop into an appropriately masculine man if he does not have the guidance of a father. Child development theories emphasizing imitation or modeling assume a child must have a same-sex model to follow. Discussion of the need for father figures has tended to arise in the context of two specific areas: child custody following divorce, which we shall examine shortly, and the "black matriarchy."

Debates over the structure of black families highlight two related issues important in understanding mothering and fathering more generally: the existence and effects of the nuclear family consisting of mother, father, and children; and the existence and effects of the patriarchal family, a more specific form consisting of a dominant father, subordinate mother, and children. Black American families are defined as "matriarchal" by people who argue that black families tend to be either single-parent maternal families or families in which a father may be present but is not the dominant adult. This matriarchal structure is said to cause many of the problems that blacks, especially black males, face.

The historical forces shaping the family life of black Americans have been very different from those exerted on whites. Slaves were owned as individuals; slave owners were under no pressure to respect the integrity of the family relationships of the people they owned, and even when the members of a black family were owned by the same person, their first duties were to the master. Despite their anguish when husbands, wives, or children were sold to other masters, black Americans learned to survive outside the nuclear family unit that whites took for granted.

The development of a black patriarchal family unit was further inhibited by an ideology at odds with the predominant beliefs of patriarchal societies that women are the weaker sex and men are the primary breadwinners. Although African cultures are very diverse and defy generalization at least as much as European cultures do, the gender norms regarding sexuality and divisions of labor of the societies from which blacks came were different from those that sent whites to America. In many of the African societies women were more economically active and men were less sexually dominant than was true in European cultures. To the degree that blacks preserved any of the values of their ancestors, their cultures were not necessarily consistent with Euro-American patriarchal values.

Moreover, the experience of black women in the United States was inconsistent with the ideology that women were weak. Indeed whites applied this ideology of frail womanhood to white women only; black women were viewed as workhorses. As slaves black women were expected to do hard labor. After emancipation black women continuted to be regarded as workhorses, and they found employment primarily in the hardest of the jobs classified as women's work, including domestic service, unskilled service work, and farm work. Black women had little opportunity to learn to see themselves as the weaker sex.

In this century, poverty, migration, and continued job discrimination against black women and men continue to mitigate against the existence of stable two-parent homes, let alone the patriarchal family. In addition, black men tend to die young, partly because of the likelihood that they will be the object of violence, so there is a large demographic imbalance between black women and men. As a result public attention in the 1960s was drawn increasingly to the black "matriarchal family." Elizabeth Almquist (1984) points out that the usual description of black families contains some gross inaccuracies, but the image that became seared into public perception was of families dominated by women who, because of their strength, "emasculated" and therefore further weakened the family. The strength of women in the family was often blamed for juvenile delinquency, failure in school, and lack of achievement motivation, especially among sons. In 1965 a government report entitled "The Negro Family: The Case for National Attention" (usually called the Moynihan Report) based its assessment of the situation of American blacks on exactly this kind of analysis.

The discussion and critique of the black matriarchy is of theoretical and political importance in a discussion of motherhood and fatherhood regardless of race. Aside from the important fact that the black matriarchy theories tend to undervalue discrimination as a source of the problems of blacks, they reveal some important and continuing assumptions about gender and parenting. The analysis does not simply point to broken or single-parent families as the reasons for difficulty in the black community; it underscores female dominance and strength. We are led to believe that black families (and, it follows, white families as well) would be better off if the male would take "his place" as the dominant authority figure in the family. Women again are the scapegoats, this time for being strong and showing a remarkable ability to cope with oppressive circumstances. Male dominance is posed as the center of gravity for a stable society. (For more discussion see Collins 1989; Zinn 1989.)

Fathers tend to do more than mothers to reinforce traditional gender ideology in children, and they are more rigid in expecting their children to conform to traditional gender norms (Johnson 1982). Children recognize at a fairly young age that men have more social power than women, and if boys especially see that part of that power means being able to expect the wife-mother to do most of the work around the house, they would be odd indeed not to try to take on that role themselves. On the other hand, child development experts suspect that one of the important aspects of a successful woman's upbringing is a close and encouraging relationship with her father.

There is a double standard in parenting. Most people are not concerned about the effects of unequal power and authority of parents when the dominant parent is the father. There is much greater concern about mother dominance, however, just as a marriage in which a wife is particularly stong tends to be ridiculed (the poor "henpecked" husband). Despite these worries it appears that more people are choosing, or finding themselves in, alternative family arrangements.

Parenting the Other 14 Million Children

Some of the discussion so far in this chapter makes an assumption that leaves out about 27 percent of America's children: the assumption that minor children live with their mothers and fathers. As the figures in Chapter 1 pointed out, a large proportion of children live with only one parent (usually the mother) or with neither parent. We will now look at some of the special problems divorce and single parenthood raise for children and parents. Both sets of problems highlight once again how closely related are questions of gender, sexuality, and economics. (For further discussion of divorce, see Chapter 10.)

WHEN A MARRIAGE BREAKS UP.   Over a century ago, when John Stuart Mill was advocating liberalization of England's very strict divorce laws, he remarked on an idea we hear very commonly today: Married couples should stay together "for the sake of the children." He believed that people should think more before they got marrried or became parents. We cannot tell whether people are now giving more thought to what they are doing at those stages of life than they were in Mill's time. What we do know is that the divorce rate has climbed dramatically and that it affects the lives of millions of children.

Child development experts are not agreed that staying together for the sake of the children is always the best rule to follow. The case in favor of divorce is most obvious when divorce removes children from scenes of physical violence. Many psychologists also support divorce to insulate children from psychological violence and discord. In her review of the effects of marital disruption on children, Mary Jo Bane (1976) concludes that concern for the welfare of children is no reason to restrict divorce reform per se but that such factors as the arrangements made for children's welfare during marriage and during and after divorce must be considered.

Treatment of children during divorce has changed considerably over the years. When the patriarchal family was more strongly enforced by law, the father had as total control over his children after divorce as he did during marriage. In a sense the mother was related to her children only by marriage; when the marriage ended so did her motherhood if that's what the head of the family wanted. Patriarchal authority was weakened in the nineteenth and early twentieth centuries as the "maternal" or "tender-years presumption" in law took hold. This presumption, held by both modern psychologists and jurists, assumes that a mother's care is needed during the tender years of childhood; all else being equal, child custody should be awarded to mothers following divorce. As a typical court decision (*Muller* v. *Muller*) stated in 1948, "The mother is the natural custodian of her child in tender years, and . . . if she is a fit and proper person, other things being equal, she should be given custody."

Mothers are judged unfit if they abuse their children or are alcoholics or if they are accused of moral faults that create what is deemed an unhealthy environment for children. Sexual activity outside of marriage has been used as grounds on which to deny women custody of their children. In 1979, for example, in *Jarrett* v. *Jarrett*, the Illinois Supreme Court threatened to deny custody to a mother for immoral conduct. The mother, who divorced her husband because of his cruelty to her, had been awarded custody of the child, but when she announced that her boyfriend was going to move in with her, the father sought custody. The court concluded that it was the policy of the state to "safeguard the moral well-being of children" and that the mother's "conduct offends prevailing public policy." Although a moral indiscretion was not sufficient grounds for denial of custody, the court feared that if the boyfriend moved in and lived with the mother, the children "may learn to disregard existing standards" of morality. Therefore the boyfriend could not reside in the house if the woman wanted to keep her children.

Lesbian activity has also been used as grounds to deny a woman custody of her children, although mere proof of lesbian inclinations is not treated as negatively by courts as it once was, and lesbian activity is coming to be treated similarly to heterosexual activity. One reason is that courts are becoming aware of research that shows that the upbringing children receive from single lesbian mothers is not very different from the upbringing they receive from single heterosexual mothers. It appears that children of lesbian mothers even learn conventional gender norms about as well as other children do (Hoeffer 1981; Kirkpatrick, Smith, and Roy 1981).

In a decision that illustrates the conflicting views about homosexuality and child custody, the Washington Supreme Court in 1978 considered the case of *Schuster* v. *Schuster,* which involved two women who had separated from their husbands to live together. The fathers had filed for divorce in a lower court, and the mothers were given custody of their children but were ordered to live apart, which they refused to do. The fathers sued to obtain custody of the children. The Supreme Court of Washington not only refused to change the custodial arrangements but also lifted the ban on the women's living together. The decision was not unanimous, however. One dissenting opinion included a quotation from a law article that illustrates the objections made to allowing lesbians custody of their children.

> In seeking to regulate homosexuality, the state takes as a basic premise that social and legal attitudes play an important and interdependent role in the individual's formation of his or her sexual destiny. A shift on the part of the law from opposition to neutrality arguably makes homosexuality appear a more acceptable lifestyle, particularly to younger persons whose sexual preferences are as yet unformed. . . . If homosexual behavior is legalized, and thus partly legitimized, an adolescent may question whether he or she should "choose" hetero-sexuality. . . . If society accorded more legitimacy to expressions of homosexual attraction, attachment to the opposite sex might be postponed or diverted for some time, perhaps until after the establishment of sexual patterns that would hamper development of traditional heterosexual family relationships. For those persons who eventually choose the heterosexual model, the existence of conflicting models might provide further sexual tension destructive to the traditional marital unit.

In this view, allowing lesbians custody of their children may not hurt the children themselves, but it could perpetuate marital instability from one generation to the next.

These cases raise a number of important issues. From the point of view of the parents involved, they highlight some of the difficulties that adults who are now single face in their personal lives because they have responsibility for children. Even if a court decision is not involved, divorced parents face particularly difficult problems in deciding how to handle their parental responsibilities.

A further question concerns the values pursued by public policy through legislation and court decisions. Few people would object to judges' attempts to act in the interests of children, especially to protect them where the parents have conflicting interests. But exactly how should the courts protect children? How far should public bodies go in deciding what is morally and socially good for a child? As the cases cited here show, safeguarding the child can mean quite profound regulation of the parents' lives and the parents' understanding of what is good for the child.

States are moving toward abolishing the maternal presumption, especially in light of the passage of equal rights amendments to state constitutions. Many people prefer to emphasize financial and other resources available in the home in determining the best outcome of custody fights. This move is not without problems, however, including those specifically relevant to the question of gender. If courts awarded judgments on the basis of parents' financial resources and abilities to provide for children, the facts of economic life would point to the father in most cases as the best care provider. One court, for example, awarded custody to the father on the grounds that the mother was intending to go to law school. The court argued that the mother would not have the appropriate amount of time to devote to her child. This decision (*Marriage* v. *Tresnak*) was reversed on appeal in 1980. It now appears that women usually gain custody of children because men do not seek custody. When men do seek custody, they are increasingly likely to win.

In recent years there have been many new developments in the way custody is handled by divorcing couples and courts. Courts take the children's views and preferences into consideration more than they once did, and they often assign an official the special task of representing the child. There is a trend away from the standard practice of awarding full custody to one parent and granting visiting rights to the other. Under joint custody rulings, children may, for example, live half the time with one parent and half with the other. This arrangement requires that the parents be able to coordinate schedules and that they live in close proximity to each other.

A more common issue than custody is what, if any, child-support payments the father will be ordered to make and whether the court order will be enforced. In most cases a divorced mother is in a weak financial position. She is likely to have considerably less earning power than the father, particularly if she has been a full-time mother and homemaker. If she has custody, she has the added financial burden of her children, including child-care costs when she must be absent from home.

In the late 1960s public policymakers became aware of a problem affecting the majority of women who were supposed to be receiving child support payments. Fathers were not paying. Within a very short time after divorce many mothers assume full responsibility for the financial support of their children. This is almost a reversal of the old patriarchal principle whereby the mother had only an indirect relationship with her child through the father. Now the father has a connection to the child only through the mother, and if his relationship with her ceases, so does his responsibility to his children. Children are regarded as the mothers' property.

For a while only sporadic attempts were made to enforce child-support payments. A man could be fairly sure to escape if he left the state in which the payments were ordered, and many did. As a result, some people charged, the only men who were actually caught were those who were poor and had real financial difficulties making payments. By the late 1970s states were computerizing their records and coordinating efforts to catch delinquent fathers, partly because the fathers' refusal to take responsibility for their children was causing the states to suffer financially. A large proportion of women seeking public assistance for their children were those who were not receiving the support payments their former husbands had been ordered to pay. This spurred the government to make greater efforts to track down delinquent fathers in the 1980s.

Child support is not the only financial aspect of divorce that affects children. They are also affected by the way in which property is divided. In Chapter 10 we saw that states use three basic methods to divide marital property after a divorce. Three states still use the common-law property assumption that ownership follows title, which leaves many women, especially homemakers, very poor. In a relatively small number of states courts are obliged to divide property equally between divorcing partners. As fair as this system may seem in the abstract, it contains what is generally regarded as a major flaw with regard to the welfare of children. If the marital home constitutes the bulk of the marital property, it has to be sold and divided. This means not only that the children must be physically uprooted, which is another disruption in their lives, but also that their standard of living will almost inevitably be substantially reduced. Even if the home is awarded in full to the custodial parent, lack of additional resources may still mean that the home must be sold and the standard of living must decline for the custodial parent to be able to afford more than the shelter itself.

Most states now allow courts discretion in apportioning marital property equitably. Equitable and flexible systems of property division increase the opportunity for courts to divide property, including the home, in ways that cause minimal disruption in the lives of children. The home in which children live is less likely to be sold out from under them in these states (Davis 1983).

SINGLE PARENTHOOD.   Nearly one-quarter of the births in America now involve single women. Regardless of whether a father lives with the mother and child or whether he assists in the support and care of the child, unless he marries the mother or follows the formal legal procedure to acknowledge paternity, the child is regarded by law as having only one parent, the mother, and is designated illegitimate. At one time this meant that although mother and child had full legal claims on each other, as far as the law was concerned father and child were strangers to each other. No claims could be made by or on behalf of the child for support, inheritance, or any other rights of the parent-child relationship.

Lawsuits involving illegitimate children and their parents raise questions about gender and sexual ideology and the influence these have on the choices people make. Part of the reason the law distinguishes between children born in and out of wedlock is that these distinctions help governments enforce certain sexual morals. However, these distinctions punish the children, who obviously cannot choose the circumstances of their births, for their parents' violation of social norms. Although the United States has not abandoned the classification of illegitimacy as some other countries have, American law is increasingly regarding discrimination between legitimate and illegitimate children as illegal and even unconstitutional under the equal protection clause of the Fourteenth Amendment. As the Supreme Court said in 1979 in the case of *Parnham* v. *Hughes*, "it is unjust and ineffective for society to express its condemnation of procreation outside the marital relationship by punishing the illegitimate child who is in no way responsible for his situation and is unable to change it."

Legitimacy laws do not discriminate among children as much as they once did, but they still discriminate against men. In *Parnham* v. *Hughes*, for example, the Supreme Court decided by a majority of one that an unwed father had no right to sue for the wrongful death of his child after the child and mother were killed in an automobile accident. The majority decided that because the father had never bothered to make the child legitimate, he could not benefit by the child's death. Another case, *Caban* v. *Mohammed* (1979), involved a child's natural mother, the mother's new husband, who did not father the child, and the child's natural father. The new husband wished to adopt the child, which by law would give the child a father. The natural father objected to the adoption. The Supreme Court ruled in favor of the husband and wife and against the natural father.

Some cases show that the law is changing, however. In the Supreme Court case of *Stanley* v. *Illinois* (1972), an unwed father found that when the mother of his child died he could not gain custodial rights, because the law assumed the child had no living parent and made the child a ward of the state. The father found that even trying to adopt the child would prove difficult because he would be treated as a stranger in the adoption proceedings. The Supreme Court concluded that, at least in this case, the needs of the child weighed more heavily than the state's desire to discourage sexual activity outside of marriage.

Herma Hill Kay points out that illegitimacy cases show that "a severe tension exists between the desire that all children be supported and the disinclination to encourage sexual promiscuity at the public expense" (1988, 381). Public policy continues to discourage what is seen as immoral sexual behavior, and the burden of this policy falls differently on men and women. Ultimately, of course, it falls on the child. The father can be inhibited from taking responsibility for his child unless he marries the mother. The child may be discouraged from having a relationship with the father, a relationship that might contribute to his or her well-being. Legitimacy laws also mean that a single woman who finds herself pregnant and cannot or does not want to have an abortion generally has to face taking full responsibility for her child.

People who become single parents by any means share many of the same problems. They must raise their children alone and find the financial means to support them. They have to balance their moral obligations to their children with their own personal needs for adult companionship. The financial problems of single mothers are particularly awesome. Single-parent households headed by women constitute a large percentage of the households that fall below the poverty line, partly because the sex/gender system continues to discriminate against women and discourages them from developing the resources to be financially independent.

Parents without Children

Sooner or later most mothers find themselves with children who no longer need or want their daily care and no longer help them fulfill the child-centered role for which they were trained. These mothers' children have grown up and may have children of their own. On the problem of mothers with grown children Pauline Bart has written:

Nowhere is [the inadequacy of traditional female roles] more apparent than when studying the super mothers suffering from Portnoy's Mother's Complaint, middle-aged depression, coming not from the hormonal changes of the menopause, but from the life cycle changes, when the children from whom the woman drew her identity depart and she has nothing to replace them with. (1975, 12)

Many writers have looked at the "empty nest syndrome," or role loss, in middle-aged women. Bart argues, "It is true that we all lose roles throughout our lives; but when we are young there are new roles to replace the old ones, and rites of passage to ease the transition. But as we age, there are usually not such new roles. . .and there are few rites of passage. There is no Bar Mitzvah for menopause" (1975, 12). We shall discuss shortly whether there are new roles for the "long-distance mother" to adopt, but the problem of loneliness and depression among some women at this stage in life is a serious one.

Bart studied over 500 women between the ages of forty and fifty-nine who had been diagnosed as depressed and had had no previous hospitalization for mental illness. In looking at the relationship between marital, maternal, and occupational role loss and depression, she found that maternal role loss was the most important predictor of these women's depression. The relationship between depression and maternal role loss was even stronger among middle-class homemakers, or women who had had "an overprotective or overinvolved relationship" with their children. Her findings seem consistent with common sense: The more a woman's life revolves exclusively around her children, the more she will suffer when they are no longer children. Gender-role norms that prescribe full-time motherhood for women throughout their younger years may lay a treacherous path for them as they age.

The problems of maternal role loss are magnified by other changes in women's situation as they age. There are different standards of beauty and attractiveness in women and men, and people in our society view aging as less attractive in women than in men. Many women also find that their marriages indeed endured only "for the sake of the children" when their husbands leave them for younger women around the time the children become independent. In addition, many women take on the new role of mother-in-law when their children leave home, a role that is itself the subject of painful stereotypes. In this role women become one of the most ridiculed and resented of our cultural figures.

One of the factors that causes problems for women with older children is the view that a woman loses her meaning when her children grow up. Critics of society's treatment of older women should not focus too long on the emptiness of life without young children. As Bart's study shows, maternal role loss depression afflicts a very special group of women, and the majority of women are now protected from it to some degree by employment, especially after their last child has entered school. In poor and working-class families grandmothers are still relatively likely to be part of the day-to-day lives of their families, at least to a greater extent than tends to be true of wealthier, more mobile families.

Changing attitudes toward aging also mitigate the effects of maternal role loss, and preventive medicine and improved health care mean that women are even more likely to be able to begin new lives and activities when children leave home. The popularity of new towns designed mainly for the "postparental" stage of life testify to the increased tendency for parents to launch new lives. Parents do not want to be cast off by their children, but increasing numbers also do not want to give up their independence to adult children in need of babysitters.

Beyond the Family

American society has made great claims about its intention to protect the family and children, especially through the instruments of law and public policy. Yet by the end of the 1970s, critics from left to right charged that in many senses America is antichild, antimother, and antifamily. Numerous conferences, including the White House Conference on Families convened by President Carter in 1980, provided forums for debate and the development of proposals. These debates highlighted contemporary uncertainty about the shape of family life and fundamental disagreement about appropriate roles for women and men in reproduction and the care of children.

Feminists and others on the left have argued that public policy regarding the family is based on and reinforces traditional gender and sexual values that place the primary burden for child care and domestic labor on women without giving them much help in performing these important tasks. They charge that public policy has not fully recognized the facts of life in modern society. Men are not the sole breadwinners in families; most women seek employment to support themselves and their dependents. A growing proportion of women are the sole heads of families.

The androcentric structure of education and the job market mean that women do not have the financial resources to provide for their children, and in too many cases the promise that fathers will provide these resources is empty. Social-welfare assistance to provide for children is inadequate and is dispensed so reluctantly as to make recipients feel degraded for turning to the government for help in raising what is claimed to be our "most valuable resource." Restrictions on abortion mean that those who are least in the position to have more children may be forced to do so.

Women who take traditional gender norms at face value and become full-time mothers and homemakers are rewarded by being the most economically and psychologically vulnerable of all women. Carolyn Adams and Kathryn Winston's comparative research led them to conclude, "The United States has the distinction of being the only major industrialized country in the world that lacks a national insurance plan covering medical expenses for childbirth and is one of few governments in industrialized nations that does not provide any cash benefits to working women to compensate for lost benefits" (1980, 33).

Unlike other nations, there is no national policy guaranteeing women maternity leave without loss of job. There is little public or private effort to provide care for the children of working mothers. In many cities families have difficulty finding a place to live because landlords refuse to rent to families with children and city governments refuse to interfere. Assistance to women and children who have been victims of abuse in the family is minimal, because the public is reluctant to interfere in the private life of the family.

In summary, feminists argue that American policy seems most supportive of motherhood and children when the husband-wife family unit is intact, the woman gets pregnant only when she wants to be pregnant, the woman is a full-time homemaker, and the husband can and does provide for the family. In other words, the American system is not supportive of the family and motherhood per se, but of a particular type of family and motherhood.

Conservatives and antifeminists see the world very differently. They focus on how much the patriarchal family has been weakened and worry about the eventual collapse of the family order. Sexuality and morality have become unconstrained by traditional morality and family values. Adults have become individualistic and self-serving, putting themselves before the interests of their families. Women are giving up devoting themselves to caring for home and children, which leaves men without incentives to be good husbands and fathers and leaves children without primary caregivers who are personally motivated.

Conservatives further argue that the incentive to provide for the family is being stripped away by the availability of tax-supported programs. Government is intruding in the family by telling parents how to care for and disipline children and how husbands and wives should treat each other. Government is also making it easier for families to break apart. The law is moving in the direction of treating heterosexuals and homosexuals, married couples and cohabiting couples all the same. Power over children is being taken away from parents, especially in education policies. In some places a fetus is as likely to be killed as to be nurtured to birth, and more marriages end than begin.

Despite the vast differences between these perspectives, both groups claim to be profamily. The differences in what the left and right define as profamily is highlighted by looking at two proposals, one from the late 1970s and one from the early 1980s, intended to help families and family members. One is the Family Protection Act, introduced into Congress by the conservative Senator Paul Laxalt in 1979. This bill was designed to strengthen the family and put a stop to policies that Laxalt and fellow conservatives felt weakened it. The proposals included increasing parental control over schools and curricula, allowing prayer in public schools, encouraging more sex segregation in school activities, requiring parents to be notified when children attempt to obtain birth-control devices and abortions, and other measures encouraging traditional family values. Related proposals by others included programs to promote chastity among single people, a constitutional ban on abortion, and incentives for women to be homemakers.

Another and very different set of proposals to strengthen and support families can be found in the agenda proposed by the White House Conference on Families in 1980. This agenda includes provisions to make it easier for women to seek employment, elimination of a tax structure that works against two-earner families, provisions for care of dependents, assistance for families with handicapped members, more equitable financial treatment of homemakers, attempts to give homemakers more respect and recognition, and development of "family impact statements" as part of the policy process regarding families. This conference was attended by both liberals and conservatives, feminists and antifeminists. Because of the influence of liberals and feminists, the conference did not limit the definition of *family* to mother, father, and children as the conservatives wished to do. Instead the conference allowed a flexible definition including, for example, single-parent households and households with unrelated adults.

Feminists and antifeminists clearly have very different views about the definition of a family and what should be done about it. Feminists emphasize the degree to which patriarchal principles still underlie family policy, and antifeminists emphasize how much that order has broken down. The red herring in the debate is the question whether there should be government interference in the family. Both sides want the government to do something about the family to support the values they are pursuing. Both sides understand that the values that shape and define the family in its various forms have profound effects on all aspects of our lives. That is why the debate is so rancorous.

The public has great power to regulate family and personal life not only through government regulations but also through incentives and disincentives. We have seen a number of examples in the justifications offered for different court decisions. Family lives and structures have changed over time. Perhaps one of the greatest changes is that we now understand that there are both individual and community decisions to be made about our familial values and policies.

One of the core issues in the continuing debate is whether or to what extent child care and the raising of children should be the work of an isolated family unit. More specifically, because of the persistence of gender divisions of labor, the issue is whether and to what degree child care and the raising of children should be the work of *women* in isolated family units. The rise of public education means that some of that duty has long since become a shared societal task. But the history of child-care provisions reveals the continuing assumption that whatever else they do, when their children are not in school women should be with them.

Mothers once relied on other women, such as their mothers, to help them, but this is less possible now.[5] Families that can afford it buy the services of babysitters or private day-care centers. Relatively few people take seriously the idea that fathers and mothers should share the responsibility for child rearing equally. Jobs, particularly men's jobs, are so structured as to make sharing difficult. This is one of the reasons that the White House Conference on families recommended proposals that would change the structure of work, including the availability of flex-time, job sharing, flexible leave, and better pay and benefits for part-time work.[6]

Day care is not a new idea in American history.[7] Early in the nineteenth century some private nurseries were set up for poor and working class women. These were merely custodial compared with the kindergartens developed later in the century, which were intended to foster child development. Limited numbers of publicly funded day-care centers were established during the Depression. There were also publicly funded day-care centers during World War II, when the nation had a specific interest in enabling women to enter the work force while men were at war. When the men came home, the funding for this relatively small program stopped. Repeated proposals to start a new program have been defeated. In 1971 a bill that would have instituted a network of federally funded and locally run child-care centers that would be available to all children who needed them passed in Congress, but President Nixon vetoed it on the grounds that it would weaken the family. Since that time a series of new and increasingly popular efforts have been aimed at trying to make the provision of healthy and high-quality day care a part of public policy. One of the most important was the introduction into Congress of the Act for Better Child Care Services (ABC).

Many businesses and local communities are beginning to sponsor day care for children, although the available spaces make only a small dent in the need. By 1987 about 5 percent of U.S. employers sponsored day-care centers or offered their employees some financial assistance for day-care. What arrangements do parents make for their children while they are at work? A study of child-care provisions for children less than five years old with mothers who are employed full-time shows that only a minority, 28 percent, attend a day-care center, nursery school, or preschool. Another 24 percent are cared for in the child's own home, by the father (11 percent), a grandparent, another relative, or a nonrelative. The largest proportion, 42 percent, are cared for in someone else's home, by a nonrelative (28 percent), a grandparent (11 percent), or another relative (U.S. Bureau of the Census 1989). This means that one of the most common ways of obtaining child care is to send the child to the home of a nonrelative, who is often running the equivalent of a small, unregulated, and uninspected day-care center. This will continue to be the primary solution until public policy changes.

The public is becoming increasingly discontented with the current situation. By the mid-1980s about 55 percent of Americans agreed that companies should share responsibility for providing day care rather than leaving it up to individual employees, and 63 percent thought that companies should make day care available to employees as part of benefits packages. There was also growing support for public provision of day care. By 1985 43 percent of the public thought that tax-supported child care should be made available to all preschool children as part of the public school system. It is no wonder that child care began to be a popular issue among politicians and legislators in the late 1980s.

Reproduction and the care of children are among the most important tasks we have as individuals and as a society. Are children, our future generation, indeed a national resource, or are they private property? Given the current structure of society, behind this question is another: What are the relative roles, responsibilities, and options of women and men in creating and caring for those future generations?

NOTES

1. Jane Brody, "Personal Health," *The New York Times,* July 13, 1989, p. 17.

2. Brody, "Personal Health," p. 17.

3. For discussion about techniques of birth control, see Hyde (1986).

4. These figures are from a *New York Times*/CBS poll taken in April 1989 and reported in *The New York Times,* April 26, 1989.

5. At the same time it is important to remember that women still do most of the child care (whether for their own children or not). In 1988 women were 97 percent of the private household child-care workers and 96 percent of other child-care workers (U.S. Department of Labor 1989).

6. Part-time work usually has a lower pay scale than full-time work and carries fewer benefits. Although part-time employment has long been regarded as a good solution to women's needs to balance income earning and domestic responsibilities (but not men's), part-time work as it is currently structured has many problems.

7. Much of the following is from Norgren (1989).

12

Work, Employment, and the Economics of Gender

WORK IS one of the most misunderstood and underestimated facets of women's lives. Until recently the dominant gender ideology led people to believe not only that women do not work as much as men but also that they are too delicate to work as much as men. Many women have tried to open people's eyes to women's labor over the years. Among the most famous was Sojourner Truth, whose 1851 speech, reported by Frances Gage, stands as one of the most powerful in the history of women's oratory:

> Look at me! Look at my arm! (and she bared her right arm to the shoulder, showing her tremendous muscular power). I have ploughed, and planted, and gathered into barns, and no man could head me! And a'n't I a woman? I could work as much and eat as much as a man—when I could get it—and bear de lash as well! And a'n't I a woman? I have borne thirteen children, and seen 'em mos' all sold off to slavery, and when I cried out with my mother's grief, none but Jesus heard me! And a'n't I a woman? (Quoted in Kerber and Mathews 1982, 203)

Sojourner Truth's experience is extraordinary because for much of her life her "occupation" was slavery. But her speech is not just about her own life but also about the lives of many women. Her experiences were shared by thousands of other women who were also owned as slaves, and much of the actual labor she did, including both fieldwork and motherwork, has been shared to some extent by millions of women both before and after her time.

Roslyn Feldberg and Evelyn Glenn (1979) argue that sociologists tend to use two entirely different models or sets of assumptions and questions depending on whether they are focusing on men or women. For men there is the "job" model; for women the "gender" model. Social scientists, they argue, assume that men's basic social

344

Sojourner Truth, an abolitionist, suffragist, and ex-slave.

relations are determined by their jobs; their sociopolitical attitudes and behavior are derived from their occupational roles and status; and their central interests and motivations in life are their employment and earnings. Men's primary connection with their families is in their role as economic providers. The job model leads us to assume that the most important thing we can know about a man is his occupation. The job model also assumes that a man's primary interests and motivations are derived from his paid occupation. The job model is not only used by social scientists but also reflected in everyday thought and language. People often use the phrase, "the ordinary working man" to refer to the average male. "The ordinary working woman" is not as common a phrase, and it does not have the same connotation as it has when applied to men.

In contrast, Feldberg and Glenn argue, women are analyzed according to a gender or (probably more appropriately) family model.[1] Social scientists assume that women's basic social relations are determined by their relationship to the family; their sociopolitical attitudes and behavior are derived from their family roles, status, and gender-role socialization; and their central interests and motivations in life revolve around the internal dynamics of family life. Women's place is the family, which is not where "work" happens. Women have only a tentative and marginal relationship with the outside occupational world. Women's class is generally defined not in terms of their relationship to production, even if they are employed, but in terms of their husbands' or fathers' occupations. Especially because domestic labor is not regarded as "real work" and is often viewed as only distantly related to the economic world, particularly the world of production, it is not seen as providing women a class status. The average woman is often referred to as the "average housewife." (For further discussion of women and class, see Chapter 13 and the section on Marxism in Chapter 2.)

The world of work and the world of the family are seen as two places that are parallel and complementary but often in conflict. In the work world people are (supposed to be) ambitious, competitive, and aggressive and are valued in the currency of money. In the family world people are (supposed to be) nurturant and more peaceful and are valued in the currency of love and loyalty. Women are assigned to one and men to the other, and their characters are defined by the worlds they are supposed to occupy.

Although the majority of women are now employed for pay, there has been less change in the conception of work and family, men and women, than might be expected. As many social scientists have pointed out, one of the reasons that women's work is so little understood is that our definition of work is androcentric. Work is what people are paid to do. For most people *work* and *employment* are synonomous. Domestic labor, except when it is performed by a paid servant, is not work. Volunteer work is not work. In other words, much of women's work is defined as something else.

This chapter examines women's work lives, gender divisions of labor, and the resulting economic situation of women. We will focus especially on the opportunities women have for making choices in their work and economic lives, and the effects of these choices, or the lack of them, on other aspects of their lives.

Making a Living versus Making a Home: Defining Differences

If we stopped people on the street and asked them whether their mothers worked when they were children, a large proportion would say "no." What they would mean, of course, is that their mothers were not employed for pay. Their mothers probably spent long hours shopping, cleaning, cooking, and performing the numerous other tasks involved in managing family life, but that is not seen as real work. Their mothers might have contributed many hours of labor to voluntary organizations but that, too, is not considered real work. Only if a woman does any of these activities for pay, is she likely to be viewed as having worked. Otherwise she is "just a housewife."

The distinction between work and family, breadwinning and homemaking, sometimes seems so obvious today that many people are surprised to learn that the very careful and apparently meaningful distinctions we make are relatively new ones and can only be applied to certain kinds of economies. In a subsistence economy, in which all members of a household labor for most of their waking hours to provide themselves with the necessities of life, there is little difference between making a home and making a living. Likewise in a small-farm agricultural society or an urban society of craftspeople, there is no workplace or market that is very distinct from the home. In these societies there are generally gender divisions of labor in which women and men perform different tasks, but it does not make sense to describe one person as a "worker" and one as "just a housewife," particularly when a large portion of the goods required in the home are produced there by women. It is true that before this century relatively few women worked outside the home. It is also true that before this century relatively few men worked outside the home.

The Rise and Fall of Homemaking

When did people begin to make a distinction between making a living and making a home? How and when did the distinct role of homemaker arise? Historians point to the rise of industrial capitalism, which increasingly moved production outside the home and provided opportunities for men to seek wage labor there. This does not mean that capitalism *created* gender divisions of labor; it certainly did not create gender inequality. Women in preindustrial American society were already governed by feudal laws that denied married women the opportunity to own property and make contracts. If the new jobs available outside the home provided opportunities primarily to men, it was partly because these jobs, as they were created, were already regarded as masculine.

What did happen was that gender divisions of labor were solidified, and men's and women's spheres became more distinct. The value of labor came to be assessed more exclusively in the currency of money, and productivity began to be defined as the amount of monetary profit one's labor returned to one's employer. Women's and men's spheres of labor became more distinct, and women's work was not generally wage labor. Since no money value could be assigned to it, it was no longer seen as productive.

348

The nature of the household and family also underwent considerable change. As Chapter 11 discussed, in the early stages of American history the structure of the family and the roles of its members were very different from what they later came to be. Children were expected to contribute their labor as soon as they could, and they were often apprenticed to other families to learn their work. As Julie Matthaei (1982) points out, if even breastfeeding could be done by a wet nurse, motherhood did not provide a central core to the meaning of homemaking. There was a division of labor, but in many cases roles overlapped and there was a continuity between many of women's and men's tasks. At harvest time people did not preserve gender roles and risk letting crops rot. Moreover the harvest season signalled not only the work of getting the crops out of the ground but also the work of preserving the food for later use. Women married to men such as sailors, whose work took them away from home for long periods of time, had to carry on all the tasks necessary to keep a household running.

The development of production and wage labor outside the household led to changes in women's and men's lives, especially in the ways people thought about work. Men's lives became fragmented into specific segments for work, family, and leisure, each with its own particular associations of times, places, and activities. The new structure of work literally and figuratively distanced men from their families. It also provided more of them with at least some opportunity to enter the labor market as individuals to "make something of themselves," and American culture began to promote the idea of the "self-made man." As Matthaei writes, "Under capitalism, men's striving in the economy became, literally, a seeking of their selves, a struggle to establish their own identities by economically competing with other men" (Matthaei 1982, 105). The measure of men's success was the wealth they were able to accumulate, and one of the important measures of masculinity became the ability to do all of the financial providing for the family; the need for a wife to enter the man's world of employment began to represent the husband's failure as a man. Because of the tie between man's work and earnings and his masculinity, men came under great pressure to deny that their wives worked.

As Matthaei and other historians show, the movement of men and production out of the home did not strip either the home or women of meaning and significance; it transformed them.

> When the development of industrial capitalism separated commodity production from the household, the family was freed from the function of organizing this production, and it was freed from the presence of strangers in the family. The household became a home, a private family place. Family relationships. . .began to gain a content of their own. (Matthaei 1982, 110)

The running of the private family place became a distinct role with distinct content. That role, homemaking, belonged to women.

The change in women's homemaking roles was not so much a matter of what specific tasks women did, although those did change. The most important change was in the significance of homemaking and the way people thought about this role. Homemaking was raised to the status of a vocation embedded in an ideology historians call the "cult of domesticity." Even if the homemaker was not valued in wages, her role slowly came to be seen as the one that held together the very fabric of society. Matthaei writes, "Women's work, as homemaking, was still the process of subordinating oneself to the needs of the family, of emptying oneself of one's own needs and of taking on instead the task of filling the needs of others, of one's family members."

Contrary to what many feminists seem to argue, taking on this new role of homemaker was not a passive process. "It demanded the active self-seeking of women as homemakers, their creative and individual responses to the needs of their families" (Matthaei 1982, 112). Women's success at home became the measure of their femininity. "Femininity began to involve as much self-expression and choice as masculinity—but whereas a man's self-seeking meant striving to subordinate other selves, a woman's self-seeking meant striving to subordinate herself to the self-advancement of her husband and children" (Matthaei 1982, 113).

By the second half of the nineteenth century people had begun to think about homemaking as a vocation and as an occupation that could and should be professionalized. For this reason homemaking was introduced as a subject of study at school, eventually even at universities. At the turn of the century experts were urging homemakers to apply in their homes management techniques that had been developed in business and industry. Homemaking, many argued, should become more scientific and efficient. Scientific homemaking would help women enter the twentieth century, as a 1912 article from the *Ladies Home Journal* demonstrates:

> I know that any woman who has once felt the comfort, satisfaction, and pride that come from the use of a systematic filing method will never return to the slipshod ways of the past. She will feel that it is just as commendable to have her home run in such a manner that a stranger can run it in the same grooves as herself as it is desirable to have the cogs in the wheels of a great railway system go right on moving, even though the fingers of the president of the road cease to write his dictates (quoted in Matthaei 1982, 161).

The image of homemaking had risen to new heights, but lurking behind this image was the hint of its fall. If homemaking could be done so scientifically and with such a set routine that a homemaker became a replaceable part, what did the homemaker gain from her task? If homemaking really did use the same principles as business and industry, why couldn't women go into business and industry?[2] This question became even more pressing as education, including college education, came to be seen as an appropriate and even necessary part of the training of homemakers who could afford it.

At first the new ideology led married women to pursue their homemaking activities in the larger community while single women increasingly took on paid jobs, such as nursing, teaching, and social work, that were regarded as consistent with domestic roles. There were many ways in which the feminine values of homemaking could be pursued in the outside world. The role of women as homemakers expanded well beyond the walls of the home. Women who had the resources to do so began to engage in "social homemaking," which meant applying their concerns and skills as homemakers to the community at large. Women's clubs and organizations worked to offset the "masculine" hardness of the outside world by protecting mothers, children, consumers, and others who fell through the cracks of an industrialized society and by working to contain alcoholism and other largely male excesses that hurt the family. As Matthaei argues,

> Their feminine morality—a concern that the needs of particular individuals be filled—was a perfect complement to capitalism's masculinity. Capitalism gave all men a chance to compete; the existence of low-wage and unemployed workers was simply a part of the game. Social homemakers, progressives, and eventually the welfare state charitably "mothered" the losers; they did not try to change the game. (1982, 177)

The movement called social homemaking has also been called "social feminism," and it included many of the best-known suffragists. (For further discussion of this tie with feminism, see Chapter 14.)

Through most of the twentieth century homemaking has remained a mandatory occupation for adult women, including those who are also employed for pay, and it remains a specifically women's role. Despite their protests to the contrary most men still do very little work in the home. At the same time, many full-time homemakers now view themselves as "just housewives," devaluing the role that society regards as especially theirs. Homemaking is in many respects invisible. Those who don't do it don't know what women do with their days.

Homemaking and housework remain central to the identities of a majority of women. When Marlene Mackie (1983) asked nearly 800 people in Calgary to provide up to twenty answers to the question, "Who am I?" 75 percent of the women and 37 percent of the men put housework somewhere on their lists. Full-time homemakers were more likely than employed women to list housework, and they put it higher on their lists. As we might expect, employed women's lists indicated that their work outside the home was more important to their senses of self than housework. Men's answers varied in a way that might surprise people: Those who were married to full-time homemakers were more likely to list housework than those married to employed women. Although the family, the marital relationship, and children remain central to people's senses of self (although more so for women), the importance of housework is diminishing, especially for people who are, or who are married to, employed women.

The Political Economy of Homemaking

Homemaking does not fit comfortably into people's understanding of the economy and world of work. Most people are aware of some of the specific tasks, such as cooking or cleaning, that homemakers perform, but few have a clear idea of how the occupation as a whole works and what roles homemakers play in the larger economy. Without this understanding it is difficult to grasp the meaning and significance of homemaking or to comprehend women's economic activities outside the household. Anyone who does not understand the economic function of homemaking has only a partial understanding of the economy as a whole.

not easily fit into our common definitions of work or, certainly, of occupations. Let us look at three reasons for this difficulty.

1. If work is something people do to earn a living—in other words, for pay— homemaking does not seem to be work. Few people have argued that home- makers should be paid for their work (although marital law does imply that when women and men marry they contract to exchange domestic services for financial support). Indeed, until recently the law stated clearly that women's household labor was required as part of the marriage contract, and therefore women could not expect direct compensation in property or salary for it.

   Today many legal experts argue that women's household labor should be taken into consideration in the division of marital property and in the social security system. But do we really want to argue that women perform the role of homemaker for financial support? This view reduces marriage to a purely economic relationship and, as Emma Goldman pointed out at the turn of the twentieth century, makes it resemble an insurance pact or prostitution (Schulman 1983). Women are supposed to do their homemaking for the love of their families and because of their nurturant, altruistic, and self-sacrificing natures, not out of economic interests. But if we accept this argument we are back at square one, saying that women's work in the home (if work is a paid occupation) is not really work.

2. Homemaking takes place not in the impersonal world of strangers and acquaint- ances in the marketplace, but in the intimate, personal, and closely bonded structure of the family. Much of the motivation for homemaking is based on the personal relations of the members of the family and not on economic interests per se; the work and the personal relationships are inseparable. Raising a child is indeed work, but it is difficult to imagine a parent who, having just helped a child walk for the first time, turns to someone else, shrugs, and says, "Well, it's a job." In arguing that household labor is an economic function and therefore is work, we would not want to argue that it is only that. There is something horrifying and inhuman about reducing one's most personal relationships to an economic equation. On the other hand, it is wrong to describe homemakers as people who are not filling an economic role.

3. The home is defined as a place for leisure rather than as a place for work. This view is in part androcentric and stems from the nineteenth-century definition of the home as a "haven in a heartless world" (Lasch 1977). The home is the place a person goes to rest, relax, and be "rehumanized" after leaving work. This understanding assumes that someone else has cleaned the house and made it comfortable, done the grocery shopping, and cooked the meals; in other words, it is based on men's experiences. It requires that women's work either be invisible or defined as something other than work. It is also consistent with the idea that the household and the work done in it are distinct and distant from the economic system.

The aspects of homemaking that make it difficult to analyze as work can, in some respects, be applied to other occupations as well. There is not as great a difference between women's domestic labor and other kinds of work as it might seem. People do not work solely to make a living; they have many motivations for doing what they do. Many people claim they would continue to work even if they did not need money and that factors other than money lead them to do the kind of work they do. Potential doctors know they can earn a lot of money, but many of them choose medicine as a profession because they want to help people and to save lives. Bricklayers may be motivated by the satisfaction of building and providing people with houses. People do develop personal relationships with and loyalties to their coworkers and occupational organizations, and these relationships can provide some of the motivation for doing a task particularly well. For many, if not most, of us a job is not just a job. Some people are more fortunate than others, of course, in being able to get paid for doing something they truly enjoy. The fact that there may be motivations for doing housework other than financial reward, or that housework is regarded as part of a personal relationship does not mean that it is not work.

ECONOMIC FUNCTIONS OF HOMEMAKING.   Homemakers provide necessary goods and services that would otherwise have to be supplied by someone else's labor. The homemaker's job responds to changes in the wealth of a family. The wealthier a family, the more a homemaker can replace some of her labor by paying someone else. This process of replacement does not necessarily mean that there is a proportionate decrease in the overall amount of work she does. A wealthier homemaker can decrease the amount of certain kinds of work she does, including physical labor, but to do this she will probably increase her management and purchasing tasks.

Homemakers have at least three important economic roles:

1. They manage household resources and are in charge of day-to-day household consumption. Homemakers do not just respond to the financial situation of a family; they also help create wealth and raise the standard of living. Because homemakers are responsible for managing the day-to-day consumption habits of the family, their skills and choices determine to a large degree what proportion of family income is depleted by day-to-day needs and what proportion can be saved or put to other uses. In a sense, a full-time homemaker determines the real value of her husband's income. So-called labor-saving devices have helped in this endeavor. They transform labor by increasing productivity, where productivity is defined as the amount of return for a given amount of time or effort. Labor-saving devices in the home serve the same function as new technology in industry that increases the productivity of workers, who experience no change in the length of their work. As Ruth Cowan (1982; 1983) has argued, just as there was an industrial revolution in industry, there was one in the household.

    Over the last century consumption has become an increasingly important aspect of homemaking. Because of their roles as chief consumers, women link the family to the rest of the economy. This is especially true in an unplanned economy, such as that of the United States, which depends to a large extent on market forces and the creation of markets. Producers depend on consumers, and women are the primary consumers. Many women have recognized their potential power in this relationship. At the turn of the twentieth century the consumer movement, composed largely of women, "attempted to constitute consumption as a productive vocation through which woman as homemaker could realize her individuality and social importance. It therefore demanded that women's work of consumption be professionalized and valued" (Matthaei 1982, 165). Among the groups women organized to pursue their interests as consumers were the National Housewives League, the National Consumer's League, and the Pure Food Association. Women continue to use their economic and political power as consumers to organize or threaten boycotts of specific products and producers.

2. Homemakers also create and maintain the labor force. Women have the primary responsibility for raising children and thereby contribute to the character of the future labor force. They also maintain the labor force on a day-to-day basis by providing essential life services to the members of the current labor force in their families (including themselves).

3. Homemakers are an auxiliary labor force. Because the homemaker has been defined through law and custom as a helpmeet to her husband, part of the homemaker's job is to make direct contributions to his work. The degree to which they do this depends on the nature of the husband's job and the economic situation of the family. Homemakers in the auxiliary labor force include wives whose husbands work as farmers, clergymen (see Chapter 6), politicians (Chapter 8), and owners of small businesses; wives of businessmen for whom home entertaining is a business affair, and even writers' wives ("I'd like to thank my wife" for typing, editorial comments, etc.).

Homemakers also serve as an auxiliary labor force in other ways. Many businesses and industries have relied on a flexible workforce of homemakers who are willing and able to do paid labor in their own homes without destroying their sense—or their husbands'—that they are still full-time homemakers. The system in which homemakers do textile work at home, for example, still exists, and in the 1980s the spread of home computers and other developments in information processing technology gave the "putting out" system new life as a means of satisfying businesses' clerical needs with home workers. Some manufacturers are also using this system. It has been popular partly because it allows employers to avoid more expensive union or salaried labor, overhead costs involved in providing workers with a place to work, the payment of benefits to regular staff employees, and the necessity of using proper procedures for hiring and firing employees. Companies such as Tupperware and Avon, which depend on telephone canvassing and sales or at-home and door-to-door sales, also rely on homemakers for their work forces.

The auxiliary labor force of homemakers can be called into action and discarded as it suits the needs of companies. Women participate in these types of jobs because of their familial roles as auxiliary earners. These jobs have been particularly important in families that need the woman's income but either cannot spare her for a regular outside job or consider it improper to do so. In many cases women's paid work at home helps the family preserve the impression that the husband is the breadwinner and does not depend on his wife's labor. Women have long found ways to earn incomes without appearing to abandon their feminine, home-based roles. In the nineteenth century many women rented spare rooms to boarders. Farm women still earn their "chicken and egg" money. Other women take in sewing or do babysitting in their homes.

Homemakers also serve as an auxiliary labor force that can substitute for men, especially their husbands, when necessary. Since colonial times widowhood has allowed women to perform work generally considered unfit for women in the abstract. Julie Matthaei correctly notes that

> such women were not destroying the sexual division of labor, or even challenging it; as widows, daughters, or sisters, they were fulfilling their womanly obligation of replacing an absent or deceased male family member at the helm of a family business. In such cases it was within their duties as women to enter into men's work, and their actions were understood as such. (1982, 191–92)

This same framework may be used to understand women's war work. Sometimes the view that women were substituting for their absent husbands was made explicit. During World War II, for example, automobile companies that had turned to war production sometimes deliberately hired the wives of men who had worked in the same plant before going off to war. It then seemed natural to the companies to fire these women at the end of the war in favor of the returning GIs (Milkman 1982).

It is very important to understand the subjective meanings of work, or people's own understanding of what they are doing. Women and men can both engage in activities that seem, at first glance, to be contradictory to gender-based expectations and stereotypes without making a great psychological break from traditional views. Here, for example, we see women doing "men's work" but being defined—and defining themselves—as "helping out" under certain appropriate circumstances. Likewise it is possible to see men doing "women's work," but defining themselves as "helping" women rather than sharing their roles.

The role of homemakers as an auxiliary labor force has limits, however. In the traditional view of gender roles a homemaker may assist her husband, bring in some extra money by doing "women's tasks" at home or part-time, or substitute for her husband while he is absent or upon widowhood until an appropriate male member of the family comes of age. The same traditional gender ideology, especially among whites, resists a women replacing an involuntarily unemployed husband in the labor force or entering the labor force because the husband's income is insufficient to meet basic needs. In other words a woman can work as an auxiliary but not as a bread-winner because that would threaten both her sense of femininity and her husband's sense of masculinity.

Before the advent of child-labor laws, children in a poor family were often sent out to work before the woman of the household was. The patterns were slightly different for white and black women. In 1900 about 3 percent of white married women were employed compared with about 23 percent of black married women. One of the reasons for this difference was that poorer black families tried to keep their children in school longer than poorer white families did. For most men, however, an employed wife was still a sign of failure.

Attitudes towad the employment of wives have changed considerably. Increasing numbers of women are choosing not to think of themselves solely as homemakers and to seek other occupations for which they can be paid. At the same time people continue to regard the wife's income as supplementary to the husband's and the idea of a woman making more money than her husband is viewed by many as odd and particularly uncomfortable for the husband. Men's sense of masculinity is still tied in part to their roles as breadwinners.

Making a Living versus Making a Home: Choices

Women have long had more choice about whether to seek employment than they have about whether to do household labor; most married women are still responsible for housework regardless of their employment status. Moreover, even when women have sought paid employment they have often had little choice except to become domestic servants; that is, to do housework, but for pay.

Many American men and women now believe that the most satisfying kind of marriage is one in which both spouses are in the labor force and both do housework and take care of children. About half of men and a somewhat greater proportion of women believe in this sharing model, as Table 12-1 shows. Although there had been some changes from the 1970s to the 1980s, a substantial proportion of the population still believed in a traditional division of labor (Simon and Landis 1989).

TABLE 12-1
Beliefs in Traditional and Sharing Marriage, 1974 and 1985

Which would give you personally the most satisfying and interesting life:

	1974		1985	
	Women	*Men*	*Women*	*Men*
Marriage where husband and wife share responsibilities. Both work and share housekeeping and child-care responsibilities	46%	44%	57%	50%
Traditional marriage; husband assumes responsibility for providing for family and wife runs house and takes care of children	50	48	37	43
Other (including remaining single, living with someone) or no opinion	5	8	6	8

Notes: Both polls were conducted by the Roper organization and included approximately 3000 women and 1000 men.
SOURCE: Simon and Landis (1989, 273).

A poll from the late 1970s showed similar proportions over all and in addition reported that the more educated or younger people were, the more they said they believed in shared marital roles. Whites were somewhat more traditional in their views than blacks and other races, and Protestants were more traditional than Jews and those who did not identify with a particular religion (reported in Matthaei 1982, 312). Despite these beliefs and the changes that have taken place in the division of domestic labor, women still do most of the housework. Women who are employed manage this double burden by purchasing child care, buying more prepared meals, and reducing their amount of leisure time (Nickols and Fox 1983).

Even if there has been less change than we might think in attitudes toward the division of domestic labor, the majority of Americans believe that married women should be able to work for wages. Yet as Table 12-2 shows, a sizable minority still disapprove.

What leads women to seek employment? We can answer the question by (1) taking a historical perspective to see when women as a group move in and out of the labor force, and (2) viewing women's life cycles and personal situations to see patterns of employment in women's individual life histories.

TABLE 12-2

Attitudes toward Employment of
Married Women, 1938–1986

Proportion approving of a married woman earning money in business or industry if she has a husband capable of supporting her:

	Women	Men	Proportion of married women in labor force
1938	25	19	15[a]
1972	66	62	42
1974	71	65	44
1975	71	69	45
1977	64	67	47
1978	74	71	48
1982	75	73	52
1983	75	75	52
1985	84	85	55
1986	76	78	55

[a]This figure is from 1940.

SOURCE: Simon and Landis (1989, 270), Hesse (1979, 53), and U.S. Bureau of the Census (1989, 385)

The typical female worker in 1900 was young, unmarried, and working class.

Women's Employment:
Historical and Aggregate Views

The proportion of women who are employed has risen dramatically over the course of this century. At the same time, because of changes in education and retirement patterns, the proportion of men who are employed has declined. As a result women now constitute over 40 percent of the civilian labor force. Why have patterns of women's labor-force participation changed over time? What has altered women's choices in their work lives?

Until this century relatively few women entered the labor market. Even when women were employed, they tended to work within familial and gender norms. At the beginning of the twentieth century the average female in the United States was young, unmarried, and from a white, working-class family. Young women worked to help support their families. Most ended their employment careers by their early twenties because marriage and employment of women were ideologically incompatible. Moreover, without electricity, stoves, refrigerators, vacuum cleaners, and so forth, a woman who could not afford to hire servants had little time or energy for employment outside the home.

The household industrial revolution made it possible for women to compress their labor enough to seek outside employment, but that opportunity alone did not push women out of the home; it could not alter the view that married women, especially those with children, should not work. The trade-off between employment and marriage is well illustrated by the lives of the growing population of college-educated women who entered professions at the turn of the century. Relatively few of them married at all because marriage would have meant the end of their careers. This trade-off was enforced by employers. Many would not hire married women or would fire female employees who married. A study of female college graduates done in 1900 showed that by the age of fifty only about half had married (Matthaei 1982, 181).

The ideology that barred married women, especially middle-class women, from employment began to fray with the development of jobs that seemed compatible with women's roles as social homemakers. As the nation needed more nurses, teachers, and social workers, women filled these jobs, partly because these occupations were regarded as incompatible with masculinity. The invention of the typewriter and the telephone created other suitably feminine jobs. The position of secretary, once an entry-level male job in business, was transformed into the dead-end female job more familiar to us today. Many factory owners favored using a labor force of compliant, unorganized females who their stereotypes told them would be good at light, repetitive work that required dexterity.

The major boosts to female employment came in the middle of the twentieth century. By 1940 the majority of households had electricity, refrigerators, stoves, washing machines, and automobiles, and women could make time for employment. During World War II employers, the government, and the mass media urged women to join the labor force. Female employment rose dramatically; in the auto industry, for example, it rose by 600 percent (Milkman 1982).

Although women were later pushed out of their war work, the expansion of the female labor force picked up steam again in the 1950s and 1960s for various reasons:

1. Many women never lost their taste for the independence of being employed, even if they left the work force temporarily to have children.
2. After the war both males and females began to stay in school longer, which provided women with greater motivation and qualification for employment.
3. The economy grew tremendously for the three decades following World War II and could accommodate, indeed demanded, massive growth in the labor force. Some of this expansion was very specifically in the female sectors of the job market. The need for clerical and sales workers ballooned. As baby-boom children reached school age in the 1950s and early 1960s, there was an even greater need for teachers. The increased wealth of the time sparked the growth of service industries such as restaurants, which frequently call for female labor. The expansion of the welfare state and the growth of the public sector created other jobs, such as clerical work, nursing, and teaching, which also called for women. Millions of women thus entered the labor market without ever competing directly with men.

Labor force participation by women was also pushed by both the rising divorce rate and women's increased control over reproduction. The growing divorce rate meant that more women found themselves in need of jobs, and the greater access to birth control meant that women could choose their child-rearing years and thus plan for the future. Finally the new enforcement of antidiscrimination legislation in the 1970s gave women greater employment opportunities.

The ideology barring wives and mothers from seeking employment has been weakened tremendously in recent years. The evidence is not simply in public opinion polls but also in people's behavior. In 1970 half of the mothers of twelve-year-olds were in the work force, and by 1975 half the mothers of seven-year-olds had joined them. In 1980 half the mothers of three-year-olds were in the labor force, and by 1983 half the mothers of two-year-olds were there, too (Waldman 1983). In 1988 half the mothers of one-year-olds were in the labor force (U.S. Bureau of the Census 1989). The "tipping point," as Jessie Bernard (1975) put it, has now been reached: Regardless of marital or maternal status, more women enter the labor force than stay out of it.

These patterns also point to another change in women's work habits. Until recently most employed women stayed in the labor force for a relatively short period of their lives. This was one of the excuses employers used for excluding women from job categories for which they desired a stable, permanent work force. This excuse is no longer valid. Women now have fewer children; they drop out of the labor force for only short periods, if at all; and they seek to remain employed for most of their adult lives.

Will these trends persist in the future? To answer this question we must make some educated guesses about the future of the forces that affect women's employment. For instance, there is no reason to believe that women's relative levels of education will decrease. Likewise, although fertility rates fluctuate over time, there is little reason to believe that women will lose the control over reproduction they now have unless abortion once again becomes illegal. Barring a major war that humanity manages to survive, there is little reason to expect a dramatic rise in birthrates. It is unlikely that we will return to a time when women expect to marry at a young age and be supported by their husbands for the rest of their lives. Moreover, we might guess that men's senses of masculinity will decreasingly be tied to their abilities to be the sole supporters of their families. Women increasingly seem to feel they need excuses to stay *out* of the labor force rather than to stay *in*.

Labor force participation of women may be most affected by the gender division of labor in the family and the kind of assistance parents receive for child care. Will women continue to accept a double burden? Will men come to accept not just women's integration into the work force but also of their own responsibilities in the family? As Chapter 11 pointed out, the United States lags behind many other nations in the availability of day care and maternity leave and benefits. Women's employment decisions are likely to depend in part on whether they can keep their jobs and seniority through the maternity period. But above all women have become aware that even if they want to withdraw from the work force for a time to have babies, their entire work life cannot be shaped by those periods. Given the current average birthrate of two closely spaced children per woman, and the view that women do not need to be home past their children's infancy, women may leave the work force to fulfill their maternal roles for only a very small fraction of the approximately fifty years between the time they leave school and the time they retire.

A final influence on the future of women's employment rates is the structure of the job market and the gender division of labor in the work force. Although we may see economic growth again, massive economic expansion like that experienced from about the end of World War II to 1973 seems unlikely. It is unlikely that the job market can tolerate another massive influx of new people, particularly if the trend toward raising or abandoning the age of mandatory retirement continues. As long as the job market remains relatively segregated, we must consider which sectors are likely to expand or contract. Women and men do not generally compete for the same jobs. At one point in the 1970s men's jobs were particularly hard hit by layoffs in the construction and automobile industries. Later on cutbacks in social services and new developments in information technology caused women's jobs to suffer.

One good example of these effects is offered by Sally Hacker's (1979) study of women's and men's employment in the American Telephone and Telegraph Company (AT&T). In 1971 the Equal Employment Opportunity Commission (EEOC) launched an investigation of sex discrimination at AT&T and filed suit against the company after concluding that it was "the largest discriminator against women in the United States." When AT&T was ordered to draw up affirmative action goals for future hiring and promotion of women, the goals it presented to the government showed a decline in the number of women they would be hiring in the future. The reason was that new technologies they expected to use in the future would eliminate the jobs of thousands of women. Because the company could not reasonably expect to hire a compensating number of women in other job categories, there was nothing the government could do.

Many women who present themselves to the labor market do not find work at all. The unemployment rate has generally been higher for women than men, and economists suspect that unemployment figures are underestimated even more for women than for men. After a period of unemployment people of either sex often become "discouraged workers"; that is, people who are so pessimistic about their job prospects that they no longer try to find work. It is likely that at this point many women who would otherwise work begin to call themselves homemakers and are therefore classified as such in government figures. This label hides the fact that they want employment but cannot get it.

Women's Employment Experiences through Life

Paid work experience generally begins for both males and females before they have finished school. Although there is little available research on patterns of work among children, it appears that boys tend to begin paid work earlier and work longer hours than girls (Greenberger and Steinberg 1983). Young unmarried men and women enter the labor force at roughly similar rates.

Marriage depresses women's employment rates somewhat, especially among less educated people, although not nearly as much as was once true. In fact some women are now pushed into the labor market by marriage. These women, who might otherwise have continued their education or training, take low-paid, low-status jobs while their husbands increase their earning potential. Relatively few husbands do the same for their wives.

Vicki Schram and Marilyn Dunsing (1981) found some evidence that husbands' attitudes continue to influence women's work choices. When a woman's husband disapproves of women being employed, the woman is likely to do volunteer work instead of paid work, thus not violating her husband's gender ideology. It is important to note, however, that this occurs in fewer and fewer families. By 1986 most married women were in the labor force, including about 70 percent of married women between the ages of twenty and forty-four.

As we have seen, women are now less likely than ever to leave the labor force when they have children. When they do leave it is for a much shorter time than used to be the case. This change has important effects on women's employment choices and opportunities. A young woman who plans to be employed throughout her adulthood is likely to make very different choices about how much she is willing to invest in training and what kind of a career she will undertake. She may be more likely to look for a career instead of just trying to find a job. As unpredictable as life may sometimes seem, planning one's work life makes a difference. Research shows that women who maintain consistent plans to be employed from their adolescence on tend to have higher wages by their mid-thirties than women who had at least some plans to be homemakers (Shaw and Shapiro 1987).

Women who delay entry into the labor force until after they have children face some special problems. Educators and employers expect good job candidates to follow the male pattern of beginning careers relatively young and are often reluctant to take on people who are over thirty, much less over forty. Some employers argue that it is not worthwhile to invest in "late starters" who will have what these employers consider relatively short careers. Women themselves often find it daunting to be surrounded by people who are much younger and have the momentum that going straight from school to career brings. When older women actually search for the first jobs, they often find the experience even more frustrating than younger people do. A substantial portion of the female unemployment rate consists of older women trying to reenter the labor market. Partly because of this, many young women are now reversing the traditional pattern and establishing themselves in careers before having children. Women's organizations have also been attentive to new laws against age discrimination in employment because of the career patterns of women.

The effect of children on labor force participation depends on the marital status of women. In 1986 16 percent of all families were maintained only by women. These mothers require employment to support their families; 63 percent of them were employed at least part-time for at least part of the year; 39 percent were employed full-time all year long. (Rix 1988; see also Johnson and Waldman 1983.) Married women with children are less likely to be employed.

As more women enter and stay in the labor force, more also face the experience of retirement. It is incorrect to assume that women fit right back into the home after retirement without any difficulty. A woman who has been employed for much of her adult life has lived a very different life from that of a full-time homemaker. The retiree may have done most of the housework as she went along, but becoming a homemaker means taking on a new role. Like retired men, women change their daily lives dramatically when they no longer spend their days on the job. Because of differences in male and female life expectancy, as well as in divorce and remarriage rates, a woman who retires is considerably more likely than a man to go home to an empty house. In 1987 about 41 percent of all women over sixty-five lived alone compared with 16 percent of all men (U.S. Bureau of the Census 1989). It is clear that a retired woman is not the same as an older homemaker.

Women's retirement experiences are somewhat different from men's. They are less prepared for retirement than men are. Men are more likely than women to have engaged in financial planning, which eases their way economically (Kroeger 1982). On the other hand, retiring women tend to draw on larger support networks of people who are close to them. Retired women also tend to belong to a relatively large number of organizations through which they can remain active and socialize with people. In this respect they are also more active than homemakers of their own age (Depner and Ingersoll 1982; Keith 1982).

No matter what aspect of women's work life we are considering, it is necessary to remember why women seek employment in the first place. Like men women seek employment to support themselves and, if they have them, their families. They work because they must. They cannot always arrange their work and family roles as they wish; they often find roadblocks in their private lives and in the world around them. The process of making choices is difficult, and unfortunately in the process of coming to grips with the choices they have made women sometimes denigrate the choices of other women. Those who seek employment belittle those who choose the domestic route; those who base themselves in the family decry the selfishness of women in the work force. These conflicts are encouraged in part by a social and economic structure that militates against combined roles (Gerson 1985).

Gender Divisions of Labor in Employment

So far in this chapter we have discussed whether and under what circumstances women work for pay. There have been considerable changes in women's lives in this respect. But are women now doing more of the same work, or has the substance of their work changed over time? What are the similarities and differences between women's and men's work and experiences?

What Is the Difference between Women's and Men's Work?

Women's and men's work are still very different. Women are concentrated into many fewer occupations than men, and the jobs in which there are a high proportion of female workers are those in which the vast majority of workers are women. Women and men in the same general job classifications or sectors are segregated into different types of work, and women's work tends to have lower status and pay. Where women are found in the same sectors, men are more concentrated in the positions of higher status and authority than women. This is true in ''women's'' jobs as well as in ''men's.'' People are well aware of gender segregation in employment. In fact people tend to exaggerate the amount of segregation there is by overestimating the number of women in ''women's'' jobs, underestimating the proportion of women in integrated jobs, and underestimating even more strikingly the number of women in ''men's'' jobs (Cooper, Doverspike, and Barrett 1985).

How much change has there been in women's work over time? There has been remarkable continuity in the types of jobs women have held over the past century. Table 12-3 lists the ten jobs employing the largest number of women for each decade from 1880 to 1980. Jobs shift position on the list from decade to decade, but overall the lists contain the same types of jobs year after year. Women clean, cook and serve food, sew, teach, and do clerical and sales work; in other words, much of the work women do for pay is the same kind of work they are expected to do as wives and mothers at home. If we move further down the list past the top ten jobs in 1980, we find many of the same occupations (or related work) that appeared on earlier lists. The jobs that held eleventh through fifteenth place in 1980 were sewing machine operators, assemblers, cooks, typists, and child-care workers.

Thus women and men work in very segregated worlds, although the amount of segregation has decreased slightly since 1970. In 1970 a majority of men (56 percent) worked in jobs with 10 percent or fewer women in them, and 75 percent worked in jobs that had 20 percent or fewer women. In 1980 53 percent of all men worked in jobs that had 20 percent or fewer women. In 1970 about 60 percent of women had jobs that had 20 percent or fewer men in them, as did 46 percent in 1980. If a thoroughly integrated occupation is one in which the ratio of one sex to the other is no more than sixty to forty, we find that in 1970 only about 5 percent of men and 8 percent of women worked in integrated jobs; in 1980 11 percent of men and 15 percent of women did (Rytina and Bianchi 1984). Few people hold jobs in which gender does not seem to make a difference in who does the work.

When women first began to move into the labor market they had few skills to take with them other than the homemaking skills they had been taught since childhood. What was called "women's work" therefore had the dual advantage of being at least somewhat familiar and seeming gender-appropriate; it allowed women to work for pay without violating norms of femininity too radically. Of course employers usually hired women only for work that required what they saw as women's natural skills. In recent years much of this "women's work" has been labelled "pink-collar" work: work that is an obvious extension of women's roles at home, particularly work involving services to other people (Howe 1978).

Clerical work is a particularly good example of pink-collar work and a good illustration of how the gender composition of jobs changes over time and how the content and structure of jobs are related to their gender composition. The history of clerical work also shows how changes in the structure of the economy affect women's work and work opportunities. Clerical work began to be feminized at the very end of the nineteenth century; until then clerical work was the bottom rung of the male business ladder.

As businesses began to grow in size and complexity, employers saw a need for maintaining larger, more specialized staffs. One way to achieve this specialization was to separate the increasingly important but routine tasks of clerical work from those of lower-level managers. After some initial resistance employers began to see women as well suited to the dead-end clerical jobs for various reasons:

1.   There was a large pool of high-school-educated women with few job opportunities who could be hired cheaply.

TABLE 12-3
The Ten Most Female Jobs, 1880–1980

1880	1890	1900	1910	1920	1930	1940	1950	1960	1970	1980
Domestic servants	Servants	Servants	Other servants	Other servants	Other servants and other domestic and personal servants	Servants (private family)	Stenographers, typists, and secretaries	Stenographers, typists, and secretaries	Secretaries	Secretaries
Agricultural laborers	Agricultural laborers	Farm laborers (family members)	Farm laborers (home farm)	Teachers (school)	Teachers (school)	Stenographers, typists, and secretaries	Other clerical workers	Other clerical workers	Sales clerks (retail trade)	Teachers (elementary school)
Milliners, dressmakers and seamstresses	Dressmakers	Dressmakers	Laundresses (not in laundry)	Farm laborers (home farm)	Stenographers and typists	Teachers (not elsewhere classified)	Saleswomen	Private household workers	Bookkeepers	Bookkeepers
Teachers and scientific persons	Teachers	Teachers	Teachers (school)	Stenographers and typists	Other clerks (except clerks in stores)	Clerical and kindred workers (not elsewhere classified)	Private household workers	Saleswomen	Teachers (elementary school)	Cashiers

TABLE 12-3 (cont.)
The Ten Most Female Jobs, 1880–1980

1880	1890	1900	1910	1920	1930	1940	1950	1960	1970	1980
Laundresses	Farmers, planters, and overseers	laundry work (hand)	Dressmakers and seamstresses (not in factory)	Other clerks (except clerks in stores)	Saleswomen	Saleswomen (not elsewhere classified)	Teachers (elementary school)	Teachers (elementary school)	Typists	Office Clerks
Cotton mill operators	Laundresses	Farmers and planters	Farm laborers (working out)	Laundresses (not in laundry)	Farm laborers (unpaid family workers)	Operators and kindred workers, apparel and accessories	Waitresses	Bookkeepers	Waitresses	Managers (not elsewhere classified)
Farmers and planters	Seamstresses	Farm and plantation laborers	Cooks	Saleswomen (stores)	Bookkeepers and cashiers	Bookkeepers, accountants, and cashiers	Bookkeepers	Waitresses	Sewers and stitchers	Waitresses
Tailoresses	Cotton mill operators	Saleswomen	Stenographers and typists	Bookkeepers and cashiers	Laundresses (not in laundry)	Waitresses (except private family)	Sewers and stitchers, manufacturing	Miscellaneous and not specified operators	Nurses, registered	Sales workers

TABLE 12-3 (cont.)
The Ten Most Female Jobs, 1880–1980

1880	1890	1900	1910	1920	1930	1940	1950	1960	1970	1980
Woolenmill operators	Housekeepers and stewards	Housekeepers and stewards	Farmers	Cooks	Trained nurses	Housekeepers (private family)	Nurses, registered	Nurses, registered	Cashiers	Nurses, registered
Hotel and restaurant employees (not clerks)	Clerks and copyists	Seamstresses	Saleswomen (stores)	Farmers (general farms)	Other cooks	Trained nurses and student nurses	Telephone operators	Other service workers (except private household)	Private household cleaners and servants	Nursing aides

Note: Categories within each year show the ten jobs that employed the largest number of women in descending order according to the U.S. Census.

SOURCE: For 1880–1970, Berch (1982, pp. 12–13); for 1980, calculated by author from U.S. Bureau of the Census (1982).

2. It seemed natural that women would willingly accept jobs that did not lead to higher positions, which were left for men.
3. After a promotion campaign by early manufacturers of typewriters using women to demonstrate their use, typewriting came to be seen as a woman's job.

Evelyn Nakano Glenn and Roslyn L. Feldberg (1989) provide figures that document the feminization of clerical work. In 1870, three years before the invention of the typewriter, women constituted about 2 percent of America's clerical workers. By 1890 they were about 17 percent, by 1900 they were 27 percent, and by 1910 they were about 36 percent of U.S. clerical workers. The "tipping point" came in the next two decades; women were 45 percent of clerical workers in 1920, and 52 percent in 1930. By 1970 three-quarters of all clerical workers were women, and in 1980 over 80 percent were women. From 1950 on secretarial work employed more women than any other job; 36 percent of all female workers were employed as clerical workers in 1987 (Glenn and Feldberg 1989, 288).

Why did women flock to clerical work? The most obvious reason is that the jobs were there and expanding, and they fit very comfortably within the definition of feminine work. Glenn and Feldberg also show that clerical work offered women advantages over blue-collar work. The work environment is relatively clean, and the work involves little physical exertion and offers women more opportunities to use their education and literacy. Traditionally, at least, clerical workers were more likely than blue-collar workers to be paid a fixed and secure salary rather than hourly and fluctuating wages, their hours were more regular, and they had greater job security and greater opportunities for advancement. Further, clerical jobs involved working with people.

Three important changes have occurred in clerical work over the course of this century:

1. The more feminized the job has become, the greater the gap between women's clerical salaries and men's blue-collar salaries. (This may also be due to the greater unionization of male blue-collar work.)
2. Secretaries have come to be seen as personal assistants to the boss, what some call the "office wife." The secretary's position is, as Glenn and Feldberg point out, defined by her attachment to the boss, and she is generally expected to perform a wide range of personal services for him. These services can reach absurd lengths and in many cases go well beyond making coffee, picking up the boss's laundry, or buying presents for his wife.
3. As the need for clerical labor has increased and having a personal secretary has increasingly become the prerogative only of high-ranking people, secretarial work has become more specialized, routine, and unskilled. (See also Davies 1983.)

Many women have broken out of female job classifications throughout women's employment history. One example is the women who have taken over their absent or deceased husbands' work. Another well-known example is women's war work. "Rosie the Riveter," the symbolic representation of women who worked in heavy industry during World War II, is often cited, but this image is misleading. Ruth

Milkman concluded from her study of women in the automobile industry that "Rosie the Riveter did a 'man's job,' but more often than not she worked in a predominantly female department or job classification" (Milkman 1982, 338). Both the automobile industry and the United Auto Workers (UAW), a generally progressive union, fought against integrating women into the plants. The industry preferred to import male workers from the South until the War Production Board forced them to stop causing migration and start hiring women. In 1943 women were 25 perent of the automobile industry's workers. Following World War II automobile companies used every means at their disposal to push women out, and within a year of the end of the war women constituted only 8 percent of the automobile company work force. The women did not go quietly, but they did go, often to other jobs (Gabin 1982). Women continued to have some amount of choice of employment, as long as they chose women's jobs.

In the 1970s and 1980s women began to enter new kinds of jobs, although again the interpretation of these changes must be made with care. Some of the change in recent decades, especially in the professions, has been more a regaining of lost ground than new gains. The proportion of professors, doctors, and lawyers who are women, for example, fell after 1930 and returned to the 1930 level only around 1970. Some social scientists and historians look at recent changes with pronounced skepticism. Bettina Berch notes that many of the job classifications in which women have increased their proportions are either industries that have undergone substantial growth and are in need of a new labor force or industries that men are leaving because they are declining (Berch 1982, 82–83). Michael Carter and Susan Carter (1981) analyzed professions in which women have most increased their proportions and found that these fields, especially the aspects of them in which women are most apparent, include jobs that have become more routine, are relatively low paying, and are undergoing a loss of power and status. In some cases, such as the traditionally male steel industry, women made gains only to see some progress lost during a recession in which layoffs took place in order of seniority, thus hurting women's new jobs especially (Deaux and Ullman 1983).

Many observers are beginning to caution that some of the progress observed in gender integration of the labor force has been an illusion. Women's employment has increased substantially in many traditionally male jobs, but sometimes it is because these have been broken down into new specialties, including new female ghettoes. Family law or medicine, residential (as opposed to commercial) real estate, and "women's" fields in university education are some examples (Patterson and Engleberg 1978). Bakers are another example. Although the proportion of women in baking shifted from 25 percent in 1970 to 48 percent in 1988, much of that is accounted for by the rise of bakeries inside supermarkets, usually staffed by women who appear to do "home baking," but in fact only heat prepackaged dough. A baker in these establishments is a lower-status, lower-paid worker than other bakers, who remain predominantly male (Reskin 1988).

These caveats underscore a most important point: The gender division of labor in employment is based both on horizontal and vertical segregation. Thus far we have looked primarily at horizontal segregation. There is also a considerable degree of vertical segregation. For example, blue-collar women are in light industry, blue-collar men are in heavy industry. Women are in auxiliary jobs. Men's jobs generally have more authority and higher status, and they are better paid.

Sometimes jobs are accorded lower status and pay *because* they are women's jobs; in other words, the fact that a job is seen as something women can and should do makes it worth less than something regarded as a man's job. The business world provides one of the clearest examples of the principle of "the higher, the fewer" with regard to women's work. In 1979 almost 99 percent of all secretaries and typists were women, while more that 98 percent of the people on the boards of directors of the *Fortune* 1300 companies were men (Schwartz 1980). No one expects secretaries to rise to the top, although most secretaries know their bosses would be lost in their own offices without them.

Gender is only one of many factors that structures inequality in the labor market. Race is another, and it is therefore important to understand the relationship between the impact of gender and race on employment experience. Inequality between women and men in the labor market is constant across racial and ethnic groups; that is, regardless of what group we consider, women and men are segregated from each other in the work force and women tend to be concentrated in lower-paying, lower-status jobs. The *degree* of gender inequality is not constant across groups, however. A study of gender effects among the eleven largest non-European racial and ethnic minorities found that there was greater gender inequality in the more affluent groups, and those with lower fertility rates; in other words, among those with more resources (Almquist 1987).

Discrimination and Gender
Divisions of Labor

Gender divisions of labor begin at a very young age. Male and female children are given different jobs at home that correspond to adult divisions of labor. The first paid work done by children and adolescents also corresponds to these divisions; boys do more manual labor, and girls do child care and clerical, sales, and service work. Even when their work is similar, girls tend to work with people and boys with things (Greenberger and Steinberg 1983; White and Brinkerhoff 1981).

As discussed in Chapter 4, educational and training institutions help sort workers into gender-appropriate jobs. As women make their job choices, they take their cues not just from what they have learned as children but also from their assessment of their chances in the labor market. If a woman knows that very few women seem to occupy one career, but many are successful in another, she is likely to choose the path most likely to lead her to success.

To see the ways in which discrimination works to keep the job market horizontally and vertically segregated, let us look at hiring and promotion processes. It is no longer legal under most circumstances for employers to refuse to hire or promote anyone, female or male, simply on the grounds of sex. Employers may not advertise jobs in ways that suggest that only men or women will be considered, and they must make good-faith efforts to consider men and women equally. Title VII of the Civil Rights Act of 1964 was the first and most important piece of congressional legislation on gender discrimination in employment. It makes it illegal to discriminate on the basis of sex in hiring, firing, "compensation, terms, conditions, or privileges of employment," or "to limit, segregate, or classify employees or applicants...in any way which would deprive or tend to deprive any individual of employment opportunities."

Most employers, employment agencies, and labor organizations are covered by this law. Title VII states that sex may be used as a criterion in employment only in "those certain instances where. . . sex . . . is a bona fide occupational qualification reasonably necessary to the normal operation of that particular business or enterprise." This phrase, the "bona fide occupational qualification," or "bfoq," is crucial to lawsuits over gender discrimination. The point is that gender cannot be used as a basis of judgment unless an employer can prove that one's gender is crucial to job performance. The question we encounter repeatedly in sex discrimination suits is what, exactly, constitutes a "bfoq"? Under what circumstances can we say that being male or being female is necessary to get the job done? The few cases that stand include (among others) jobs for actors and actresses, sopranos and basses, bathroom attendants, and prison guards under certain circumstances.

Although Title VII of the 1964 Civil Rights Act technically went into effect in 1965, the law had very little real impact until the early 1970s. The first case about the meaning of that law with regard to women was decided by the Supreme Court in 1971. Just as importantly in 1972 Congress gave the Equal Employment Opportunity Commission (EEOC) the power to sue employers under Title VII. Before that time the EEOC did not have this power, and victims of discrimination had to assume the burden of suing. Governmental procedures can make a great difference in how thoroughly a law is enforced. The EEOC's first major success came in 1973, when a suit against AT&T resulted in the award of millions of dollars of back pay to women employees who had suffered discrimination.

The courts have extended and refined the meaning of Title VII considerably. In the first, 1971 Supreme Court case, *Phillips* v. *Martin Marietta,* the Court concluded that a policy of refusing employment to mothers of preschool children but not to fathers of preschool children violated Title VII. The Martin Marietta Corporation claimed it was not discriminating against women, but rather against a certain classification of women: mothers. The company thought that because mothers but not fathers of small children are likely to take time off from work because of children's illnesses and holidays, it would be fair to say that mothers (but not fathers) were bad risks as employees. The Court rejected this argument, observing that the company had "one hiring policy for women and another for men—each having preschool aged children." The company had not shown that not being a mother of preschool children was a bfoq. Discrimination of the "sex plus" type (in this case, sex plus parenthood) is illegal, a decision reinforced in later cases, including one that condemned a company that discriminated against married women, but not married men (*Sprogis* v. *United Airlines,* 1971).

If an employer discriminates against pregnant women, is this a case of sex discrimination? For a while the answer was no because, as the Supreme Court reasoned, there is no such thing as a pregnant man, and therefore there is no sex discrimination. For pregnancy discrimination to be *sex* discrimination, the Court reasoned, we would have to see different treatment of women and men in a similar condition: pregnant (*General Electric Co.* v. *Gilbert,* 1976).

Congress took care of this problem by passing the Pregnancy Discrimination Act, which amended Title VII of the 1964 Civil Rights Act to say that discrimination on the basis of pregnancy is sex discrimination. (For a more extensive discussion, see Chapter 5.)

It is important to remember that Title VII applies to men as well as to women. In *Diaz* v. *Pan American Airways,* a 1971 case involving discrimination against a man, a federal court found that Pan Am violated Title VII by refusing to hire men as cabin attendants. The company had argued that passengers prefer female attendants, but the Court said a company cannot justify discrimination on the grounds that it pleases clients.

In 1967 a new policy mechanism was applied to women in an attempt to enforce the spirit of Title VII. This mechanism, introduced by an executive order of President Lyndon Johnson and later extended by President Nixon, was called affirmative action. In 1961 President Kennedy had issued an executive order stating that certain employers must "take affirmative action to ensure that applicants are employed, and that employers are treated during employment, without regard to race, creed, color, or national origin."

Affirmative action policy has been one of the most widely misunderstood of all policies used to combat discrimination. The purpose and underlying theory of affirmative action as it was designed are quite simple. Antidiscrimination policy had hitherto been couched in negative terms; it concentrated on telling employers what they should not do. In contrast the affirmative action policy tells employers what positive steps they must take to eliminate discrimination, and that they must make "every good-faith effort" to provide equal employment opportunity by participating in an affirmative action program.

What is an affirmative action program to combat discrimination against women? How does an employer engage in good-faith efforts to combat discrimination? The heart of affirmative action is the development of goals and timetables for employers to use to achieve equal opportunity in employment policies and practices. Employers are required to do a utilization analysis, which consists of determining for themselves how many women are being used in what capacities and comparing that with an estimate of the number of women available locally who have appropriate skills or who could be given these skills by the employer in a reasonable time and might, therefore, be employed to do a certain job. This comparison allows employers to determine in what capacities women are being underutilized. Once this is done, employers are required to develop a target number of women they think they will be able to hire within a time frame they specify for themselves. Goals and timetables are drawn up according to the employer's own assessment of the available work force and the vacancies the employer is likely to have in the specified time. The original design of the program makes it very clear that "goals may not be rigid and inflexible quotas which must be met, but must be targets reasonably attainable by means of applying every good-faith effort to make all aspects of the entire affirmative action program work."

If a company does not meet its goals in the time projected, the government investigates to see whether the company appears to be making good-faith efforts to grant equal opportunity. If the company seems earnest in its efforts, it cannot be punished, even if it has made no real changes at all. In fact most organizations under investigation have passed this test to the satisfaction of the government. The worst punishment available under the policy is withdrawal of all government contracts from that institution. This threat is obviously more serious to some institutions than to others, but it is rarely carried out.

Some courts and employers have attempted to use quotas rather than goals as a specific form of affirmative action. In some cases an employer has been found utterly lacking in good-faith actions—for example, an employer that intentionally discriminates against women or minorities—and the courts have ordered the employer to hire a certain number of the group discriminated against by a specific date. The power of the courts to order quotas rather than invoke the punishment of contract withdrawal has generally been upheld as a way of correcting intransigent employers.

The courts have not been favorable to employers who establish their own private program of preferential treatment of women or minorities, because such programs are held to be in violation of Title VII, which forbids discrimination in employment. They have, on the other hand, accepted the idea of taking gender into account as one of the characteristics employers are looking for, if taking gender into account is part of a plan to pursue more equality in the work force (*Johnson* v. *Transportation Agency, Santa Clara County,* 1987). They have also tended to allow private companies to develop quota-based affirmative action plans, particularly if these plans are part of a contract bargained with a labor union. Even stricter nondiscrimination standards are used with public employers, who have usually been forbidden to use quota-based affirmative action programs.

As one result of the widespread misunderstanding of affirmative action policies many people believe that it is difficult for white males to get jobs and that the women and minorities who are being hired are unqualified. As we have seen, there is already a tendency for women and men and their levels of success to be evaluated differently. This misperception of affirmative action policies reinforces that tendency and leads people to assume that many women have their jobs not because they deserve them but because of preferential treatment.

Although enforcement of antidiscrimination law has become more rigorous, it is not easy for women who feel they are victims of discrimination to seek and gain relief. A person suffering discrimination is extremely vulnerable. The process of litigation is time-consuming, wearing, and expensive. Even when the EEOC takes on the case for the victimized person, it is under its own constraints. Because the EEOC is a part of the executive branch of the government, its effectiveness is ultimately determined by the person who happens to be president at the time. If an administration is unsympathetic to the idea of devoting great efforts to fighting sex discrimination, the EEOC can be rendered ineffective.

If a discrimination case goes to court, the burden of providing proof is on the plaintiff, the person claiming to be a victim. The plaintiff must prove that there is discriminatory intent, which is generally very difficult to do, or that employment requirements do not constitute a bfoq, which also can be difficult. Meanwhile, although it is illegal for employers to punish employees for litigating discrimination cases, it is unlikely that such employees or job candidates will be viewed favorably by employers.

More on Discrimination and Antidiscrimination Policy

There are many problems women face in employment that have only been partially resolved, and there are some for which there is no clear solution. We will look at three: (1) the special problems of women who begin their careers late, (2) sexual harassment and hostility, and (3) nonconscious discrimination.

Age and Sex Discrimination

We have already looked at the different work-life patterns of women and men. Women have tended to begin their careers later than men either because they delay until their children are in school or because they realize a need to become financially

Old age did not stop astronomer Maria Mitchell, a professor at Vassar
from 1865–1888.

independent after divorce or widowhood. In most male-dominated occupations employers expect their employees to start their careers young because that is what men generally do. Therefore women have often been ruled out of male occupations not because they are women but because they are viewed as too old. The Age Discrimination Act of 1967, which bars discrimination against people between forty and seventy years old, provides some relief, but it is not sufficient to cover the problems of women who have been housewives.

One common problem women face is that they have little or nothing to put down under the heading "prior relevant experience" on employment applications that will be considered seriously. Most employers expect to see a listing of the applicant's prior work experience, and as we have seen, work is usually defined as something one is paid to do. The skills and experiences a woman has gained through homemaking or volunteer work usually do not count, even if a woman's volunteer work has amounted to a nearly full-time job with considerable responsibility. Employers are now being urged to look at these experiences more seriously and carefully.

Another problem faced by many women who have been married homemakers is that they find themselves in need of a job suddenly and unexpectedly because of divorce or widowhood. They must find a job quickly, and they have little opportunity for learning what might be available or for undertaking necessary training. Many communities have now developed programs designed to help such "displaced homemakers."

Sexual Harassment

Chapter 10 discussed the problems of sexual harassment and the difficulties women face in being subjected to systematic, unwanted sexual advances. Many feminists and attorneys have argued that sexual harassment in the workplace is a form of sex discrimination and should be treated as such by the law. Harassment can involve making sexual activity or at least toleration of insults a job requirement. Many women feel that the only way to avoid harassment is to quit, and many have been fired or blocked from promotion because they did not respond appropriately in the eyes of their employers. Moreover, the pressures of harassment may make it difficult for the woman to work effectively, which has a negative impact on the quality of the woman's work and decreases her employment opportunities. Indeed a federal government study has estimated that the amount of job turnover, medical insurance claims, absenteeism, and reduced productivity due to sexual harassment may cost the economy $189 million over a two-year period (Livingston 1982).

At first women who tried to seek legal remedies to harassment through the courts were usually unsuccessful. Most people, including judges, thought sexual harassment was really a personal matter based on sexual attraction and that it had little if anything to do with the job. Men, who predominate as judges, are not as convinced as women that harassment is a problem, as shown by large-scale studies of federal employees (U.S. Merit Systems Protection Board 1981) and business executives (Collins and Blodget 1981). The survey of federal employees shows that although less than 25 percent of the female employees think reports of harassment have been exaggerated, more than 40 percent of the male employees do (Tangri, Burke, and Johnson, 1982).

Catherine Mackinnon (1979) argues that there are two types of sexual harassment. The first is the "quid pro quo" type, in which sexual favors are required for a raise, promotion, or good evaluation or simply to retain one's job. Courts have slowly moved toward recognizing this form as illegal. In the 1970s employers were held responsible for sexual harassment by employees or others at the workplace only if the employer had a policy or practice compelling workers to submit to harassment. Employers are now held more responsible: They must show they have policies and procedures to stop harassment, and they must take prompt action when harassment problems are called to their attention.

An important advance was made when courts began to interpret at least some sexual harassment as a violation of Title VII. The following passage from a 1977 U.S. Court of Appeals case, *Barnes* v. *Castle,* shows how courts justify claiming that sexual harassment is sex discrimination:

> *But for her womanhood*. . . her participation in sexual activity would never have been solicited. To say, then, that she was victimized in her employment simply because she declined the invitation is to ignore the asserted fact that she was invited only because she was a woman subordinate to the inviter in the hierarchy of agency personnel. Put another way, she became the target of her superior's sexual desires because she was a woman and was asked to bow to his demands as the price for holding her job [emphasis added].

The precedent set in *Barnes* v. *Castle* raises an interesting problem. Its logic applies when a heterosexual male harasses a woman, when a heterosexual woman harasses a man, or when a homosexual man or woman harasses someone of his or her own sex. In each case the rule applies: But for the victim's sex he or she would not have been victimized. But what about a bisexual perpetrator? They are exempt from the logic of this decision.

The second type of harassment that Mackinnon describes is a constant and negative aspect of the work environment. Consider the secretary who is never asked directly or indirectly to trade sexual services for job benefits but is subjected to a constant flow of sexual remarks and nonverbal innuendos. Throughout the 1970s, a woman had to point to tangible negative repercussions to make a successful case that she was the victim of harassment. She had to show that her job was affected in a direct and material way; showing that the perpetrator created a job environment that caused psychological distress was not sufficient. Courts began to change their attitudes in the 1980s. For example, in *Bundy* v. *Jackson* (1981) a federal court compared sexual harassment to the situations of workers exposed to constant racial or ethnic slurs at their workplaces:

> The relevance of these "discriminatory environment" cases to sexual harassment is beyond serious dispute. Racial or ethnic discrimination against a company's minority clients may reflect no intent to discriminate directly against the company's minority employees, but in poisoning the atmosphere of employment it violates Title VII. . . . How. . . can sexual harassment, which injects the most demeaning sexual stereotypes into the general work environment and which always represents an intentional assault on an individual's innermost privacy, not be illegal?

The court pointed out that Title VII covers discrimination in the "terms, conditions, or privileges of employment," and therefore harassment, by poisoning the work environment selectively on the basis of sex, is a violation of the law. In 1986 the Supreme Court agreed unanimously that sexual harassment violates antidiscrimination law and further that employers can be held responsible if their supervisory personnel engage in harassment (*Meritor Savings Bank* v. *Vinson*).

Sexual harassment remains one of the thorniest employment problems to solve. How can harassment be distinguished from "legitimate" attraction of one person to another that happens to occur in the workplace? Most people argue that the test is whether the activity is persistent and continues despite lack of encouragement on the part of the victim. But who is to judge what persistence and lack of encouragement are? As Chapter 10 showed, men tend to interpret women's friendliness as sexual encouragement. If the perpetrator is a superior in the workplace hierarchy, the victim is understandably likely to be reluctant to appear nasty or insubordinate. Feminists argue that in the normal course of events sexual advances are simply out of place at work, and that superiors have the extra burden of responsibility in making sure their behavior toward subordinates is judicious.

Harassment raises the related issue of hostility toward female employees, especially those in traditionally masculine jobs. It is clear that some harassment is based in male hostility toward the female invader. Sometimes the hostility takes apparently sexual forms. It is not uncommon for women in male-dominated jobs to receive messages with threatening sexual innuendos. Women sometimes are subject to hazing or initiation processes by their male colleagues. Female police officers, for example, report cases in which male colleagues have refused to answer their calls for assistance or have cut the wires to their radios. When a woman objects to such hazing, she may be accused of being oversensitive and not having a sense of humor.

Studies of women in nontraditional blue-collar jobs reveal that more than 25 percent feel hostility directed against them by male coworkers. Such disapproval poisons the work environment for women, who then experience less job satisfaction than those who are not exposed to coworker hostility (O'Farrell and Harlan 1982). This problem is not limited to blue-collar workers. Female professionals in traditionally male occupations also find a significant number of male colleagues who, if not openly hostile and harassing, show obvious discomfort in their presence and confusion about how to deal with them. In some cases the problem extends beyond the workplace. Female police officers, firefighters, and miners know that quite often the wives of their male colleagues are hostile toward them, partly because of the close physical contact required by these jobs and partly because they do not feel comfortable entrusting their husband's safety to a woman (Hammond and Mahoney 1983). Often the burden is on the "newcomer" to make those around her feel comfortable, a responsibility that cannot ease her integration into a new job.

Nonconscious Discrimination

Employers are not always aware that they are discriminating against women. Personnel assessment is not an exact science, and there is much room for bias in perception and judgment by employers and employees who may act on gender-related cues. This book has cited numerous experimental studies that show evidence of nonconscious gender bias in evaluation of men and women.[3] Some of these apply specifically to employment, and some use business people as subjects.

A study by Mary Wiley and Arlene Eskilson (1982) showed that when managers evaluated reports about a fictitious man or woman, they evaluated men who used power strategies at work more favorably and as more effective than women who used similar strategies. They were also more likely to believe that a woman rather than a man was a subordinate. Another experimental study of managers in a large corporation investigated hiring for two different kinds of engineering jobs, one of which also involved some managerial duties. For the job involving managerial duties women were rated lower than men with the same qualifications; they were even rated lower than women applying for the technical engineering job without the management component.

Employers are less likely to help female than male job candidates who have spouses that need employment, and men with families are rewarded with higher pay than women with families (Osterman 1979). Businessmen view male candidates as more likely to remain with a company (Rosen, Jerdee, and Prestwick 1975), and women are expected to hold their jobs for briefer periods than men (Gerdes and Garber 1983).

Not all discrimination is nonconscious, and some occurs so early in the hiring process that employers avoid even considering women or men for nontraditional jobs. Richard Levinson (1975) did an experiment in which men and women phoned employers to inquire about jobs advertised in local newspapers. They selected advertisements for jobs that were clearly traditionally male or female, and initially only someone of the ''wrong'' sex made an enquiry. When a person of the ''wrong'' sex was told on the telephone that the job was already filled, a person of the ''right'' sex telephoned soon after to find out whether the response was the same. In many cases the experimenters were directly told that they were the wrong sex for the job. When the responses were tallied, Levinson found that in about 35 percent of the cases there was clear-cut sex discrimination, in 27 percent of the cases the situation was ambiguous, and in 31 percent of the cases there was no evidence of discrimination.

No law or policy can cancel out the effects of nonconscious discrimination. It is often very difficult for a person to know when she or he has been the victim of such discrimination. This is of particularly great significance in light of other research showing that women tend to attribute their failure to lack of skill. Nonconscious discrimination can depress the aspirations of women who have no ready explanation for their lack of success other than lack of ability.

There is evidence that nonconscious discrimination has even been activated by attempts to end sex discrimination. Reminding personnel departments that they are obliged to consider women and men equally for jobs can cause resentment or stimulate the belief by people in authority that women are people with special, and inferior, characteristics. In his experimental study William Siegfried (1982) found that when men were given standard equal opportunity warnings, they tended to find male candidates more likable than females and to hire them more often. Rosen and Mericle (1979) found that strong warnings had no effect on whether men or women were hired but did result in women being hired at lower starting salaries than men. Such evidence makes it clear that job equity will evolve only when sexist beliefs and attitudes disappear. Unfortunately it is difficult to imagine these attitudes disappearing until women have proven themselves in the positions in which they now face discrimination.

Pay for Work

Women may be increasing the amount of time they spend in employment, but they continue to earn considerably less than men do. In 1985 women who worked full-time, year-round earned 68 percent of what men earned; in other words the average American woman earned less than 70 cents for every dollar the average male earned. Women are twice as likely to have salaries at or below the minimum wage (Mellor 1987).

The gap in pay is not simply due to differences in the positions held by women and men or differences in their levels of experience. There are also differences in the pay received by women and men in similar jobs. A study done in the early 1980s highlighted this disparity. At that time the median salary of female Ph.D.s in science and social science fields, for example, was 77 percent of the median salary of male Ph.D.s in those fields. The median salary of female Ph.D.s in chemistry was 81 percent of the median salary of male Ph.D.s in chemistry, and the median salary of female Ph.D.s in chemistry with six to ten years' job experience was 82 percent of the median salary of male Ph.D.s in chemistry with six to ten years' job experience (Berch 1982, 14–15). And the earnings gap is relatively small in the professions compared to that in other fields.

Sex discrimination in pay is illegal and has been since the Equal Pay Act of 1963. That law says, "No employer...shall discriminate...between employees on the basis of sex by paying wages to employees...at a rate less than the rate at which he pays wages to employees of the opposite sex...for equal work on jobs the performance of which requires equal skill, effort, and responsibility, and which are performed under similar working conditions...." Labor unions were also covered by the law.

Employers reacted quickly to this law. Realizing that "equal pay for equal work" could be very costly, especially because employers could not reduce anyone's salary to comply with the Equal Pay Act, many of them made sure that men and women in their companies had different job titles so that they could justifiably be paid differently. Some employers also made sure there was something slightly different about the actual work that men and women did so that their work could be proven to be of unequal value. A turning point came in 1970 when a federal court decided that in ordering equal pay for equal work Congress "did not require that the jobs be identical, but only that they must be substantially equal. Any other interpretation would destroy the remedial purposes of the Act" (*Schultz* v. *Wheaton Glass Co.*). Thus women and men are supposed to be paid the same for doing *substantially similar* work.

However, women and men continue to be paid somewhat differently for the same work. In most jobs pay is based partly on subjective evaluations of the worker by a supervisor, and in this area conscious and nonconscious discrimination takes its toll. An even greater problem is that women and men for the most part do not do the same or even "substantially similar" work because of vertical and horizontal segregation. Women and men occupy different jobs, and therefore "equal pay for equal work" is, practically speaking, meaningless, unless *equal* is defined to mean something other than similarity in the substance of the job.

This observation has led many experts in the 1980s to look to the principal of *comparable worth* or *pay equity* as the standard for identifying sex discrimination in pay. A comparable worth policy requires assessment of the relative amounts of skill, training, experience, and other valued characteristics required to do different jobs to determine the relative worth of different jobs in terms of pay. Without this kind of policy the only way to determine whether there is gender bias in pay is to compare women and men holding substantially similar jobs. Under pay equity we would compare the pay of women and men holding jobs that we think should be valued equally.

The logic of comparable worth suggests, among other things, that "women's work" is often paid less than "men's work" not because it is of different intrinsic value, but simply because it is done by women rather than by men. The implementation of policies based on the notion of comparable worth would transform the process of determining pay and would cost business considerable sums of money. Despite resistance from business the 1980s witnessed some movement toward acceptance of the idea of comparable worth. (Brenner 1987; Evans and Nelson 1989; Hartmann 1985; Steinberg 1987)

Gender-role choices affect potential earnings. Marnie Mueller (1982) discusses women's work and earnings in terms of human capital theory. According to this theory, earnings are a function of the amount of schooling and experience an individual worker has; in other words, the investment of time, effort, and money ("human capital") should pay off in earnings. As Mueller points out, this theory has generally been applied to male workers. Those who have investigated women have found that women get less for their investment. Mueller, therefore, refined the human capital theory on the basis of observation of women's behavior. She points out that a large proportion of women spend some time out in the labor market to raise children. During this period their skills, and therefore their human-capital investment, depreciate in value, that is, women's education and experience *lose their value* if they are not "used."

Mueller cites evidence to show that the depreciation of value is greatest among the most educated women, which means that the gender-based decision to stay out of the labor market to raise children ultimately reduces some of the relative advantages of women of one class over another when they attempt to secure jobs later. We need only consider the experience of middle-aged, college-educated, displaced homemakers to see how this works. Mueller also looked at women's alternative to paid labor, volunteer work, and found that if she calculated what the volunteer worker would be paid if her labor were not being donated, the human-capital theory still applies. Even when women are not being paid, the value of their labor outside the home depends on their education and prior experience. If a highly educated woman stays out of the labor market and takes on volunteer work that could command relatively high wages if it were paid, because she is out of the labor market her market value still declines. Many women, therefore, can find work that is more suitable to their skills if they do not seek paid work. Challenging and interesting volunteer work, however, does not put dinner on the table.

Many women seek part-time work in order to balance family and economic responsibilities or because it is more consistent with conceptions of women's roles.

As the economy is currently constructed, this also results in a financial loss for women. Part-time employees are generally paid on a lower scale than full-time employees and often do not receive the fringe benefits of full-time employees, including valuable health and other insurance coverage. Part-time employees do not usually have the same opportunities for promotion that full-time employees have. Moreover, part-time work is often less challenging and interesting than the volunteer work that is available. Some social scientists argue that many women use their human-capital investment to buy fewer hours of work rather than more pay because of their domestic responsibilities (Quester and Olson 1978). Men are not forced to do this and have more opportunity to reap the benefits of their education and experience.

It is important to remember that most women do a considerable amount of work that is valuable but for which they receive no pay: household labor. It is difficult to assess the financial value of women's domestic labor, although many people have tried. What is this work worth in money? Bettina Berch (1982) writes that two methods of analysis can be used to arrive at a dollar value for women's household labor: opportunity cost and replacement cost.

Using the *opportunity cost* approach, the value of the household labor is calculated according to what a woman could be earning if, instead, she held a paid job. In this case housework's value is calculated in the lost opportunity to earn income. There are two problems with this approach:

1. The value of the labor has nothing to do with the labor itself; domestic work remains, in an important sense, valueless labor.
2. Unpaid domestic labor is not an alternative to employed labor for married women. There are many women who do unpaid domestic labor and do not have paid jobs, but most employed married women also do most of the domestic labor.

Using the *replacement cost* approach the cost of paying someone else to do house-work is calculated. Insurance companies use this method in calculating how much to compensate a widower who insured his wife's value as a housewife. With this approach, the value of housework is tied to the housework itself. In the early 1980s the average replacement cost of a housewife was calculated to be more than $12,000.

Some people have even suggested that women should receive wages for house-work (Malos 1980). This proposal has serious theoretical and practical problems. The main question is, who would pay? Who could pay? Do we want our family and personal lives to be judged by market standards?

Other Means of Support

Salaries are not the only sources of income for men or women. The poor, disabled, unemployed, and retired, for instance, may depend on various types of public benefits. The wealthy may receive income from investments. In analyzing the economic situations of women and men it is necessary to look at all the different sources of financial support for individuals and families.

Assistance to the poor is a woman's issue because women appear in dispropor-tionately large numbers among the poor. Numerous social scientists point to the

TABLE 12-4

Proportion of Families that Fall Below
the Poverty Line, 1987

Family Type	White	Black	Hispanic
Married couple	5.2	12.3	18.1
Male householder	10.3	24.3	15.7
Female householder	26.7	51.8	51.8

Note: This table includes only families with children.

SOURCE: U.S. Department of Labor (1989)

"feminization of poverty," or the increasing tendency for poor populations in the United States to be composed of women. Table 12-4 shows the degree to which poverty is concentrated by gender, race, and family status. Poverty rates are higher among blacks and Hispanics than among whites, higher among single-parent families, and higher among families maintained by women than among those maintained by men. More than half the single-parent families maintained by black and Hispanic women are poor.

What do people live on other than income? How much do they depend on other sources of income? Table 12-5 shows the dependence of black and white families on different types of income. The first is job earnings. The second, labeled "transfer," includes government payments such as AFDC, Social Security, unemployment compensation, pension income, and child support. The third category includes primarily "unearned" income, such as dividends and interest. The figures reveal a number of important patterns. In dual-earner families, wives contribute a substantial proportion to family income, particularly among black families. Married couple families in which the wife is not employed are worse off financially than those in which women are employed, particularly among black families. Clearly married women are employed in order to support their families.

The relative importance of transfer payments rises among married couple families if the wife is not employed, particularly among black families, which reflects the higher poverty rates shown earlier in Table 12-4. Almost 25 percent of those families live in poverty. The heaviest dependence of all on transfer payments, however, is in female-headed households, in which a little over 25 percent of the income of the family comes from transfers. It is also important to notice that at least in this regard, the impact of being a single mother appears to eliminate the usual race differences.

The problems of families headed by women are particularly dire. Research on the impact of divorce on women and children shows part of the process by which poverty takes its toll. As we have already seen, the divorce rate in the United States has been climbing in recent decades. What happens to women financially after divorce? Women's standard of living tends to decline steeply, especially when they are caring for children. Robert S. Weiss's 1984 study of the economic effects of divorce shows that the steepest decline was experienced by women whose marital income

TABLE 12-5

Sources of Family Income, by Race and Family Type, 1985

	White		
	Married Couple		
	Working Wife	Nonworking Wife	Single Mother
Mean income in 1985 dollars	$36,805	$29,320	$11,644
Percentage of income due to:			
Husband's earnings	62.9	83.3	0.0
Wife's earnings	29.6	0.0	70.6
Transfer	3.2	8.4	25.5
Dividend, interest, other	4.3	8.3	3.8

	Black		
	Married Couple		
	Working Wife	Nonworking Wife	Single Mother
Mean income in 1985 dollars	$30,777	$17,315	$8,672
Percentage of income due to:			
Husband's earnings	53.5	78.0	0.0
Wife's earnings	40.3	0.0	73.3
Transfer	5.0	18.6	26.2
Dividend, interest, other	1.2	3.4	0.5

Note: "Transfer" includes government transfers (AFDC, Social Security, unemployment compensation, etc.), pension income, and child support.
SOURCE: Rix, 1988, Tables 3.3, 3.5

had been the highest. In other words, divorce has a leveling effect on women, reducing the financial differences among them. Weiss looked at women's reliance on welfare payments and food stamps and found that in the first year after divorce 71 percent of women who had had lower marital income used these sources of support as did 25 percent of middle-income and 4 percent of higher-income divorcées. Even more shocking is the fact that in the first year after divorce welfare and food stamps constituted 60 percent of the income of lower-income women, 37 percent of the income of middle-income women, and 26 percent of the income of higher-income women.

One of the greatest problems of women following divorce is the tendency for their former husbands to default on court-ordered child–care payments. In 1985, for example, about half of the 8.8 million women responsible for children with absent fathers should have been receiving child support payments from the fathers. About 26 percent of them were not actually receiving any of the money owed. Only 48 percent were receiving the full court-ordered payment. (Rix 1988) If we combine these problems with the generally lower earning capacity of women and the need for child-care to seek work or further training, it is obvious why poverty is a special problem for women, and why sources of support other than wages are necessary.

Of course divorce is not the only source of poverty for women. Single mothers in general face economic hardship. But even when women are married and share poverty with their husbands, whether in the inner cities or rural areas, as long as women are responsible for the primary care of children, women's poverty is a special problem. Women's poverty, combined with the high cost of health care and lack of universal health-care coverage is a danger not just to the women themselves but also to future generations. Low-income women are much less likely to receive health care during the terms of their pregnancy, which is part of the reason that infant and maternal mortality rates are higher in the United States than in many other nations.

The public aid that is available is remarkably ineffective in helping people out of poverty. The federal program Aid to Families of Dependent Children (AFDC) is a case in point. AFDC began in 1935 as a program to aid impoverished children cared for by one-parent families. It is estimated that about 25 percent of all American children receive AFDC at some time in their lives, and the vast majority of these children live with their mothers. The AFDC program slowly grew until the Reagan administration began cutting it in 1981. Even before these cutbacks, however, only in Alaska was a combination of AFDC and food stamps likely to raise the children these programs serve above the poverty level. In the past many welfare programs were explicitly oriented toward helping men out of poverty on the grounds that they could then help women out. In fact in the 1960s more male-headed than female-headed families were brought out of poverty by government programs.[4]

One of the problems poor women face is negative public attitudes toward public assistance programs and those who depend on them. Although surveys reveal Americans claim sympathy with "the poor," they are highly critical of "people on welfare" (Smith 1987). About 40 percent of the public believe that most people who receive welfare could get along without it if they tried, and 32 percent favored decreasing spending on Food Stamps, a program used disproportionately by women and children (Shapiro et al. 1987).

A persistent charge aimed at poor women is that they have children in order to obtain or stay on welfare. A study of recipients of AFDC, Food Stamps, and Medicaid proves the charge baseless. After controlling for factors such as race, education, and age, analysis showed women on welfare had a substantially lower fertility rate than other women, and the longer they remained on welfare the lower the fertility rate became (Rank 1988).

Organization of Women in the Work Force

Julie Matthaei wrote about the entrance of women into the labor force at the turn of the century, "Men and women entered the labor force differently; a man seeking to establish himself as a successful man and head of household, a woman as a daughter or homemaker seeking money to aid her family" (1982, 214). Matthaei claims that women just wanted to earn a wage; as women with no desire to forsake what was labeled their femininity, they presented employers with what Matthaei calls an "invitation to exploitation."

Women entered the labor force in large numbers at the same time that male labor was organizing and seeking recognition and the power to fight for its growing membership. Although the proportion of the U.S. labor force that is unionized is one of the smallest among Western democracies, unions have been successful in improving working conditions and benefits (including pay) in the workplace through collective bargaining and lobbying the government. What has been women's relationship to labor organization? What role have such organizations played in the history of gender segregation and equity in the work place?

Most labor organizations were male dominated and androcentric from their inception. The history of the American Federation of Labor (AFL) shows the degree to which labor tended to hold the woman worker at arm's length. Before its official founding in 1886, the AFL had approved the organization of working women and policies of equal pay. Union members and leaders, however, were skeptical of women as workers. Women who had been barred from some kinds of employment because unions excluded them were sometimes used as strikebreakers. Samuel Gompers, the head of the AFL, was particularly opposed to women workers on the grounds that they took jobs from men, reduced men's wages, and destroyed the family. As a result, soon after the first official woman delegate went to an AFL convention in 1890, the AFL supported protective labor legislation. Part of the rationale was that employers would be loathe to hire women—and in some cases would be prohibited from hiring them—if women were "protected" by the law. Gompers went even further and in 1898 unsuccessfully urged the government to place an outright ban on employment of women in government. The female membership of unions declined from 4.6 percent in 1895 to 2.9 percent in 1908 (Berch 1982).

Despite considerable opposition many women tried to organize workers and force labor unions to consider women's needs and interests. One of the best-known efforts was the founding of the National Women's Trade Union League (NWTUL) in 1903 at an AFL meeting. The NWTUL involved working union members and their allies, wealthy women who were sympathetic to the plight of working women. Unfortunately it was the wealthy women who had the time to contribute to the NWTUL, so the policies of that group did not reflect the interests of the workers as much as they might have. The women of the NWTUL fell in behind the cause of protective labor legislation for women.

Women have remained weak within the union movement throughout the twentieth century. Until recently unions have not worked very hard to organize workers in "women's" jobs (with certain important exceptions, such as those in the textile trade) and have not been very supportive of women's special interests. Women have tended to view labor unions as inappropriate to their types of jobs. In 1960 women were 18 percent of all union members; by 1980 they were 30 percent, and in 1987 they were 35 percent. Black women are somewhat more likely to be union members than white or Hispanic women. In 1988 about 12 percent of both white and Hispanic women were members, compared with 20 percent of black women workers (U.S. Department of Labor 1989, 225).

Women appear in very small numbers in national union leadership. They have made more gains at the regional, district, and local levels. Some people argue that women would not have made even this much progress were it not for the founding in 1974 of the Coalition of Labor Union Women (CLUW), a women's caucus in the AFL-CIO.

Despite these problems women have made gains through the unions. There are still tensions over the unions' staunch support of the principle of seniority, or "last hired, first fired," which in most occupations means more job losses for women than for men. On the other hand, some unions work with feminist organizations and support feminist positions on various issues.

Although men earn more than women in all occupational sectors, the gap is generally much smaller between unionized men and women than between non-unionized men and women. Regardless of sex workers earn more if they are unionized than if they are not, and in some sectors the gain for women who join unions is even greater than the gain for men (Berch 1982, 162). There are alternative organizations for women workers. Some of the largest are employee associations such as the American Nurse's Association and the National Educational Association. These associations are female dominated in membership, and some, such as the two just mentioned, also have a preponderance of women leaders.

A more recent trend is toward organizations composed specifically of women workers. Among the best known of these is 9 to 5, an organization of secretaries, and Women Office Workers (WOW). Most occupations now have caucuses or organizations of women who seek to promote their own interests. There are also many organizations, such as those concerned with sexual harassment on the job, oriented to special problems of working women rather than to specific occupations. Women are not waiting for other people to organize them or tell them what is in their best interests.

The Uneasy Balance

People have long been worried about conflicts between work and family in the lives of women. Many of these fears were unfounded. Work as such need not conflict with women's traditional family roles or senses of femininity, because women's family roles constitute much of their work. Moreover, as women expanded their work to locations outside the home and began to receive pay, they did so in ways that stretched rather than disregarded the meaning of femininity. Eventually the main issue was not whether women worked for pay, but how they did so.

Women's employment has not destroyed the family, as some people thought might happen. Many women, of course, seek employment because they do not have a husband to support them, but married women who are employed have tended to stay within the bounds of "appropriate" gender roles.

Women's employment, however, does not leave gender and familial roles and ideology untouched. Research shows that among married couple families, those in which both husband and wife work for pay are more egalitarian. Husbands and wives are more likely to share power in the home, and husbands respect their wives more (Blumstein and Schwartz 1983; Huber and Spitze 1981).

Women's employment does lead to confusion and problems under some circumstances. Not everyone feels that married women should work for pay; for example, one quarter of the wives and one third of the husbands in Blumstein and Schwartz's couples study did not think that husbands and wives should both be employed (1983, 118). One study shows that the effects of employment on husbands and wives depends on their attitudes toward women's employment in the first place. Among husbands who are not in favor of working wives, a man's wife's employment increases the likelihood that he will experience psychological depression. Likewise wives who would prefer to be housewives tend to show more signs of depression if they are employed. Wives who would prefer to be employed show more signs of depression if they are homemakers. A wife's employment status makes no difference to husbands who are in favor of working wives (Ross, Mirowsky, and Huber 1983).

Divisions of domestic labor also affect how husbands and wives view themselves and their relationships. Women show fewer signs of depression when their husbands do some housework. This is true regardless of whether the women themselves are employed (Ross, Mirowsky, and Huber 1983). On the other hand, "When husbands do a lot of homework, married couples have greater conflict" (Blumstein and Schwartz 1983, 146). Men appear to believe a successful partner should not have to do housework (151). When wives are employed, husbands and wives also argue more about how children should be raised (Blumstein and Schwartz 1983, 135). These different studies suggest that life may be more peaceful when there is a traditional division of labor in which the man has his world of work outside the home and the woman has hers inside. The reason this division of labor may foster harmony is because husbands and wives live basically separate, unshared lives, and because there is a clearer division of labor and of power, authority, and respect within the family.

The amount of time women spend working for pay has greatly increased, but women spend only slightly less time doing free domestic labor now than they did formerly (especially if they are employed). Women have increasing incentives to enter the labor force, but is is less clear what will motivate men to do more domestic labor. Many employed women find it easier to avoid conflicts and continue to do the housework themselves. But is this wise, especially in the long run?

NOTES

1.   Although Feldberg and Glenn talk about the job model for men and gender model for women, in fact both are gender models because both are shaped by gender. For this reason, I use *job model* to refer to the gender-based model used for men, and *family model* to refer to the gender-based model used for women.

2.   For more on the development of scientific homemaking, see Cowan (1983).

3.   For a review of experimental research on sexism in personnel decision making, see Cash, Gillen, and Burns (1977).

4.   For more reading on women, poverty, and social welfare, see Fraser (1987), Gordon (1988b), Nelson (1984), Pearce (1989), Piven and Cloward (1988), Shortridge (1989), and Zinn (1989).

PART FOUR

Unity, Division, and Feminism

EACH CHAPTER of this book thus far has considered some of the ways in which women have acted individually and together to try to improve their life options and the quality of their lives. In this final section we turn specifically to the questions of feminism and united action among women. We will purposely take a difficult route and focus first on the differences that divide women and make many people dubious about any possibility for a united feminism. Only when these differences among women have been examined can we see the significance of feminism in the past and its potential for the future.

Reflect Before You Read

1. Construct a list of the five most important problems facing people like you today. Who did you define as *people like you?* Why? What other choices might you have made in defining *people like you?* How many of the problems you selected truly affect women and men in the same way? What role can or does feminism play in the solutions to these problems?

2. Construct a list of the five most important problems facing women today. Now think about the relationship of these problems to different kinds of women. Do women of different classes face these problems in the same way? Women of different races? Ages? Religions? Sexual orientation? How did your own personal situation and experiences affect the way you defined the problems of women?

3. What changes in the status and roles of women and men do you think need to be made in the future? How can these best be accomplished? What role will you play? Why?

4. You are probably aware of the many different strategies women use to become involved in questions raised by feminism. Some women actively oppose feminist organizations. Some do the best they can individually. Some become involved in organizations that work through conventional political means. Some become involved

in radical kinds of action. Why do you think people choose each of these different paths? Which path are you following? Why? If you have remained aloof from them all, why?

5. Do you think of yourself as a feminist? Why/Why not? What is a feminist?

13

Commonality and Difference among American Women

I don't see how you can make generalizations about women's condition—after all, we're all so different!

A feminist movement can't possibly benefit all women. Women of one class have more in common with the men of their class than they do with the women of another class.

The feminist movement is based on the interests of white, middle-class women.

Oh, I'm too old to change my ways. Feminism is for young women.

THESE ARE some of the comments one hears over and over when discussing women's situation and the potential for feminism. Women's lives do indeed differ; a poor woman's life certainly is not the same as a rich woman's, and a twenty-one-year-old woman's life is not much like an eighty-one-year-old's. But does this mean that women's studies and feminism are illusions? Some people answer yes and argue that women's studies and feminism necessarily serve the interests of only a few women against the interests of most. It is impossible to analyze feminism, the task of Chapter 14, until we focus directly on the significance of difference and diversity among women. That is what we will do here.

This chapter draws on both material presented earlier and some new material to analyze the degree and meaning of difference and commonality among women. It begins with a discussion of what can be learned when students of women's studies emphasize differences among women, and what problems there are in attempting to do so. The remainder of the chapter focuses on particular social categories—age, class, race and ethnicity, and geography—that are said to divide women.

Social scientists have long been interested in the impact of class, religion, and race on people's lives. Even though our primary focus is the nature of sex/gender systems, there are a number of reasons for analyzing these social divisions: (1) to understand the variety of lives women lead, (2) to evaluate the different ways that sex/gender systems affect people, (3) to untangle the effects of different stratification systems on people, and (4) to construct the possibility of a feminism that is not limited to specific groups of women. We will discuss the first three here and turn to the fourth at the end of the chapter.

Her Infinite Variety

Feminists charge that those with androcentric perspectives simplistically and falsely see women as basically the same. They apply stereotypes to women as a group and as individuals and ignore women's individual characters and abilities. Those with feminist perspectives can fall prey to the same problem and view all women as pitiful unhappy creatures suffering from the same oppression, or as earth mother goddesses and brave heroines. The obvious truth is that women live many different kinds of lives, and these must be considered when viewing the experience of women as a group.

Adrienne Rich's (1979) essay on racism points out one trap many feminists fall into because of the nature of feminism and the genesis of the contemporary feminist movement. Feminists emphasize sisterhood and focus on the commonalities of women's lives. Because the contemporary women's movement is partly rooted in the 1960s movement for black civil rights, many white feminists have been so eager to emphasize their sisterhood with black women and the underlying similarities of their lives that they have ignored or denied any differences. Progressive white parents teach their children "there's no difference between black and white." The problem is, as Rich suggests, that there are differences, although not of the type that racists see. American blacks and whites have a different history and thus a somewhat different culture; they have different amounts of power; and they face different opportunities and limitations within society. These different experiences have to be considered equally as part of women's history, including recognition that some women have been slaves, and others have been those slaves' masters.

A similar misplaced sense of sisterhood can create ignorance of other aspects of women's lives. Gender structures women's lives in many ways, but it does not make women's lives all the same. Ignorance creates a distance among different groups that can blind us to the differences among women who hold views at odds with ours. At a distance, be it physical or social, people of another group "all look alike" (Frable and Bem 1985).

The Differential Effects of Sex/Gender Systems

Analyzing and comparing women in different social groups can reveal commonalities in women's lives that might otherwise be ignored. However, to argue that there is a sex/gender system that structures women's experiences is not the same as saying that all women are affected by this system in the same way. Consider a few examples discussed in earlier chapters.

Chapter 10 pointed out how gender norms governing sexuality affect women regardless of their sexual orientation. If women are rewarded for being dependent on and deferential toward men, both women who conform to that norm and women who do not are caught in that same system; they are treated differently and their experiences are different because of it. Some of the differences between the experiences of heterosexual and homosexual women are shaped by the same values. Heterosexual women are rewarded for accepting them, and lesbians are punished for violating them.

The discussion of the so-called black matriarchy in Chapter 11 pointed out the central role of patriarchal gender norms in an analysis of the situation of American blacks. By some reports one of the major causes of the social problems blacks face is the lack of a dominant father in the household. This argument implies that one of the good things about white society is an apparently widespread presence of dominant males in the household. In this respect both black and white women—and, more generally, black and white society—are being judged by the same gender norms, although with different effects.

Chapter 9 showed how male and female patterns of speech differ and how the speech pattern men use is preferred and of higher status. In the United States, for example, men tend to speak more directly and forcefully and are regarded as better and more effective speakers. There is at least one society in which the preferred, higher-status mode of speech is indirect and subtle. In that culture it is the women who speak in a way Americans would regard as more forceful and direct. Because it is women who use it, however, the society regards this mode as inferior. By comparing the American and cultures, which are very different in some respects, we can see how androcentric sex/gender systems can vary considerably in detail.

Chapter 12 showed that women who are employed and those who are not are similarly affected by gender norms defining femininity and "women's work." The majority of women who are employed have jobs that are consistent with the domestic roles women are supposed to perform. A comparison of women in different situations and cultures shows that (1) there is nothing essentially or naturally feminine about specific jobs, and (2) the same gender norms can have very different effects on women, depending on the situation. In the United States nursing is seen as consistent with women's roles as nurturers, and doctoring is seen as a male role because it is an authoritative and scientific job. In the Soviet Union most nurses are women, but the majority of medical doctors are also women. A closer look, however, reveals that in the Soviet Union doctors are women because doctoring is regarded as consistent with women's abilities to nurture.

One of the most interesting and revealing cases in which apparent differences mask similarities is the view of feminist organizations taken by different social movements and interest groups. Time after time women's movements have been seen as secondary to other movements and groups or as divisive and detrimental to the general good. Workers' organizations historically have argued that separate women's organizations are divisive to organization of the working class, and that women's problems will be solved anyway with the overthrow of the capitalist system. Many American black leaders have argued that separate black women's organizations are divisive to the organization of blacks, and the black women's problems will be solved anyway when blacks as a group become free and equal to whites. The same argument has been made within the Chicano movement (Mirandé and Enríquez 1979). Leaders of primarily white and middle-class groups use similar arguments when they claim that the most important social ills are human problems, and that distinct organizations of women are divisive and misguided.

Many leaders of various movements argue that the "woman problem" may be a problem for other social groups but not theirs. Middle-class representatives argue that working-class families suffer the most patriarchal norms, and working-class activists claim that the middle class foists the ideal of feminine fragility on women. Black activists point to the long history of black female employment and the image of the strong black mother to show that feminism is a white problem. Chicano activists claim that behind the stereotype of machismo is veneration for the Chicana who holds social life and the family together as the Anglo mother no longer does. Christians attempt to prove that theirs is the liberated group by pointing to the New Testament declaration that there is "neither male nor female," and Jews point out that because Judaism is a home-based religion women's leadership in the home gives them a unique power and authority.

Meanwhile, in none of these groups do women have the range of opportunities men have, and in none of them are women who are trying to support themselves and their families paid as much as men are. These varying groups seem to be able to agree about one thing: Women who try to organize women on behalf of their own quality of life are out of line.

At the same time that we emphasize the problems women face across different groups it is important to recognize the different and special kinds of power women have had and contributions they have made in different groups. Women's story is not purely a story of victimization. Stereotypes of specific groups of women tend to paint them as particularly oppressed, passive, and victimized. In contrast to the racist stereotype of the silent squaw, research on Native American women paints a very different picture (e.g., Lynch 1986; Albers and Medicine 1983). Resistance can take many forms, including apparant passivity and acquiescence, as research on black women slaves and sharecroppers shows (Hine 1989; Jones 1985). Work on women of other ethnic groups also reveals the faults in ethnic stereotypes of women (Diner 1983; Deutsch 1987).

Untangling Oppression

Three women are standing before a covered mirror. At a given signal the cover will be removed and the following question will be put to them:
Mirror, mirror on the wall
What is the greatest oppressor of us all?
The mirror is unveiled and all three see their reflections bouncing back. Woman number one sees her Blackness. "It is my blackness that is most dominant. That is what makes for my oppression. And who oppresses blacks? Whites. So it is White Racism that is the greatest oppressor. . . ."

Woman number two says, "I see myself as female, and as such, dominated and controlled by men. Men and their sexism oppress women so sexism is the greatest oppressor of them all."

Woman number three observes her reflection and sees her gender, race, and class. "My femaleness, my color, and my class are sources of exploitation. Who is exploiting me? The question deserves serious consideration. An immediate response will not do" (Joseph and Lewis 1981, 19).

Gender is only one of many social facts on which stratification systems are based. We are all members of many different social groups, some of which form the basis of status rankings and the opportunities available to us. Any given individual has not only gender but also race, class, nationality, place of residence, age, and perhaps religion. It is important to untangle the effects of all these different characteristics on the individual. It seems obvious to most people that a poor Native American woman has low status and relatively meager life chances in the United States, and a wealthy white Episcopalian businessman has high status and a great opportunity to shape his life and the lives of others. But what are the relative effects of these different social characteristics? Specifically, what role does gender play vis-à-vis others in shaping people's lives? This question is difficult to answer because each individual may acquire characteristics from different rungs of the social ladder.

It is extremely difficult to untangle the different sources of inequity. There is little point in debating whose oppression hurts more; such debates tend to lead people almost to express pride in their oppression. The "whose oppression is bigger" debate defeats the whole purpose of comparing women's lives, because it tends to lead the participants to reject or downplay the claims of other women. Moreover, attempts to rank oppressions is for many women an exercise in self-fragmentation. Individual women have many different social identities. How does a woman decide which bit of her is the source of her oppression? Cheryl Clarke, a black radical feminist, arrives at perhaps the only sane response to women's self-fragmentation when she writes, "So, all of us would do well to stop fighting each other for our space at the bottom, because there ain't no more room. We have spent so much time hating ourselves. Time to love ourselves" (1981, 137).

If we think of status simply in terms of wealth and income, it is possible to analyze the relative impact of, for example, gender and race to determine what contribution each makes to raise or lower income. Within any given class or job, research shows that on average a person's salary will be lower if that person is a female rather than a male and lower still if the woman is black or Hispanic rather than white. Both black and white women earn less than both black and white men, even if we control for their levels of education. Within each sex, blacks earn less than whites, although the gap is much wider among men than among women. The conclusion economic research allows us to make is that apart from education, training, and skill, both gender and race and ethnicity have *independent* effects on where people stand on the economic ladder. The effects of gender are slightly different for blacks and whites, and the effects of race and ethnicity are slightly different for women and men.

But depicting social status and stratification simply in financial terms is also misleading. Inequality and oppression are better thought of as both qualitative and quantitative differences in the types of lives people lead, the amount of control they have over their lives, and the amount of respect and dignity accorded them by others. This makes sorting out the sources of oppression very difficult indeed. Untangling the effects of social classifications on income is complicated, but in terms of research methods and skills it is relatively straightforward compared with trying to sort out their effects on such intangibles as "respect" and "freedom."

Let us look at an example of both the need for and the difficulty of untangling different sources of oppression. As earlier chapters have emphasized, women are defined by traditional gender ideology as sexual objects and breeders. Although passivity is an important element of traditional views of women's sexuality, woman has long been seen as the seductive Eve or the Siren, temptresses who caused the fall of man. The belief in female passivity allows men the sexual right-of-way discussed in Chapter 10. The belief in women as evil temptresses allows men to deny responsibility for their own actions when they engage in rape, harassment, or other forms of sexual violence. As considerable research shows, the idea that a woman who is raped is generally guilty of causing the rape is an important feature of the mentality of rapists. This combination of sexual and gender ideology also helps explain why prostitutes and promiscuous women are condemned more than prostitutes' clients and promiscuous men. The woman's "misplaced" or "excessive" sexuality is interpreted as providing the conditions for illicit sex.

If we want a more complete understanding of the historical place of sexuality and especially rape within systems of oppression, it is necessary to look beyond gender. Gender is one of the important factors that determine the degree to which women are regarded and treated as sex and rape objects, but their race, ethnicity, class, and whether they are recent immigrants are also important. In other words, the lower a woman's status is by almost any measure, the more likely she is to be a target of sexual violence. Some examples of how this works follow.

Bell Hooks (1981) offers a powerful analysis of the intertwined effects of race and gender on sexual oppression. Rape was an integral part of the female slave experience beginning with the sea voyage, during which the slavers did what they could to break the Africans' spirits and make them passive and compliant. For the women this process included rape. As Bell Hooks shows, neither race nor gender alone account for the experience of slavery because, "While racism was clearly the evil that had decreed black people would be enslaved, it was sexism that determined that the lot of the black female would be harsher, more brutal than that of the black male slave" (43). Women were subjected to the same condition of slavery because of their race, but they were also used as sexual objects and as breeders because of their sex. The situation is not limited to blacks; the same was true for the Indians held as slaves in the Southwest (Mirandé and Enríquez 1979).

Race and gender also combined to affect the experience of slave owners. White men could own slaves because of their race and gender. Their sex gave them the right to own property in the first place, and their race gave them the right to own human beings. In one sense this gender difference among whites is little more than a technical nicety; white women had great power over their husband's slaves. On the other hand, gender did distinguish white slave holders in one important respect: White women knew about their husbands', brothers', and sons' sexual treatment of their slaves and that the fathers of the progeny of rapes were their "loved ones." This knowledge motivated some white women like the Grimké sisters to become abolitionists, but many others simply resented the situation. Many also resented and blamed the black women. Hooks adds a possible facet of the gender division of white slave owners when she speculates, "Surely it must have occurred to white women that were enslaved black women not available to bear the brunt of such intense anti-woman male aggression, they themselves might have been the victims" (1981, 38).

The belief in victim precipitation played a role in the sexual exploitation of female slaves. White men and women alike often held female slaves responsible for their own sexual exploitation. Even those who wished to expose the evils of slavery often referred to the "prostitution" of female slaves when they were actually talking about rape. The use of the word *prostitution* suggests that the women not only were at least partly responsible for what occurred but also might have profited by it.

The idea that woman precipitate attacks on themselves plays a special role where racial and ethnic differences are concerned. Women of low-status groups, especially those perceived as alien, are often regarded as excessively sexual and even animal-like. Hooks explains the implications of this view of black women by whites:

> The designation of all black women as sexually depraved, immoral, and loose had its roots in the slave system. White women and men justified the sexual exploitation of enslaved black women by arguing that they were the initiators of sexual relationships with men. From such thinking emerged the stereotype of black women as sexual savages, and in sexist terms a sexual savage, a nonhuman, an animal cannot be raped. (1981, 52)

The same principle applied to Hispanic and Indian women (Mirandé and Enríquez 1979). Likewise, one of the most commonly voiced objections to immigration in the late nineteenth and early twentieth centuries was the belief that specific groups of immigrant women—Irish, Italian, Jewish, or whatever—were especially promiscuous and likely to ruin the morals of innocent American men. Young immigrant women, especially those helping to support their families, were constantly subjected to sexual harassment and exploitation and then labeled promiscuous. In each of these cases the primary basis on which the sexual exploitation occurred was gender, but the specific conditions of the exploitation and the explanations offered for the women's sexual experiences were based on their other social characteristics such as race, ethnicity, and class.

Esther Ngan-Ling Chow (1987) offers a further example from the stereotyped view of Asian-American women. She points out that Asian-American women's experience in the United States is shaped not just by sexism or racism but also by ethnic sexism. The stereotypes of non-Asians define Asian-American women in a variety of closely related roles: Suzie Wong, geisha, picture bride, and sexpot. In each case, the definition of the Asian-American woman depends on both race and sex. Stereotypes of the Jewish-American princess (JAP) are based on both gender and ethnicity. Neither gender nor race or ethnicity are sufficient to understand her situation.

These examples demonstrate that the forms of gender-based oppression and exploitation people experience depend in part on their other social characteristics, and that the forms of oppression and exploitation that structure social relations, such as those based on race or class, depend in part on gender (See also Hurtado 1989; Mann 1989). In fact, we can argue that the exploitation of gender relations is often a means of enforcing other types of oppression.

As Chapter 10 showed, the state's control over marriage and sexual relations gives it leverage to pursue many different goals. Consider the case of a racist society. If a society wishes to preserve the social superiority of particular racial or ethnic groups, it must drive a wedge between them and others and make sure they do not mix in an intimate and equal manner; they cannot become kin with the full mutual loyalty and commitment owed to family members. To guard against such a breakdown of social hierarchy societies such as the United States in earlier years and South Africa today make it illegal for people of different races to marry.

These laws may seem to fall equally on the shoulders of women and men, but they do not. As the previous discussion pointed out, higher-status men maintain sexual rights over lower-status women, or at least they are not punished as severely as their partners in sexual mixing of races. In the American past sexual relations between white women and nonwhite men were punished more severely than relations between white men and nonwhite women. The first American antimiscengenation law, for example, was passed in 1664 in Maryland and declared that any white woman who had sexual relations with an enslaved black male would herself become a slave. No such law applied to white men.

Pressures within hierarchical societies lead them to regulate the sexual behavior of high-status females and low-status males. If a low-status female becomes pregnant by a high-status male, it has little effect on their relative status. Patriarchal ideology means that the male remains in control; if the woman makes too many claims he can abandon and reject her with relatively little social cost, partly because he can accuse her of promiscuity. A situation involving a low-status male and high-status female is very different. For example, a baby of mixed-race parentage born to a white woman has been regarded as a pollution of the white race. Because women are regarded as the property of male protectors in a patriarchal society, a nonwhite male who has sexual relations with a white woman is ultimately seen as taking something from or showing a weakness in white men. The effects of this dual system of racial and sexual oppression lasted long after the end of slavery. Public and legal reactions to interracial rape, for example, show that rape of a white woman by a nonwhite male is regarded as the most serious type of heterosexual rape.

Gender relations can also maintain class structures. Until recently property ownership and distribution from one generation to the next was governed very strictly by patriarchal norms. The principle that once did more than almost any law to ensure the continuation of a landed aristocracy was *primogeniture,* the inheritance of property by the first son. A patriarchal gender ideology has also offered women to the economy as marginal and auxiliary workers. Thus women have rarely made the types of economic demands they might have made if employment had been seen as a normal, necessary, and integral part of women's lives. Women have been developed as a stable core of consumers necessary to soak up the output of the economy.

It can be argued that women's place in patriarchal families has helped make working-class men less demanding than they might have been in two respects.

1. As Chapter 12 discussed, women's domestic labor inflates the real value of their husbands' wages. It is women's virtually invisible work that determines whether their husbands' low wages buy a tolerable or intolerable quality of life.
2. Insofar as masculinity depends on men's ability to support their dependent wives, men may be very reluctant to risk their jobs to fight for better working conditions and pay. They would be less hesitant if their wives were also regarded as breadwinners.

Almost a generation ago women's studies researchers began to emphasize the need to take gender into account to understand important social issues. In recent years they have been demanding still more sophistication and arguing that gender analysis cannot be complete if it is not integrated with an understanding of other structural bases of social life. Maxine Baca Zinn offers a good example in her writing on the family and poverty (1989). She shows that efforts to understand and solve the problems of poverty are doomed to failure if we look only at culture or race and class or gender structures. Society and social relations are constructed of all of these.

Some Sketches of Unity and Diversity

This chapter has focused on general questions of comparison, commonality, and difference across different social groups. This part briefly examines some of the questions about gender that can be addressed by looking at specific aspects of difference and diversity. The categories considered here are age, class, race and ethnicity, and geographic community. Many other equally important social categories could be treated; among those that received special attention earlier in this book are religion (see Chapter 6), sexual orientation (see Chapter 10), marital status (see Chapter 10), maternal status (see Chapter 11) and employment status (see Chapter 12). The categories discussed here were chosen primarily because the points raised about them have been dispersed throughout the book. Discussion in each case emphasizes the questions asked earlier in this chapter: What is unique about each special category of women? How does understanding of each special category deepen our understanding of gender, oppression, and liberation? The discussion will underscore the point that, when people talk about women as a group, they are often referring to a specific group of women.

Age

When people discuss the problems and roles of women, they tend, sometimes unwittingly, to talk primarily about females of particular ages. Writings about women and society usually place considerable emphasis on childhood because that is presumably the time of life when the basic framework of gender identity, roles, and ideology is set. By the time people become adults they know what femininity and masculinity are supposed to be, and they have already made many of the important gender-relevant choices, or been pushed into many of the gender-relevant tracks, that will shape their future lives.

The early stages of adulthood are also common objects of attention because that is the time at which people most clearly become "men" and "women." When we refer to the choices people make about their work lives or whether to get married or have children, we are referring primarily to the time between the ages of 18 and 40. The choices faced by women with dependent children occur when most of those women are relatively young (by adult standards), and therefore most discussions of how women can balance career and home life or single parenthood actually focus on women within a particular range of ages.

Women in later stages of life are considered much less often, apart from examination of middle-aged depression and menopause, although more attention is now being paid to widowhood and retirement, sexuality among older adults, and the special problems of poverty for the aged. Some of these issues were touched on in earlier chapters. In this section we shall show how focusing on older women can help us understand the structure of sex/gender systems more generally.[1]

Older women's lives are important illustrations of the workings of gender ideology because such women do not fulfill cultural definitions of femininity. They are not treated as sex objects because American culture defines attractive females as young. Most are not full-time mothers because they have no dependent children. Their lives are not as likely as younger women's to revolve around men; the older a woman is, the fewer men of her age there are. Although the aged suffer from dependencies

A volunteer worker at a child-care center bridging the generation gap.

due to health and financial circumstances, there is a sense in which older women are among the most self-reliant of people; a large proportion of them live on their own. Regardless of how women spend their younger adult years, there comes a time in most women's lives when they do not conform to some of the stereotypes of womanhood and femininity because these are built around age-specific norms.

The incongruity between stereotypes of womanhood and the situation of older women has conflicting implications for their experiences and status. Because older women do not easily fit into traditional definitions of womanhood, they are often viewed as though they are not real women but a kind of third sex (somewhere between male and female) or, worse, sexless. Many women react to menopause not just with the common anxiety most of us feel when confronted with the realization of our aging and mortality, but also with depression over a loss of femininity.

If women in general are misrepresented in the mass media (see Chapter 7), older women are treated even worse. They rarely appear in television programs, for example, and when they do they are almost always comic characters with neither brains nor beauty or they are nasty and bothersome mothers-in-law. Not until the late 1980s was there a television show (''Golden Girls'') that sometimes asked us to laugh with rather than at older women. The treatment of older women provides additional evidence that gender stereotypes regulate both women who conform to them and women who do not. Many negative aspects of the way older women are treated stem from the fact that they do not conform to stereotypes, and they therefore are rejected as useless and extraneous. (A parallel process affects men, although not to the same degree. For example, the term *old man* is used as an epithet to indicate that a man is weak and not in command; in other words, not masculine enough.) Degrading treatment of older people is based primarily on age but also on gender norms.

Old age also releases women from some of the problems faced at younger ages. In some cultures women gain respect and power only with age. Although the structure of American families has changed as people have become more geographically mobile, the matriarch of a family is still often regarded as the center of the extended kinship network and the person who defines and holds the family together.

Women often remark on some very specific freedoms they gain as they grow older. Whereas some people emphasize loss and depression at menopause, many women find their sense of enjoyment of sex and sexuality increases at that time because they no longer have to worry about getting pregnant. Women also have more opportunity to concentrate on their own interests and pursuits because they no longer have to balance these against the demands of dependent children. Many women also readily admit, at least to each other, that they feel freer to act, speak, and dress as they wish because they feel less pressure to conform to the stereotypes of femininity.

Old-age interest groups such as the Grey Panthers, long led by Maggie Kuhn, and the women's movement in general have sought changes in the material conditions of older women. The poverty of America's aged population, especially of women, is astounding. In 1981 the proportion of women over sixty-five who lived in poverty was 16 percent among whites, 27 percent among Hispanics, and 44 percent among blacks (Muller 1983). Policies affecting marital property, especially the disposition of property after widowhood or divorce, have direct effects on the situation of elderly women. Pension schemes and social security benefits, which in the past discriminated against female retirees and dependent homemakers, are slowly being changed to raise the living standard of older women.

The more difficult battle to be waged is against cultural stereotypes and social relations among people of different ages. It is not polite to refer to someone as an old woman or man because being old has many negative connotations. When someone says ''I am old,'' it is likely said in a tone of defeat. Instead we use such euphemisms as *senior citizen, golden ager, mature,* or perhaps *aging* or *older*. It will take much work to make *old* a proud word.

Class

It is difficult to assess the impact of class on women's lives because it is difficult to formulate a definition of *class* that applies to women in a meaningful way. This does not suggest that it is irrelevant to look at the interaction of class and gender; the very problem with the concept of class is one of the reasons it is important and revealing to consider this relationship.

Class is usually defined according to the occupation one pursues or, for children, the occupation one's father pursues. There are several ways class can be defined more specifically. Most analyses of class use a basic framework of blue-collar, white-collar, and professional or managerial occupations. The problem with definitions of class from the point of view of women is that class designations are often applied patriarchally; that is, a married woman's class is judged by her husband's occupation. This procedure makes no sense from the Marxist perspective, although most Marxists use it, because it does not tell us anything about a woman's relationship to the mode of production. Indeed it makes little sense from any perspective of occupational or economic analysis. Most people argue that a married homemaker's class should be identified according to her husband's occupation because she has no occupation to measure. This assumes that homemaking is not an occupational or economic role and does not help define a woman's status or the standard of living of the woman or her family. We have already questioned these assumptions in Chapter 12.

These definitional problems highlight some important points about the nature of women's social roles and status. As Feldberg and Glenn (1979) have argued, whereas men's status and economic worth are defined largely by their work, women's are defined by their marital status and, if they are married, by their husband's work. Women's employment is defined as secondary to their family roles, which is the reason a married woman's class status is often judged by her husband's work even if she is employed. Women's domestic work is not defined as real work, or at least not the kind that shapes her place in socioeconomic and class relations.

If we think of class in terms of wealth and control over economic resources, we find again that women's class status is determined somewhat differently from men's. It is much more vulnerable to change and depends more on family relationships. Regardless of the wealth of the family in which women were raised, women are much more vulnerable to a descent into poverty than men are. As Chapter 12 showed, women comprise a disproportionately large share of the poor. The reasons have as much to do with aspects of women's lives other than their own employment as they do with employment per se. Of equal importance are their responsibility for children, their experiences after divorce, and their relative longevity.

The usual class definitions of occupations are not adequate to inform us about the nature of women's work, and they obscure some of the most important aspects of the structure of women's work and its function in the economic system and economic relations. Traditional categorizations of class distinguish among farm, blue-collar, white-collar, business/managerial, and professional work, but they do not distinguish the type of work within each of these categories that most clearly marks women's work: pink-collar or auxiliary service work. Unpaid housewives, blue-collar service workers, pink-collar clerical workers, and professionals in such traditional women's occupations as nursing and social work must all be viewed differently. Moreover, class as conventionally defined cannot account for one of the dynamics of the workplace that so crucially affects women's working conditions and the work environment: sexual harassment and domination.

Women's roles do not fit neatly into class designations developed primarily with men's work in mind, and feminist scholars' efforts to construct new definitions have provoked controversy (Abbott and Sapsford 1988). Examining the concept of class as it applies to women reveals how important gender is in governing social and economic relations.

Despite the difficulty of developing an adequate definition of class, many people have fruitfully used different definitions to show the commonalities and differences in the experiences of women of different classes. The history of gender roles for women of different social classes, for example, has differed greatly. When we say that women are increasingly entering the labor market we are not referring to the poorest women; they have always had to work for pay to survive. Much more attention has been given to women breaking into traditionally male middle-class jobs than to those breaking into working-class jobs, and less progress has been made in the latter than in the former.

Research by Theodore Caplow and Bruce A. Chadwick (1979) offers an interesting picture of class-based changes in women's roles during the twentieth century. In 1929 and 1937 sociologists Robert and Helen Lynd published two very influential books based on studies of life in "Middletown," a fictional name for Muncie, Indiana. Caplow and Chadwick's research examined some of the differences between working- and middle-class women in Middletown in 1978 against the backdrop of the Lynds' findings in the 1920s. They found that many changes had occurred in half a century, one of the most notable being the convergence in the lives of working- and middle-class women.

In the 1920s working-class women did much more domestic labor than middle-class women did. Middle-class women did very little washing and ironing, and they did less sewing, mending, and baking than working-class women did. In 1924 95 percent of the working-class women but only 10 percent of the middle-class women had no paid help in the home; 33 percent of the middle-class women and none of the working-class women had full-time paid help.

The picture was very different 50 years later, largely because of the increase in the amount of domestic labor done by middle-class women. By 1978 working-class and middle-class women did essentially equivalent amounts of housework, including each of the tasks mentioned earlier. In the 1970s women, especially middle-class women, did more laundry than they did earlier in the century, and they were more likely to bake bread than they were earlier. In 1978 91 percent of working-class women and 83 percent of middle-class women had no paid domestic help; 1 percent of both middle-class and working-class women had full-time help. Caplow and Chadwick also found there was no longer any difference in the educational aspirations middle- and working-class women had for their children. Surprisingly, perhaps, especially for those who romanticize the traditional family, both mothers and fathers reported spending more time with their children in 1978 than they did in the 1920s.

Analysis of public opinion poll data repeatedly shows that the higher an individual's social class, the more likely the person is to have more progressive and feminist attitudes toward women's public and private roles and, more generally, the family and sexuality. However, Anne Locksley's (1982) research shows that some of these differences are due not so much to occupational social class as to differences in education.

There are some important class differences in how women view the balance between family and occupation. A CBS/*New York Times* poll conducted in 1983 showed that although only about one-third of the employed women would become full-time homemakers if they had a choice, almost half of the women in blue-collar jobs would prefer to be full-time homemakers. (As Table 13-1 shows, occupational social class does not seem to make a difference in men's preference for employment or family life.) The blue-collar women were different from the higher-status women in certain other respects as well, as the *New York Times* article that reported these data explained. Most of the blue-collar women were mothers, "and many of them divorced or widowed or supporting unemployed husbands. Unlike the professional and business women, and clerks and secretaries, most of these women said they worked for money, not satisfaction." [2] The report offered a typical statement made by a blue-collar woman, in this case a member of the Pima Indian tribe who worked as a cleaning woman in a school system to support her husband and daughter. "My job's OK, but it's getting tiresome. My daughter is starting high school and I've never been home with her. We're drawing apart."

The attitudes of blue-collar women are distinguished from those of other employed women for a number of reasons. As Locksley reminds us, their levels of education differ. Their socioeconomic situations also differ. Women with lower levels of education and from lower social classes tend to marry younger, have children younger, and divorce earlier. They assume responsibility for caring for a family at a younger age, when women with more resources and higher status have only abstract ideals of home and family rather than real-life adult experience. Because of their economic vulnerability they are especially likely to be working because of financial necessity rather than other motives. The nonmonetary rewards working-class women receive from their employment, particularly when compared with the rewards they might receive from being homemakers, may not be as great as they are for other women because of the nature of the jobs open to them.

Myra Marx Feree (1980) studied 135 working-class women in Boston to discover their attitudes toward feminism and women's roles. Employment seemed to be an important determinant of their attitudes, although the impact of employment

TABLE 13-1

403

Chapter 13:
Commonality and
Difference among
American Women

Attitudes Toward Work versus Staying at Home

If you were free to do either, would you prefer to have a job outside the home, or would you prefer to stay at home and take care of your house and family?

	Prefer job		Prefer to stay home	
	Women	Men	Women	Men
Total	45	72	47	21
Employment status				
Employed	58	72	33	21
Not employed	31	73	62	21
Occupation				
Professional and managerial	63	70	27	21
Other white collar	65	—	26	—
Blue collar	43	70	49	22
Income				
Below $10,000	53		36	
$10,000–20,000	62	68[a]	32	24[a]
Over $20,000	62	77	28	17

Note: Figures show proportion of women or men in each category saying they would prefer to have a job or stay home.
[a]These figures combine the income brackets "Below $10,000" and "$10,000–20,000."
SOURCE: CBS/*New York Times* Poll conducted November 11–20, 1983. Reported in *The New York Times,* December 4, 1983.

depended on the reasons the women had for being employed. Of the women Feree interviewed, the most feminist were those who were employed for personal reasons such as fulfillment. The second most feminist group were those who said they were employed for financial reasons. The least feminist group were the homemakers.

Scholars have painted many different pictures of working-class women's lives. In some cases working-class women appear as oppressed members of the most patriarchal kinds of families (Rubin 1976); in others they are brave, tough people with magnificent coping reactions (Seifer 1976). Most people who discuss class and gender emphasize the differences among women of different classes. Some of these are profound. But just as the effects of class are sometimes ignored, they can be exaggerated.

Race and Ethnicity

Race might seem easier to analyze than class because it should be easier to define. Any appearance of simplicity, however, is a pernicious illusion. As Michael Banton

(1983) shows in his history of racial definition, different societies at different times vary considerably in how they define race. Race is not a biological classification, even though is is built around biological characteristics such as parentage or skin pigmentation. It is a social category defined by cultural norms.

A few brief examples illustrate how elusive the concept of race is. Some cultures define Jews as a race, others do not. At one time most Hispanic leaders in the United States objected to being categorized as a race distinguished from "white," but by the late 1970s many Hispanic leaders wished to be regarded as a race. Even so, this demand is made only by some people of Latin American ancestry, notably those of Mexican heritage. A very large proportion of American blacks are descended from the union of white slave masters of European ancestry with black slaves of African ancestry. The children of a black-white union have generally been regarded and, most importantly, treated as a black even if their gene pools come from white parentage as much as black. As in other cases in which one race is regarded as inferior to another, it takes only a small fraction of the blood of the lower-status race for an individual to be treated as a part of that race. Thus the relevance of race to an individual's life is ultimately determined not by biology but by how societies deal with a clue that biology gives them.

Ethnicity is an even more subjective cultural concept, especially in a society in which there is a relatively high degree of intermarriage. Ethnicity is largely, although not entirely, defined by the nationality of one's forebears. The significance of ethnicity in the United States is unique, not because there are diverse and recognizable ethnic groups, but because of the concept of the "hyphenated American"—the Irish-American, the Italian-American, and so on—that seems so normal in the United States and is regarded as curious abroad.

Most of the writing on race and gender has concentrated on blacks and comparison of black with whites.[3] Other than biographies and literary works, there have been relatively few serious and systematic treatments of other nonwhite women, especially from the perspective of the social sciences, and few that focus on specific ethnic groups and comparisons. This neglect constitutes an important gap in the field of women's studies. This section concentrates on black women and black-white comparisons because the available literature makes it possible to make more than broad statements, and because black women have played a special role in writings on gender.

Much of the writing on American women pays little attention to black women and sometimes makes sweeping generalizations about women and their histories that simply do not apply to black women. This pattern is sometimes only partially improved by the treatments of black women that do appear in general books on women. There is a tendency to restrict recognition of racial differences to a special section or chapter on black women, which often seems to suggest that unless otherwise specified, the work is about white women. This tendency toward generalization is not, of course, limited to the treatment of one group.

Bell Hooks provides examples that reveal special problems when analysts compare the history and situation of women as a group with that of blacks: "When black people are talked about the focus tends to be on black *men;* and when women are talked about the focus tends to be on *white* women" (1981, 7). For example, discussions of post–Civil War movements to broaden the franchise commonly mention the debates over whether reformers should fight to secure the vote for women as well as blacks or just for blacks. In the end, we are told, blacks were given the legal right to vote. In fact, of course, "blacks" were not given the legal right to vote; it was black men whose legal rights had technically changed.

Focusing on black women is particularly revealing of the nature of sex/gender systems in America because black women's lives and experiences defy dominant stereotypes of femininity. Black women have never been defined as frail, dependent, and submissive creatures. They have worked at hard physical labor and have been the primary breadwinners in their families in larger proportions than most other groups of American women. These aspects of black women's lives have often served as the basis for accusations that black women "emasculate" black men (Collins 1989b).

We have already touched on the debates about the black matriarchy and the emasculation thesis (see Chapter 11). Just as the view that true women should not be breadwinners kept women who could afford not to work from seeking employment, it allows people to point the accusing finger at women who have to work or were forced to do so. Bonnie Dill reminds us that

> it is a cruel irony that the black woman's role as a worker has been used to represent dominance over and emasculation of black men. This predisposition ignores both historical and socioeconomic realities. Black workers were brought to this country for two economic reasons: to work and to produce workers. Although they were valued for their reproductive function, as were white women settlers, it was only of equal importance to their labor (1979, 550).

Bell Hooks points out that an important aspect of the process of enslaving women was the requirement that they do labor regarded in America as men's work. Male slaves were less often subjected to the complementary treatment of being required to do women's work (1981, 20; Mann 1989, 780).

As Hooks argues, the fact that most nineteenth-century black women could not live the life that many white women led does not mean they were unaffected by the cult of domesticity; the image of the woman fostered by this view became an unreachable goal to which black women aspired (1981, 48; see also Perkins 1983). Attempts to take for themselves the predominant definition of femininity after emancipation were met by the racial hatred of whites. As Hooks observes, "A black woman dressed tidy and clean, carrying herself in a dignified manner, was usually the object of mudslinging by white men who ridiculed and mocked her self-improvement efforts" (1981, 55). Black women have historically been caught in a crossfire of demands based on the interplay of gender and racial politics. They have been exploited by white society for their ability to depart from feminine roles and slapped down by the same society for attempting to conform to the dominant norms of femininity. In recent years many black male leaders have demanded that they step back and act out more patriarchal definitions of femininity on the grounds that the real crime of white society against blacks in general is that it has stripped black men of their masculinity, or their ability to be patriarchs.

The historical experiences of black as compared with white women has been playing another role in literature on gender and race in recent years. As the realities of black women's experiences are finally being examined more extensively, they are serving as the basis for a new symbolism and mythology. Just as blacks in general have become the American symbol of poverty and oppression, in feminist and black writing the black woman has become the symbol of strength against odds, the wonder woman.

Pride in the history and strength of black women marks a happy turn in American cultural history. On the other hand, turning black women into romantic symbols has its dangers. Many black women and men, for example, have argued that dwelling on sex/gender systems and the liberation of women is irrelevant to black women. They argue that black women need to be liberated not as women but as blacks, because their lives have defied stereotypes of femininity. As we have seen, however, defying stereotypes does not mean one is unhurt by them. Further, if liberation means having choice and control over one's life, black women have had precious little liberation as either blacks or women. Bell Hooks is wary of those who romanticize the historical display of strength among black women and claims "they ignore the reality that to be strong in the face of oppression is not the same as overcoming oppression,

Women such as Whoopi Goldberg are finding ways to express pride in themselves as both women and members of their cultural communities.

that endurance is not to be confused with transformation" (1981, 6). None of these observations reduces the achievements of black women; they are great enough in real life not to need embellishment. The romanticizing of any women's lives, however, and especially their oppression, can lead to complacency.

White women in the women's movement have been particularly prone both to romanticize black women and to use the black woman as a symbol for their own purposes. Hooks points out an irony in this treatment in her observation that

> when the women's movement was at its peak and white women were rejecting the role of breeder, burden bearer, and sex object, black women were celebrated for their unique devotion to the task of mothering; for their "innate" ability to bear tremendous burdens; and for their ever-increasing availability as sex objects. (1981, 6)

This apparent hypocrisy, which stems largely from good intentions and is often called "liberal guilt," is a double standard. Hooks also points out that although white feminists have rarely devoted much effort to learning about or from black women's lives, they have long used the analogy of black oppression and struggle to underscore the oppression of women. One of the earliest writings of the contemporary women's movement, for example, was entitled *The Woman as Nigger* (Gallion 1970). There are many parallels, but Hooks argues, "A white woman who has suffered physical abuse and assault from a husband or lover, who also suffers poverty, need not compare her lot to that of a suffering black person to emphasize that she is in pain" (1981, 142).

Neither black nor white women in America can be understood without reference to both race and sex. Examining privileges of white women vis-à-vis black women is as necessary to understand white women's lives as it is to understand black women's. White women continue to have wider opportunities than black women, but this is not all: White women have also had power over black women, a point that black women do not forget even when white women do. Although white women have lived under the control of white men, black slaves of either sex lived under the control of white women. In this respect, at least, one cannot argue that white women were completely powerless, even in the patriarchal Old South.

This social division between black and white offers one of the clearest examples of the complex workings of sex/gender systems. On the one hand black women are doubly caught at the bottom of both race and gender stratification. On the other hand white women are caught at the bottom of gender stratification but have been granted relative status, power, and privilege through their position at the upper level of race stratification.

Relations between white and black women are marked by a considerable degree of both commonality and division. Margaret Simons is correct when she argues that "the notion of an absolute patriarchy can obscure the reality, all too familiar to minority women, that some white women have historically had access to power which they have at times wielded against both minority men and women" (1979, 338). It is not contradictory to Simons' point to say, however, that focusing only on racial divisions can obscure the reality that black and white women, as well as women of other races and different ethnic groups, have suffered because of the power wielded against them on the basis of gender.

Any student of American history knows that one of the most important sources of division has been geography. American history is marked by economic and political struggles for power between, for example, different regions of the country and between urban and rural interests. There are obvious differences between living in rural Nebraska and living in New York City. Despite great geographic mobility and the pervasiveness of the mass media, the regions of the country continue to differ considerably in economic structure, culture, and demography. Consider these characteristics of the residents of different regions in 1980: In the Pacific states 47 percent of people had at least some college education, compared with 25 percent in the East South Central states. While 14 percent of the residents of the South Atlantic states had ancestors who came from Africa, less than 1 percent of those in the Mountain states did. Although 16 percent of all New Englanders had Italian background, only 1 percent of the people in the East and West South Central area did. And 89 percent of the people in the East South Central states were Protestant, compared with 26 percent of all New Englanders.[4]

Public opinion surveys show that attitudes toward gender and sexual issues differ by region. As Table 13-2 shows, the New England and Pacific states are more liberal than people in other regions on almost all issues; people in Southern states are more likely to be conservative in their opinions, but the South is not homogeneous. Some of the patterns can be accounted for by differences in education, religion, ethnicity, and so forth. Although there have been many changes in all regions in this century, it is interesting to note that one of the best predictors of how quickly a state approved the Equal Rights Amendment in the 1970s was how quickly the states supported giving women the right to vote.

One of the interesting aspects of American women's history is the regional variation. Some of the differences are obvious. The story of women under slavery is a story of the South, the story of immigrant women working in sweatshops is a story primarily of the Northeast. Parts of the country found it in their interest to encourage women to be property holders, even when this wasn't the case elsewhere. The territory of Oregon, for example, offered single women settlers (but not single men) a large parcel of free farmland because it was thought that would encourage both men and women to settle and develop the territory. The Midwest was particularly quick to develop coeducational higher education, first at private colleges such as Oberlin in Ohio and Lawrence in Wisconsin, and then at the public land-grant colleges that are now state universities.

As in other cases we have examined, observers sometimes exaggerate regional variation and sometimes minimize it. Life in the Old South (including gender norms) was undoubtedly different from that in other parts of the country. But the stereotype of the white Southern belle is an overdrawn portrait that historians have labored to correct. Most white Southern women were not ladies of the manor; they were farm women. D. Harland Hagler (1980) traced the record of Southern history to find that for most white men the ideal wife was not a delicate lady, but a woman who could carry her weight in helping to run farm and family. Regardless of region the ideal of the lady was a luxury only the wealthy could afford. In her history of Southern women, Anne Firor Scott (1970) focuses on the much-neglected story of

TABLE 13-2

Regional Differences in Attitudes toward Gender and Society

	New England	Mid Atlantic	E.N. Central	W.N. Central	S. Atlantic	E.S. Central	W.S. Central	Mountain	Pacific
Favor E.R.A.:	66	61	45	54	50	47	51	51	68
Agree that women should run their houses and leave running the country to men:	20	29	29	32	43	43	35	28	26
Agree that it should be legal to obtain an abortion for any reason:	51	48	30	34	29	28	36	42	55
Agree that sex before marriage is always/almost always wrong:	30	27	40	42	53	53	44	44	29
Agree that homosexual relations are always/almost always wrong:	66	73	80	77	87	91	87	77	67

SOURCE: NORC surveys from 1977 to 1982, reported in *Public Opinion* February–March 1983, 26–27.

women who became involved in politics and struggles for change. Gerda Lerner's (1971) biography of the Grimké sisters, who devoted themselves to abolition and women's rights, shows the determination of these women to fight against a system their own family helped perpetuate.

Most women's studies scholars now accept the charge that the field has been dominated by the experiences of middle-class white women. Less well recognized is a charge articulated by southern scholars such as Jacquelyn Dowd Hall: Women's studies is "New Englandized," or based largely on the experiences and perspectives of women from the Northeast. Hall points out that the interpretive framework used most often for American women's history

> turned on the industrial revolution, which, beginning in the 1830s, severed work from life, the public from the private sphere, and transformed the household from a unit of production to a woman-dominated haven from a heartless world. Women lost their productive roles but gained access to education and a conviction of moral superiority. Above all they acquired the sense of grievance and group identity that would inspire them to form voluntary associations, oppose slavery, and launch a movement for women's rights. (Hall 1989, 904)

This story is not exclusively of the Northeast, but it is certainly not an adequate rendition of conditions in the South of that period.

Comparing women in urban and rural settings offers another example of the way in which attention to commonalities and differences among women helps create a more complete picture of the meaning of gender in America. In Chapter 12, for example, we noted that the growth of cities and the development of suburbs both changed the structure and effects of gender roles. Many experts in policy and planning are coming to realize that the structure and design of communities has a special impact on women because of their gender roles, and that women's needs must be given more attention in urban planning, for example ("Women and the American City" 1980).

Although cities are often the base of progressive attitudes and social change, we cannot ignore the role of rural areas. For example, the nineteenth-century cult of domesticity (the set of beliefs that counterposed the rough and tumble world of male commerce with the serene woman's domain of the home) or the Victorian image of the frail, swooning lady had little relevance to—indeed could provoke economic disaster in—the farmlands. In fact many rural women have found it difficult to relate to the problems that urban reformers have fought to solve. Some of the almost entirely agricultural midwestern states were among the first to grant women the right to vote. In some cases unusual coalitions have been formed among women from different areas; in the 1960s and 1970s, for example, many conservative Republican farm women were attracted to feminist organizations such as the National Organization for Women by their desire to change marital property laws that often took their farms from them upon widowhood.

One other type of cultural and geographic division among women should be considered. Although this book is about the United States, it is important to know whether the evidence provided by the American experience is similar to that found in other countries, and what aspects of the American experience are unique to this society. The question of how much change has occurred and how much change can occur is a relative one. How do the types and degrees of change that have occurred in the United States compare with those that have occurred elsewhere? It is impossible to make more than a few brief comments here, but these will indicate directions for further inquiry.[5]

Writings about women in the United States and in other industrialized nations are striking in their similarities. Although employment rates of women in the United States are among the highest in the industrialized, non-Communist world, the degree of occupational segregation is similar, and in some countries—France and West Germany, for example—the earnings gap between women and men is smaller than in the United States. Even in Scandinavian countries, which are generally considered more progressive than the United States, feminists are quick to point out how much job segregation remains; indeed, Scandinavian feminists often regret the degree to which American feminists, among others, romanticize the Scandinavian situation.[6] Comparative studies of the proportion of domestic labor done by women also show very striking similarities among the different countries.

Just as the United States in general tends to compare favorably with other countries in terms of policies supporting individual civil rights and liberties and somewhat less favorably in terms of social-welfare policies, so it is with policies directly affecting women. The achievements and implementation of antidiscrimination legislation have been very impressive in the United States compared to other countries. European nations differ in their approaches to these issues, but the European Community and European Parliament have been making efforts in recent years to improve the situations in member nations. The United States, on the other hand, lags behind other nations in policies providing for the material welfare of women, especially pregnant women and mothers.

Industrial wealth, modernization, and democratic government do not ensure gender equality across nations. Traditional attitudes and cultural differences play a large role as well. Table 13-3 reveals some interesting differences in public opinion among the member nations of the European Community. People in these countries have different attitudes toward women's and men's roles. Further, the degree to which women and men agree or disagree with each other depends on the country in which they live.

Japan offers a clear example of the importance of traditional culture compared with the general structure of the political economy and modernization. One of the most advanced industrial states in the world, Japan has retained much of its very hierarchical sex/gender system. Although life for Japanese women is not the same as it was before World War II, women in Japan are still expected to leave employment when they marry, and the general business policy of paying women on explicitly lower scales than men is rarely questioned. The Japanese constitutional guarantee of equality for women and men means very little in practice.

It is difficult to compare the situation of women in Communist nations with that of women in capitalist/democratic nations.[7] Discussing employment opportunity as a civil right, for example, makes little sense in the Soviet Union, in which working is declared a civil duty in the constitution. Centrally planned economies in which

TABLE 13-3

European Attitudes toward Gender Roles and Feminism, 1978

	Denmark		W. Germany		France		Ireland		Italy		United Kingdom	
	Women	Men	Women	Men	Women	Men	Women	Men	Women	Men	Women	Men
Household tasks it is reasonable for men to do frequently (percent agreeing)												
Shopping	63	67	76	77	74	71	65	63	69	71	74	74
Washing dishes	64	62	50	47	51	53	74	67	20	21	86	85
Organizing meals	43	37	30	28	38	40	40	40	42	43	53	62
Cleaning house	49	46	30	29	36	44	42	39	28	29	47	57
Staying home with sick child	31	31	19	17	32	30	27	27	40	37	28	37
Changing diapers	28	25	10	8	22	17	25	15	17	13	30	30
Ironing	18	19	11	7	10	14	12	11	11	6	22	29
None of these	16	20	11	12	8	9	8	10	14	11	3	3
Men and women in parliament												
Would have more confidence in a man	21	28	31	56	31	33	45	63	39	54	35	48
Would have more confidence in a woman	12	2	11	2	13	7	27	7	22	9	20	8
Would have equal confidence in a man or a woman	62	66	50	39	48	54	23	25	35	33	37	39
Percent having positive attitude toward women's liberation movement	52	48	41	35	57	55	47	43	46	44	41	43

SOURCE: Commission of the European Community, 1979.

virtually all industry is publicly owned work very differently from market-based economies. Finally the structure of feminist politics must differ in countries that tolerate little dissent and no political organization apart from what is officially sanctioned.

Communist nations are as diverse as non-Communist nations. Research on the Soviet Union and East Germany suggests that the material gap between women and men is relatively small in comparison to the West, partly because of the structure of employment and partly because of the programs of public benefits, especially for pregnant women and mothers. Some of the special problems of centrally planned economics fall on the shoulders of women who, in most parts of the Communist world, continue to do most of the domestic labor, just as their sisters in the West do. The deemphasis on consumer goods in favor of heavy industrial goods means that women spend many hours waiting to obtain household necessities in addition to the work they do for their employers and at home. In the Soviet Union the lack of consumer goods includes lack of contraceptives, which means that free abortion is virtually the sole means of contraception for most women.

Most Communist countries have devoted much attention to policy issues directly affecting women, although with different intents and results. The Soviet Union and China, for example, have had population problems the United States has never experienced. In China, which faces severe overpopulation, for a while government policy limited the number of births per family to one. In contrast the Soviet Union,

413

Chapter 13:
Commonality and
Difference among
American Women

While China enforced a one-child policy to combat overpopulation in the 1970s, the government found it also had to campaign against selective abortion of female fetuses.

which had its population seriously depleted by its own revolution and two world wars, has developed a series of policies aimed at increasing population. One Communist nation that appears to have paid special attention to the status of women is Cuba, which began working to eliminate the literacy gap between women and men and later launched other programs to equalize the roles and status of women and men. Cuba is unique in attempting to use law and policy to eliminate women's double burden partly by trying to encourage men to take up more of their share of domestic labor.

Once again, we find considerable commonality and, of course, considerable difference. Although nationalism and parochialism drive deep wedges between the women of different countries, the international feminist movement (discussed in Chapter 14) has often revealed and fruitfully used the common experiences of women around the world.

Diversity and Feminism

Understandably the claims of various feminist movements to represent the interests of women as a group sometimes seem pretentious and, to some groups of women, annoying. Over and over the women's movement has been accused of being limited to the concerns of only some women, especially those who are white, middle class, and urban. Chapter 14 will look more specifically at the composition, strategies, and goals of American feminism to determine just how we should characterize it. Here we will ask a more general and speculative question: Given the undeniable diversity among women, what are the grounds for arguing that there can be such things as ''women's studies'' or a ''women's movement''?

The answer to the first part of this question is relatively easy. To argue that there is a field of study called women's studies or that sex/gender systems are integral parts of the structure of society does not imply that all women live the same lives or that sex/gender systems and gender ideology affect all groups of women the same way. As this chapter has shown, a gender ideology is a complex set of beliefs and ideas; if it were not, it might be easier to change. A single rule affects the conformist and the nonconformist equally, though differently. Because commonality does not mean sameness, only a careful exploration of the diversity of women will reveal how much commonality there really is.

The second part of the question is more difficult to answer. One can imagine constructing a feminist movement that considers and is based on commonality within diversity. This need not mean finding the lowest common denominator: a few issues that affect most women in the same way. A diverse feminist movement requires tackling the aspects of sex/gender systems that affect women, but differently. Such a movement would require women to become interested in issues that might seem to affect others more than themselves.

The major obstacle is the reality of the political world. It is easy to say that a movement should be all things to all people, but people have only limited amounts of time, energy, and resources to devote to social action, and they must make choices about what actions they want to take. A united and diverse feminist movement cannot develop if some women sit on the sidelines because they do not see enough other women tackling the problems that concern them most. On the other hand, women already involved in the women's movement cannot feel content to restrict their actions to interests that seem to affect them directly while ignoring the needs of other women. This process of coming together is painful, and involves anger and frustration as well as the joy of discovery. The process is often frightening because women say and hear words they have not dared to express before, at least to each other.[8] But many feminists who are committed to building connections among women argue that the politeness and silence that is the alternative to confrontation is a means of avoiding the truth—of lying (Rich 1979).

Optimistic words are merely that, but perhaps the best observation of the meaning of social divisions and feminism was made by Sojourner Truth, whose life under slavery taught her she could not neglect either her blackness or her womanhood, because no one else would:

> Wall, chilern, whar dar is so much racket dar must be somethin' out o' kilter. I tink dat' twixt de niggers of de souf and de womin at de Norf, all talkin' 'bout rights, de white men will be in a fix pretty soon (quoted in Kerber and Mathews 1982, 20).

NOTES

1. For convenience, this discussion will focus on women who are at least in their sixties.
2. *New York Times,* December 4, 1983.
3. The literature on black women is now very large. Among the best-known works are books by Ladner (1971), Reid (1975), Stack (1974), Davis (1981), Hooks (1981), Joseph and Lewis (1981), Giddings (1984), Jones (1985), and White (1985) and anthologies by Cade (1970), Lerner (1973), and Harley and Terborg-Penn (1978).
4. *Public Opinion,* February–March 1983. Here and elsewhere regional breakdowns are as follows: New England (Connecticut, Massachusetts, Maine, New Hampshire, Vermont), Middle Atlantic (New Jersey, New York, Pennsylvania), South Atlantic (Delaware, Florida, Georgia, Maryland, North Carolina, South Carolina, Virginia, West Virginia), East North Central (Illinois, Indiana, Michigan, Ohio, Wisconsin), East South Central (Alabama, Kentucky, Mississippi, Tennessee), West North Central (Iowa, Kansas, Minnesota, Missouri, Nebraska, North Dakota, South Dakota), West South Central (Arkansas, Louisiana, Oklahoma, Texas), Mountain (Arizona, Colorado, Idaho, Montana, New Mexico, Nevada, Utah, Wyoming), and Pacific (Alaska, California, Hawaii, Oregon, Washington).
5. This discussion will be limited to industrialized communist and noncommunist countries, those most commonly compared with the United States.
6. For discussion of women and feminism in Scandinavia, see Haavio-Mannila et al. (1985).
7. For some writing on women in Communist countries, see Wolchik and Meyer (1985).
8. One of the most provocative and evocative efforts of this sort is found in Moraga and Anzaldúa (1981).

14

Feminism and the Future

A GROUP OF people are standing together in a room. Over there is Abigail Adams, wife of a revolutionary who will later become the second president of the United States. Adams is telling her husband (half jokingly) that the ladies are bound to foment a revolution if they are not remembered in the design of the new government. Standing nearby is Elizabeth Cady Stanton, who spent half a century pushing for expansion of women's rights. She is arguing with Ida B. Wells, who exposed the prevalence of lynching at the turn of the century and also pointed out the special sexual oppression of black women. Wells is angry with Stanton for her racist remarks and belief that it is more important for white women than black men to have the vote. There is a young Jewish immigrant who has spent the last fourteen hours at a factory sewing machine working to support her family. She is about to strike in support of higher wages and a ten-hour working day. She is gazing at a wealthy patron of the arts who has helped build a concert hall where women's music can be heard. A curious conversation is taking place between Valerie Solanas of the Society for Cutting Up Men (SCUM) and Phyllis Schlafley, who vigorously opposes the Equal Rights Amendment and supports policies she thinks will maintain the dignity of women's roles in the family. Catherine Beecher, looking on, is partly sympathetic and points out that she devoted considerable effort to the task of improving the status of women, although she saw no need for women to vote. One woman is walking away from one of the few men in the room because she can't imagine what he would have to say to her about women's rights that would be useful. She has argued that the only way to seek freedom for women is by working with other women to figure out what they need. John Stuart Mill shakes his head sadly, thinking about the hours he spent trying to convince his colleagues in Parliament to support giving women the franchise. Three women stand at the edge of the room. One is thinking that she certainly is not a feminist, but she does believe women should have a better chance to earn a living and do the things they want to do. Another thinks she has no time for these arguments because she is too busy working with her welfare rights organization fighting for higher benefits for single mothers. Another impatiently thinks that she has no time for feminism because she works fifteen hours a day as the first female head of a corporation in her industry.[1]

Which of these people are feminists? Nearly 200 years separate their birthdates; they are of different sexes, races, religions, and classes; and they would find few points of agreement. Each, however, has argued for what she or he saw as improvements in the status of women, has done things that might have direct and special benefits for women, or has lived in defiance of stereotypes of women. After all is said and done, what is feminism? Who are feminists? When and how do feminist movements happen, and what is their social significance? These are the questions this chapter explores.

What Is Feminism?

As is the case with so many other words describing important social phenomena, *feminist* and *feminism* are extremely difficult to define. Ever since the word *feminism* was coined near the end of the nineteenth century, those attached to it and those antagonistic toward it have been struggling among and between themselves to define it (Cott 1987; Offen 1988).

Why would people who are not bookish academics struggle over the meaning of a word? The answer to this question begins to point us toward the nature of feminism. Feminism has an inseparably dual character, involving both theory and practice. Feminism is both a way of thinking about the world and a way of acting in it. The meaning of feminism is derived not just from footnote-dotted books but also from the decisions and actions of people claiming to act on its behalf. So disagreement over the definition of *feminism* is a disagreement over how people should act and interact.

Let us start with a general working definition and then turn briefly to some alternative contemporary feminist theories to see what some of the disagreements are. If we sort through all these different perspectives, we can find a core of characteristics about which most agree.

Feminism is a perspective that views gender as one of the most important bases of the structure and organization of the social world. Feminists argue that in most known societies this structure has granted women lower status and value than men, more limited access to valuable resources, and less autonomy and opportunity to make choices about their lives. Feminists further believe that although this gender-based world may be organized around certain biological facts, such as the exclusive capacity of men to create sperm and the exclusive capacity of women to bear children, gender inequality is rooted in the social construction of human experience, which means that it should be possible to eradicate it. Finally feminists believe that these inequities should be eliminated and that to do this, feminists cannot simply try to do better as individuals in the social world as it exists but must work together to change the structure of the social world. Any other action means making the best of an unjust situation.

This general working definition provides only the common denominator in definitions of feminism. Further refinement requires examining various traditions and types of feminism. As in other ideologies and approaches to the social world there are different schools of thought and action. To discuss these alternatives it is necessary to look back to Chapters 2 and 3. Those two chapters presented different types of theories that have been offered to explain why societies develop particular sex/gender systems and how individuals in any given society come to fit into those societies. That discussion pointed out that both feminist and nonfeminist theorists form a part of each tradition. Although both feminists and nonfeminists have used the basic structure of liberal, Marxist, and other theories, they interpret them and use them in different ways and reach different conclusions. Here we will compare three different approaches to feminist theory and action that form parts of current American feminism: liberal, socialist, and radical feminism. Although any brief outline is bound to be an oversimplification, this discussion will suggest some of the different ways feminists understand both the social world as it exists and the possibilities for change.[2]

Liberal Feminism

Liberal feminism has been the predominant form in the United States or, for that matter, in most of the best-known feminist movements throughout the world (see Chapter 2).[3] The earliest explication of a liberal feminist theory can be found in Mary Wollstonecraft's *Vindication of the Rights of Woman* ([1792], 1975), although it was left to later liberal feminists to develop the structure of liberal feminist political action.

The underlying emphasis of liberal feminism is best illustrated by the Declaration of Rights and Sentiments drawn up at the 1848 Seneca Falls Convention. That document took the logic of the American Declaration of Independence and translated it into feminist terms, beginning with one of its most famous lines: "We hold these truths to be self-evident: that all men and women are created equal, that they are endowed by their creator with certain inalienable rights, that among these are life, liberty, and the pursuit of happiness." Although liberal feminism has changed in detail over time and differs in certain respects from one place to another, its vision is based on liberal democratic principles. Its complaint about the world is, as Alison Jaggar observes, "that the treatment of women in contemporary society violates, in one way or another, all of liberalism's political values, the values of equality, liberty, and justice" (1983, 175–76).

Liberal feminists argue that women are not given the same opportunities as men to pursue their individual interests, because women as a group are blocked by informal and formal discrimination and an ideology learned through socialization that views women differently from men. They argue not that men's lives are necessarily free and fulfilled, but that the privileges, rights, and powers that allow individuals to pursue freedom and fulfillment are unequally distributed and give men a disproportionate share of control over themselves and women.[4] Liberal feminists do not want to change liberal democratic principles of individual freedom and autonomy; they want these principles applied to women and men equally.

The history of feminism shows how the liberal feminist interpretation of society has shaped the political action pursued by its proponents. The method of liberal feminism is to survey the quality and quantity of rights and privileges granted to women and men, pinpoint the areas of inequality, and then set about making adjustments to create equality of opportunity. The liberal feminist agenda is derived in large part from the more general agenda of liberalism and therefore has focused on extending to women the rights that men have gained in education, employment, and civic and political life. Above all, liberal feminists emphasize the importance of sexist ideology and ignorance as the basis for the inequality and oppression of women. They argue that the real key to liberation is changing people's values and beliefs with respect to gender. If people can be resocialized to believe that women and men are equal, they will treat them that way.

Socialist Feminism

A second major branch of feminism is socialist feminism, which developed within the framework of Marxist thought as a critique of liberal reformist views. It also, however, criticizes some of the traditional Marxist understanding of "the woman question" (see Chapter 2). Because socialist feminism is still in the early stages of formulation, and because the premises of liberal feminism are probably familiar to most readers, this discussion will define socialist feminism by pointing out some of the ways in which it most clearly diverges from liberal feminism.[5]

Socialist feminists argue that because the liberal framework does not account for the sources and processes of oppression and liberation, liberal feminism is necessarily misguided in its strategies. Socialist feminists focus on the relationship between the material conditions of societies and the social structures and ideologies that flow from them. The socialist framework leads feminists not just to ask whether women have the same opportunities as men within given social institutions but also to look more deeply at the structure and relationship of the institutions themselves. They do not take specific institutions such as the workplace or the family as givens but view them as historically changing social relationships created and recreated by people, especially those in power, to meet changing material needs and capacities. Above all socialists focus on people not just as individuals with abstract rights but as essentially social beings whose meaning depends on historical context and social relations.

Because liberal feminists argue from the perspective of individual abstract rights, they are very much bound to strategies that tear down specific barriers. Socialists argue that this is not enough. Because they believe that the central feature of human life is social relations, socialist feminists must look not just at what is good for given individuals but also at what is good for people as part of a community. Socialist feminism therefore includes in its strategy the distribution of both specific rights and obligations and the alteration of the individual's relationship to others.

The issue of day care for children offers a good example of the difference between liberal and socialist feminists. Both argue that day care should be more readily available and that more public money should be devoted to these arrangements. These proposals are more central to socialist feminist theory and are easier to justify by socialist arguments. The following discussion shows why.

Liberal feminists generally argue for day care in terms of individual rights: Day care should be made available because without it women have less opportunity to seek employment than men have; provision of day care can help break down barriers to equal opportunity. Liberal feminism, however, provides little justification for claiming that those who don't need such services should be required to pay for them, which is necessary if day-care centers are to be publicly funded. Liberal views also reinforce the idea that children are the private property of individual families, and that child care is women's job. There is a trade-off between women's employment and child care, and women will be responsible for child care in their families unless help is provided from the outside.

Socialist feminists take a different approach. They begin with the premise that reproduction, including the care and nurturing of children, is a social activity and responsibility, not an individual one determined by biological ties. Society can and has cared for its children in many different ways. As Chapter 11 noted, the structure of child care has varied even within American history. For different historical reasons, child care has been done sometimes by women only and sometimes by women and men; sometimes by biological parents and sometimes by others; sometimes by single individuals and sometimes by many different people. What is valued in child care also differs from time to time. Socialists start with this historical view and ask what arrangements most benefit the community as a whole, where community refers to individuals in their different social relations and to the social relations themselves. The answer socialist feminists arrive at is that child rearing should be a communal responsibility shared by women and men, parents and nonparents alike.

Many socialists use the concept of alienation to argue that the current arrangement of responsibility for child care is alienating to men, women, and children. It is alienating to men because they are separated both from the vital human task of child care and from the mothers of their children because of the strict division of domestic labor. It is alienating to women because, although they do most of the work of reproducing human life, they do not "control the conditions of their motherhood." They are thus engaged in "alienated labor" in the Marxist sense (Jaggar 1983, 310). In brief, women's motherhood has been used as an excuse to limit their activities and resources.

These observations suggest to social feminists that current child-raising arrangements are also alienating to children. It breeds hostility between child and mother, distance between child and father, and incomplete bonds between child and society. To socialist feminists, then, the argument for the provision of day care is that it is a mechanism for organizing the task of child care into a truly social endeavor.

The perspective of socialism thus focuses primarily on social relations rather than on individual rights, and it suggests that the entire structure of institutional arrangements must be questioned, not just the apparent inequities within these arrangements. It also suggests that although feminists must focus on questions of gender, the problems women face are also rooted in other social structures—primarily class—that alienate people from their own labor and human society.

Radical Feminism

A third branch of feminism is radical feminism.[6] Radical feminists define sexual relations and sexuality as the center of their feminist framework and argue that societies as they are currently arranged are patriarchal; they are run, organized, and defined by men for their own benefit. In men's societies women serve as a colonized people. They are made dependent on men and are not only forced to serve the interests of men but also tricked into regarding what amounts to sexual slavery as in their own interest. Men accomplish this trickery by perverting the bond of love through "compulsory heterosexuality," which makes women dependent on men and separates them from other women, and by coercing women into repressive forms of motherhood.

Radical feminists see rape and other forms of sexual violence as mechanisms men use to enforce their rule. Some radical feminists, such as Mary Daly (1978), say that although different male cultures appear to vary, such practices as Chinese foot binding, Indian suttee, European witch burning, African genital mutilation, and American gynecological practices all are variations of the same thing: violent or coercive control of women by men. Daly argues that the fact that women appear to accept these practices (for example, when mothers make sure their daughters undergo the rites of foot binding or genital mutilation, when widows throw themselves on the burning pyres of their husbands, or when female nurses participate in medical violence) only shows how insidious male culture and its colonization of women is. According to this view, in societies in which men have any power over women, the practices are different but the meaning is the same: Women are oppressed by men in much the same way.

The solution radical feminists offer is the rebellion of the colonized against the colonizer; in other words, unity among women against male authority. The task of women is to look among themselves to discover their own feelings and interests and their own culture and to refuse to participate in the male order. The problem they see is not that women's opportunities have differed from men's, but that women have been coerced into thinking in a way that serves male interests and not their own. For this reason many radical feminists use the rallying cry, "the personal is the political." They argue that the governing of women by men means that women have sung their own songs, written their own words, and felt their own feelings only at great risk to themselves.

According to radical feminists women must fight back first by seizing control of their own bodies, both by liberating them from the control of men and by liberating themselves to be able to share intimacy with other women. Most radical feminists do not believe it is possible for women to free themselves if they remain sexually involved with men, because men use sexuality to control women. They also believe it is impossible for women to free themselves and discover a female reality and culture if barriers to intimacy among women remain. For this reason many radical feminists describe lesbians as the vanguard of feminism.

Some radical feminists advocate a life-style and strategy of separatism, although they disagree about how much separatism is necessary. By separatism radicals mean not just sexual separation of women from men but also a wider separation from male culture and institutions. If the social institutions and dominant culture are patriarchal, women cannot free themselves by accepting and working within them. Many radicals also believe that women and men have different natures, or at least that women working together would create a society and culture different from any created by men. Separatism therefore also means working together to create or rediscover a "woman culture" based on what radicals regard as the specifically female virtues of nurturance, sharing, and intuition. Radical feminists seek to rediscover the lost and devalued aspects of women's culture and to create their own alternative organizations and communities.

Radical feminist strategy differs from other forms of feminism in other ways as well. Radical feminists claim that it is no coincidence that most social institutions are hierarchically organized. Hierarchy, they claim, is a key ingredient of male culture. Radicals therefore try to organize themselves nonhierarchically, communally, and democratically. They often also reject the values they see as perpetrated by male culture, especially the view that scientific and analytic reasoning (which they sometimes describe as elitist) is superior to intuition and knowledge gained from personal experience. In many ways radical feminism is based on a transformation of the old view that equates male with mind and female with body and nature.

Because of the radical feminist view that political institutions as they are generally defined are patriarchal and that "the person is the political," radical feminists often eschew strategies to influence law and policy and concentrate on what is sometimes called "witness politics." The arena for political action is personal life, so changing one's way of life is political activity.

Multicultural Feminism

One of the most important changes in feminism and feminist theory in the 1980s was a shift toward a *multicultural* feminism. Up to that point the search for, or emphasis on, commonality among women made it difficult for feminist theory and practice to take full account of the differences among women. This is not to say that feminist movements and organizations were homogeneous. There were feminist writers, activists, and organizations of all different types in most nations around the world. However, there was little sense of coherence or relationship among these different people and groups. More importantly, even if feminism was heterogeneous, it was dominated by white, middle-class, well-educated women (especially those based on campuses), leaving the voices and contributions of other women more marginal.[7]

Two developments effected a shift in the frame and terms of feminist discussion and debate.

1. International contact among women concerned with the condition of women increased. The United Nations International Women's Decade (1975–1985) was only the largest and best-known of many efforts to bring together women from around the world. Feminism organized most quickly in the United States in the 1960s and 1970s, but by the 1970s and 1980s there were many large or well-organized feminist movements around the world. Feminism began to have a major impact on theory and scholarship in different countries. The feminist practice and theory that developed around the globe was different from country to country because of their various histories, cultures, social structures, and problems. As the growth of feminist organization and influence within different countries facilitated contact across countries, the debates among feminists that highlighted differences among women's situations became important. Increased contact between First and Third World feminists enriched feminism considerably.

2. Increased feminist activism and involvement of women of color, poor women, and others whose experiences had been marginalized forced feminists to take account of the differences among women's social circumstances. The growing strength of organization among black and Hispanic women and those in the battered woman's movement, for example, became important forces within feminism and demanded greater reckoning with the diversity of women's lives from everyone involved.

Thus multicultural feminism recognizes that women live in many different kinds of situations, and it is a form of feminism that is shaped by those differences. It not only looks for the obvious similarities in women's lives but also analyzes the varying effects of androcentric sex/gender systems, as Chapter 13 suggested. Multicultural feminism may draw from arguments of the liberal, socialist, or radical traditions in feminist theory. It adds an element that might otherwise be missing. We cannot really understand the role of gender in people's lives unless we also understand its relationship to such other aspects of social life as race and class. Because of the importance of highlighting diversity in multicultural feminism it also recognizes conflict among women, even those who consider themselves feminists. This is unusual in social movements, which usually emphasize a kind of solidarity among their members that attempts to minimize difference and conflict. In multicultural feminism the recognition of diversity and acceptance of some conflict is interpreted as part of a healthy political process.[8]

It is important to note that a piece of feminist writing about women of different cultures or social groups is not necessarily multicultural, while a piece of writing about women of one culture or social group is not necessarily *non*multicultural feminism. Merely adding some focus on women of color to thinking that is otherwise dominated by the experience of whites does not make it multicultural just as simply adding some focus on women to otherwise androcentric thinking does not make it feminist. Multiculturalism depends on the framework and method of analysis. Patricia Hill Collins' effort to construct an Afrocentric or black feminist thought incorporates different and conflicting ways of understanding African-American women without "trying to synthesize competing worldviews that . . . may defy reconciliation" (Collins 1989a, 773). She does not try to make single what is multiple.

Bell Hooks emphasizes the importance of understanding the differing relationships to domination each individual can have.

> I understand that in many places in the world oppressed and oppressor share the same color. I understand that right here in this room, oppressed and oppressor share the same gender. Right now as I speak, a man who is himself victimized, wounded, hurt by racism and class exploitation is actively dominating a woman in his life—that even as I speak, women who are ourselves exploited, victimized, are dominating children. (1988, 20–21)

She argues that "To understand domination, we must understand that our capacity as women and men to be either dominated or dominating is a point of connection, of commonality" (1988, 20). Her argument is part of a multicultural feminism because it is her awareness of difference among women that helps her understand gender relations and because she "shifts the center" of her focus and tries to take account of the multiple standpoints and experiences of the people she talks about.

The Feminist Umbrella

Liberal, socialist, radical, and multicultural feminism are only umbrella terms for a wide range of different viewpoints. None of the branches of feminism has a catechism or list of articles of faith; the many different organizations of women have developed certain shared perspectives and certain clear differences of opinion during the course of their thinking, talking, and acting. In fact these perspectives cannot always be distinguished because each has contributed to what constitutes feminism today. Any given feminist might, for example, participate in one of the liberal feminist organizations that have been so effective in achieving legal and policy reforms, yet at the same time accept the need for more fundamental changes in social structure, agree that feminists must learn to be more "woman identified," and understand the flaws of generalizing from the experience of particular groups of women.

The reality of feminist theory and practice is that it is a constant discussion among many perspectives and continues to change over time. Ideas that seem radical at one time seem downright conservative at another. As long as feminism has stayed alive it has responded to changed historical circumstances.

Outsiders sometimes paint the arguments among feminists as petty bickering typical of females. This characterization is no more appropriate than it would be to say that the arguments between John Adams and Thomas Jefferson, between one branch of the trade union movement and another, or between the NAACP and the Black Muslims were petty bickering typical of males. They are serious arguments among people trying to define as accurately and effectively as possible the problems they see and the best means to solve them.

American Feminism

Like most social movements, feminist movements are not spontaneous uprisings that occur randomly. A social movement is a collective effort by a large group of people to solve a set of problems they think they share. Participants in social movements generally do not have the political power to achieve the changes they desire through regular governmental channels and procedures, which is why they turn to collective action. But how do these groups of people come together in the first place? Why do they come together when they do? What makes them decide that they share common problems and that they can solve these problems through collective action? How do they choose the particular strategies they do? How and why do they succeed or fail? Historians and social scientists disagree about details, but their study of past social movements does point to some answers.[9]

Social movements do not necessarily begin because a group faces a new problem; they begin when a group arrives at a new perception of its problems and the possibilities for change. The women's movement of the 1960s did not arise because inequality in employment or education or marital law and policy had just developed, but because enough women came to a special awareness of these inequities. In fact some theorists and social scientists argue that social movements often begin just when a group's situation is starting to improve.

A social movement is often incited by a precipitating event that sparks a special awareness or new consciousness on the part of a relatively small group of people, who in turn organize and attempt to mobilize others they think should share this consciousness. The success of organization and mobilization generally seem to depend on two factors:

1. The early leaders must be able to draw on some prior frustration or discontent experienced by their potential followers, even if that discontent has not yet been expressed in the specific form the new social movement will give it. In the 1950s, for example, Betty Friedan witnessed the "problem that had no name," a feeling of personal discontent on the part of middle-class women that no one seemed to understand.
2. Social movements generally do not start from scratch but develop from and build on existing networks and organizations. Jo Freeman (1975) shows how the contemporary women's movement was built from earlier networks, and many historians of nineteenth-century feminism show the same pattern in the suffrage movement.

The task of mobilizing recruits is the most crucial and difficult aspect of social movements. In the early stages of any given movement's history, which is when movements are most likely to fail, mobilization is at least as important as attempting to influence those in power. Social movements rely on numbers, and they cannot make a credible case, or credible threats, to power holders if they include only a tiny proportion of the group that claims to have a grievance. Mobilization of potential members of a social movement involves identifying those people who share an interest and convincing them that they have a problem, that it is a shared problem with a shared solution, and that it is in their personal best interest to join the movement. The already converted sometimes underestimate the difficulty of doing this.

A social movement that is successful in growing is susceptible to change and fragmentation as it grows for a number of reasons:

1. The methods and strategies appropriate to a large movement are different from those appropriate to a new and small movement. A large group has different resources, is more diverse, and does not need to devote as much effort to consciousness raising among potential members.
2. As a movement grows its actions must adjust to the changing reactions of outsiders and to changes in historical circumstances. The suffrage movement, for example, used different strategies and approaches at the close of the Civil War than it did on the eve of World War I, just as the contemporary women's movement, born in a time of prosperity and optimism in the 1960s, had to adjust to the economic hard times of the 1970s and early 1980s. In both cases even the technological supports for political activities changed dramatically. The later

suffragists had modes of transportation and communication not available to their predecessors, and current feminists can use computers, which were not as widely available earlier.

3. The characteristics of the people involved change. Early participants gain experience, learn, and are sometimes left behind by the changes that take place within their own organizations. Elizabeth Cady Stanton was a young woman of thirty-three when she organized the Seneca Falls Convention; she was seventy-five years old when she served her last term as president of a national suffrage organization. Many of the women who first came together at the beginning of the contemporary women's movement are still active, but they are not the same as they were two decades ago. New women with new experiences, motivations, and skills enter a movement in its later stages. They bring with them new ideas of what is to be done and how, and they sometimes feel considerable frustration with the old guard, who seem reluctant to change.

As we look at the history of American feminism we can see some of these patterns and others. Although a detailed history of American feminism would fill volumes, even the brief sketch provided here points out how varied and continuous the history of feminism in America has been. We will look at four phases in this history: the period before the Civil War, often characterized as the era of the women's rights movement; the period from the Civil War to the ratification of the Nineteenth Amendment in 1920, most remembered for the suffrage movement; the period from 1920 to the establishment of presidential commissions on women's status in 1961, when there was no unified national women's movement; and the era from the early 1960s to the present, when the contemporary women's movement has grown and gained force.

Before the Civil War

If feminism is a self-conscious, collective effort to improve the condition of women, there was little feminism as such before the Civil War.[10] There was no mass movement that attacked the oppression of women as a group, although many individuals and organizations worked to alleviate certain specific problems that particular groups of women faced. By the middle of the nineteenth century, however, advocates of women's rights had laid the groundwork for the post–Civil War surge in feminism and had contributed to a change in the consciousness of many women that provided the breeding ground for a more comprehensive feminist ideology and action.

In the first decades of the Republic, discussion of the roles and status of American women was part of the more general attempt by intellectuals and other leaders to define the nature of the new nation and its members (Kerber 1986). Mary Wollstonecraft's *Vindication* made the rounds in these circles, and at about the same time, an American named Judith Sargent Murray wrote a series of essays under the pen name Constantia that pointed out the need for better education for women (see Rossi 1988). Newspapers often served as a forum for discussion of needed improvements. From the early colonial period up to the nineteenth century there were isolated attempts by individual and groups of women to remedy specific problems they personally suffered because of unequal treatment of women and men, but these actions did not form the basis of any wider collective action or change in attitudes.

Nevertheless it would be incorrect to say that no one actively fought for the rights of women before the rise of nineteenth-century women's movements. Action oriented toward change became more common in the early nineteenth century. The predominant focus of attention was female education, and it was often promoted by one person or a small group of people working to establish schools for females (see Chapter 4). Emma Willard (1787–1870), for example, established the Troy Female Seminary in 1821 and successfully lobbied to get partial public funding for her school. Her success is particularly notable because the idea of the public school was still in its infancy. People such as Willard and Mary Lyon (1797–1849), who founded Mt. Holyoke in 1837, pursued the principle of women's rights by spreading their ideas and attempting to fulfill their own dreams in individual ways.

Although they had no notion of founding a mass movement, women like Willard and Lyon inspired the women who later led the feminist movement. Lucy Stone (1818–1893), for example, seems to have awakened to feminist ideas as she sat in a sewing circle working to provide the income for a young man to pursue his studies (as many young women did). While she sewed she listened to Mary Lyon speaking of women's education. Stone apparently left her sewing thinking, "Let these men with broader shoulders and stronger arms earn their own education while we use our scantier opportunities to educate ourselves" (Flexner 1975, 34). Stone went on to become one of the first female graduates from Oberlin College and a moving force in American feminism.

Women did get involved in two widespread social movements that transformed their ideas about the condition of women and thus provided the country with a core of feminist leaders and organizers. These were the moral reform movement and the abolitionist movement.

Barbara Berg (1978) provides an account of the growth of female moral reform societies during the first half of the nineteenth century and of their evolutionary role in transforming many women's views of their own conditions. Like other historians, Berg reminds us that the growth of female social activism and feminine—and ultimately feminist—consciousness occurred during a time of widespread social change and redefinition. On one hand there was the growth of an urban culture and pressures for democratization; on the other there was a groping for security best exemplified by the pursuit of a romantic, orderly, pastoral ideal. That ideal included the cult of domesticity and the belief that woman's place is in the home. The home came to be seen as a place distinct from the public world of politics and markets, and woman, the guardian and symbol of the home, came to be seen as having a character distinct from that of man.

Berg argues that not just the home but also this emerging perception of woman's character provided a base of security to white urban men in a confusing and dynamic world.

Woman's nature, then, perceived as the opposite of man's gave clear expression to the elusive male identity. Moreover, the alleged and exaggerated difference between the sexes substituted for the absence of rigid class distinctions in the first part of the nineteenth century. Because masculine security depended so heavily on the distance man set between himself and woman, every effort had to be made to indicate vast differences in the nature of the two sexes (Berg 1978, 73–74).

The result was the creation of a relatively rigid theory of sex distinction, as well as a class of women with very little to do. (For further discussion, see Chapter 12.)

Many women turned their attentions to social activities that seemed appropriate for ladies. In some cases these were clubs and literary societies. Many women organized and became active in benevolent and moral reform societies. Because they had no intention of defying social mores, most of their good works involved helping other women. The result, however, was a growing awareness that there was something especially oppressive about women's lives. As Berg writes (1978, 170):

> Voluntarism exposed many facets of woman's oppression. It brought into sharp focus those abuses that generally had the greatest impact on the lives of poorer women. Whether they distributed firewood to widows, shelter to orphans, medicine to the sick, Bibles to the unconverted or education to young girls, the women in philanthropic organizations visited with and listened to hundreds of thousands of destitute females in cities across the country. Their collective experiences vivified the depth and extent of feminine suffering.

The two aspects of women's lives that were underscored most clearly to them were economic inequality and women's "subjugation to masculine brutality." Berg further argues that as the volunteer women began to work more closely with those less fortunate, such as poor women, widows, prostitutes, imprisoned women, and the wives of drunkards, many began to see considerable similarity between themselves and these other women. Berg suggests that because the ideology of the time was that men and women have distinct and opposite natures, it was a small step for these early social workers to feel a certain unity with women in apparently very different circumstances.

Some activists began to speak and act in ways that would seem very familiar to feminists today. In New York, for example, members of the Moral Reform Society kept vigil at brothels and reported their findings in their journal. They identified some patrons of the brothels publicly and threatened to do the same to others (Berg 1978, 185). The writing in moral reform periodicals could be very biting:

> Women have so long been called "angels" that men seem to have come to the conclusion that they have no persons to protect; and as for property, they say women do not know enough to take care of it, and therefore the laws and customs of society virtually say they shall have none to protect. . . the law in its kind care for women. . . takes away every cent from her. This is not exactly burning a woman on the funeral pile of her husband, but is rather a refinement on the Asiatic cruelty (Berg 1978, 209).

Above all, the reformers came to believe that women had to take responsibility for themselves and, as they said repeatedly, to think for themselves. Their work in women's organizations gave many women a new respect and affection for women and their abilities (Degler 1980, 301).

Women in moral reform and related organizations focused on several specific issues. Some concentrated on marital property reform, especially in the 1830s and 1840s, and others concentrated on the conditions of working women. A large proportion focused on the poor, widows, and orphans. Many of their efforts were aimed at protecting women from male exploitation and brutality, through, for example, temperance and birth control (women's right to refrain from sex), and helping "fallen women," who had already been prey to such exploitation and brutality. Finally many women became active in the abolitionist movement.

The abolition movement gave many black and white women their first real taste of social and political action. As in the moral reform movement, they did not simply talk but also engaged in action, which in this case could be extremely dangerous, especially when they served as conductors or provided stations on the Underground Railway. As white women worked toward emancipation of black slaves they began to see some aspects of their own condition as women more clearly. For example, Sarah (1792–1873) and Angelina (1805–1879) Grimké, argued that women had a special role to perform in emancipation work and began to talk about women's roles as well (Lerner 1971; Rossi 1988). In 1870, more than thirty years after Angelina's "Appeal to Christian Women of the South," both sisters cast symbolic ballots in special ballot boxes in Massachussetts to demonstrate their support for the female vote.

It is often said that nineteenth-century feminism, especially the suffrage movement, was born of the abolition movement. Although more of the white women who became involved in the later feminist movements probably came through moral reform organizations, abolition provided the original cadre of suffrage leaders, and it gave shape to midcentury feminist organizations.

The early link between abolition and feminism is direct and well known. In 1833 the "men only" American Anti-Slavery Society was founded in Philadelphia. Undaunted by the fact that they were not allowed to join, interested women formed the Philadelphia Female Anti-Slavery Society. Their separatism was foisted upon them; unwilling to pick a leader from their midst, they chose a black freedman as the head of their organization. At the first convention of the National Female Anti-Slavery Society in 1837, however, the members made it clear that women were quite capable of managing without male leaders such as Theodore Weld (the man Angelina Grimké later married).

In 1840 the World Anti-Slavery Convention in London excluded women, including abolitionist activists Lucretia Mott (1793–1880), one of the founders of the Female Anti-Slavery Society, and Elizabeth Cady Stanton (1815–1902). The two women walked around London angrily discussing their plight, but they went their separate ways for the next eight years, although they stayed in contact. Eventually Stanton and her husband settled in the small town of Seneca Falls, New York, where she found herself growing increasingly discontented with her own limited domestic roles and with the roles assigned to women in general.

The general discontent I felt with woman's portion . . . impressed me with the strong feeling that some active measures should be taken to remedy the wrongs of society in general and of women in particular. My experience at the World Anti-Slavery Convention, all I had read of the legal status of women, and the oppression I saw everywhere, together swept across my soul, intensified now by many personal experiences. It seemed as if all the elements had conspired to impel me to some onward step. I could not see what to do, or where to begin—my only thought was a public meeting for protest and discussion (quoted in Flexner 1975, 73–74).

The same pattern occurred repeatedly both at that time and later: A woman or group of women is struck by a combination of personal experiences and events that demand action. But what action? The first step for Stanton, as for others, was to call a meeting to share observations with other women and figure out what needed to be done.

In the summer of 1848 Stanton met with Mott and four other women and "poured out, that day, the torrent of my long accumulating discontent, with such vehemence and indignation that I stirred myself, as well as the rest of the party, to do and dare anything" (Flexner 1975, 74). The meeting they planned came to be known as the Seneca Falls Convention, and ended in the signing of the Declaration of Sentiments and Resolutions. Elizabeth Cady Stanton's feelings at that time kept her active for more than a half century more. Only one woman present at the meeting, which issued the first tentative call for women's suffrage, lived to vote as a result of the Nineteenth Amendment to the Constitution.

Activists continued their abolitionist work until the Civil War, and added to it their commitment to the rights of women. In 1850 an important women's rights convention held in Worcester, Massachusetts gained international fame through the writings of Harriet Taylor in England (see Rossi 1988). In fact conventions were held nearly every year until 1861. The overlap between the abolitionist and women's rights movement is well illustrated by the names of the key leaders who spoke and acted for both. Although Elizabeth Cady Stanton, Susan B. Anthony (who joined Stanton in 1851), Lucretia Mott, and Lucy Stone are usually associated with women's rights, and Sojourner Truth (1797?–1883), Theodore Weld, Wendell Phillips, and William Lloyd Garrison are generally associated with abolitionism, in fact all of these people devoted their efforts to both. Sojourner Truth's most famous speech was delivered to a woman's rights convention in Akron, Ohio, in 1851.

The women's movement was not yet a very large social movement; it consisted of various groups of political activists pursuing different, discrete goals, often tied to other concerns such as moral reform or abolition. Small as the movement was, the group was criticized for doing nothing but talk. The historian Eleanor Flexner answers the charge as follows:

At this stage, there was not much else they could do. Having stated their dissatisfaction with things as they were, they had to agree on what they wanted to achieve, and to develop an ideology which would serve to refute their critics and win them new adherents. What was the proper condition of married women? What should be women's place in the church, the community, the professions, the state? On what basis should divorce be permitted . . . ? From the gatherings where these issues were thrashed out there emerged a body of thought, new and dedicated leadership, wide publicity, and new recruits (1975, 81–82).

Many of the feminists began to write about these issues, and some started their own periodicals. There was some attempt to coordinate feminist activity nationally. A central committee was formed in the 1850s with delegates from any state in which there was women's rights activity. Flexner notes that at that time activists had little desire for greater organization for much the same reasons that later feminists were wary of too much organization: They feared that it would stultify growth and inhibit rather than promote action (1975, 83). The intentional building of a strong movement had to wait until after the Civil War.

Fifty Years and More: From Civil War to Suffrage [11]

The Civil War offered women new avenues for their social concern and activism. Many social activists turned their attention to new organizations, such as the Sanitary Commission, which did war relief and nursing work. The more politically minded put their efforts to a new task: fighting in Congress for passage of a constitutional amendment that would forever ban slavery in the United States. Elizabeth Cady Stanton and Susan B. Anthony gained their national political organizing skills through their positions as officers in the National Women's Loyal League, which in 1864 presented to Congress a petition with over 300,000 signatures supporting an amendment to ban slavery.

The text that eventually became the Fourteenth Amendment to the Constitution both sparked the organization of a full-blown women's suffrage movement and deeply divided it as it was forming. That amendment, which was to become critical in defining citizenship, contained the first and only use of the word *male* in the U.S. Constitution; it levied a punishment against states that interfered with the voting rights of "male citizens." Activists such as Stanton and Anthony were infuriated and wanted, at least, that the word *male* be removed. But they went further and added their voices to the discussion of another proposed amendment (eventually the fifteenth), which would guarantee the right to vote regardless of race. They wanted it also to guarantee the right to vote regardless of sex.

The rift that ensued broke up the Equal Rights Association, which had been organized at the end of the war to pursue the rights of women and blacks. The rift focused on two related questions:

1. Should the Association fight to get what it could, which might mean legal guarantees of rights for blacks (or at least black men) and not women, or should it press for rights for women as well?
2. Which was the more pressing need: legal guarantees for blacks or for women? This type of insidious question is often faced by different oppressed groups attempting to work in coalition.

The Equal Rights Association chose rights for blacks as their primary goal. In contrast many of the women present agreed with Sojourner Truth's argument:

I feel that I have a right to have just as much as a man. There is a great stir about colored men getting their rights, but not a word about the colored women;

and if colored men get their rights, and not colored women theirs, the colored men will be masters over the women, and it will be just as bad as it was before. So I am for keeping the thing going while things are stirring; because if we wait till it is still, it will take a great while to get it going again. (Sterling 1984, 411–12)

In 1869 Stanton and Anthony broke away to form the National Woman Suffrage Association, which was only open to women, because they believed that the men of the Equal Rights Association were selling out and duping the women of that organization. The National became dedicated to a constitutional amendment for women's suffrage. Later that year Lucy Stone and others formed the American Woman Suffrage Association, which restricted its membership to delegates and preferred the more conservative strategy of pursuing women's rights on a state-by-state basis. The national organization for the late-nineteenth-century women's movement was in place, but it remained split for the next 20 years.

The breakup of the Equal Rights Association caused unforgettable tension between black and women leaders. Stanton and Anthony embellished their break with many racist remarks, just as many later suffragists pitted blacks against whites and "native women" (native-born Americans of European stock) against immigrants. Although these events are often discussed as if they involved only black men and white women, they also involved white men and black women. The white men of the Equal Rights Association by and large stuck with the argument, "this is the Negro's hour," and black women faced a most difficult dilemma. An amendment that barred discrimination on the basis of race alone would not give black women the vote. But if clear incursions into racism were not made, no amount of women's rights legislation would help them because it would not apply to them.

The ambivalence of black women lasted throughout the century because they were "placed in a double bind; to support women's suffrage would imply that they were allying themselves with white women activists who had publicly revealed their racism, but to support black male suffrage was to endorse a patriarchal social order that would grant them no political voice" (Hooks 1981, 3). Despite the number of times white suffragists made racist statements and discriminated against black suffragists, many black women fought for women's rights throughout the end of the nineteenth century and into the beginning of the twentieth, sometimes in their own organizations, and sometimes in integrated organizations. In the split between the NWSA and AWSA most black suffrage leaders, including Sojourner Truth and Harriet Tubman (1820–1913) chose to stay with Stanton and Anthony in the NWSA.

The suffrage movement remained active throughout the rest of the nineteenth century. It mobilized women by drawing on those involved in other kinds of women's organizations. Women's organizations in the postwar period were even more active than they had been before the war. Social activists, including many of the leading suffragists, increased their efforts to influence the morals and social life of the nation, especially as they affected women and children. These efforts in the last decades of the nineteenth century are often called the "social purity" movement.

One of the best known of the social purity organizations was the Women's Christian Temperance Union, which was founded in 1874 and became the largest single women's organization in the nation. Under the leadership of Frances Willard

(1839–98) it was also linked to the suffragist cause, although many people worried about whether the two issues should be mixed. Willard herself took care not to be associated with the so-called radicals in the suffragist movement, such as Stanton and Anthony. To most other temperance suffragists (such as Anthony herself) the reason for mixing temperance and suffrage seemed obvious. If men would stop spending their wages on drink and coming home to be useless fathers and husbands or worse, women would be better able to provide themselves and their children with good and healthful lives. If women had the vote, they would also have the political leverage to provide themselves and their children with good and healthful lives, as well as a means to spread their own moral influence.

By the end of the century the movement was also drawing from other sources: women who were receiving advanced degrees and were becoming professionals, some of the women of the new labor movement, and some of the women of the West who had become involved in the labor movement and in populist uprisings and organizations such as the Grange clubs. Even if the suffragist movement began as an alliance primarily of homemakers who had the time to devote to social house-keeping and reform causes, by the end of the century it included many working women who were drawn in not as individuals but as members of work-related groups.

The late-nineteenth-century suffragists used various strategies to pursue their goals. They lobbied, spoke, organized petitions, and got involved in state referendum campaigns. The National worked on increasing congressional support for a constitutional amendment. Suffragists also engaged in protest and direct actions such as attempting to cast ballots in elections, as they did across the country in the early 1870s. They tried to use the courts, but two famous cases—those of Susan Anthony in New York and Virginia Minor (1824–94) in the Supreme Court—made it clear that the judicial system could not be used to gain women the vote. Both women attempted to vote and sued unsuccessfully when they were barred from doing so. Other participants in the protest, such as Sojourner Truth, were turned away before they could obtain ballots. (For further discussion, see Chapter 8.) By the end of the century only a handful of states and local areas had given women the right to vote, and Congress did not seem to be moving toward support for an amendment. The differences between the two major suffragist organizations (the National and the American Woman Suffrage Associations) blurred, and in 1890 the two groups merged to form the National American Woman Suffrage Association (NAWSA).

By the turn of the century the early suffrage activists were very old. The last of the original leaders, Stanton and Anthony died in the early 1900s. The new leaders and activists were very different from their predecessors. Carrie Chapman Catt (1859–1947) did not fear organization as earlier feminists had. Catt, who engineered the final successful stage of the campaign, brought with her a modern sense of political organization. Elizabeth Cady Stanton's daughter, Harriot Stanton Blatch (1856–1940), had spent twenty years in England and imported some of the techniques she had witnessed there. She formed a new organization and tried new strategies such as holding open-air meetings and marches and working with trade unions. She captured for suffrage work some of the brightest and eventually best-known women of the era, including Charlotte Perkins Gilman (1860–1935) and Florence Kelley (1859–1932) (Flexner 1975, 261). The movement drew women of all types and classes, from trade union women of the garment district to wealthy wives of bankers and industrialists. Women of all political parties—Democrats, Republicans, Socialists, and Progressives, a new party that endorsed women's suffrage in 1912—were involved. At the same time, the size and complexity of the movement meant that agreement on a single plan was difficult to achieve, and the movement was often torn by disagreements about tactics.

One woman who both breathed new life into the movement and fostered a schism in it was Alice Paul (1885–1977), a young woman who had spent some time in England before coming home to the United States to complete her Ph.D. She was much impressed with the radical activities of the Pankhursts (a woman and her two daughters who led the English suffrage movement) and thought she could use the same techniques to call attention to women's plight in America. When she became head of the Congressional Committee of the NAWSA one of her first acts was to organize a parade of 5000 women in Washington the day before Woodrow Wilson's inauguration, which sparked a near riot (Flexner 1975, 272–73).

Alice Paul's radicalism led to a separation of her group from the NAWSA. Paul wanted to hold whichever political party happened to be in power responsible for the lack of the federal amendment granting suffrage to women. NAWSA opposed this position because this would mean working against some prosuffragist candidates. Paul's group, the Congressional Union, worked in the 1914 election campaigns to punish the party in power at that time, the Democrats. Their activities succeeded in bringing the amendment to a vote, but it was at first defeated.

Paul and her organization then became more militant. In 1917 the Congressional Union picketed the White House, the first time any political group had done so. It changed its name to the National Women's Party and added anti-war slogans to its rhetoric. These demonstrations provoked violence by onlookers, and the women demonstrators (not the violent onlookers) were arrested. Eventually the women held a new kind of protest inspired by the English feminists. They demanded to be called political prisoners and went on a hunger strike in prison. Prison officials reacted by force-feeding them, which caused a public outcry that eventually led to the release of the women.

Many people argued that these radical actions hurt more than they helped and made people unwilling to join the suffragists. This argument is still used against militancy in social movements. The criticism, however, is often launched by people who have not been drawn into the movement by more conservative strategies either. Analysis of the effects of different wings of the suffrage and other feminist movements suggests that the combined or parallel actions of the moderate and radical wings allows more widespread participation and more varied strategies.

Alice Paul's actions called attention to the resolve of the feminists in a way other strategies did not; they showed that women were willing to risk their lives and careers for suffrage. Many people would have been quite unaware of the suffrage movement were it not for the headlines that Alice Paul and her group provoked, and the public was appalled by the violence with which the states fought against them. Meanwhile Carrie Chapman Catt's "Winning Plan," as she labeled her strategy of intense but more conventional political campaigning, did in the end achieve passage and ratification of the Nineteenth Amendment. The irony is that it is in large part the strategies

Alice Paul, a suffragist and feminist.

of people like Alice Paul who made Catt's strategies appear conventional, conservative, and reasonable. Until that time the political tactics NAWSA was using may have been conventional for men, but they were very unconventional for women.

An interesting perspective on this question of moderation versus radicalism in strategy is offered by Arvonne Fraser, an activist who became a leader in mainstream feminist groups in the 1960s and 1970s, including the Women's Equity Action League. She writes (1983, 122):

> radical feminists identified and publicized "the system's" oppression of women. They also made it respectable for women to work on women's issues. Eventually, establishment women began to work within the system to change laws and regulations and their task was made easier by these earlier efforts. Our group and others like it would never have been formed if the women's liberation groups had not staked out a more extreme position.

It is difficult to ascertain whether success would have come if only one strategy had been used. It is even more difficult to know the answer to such a question when one is in the middle of the battle.

Many casual observers paint the suffrage amendment and the feminist movement that supported it as failures for two reasons:

1. They say the feminist goals were too narrowly focused on getting the vote.
2. They maintain that the feminist movement disappeared after 1920.

We will consider the first criticism here and turn to the second in the next section.

The vote was no small goal to achieve. It is the symbol of the free citizen, and without it women could not be seen as free citizens. Political leaders often explicitly argued that women's rights did not matter because after all they could not vote. Leaders have no practical reason to be responsible to anyone but the voting public. Other rights are contingent on voting either by law or custom, including holding certain types of political offices and sitting on juries. The vote is an instrument to be used to pursue other goals, and this is how most suffragists saw it.

Although suffrage is the best-known goal of feminists of this period, it was not the only one. We have already seen that the social purity movement was based on the belief that women should have increased control over their destinies. The specific goals of this movement may seem conservative to today's feminists, but they were nonetheless intended to free women. A new and more radical birth control movement developed after the turn of the century, as women like Margaret Sanger (1883–1966) and Emma Goldman (1869–1940) fought to make contraception more widely available.

The same era witnessed the rise of organizations oriented toward alleviating the plight of working women. The Women's Trade Union League (WTUL) was formed in 1903 because of the failure of male-dominated unions to work for women. Although this group, like some other groups oriented toward women workers, involved both working-class and wealthy women, it came to be dominated by the wealthier, more conservative members, who supported paternalistic strategies such as protective labor legislation that restricted women's entry into jobs. A related effort was the National Consumer's League established in 1899, which originally worked to alert consumers about whether the products they were buying were made in shops with proper working conditions. Meanwhile women who had entered various professions formed organizations to fight for women's rights within their own groups.

It is difficult to identify an area of life that was not in some way touched by feminism in the late nineteenth and early twentieth centuries. There were attempts at dress reform for women and continuing debates over women's health and education. There is a rich feminist literature from that time produced by feminists in the social sciences, journalism, and the literary arts. Women's groups intensified their efforts to help immigrants and the poor. Women's organizations within various racial, religious, and ethnic groups focused on some of the special problems these groups faced. Some concentrated on the role of women in religion; in the 1880s a committee headed by Elizabeth Cady Stanton turned their pens to the task of criticizing and revising the Bible to develop what we would now call a nonsexist religion. Increasingly after the turn of the century the various feminist organizations also threw their support behind suffrage, much as the widely divergent feminist groups in the 1970s added their voices and efforts to support of the Equal Rights Amendment.

Suffrage was not the only goal of turn-of-the century feminism; it was not even the only goal of most suffragists. It was only the most widely accepted one (and the only one that many people now remember).

The Quiet Time: From Suffrage to Presidential Commissions[12]

Did feminism disappear after 1920 as so many people charge? If the question is whether a large, well-coordinated movement of women persisted after the vote was won, feminism did indeed disappear. But if the question is whether all the feminists packed their intellectual and activist bags and went home, feminism did not disappear, at least not immediately.

To explain these two answers it is necessary to analyze the forty-year period following 1920 by asking two questions:

1. What happened to the large suffrage organizations?
2. What other forms did feminism take during the postsuffrage period?

The presuffrage feminists in no sense thought their war was over when they won the suffrage battle. To understand what happened to them and their movement, it is important not just to look at the events that followed but also to understand the sociology of social movements.

As this chapter has emphasized throughout, mass social movements are fragile coalitions of different types of people with different motivations pursuing similar goals. The suffrage movement was a carefully constructed coalition of people who agreed that women should have a basic right of citizens: the vote. They disagreed considerably over what other issues they should pursue. Should they work for temperance? for birth control? for equal pay or for protective legislation? for marital and divorce reform? How should they structure their organizations? Should whites and blacks work together, even if that alienated a large block of legislators and white suffragists? Should they work in as ladylike and feminine a manner as possible, or should they display their anger and frustration and use threats and coercion to achieve their ends? Should they focus on the national or state and local levels? It is often more surprising when the coalitions in social movements hang together than it would be if they fell apart. Feminism is one of the largest and longest-lived movements in American history, and although it had its failures, its longevity is an indication of its relative strength and success compared with other American movements. In part what happened as the suffrage battle was won was an intense and active rethinking of the terms of feminism and feminist action (Cott 1987).

The suffrage coalition weakened and eventually fell apart after the vote was gained because those involved did not agree on their next major goals or the strategies they should use to reach them. The goals of different individuals and organizations overlapped, but that was not enough, and other events of the period put obstacles in their path.

Leaders of the suffrage movement did not wait for ratification to begin planning for the future. Alice Paul and Carrie Chapman Catt began to transform their respective organizations before the Nineteenth Amendment was in place on the assumption that they should be prepared for the inevitable time when their constituents would be voters. The difference between their new organizations reflects an important underlying difference in their definitions of feminist goals and strategies.

Alice Paul's Congressional Union became the National Women's Party (NWP), whose offices still stand two blocks from the national Capitol. As the name implies, Paul had visions of an explicitly feminist political party that would continue its battle for women's rights at the highest levels of government. Still believing in the most direct and vigorous route to equality, Alice Paul proposed in the early 1920s that the Constitution should be amended to contain a clause making discrimination on the basis of sex unconstitutional. The wording of the amendment has changed only slightly over time. The most recent version states simply "Equality of rights under the law shall not be denied or abridged by the United States or by any state on account of sex." This proposal has been the main goal of the NWP since 1923 (Cott 1987; Rupp 1985).

For most of its history the NWP has stood relatively isolated in its support of an equal rights amendment, although more recently other important organizations have joined with the NWP. In 1935 the National Association of Women Lawyers endorsed the amendment, and two years later the 90,000-member National Federation of Business and Professional Women's Clubs added their support as well. In the 1940s the NWP gained important allies when the amendment was endorsed by the General Federation of Women's Clubs (GFWC), the National Education Association, five women's service organizations (Soroptimists, Altrusa, Pilot, Quota, and Zonta), and even the Republican and Democratic Parties (Rawalt 1983).

Although the Equal Rights Amendment was introduced in Congress in 1923 and in every successive Congress, it did not pass until nearly fifty years later in 1972. Ten years later the necessary number of states had not ratified it, and the proposal died—for the time being.

This was not the only focus of the NWP's attention, however. The post–World War I period was a time of international conferences on law and human rights, and Alice Paul fought to make equality of the sexes part of international law. The NWP took a leading role in the fight to allow women their own independent nationalities and to pass nationality on to their children. As they pointed out, gaining the right to vote in 1920 did not make women full citizens because if an American woman married a foreigner, she was stripped of her citizenship and if she had a child by an alien, the child was an alien. Members of the NWP, many of them also members of the feminist Women Lawyers Association, continuously lobbied and testified to Congress until their demands were won in 1934 (Becker 1981, 1983; Sapiro 1984).

The NWP met opposition in the feminist community primarily because their goals were incompatible with protective labor legislation. This opposition reflects a fundamental disagreement within feminist theory at the time. Alice Paul and her group wanted equal opportunity and equal treatment for women and men. Most other feminists thought that equal treatment, especially in the labor market, would maintain a system of laissez-faire economics in which women were a cheap and exploited labor force and no extra care was given to mothers and children.

Most feminist also continued to see Paul's goals and strategies as too radical and militant, and most rejected a separate women's party on two grounds:

1. They wanted an integrated system in which women and men worked together as responsible citizens for the betterment of all.
2. If women wanted power in the political system, many argued, they would do better to make inroads into the main political system than to form a party of their own.

As head of NAWSA Carrie Chapman Catt was the leader of the more widely accepted brand of feminism. She transformed the NAWSA into the League of Women Voters. Catt's idea was that the League would be a nonpartisan training ground for female political activities and citizenship. It would be a place where women could develop their political agenda. They could then fight for their goals through the regular political parties and processes as equals. The League was intended to promote women in politics much as the National Women's Political Caucus (NWPC) is today. In its first few years the League drew up an impressive agenda of policy goals covering democratization in government; improvement in health, education, consumer, and welfare policy; better care for children and mothers; and protective labor legislation for women.

The League was strengthened when it initiated an even wider coalition of feminist groups. In 1920 the League became aware that it might be stepping on the toes of other women's groups, such as the GFWC and the WTUL, because its program and leadership overlapped with theirs. Under the leadership of Maud Wood Park the League negotiated the formation of the Women's Joint Congressional Committee (WJCC). Any federal bill supported by at least three of the member organizations was backed by the financial and labor resources of the WJCC.

The greatest early victory of the WJCC was the passage of the Sheppard Towner Act in 1921, which had been drafted by Julia Lathrop (1858–1932), a League of

Women Voters member and director of the Children's Bureau, and introduced into Congress by Senator Jeanette Rankin (1880–1973) in 1917. The Sheppard Towner Act, which provided federal funding for child and maternal health care, was an early breakthrough in the development of federal welfare policies. This early success, however, also contributed to the eventual weakening of the coalition responsible for it. The women's groups were caught in the middle of the first "red scare" of this century and a subsequent wave of anticommunism.

Feminists had long been accused of being socialists or Communists; indeed, some feminist leaders were socialists. Such accusations became very serious matters after the 1917 Russian Revolution when many radicals, including Emma Goldman, were deported. In the 1920s anticommunism and xenophobia in general played important roles in American politics. The Sheppard Towner Act, widely regarded as the first step toward socialism in America, was the final proof to many people that feminists were insidious Bolshevik radicals. Different scare tactics were used against the WJCC, including the drawing of a spider web showing the connections between feminism, socialism, and Moscow (Lemons 1972; Cott 1987). This spider web suggested a dangerous conspiracy that could trap the innocent. The resulting backlash helped weaken the coalition and forced many of the women's groups, including the League, to put their heads down to survive.

Other factors aided in the demise of widespread, united feminism. The political parties were resentful of groups such as the League, arguing that no matter what they claimed, they were trying to compete with the parties. Women who were party activists found their loyalties tested, and the League's hold on many of its members was strained by the greater power of the political parties. Many members were also overstretched and had to reevaluate their commitments.

The feminist activists of the 1920s and 1930s were different from their predecessors in one important respect. They were, for the most part, employed as professionals or as blue- or white-collar workers. Some worked in government. They had limited time for activism and many devoted time to the organizations relevant to their jobs. The specific political goals that dominated their interests diverged— many goals were compatible but different—and the feminist movement became more fragmented. Unfortunately the breakdown of a coalition can also weaken its constituent parts.

In the 1920s feminists had difficulty attracting young women to their cause. The young women, especially those who were college educated, believed that there was no battle left to fight, or at least not one that was significant enough to join. They could vote, drink, smoke, and, it seemed, dress as they liked. Many believed that women had gained their freedom, and the public press agreed with them. The flapper and the movie star were more glamorous than the tiresome, serious feminist. The feminist movement thus lost an important pool of new recruits. Finally the stock market crash of 1929 and the ensuing depression overshadowed the demands of feminists.

Between the two world wars, some women continued to fight for feminist reforms through their jobs or through women's organizations or religious and ethnic associations. Many women in government and journalism pushed for reforms. The New Deal programs of President Franklin Roosevelt offered a special opportunity for women to achieve some of the types of programs they supported and to participate in their administration. Eleanor Roosevelt (1884–1962) associated herself with women's interests and organizations and, in her position as the first activist First Lady, provided an important support for women. People such as Margaret Sanger continued their work on birth control, and trade union women continued to organize women. Women in groups such as the International League for Peace and Freedom, many of whom also had been active in other feminist groups, continued their efforts to avert war. At the same time, women began to take their places in formerly male domains of economic and social life. The early 1930s saw a peak in the proportion of higher degrees and some professional jobs held by women. That record was not matched again until the 1970s.

The story of World War II and its effects on women has been told throughout this book. Women plunged into war work at home and abroad, and many gained a new consciousness of their potential and the social inhibitions placed on it. Surveys showed that most women did not want to ''go home'' after the war, and in some industries women struggled together to keep their jobs (Gabin 1982). The systematic attempt to demobilize women, or at least to bump them down into lower-paying and more traditionally gender-appropriate jobs, proved too strong for them, however (Tobias and Anderson 1982). By the 1950s, feminism was a word associated with what seemed to be ancient history, and as Betty Friedan suggested, women didn't even have a name for the problems they faced (Friedan 1963).

Events of the early 1960s, however, provide evidence that feminism never entirely disappeared. The NWP and some other women's groups had continued to push for an equal rights amendment, which the Senate had passed in 1950 and 1953, and both major parties had supported the ERA in their platforms since 1944. As a liberal Democrat President John F. Kennedy could not ignore the issue of women's rights, and he established a presidential commission on the status of women to look into the matter. He also urged the states to establish their own commissions, which all had done by 1967. This series of study commissions set the stage for the rise of the new women's movement in the 1960s.

The Rebirth of Feminism: Emma Said It in 1910/Now We're Going to Say It Again [13]

If the birth of social movements generally depends on changing perceptions of a group's situation, an established network among potential leaders, and an event that precipitates action, the women's liberation movement fits the pattern very well. The postwar economic boom drew women into education and jobs at an unprecedented rate in the late 1950s and 1960s. Divorce rates began to rise in the early 1960s following a decline from a postwar peak. Finally, although America was increasingly affluent and its growth potential seemed unlimited, new social movements were asking people to question whether life was as good as it could be. The black civil rights movement; the ban-the-bomb and antiwar movements; and the early 1960s Free Speech Movement, which sparked student activism nationwide, were all part of the new social ferment of the times and provided the training ground for many young social activists who went on to lead the women's liberation movement.

The first decisive event in the history of the new movement occurred in 1966 after both the Equal Pay Act and Civil Rights Act had already been passed and the Equal Employment Opportunity Commission (EEOC) had been established. At the annual meeting of the National Conference of State Commissions some of the delegates became angry when they found that they would not be allowed to do anything to correct the problems they had been assigned to study. A group of women met in the hotel room of Betty Friedan, one of the delegates, to decide what to do. After this and a series of later meetings, the National Organization for Women (NOW) was founded in October 1966 with 300 members and Betty Friedan as president.

NOW has sometimes been known as the more conservative wing of the feminist movement. Certainly many of its early members had been active in politics, including women's politics, for many years. As Jo Freeman (1975) argues, however, the difference among the various feminist organizations is at least as much one of style as of substance. NOW has a formal organizational structure and paid officers. It has concentrated on legal and policy changes and has become one of the foremost lobbyists for the women's movement. Even though NOW has been criticized as conservative by more radical feminists, this has not necessarily been the view of the larger society. Some of the first women to break away from NOW formed their own feminist groups because they worried about NOW's radicalism and its strong ideological stance. Some trade union women withdrew their support at first because NOW supported the ERA and their own unions did not. The Women's Equity Action League (WEAL) was formed as a separate organization in 1968 because it wanted to concentrate on sex discrimination and feared that NOW's proabortion stand would damage its effectiveness. However, NOW was particularly visible as it spearheaded the drive for the ratification of the Equal Rights Amendment through the 1970s, and it remains the largest and best-known feminist organization.

At the same time that NOW and other nationally organized groups were developing, very different types of feminist groups emerged (for parallel reasons) at the local level from the political organizations of the New Left. In the early 1960s women in New Left organizations such as the Student Non-Violent Coordinating Committee (SNCC) and the Students for a Democratic Society (SDS) began to discuss among themselves the problems that women faced. As the women became more conscious of the status of women in society, they concluded that altering this status should be part of the agenda of the New Left groups that claimed to be fighting for a more egalitarian and democratic society. The women who presented their demands to SDS meetings in 1965 and 1966 and to a national meeting of New Left groups in 1966 were greeted with jeers and verbal violence. The same happened to women in other New Left and antiwar organizations across the country. Like Elizabeth Cady Stanton over a century earlier and the organizers of NOW, these women reacted with rage, confusion, and the desire to meet separately to plan a course of action. The result was the formation of small feminist groups across the country based on the politics of the New Left.

The contemporary women's movement therefore began not as a single organization but as a complex network of very different groups, much as the women's suffrage movement had developed from parallel and sometimes conflicting organizations. At times the differences have seemed to overshadow the similarities. The more radical groups' antipathy toward formal structure and hierarchy has led them to experiment with leaderless structures in an attempt to create a more thoroughly consensual democracy. In the early days many small local groups emphasized consciousness-raising sessions to awaken women to their situations and help them translate their discontent into political action. As women in consciousness-raising sessions discussed their own personal problems, they became aware that these same problems were commonly faced by other women, and this helped mobilize many women to action. Other groups assumed the task of providing services, such as child-care centers and counseling and assistance services for victims of rape and wife battery.

Feminists quickly began to organize demonstrations to attract national attention to their demands. One of the most infamous was a protest staged at the 1968 Miss America contest, where a Freedom Trash Can was set up to dispose of ''women's garbage,'' and a sheep was crowned Miss America. Despite the fact that no one seems to recall the burning of any bra, from that date feminists were given the trivializing name ''bra burners.'' Certainly feminists burned no bras after that date, if only to avoid adding more fuel to the fires of antifeminism. The next major demonstration—

Demonstrations at the 1968 Miss America contest protested definition of women as sex objects. The poster was of a well-known restaurant advertisement.

on the fiftieth anniversary of women's suffrage, August 26, 1970—was the Women's Strike for Equality, which involved feminists of all views.

As the feminist movement grew, it developed the rifts and fragmentation common to most social movements. These rifts were apparent both within and across organizations. Because of the growth in the membership of the movement, feminists could specialize in particular concerns—abortion, day care, employment discrimination, sexuality—which made the movement more comprehensive and effective but also made coordination and consensus more difficult to attain. Some women felt their concerns were being neglected, and some argued that concentration on such issues as professional employment, higher education, and women's studies was elitist and of little relevance to most women. Others argued that the tactics of such radical women as the lesbian separatists would scare off the more conservative women who most needed the movement. Some objected to the emphasis on abortion rights.

It is one thing for a social movement to appear united when it consists of a relatively small group of people with an apparently simple demand such as "equality" or "equal pay for equal work"; it is quite another when the movement is large and increasingly precise in its identification of problems and solutions. Because many people mistakenly think that disagreement within a social movement is necessarily a sign of failure, many assumed that the women's movement was about to fall apart, even as it was growing larger.

The history of NOW is a microcosm of the larger movement. As some of its associates moved away because they feared such issues as abortion, others grew dissatisfied because they thought NOW too conservative. The arguments, which at times threatened the organization's existence, revolved around NOW's hierarchical structure, the distribution of power in the organization, and the low priority given to lesbian issues. In the early 1970s the battle between lesbian activists and the NOW leadership reached its height and caused what many described as a purge of the lesbian leaders. Although NOW later added support for lesbian women to its platform, scars remained. Despite these disagreements, NOW's membership and the membership of the thousands of other women's groups across the country grew tremendously into the middle of the 1980s, and the number of groups multiplied until it is now impossible to list all that exists. It is probably safe to say that a feminist group exists for every social category or interest.

Despite differences in views and strategies, the feminist movement has been remarkably cohesive. The different branches and organizations have learned much from each other, to the point where some earlier differences have become obscured. The move toward multiculturalism has changed the character of the movement. As forces such as the Moral Majority, the policies of the Reagan administration, and the new conservatism of the Supreme Court threatened to eliminate the gains of the previous decade, the women's movement experienced a renewed surge of motivation and activity.

The new women's movement is about a quarter of a century old now and larger than ever. The number of people involved is incalculably large. Besides the well-known national groups, there are hundreds of smaller ones, and many feminist activists press their demands in other types of organizations. Many of the early and prominent organizations of the new women's movement are still influential. These include NOW; the National Women's Political Caucus (NWPC), which was formed in 1971 to promote women in politics; and the Coalition of Labor Union Women (CLUW), which was formed in 1974. There are feminist groups and caucuses in nearly every occupational group containing women, in every field of study, and in most religious denominations. Most major towns and cities have at least some community services run by and for women. Some older women's organizations, such as the League of Women Voters, that had once lost their feminist base are now part of feminist coalitions. Even groups like the YWCA and the Girl Scouts of America occasionally join the feminist alliance. Although many feminist periodicals have been short-lived, their overall number has continued to rise. The history of this phase of the feminist movement is not yet complete.

International Feminism

Because feminism is a worldwide movement, American feminism must be understood in this context. American feminists have often learned from their sisters abroad, and they have often influenced the feminists of other nations. Feminism has long crossed national borders as women from different nations have worked together for their common cause.

American feminists have been influenced by those from other nations since the eighteenth century. They found their intellectual roots, for example, in the writings of people such as Mary Wollstonecraft, an Englishwoman. Late nineteenth and early twentieth century feminists like Margaret Sanger, Harriot Stanton Blatch, and Alice Paul gained considerable training and inspiration from European activists during travels abroad. American feminists have also been effective in exporting their ideas and strategies to the outside world through their travels, their publications, and the impressions they have made on foreign women who have traveled in the United States.

The turn of the twentieth century witnessed the rise of international organizations of feminists, including the International Woman Suffrage Alliance (IWSA) and international meetings of trade unionists. At these meetings women exchanged ideas about goals and strategies to support each other in their struggles at home. Carrie Chapman Catt was particularly active in these efforts and, through her, the NAWSA agreed to contribute to the IWSA.

The 1930s were a time of heightened international feminist activity. Governments and international lawyers made numerous efforts to construct a more coherent and enlightened system of international law, particularly as it concerned human rights. Women quickly seized the opportunity to advocate women's rights, as they did at the Montevideo international conference on women's rights in 1933. The National Women's Party was particularly active in this regard. The United Nations and its agencies have continued to promote international agreements and conventions on women's rights, as have the Organization for Economic Cooperation and Development (OECD), of which the United States is a member, and the European Community, a confederation of western European nations.

Changes in transportation and communications technology have facilitated the coordination of international feminist organizations. International women's conferences are held yearly around the world, and women's caucuses meet in the context of larger international meetings and organizations. These international efforts are important not just because they offer an opportunity for feminists to compare notes but also because it has become increasingly obvious that women's problems are not local in origin and sometimes arise from countries' foreign policies. For example, some dangerous birth control drugs or devices banned by the U.S. Food and Drug Administration have been channeled to women in countries without such strong consumer protections. American feminists have fought such policies and have sought less sexist and discriminatory administration of American foreign aid programs (Jaquette and Staudt 1985; Staudt 1985). A nation's defense policy also has special effects on women (Enloe 1983). In a world that is as economically interdependent as ours feminism must look beyond national borders.

International feminism has its own special problems. The three international conferences held in 1975, 1980, and 1985 as part of International Women's Decade made some of these problems painfully clear. In 1975 the United Nations sponsored an International Women's Year Conference in Mexico City. When it became clear that some women delegates were being used to foster their governments' own aims, an alternative meeting, called the Tribune, was convened. Most of the feminist activists went to this other meeting rather than the official meeting. In 1980 a meeting was held in Copenhagen to evaluate progress since 1975. That meeting was also disrupted by official delegates less concerned with feminism than with their countries' nationalistic goals. Some delegates went so far as to try to bar and censure women from certain countries simply because of their nationalities. Many feminist delegates left bitter and skeptical about the potential of international efforts, especially those organized through official governmental bodies. Nevertheless, feminists of different nations met again in Nairobi in 1985—more successfully this time—and continue to cooperate where they can.[14]

Opposition

There is considerable continuity in the arguments used against feminism and feminist movements over the course of American history. Some of the attacks made on today's feminism were made against the suffragists. The antifeminist arguments are as varied as those of the feminists.

One of the chief arguments against feminism has been that if women are given equal treatment and opportunities in society, they will lose their protection and become more overburdened than they already are. Antisuffragist women and men used this argument in the nineteenth and early twentieth centuries, and antifeminists continue to use it today. They claim that equality will, in fact, result in injustice for women.

Much opposition throughout the history of feminism has come from religious groups and leaders. These groups are distressed by feminist attacks on what they see as the moral order of male and female difference and changes in familial, sexual, and reproductive mores.[15]

Some opposition is based on economic arguments. Various business interests, including railroads and liquor producers, opposed suffrage because they feared what women would do with their votes (Flexner 1975). In the 1970s insurance companies opposed feminist causes because of the money they would lose if they had to treat women and men equally. The National Association of Manufacturers (NAM), which opposes any governmental restraint on business, opposed feminist demands that they prove they treat employees fairly and equitably.

Some opponents to feminism have worried about the domino effect of social change: If changes are accepted for women, who will want changes next? During the later years of the suffrage movement many political leaders worried that if women were granted new rights, there would be little justification for denying the same rights to blacks or immigrants.

Sometimes the opposition has framed its argument not in terms of feminism or women's roles per se, but in terms of the effects any changes might have on the larger society. Because feminists have tended to look to the federal government for assistance, supporters of state rights have tended to be antagonistic to feminism. Feminist proposals support government interference with husbands' traditional abilities to overpower their wives financially and physically. Many opponents see these proposals as demands for big government to expand still further and thus interfere with private rights of commerce and personal relations. Feminist proposals have also tended to call for the expansion of social services, which stirs up opposition on the part of those who see these proposals as socialist or as too costly.

Opposition also comes from those who quite simply think that society has been well structured in the past, works well, and is in no need of tampering. Those who believe that American social institutions have operated in a fair and open way in the past regard any effort to change their gender composition as an attack on "merit" systems. They argue that women are underrepresented or receive less reward because they have not wanted or been good enough to do better. Conservative critics of feminist efforts to alter the emphasis of research and education argue that these efforts will result in research agendas and curricula based on political decisions rather than merit decisions. They believe that an objective market of ideas (not men raised in androcentric cultures, even if well educated) has determined that women and their creations are not worth much attention.

Explicit antifeminist activity tends to emanate from the most conservative sectors of society. Throughout this century feminists have been accused by their opponents of being socialist and anti-American, particularly because they support social programs to help the needy and governmental regulation of industry to benefit the consumer and worker. Studies in the 1970s showed that antifeminist activists tended to be particularly fearful about the spread of communism in the United States.

The argument between feminists and antifeminists has generally not been a battle of equal and opposing parties appealing to the government for change. The battle has usually been between groups of mostly women (and generally led by women) on the one hand; and the mostly male leaders of government, business, and religion on the other. Of course many women are opposed to feminism, including members of such women's organizations as Phyllis Schlafley's Stop-ERA and Women Who Want to Be Women (WWWW). In the nineteenth century many of the most active female opponents were wives of men in government or business who had power to maintain the old system of discrimination and oppression. The most effective opposition then and now is from those who are in power.

It is generally easy to see why these institutional leaders want to forestall change: It is costly to those already in power. Although men can derive many benefits from feminism, women who argue that men can ''only benefit'' by equality for women are naive, and most men know it.

The contemporary women's movement may be the first in American history to face the opposition of an organized antifeminist social movement. From the mid-1970s to the 1980s, a coalition of groups calling themselves profamily, prolife, and anti-ERA emerged. These groups, which drew from right-wing political organizations and the Moral Majority, were formed in reaction to feminist successes in reproductive, family, and antidiscrimination policies. These antifeminists use all the opposition arguments already mentioned, but they focus on the ''protection'' of women and the preservation of what they define as traditional Christian moral values.

Antifeminist women are not generally opposed to women's holding jobs or engaging in political activity; many of them do the former and all, by their involvement in the antifeminist movement, are doing the latter. They are willing to use all the political rights won for them by earlier feminists: They organize, demonstrate, petition, lobby, litigate, vote, and hold office. Some even use violence, for example, firebombing abortion clinics or physically harassing women going in and out of these clinics. They use these means to defend what they define as women's interests, just as feminists use most of these tactics (except violence against women) to defend what they define as women's interests. How can antifeminist women reconcile their opposition to demands for equality and liberation with their claims that they are fighting for women?

A clue to the answer lies in what we now define as nineteenth-century feminism, where women's rights activists and moral and social purity campaigners were often one and the same because these were seen as two sides of the same equation. Moral and social purity, they claimed, could give women the dignity and protection they needed from the brutal masculine world and the men in it. Men, they argued, are not trustworthy. They will exploit, neglect, and hurt their families if left to their own devices. Women need protection from men, and men need protection from themselves. Giving women more strength as women to spread their influence as nurturers and preservers of traditional values was seen as a key to the solution.

Contemporary antifeminists often use much the same argument, except they argue that contemporary feminists have gone too far in the wrong direction. Today's antifeminists say that by emphasizing a social structure of genderless individuals with precisely the same rights, roles, and characters and by destroying the foundations of familial morality, the feminists are taking away men's motivation to remain loyal to their families and women's motivation to be anything but self-seeking, individually competitive people, just like men. If feminist goals are achieved, they argue, women, children, old people, and others will be left unprotected or taken care of by sterile, bureaucratic public institutions.

Just as many conservatives of today resemble nineteenth-century liberals, many antifeminist activists of today resemble nineteenth-century feminists. They reject the overwhelming emphasis modern liberal feminists place on individualism, they distrust reliance on public institutions, and although they agree in a sense with the radical feminist view that women and men have different characters, they reject segregation and separation because it necessitates rejecting traditional family and moral values.[16]

Myra Marx Feree's study of attitudes among working-class women (1983) shows that feminists and antifeminists, whether activist or not, not only disagree about specific issues but also look at feminism in different ways. Among the women Feree interviewed, those who favored the feminist movement emphasized its contributions to women's senses of self-worth and entitlement. Those who opposed the movement emphasized its effects on sexual morality and the belief that it fostered social segregation of the sexes. Those who were mildly sympathetic—most of Feree's sample— emphasized the benefits it offered to future generations of women.

Feree's research and that of others indicates that feminists and antifeminists focus on quite different aspects of feminist issues. Those who wish to restrict or prohibit abortion, for example, tend to focus on moral questions concerning the life of the conceived but unborn, and those who want abortion to remain relatively unrestricted focus on the rights of women to determine their own reproductive lives. The two sides do not simply disagree about what should be done about abortion, they disagree about what the key issues are.

The language people use to talk about issues influences how people react to them. The answers people give to questions about their attitudes toward abortion, for example, depend on how such questions are worded. This is because slightly different wording makes people think about slightly different aspects of the issue.

When Marsha Jacobson (1979) asked a sample of women and men how they felt about feminism, but used different terms for feminism with different people, she evoked different reactions depending on the terms used. People responded most favorably when she asked how they felt about equal rights for women, slightly less favorably when questioned about "women's lib" and "feminism," and least favorably when questioned about "women's liberation." It is probably that people understood "equal rights for women" as a moderate and enlightened goal, while they associated "women's liberation" with the mass media image of bra-burning, man-hating radicals.

Some research has explored the sectors of society from which feminism and antifeminism draw support. Val Burris (1983) analyzed the results of a 1980 nationwide survey of adults to find out who favored the Equal Rights Amendment. Among both women and men, blacks were more favorable than whites, people from the east and west coasts were more favorable than people from other parts of the country, and people who attended church regularly were less favorable than people who did not. Men subscribing to fundamentalist religious beliefs were less favorable than men who did not, and women who were more educated or who lived in cities were more favorable than women who were less educated or from rural areas. Most surveys also show that younger people are more favorable toward feminism and the feminist movement than older people.

A study of pro- and anti-ERA activists revealed similar findings: Pro-ERA activists had higher education and income than did ERA opponents, and they were more likely to come from urban areas (Tedin 1978). A study of Massachusetts activists for and against the ERA found that pro-ERA activists were younger, more liberal, less religious, more likely to be single and employed, and if employed more likely to be professionals (Mueller and Dimieri 1982). Some researchers, such as Myra Marx Feree (1980), find that women who are employed have more favorable attitudes toward feminism than women who are not.

It is important to understand not just the social bases of the conflict over women's status, but also how people perceive the conflict itself. If people believe the real battle is between men and women, for example, they might hold different views than if they think it is between older and younger generations of people. One study (Sapiro 1980) investigated these perceptions using a 1976 national survey in which people were asked how they felt about equal social roles for women and men and then how they thought most women, most men, most young people, and most older people felt. There was considerable agreement between men and women on the general question of women's roles: They tended to agree that women and men should have equal roles in society and to reject the idea that woman's place is in the home. Younger people were more egalitarian in their attitudes than were older people.

Regardless of their own age or sex, people believed there was considerable conflict between the sexes and generations over women's rights. They thought that most women were more egalitarian than most men, and that most younger people were more egalitarian than most older people. Men saw about equal levels of sex and age conflict, and women tended to see more conflict between the generations than between the sexes. Most people thus viewed conflict between women and men as only half the problem at most.

How did people see themselves in relation to sex and generational conflict? Most tended to place themselves on what they saw as the more progressive side: in alliance with women and the young. Women identified themselves as agreeing with most women and most younger people and as much more egalitarian than most men and older people. Although most men thought they were slightly less egalitarian than most women, they saw themselves as agreeing with most young people and as much more egalitarian than most men and most older people. They seemed to be saying, "Most men aren't as egalitarian as they might be, but I'm okay."

There are many ways of thinking about why people are feminists or antifeminists, why people join one movement or the other or simply remain aloof. Probably the least useful way is to regard the opposition (be it feminist or antifeminist) as evil or ignorant. One of the most important writings along these lines was contributed by Robyn Rowland (1984). Rowland wrote to many different women around the world, feminist and antifeminist, and asked them to write about their understanding of and attitudes toward feminism. These essays, collected under the title *Women Who Do and Women Who Don't Join the Women's Movement,* offers an unparalleled opportunity to hear many different women speak for themselves. The number of different paths they took to reach their conclusions is striking.

Feminism and the Future

During the past two centuries there seem always to have been at least some people thinking about and working to improve the status of women. At some times there have been large mass movements, and at others there have been only isolated actions by individuals and small groups. In each generation people have continued the debate over what equality or liberation would mean and how it could best be achieved. In each generation there have been many women who were frightened by the changes proposed or thought that they had all the choice and freedom they needed. In each generation there have been masses of people who have remained ignorant both about their own history and about the turmoil of the present.

As feminism has achieved some goals and failed to meet others, its agenda for the future has grown longer rather than shorter. The solutions to problems always seem to reveal many other problems. Each turning point in feminist history has revealed the degree to which gender continues to be used to restrict people's options. Moreover, as human societies change over time and develop new ways of making their lives better and worse, women's situation changes.

Anyone who needs confirmation that there is still much to be done need only consider that many people regard feminism and women's studies as frivolous and of only peripheral importance. Women who take an interest in their own status and roles in society are seen as selfish or divisive, and men who take an interest in women's status and roles in society are seen as odd or even pitiful. Nevertheless many women and men persevere.

There has been much change in the definition of female and male gender in recent centuries. As we have seen, many of the changes have been liberating, and some have not. What is left to be done? This book is filled with suggestions that come from today's feminism and social analysis. Beyond this, future generations will have to decide for themselves.

NOTES

1. My thanks to Sarah Slavin, who suggested this approach to the differences and commonalities among different thinkers (see Schramm 1979).

2. Feminist theorists have offered many different ways of viewing and categorizing feminist theory. As most would admit, there are problems with any attempt at classification. I have not, for example, included discussion of postmodern and psychoanalytic feminism because those are influential primarily as intellectual and scholarly movements and have relatively little impact on the mass politics of the women's movement or on feminist policy development. For discussion of these approaches see Marks and de Courtivron (1980), Gallop (1982), Eisenstein and Jardine (1985), Moi (1985), Flax (1987), Spivak (1987), Alcoff (1988), and Diamond and Quinby (1988).

3. For further discussion of liberal feminism, see Eisenstein (1981), Okin (1979), Jaggar (1983), and Pateman (1988).

4. Those who object to feminism often argue that men can be oppressed by their gender as well; for example, men are not supposed to cry, and they are under great pressure to perform economically and sexually. This is true, but as feminists have been arguing at least since Margaret Fuller's time in the early nineteenth century, men have long dominated most positions of societal power and authority, so they have been in a better position to change their situations. They have never had to petition women to grant them rights. (See Fuller [1845] 1971; also extracted in Rossi 1988.)

5.   For further discussion of socialist feminism see Jaggar (1983), Barrett (1988), Editors of *Quest* (1981), Sargent (1981), and Sayers (1987).

6.   For further discussion of radical feminism see *Quest* (1981), Daly (1978), Jaggar (1983), Morága and Anzaldúa (1981), and Bunch (1987).

7.   It would be a mistake to think of even this group as homogeneous. Too often people forget there are sharp and crucial differences even among "middle-class, college-educated, white women." They are diverse in ethnicity and religion, family history and experience, sexual orientation, and exposure to violence against women, to name just a few things that would make a difference in their understanding of women's situation.

8.   Multicultural feminism is a name I have chosen for this new turn in feminist theory. It is important to note that even at the beginning of this century many feminists were struggling with questions of diversity (Cott 1987). For some examples of multicultural feminism, see Aptheker (1982), Morága and Anzaldúa (1981), Hooks (1981; 1984; 1989), Collins (1989a), Hurtado (1989), Spivak (1987), and Minh-ha (1989).

9.   For works on social movements see Tilly (1978) and Jenkins (1981).

10. For more reading on feminism in this period, see Berg (1978) and Flexner (1975).

11. The literature on this period of feminism is voluminous. For some different approaches, see Flexner (1975), DuBois (1978), Stanton, Anthony, and Gage ([1881] 1969), Kraditor (1965), and Sochen (1972).

12. For further reading on this period see Lemons (1972), Sochen (1973), Becker (1981), Ware (1981; 1983), Hartman (1983), Scharf and Jensen (1983), Honey (1984), Kaledin (1984), and Higgonet, et al. (1987).

13. For further reading on this period, see Freeman (1975), Boles (1979), Evans (1979), Hole and Levine (1971), and Klein (1984).

14. For reading on international feminism, see Bassnett (1986), Bouchier (1984), Chafetz and Dworkin (1986), Dahlerup (1986), O'Barr et al. (1986), and Rowland (1984).

15. At the same time many religious organizations have worked as part of the feminist coalition. Among the principal supporters of the ERA were the American Association of Women Ministers, the American Jewish Committee, Disciples of Christ, Lutheran Church in America, National Council of Churches, Union of American Hebrew Congregations, United Church of Christ, United Jewish Congress, United Methodist Church, and the United Presbyterian Church, plus a number of Catholic organizations and many women's organizations in numerous denominations.

16. For works on or by antifeminists, see Andelin (1974), Decter (1973), Morgan (1975), Petchesky (1981), Gilder (1973), Dworkin (1983), and Conover and Gray (1983).

Bibliography

Abbott, Pamela and Roger Sapsford. 1988. *Women and Social Class*. New York: Routledge.

Abbey, Antonia. 1982. "Sex Differences in Attributions for Friendly Behavior: Do Males Misperceive Females' Friendliness?" *Journal of Personality and Social Psychology* 42 (May): 830–38.

Abel, Emily. 1981. "Collective Protest and the Meritocracy: Faculty Women and Sex Discrimination Lawsuits." *Feminist Studies* 7 (Fall): 505–38.

Abramowitz, Stephen I., Christine V. Abramowitz, Carolyn Jackson, and Beverly Gomes. 1973. "The Politics of Clinical Judgment: What Non-Liberal Examiners Infer about Women Who Don't Stifle Themselves." *Journal of Consulting and Clinical Psychology* 41:385–91.

Adams, Carolyn Teich, and Kathryn T. Winston. 1980. *Mothers at Work*. New York: Longman.

Adams, Karen L., and Norma C. Ware. 1989. "Sexism and the English Language: The Linguistic Implications of Being a Woman." In *Women: A Feminist Perspective,* edited by Jo Freeman, 470–84. Mountain View, Calif.: Mayfield.

Adams, Kathryn A. 1980. "Who Has the Final Word? Sex, Race, and Dominance Behavior." *Journal of Personality and Social Psychology* 38 (January): 1–8.

Adler, Freda. 1975. *Sisters in Crime*. Lexington, Mass.: D.C. Heath.

Albers, Patricia, and Beatrice Medicine, eds. 1983. *The Hidden Half: Studies of Plains Indian Women*. Lanham, Md.: University Press of America.

Alcoff, Linda. 1988. "Cultural Feminism versus Post-Structuralism: The Identity Crisis in Feminist Theory." *Signs* 13 (Spring), 405–46.

Allgeier, A.R. 1983. "Sexuality and Gender Roles in the Second Half of Life." In *Changing Boundaries: Gender Roles and Sexual Behavior,* edited by Elizabeth Rice Allgeier and Naomi B. McCormick, Palo Alto, Calif.: Mayfield, 135–57.

Almquist, Elizabeth. 1975. "Untangling the Effects of Race and Sex: The Disadvantaged Status of Black Women." *Social Science Quarterly* 56 (June): 129–42.

———. 1984. "Race and Ethnicity in the Lives of Minority Women." In *Women: A Feminist Perspective,* edited by Jo Freeman, Palo Alto, Calif.: Mayfield, 423–53.

———. 1987. "Labor Market Gender Inequality in Minority Groups." *Gender and Society* 1 (December): 400–14.

Andelin, Helen. 1974. *Fascinating Womanhood.* New York: Bantam.

Anderson, Lynn R., Martha Finn, and Sandra Leider. 1981. "Leadership Style and Leader Title." *Psychology of Women Quarterly* 5:661–69.

Andrade, Vibiana M. 1981. "The Toxic Workplace: Title VII Protection for the Potentially Pregnant Woman." *Harvard Women's Law Journal* 4 (Spring): 71–104.

Aptheker, Bettina. 1982. *Woman's Legacy: Essays in Race, Sex, and Class.* Amherst: University of Massachusetts Press.

Aquinas, Saint Thomas. 1945. "Question XCII: The Production of Women." In *Basic Writings of Saint Thomas Aquinas,* edited by Anton C. Pegis, 879–84. New York: Random House.

Archer, John, and Barbara Lloyd. 1982. *Sex and Gender.* New York: Penguin.

Aries, Philippe. 1942. *Centuries of Childhood.* London: Jonathan Cape.

Ashby, Marylee Stoll, and Bruce C. Whittmaier. 1978. "Attitude Changes in Children after Exposure to Stories about Women in Traditional or Nontraditional Occupations." *Journal of Educational Psychology* 70 (December): 945–49.

Aslin, Alice. 1977. "Feminist and Community Mental Health Center Psychotherapists' Expectations of Mental Health for Women." *Sex Roles* 3 (December): 537–44.

Backhouse, Constance, and Lea Cohen. 1981. *Sexual Harassment on the Job.* Englewood Cliffs, N.J.: Prentice-Hall.

Baker, Ross K., Laurily K. Epstein, and Rodney D. Forth. 1981. "Matters of Life and Death: Social, Political, and Religious Correlates of Attitudes on Abortion." *American Politics Quarterly* 9 (January): 89–102.

Bane, Mary Jo. 1976. "Marital Disruption and the Lives of Children." *Journal of Social Issues* 32 (Winter): 103–17.

Bank, Barbara J., Bruce J. Biddle, and Thomas L. Good. 1980. "Sex Roles, Classroom Instruction, and Reading Achievement. *Journal of Educational Psychology* 72 (April): 119–32.

Banton, Michael. 1983. *Racial and Ethnic Competition.* New York: Cambridge University Press.

Barrett, Michelle. 1988. *Women's Oppression Today: Problems in Marxist Feminist Analysis.* London: Verso.

Bart, Pauline B. 1971. "Depression in Middle Aged Women." In *Women in Sexist Society,* edited by Vivian Gornick and Barbara K. Moran, 99–117. New York: Basic Books.

———. 1975. "Emotional and Social Status in the Older Woman." In *No Longer Young: The Older Woman in America,* 3–22. Ann Arbor: Institute for Gerontology, University of Michigan.

Bart, Pauline B., and Patricia H. O'Brien. 1984. "Stopping Rape: Effective Avoidance Strategies." *Signs* 10 (Autumn): 83–101.

Barth, Robert J., and Bill N. Kinder. 1988. "A Theoretical Analysis of Sex Differences in Same-Sex Friendships." *Sex Roles* 19 (September): 349–63.

Basow, Susan A., and Nancy T. Silberg. 1987. "Student Evaluations of College Professors: Are Female and Male Professors Rated Differently?" *Journal of Education Psychology* 79:308–14.

Bassnett, Susan. 1986. *Feminist Experiences: The Women's Movement in Four Cultures.* New York: Allen & Unwin.

Baxter, Sandra, and Marjorie Lansing. 1980. *Women and Politics: The Invisible Majority.* Ann Arbor: University of Michigan Press.

Bebel, August. [1910] 1970. *Women and Socialism.* New York: Schocken.

Becker, Susan D. 1981. *The Origins of the Equal Rights Amendment: American Feminism between the Wars.* Westport, Conn.: Greenwood.

———. 1983. "International Feminism between the Wars: The National Women's Party versus the League of Women Voters." In *Decades of Discontent,* edited by Lois Scharf and Joan M. Jensen, 223–43. Westport, Conn.: Greenwood.

Beecher, Catharine. [1841] 1977. *A Treatise on Domestic Economy.* New York: Schocken.

Bem, Sandra Lipsitz. 1975. "Sex Role Adaptability: One Consequence of Psychological Androgyny." *Journal of Personality and Social Psychology* 31:634–43.

———. 1983. "Gender Schema Theory and Its Implications for Child Development: Raising Gender-Aschematic Children in a Gender-Schematic Society." *Signs* 8 (Summer): 596–616.

Benson, John M. 1981. "The Polls: A Rebirth of Religion?" *Public Opinion Quarterly* 45 (Winter): 576–85.

Berch, Bettina. 1982. *The Endless Day: The Political Economy of Women and Work.* New York: Harcourt, Brace, Jovanovich.

Berg, Barbara. 1978. *The Remembered Gate: Origins of American Feminism: The Woman and the City, 1800–60.* New York: Oxford University Press.

Berlo, Janet Catherine. 1976. "The Cambridge School: Women in Architecture." *Feminist Art Journal* 5 (Spring): 27–32.

Bernard, Jessie. 1972. *The Future of Marriage.* New York: Bantam.

———. 1975. *Women, Wives, Mothers: Values and Options.* Chicago: Aldine.

Bernstein, Barbara, and Robert Kane. 1981. "Physicians' Attitudes toward Female Patients." *Medical Care* 19 (June): 600–608.

Bethune, Mary McLeod. [1941] 1982. "How the Bethune-Cookman College Campus Started." In *Women's America,* edited by Linda K. Kerber and Jane De Hart Mathews, 260–62. New York: Oxford University Press.

Birnbaum, Judith A. 1975. "Life Patterns and Self-Esteem in Gifted Family Oriented and Career Committed Women." In *Women and Achievement: Social and Motivational Analyses,* edited by Martha T. Mednick, Sandra Tangri, and Lois Hoffman, 396–419. New York: Wiley.

Blau, Francine D., and Anne E. Winkler. 1989. "Women in the Labor Force: An Overview." In *Women: A Feminist Perspective,* edited by Jo Freeman, 265–86. Mountain View, Calif.: Mayfield.

Bleier, Ruth. 1984. *Science and Gender: A Critique of Biology and Its Theories on Women.* New York: Pergamon.

Blumstein, Philip W., and Pepper Schwartz. 1977. "Bisexuality: Some Social Psychological Issues." *Journal of Social Issues* 33 (Spring): 30–45.

———. 1983. *American Couples: Money, Work, Sex*. New York: William Morrow.

Boles, Janet. 1979. *The Politics of the Equal Rights Amendment*. New York: Longman.

Bonafede, Dom. 1982. "Women's Movement Broadens the Scope of Its Role in American Politics." *National Journal*, 11 December, 2108–11.

Borden, Richard J., and Gorden M. Homleid. 1978. "Handedness and Lateral Positioning in Heterosexual Couples: Are Men Still Strongarming Women?" *Sex Roles* 4 (February): 67–73.

Boston Women's Health Book Collective. 1985. *Our Bodies, Ourselves*. New York: Simon & Schuster.

Bouchier, David. 1984. *The Feminist Challenge: The Movement for Women's Liberation in Britain and the USA*. New York: Schocken.

Brabeck, M. 1983. "Moral Judgment: Theory and Research on Differences between Males and Females." *Developmental Review* 3:274–91.

Breines, Wini, and Linda Gordon. 1983. "New Scholarship on Family Violence." *Signs* 8 (Spring): 490–531.

Brenner, Johanna. 1987. "Feminist Political Discourse: Radical versus Liberal Approaches to the Feminization of Poverty and Comparable Worth." *Gender and Society* 1 (December): 447–65.

Briggs, Kenneth A. 1983. "Women and the Church." *New York Times Magazine*, 6 November.

Brooks-Gunn, Jeanne, and Diane K. Ruble. 1982. "The Development of Menstrual-Related Beliefs and Behaviors during Early Adolescence." *Child Development* 53: 1567–77.

Broverman, Inge K., Donald M. Broverman, Frank E. Clarkson, Paul S. Rosencrantz, and Susan R. Vogel. 1970. "Sex Role Stereotypes and Clinical Judgments of Mental Health." *Journal of Consulting and Clinical Psychology* 34:1–7.

Brown, Charles Brockden. 1970. *Alcuin*. New York: Grossman.

Brown, Diane Robinson, and Lawrence E. Gray. 1988. "Unemployment and Psychological Distress among Black American Women." *Sociological Focus* 21:209–22.

Brownmiller, Susan. 1975. *Against Our Will: Men, Women, and Rape*. New York: Simon & Schuster.

Bruch, Hilde. 1978. *The Golden Cage: The Enigma of Anorexia Nervosa*. Cambridge: Harvard University Press.

Buckley, Thomas, and Alma Gottlieb, eds. 1988. *Blood Magic: The Anthropology of Menstruation*. Berkeley: University of California Press.

Bunch, Charlotte. 1979. "Learning from Lesbian Separatism." In *Issues in Feminism: A First Course in Women's Studies*, edited by Sheila Ruth, 551–56. Boston: Houghton Mifflin.

———. 1981. "Not for Lesbians Only." In *Building Feminist Theory: Essays from Quest*, 67–73. New York: Longman.

———. 1987. *Passionate Politics: Feminist Theory in Action*. New York: St. Martin's.

Burris, Val. 1983. 'Who Opposed the ERA? An Analysis of the Social Bases of Anti-Feminism." *Social Science Quarterly* 64 (June): 305–17.

Burt, Martha R. 1980. "Cultural Myths and Supports for Rape." *Journal of Personality and Social Psychology* 38 (February): 217–30.

Buss, David M. 1981. "Sex Differences in the Evaluation and Performance of Dominant Acts." *Journal of Personality and Social Psychology* 40 (January): 147–54.

Bussey, Kay, and Betty Maughan. 1982. "Gender Differences in Moral Reasoning." *Journal of Personality and Social Psychology* 42 (April): 701–6.

Cade, Toni, ed. 1970. *The Black Woman.* New York: Signet.

Campbell, Angus, Philip E. Converse, and William L. Rodgers. 1976. *The Quality of American Life: Perceptions, Evaluations, and Satisfaction.* New York: Russell Sage.

Cantor, Muriel. 1978. "Where Are the Women in Public Broadcasting?" In *Hearth and Home: Images of Women in the Mass Media,* edited by Gaye Tuchman, Arlene Kaplan Daniels, and James Benet, 78–89. New York: Oxford University Press.

Caplow, Theodore, and Bruce A. Chadwick. 1979. "Inequality and Life-Styles in Middletown, 1920–78." *Social Science Quarterly* 60 (December): 367–86.

Carlsson, Marianne, and Pia Jaderquist. 1983. "Note on Sex Role Opinions as Conceptual Schemata." *British Journal of Social Psychology* 22 (February): 65–68.

Carpenter, Eugenia S. 1980. "Children's Health Care and the Changing Role of Women." *Medical Care* 18 (December): 1208–18.

Carroll, Jackson W., Barbara Hargrove, and Adair T. Lummis. 1981. *Women of the Cloth: A New Opportunity for the Churches.* New York: Harper & Row.

Carroll, Susan, 1985. *Women as Candidates in American Politics.* Bloomington: Indiana University Press.

Carter, Michael J., and Susan Boslego Carter. 1981. "Women's Recent Progress in the Professions, or Women Get a Ticket to Ride after the Gravy Train Has Left the Station." *Feminist Studies* 7 (Fall): 477–504.

Cash, Thomas F., Barry Gillen, and D. Steven Burns. 1977. "Sexism and Beautyism in Personnel Consultant Decision Making." *Journal of Applied Psychology* 62:301–10.

Chafetz, Janet Saltzman, and Anthony Gary Dworkin. 1986. *Female Revolt: Women's Movements in World and Historical Perspective.* Totowa, N.J.: Rowman & Allanheld.

Chavkin, Wendy, ed. 1984. *Double Exposure: Women's Health Hazards on the Job and at Home.* New York: Monthly Review Press.

Cherry, Frances. 1983. "Gender Roles and Sexual Violence." In *Changing Boundaries: Gender Roles and Sexual Behavior,* edited by Elizabeth Rice Allgeier and Naomi B. McCormick, 245–60. Palo Alto, Calif.: Mayfield.

Chesler, Phyllis. 1971. "Patient and Patriarch: Women in the Psychotherapeutic Relationship." In *Women in Sexist Society,* edited by Vivian Gornick and Barbara K. Moran, 251–75. New York: Basic Books.

Chodorow, Nancy. 1978. *The Reproduction of Mothering: Psychoanalysis and the Sociology of Gender.* Berkeley and Los Angeles: University of California Press.

Chodorow, Nancy, and Susan Contratto. 1982. "The Fantasy of the Perfect Mother." In *Rethinking the Family: Some Feminist Questions,* edited by Barrie Thorne and Marilyn Yalom, 54–72. New York: Longman.

Chow, Esther Ngan-Ling. 1987. "The Development of Feminist Consciousness among Asian-American Women." *Gender and Society* 1 (September): 284–99.

Christ, Carol, and Judith Plaskow, eds. 1979. *Womanspirit Rising: A Feminist Reader in Religion.* New York: Harper & Row.

Christensen, Dana, and Robert Rosenthal. 1982. "Gender and Nonverbal Decoding Skill as Determinants of Interpersonal Expectancy Effects." *Journal of Personality and Social Psychology* 42 (January): 75–87.

Christoplos, Florence, and JoAnn Borden. 1978. "Sexism in Elementary School Mathematics." *The Elementary School Journal* 78 (March): 275–77.

Cixous, Hélène. 1976. "The Laugh of the Medusa." *Signs* 1 (Summer): 875–94.

Clarke, Cheryl. 1981. "Lesbianism: An Act of Resistance." In *This Bridge Called My Back: Writings by Radical Women of Color,* edited by Cherrie Morága and Gloria Anzaldúa, 128–37. Watertown, Mass.: Persephone Press.

Cobb, Nancy J., Judith Stevens-Long, and Steven Goldstein. 1982. "The Influence of Televised Models in Toy Preference in Children." *Sex Roles* (October): 1075–80.

Cohen, Claudia. 1981. "Person Categories and Social Perception: Testing Some Boundaries of the Processing Effects of Prior Knowledge." *Journal of Personality and Social Psychology* (March): 441–52.

Cole, C. Maureen, Frances A. Hill, and Leland J. Daly. 1983. "Do Masculine Pronouns Used Generically Lead to Thoughts of Men?" *Sex Roles* 9 (June): 737–50.

Cole, Johnetta B., ed. 1986. *All American Women: Ties That Divide, Ties that Bind*. New York: Free Press.

Collins, Eliza G.C., and Timothy Blodget. 1981. "Sexual Harassment...Some See It...Some Won't." *Business Review* 59 (March–April): 76–94.

Collins, Patricia Hill. 1989a. "The Social Construction of Black Feminist Thought." *Signs* 14 (Summer): 745–73.

———. 1989b. "A Comparison of Two Works on Black Family Life." *Signs* 14 (Summer): 875–84.

Colwill, Nina. 1982. *The New Partnership: Women and Men in Organizations*. Palo Alto, Calif.: Mayfield.

Commission of the European Community. 1979. *European Men and Women, 1978*. Brussels: European Community.

Conover, Pamela, and Virginia Gray. 1983. *Feminism and the New Right: Conflict over the American Family*. New York: Prager.

Cook, Alice H., Val R., Lorwin, and Arlene Kaplan Daniels, eds. 1984. *Women and Trade Unions in Eleven Industrialized Countries*. Philadelphia: Temple University Press.

Cook, Ellen Piel. 1985. *Psychological Androgyny*. New York: Pergamon.

Cooper, Elizabeth A., Dennis Doverspike, and Gerald V. Barrett. 1985. "Comparison of Different Methods of Determining the Sex Type of American Occupations." *Psychological Reports* 57 (December): 747–50.

Cooperstock, R. 1971. "Sex Differences in the Use of Mood Modifying Drugs: An Exploratory Model." *Journal of Health and Social Behavior* 12:238–44.

Cott, Nancy F. 1987. *The Grounding of American Feminism*. New Haven: Yale.

Cowan, Gloria, Carole Lee, Danielle Levy, and Debra Snyder. 1988. "Dominance and Inequality in X-Rated Videocassettes." *Psychology of Woman Quarterly* 12:299–311.

Cowan, Ruth Schwartz. 1982. "The 'Industrial Revolution' in the Home: Household Technology and Social Change in the Twentieth Century." In *Women's America: Refocusing the Past,* edited by Linda Kerber and Jane De Hart Mathews, 324–38. New York: Oxford University Press.

———. 1983. *More Work for Mother: The Ironies of Household Technology from the Open Hearth to the Microwave*. New York: Basic.

Dahlerup, Drude, ed. 1986. *The New Woman's Movement: Feminism and Political Power in Europe and the USA*. Newbury Park, Calif.: Sage.

Daly, Mary. 1973. *Beyond God the Father: Toward a Philosophy of Women's Liberation*. Boston: Beacon.

———. 1975. *The Church and the Second Sex*. New York: Harper & Row.

———. 1978. *Gyn/Ecology: The Metaethics of Radical Feminism*. Boston: Beacon.

Darcy, R., Susan Welch, and Janet Clark. 1987. *Women's Elections and Representation*. New York: Longman.

D'Augelli, Judith Frankel, and Anthony R. D'Augelli. 1977. "Moral Reasoning and Premarital Sexual Behavior: Toward Reasoning about Relationships." *Journal of Social Issues* 33 (Spring): 46–66.

Davies, Margery. 1983. *Women's Place Is at the Typewriter: Office Work and Office Workers: 1870-1930*. Philadelphia: Temple University Press.

Davis, Angela. 1981. *Women, Race, and Class*. New York: Random House.

Davis, Martha F. 1983. "The Marital Home: Equal or Equitable Distribution?" *The University of Chicago Law Review* 50 (Summer): 1089–1115.

Dawson, Debra L.A. 1988. "Ethnic Differences in Female Overweight: Data from the 1985 National Health Interview Study." *American Journal of Public Health* 78:1326–29.

Dayhoff, Signe. 1983. "Sexist Language and Person Perception: Evaluation of Candidates from Newspaper Articles." *Sex Roles* 9 (April): 527–40.

Deaux, Kay. 1976. *The Behavior of Women and Men*. Monterey, Calif.: Brooks/Cole.

Deaux, Kay, and Joseph C. Ullman. 1983. *Women of Steel: Female Blue-Collar Workers in the Basic Steel Industry*. New York: Praeger.

De Beauvoir, Simone. 1952. *The Second Sex*. New York: Knopf.

Deckard, Barbara Sinclair. 1979. *The Women's Movement: Political, Socioeconomic, and Psychological Issues*. New York: Harper & Row.

Decter, Midge. 1973. *The New Chastity and Other Arguments against Women's Liberation*. New York: Coward, McCann, and Geoghegan.

Degler, Carl N. 1980. *At Odds: Women and the Family in America from the Revolution to the Present*. New York: Oxford University Press.

Delaney, Janice, Mary Jane Lupton, and Emily Toth, eds. 1988. *The Curse: A Cultural History of Menstruation*. Urbana: University of Illinois.

DeLoache, Judy S., Deborah J. Cassidy, and C. Jan Carpenter. 1987. "The Three Bears Are All Boys: Mothers' Gender Labelling of Neutral Picture Book Characters." *Sex Roles* 17:163–78.

de Monteflores, Carmen, and Stephen J. Schultz. 1978. "Coming Out: Similarities and Differences for Lesbians and Gay Men." *Journal of Social Issues* 34 (Summer): 59–72.

de Pauw, Linda Grant. 1975. *Founding Mothers: Women of America in the Revolutionary Era*. Boston: Houghton Mifflin.

Depner, Charlene, and Berit Ingersoll. 1982. "Employment Status and Social Support: The Experience of Mature Women." In *Women's Retirement: Policy Implications of Recent Research,* edited by Maximiliane Szinovacz, 77–91. Beverly Hills: Sage.

Deutsch, Francine M., Dorothy LeBaron, and Maury March Fryer. 1987. "What's in a Smile?" *Psychology of Women Quarterly* 11:341–52.

Deutsch, Sarah. 1987. "Women and Intercultural Relations: The Case of Hispanic New Mexico and Colorado." *Signs* 12 (Summer): 719–39.

Diamond, Irene, and Lee Quinby, ed. 1988. *Feminism and Foucault: Reflections on Resistance*. Boston: Northeastern.

Dibble, Ursula, and Murray Straus. 1980. "Some Social Structure Determinants of Inconsistency Between Attitudes and Behavior: The Case of Family Violence." *Journal of Marriage and the Family* 42 (February): 71–82.

Dill, Bonnie Thornton. 1979. "The Dialectics of Black Womanhood." *Signs* 4 (Spring): 543–55.

Diner, Hasia R. 1983. *Erin's Daughters in America: Irish Immigrant Women in the Nineteenth Century.* Baltimore: John Hopkins University Press.

Doering, Charles H., H.K.H. Brodie, H. Kramer, H. Becker, and D.A. Hamburg. 1974. "Plasma Testosterone Levels and Psychologic Measures in Men Over a Two Month Period." In *Sex Differences in Behavior,* edited by R. Friedman, R. Richart, and R. Vande Wiele, 413–31. New York: Wiley.

Donahue, Thomas J., and James W. Costar. 1977. "Counselor Discrimination against Young Women in Career Selection." *Journal of Counseling Psychology* 24 (November): 481–86.

Douglas, Ann. 1977. *The Feminization of American Culture.* New York: Alfred Knopf.

Downing, Mildred. 1974. "Heroine of the Daytime Serial." *Journal of Communication* 24 (Spring): 130–32.

DuBois, Ellen Carol. 1978. *Feminism and Suffrage: The Emergence of an Independent Women's Movement in America, 1848–69.* Ithaca, N.Y.: Cornell University Press.

Durio, Helen F., and Cheryl A. Kildow. 1980. "The Nonretention of Capable Engineering Students." *Research in Higher Education* 13:61–71.

Dweck, Carol S., William Davidson, Sharon Nelson, and Bradley Enna. 1978. "Sex Differences in Learned Helplessness." *Developmental Psychology* 14 (May): 268–76.

Dworkin, Andrea. 1983. *Right Wing Women.* New York: G.P. Putnam's Sons.

Dwyer, Carol A. 1974. "Influence of Children's Sex Role Standards on Reading and Arithmetic Achievement." *Journal of Educational Psychology* 66:811–16.

Dwyer, Johanna, and Jean Myer. 1968. "Psychological Effects of Variations in Physical Appearance during Adolescence." *Adolescence* 3 (Winter): 353–80.

Eagly, Alice H., and L.L. Carli. 1981. "Sex of Researchers and Sex-Typed Communications as Determinants of Sex Differences in Influenceability: a Meta-Analysis of Social Influence Studies." *Psychological Bulletin* 90:1–20.

Eakins, Barbara Westbrook, and R. Gene Eakins. 1978. *Sex Differences in Human Communication.* Boston: Houghton Mifflin.

Eaton, W.O., and L.R. Enns. 1986. "Sex Differences in Human Motor Activity." *Psychological Bulletin* 100:19–28.

Ebaugh, Helen, Rose Fuchs, and C. Allen Haney. 1980. "Shifts in Abortion Attitudes, 1972–78." *Journal of Marriage and the Family* 42 (August): 491–500.

Editors of *Quest,* eds. 1981. *Building Feminist Theory: Essays from Quest.* New York: Longman.

Ehrenreich, Barbara, and Dierdre English. 1979. *For Her Own Good: One Hundred Fifty Years of the Experts' Advice to Women.* Garden City, N.Y.: Doubleday.

Eichler, Margrit. 1980. *The Double Standard: A Feminist Critique of Feminist Social Science.* New York: St. Martin's.

———. 1988. *Nonsexist Research Methods: A Practical Guide.* Boston: Allen & Unwin.

Eisenberg, N., and R. Lennon. 1983. "Sex Differences in Empathy and Related Capacities." *Psychological Bulletin* 94:100–31.

Eisenstein, Hester, and Alice Jardine, eds. 1985. *The Future of Difference*. New Brunswick: Rutgers University Press.

Eisenstein, Zillah. 1981. *The Radical Future of Liberal Feminism*. New York: Longman.

Elder, Ruth Gale, Winnefred Humphreys, and Cheryl Laskowski. 1988. "Sexism in Gynecology Textbooks: Gender Stereotypes and Paternalism, 1978–1983." *Health Care for Women International* 9:1–17.

Engels, Friedrich. ([1884] 1972). *The Origin of the Family, Private Property, and the State*. New York: Pathfinder.

English, Jane. 1982. "Sex Equity in Sports." In *"Femininity," "Masculinity," and "Androgyny": A Modern Philosophical Discussion*, edited by Mary Vetterling-Braggin, 259–67. Totowa, N.J.: Littlefield, Adams.

Enloe, Cynthia. 1983. *Does Khaki Become You? The Militarization of Women's Lives*. Boston: South End.

Estler, Suzanne. 1975. "Women as Leaders in Public Education." *Signs* 1 (Winter): 363–85.

Etaugh, Claire, and Ethel Foresman. 1983. "Evaluations of Competence as a Function of Sex and Marital Status." *Sex Roles* 9 (July): 759–65.

Evans, Sara. 1979. *Personal Politics: The Roots of Women's Liberation in the Civil Rights Movement and the New Left*. New York: Vintage.

Evans, Sara M., and Barbara J. Nelson. 1989. *Wage Justice: Comparable Worth and the Paradox of Technocratic Reform*. Chicago: University of Chicago Press.

Ewen, Elizabeth. 1980. "City Lights: Immigrant Women and the Rise of Movies." *Signs* 5 (Spring): 45–66.

Ewen, Stuart. 1976. *Captains of Consciousness: Advertising and the Social Roots of Consumer Culture*. New York: McGraw Hill.

Falbo, Toni. 1977. "Relationship between Sex, Sex Role, and Social Influence." *Psychology of Women Quarterly* 2 (Fall) 62–72.

Falbo, Toni, Michael D. Hazen, and Diane Linimon. 1982. "The Costs of Selecting Power Bases or Messages Associated with the Opposite Sex." *Sex Roles* 9 (Fall): 147–57.

Feldberg, Roslyn K., and Evelyn Nakano Glenn. 1979. "Male and Female: Job versus Gender Models in the Sociology of Work." *Social Problems* 26 (June): 524–38.

Feldman, Harold. 1981. "A Comparison of Intentional Parents and Intentionally Childless Couples." *Journal of Marriage and the Family* 43 (August): 593–600.

Feldstein, Jerome H., and Sandra Feldstein. 1982. "Sex Differences in Televised Toy Commercials." *Sex Roles* 8 (June): 581–88.

Feree, Myra Marx. 1980. "Working Class Feminism: A Consideration of the Consequences of Employment." *Sociological Quarterly* 21 (Spring): 173–84.

———. 1983. "The Women's Movement in the Working Class." *Sex Roles* 9 (April): 493–505.

Ferrante, Carol L., Andrew M. Haynes, and Sarah M. Kingsley. 1988. "Images of Women in Television Advertising." *Journal of Broadcasting and Electronic Media* 32:231–37.

Field, Martha A., 1988. *Surrogate Motherhood*. Cambridge, Mass.: Harvard University Press.

Finlay, Barbara Agresti. 1981. "Sex Differences in Correlates of Abortion Attitudes among College Students." *Journal of Marriage and the Family*. 43 (August): 571–82.

Fisher, William A. 1983. "Gender, Gender Role Identification, and Response to Erotica." In *Changing Boundaries: Gender Roles and Sexual Behavior,* edited by Elizabeth Rice Allgeier and Naomi B. McCormick, 261–84. Palo Alto, Calif.: Mayfield.

Flax, Jane. 1987. "Postmodernism and Gender Relations in Feminist Theory." *Signs* 12 (Summer): 621–43.

Flexner, Eleanor. 1975. *Century of Struggle: The Women's Rights Movement in the United States.* Cambridge, Mass.: Harvard University Press.

Foner, Philip S. 1982. *Women and the American Labor Movement: From the First Trade Unions to the Present.* New York: Free Press.

Ford, M.R., and C.R. Lowery. 1986. "Gender Differences in Moral Reasoning: A Comparison of the Justice and Care Orientations." *Journal of Personality and Social Psychology* 50:777–83.

Foreit, Karen G., et al. 1980. "Sex Bias in the Newspaper Treatment of Male-Centered and Female-Centered News Stories." *Sex Roles* 6 (June): 475–80.

Forrest, Jacqueline Darroch, and Richard R. Fordyce. 1988. "U.S. Women's Contraceptive Attitudes and Practice: How Have They Changed in the 1980s?" *Family Planning Perspectives* 20:112–18.

Foster, Martha A., Barbara Strudlar Wallston, and Michael Berger. 1980. "Feminist Orientation and Job Seeking Behavior among Dual Career Couples." *Sex Roles* 6 (February): 59–65.

Fox, Mary Frank. 1989. "Women and Higher Education: Gender Differentials in the Status of Students and Scholars." In *Women: A Feminist Perspective,* edited by Jo Freeman, 217–35. Mountain View, Calif.: Mayfield.

Fox, Mary Frank, and Sharlene Hesse-Biber. 1984. *Women at Work.* Palo Alto, Calif.: Mayfield.

Frable, Deborah E.S., and Sandra Lipsitz Bem. 1985. "If You Are Gender Schematic, All Members of the Opposite Sex Look Alike." *Journal of Personality and Social Psychology* 49 (August): 459–68.

Frank, Dana. 1985. "Housewives, Socialists, and the Politics of Food: The 1917 New York Cost-of-Living Protests." *Feminist Studies* 11 (Summer): 255–86.

Franzwa, Helen. 1978. "The Image of Woman in Television: An Annotated Bibliography." In *Hearth and Home: Images of Women in the Mass Media,* edited by Gaye Tuchman, Arlene Kaplan Daniels, and James Benet, 274–99. New York: Oxford University Press.

Fraser, Arvonne S. 1983. "Insiders and Outsiders." in *Women in Washington: Advocates for Public Policy,* edited by Irene Tinker, 120–39. Beverly Hills, Calif.: Sage.

Fraser, Nancy. 1987. "Women, Welfare, and the Politics of Need." *Thesis Eleven* 17: 88–106.

Fratto, Toni Flores. 1976–77. "Samplers: One of the Lesser American Arts." *Feminist Art Journal* 5 (Winter): 11–15.

Freedman, Estelle. 1979. "Separatism as Strategy: Female Institution Building and American Feminism, 1870–1930." *Feminist Studies* 5 (Fall): 512–29.

Freeman, Jo. 1975. *The Politics of Women's Liberation.* New York: Longman.

Freud, Sigmund. [1930] 1961. *Civilization and Its Discontents.* New York: Norton.

———. [1933] 1965. "Femininity." In Sigmund Freud, *New Introductory Lectures in Psychoanalysis,* 112–35. New York: Norton.

Friday, Nancy. 1977. *My Mother/Myself.* New York: Delacorte.

Friedan, Betty. 1963. *The Feminine Mystique.* New York: Dell.

Fritz, Kathlyn Ann, and Natalie Kaufman Hevener. 1979. "An Unsuitable Job for a Woman: Female Protagonists in the Detective Novel." *International Journal of Women's Studies* 2 (March-April): 105–29.

Frost, J. William. 1973. *The Quaker Family in Colonial America.* New York: St. Martins.

Fulenwider, Claire. 1980. *Feminism in American Politics: A Study of Ideological Influence.* New York: Praeger.

Fuller, Margaret. [1845] 1971. *Women in the Nineteenth Century.* New York: Norton. Also excerpted in Rossi, 1988.

Gabin, Nancy. 1982. "They Have Placed a Penalty on Womanhood: The Protest Actions of Women Auto Workers in Detroit Area UAW Locals, 1945–47." *Feminist Studies* 8 (Summer): 373–98.

Gage, Matilda Joslyn. [1900] 1972. *Women, Church, and State: A Historical Account of the Status of Women through the Christian Ages, with Reminiscences of the Matriarchate.* New York: Arno Press.

Gallagher, Janet. 1985. "Fetal Personhood and Women's Policy." In *Women, Biology, and Public Policy* edited by Virginia Sapiro, 91–116. Beverly Hills, Calif.: Sage.

Gallion, Jane. 1970. *The Woman as Nigger.* Canoga Park, Calif.: Weiss, Day, and Lord.

Gallop, Jane. 1982. *The Daughter's Seduction: Feminism and Psychoanalysis.* Ithaca: Cornell University Press.

Garfinkle, Ellen M., and Stephen F. Morin. 1978. "Psychologists' Attitudes toward Homosexual Psychotherapy Clients." *Journal of Social Issues* 34 (Summer): 101–12.

Gelb, Joyce, and Marian Palley. 1987. *Women and Public Policies.* Princeton: Princeton University Press.

Geller, Laura. 1983. "Reactions to a Woman Rabbi." In *On Being a Jewish Feminist,* edited by Susannah Heschel, 210–13. New York: Schocken.

Gelles, Richard J. 1980. "Violence in the Family: A Review of Research in the 1970's." *Journal of Marriage and the Family* 42 (November): 873–76.

Gerbner, George. 1978. "The Dynamics of Cultural Resistance." In *Hearth and Home: Images of Women in the Mass Media,* edited by Gaye Tuchman, Arlene Kaplan Daniels, and James Benet, 46–50. New York: Oxford University Press.

Gerdes, Eugenia Proctor, and Douglas M. Garber. 1983. "Sex Bias in Hiring: Effects of Job Demands and Applicant Competence." *Sex Roles* (March): 307–19.

Gersh, Eileen S., and Isadore Gersh. 1981. *The Biology of Women.* London: University Parl Press.

Gerson, Kathleen. 1985. *Hard Choices: How Women Decide about Work, Career, and Motherhood.* Berkeley: University of California Press.

Gertzog, Irwin, and Michele Simard. 1980. "Women and 'Hopeless' Congressional Candidates: Nomination Frequency 1916–78." *American Politics Quarterly* 9 (October): 449–66.

Giddings, Paula. 1984. *When and Where I Enter: The Impact of Black Women on Race and Sex in America.* New York: Bantam.

Giele, Janet Zollinger, and Audrey Roberts Smock, eds. 1977. *Women: Roles and Status in Eight Countries.* New York: Wiley.

Gilder, George. 1973. *Sexual Suicide.* New York: Quadrangle.

Gilligan, Carol. 1982. *In a Different Voice: Psychological Theory and Women's Development.* Cambridge, Mass.: Harvard University Press.

Gilman, Charlotte Perkins. [1898] 1966. *Women and Economics.* New York: Harper & Row.

———. 1911. *The Man-Made World: Our Androcentric Culture.* New York: Charlton.

———. [1915] 1979. *Herland.* New York: Pantheon.

Glenn, Evelyn Nakano, and Roslyn L. Feldberg. 1989. "Clerical Work: The Female Occupation." In *Women: A Feminist Perspective,* edited by Jo Freeman, 287–312. Mountain View, Calif.: Mayfield.

Glenn, Norval D., and Sara McLanahan. 1982. "Children and Marital Happiness: A Further Specification of the Relationship." *Journal of Marriage and the Family* 44 (February): 63–72.

Glick, Peter, Cari Zion, and Cynthia Nelson. 1988. "What Mediates Sex Discrimination in Hiring Decisions?" *Journal of Personality and Social Psychology* 55:178–86.

Goldberg, Philip. 1968. "Are Women Prejudiced Against Women?" *Transaction* 4:28–30.

Goldman, Ronald, and Juliette Goldman. 1982. *Children's Sexual Thinking.* Boston: Routledge & Kegan Paul.

Goldstein, Leslie Friedman. 1988. *The Constitutional Rights of Women: Cases in Law and Social Change.* Madison, Wis.: University of Wisconsin Press.

Gordon, Linda. 1977. *Woman's Body, Woman's Right: A Social History of Birth Control in America.* New York: Viking.

———. 1982. "Why Nineteenth Century Feminists Did Not Support 'Birth Control' and Twentieth Century Feminists Do: Feminism, Reproduction, and the Family." In *Rethinking the Family: Some Feminist Questions,* edited by Barrie Thorne and Marilyn Yalom, 40–53. New York: Longman.

———. 1988a. *Heroes of Their Own Lives: The Politics and History of Family Violence, Boston 1880–1960.* New York: Viking Press.

———. 1988b. "What Does Welfare Regulate?" *Social Research* 55 (Winter): 609–30.

Gordon, Margaret T., and Stephanie Riger. 1989. *The Female Fear.* New York: Free Press.

Gove, Walter R. 1972. "The Relationship between Sex Roles, Marital Status, and Mental Illness." *Social Forces* 51 (September): 34–44.

Granberg, Donald, and Beth Wellman Granberg. 1981. "Pro-Life versus Pro-Choice: Another Look at the Abortion Controversy in the United States." *Sociology and Social Research* 65 (July): 424–33.

Green, Susan K., and Philip Sanders. 1983. "Perceptions of Male and Female Initiators of Relationships." *Sex Roles* 9 (August): 849–52.

Greenberger, Ellen, and Laurence D. Steinberg. 1983. "Sex Differences in Early Labor Force Experience: Harbinger of Things to Come." *Social Forces* 62 (December): 467–86.

Gross, Neal, and Anne Trask. 1976. *The Sex Factor and the Management of Schools.* New York: Wiley.

Gruhl, John, Cassia Spohn, and Susan Welch. 1981. "Women as Policy Makers: The Case of Trial Judges." *American Journal of Political Science* 25 (May): 308–22.

Haavio-Mannila, Elina, et al., eds. 1985. *Unfinished Democracy: Women in Nordic Politics.* New York: Pergamon.

Hacker, Sally L. 1979. "Sex Stratification, Technology, and Organizational Change: A Longitudinal Case Study of AT&T." *Social Problems* 26 (June): 539–57.

Hafkin, Nancy J., and Edna G. Bay, eds. 1976. *Women in Africa: Studies in Social and Economic Change*. Stanford, Calif.: Stanford University Press.

Hagler, D. Harland. 1980. "The Ideal Woman in the Antebellum South: Lady or Farmwife?" *Journal of Southern History* 46 (August): 405–18.

Hall, Elaine J. 1988. "One Week for Women? The Structure of Inclusion of Gender Issues in Introductory Textbooks." *Teaching Sociology* 16:431–42.

Hall, Jacqueline Dowd. 1989. "Partial Truths." *Signs* 14 (Summer): 902–11.

Hall, Judith A. 1978. "Gender Differences in Decoding Nonverbal Cues in Conversation." *Psychological Bulletin* 85 (July): 845–57.

Halperin, Marcia S., and Doris L. Abrams. 1978. "Sex Differences in Predicting Final Examination Grades: The Influence of Past Performance, Attributions, and Achievement Motivation." *Journal of Educational Psychology* 70 (October): 763–71.

Hammond, Judith A., and Constance W. Mahoney. 1983. "Reward-Cost Balancing among Women Coalminers." *Sex Roles* 9 (January): 17–29.

Hare-Mustin, Rachel T., Sheila Kaiser Bennett, and Patricia C. Broderick. 1983. "Attitudes Toward Motherhood: Gender, Generational and Religious Comparisons." *Sex Roles* 9 (May): 643–61.

Harley, Sharon, and Rosalyn Terborg-Penn, eds. 1978. *The Afro-American Woman: Struggles and Images*. Port Washington, N.Y.: Kennikat.

Harrison, James. 1978. "Warning: The Male Sex Role May Be Dangerous to Your Health." *Journal of Social Issues* 34 (Winter): 65–86.

Hartmann, Heidi, ed. 1985. *Comparable Worth: New Directions for Research*. Washington, D.C.: National Academy Press.

Hartmann, Susan M. 1983. *The Home Front and Beyond: American Women in the 1940's*. Boston: Twayne.

Hartz, Louis. 1955. *The Liberal Tradition in America*. New York: Harcourt, Brace, and World.

Harvey, S. Marie, and Susan C.M. Scrimshaw. 1988. "Coitus-Dependent Contraceptives: Factors Associated with Effective Use." *Journal of Sex Research* 25:364–78.

Hatfield, Elaine. 1983. "What Do Women and Men Want from Love and Sex?" In *Changing Boundaries: Gender Roles and Sexual Behavior*, edited by Elizabeth Rice Allgeier and Naomi B. McCormick, 106–34. Palo Alto, Calif.: Mayfield.

Havens, Beverly, and Ingrid Swenson. 1988. "Imagery Associated with Menstruation in Advertising Targeted to Adolescent Women." *Adolescence* 23:89–97.

Hayes, Kathryn E., and Patricia L. Wolleat. 1978. "Effect of Sex in Judgments of a Simulated Counseling Interview." *Journal of Counseling Psychology* 25 (March): 164–68.

Hayghe, Howard. 1983. "Married Couples: Work and Income Patterns." *Monthly Labor Review* 106 (December): 26–34.

Hedges, Elaine. 1980. "Quilts and Women's Culture." In *In Her Own Image: Women Working in the Arts*, edited by Elaine Hedges and Ingrid Wendt, 13–19. New York: McGraw-Hill.

Hedges, Elaine, and Ingrid Wendt, eds. 1980. *In Her Own Image: Women Working in the Arts*. New York: McGraw-Hill.

Henley, Nancy M. 1977. *Body Politics: Power, Sex, and Nonverbal Communication*. Englewood Cliffs, N.J.: Prentice-Hall.

Heschel, Susannah, ed. 1983. *On Being a Jewish Feminist*. New York: Schocken.

Hesse, Sharlene. 1979. "Women Working: Historical Trends." In *Working Women and Families,* edited by Karen Wolk Feinstein, 35–62. Beverly Hills: Sage.

Higgonet, Margaret Randolph, et al., eds. 1987. *Behind the Lines: Gender and the Two World Wars.* New Haven: Yale.

Hill, Charles T., Zick Rubin, and Letitia Anne Peplau. 1976. "Breakups before Marriage: The End of One Hundred Three Affairs." *Journal of Social Issues* 32 (Winter): 147–68.

Hine, Darlene Clark. 1989. "Rape and the Inner Lives of Black Women in the Middle West: Preliminary Thoughts on the Culture of Dissemblance." *Signs* 14 (Summer): 912–20.

Hite, Shere. 1976. *The Hite Report: A Nationwide Study of Female Sexuality.* New York: Macmillan.

———. 1981. *The Hite Report on Male Sexuality.* New York: Alfred Knopf.

Hoeffer, Beverly. 1981. "Children's Acquisition of Sex-Role Behavior in Lesbian-Mother Families." *American Journal of Orthopsychiatry* 51 (July): 536–44.

Hole, Judith, and Ellen Levine. 1971. *Rebirth of Feminism.* New York: Quadrangle.

Holmes, Douglas S., and Bruce Jorgensen. 1971. "Do Personality and Social Psychologists Study Men More Than Women?" *Representative Research in Social Psychology* 2 (January): 71–76.

Holsti, Ole, and James N. Rosenau. 1981. "The Foreign Policy Beliefs of Women in Leadership Positions." *Journal of Politics* 43 (May): 326–47.

Honey, Maureen. 1984. *Creating Rosie the Riveter: Class, Gender, and Propaganda during World War II.* Boston: Northeastern University Press.

Hooks, Bell. 1981. *Ain't I a Woman: Black Women and Feminism.* Boston: South End Press.

———. 1984. *Feminist Theory: From Margin to Center.* Boston: South End.

———. 1989. *Talking Back: Thinking Feminist, Thinking Black.* Boston: South End.

Horgan, Dianne. 1983. "The Pregnant Woman's Place and Where to Find It." *Sex Roles* 9 (March): 333–39.

Hornbrook, Marc C., and Marsha G. Goldfarb. 1981. "Patterns of Obstetrical Care in Hospitals." *Medical Care* 19 (January): 55–67.

Horney, Karen. 1967. *Feminine Psychology.* New York: Norton.

Hornung, Carlton A., Claire McCullough, and Taichi Sugimoto. 1981. "Status Relationships in Marriage: Risk Factors in Spouse Abuse." *Journal of Marriage and the Family* 42 (February): 71–82.

Hoskin, Fran P. 1980. "Women and Health: Genital and Sexual Mutilation." *International Journal of Women's Studies* 3 (May–June): 300–316.

Howe, Lucy Kapp. 1978. *Pink Collar Workers.* New York: Avon.

Huber, Joan, and Glenna Spitze. 1981. "Wives' Employment, Household Behaviors and Sex-Role Attitudes." *Social Forces* 60 (September): 150–69.

Hurtado, Aida. 1989. "Relating to Privilege: Seduction and Rejection in the Subordination of White Women and Women of Color." *Signs* 14 (Summer): 833–55.

Hyde, Janet Shibley. 1984. "How Large Are Gender Differences in Aggression? A Developmental Meta-Analysis." *Development Psychology* 20:722–36.

———. 1986. *Understanding Human Sexuality.* New York: McGraw-Hill.

Hyde, Janet Shibley, Elizabeth Fennema, and Susan J. Lamon. 1990. "Gender Differences in Mathematic Performance: A Meta-Analysis." *Psychological Bulletin* 106 (forthcoming).

Instone, Debra, Brenda Major, and Barbara A. Bunker. 1983. "Gender, Self Confidence, and Social Influence Strategies: An Organizational Simulation." *Journal of Personality and Social Psychology* 44 (February): 322–33.

Irvine, Jacqueline Jordan. 1986. "Teacher-Student Interactions: Effects of Student Race, Sex, and Grade Level." *Journal of Educational Psychology* 78 (February): 14–21.

Jacobson, Marsha B. 1979. "A Rose by Any Other Name: Attitudes toward Feminism as a Function of Its Label." *Sex Roles* 5 (June): 365–71.

Jaggar, Alison M. 1983. *Feminist Politics and Human Nature.* Totowa, N.J.: Littlefield, Adams.

Jaquette, Jane S., and Kathleen A. Staudt. 1985. "Women as 'At Risk' Reproducers: Biology, Science, and Population in U.S. Foreign Policy." In *Women, Biology, and Public Policy,* edited by Virginia Sapiro, 235–68. Beverly Hills, Calif.: Sage.

Jaskoski, Helen. 1981. "'My Heart Will Go Out': Healing Songs of Native American Women." *International Journal of Women's Studies* 4 (March–April): 118–34.

Jeffrey, Julie Roy. 1979. *Frontier Women: The Trans-Mississippi West, 1840-1880.* New York: Hill & Wang.

Jenkins, J. Craig. 1981. "Sociopolitical Movements." In *The Handbook of Political Behavior,* edited by Samuel L. Long, 81–153. New York: Plenum.

Jennings, M. Kent. 1979. "Another Look at the Life Cycle and Political Participation." *American Journal of Political Science* 23 (November): 755–71.

Jennings, M. Kent, and Barbara G. Farah. 1981. "Social Roles and Political Resources: An Over-Time Study of Men and Women in Party Elites." *American Journal of Political Science* 25 (August): 462–82.

Jensen, Inger W., and Barbara A. Gutek. 1982. "Attributions and Assignment of Responsibility in Sexual Harassment." *Journal of Social Issues* 38 (Winter): 121–36.

Jepson, Barbara. 1975–76. "American Women in Conducting." *Femininst Art Journal* 4 (Winter): 13–18.

Johnson, Beverly L., and Elizabeth Waldman. 1983. "Most Women Who Maintain Families Receive Poor Labor Market Returns." *Monthly Labor Review* 106 (December): 30–34.

Johnson, C.L., and F.A. Johnson. 1977. "Attitudes toward Parenting in Dual Career Families." *American Journal of Orthopsychiatry* 51 (July): 536–44.

Johnson, Miriam M. 1982. "Fathers and 'Femininity' in Daughters: A Review of the Research." *Sociology and Social Research* 67 (October): 1–17.

Johnson, Paula. 1976. "Women and Power: Toward a Theory of Effectiveness." *Journal of Social Issues* 32 (Summer): 99–110.

Jones, Jacqueline. 1980. "Women Who Were More Than Men: Sex and Status in Freedman's Teaching." *History of Education Quarterly* 19 (Spring): 47–60.

———. 1985. *Labor of Love, Labor of Sorrow: Black Women, Work, and the Family from Slavery to the Present.* New York: Basic.

Jones, Warren H., Mary Ellen Chernovetz, and Robert O. Hansson. 1978. "The Enigma of Androgyny: Differential Implications for Males and Females?" *Journal of Consulting and Clinical Psychology* 46 (April): 298–313.

Jones, W.T. 1963. *Masters of Political Thought.* Vol. 3. London: George Harrap.

Joseph, Gloria, and Jill Lewis. 1981. *Common Differences: Conflicts in Black and White Feminist Perspectives.* Garden City, N.Y.: Doubleday.

Kaledin, Eugenia. 1984. *Mothers and More: American Women in the 1950's*. Boston: Twayne.

Kalmuss, Debra S., and Murray A. Strauss. 1982. "Wife's Marital Dependency and Wife Abuse." *Journal of Marriage and the Family* 44 (May): 277–86.

Kanin, E.G., K.D. Davidson, and S.R. Scheck. 1970. "A Research Note on Male/Female Differentials in the Experience of Heterosexual Love." *Journal of Sex Research* 6:64–72.

Kay, Herma Hill. 1988. *Sex Based Discrimination*. St. Paul, Minn.: West.

Keith, Pat M. 1982. "Working Women versus Homemakers: Retirement Resources and Correlates of Well Being." In *Women's Retirement: Policy Implications of Recent Research*, edited by Maximiliane Szinovacz, 77–91. Beverly Hills, Calif.: Sage.

Kellerman, Jonathan. 1974. "Sex Role Stereotypes and Attitudes toward Parental Blame for the Psychological Problems of Children." *Journal of Consulting and Clinical Psychology* 42: 153–54.

Kellerman, Jonathan, and Ernest R. Katz. 1978. "Attitudes toward the Division of Child-Rearing Responsibility." *Sex Roles* 4:505–12.

Kerber, Linda K. 1982. "The Daughters of Columbia: Educating Women for the Republic, 1787–1805." In *Women's America*, edited by Linda K. Kerber and Jane De Hart Mathews, 82–94. New York: Oxford University Press.

———. 1986. *Women of the Republic: Intellect and Ideology in Revolutionary America*. New York: WW Norton.

Kerber, Linda K., and Jane De Hart Mathews. 1982. *Women's America: Refocusing the Past*. New York: Oxford University Press.

Kerber, Linda K., et al. 1986. "On *In a Different Voice:* An Interdisciplinary Forum." *Signs* 11 (Winter): 304–33.

Kessler-Harris, Alice. 1982. *Out to Work: A History of Wage-Earning Women in the United States*. New York: Oxford.

Key, Mary Ritchie. 1975. *Male/Female Language*. Metuchen, N.J.: Scarecrow Press.

Kinsey, Alfred C., Wardell B. Pomeroy, and Clyde E. Martin. 1948. *Sexual Behavior in the Human Male*. Philadelphia: W.B. Saunders.

Kinsey, Alfred C., Wardell B. Pomeroy, Clyde E. Martin, and Paul A. Gebhart. 1953. *Sexual Behavior in the Human Female*. Philadelphia: W.B. Saunders.

Kirkpatrick, Martha, Catherine Smith, and Ron Roy. 1981. "Lesbian Mothers and Their Children: A Comparative Study." *American Journal of Orthopsychiatry* 51 (July): 545–51.

Klein, Dori. 1982. "The Dark Side of Marriage: Battered Wives and the Domination of Women." In *Judge, Lawyer, Victim, Thief: Women, Gender Roles, and Criminal Justice.* edited by Nicole Hahn Rafter and Elizabeth Anne Stanko, 83–110. Boston: Northeastern University Press.

Klein, Ethel. 1984. *Gender Politics*. Cambridge: Harvard University Press.

Koehler, Lyle. 1982. "The Case of the American Jezebels: Anne Hutchinson and Female Agitation During the Years of Antinomian Turmoil, 1636–40." In *Women's America*, edited by Linda K. Kerber and Jane De Hart Mathews, 36–51. New York: Oxford University Press.

Kohlberg, Lawrence. 1966. "A Cognitive-Development Analysis of Children's Sex Role Concepts and Attitudes." In *The Development of Sex Differences*, edited by Eleanor Maccoby, 82–173. Stanford, Calif.: Stanford University Press.

Komarovsky, Mirra. 1967. *Blue Collar Marriage*. New York: Vintage.

———. 1976. *Dilemmas of Masculinity: A Study of College Youth.* New York: Norton.

Kraditor, Aileen S. 1965. *The Ideas of the Woman Suffrage Movement, 1890–1920.* New York: Columbia.

Kraditor, Aileen, ed. 1968. *Up from the Pedestal: Selected Writings in the History of Feminism.* New York: Quadrangle.

Krauskopf, Joan M. 1977. "Partnership Marriage: Legal Reforms Needed." In *Women into Wives,* edited by Joan Roberts Chapman and Margaret Gates, 93–122. Beverly Hills, Calif.: Sage.

Kravetz, Diane, and Linda E. Jones. 1981. "Androgyny as a Standard of Mental Health." *American Journal of Orthopsychiatry* 51 (July): 502–509.

Kroeger, Naomi. 1982. "Preretirement Preparation: Sex Differences in Access, Sources, and Use." In *Women's Retirement: Policy Implications of Recent Research,* edited by Maximiliane Szinovacz, 95–112. Beverly Hills, Calif.: Sage.

Ladner, Joyce. 1971. *Tomorrow's Tomorrow.* Garden City, N.Y.: Doubleday.

Lakoff, Robin. 1975. *Language and Women's Place.* New York: Harper & Row.

Lamke, Leanne K. 1982. "The Impact of Sex Role Orientations of Self-Esteem in Early Adolescence." *Child Development* 53 (December): 1530–35.

Lander, Louise. 1988. *Images of Bleeding: Menstruation as Ideology.* New York: Orlando Press.

Lasch, Christopher. 1977. *Haven in a Heartless World: The Family Besieged.* New York: Basic.

Leach, William. 1980. *True Love and Perfect Union: The Feminist Reform of Sex and Society.* New York: Basic.

Leavitt, Judith Walzer. 1980. "Birthing and Anesthesia: The Debate Over Twilight Sleep." *Signs* 6 (Autumn): 147–64. Also in Leavitt, 1984.

———. 1983. "'Science' Enters the Birthing Room: Obstetrics in America Since the Eighteenth Century." *Journal of American History* 70 (September): 281–304.

———. 1986. *Brought to Bed: Childbearing in America, 1750–1950.* New York: Oxford.

Leavitt, Judith Walzer, ed. 1984. *Women and Health in America: Historical Readings.* Madison: University of Wisconsin Press.

Leavitt, Judith Walzer, and Whitney Walton. 1982. "Down to Death's Door: Women's Perceptions of Childbirth in America." In *Proceedings of the Second Motherhood Symposium: Childbirth: The Beginning of Motherhood,* edited by Sophie Colleau, 113–36. Madison, Wis.: Women's Studies Program. Also in Leavitt 1984.

Lee, Marcia Manning. 1977. "Towards Understanding Why Few Women Hold Political Office." In *A Portrait of Marginality,* edited by Marianne Githens and Jewel Prestage, 118–38. New York: Longman.

Leinhardt, Gaea, Andrea Mar Seewald, and Mary Engel. 1979. "Learning What's Taught: Sex Differences in Instruction." *Journal of Educational Psychology* 71 (August): 432–39.

Lemon, Judith. 1978. "Dominant or Dominated? Women in Prime-Time Television." In *Hearth and Home: Images of Women in the Mass Media,* edited by Gaye Tuchman, Arlene Kaplan Daniels, and James Benet, 51–68. New York: Oxford University Press.

Lemons, Stanley. 1972. *The Woman Citizen: Social Feminism in the 1920's.* Urbana: University of Illinois Press.

Lerner, Gerda. 1971. *The Grimké Sisters from South Carolina: Pioneers for Women's Rights and Abolition.* New York: Schocken.

Lerner, Gerda, ed. 1973. *Black Women in White America.* New York: Vintage.

Levine, Martine P., and Robin Leonard. 1984. "Discrimination against Lesbians in the Workforce." *Signs* 9 (Summer): 700–10.

Levinson, Richard M. 1975. "Sex Discrimination and Employment Practices: An Experiment with Unconventional Job Inquiries." *Social Problems* 22:533–43.

Levitt, Eugene E., and Albert D. Klassen. 1974. "Public Attitudes toward Homosexuality." *Journal of Homosexuality* 1:29–47.

Levy, A.H. 1983. "Double-Bars and Double Standards: Women Composers in America, 1880–1920." *International Journal of Women's Studies* 6 (March–April): 162–745.

Lewis, Robert A. 1978. "Emotional Intimacy Among Men." *Journal of Social Issues* 34 (Winter): 108–21.

Lifton, P.D. 1985. "Individual Differences in Moral Development: The Relation of Sex, Gender, and Personality to Morality." *Journal of Personality* 53:306–34.

Linn, M.C., and A.C. Peterson. 1985. "Emergence and Characterization of Gender Differences in Spatial Ability: A Meta-analysis." *Child Development* 56:1479–98.

Linz, Daniel G., Edward Donnerstein, and Steven Penrod. 1988. "Effects of Long-Term Exposure to Violent and Sexually Degrading Depictions of Women." *Journal of Personality and Social Psychology* 55 (November): 758–68.

Lips, Hilary M. 1981. *Women, Men, and the Psychology of Power.* Englewood Cliffs, N.J.: Prentice-Hall.

———. 1988. *Sex and Gender: An Introduction.* Mountain View, Calif.: Mayfield.

Livingston, Joy A. 1982. "Responses to Sexual Harassment on the Job: Legal, Organizational, and Individual Actions." *Journal of Social Issues* 38 (Winter): 5–22.

Locksley, Anne. 1982. "Social Class and Marital Attitudes and Behavior." *Journal of Marriage and the Family* 44 (May): 427–40.

Lopata, Helena Z. 1971. *Occupation: Housewife.* New York: Oxford University Press.

Lorde, Audre. 1984. "Man Child." In Lorde, *Sister Outsider.* Trumansburg: Crossing Press.

Lott, Dale F., and Robert Sommer. 1967. "Seating Arrangements and Status." *Journal of Personality and Social Psychology* 7:90–95.

Lull, James, Catherine A. Hanson, and Michael J. Marx. 1977. "College Students' Recognition of Female Stereotypes in Television Commercials." *Journalism Quarterly* 54 (Spring): 153–57.

Lull, James, Anthony Mulack, and Shelly Lisa Rosen. 1983. "Feminism as a Predictor of Mass Media Use." *Sex Roles* 9 (February): 165–78.

Lynch, Robert N. 1986. "Women in Northern Paiute Politics." *Signs* 11 (Winter): 352–66.

Lynd, Robert S., and Helen Merrell Lynd. 1929. *Middletown: A Study of American Culture.* New York: Harcourt & Brace.

———. 1937. *Middletown in Transition: A Study in Cultural Conflict.* New York: Harcourt & Brace.

Lynn, Naomi. 1979. "American Women and the Political Process." In *Women: A Feminist Perspective,* edited by Jo Freeman, 404–29. Palo Alto, Calif.: Mayfield.

Lyons, Judith A., and Lisa A. Serbin. 1986. "Observer Bias in Scoring Boys' and Girls' Aggression." *Sex Roles* 14 (March): 301–13.

Maccoby, Eleanor, and Carol Jacklin. 1974. *The Psychology of Sex Differences.* Stanford, Calif.: Stanford University Press.

McCormick, Naomi B., and Clinton J. Jesser. 1983. "The Courtship Game: Power in the Sexual Encounter." In *Changing Boundaries: Gender Roles and Sexual Behavior,* edited by Elizabeth Rice Allgeier and Naomi B. McCormick, 64–86. Palo Alto, Calif.: Mayfield.

McCourt, Kathleen. 1977. *Working Class Women and Grassroots Politics.* Bloomington: Indiana University Press.

McDonough, Eileen. 1982. "To Work or Not to Work: The Differential Aspect of Achieved and Derived Status upon the Political Participation of Women, 1956–76." *American Journal of Political Science* 26 (May): 280–97.

McGhee, Paul E., and Terry Frueh. 1980. "Television Viewing and the Learning of Sex Role Stereotypes." *Sex Roles* 6 (April): 179–88.

McGlen, Nancy. 1980. "The Impact of Parenthood on Political Participation." *Western Political Quarterly* 33 (September): 297–313.

McGuinnes, Kate, and Trish Donahue. 1988. "Women in Law Enforcement." In *The American Woman, 1988–89: A Status Report,* edited by Sara E. Rix, 252–57. New York: WW Norton.

Mackie, Marlene. 1983. "The Domestication of Self: Gender Comparisons of Self-Imagery and Self-Esteem." *Social Psychology Quarterly* 45 (December): 343–50.

Mackinnon, Catharine. 1979. *The Sexual Harassment of Working Women.* New Haven: Yale University Press.

Macklin, Eleanor D. 1980. "Nontraditional Family Forms: A Decade of Research." *Journal of Marriage and the Family* 42 (November): 905–22.

Macklin, M. Carole, and Richard G. Kolbe. 1984. "Sex Role Stereotyping in Children's Advertising." *Journal of Advertising* 13:34–42.

McManus, Karen A., Yvonne Brackbill, Lynn Woodward, Paul Doering, and David Robinson. 1982. "Consumer Information about Prenatal and Obstetric Drugs." *Women and Health* 7 (Spring): 15–29.

Major, Brenda. 1981. "Gender Patterns in Touching Behavior." In *Gender and Nonverbal Behavior,* edited by Clara Mayo and Nancy Henley, 15–38. New York: Springer-Verlag.

Malamuth, Neil M. 1981. "Rape Proclivity among Males." *Journal of Social Issues* 37 (Fall): 138–57.

Malos, Ellen, ed. 1980. *The Politics of Housework.* New York: Schocken.

Mamay, Patricia D., and Richard L. Simpson. 1981. "Three Female Roles in Television Commercials." *Sex Roles* 7 (December): 1223–32.

Mandelbaum, Dorothy Rosenthal. 1978. "Women in Medicine." *Signs* 4 (Autumn): 136–45.

Mann, Susan A. 1989. "Slavery, Sharecropping, and Sexual Inequality." *Signs* 14 (Summer): 774–98.

Marks, Elaine, and Isabelle de Courtivron, eds. 1980. *New French Feminisms: An Anthology.* Amherst: University of Massachusetts Press.

Markus, Hazel, et al. 1982. "Self-Schemas and Gender." *Journal of Personality and Social Psychology* 42 (January): 38–50.

Martin, Elaine. 1984. "Power and Authority in the Classroom: Sexist Stereotypes in Teaching Evaluations." *Signs* 9 (Spring): 482–92.

Marx, Karl, and Friedrich Engels. 1947. *The German Ideology.* New York: International.

Marzolf, Marion. 1977. *Up from the Footnote: A History of Women Journalists*. New York: Hastings House.

Matheson, Kimberly, and Connie M. Kristensen. 1987. "The Effect of Sexist Attitudes and Social Structures on the Use of Sex-Biased Pronouns." *Journal of Social Psychology* 127 (August): 395–401.

Matthaei, Julie A. 1982. *An Economic History of Women in America: Women's Work, The Sexual Division of Labor, and the Development of Capitalism*. New York. Schocken.

Mayer, Steven E., and Anita I. Bell. 1975. "Sexism in Ratings of Personality Traits." *Personnel Psychology* 28:239–49.

Mazey, Mary Ellen, and David R. Lee. 1983. *Her Space, Her Place: A Geography of Women*. Washington, D.C.: Association of American Geographers.

Mechanic, David. 1978. *Medical Sociology*. New York: Free Press.

Mellor, Earl F. 1987. "Workers at the Minimum Wage or Less." *Monthly Labor Review* 110 (July): 34–38.

Metz, Robert. 1975. *CBS: Reflections in a Bloodshot Eye*. New York: New American Library.

Milkman, Ruth. 1982. "Redefining 'Women's Work:' The Sexual Division of Labor in the Auto Industry During World War II." *Feminist Studies* 8 (Summer): 337–72.

Miller, Dorothy C. 1983. "AFDC: Mapping a Strategy for Tomorrow." *Social Service Review* 57 (December): 599–613.

Miller, Patrice M., Dorothy L. Danaher, and David Forbes. 1986. "Sex-Related Strategies for Coping with Interpersonal Conflict in Children Aged 5 to 7." *Developmental Psychology* 22 (July): 543–48.

Millett, Kate. 1970. *Sexual Politics*. Garden City, N.Y.: Doubleday.

Milliren, John W. 1977. "Some Contingencies Affecting the Utilization of Tranquilizers in Long-Term Care of the Elderly." *Journal of Health and Social Behavior* 18 (June): 206–11.

Mills, Elizabeth Anne. 1982. "One Hundred Years of Fear: Rape and the Medical Profession." In *Judge, Lawyer, Victim, Thief: Women, Gender Roles, and Criminal Justice*, edited by Nicole Hahn Rafter and Elizabeth Anne Stanko, 29–62. Boston: Northeastern University Press.

Milman, Barbara. 1980. "New Rules for the Oldest Profession: Should We Change Our Prostitution Laws?" *Harvard Women's Law Journal* 3 (Spring): 1–82.

Minh-ha, Trinh T. 1989. *Woman, Native, Other: Writing Postcoloniality and Feminism*. Bloomington: Indiana University Press.

Mirandé, Alfredo, and Evangelina Enríquez. 1979. *La Chicana: The Mexican-American Woman*. Chicago: University of Chicago Press.

Mitchell, Juliet. 1974. *Psychoanalysis and Feminism*. New York: Pantheon.

Moi, Toril. 1985. *Sexual/Textual Politics: Feminist Literary Theory*. New York: Methuen.

Moraga, Cherrie, and Gloria Anzaldúa, eds. 1981. *This Bridge Called My Back: Writings by Radical Women of Color*. Watertown, Mass.: Persephone.

Morgan, Edmund S. [1944] 1978. "The Puritans and Sex." In *The American Family in Historical Perspective*, edited by Michael Gordon, 363–73. New York: St. Martin's.

Morgan, Marabelle. 1975. *The Total Woman*. Old Tappan, N.J.: Revell.

Morin, Stephen F., and Ellen M. Garfinkle. 1978. "Male Homophobia." *Journal of Social Issues* 34 (Winter): 29–47.

Mueller, Carol, and Thomas Dimieri. 1982. "The Structure of Belief Systems among Contending ERA Activists." *Social Forces* 60 (March): 657–75.

Mueller, Claus. 1973. *The Politics of Communication: A Study in the Political Sociology of Language, Socialization, and Legitimation.* New York: Oxford University Press.

Mueller, Marnie W. 1982. "Applying Human Capital Theory to Women's Changing Work Patterns." *Journal of Social Issues* 38 (Spring): 89–96.

Mulac, Anthony, and Torborg Louisa Lundell. 1986. "Linguistic Contributors to the Gender-Linked Language Effect." *Journal of Language and Social Psychology* 5:81–101.

Muller, Charlotte. 1983. "Income Supports for Older Women." *Social Policy* 14 (Fall): 23–31.

Musa, Kathleen E., and Mary Ellen Roach. 1973. "Adolescent Appearance and Self Concept." *Adolescence* 8 (Fall): 385–94.

Nelson, Barbara J. 1984. "Women's Poverty and Women's Citizenship: Some Political Consequences of Economic Marginality." *Signs* 10: 209–31.

Newberry, Phyllis, Myrna Weissman, and Jerome K. Myers. 1979. "Working Wives and Housewives: Do They Differ in Mental Status and Social Adjustment?" *American Journal of Orthopsychiatry* 49 (April): 282–91.

New Jersey Supreme Court Task Force. 1986. "The First Year Report of the New Jersey Supreme Court Task Force on Women in the Courts—June 1984." 1986. *Women's Rights Law Reporter* 9 (Spring), 129–75.

Nichols, Patricia C. 1978. "Black Women in the Rural South: Conservative and Innovative." *International Journal of the Sociology of Language* 17:45–54.

Nickols, Sharon Y., and Karen D. Fox. 1983. "Buying Time and Saving Time: Strategies for Managing Household Production." *Journal of Consumer Research* 10 (September): 197–208.

Nochlin, Linda. 1971. "Why Are There No Great Women Artists?" In *Women in Sexist Society,* edited by Vivian Gornick and Barbara K. Moran, 480–510. New York: New American Library.

Norgren, Jill. 1989. "Child Care." In *Women: A Feminist Perspective,* edited by Jo Freeman, 176–96. Mountain View, Calif.: Mayfield.

O'Barr, Jean, et al. 1986. "Reflections on Forum '85 in Nairobi, Kenya: Voices from the International Women's Studies Community. *Signs* 11 (Spring): 584–608.

O'Farrell, Brigid, and Sharon L. Harlan. 1982. "Craft Workers and Clerks: The Effects of Male Co-Worker Hostility on Women's Satisfaction with Non-traditional Jobs." *Social Problems* 23 (February): 252–65.

Offen, Karen. 1988. "Defining Feminism, A Comparative Historical Approach." *Signs* 14 (Autumn): 119–57.

Office for Economic Cooperation and Development. 1988. *Labor Force Statistics.* Paris: OECD.

Okin, Susan Moller. 1979. *Women in Western Political Thought.* Princeton, N.J.: Princeton University Press.

Oldham, Sue, Doug Farmill, and Ian Bell. 1982. "Sex Role Identity of Female Homosexuals." *Journal of Homosexuality* 8 (Fall): 41–46.

O'Malley, K.M., and S. Richardson. 1985. "Sex Bias in Counseling: Have Things Changed?" *Journal of Counseling and Development* 63:294–99.

Orenstein, Gloria Feman. 1975. "Art History." *Signs* (Winter): 505–25.

Osterman, Paul. 1979. "Sex Discrimination in Professional Employment: A Case Study." *Industrial and Labor Relations Review* 32 (July): 451–64.

Owen, Diana, and Jack Dennis. 1988. "Gender Differences in the Politicization of American Children." *Women and Politics* 8:23–44.

Paige, Karen E., and Jeffrey M. Paige. 1981. *Politics of the Reproductive Rituals.* Berkeley: University of California Press.

Parisi, Nicolette. 1982a. "Exploring Female Crime Patterns: Problems and Prospects." In *Judge, Lawyer, Victim, Thief: Women, Gender Roles, and Criminal Justice,* edited by Nicole Hahn Rafter and Elizabeth Anne Stanko, 111–30. Boston: Northeastern University Press.

———. 1982b. "Are Females Treated Differently? A Review of the Theories and Evidence on Sentencing and Parole Decisions." In *Judge, Lawyer, Victim, Thief: Women, Gender Roles, and Criminal Justice,* edited by Nicole Hahn Rafter and Elizabeth Anne Stanko, 205–29. Boston: Northeastern University Press.

Parsons, Jacqueline Eccles. 1983. "Sexual Socialization and Gender Roles in Childhood." In *Changing Boundaries: Gender Roles and Sexual Behavior,* edited by Elizabeth Rice Allgeier and Naomi B McCormick, 19–48. Palo Alto, Calif.: Mayfield.

Parsons, Talcott. 1951. *The Social System.* New York: Free Press.

Pateman, Carole. 1980. "Women and Consent." *Political Theory* 8 (May): 149–68.

———. 1988. *The Sexual Contract.* Stanford: Stanford University Press.

Patterson, Michelle, and Laurie Engleberg. 1978. "Women in Male Dominated Professions." In *Women Working: Theories and Facts in Perspective,* edited by Anne H. Stromberg and Shirley Harkness, 266–92. Palo Alto, Calif.: Mayfield.

Pearce, Diana M. 1989. "Farewell to Alms: Women's Fare under Welfare." In *Women: A Feminist Perspective,* edited by Jo Freeman, 493–506. Mountain View, Calif.: Mayfield.

Pedersen, Darhl M., Martin M. Schinedling, and Dee L. Johnson. 1968. "Effects of Sex of Examiner and Subject Taught on Children's Quantitative Test Performance." *Journal of Personality and Social Psychology* 10:251–54.

Peplau, Letitia Anne, Susan Cochran, Karen Rook, and Christine Padesky. 1978. "Loving Women: Attachment and Autonomy in Lesbian Relationships." *Journal of Social Issues* 34 (Summer): 7–27.

Peplau, Letitia Anne, and Steve Gordon. 1983. "The Intimate Relationships of Lesbian and Gay Men." In *Changing Boundaries: Gender Roles and Sexual Behavior,* edited by Elizabeth Rice Allgeier and Naomi B. McCormick, 226–44. Palo Alto, Calif.: Mayfield.

Peplau, Letitia Anne, Zick Rubin, and Charles Hill. 1977. "Sex Intimacy in Dating Relationships." *Journal of Social Issues* 33 (Spring): 96–109.

Perkins, Jerry, and Diane L. Fowlkes. 1980. "Opinion Representation versus Social Representation: Or, Why Women Can't Run as Women and Win." *American Political Science Review* 74 (March): 92–103.

Perkins, Linda M. 1983. "The Impact of the 'Cult of True Womanhood' on the Education of Black Women." *Journal of Social Issues* 39 (September): 17–28.

Petchesky, Roslyn P. 1981. "Antiabortion, Antifeminism, and the Rise of the New Right." *Feminist Studies* 7 (Summer): 206–46.

———. 1984. *Abortion and Women's Choice: The State, Sexuality, and Reproductive Freedom.* New York: Longman.

Peterson, Susan Rae. 1977. "Coercion and Rape: The State as a Male Protection Racket." In *Feminism and Philosophy,* edited by Mary Vetterling-Braggin, Frederick A. Elliston, and Jane English, 313–32. Totowa, N.J.: Littlefield, Adams.

Phillips, E. Barbara. 1978. "Magazines' Heroines: Is *Ms.* Just Another Member of the *Family Circle?*" In *Hearth and Home: Images of Women in the Mass Media,* edited by Gaye Tuchman, Arlene Kaplan Daniels, and James Benet, 116–29. New York: Oxford University Press.

Piercy, Marge. 1974. "Looking at Quilts." In *Living in the Open,* edited by Marge Piercy, 86–87. New York: Alfred A. Knopf.

Pistrang, Nancy. 1984. "Women's Work Involvement and Experience of New Motherhood." *Journal of Marriage and the Family* 46 (May): 433–47.

Piven, Frances Fox, and Richard A. Cloward. 1988. "Welfare Doesn't Shore Up Traditional Family Roles: A Reply to Linda Gordon." *Social Research* 55 (Winter): 631–47.

Poole, Debra A., and Anne E. Tapley. 1988. "Sex Roles, Social Roles, and Clinical Judgments of Mental Health." *Sex Roles* 19 (September): 265–72.

Porter, Natalie, and Florence Geis. 1981. "Women and Nonverbal Leadership Cues: When Seeing Is Not Believing." In *Gender and Nonverbal Behavior,* edited by Clara Mayo and Nancy Henley, 39–62. New York: Springer-Verlag.

Prather, J., and Linda S. Fidell. 1975. "Sex Differences in the Control and Style of Medical Ads." *Social Science and Medicine* 9:23–26.

Quester, Aline O., and Janice Olson. 1978. "Sex, Schooling, and Hours of Work." *Social Quarterly* 58 (March): 566–82.

Rafter, Nicole Hahn. 1982. "Hard Times: Custodial Prisons for Women and the Example of the New York State Prison for Women at Auburn, 1893–1933." In *Judge, Lawyer, Victim, Thief: Women, Gender Roles, and Criminal Justice,* edited by Nicole Hahn Rafter and Elizabeth Anne Stanko, 237–60. Boston: Northeastern University Press.

Rafter, Nicole Hahn, and Elizabeth Anne Stanko, eds. 1982. *Judge, Lawyer, Victim, Thief: Women, Gender Roles, and Criminal Justice.* Boston: Northeastern University Press.

Randall, Vicki. 1987. *Women and Politics.* Chicago: University of Chicago Press.

Rank, Mark R. 1988. "Fertility among Women on Welfare: Incidence and Determinants." *American Sociological Review* 54 (April): 296–304.

Rawalt, Marguerite. 1983. "The Equal Rights Amendment." In *Women in Washington: Advocates for Public Policy,* edited by Irene Tinker, 49–78. Beverly Hills, Calif.: Sage.

Reid, Inez Smith. 1975. *Together Black Women.* New York: Emerson Hall.

Reiss, Harry T., and Linda A. Jackson. 1981. "Sex Differences in Reward Allocation: Subjects, Partners, and Tasks." *Journal of Personality and Social Psychology* 40 (March): 465–78.

Reskin, Barbara F. 1988. "Bringing the Men Back In: Sex Differentiation and the Devaluation of Women's Work." *Gender and Society* 2 (March): 58–81.

Resnick, Michael D. 1984. "Studying Adolescent Mothers' Decision Making about Adoption and Parenting." *Social Work* 29 (January–February): 5–10.

Reuther, Rosemary, ed. 1974. *Religion and Sexism: Images of Women in the Jewish and Christian Traditions.* New York: Simon and Schuster.

Rich, Adrienne. 1976. *Of Woman Born: Motherhood as Experience and Institution.* New York: Norton.

———. 1979. *On Lies, Secrets, and Silence.* New York: Norton.

———. 1980. "Compulsory Heterosexuality and Lesbian Existence." *Signs* 5 (Summer): 631–60.

Rickel, Annette U., and Linda M. Grant. 1979. "Sex Role Stereotypes in the Mass Media and Schools: Five Consistent Themes." *International Journal of Women's Studies* 2 (March/April): 164–79.

Rix, Sara E. 1987. *The American Woman, 1987–88: A Report in Depth.* New York: Norton.

———. 1988. *The American Woman, 1988–89: A Status Report.* New York: Norton.

Robbins, James. 1980. "Religious Involvement, Asceticism, and Abortion among Low Income Black Women." *Sociological Analysis* 41 (Winter): 365–74.

Robinson, John P. 1980. "Household Technology and Household Work." In *Women and Household Labor,* edited by S.F. Berk, 29–52. Beverly Hills, Calif.: Sage.

Rohrbaugh, Joanna Bunker. 1980. *Women: Psychology's Puzzle.* Brighton: Harvester Press.

Rook, Karen S., and Constance Hammer. 1977. "A Cognitive Perspective on the Experience of Sexual Arousal." *Journal of Social Issues* 33 (Spring): 7–29.

Rosen, Bernard, Thomas H. Jerdee, and Thomas L. Prestwick. 1975. "Dual-career Marital Adjustments: Potential Effects of Discriminatory Managerial Attitudes." *Journal of Marriage and the Family* 37 (August): 565–72.

Rosen, Bernard, and M.F. Mericle. 1979. "Influence of Strong versus Weak Fair Employment Policies and Applicant's Sex on Selection Decisions and Salary Recommendations in a Management Simulation." *Journal of Applied Psychology* 64:435–39.

Rosenkrantz, Paul, Susan R. Vogel, Helen Bee, and Donald Broverman. 1968. "Sex Role Stereotypes and Self-Concept in College Students." *Journal of Consulting and Clinical Psychology* 32:287–95.

Ross, Catherine E., and John Mirowsky. 1988. "Child Care and Emotional Adjustment to Wives' Employment." *Journal of Health and Social Behavior* 29:127–38.

Ross, Catherine E., John Mirowsky, and Joan Huber. 1983. "Dividing Work, Sharing Work, and In-between: Marriage Patterns and Depression." *American Sociological Review* 48 (December): 809–23.

Ross, Joanna, and James B. Kahan. 1983. "Children by Choice or by Chance: The Perceived Effects of Parenthood." *Sex Roles* 9 (January): 69–77.

Ross, Laurie, Daniel R. Anderson, and Patricia A. Wisocki. 1982. "Television Viewing and Adult Sex-Role Attitudes." *Sex Roles* 8 (June): 589–92.

Rossi, Alice. 1965. "Barriers to the Career Choice of Engineering, Medicine, or Science among American Women." In *Women and the Scientific Professions,* edited by J.A. Mattfield and C.G. Van Aken, 51–127. Cambridge: MIT Press.

Rossi, Alice, ed. 1970. *Essays in Sex Equality: John Stuart Mill and Harriet Taylor Mill.* Chicago: University of Chicago Press.

———. 1988. *The Feminist Papers: From Adams to de Beauvoir.* Boston: Northeastern University Press.

Rothman, Barbara Katz. 1982. *In Labor: Women and Power in the Birthplace.* New York: Norton.

Rowland, Robyn, ed. 1984. *Women Who Do and Women Who Don't Join the Women's Movement.* Boston: Routledge & Kegan Paul.

Rubin, Gayle. 1974. "The Traffic in Women: Notes on the 'Political Economy' of Sex." In *Toward an Anthropology of Women* edited by Rayna Reiter, 157–210. New York: Monthly Review Press.

Rubin, Jeffrey Z., Frank J. Provenzano, and Zella Luria. 1974. "The Eye of the Beholder: Parents' Views on Sex of Newborns." *American Journal of Orthopsychiatry* 44:512–19.

Rubin, Lillian B. 1976. *Worlds of Pain: Life in the Working Class Family.* New York: Basic Books.

Ruddick, Sara. 1982. "Maternal Thinking." In *Rethinking the Family: Some Feminist Questions,* edited by Barrie Thorne and Marilyn Yalom, 76–94. New York: Longman.

Ruddick, Sara, and Pamela Daniels, ed. 1977. *Working It Out: Twenty-three Women Writers, Artists, Scientists, and Scholars Talk about Their Lives and Work.* New York: Pantheon.

Rupp, Leila. 1985. "The Woman's Community in the National Woman's Party, 1945 to the 1960s." *Signs* 10 (Summer): 715–40.

Ruth, Sheila. 1980. *Issues in Feminism: A First Course in Women's Studies.* Boston: Houghton Mifflin.

Ryan, Mary P. 1979. "The Power of Women's Networks: A Case Study of Female Moral Reform in Antebellum America." *Feminist Studies* 5 (Spring): 66–85.

Rytina, Nancy E., and Suzanne M. Bianchi. 1984. "Occupational Reclassification and Distribution by Gender." *Monthy Labor Review* 107 (March): 11–17.

Sadker, Myra Pollack, and David Miller Sadker. 1980. "Sexism in Teacher Education Texts." *Harvard Education Review* 50 (February), 36–46.

Salzinger, Suzanne, Sandra Kaplan, and Connie Artmeyeff. 1983. "Mothers' Personal Social Networks and Child Maltreatment." *Journal of Abnormal Psychology* 92 (February): 68–76.

Sanday, Peggy Reeves. 1981. "The Socio-Cultural Context of Rape: A Cross-Cultural Study." *Journal of Social Issues* 37 (Fall): 5–27.

Sanders, Marlene, and Marcia Rock. 1988. *Waiting for Prime Time: The Women of Television News.* Urbana: University of Illinois Press.

Sapiro, Virginia. 1979. "Women's Studies and Political Conflict." In *The Prism of Sex: Essays in the Sociology of Knowledge,* edited by Julia Sherman and Evelyn Beck, 253–65. Madison: University of Wisconsin Press.

———. 1980. "News from the Front: Inter-Sex and Intergenerational Conflict over the Status of Women." *Western Political Quarterly* 33 (June): 260–77.

———. 1982a. "Public Costs of Private Commitments or Private Costs of Public Commitments: Family Roles versus Political Ambition." *American Journal of Political Science* 26 (May): 265–79.

———. 1982b. "If U.S. Senator Baker Were a Woman: An Experimental Study of Candidate Images." *Political Psychology* 3 (Spring-Summer): 61–83.

———. 1983. *The Political Integration of Women: Roles, Socialization and Politics.* Urbana: University of Illinois Press.

———. 1984. "Women, Citizenship, and Nationality: Immigration and Nationalization Policies in the United States." *Politics and Society* 13:1–26.

———. 1986. "The Gender Basis of American Social Policy." *Political Science Quarterly* 101:221–38.

———. 1989. "The Women's Movement and the Creation of Gender Consciousness: Social Movements as Socialization Agents." In *Political Socialization for Democracy,* edited by Orit Ichilov. New York: Teachers' College Press.

Sapiro, Virginia, and Barbara G. Farah. 1980. "New Pride and Old Prejudice: Political Ambitions and Role Orientations among Female Partisan Elites." *Women and Politics* 1 (Spring): 13–36.

Sargent, Lydia, ed. 1981. *Women and Revolution: A Discussion of the Unhappy Marriage of Feminism and Marxism.* Boston: South End Press.

Sayers, Janet. 1982. *Biological Politics: Feminist and Anti-feminist Perspectives.* New York: Tavistock.

Sayers, Janet, ed. 1987. *Engels Revisited: New Feminist Perspectives.* New York: Routledge.

Scharf, Lois, and Joan M. Jensen, eds. 1983. *Decades of Discontent.* Westport Conn.: Greenwood.

Schneider, Joseph W., and Sally L. Hacker. 1973. ''Sex Role Imagery and the Use of Generic 'Man' in Introductory Texts.'' *American Sociologist* 8 (February): 12–18.

Schram, Vicki R., and Marilyn M. Dunsing. 1981. ''Influences on Married Women's Volunteer Work Participation.'' *Journal of Consumer Research* 7 (March): 373–79.

Schramm, Sarah Slavin. 1979. *Plow Women Rather than Reapers: An Intellectual History of Feminism in the United States.* Metuchen, N.J.: Scarecrow Press.

Schwartz, Felice N. 1980. '' 'Invisible' Resource: Women for Boards.'' *Harvard Business Review* 58 (March–April): 6–19.

Scott, Anne Firor. 1970. *The Southern Lady: From Pedestal to Politics.* Chicago: University of Chicago Press.

Scott, Ronald L., and Laurie A. Tetrault. 1987. ''Attitudes of Rapists and Other Violent Offenders toward Women.'' *Journal of Social Psychology* (August): 375–80.

Scully, Diana, and Pauline Bart. 1973. ''A Funny Thing Happened on the Way to the Orifice: Women in Gynecology Textbooks.'' *American Journal of Sociology* 78 (January): 1045–50.

Seiden, Ann M. 1976. ''Overview: Research on the Psychology of Women: Gender Differences in Sexual and Reproductive Life.'' *American Journal of Psychiatry* 133:995–1007.

Seidenberg, Robert. 1971. ''Advertising and Abuse of Drugs.'' *New England Journal of Medicine* 284:789–90.

Seifer, Nancy. 1976. *Nobody Speaks for Me: Self-Portraits of American Working Class Women.* New York: Simon & Schuster.

Seller, Maxine. 1982. ''The Education of Immigrant Women, 1900–35.'' In *Women's America,* edited by Linda K. Kerber and Jane De Hart Mathews, 242–56. New York: Oxford University Press.

Serbin, Lisa A., Daniel K. O'Leary, Ronald M. Kent, and Ilene J. Tonick. 1973. ''A Comparison of Teacher Response to the Preacademic and Problem Behavior of Boys and Girls.'' *Child Development* 44:796–84.

Settin, Joan M., and Dana Bramel. 1981. ''Interaction of Client Class and Gender Biasing in Clinical Judgement.'' *American Journal of Orthopsychiatry* 51 (July): 510–20.

Shaffer, David R., and Thomas Case. 1982. ''On the Decision to Testify on One's Own Behalf: Effects of Withheld Evidence, Defendents' Sexual Preferences, and Juror Dogmatism on Juridic Decisions.'' *Journal of Personality and Social Psychology* 42 (February): 335–46.

Shapiro, Robert Y., et al. 1987a. ''The Polls: Employment and Social Welfare.'' *Public Opinion Quarterly* 51 (Summer): 268–81.

———. 1987b. ''The Polls: Public Assistance.'' *Public Opinion Quarterly* 51 (Spring): 120–30.

Shaver, Philip, and Jonathan Freedman. 1976. ''Your Pursuit of Happiness.'' *Psychology Today* 10 (August): 26–32.

Shaw, Lois B., and David Shapiro. 1987. "Women's Work Expectations and Actual Experience." *Monthly Labor Review* 110 (November): 7–13.

Shaw, Nancy Stoller. 1982. "Female Patients and the Medical Profession in Jails and Prisons: A Case of Quadruple Jeopardy." In *Judge, Lawyer, Victim, Thief: Women, Gender Roles, and Criminal Justice,* edited by Nicole Hahn Rafter and Elizabeth Anne Stanko, 261–73. Northeastern University Press.

Shepherd, R. 1982. "EEG Correlates of Sustained Attention: Hemispheric and Sex Differences." *Current Psychological Research* 2 (January–March): 1–19.

Sherman, Julia. 1980. "Mathematics, Spatial Visualization, and Related Factors: Changes in Boys and Girls, Grades 8-11." *Journal of Educational Psychology* 72 (August): 476–82.

Sherman, Julia, Corinne Koufacos, and Joy A. Kenworthy. 1978. "Therapists: Their Attitudes and Information about Women." *Psychology of Women Quarterly* 2:299–313.

Shorter, Edward. 1982. *A History of Women's Bodies.* New York: Basic.

Shortridge, Kathleen. 1989. "Poverty Is a Woman's Problem." In *Women: A Feminist Perspective,* edited by Jo Freeman, 485–92. Mountain View, Calif.: Mayfield.

Shotland, R. Lance, and Jane M. Craig. 1988. "Can Men and Women Differentiate between Friendly and Sexually Interested Behavior?" *Social Psychology Quarterly* 51:66–73.

Shulman, Alix Kates. 1983. *Red Emma Speaks.* New York: Schocken.

Siegfried, William D. 1982. "The Effects of Specifying Job Requirements and Using Explicit Warnings to Decrease Sex Discrimination in Employment Interviews." *Sex Roles* 8:73–82.

Simon, Rita J. 1975. *Women and Crime.* Lexington, Mass: D.C. Heath.

Simon, Rita J., and Jean M. Landis. 1989. "Report: Women's and Men's Attitudes about a Woman's Place and Role." *Public Opinion Quarterly* 53 (Summer): 265–76.

Simons, Margaret. A. 1979. "Racism and Feminism: A Schism in the Sisterhood." *Feminist Studies* 5 (Summer): 384–401.

Sklar, Kathryn Kish. 1982. "Catharine Beecher: Transforming the Teaching Profession." In *Women's America,* edited by Linda K. Kerber and Jane De Hart Mathews, 140–48. New York: Oxford University Press.

Sloane, Ethel. 1980. *Biology of Women.* New York: Wiley.

Smith, Tom W. 1987. "That Which We Call Welfare by Any Other Name Would Smell Sweeter: An Analysis of the Impact of Question Wording on Response Patterns." *Public Opinion Quarterly* 51 (Spring): 75–83.

Smith-Lovin, Lynn, and Charles Brody. 1989. "Interruptions in Group Discussions: The Effects of Gender and Group Composition." *American Sociological Review* 54 (June): 424–35.

Smith-Rosenberg, Carroll. 1975. "The Female World of Love and Ritual: Relations between Women in Nineteenth Century America." *Signs* 1 (Autumn): 1–29. Also in Kerber and Mathews 1982, and Leavitt 1984.

Sniezek, Janet A., and Christine H. Jazwinski. 1986. "Gender Bias in English: In Search of Fair Language." *Journal of Applied Social Psychology* 16:642–62.

Snyder, Mark, and Seymour W. Uranowitz. 1978. "Reconstructing the Past: Some Cognitive Consequences of Person Perception." *Journal of Personality and Social Psychology* 36 (September): 941–50.

Sochen, June. 1972. *The New Woman: Feminism in Greenwich Village, 1910-20.* New York: Quadrangle.

———. 1973. *Movers and Shakers: American Women Thinkers and Activists, 1900–70*. New York: Quadrangle.

———. 1981. *Herstory: A Record of the American Woman's Past*. Sherman Oaks, Calif.: Alfred.

Sommers, Paul M., and Laura S. Thomas. 1983. "Restricting Federal Funds for Abortion: Another Look." *Social Science Quarterly* 6 (June): 40–46.

Spiegel, David. 1982. "Mothering, Fathering, and Mental Illness." In *Rethinking the Family: Some Feminist Questions*, edited by Barrie Thorne, 95–110. New York: Longman.

Spivak, Gayatri Chakravorty. 1987. *In Other Worlds: Essays in Cultural Politics*. New York: Routledge.

Sprafkin, Joyce N., and Robert M. Liebert. 1978. "Sex Typing and Children's Television Preferences." In *Hearth and Home*, edited by Gaye Tuchman, Arlene Kaplan Daniels, and James Benet, 228–39. New York: Oxford University Press.

Stack, Carol. 1974. *All Our Kin: Strategies for Survival in a Black Community*. New York: Harper & Row.

Stake, Jayne, and Charles R. Granger. 1978. "Same Sex and Opposite Sex Teacher Model Influences on Science Career Commitment among High School Students." *Journal of Educational Psychology* 70 (April): 180–86.

Stanko, Elizabeth Anne. 1982. "Would You Believe This Woman? Prosecutorial Screening for 'Credible' Witnesses and a Problem of Justice." In *Judge, Lawyer, Victim, Thief: Women, Gender Roles, and Criminal Justice*, edited by Nicole Hahn Rafter and Elizabeth Anne Stanko, 63–82. Boston: Northeastern University Press.

Stanton, Elizabeth Cady. [1895] 1974. *The Woman's Bible*. New York: Arno Press.

Stanton, Elizabeth Cady, Susan B. Anthony, and Mathilda J. Gage. [1881] 1969. *History of Women's Suffrage*. New York: Arno.

Stanworth, Michelle. 1983. *Gender and Schooling*. London: Hutchison.

Staudt, Kathleen A. 1985. *Women, Foreign Assistance, and Advocacy Administration*. New York: Praeger.

Steck, Loren, Diane Levitan, David McLane, and Harold H. Kelley. 1982. "Care, Needs, and Conceptions of Love." *Journal of Personality and Social Psychology* 43 (September): 481–91.

Steffensmeier, Darrell J. 1981. "Patterns of Female Property Crime 1960–78: A Postscript." In *Women and Crime in America*, edited by Leo Bowker, 39–64. New York: Macmillan.

Steinberg, Ronnie. 1987. "Radical Challenges in a Liberal World: The Mixed Success of Comparable Worth." *Gender and Society* 1 (December): 466–75.

Stellman, Jeanne Mager. 1977. *Women's Work, Women's Health*. New York: Pantheon.

Sterling, Dorothy, ed. 1984. *We Are Your Sisters: Black Women in the Nineteenth Century*. New York: Norton.

Stimpson, Catherine R. 1979. "The Power to Name: Some Reflections on the Avant Gard." In *The Prism of Sex: Essays in the Sociology of Knowledge*, edited by Julia Sherman and Evelyn Beck, 55–78. Madison: University of Wisconsin Press.

———. 1980. "Power, Presentations, and the Presentable." In *Issues in Feminism*, edited by Sheila Ruth, 426–40. Boston: Houghton Mifflin.

Strober, Myra H., and David Tyack. 1980. "Why Do Women Teach and Men Manage? A Report on Research on Schools." *Signs* 5 (Spring): 494–503.

Strube, Michael J., and Linda S. Barbour. 1983. "The Decision to Leave an Abusive Relationship: Economic Dependence and Psychological Commitment." *Journal of Marriage and the Family* 45 (November): 785–93.

Swim, Janet, Eugene Borgida, Geoffrey Maruyama, and David G. Myers. 1989. "Joan McKay versus John McKay: Do Gender Stereotypes Bias Evaluations?" *Psychological Bulletin* 105:409–29.

Taffel, Selma M., Paul J. Placek, and Teri Less. 1987. "Trends in the United States Cesarean Section Rate and Reasons for the 1980–85 Rise." *American Journal of Public Health* 77:955–59.

Tangri, Sandra S., Martha R. Burke, and Leanor B. Johnson. 1982. "Sexual Harassment at Work: Three Explanatory Models." *Journal of Social Issues* 38 (Winter): 33–54.

Tanney, Mary Faith, and Janice M. Birk. 1976. "Women Counselors for Women Clients? A Review of the Research." *The Counseling Psychologist* 6:28–32.

Tavris, Carol, and Carole Offir. 1977. *The Longest War: Sex Differences in Perspective.* New York: Harcourt, Brace, Jovanovich.

Tedin, Kent. 1978. "Religious Preference and Pro-Anti Activism on the ERA Issue." *Pacific Sociological Review* 21 (January): 55–66.

Thompson, Kenrick S. 1980. "A Comparison of Black and White Adolescents' Beliefs about Having Children." *Journal of Marriage and the Family* 42 (February): 133–39.

Thompson, Victor A. 1961. *Modern Organization.* New York: Alfred A. Knopf.

Thorne, Barrie, Cheris Kramarae, and Nancy Henley, eds. 1983. *Language, Gender, and Society.* Rowley, Mass.: Newbury House.

Tidball, M. Elizabeth. 1980. "Women's Colleges and Women Achievers Revisited." *Signs* 5 (Spring): 504–17.

Tiger, Lionel. 1969. *Men in Groups.* New York: Vintage.

Tilly, Charles. 1978. *From Mobilization to Revolution.* Reading, Mass.: Addison-Wesley.

Tobias, Sheila, and Lisa Anderson. 1982. "What Really Happened to Rosie the Riveter? Demobilization and the Female Labor Force, 1944–47." In *Women's America: Refocusing the Past,* edited by Linda K. Kerber and Jane De Hart Mathews, 354–73. New York: Oxford University Press.

Tobias, Sheila, and Carol Weissbrod. 1980. "Anxiety and Mathematics: An Update." *Harvard Educational Review* 50 (February): 63–70.

Toth, Emily. 1980. "The Fouler Sex: Women's Bodies in Advertising." In *Issues in Feminism: A First Course in Women's Studies,* edited by Sheila Ruth, 107–14. Boston: Hougton Mifflin.

Treichler, Paula A. 1984. "Women, Language, and Health Care: An Annotated Bibliography." *Women and Language News* 7 (Spring): 7–19.

Tuchman, Gaye. 1978. "Introduction." In *Hearth and Home: Images of Women in the Mass Media,* edited by Gaye Tuchman, Arlene Kaplan Daniels, and James Benet, 3–38. New York: Oxford University Press.

———. 1979. "Women's Depiction in the Mass Media." *Signs* 4 (Spring): 528–42.

Tuchman, Gaye, Arlene Kaplan Daniels, and James Benet, eds. 1978. *Hearth and Home: Images of Women in the Mass Media.* New York: Oxford University Press.

Tudor, William, Jeanette F. Tudor, and Walter R. Gove. 1977. "The Effects of Sex Role Differences on the Social Control of Mental Illness." *Journal of Health and Social Behavior* 18 (June): 98–112.

Turow, Joseph. 1974. "Advising and Ordering: Day Time, Prime Time." *Journal of Communication* 24:138–41.

Ulbrich, Patricia, and Joan Huber. 1981. "Observing Parental Violence: Distribution Effect." *Journal of Marriage and the Family* 43 (August): 623–32.

Unger, Rhoda K. 1979. *Female and Male: Psychological Perspectives*. New York: Harper & Row.

U.S. Bureau of the Census. 1980. *Statistical Abstract of the United States*. Washington, D.C.: Government Printing Office.

———. 1982. *Statistical Abstract of the United States*. Washington, D.C.: Government Printing Office.

———. 1987a. *A Statistical Abstract of the United States*. Washington, D.C.: Government Printing Office.

———. 1987b. *Current Population Reports Series P-70, No. 10: Male-Female Differences in Work Experience, Occupation, and Earnings, 1984*. Washington, D.C.: Government Printing Office.

———. 1989. *A Statistical Abstract of the United States*. Washington, D.C.: Government Printing Office.

U.S. Commission on Civil Rights. 1979. *Window Dressing on the Set: An Update*. Washington, D.C.: Government Printing Office.

U.S. Congress, House of Representatives Committee on Immigration and Naturalization. 1930. "Supreme Court Decision, Citations, Comment, etc. *In re* Rosika Schwimmer and Martha Jane Graber." 71st Congress, 2d Session, 6 March.

U.S. Department of Education. 1987. *Trends in Bachelor's and Higher Degrees, 1975–85*. Washington, D.C.: Government Printing Office.

———. 1988. *Digest of Education Statistics, 1988*. Washington, D.C.: Government Printing Office.

U.S. Department of Labor. 1980. *Perspectives on Working Women: A Databook*. Washington, D.C.: Government Printing Office.

———. 1989. *Employment and Earnings (January 1989)*. Washington, D.C.: Government Printing Office.

U.S. Merit Systems Protection Board. 1981. *Sexual Harassment in the Federal Workplace: Is It a Problem?* Washington, D.C.: U.S. Government Printing Office.

Valeska, Lucia. 1975. "If All Else Fails, I'm Still a Mother." *Quest* 1 (Winter): 52–63.

Vanek, Joann. 1980. "Household Work, Wage Work, and Sexual Equality." In *Women and Household Labor,* edited by Sarah Fenstermaker Berk, 275–92. Beverly Hills, Calif.: Sage.

Ventura, Jacqueline N., and Pauline G. Boss. 1983. "The Family Coping Inventory Applied to Parents with New Babies." *Journal of Marriage and the Family* 45 (November): 867–75.

Verna, Mary Ellen. 1975. "The Female Image in Children's TV Commercials." *Journal of Broadcasting* 19:301–9.

Vladeck, Judith P. 1981. "Sex Discrimination in Higher Education." *Women's Rights Law Reporter* 7 (Fall): 27–38.

Voydanoff, Patricia. 1984. *Work and Family: Changing Roles of Men and Women*. Palo Alto, Calif.: Mayfield.

Waelti-Walters, Jennifer. 1979. "On Princesses: Fairy Tales, Sex Roles, and Loss of Self." *International Journal of Women's Studies* 2 (March/April): 180–88.

Waldman, Elizabeth. 1983. "Labor Force Statistics from a Family Perspective." *Monthly Labor Review* 106 (December): 16–20.

Walker, Lawrence. 1984. "Sex Differences in the Development of Moral Reasoning: A Critical Review." *Child Development* 55:667–91.

Walsh, Mary Roth. 1979. "The Rediscovery of the Need for a Feminist Medical Education." *Harvard Education Review* 49 (November): 447–66.

Ware, Susan. 1981. *Beyond Suffrage: Women in the New Deal.* Cambridge, Mass.: Harvard University Press.

———. 1983. *Holding Their Own: American Women in the 1930's.* Boston: Twayne.

Warner, Marina. 1976. *Alone of All Her Sex: The Myth and the Cult of Mary.* New York: Random House.

Weeks, Jeffrey. 1977. *Coming Out: Homosexual Politics in Britain, from the Nineteenth Century to the Present.* London: Quartet.

Weeks, M. O'Neal, and Darla R. Botkin. 1987. "A Longitudinal Study of the Marriage Role Expectations of College Women: 1961–84." *Sex Roles* 17:49–58.

Weinberg, Martin S., and Colin J. Williams. 1980. "Sexual Embourgeoisment? Social Class and Sexual Activity, 1938–48." *American Sociological Review* 45 (February): 33–48.

Weisfeld, Carol C., Glenn E. Weisfeld, and John W. Callaghan. 1982. "Female Inhibition in Mixed Sex Competition among Young Adolescents." *Ethnology and Sociobiology* 3:29–42.

Weiss, Robert S. 1984. "The Impact of Marital Dissolution on Income and Consumption in Single-Parent Households." *JMF* 46 (February): 115–28.

Weitzman, Leonore J. 1979. *Sex Role Socialization.* Palo Alto, Calif.: Mayfield.

———. 1985. *The Divorce Revolution: The Unexpected Social and Economic Consequences for Women and Children in America.* New York: Free Press.

Welch, Susan. 1978. "Recruitment of Women to Public Office: A Discriminant Analysis." *Western Political Quarterly* 31 (September): 372–80.

Welch, Susan, and Alan Booth. 1977. "Employment and Health among Married Women with Children." *Sex Roles* 3 (August): 385–98.

Welter, Barbara. 1966. "The Cult of True Womanhood, 1830–1860." *American Quarterly* 18 (Summer): 151–74.

Wertheimer, Barbara M., and Anne H. Nelson. 1982. "Education for Social Change: Two Roads." *Economic and Industrial Democracy* 3 (November): 483–513.

———. 1989. "'Union Is Power': Sketches from Women's Labor History." In *Women: A Feminist Perspective,* edited by Jo Freeman, 312–28. Mountian View, Calif.: Mayfield.

West, Candace. 1984. "When the Doctor Is a 'Lady:' Power, Status, and Gender in Physician-Patient Encounters." *Symbolic Interaction* 7 (Spring):87–106.

West, Candace, and Don. H. Zimmerman. 1987. "Doing Gender." *Gender and Society* 1 (June): 125–51.

Wheeler, Ladd, and John Nezlek. 1977. "Sex Differences In Social Participation." *Journal of Personality and Social Psychology* 35 (October): 742–54.

White, Deborah Gray. 1985. *"Ar'n't I a Woman?" Female Slaves in the Plantation South.* New York: Norton.

White, Gregory L., Sanford Fishbein, and Jeffrey Rutstein. 1981. "Passionate Love and Misattribution of Arousal." *Journal of Personality and Social Psychology* 41 (July): 56–62.

White, Lynn K., and David B. Brinkerhoff. 1981. "The Sexual Division of Labor: Evidence from Childhood." *Social Forces* 60 (September): 170–81.

Whittaker, Susan, and Ron Whittaker. 1976. "Relative Effectiveness of Male and Female Newscasters." *Journal of Broadcasting* 20: 177–84.

Wilbanks, William. 1982. "Murdered Women and Women Who Murder: A Critique of the Literature." In *Judge, Lawyer, Victim, Thief: Women, Gender Roles, and Criminal Justice,* edited by Nicole Hahn Rafter and Elizabeth Anne Stanko, 151–80. Boston: Northeastern University Press.

Wiley, Mary G., and Arlene Eskilson. 1982. "The Interaction of Sex and Power Based on Perceptions of Managerial Effectiveness." *Academy of Management Journal* 25 (September): 671–77.

Wilson, E.O. 1975. *Sociobiology: A New Synthesis.* Cambridge, Mass.: Harvard University Press.

Wise, Erica, and Janet Rafferty. 1982. "Sex Bias and Language." *Sex Roles* 8 (December): 1189–96.

Wolchik, Sharon L., and Alfred G. Meyer, eds. 1985. *Women, State, and Party in Eastern Europe.* Durham, N.C.: Duke University Press.

Wolfe, J., and V. Baker, 1980. "Characteristics of Imprisoned Rapists and Circumstances of Rape." In *Rape and Sexual Assault,* edited by Carmen G. Warner. Germantown, Md.: Aspen Systems.

Wollstonecraft, Mary. [1792] 1975. *A Vindication of the Rights of Woman.* Baltimore, Md.: Penguin. Excerpted in Rossi, 1988.

"Women and the American City." 1980. *Signs* 5 (May): entire issue.

Women on Words and Images. 1972. *Dick and Jane as Victims.* Princeton, N.J.: Know, Inc.

Wood, Marion M. 1966. "The Influence of Sex and Knowledge of Communication Effectiveness on Spontaneous Speech." *Word* 22:112–37.

Woods, Laurie. 1981. "Litigation on Behalf of Battered Women." *Women's Rights Law Reporter* 7 (Fall): 39–46.

Worcester, Nancy, and Mariamne H. Whatley. 1988. "The Response of the Health Care System to the Women's Health Movement: The Selling of Women's Health Centers." In *Women's Health: Readings on Social, Economic, and Political Issues,* edited by Nancy Worcester and Mariamne H. Whatley, 17–24. Dubuque: Kendall/Hunt.

Wylie, Philip. 1942. *A Generation of Vipers.* New York and Toronto: Farrar & Rinehart.

Yee, Doris K., and Jacquelynne S. Eccles. 1988. "Parent Perceptions and Attributions for Children's Math Achievement." *Sex Roles* 19 (September): 317–33.

Zeldow, Peter B. 1976. "Effects of Nonpathological Sex Role Stereotypes on Student Evaluations of Psychiatric Patients." *Journal of Consulting and Clinical Psychology* 44:304.

Zellman, Gail L., and Jacqueline D. Goodchilds. 1983. "Becoming Sexual in Adolescence." In *Changing Boundaries: Gender Roles and Sexual Behavior,* edited by Elizabeth Rice Allgeier and Naomi B. McCormick, 49–63. Palo Alto, Calif.: Mayfield.

Zimmerman, Don. H., and Candace West. 1975. "Sex Roles, Interruptions, and Silences in Conversation." In *Language and Sex,* edited by Barrie Thorne and Nancy Henley, 105–29. Rowley, Mass.: Newbury House.

Zinn, Maxine Baca. 1989. "Family, Race, and Poverty in the Eighties." *Signs* 14 (Summer): 856–74.

ILLUSTRATION CREDITS

Page 18: Elizabeth Crews/The Image Works
Page 21: Barbara Alper/Stock Boston
Page 36: Harriet Gans/The Image Works
Page 44: Peter Menzel/Stock Boston
Page 51: Culver Pictures
Page 57: Wyoming State Archives, Museums and Historical Department
Page 70: Wayne Glusker
Page 73: The Bettmann Archive
Page 82: Alan Carey/The Image Works
Page 101: Courtesy of Bethune-Cookman College
Page 104: Sophia Smith Collection, Smith College, photograph by A. J. Schillare
Page 112: Sophia Smith Collection, Smith College, photograph by Katherine E. McClellan
Page 124: Culver Pictures
Page 140: Brown Brothers
Page 149: Museum of the City of New York
Page 159: Sophia Smith Collection, Smith College
Page 166: Kevin Horan/Picture Group
Page 174: UPI/Bettmann Newsphotos

Page 184: AP/Wide World Photos
Page 192: Brown Brothers
Page 200: Wide World Photos
Page 208: Brown Brothers
Page 214: AP/Wide World Photos
Page 245: Rick Smolan/Stock Boston
Page 260: Michael A. Keller/FPG International
Page 268: UPI/Bettmann Newsphotos
Page 272: Mark Antman/The Image Works
Page 291: Elizabeth Crews/Stock Boston
Page 310: Staten Island Historical Society
Page 314: Brown Brothers
Page 323: Sue Owrutsky/Picture Group
Page 324: AP/Wide World Photos
Page 345: Sophia Smith Collection, Smith College
Page 357: International Museum of Photography at the George Eastman House
Page 373: Courtesy, Vassar College Library
Page 398: David Wells/The Image Works
Page 406: Laura Luongo/Picture Group
Page 413: Owen Franken/Stock Boston
Page 435: Brown Brothers
Page 443: AP/Wide World Photos

Subject Index

American Medical Association (AMA), 148
American Nurse's Association, 385
American Psychological Association, 121, 288
American Social Science Association, 102
American Telephone and Telegraph (AT&T), 360, 370
American Woman Suffrage Association (AWSA), 432, 433
Androcentrism, 1–2, 79, 122, 125, 126, 143, 166, 202, 205 217, 221, 263, 265, 275, 277, 281, 289, 306, 340, 346, 351, 384, 390, 423
  definition, 1
Androgyny, 30–31, 143–144, 157, 259, 261–262, 284, 311
  See also Femininity; Masculinity
Anorexia nervosa
  See Health and disease
Anthropology and anthropologists
  See Social science
Antifeminism, 56, 60, 62, 63, 64, 68, 77, 226, 289, 341–342, 443, 446–450
  arguments of, 56, 60, 446–447
  characteristics of antifeminists, 449–450
  reasons for, 448
  See also Feminism; Feminism, history of; Social movements
Architecture, 22, 71, 195
Arts and artists, 68, 177, 193–202, 416
  and crafts, 197–199
  and feminism, 197
  dance, 139, 142, 198
  degrees awarded, 22
  detective fiction, 199
  discrimination, 195–196
  education and training, 96, 111, 195, 196
  film, 139, 141, 194, 199, 201
  gender as subject of, 199–201
  graphic, 177, 195–196, 198, 200, 244, 308
  literature and literacy criticism, 22, 98, 177, 179, 186, 194–195, 198, 244

music, 22, 96, 189, 195, 196, 198, 370
samplers, 198
theater, 189, 194, 199, 370
Asian Americans
  See Race and ethnicity
Association for Women in Psychology, 150
Authority
  See Power

Baker v. *Nelson* (1971), 302
Bakers, 368
Ballard v. *U.S.* (1946), 3, 211
Barnard College, 100, 101
Barnes v. *Castle* (1977), 375
Beal v. *Doe* (1977), 322
Beauty, 62, 96, 139–143, 339, 398
  See also Dress and fashion; Health and disease
Bellevue Hospital, 149
Bem Sex-Role Inventory Scale (BSRI), 143–144, 284
Bethune-Cookman College, 100
Bible, 45, 96, 156, 158, 159, 160–161, 164, 165, 175, 437
  different interpretations of, 160, 175
  See also Religion
Biology, 7, 42–45, 59, 63, 66, 67–74, 81, 87, 127, 135, 198, 135, 251, 404
  brain, 66, 71–73, 135
  genes and genetics, 59, 62–63, 67–68, 69–71, 404
  hormones, 43, 66, 67–68, 69, 72–74, 127, 338
  instincts, 63, 81
  selfish gene, 62–63
  See also Evolution; Science; Sex and sex difference; Sociobiology
Biological sciences
  See Science
Birth control
  See Contraception
Bisexuality
  See Sexuality

Blacks
  See Race and ethnicity
Bonding
  See Motherhood; Social relationships
Bowers v. *Hardwick* (1986), 288
Bradwell v. *Illinois* (1873), 207–208
Brain
  See Biology
Bryn Mawr College, 100
Bundy v. *Jackson* (1981), 375
Business and commerce, 20, 22, 24, 25, 91, 98, 106, 180, 229, 301, 343, 349, 363, 368, 369, 377, 379, 401, 410, 447
  education and training, 22
  executives, 20, 25, 28, 91, 252, 254, 260, 353, 369, 374, 402, 447
  insurance companies, 447
  sales workers, 24, 25, 363, 364, 365, 366, 369
  See also Clerical work; Commercial media and advertising

Caban v. *Mohammed* (1979), 338
Capitalism
  See Economics and economies
Carey v. *Population Services International* (1977), 309, 316
Castration
  See Reproductive system
Censorship, 194, 283
Chastity belts, 124, 125
Child care, 25, 43, 131, 132, 135–136, 151, 215, 216, 218, 263, 342–343, 356, 359, 369, 383, 419–420, 443, 444
  availability, 135–136, 342–343
  justifications for, 419–420
  public opinion, 343
  workers, 25, 132, 215, 363
  See also Homemaking; Motherhood
Child custody, 152, 206
  See also Divorce
Children, 9, 19, 46, 71–72, 75–76, 79, 80–86, 90, 104, 105,

487

See also Marriage and marital roles; Sexuality

Courts, 3, 28, 43–44, 120, 136–137, 138, 156, 184, 204, 205, 220, 221, 223–224, 244, 300, 321, 334–336, 372
    judges, 28, 218, 222, 224, 210, 232, 299, 374
    juries, 3, 206, 211–212, 221, 222, 287, 436
    Supreme Court, 3, 28, 43–44, 136–137, 138, 156, 184, 205, 207–209, 210–214, 233, 288, 316, 319–321, 322, 337–338, 370, 372, 433, 444
    See also Crime and Criminal justice; Law and policy

Crime and criminal justice, 19, 27, 28, 42, 62, 63, 69, 79, 103, 121, 126, 133, 134, 146, 148, 151, 180, 189, 199, 201, 206, 216–224, 229, 288, 318
    against property, 217
    and mass media, 180, 217
    crime and arrest rates, 27, 216–218, 220
    juvenile delinquency, 103, 332
    murder, 19, 27, 121, 180, 217, 220–221, 222, 223, 323
    police, 28, 134, 189, 220, 221, 223, 278, 376
    prisons, 27, 28, 69, 216, 218–219, 220, 370, 428, 434
    prosecutors, 218, 222, 223
    prostitution, 27, 103, 199, 216, 219–220, 351, 394, 395, 428
    reporting, 221, 278
    self-defense, 220, 221, 222
    sentencing, 218
    victim precipitation, 222, 278, 281, 394
    weapons, 216, 217, 220, 221, 224
    witness, 223
    woman battering, 27, 62, 63, 133, 215, 216, 220, 221–223, 282, 443
    women as criminals, 27, 103, 199, 216–221

women as victims, 27, 42, 62, 63, 79, 126, 133, 146, 201, 215, 216, 217, 219, 220–224, 274, 275, 277–282, 283, 322, 323, 394–395, 421, 443
See also Courts; Rape; Violence

Cross-cultural comparison, 4, 23, 28, 29, 47, 68, 125, 130, 139, 141, 156, 232, 252, 277, 294, 319, 332, 359, 383, 384, 391, 396, 410–414, 421, 422–424, 445–446
    Africa, 125, 332, 396
    Canada, 23, 156
    childbirth, 68, 413
    child care, 359
    China, 139, 141, 413, 421
    domestic labor, 412
    Eastern Europe, 413
    Europe, 4, 139, 332
    European community, 411
    feminism, 412, 413, 422–424, 445–446
    Japan, 139, 411
    labor force and employment, 23, 391, 411
    law and policy, 411–412
    politics, 28, 29, 412
    religious beliefs, 156
    rape, 277
    sexuality, 294
    Scandinavia, 23, 294, 319, 411
    Soviet Union, 391, 411, 413
    Western Europe, 23, 47, 130, 156

Cult of domesticity, 349, 405, 410, 427
    and black women, 405

Cult of true womanhood, 53, 168, 179

Day care
    See Child care

Declaration of Independence, 47, 178, 205, 418

Declaration of Sentiments and Resolutions, 205, 418, 430
    See also Feminism, history of; Seneca Falls convention

Deity, 1, 42, 45–47, 60, 157–158, 160, 161, 164, 165, 167, 207, 390
    gods, 1, 42, 45–47, 60, 157–158, 160, 161, 164, 165, 167, 207
    goddesses, 60, 167, 390
    See also Religion

Democracy, 39, 97, 168, 204, 205, 206, 207, 209, 210, 232–233, 418, 439, 442, 443

Dentistry
    See Health practitioners

Dependence
    See Independence and dependence

Devil, 158, 162, 166

The Dial, 99

Diaz v. Pan American Airways (1971), 371

Difference, 35–39, 55, 66, 389–415, 422–424
    and feminism, 414–415, 422–424
    reasons for studying, 35–39, 390–397
    See specific bases of difference

Dinner Party, 200–201

Discrimination, 48, 52, 67, 89–91, 104–105, 116, 117, 119–120, 136, 137, 138, 148, 172, 180, 181–182, 195–197, 205, 207–208, 210–211, 213–214, 215, 229, 244, 287, 288, 304, 322, 332, 333, 360, 369–377, 375–377, 378, 411, 418, 432, 442, 444, 448
    definition, 89
    discriminatory environment, 375–376
    education, 89, 91, 104–105, 116, 117, 119–120, 148, 196, 210, 215
    employment, 48, 52, 89, 90, 91, 136, 137, 138, 172, 180, 181–182, 196, 207–208, 210–211, 215, 288, 360, 369–377, 378, 444
    military, 213–214
    nonconscious, 376–377, 378, 448

Diversity
    See Difference

Family *continued*
"family model," 346, 386
history, 348–349
law and policy, 215, 448
protection of, 216, 223
single parent, 20, 26, 133, 152, 381
See also Fatherhood; Marriage and marital roles; Mothers and motherhood; Parenthood
Fathers and fatherhood, 19, 32, 45, 46–47, 77, 82, 131, 152, 157–158, 167, 209, 213, 227, 271, 300, 308, 310, 311, 313, 327, 328, 329, 330, 331, 333, 334, 336, 337–338, 370, 382–383, 391, 395, 400
relationship with children, 77, 82, 402
See also Parenthood
Femininity, 28–32, 53, 66, 74, 76–77, 80, 85, 88, 108, 109, 122, 139, 142, 143–144, 146, 157, 179, 207, 210, 218, 238, 244, 259, 261–262, 264, 282, 288, 349, 354, 363, 367, 385, 391, 392, 397, 399, 405, 438
See also Androgyny; Masculinity; Stereotypes
Feminism, 7, 8–9, 49, 54–55, 56, 60, 62, 64, 68, 77, 79, 87, 99, 102, 125, 134, 154, 160, 172, 174, 179, 181, 185, 186, 187, 188, 189, 197, 202, 205, 216, 228, 232, 233, 262, 263, 267, 270, 277, 281, 289, 294, 297, 307, 316, 340–342, 349, 350, 374, 376, 389, 390, 393, 402–403, 409, 411, 412, 414–415, 416–452
and anticommunism, 440
attitudes toward, 402–403, 409, 412, 449–450
causes of, 54–55
characteristics of feminists, 440, 449–450
definition, 417–418
international, 411, 414, 422–424, 445–446
liberal, 418–419, 420, 423, 424

multicultural, 422–424, 444
racial tensions within, 431–432
radical, 77, 197, 289, 393, 420–422, 423, 424, 434–436, 439, 442, 443, 444
social feminism, 350
socialist, 419–420, 423, 424
terms for, 449
See also Antifeminism; Feminism, history of; Organizations; Social movements
Feminism, history of
1920–1960, 437–441
contemporary, 390, 407, 424–425, 441–451
Civil War to suffrage, 410, 425, 431–437, 448
pre-Civil War, 426–431
See also Antifeminism; Feminism; Organizations; Social movements
Feudalism, 347
Food stamps
See Social welfare
Friendship
See Social relationships

Gender, 87–89, 156, 175, 178, 189, 199–201, 216, 238–249, 284, 417
"doing gender," 88–89
definition, 67–69
development of, 67, 74–92
model, 344–345, 386
See also Femininity; Gender difference; Gender roles; Identity; Ideology; Masculinity; Sex and sex difference; Sex/gender system
Gender difference, 3–4, 9–10, 17–39, 58–59, 70, 80–85, 90, 104–107, 109–110, 113, 114–116, 118, 131–132, 138, 150, 151–152, 171–175, 217–219, 220, 221, 225, 226, 227, 229–232, 244, 246, 249–263, 271, 274, 275, 276–277, 278, 281, 283, 286, 290–291, 292–293, 294–295, 308, 311, 324–326, 327, 328,

329, 333, 336, 350, 355, 360, 362, 367, 373, 374, 377, 378–379, 383–384, 385, 394, 403, 419, 450
crime, 9–10, 27, 217–219, 220, 221
definition, 34–35
demographic, 17–27
economic and work roles, 9, 22–25, 58, 118, 138, 150, 294–295, 360, 362, 363, 367, 373, 377, 378–379, 383–384, 385, 403
education, 21–22, 104–107, 109–110, 113, 114–116, 118
family roles, 19–21, 131–132, 151–152, 271, 294–295, 308, 311, 327, 328, 329, 333, 336, 355
health, 18, 19, 131–132, 138
language use, 244, 246, 249–263, 274
politics, 225, 226, 227, 229–232
power and authority positions, 28, 29, 173–174
psychological, 3, 31–33, 80–85, 350
religious roles, 171–175
sexuality, 275, 276–277, 278, 283, 286, 290–291, 292–293
use of space, 252–255
See also Difference; Perception; Sex and sex difference; specific topics
Gender roles, 5, 53, 68, 86–87, 108, 122, 142, 144, 193, 215, 225, 259, 284, 331, 397, 401
defined, 68
See also Gender; Gender difference; specific roles
Gender schema, 87–89
definition, 87
General Electric Co. v. *Gilbert* (1976), 138, 370
General Federation of Women's Clubs (GFWC), 226, 438, 439
Genes and genetics
See Biology
Geography and geographical difference, 9, 53, 99, 128, 131,

History *continued*
of motherhood, 308–309
of citizenship rights and
obligations, 205–214
theories of, 41–65
Home, 84, 128, 132, 145, 151,
152–153, 169, 198, 253, 282,
347, 348, 392
See also Family; Homemakers and
homemaking; Space
Home economics, 22, 58, 86, 103,
108–109, 111, 151, 191, 349
Homemakers and homemaking, 6,
21, 39, 53, 54, 56, 58, 71, 86,
87, 97, 103, 108–109, 111,
131–132, 135–136, 137, 168,
170, 186, 191–193, 212, 227,
241, 248–249, 253, 290,
294–295, 301, 302, 303, 336,
337, 339, 340, 341, 346,
347–356, 361, 362, 363, 374,
379, 380, 382, 384, 386, 391,
397, 400, 401–403, 411–412,
413, 414, 433
definition, 350–352
displaced, 303, 374, 379
domestic labor, 58, 87, 103, 111,
131–132, 191–193, 248–249,
253, 294–295, 301, 346,
351–352, 356, 363, 380, 386,
391, 397, 401–402, 411, 412,
413, 414
economics, 21, 52, 54, 304,
350–355
history, 309, 347–350, 401, 402
homemakers compared with
employed women, 39, 86,
135–136, 294, 339, 362, 382,
402–403
men and, 131, 135, 193, 386
scientific, 191–192, 349
social homemaking, 349–350, 357,
433
technology and, 6, 352, 357
value of, 380
See also Family; Employment and
occupations; Motherhood;
Work
Homophobia
See Sexuality

Homosexuality
See Sexuality
Hormones
See Biology
Hospitals and clinics
See Health care
Hoyt v. *Florida* (1961), 211
Hyde Amendment, 322
Hysteria, 43, 125, 146, 220
See also Health and disease

Id, 74–75, 79
Identity, 67, 80, 81–83, 87, 89,
283–287, 306, 311, 350, 397
gender, 81–83, 283, 397
sexual, 283–286
Ideology, 47, 48, 49, 50, 53, 54–55,
66, 68, 72, 79, 97, 119, 124,
144, 146, 148, 152, 153, 156,
158, 163, 172, 194, 195, 202,
206, 207, 215, 216, 217, 224,
225, 226, 230, 263, 272, 273,
275, 277, 278, 279–280, 281,
282, 287, 289, 291, 294, 295,
306, 311, 317, 325, 326, 331,
332, 333, 337, 341, 344, 349,
354, 358, 385, 394, 396, 397,
398, 414, 418, 419, 430, 446,
447, 450
gender, 72, 124, 146, 148, 152,
153, 202, 217, 224, 225, 226,
263, 273, 277, 281, 287, 289,
294, 295, 306, 311, 326, 331,
332, 333, 337, 344, 354, 394,
397, 398, 414
political, 47, 49, 144, 195, 325,
326, 341, 447
sexual, 272, 273, 275, 277, 278,
279–280, 282, 291, 294, 317,
337, 394, 446
Immigration and immigrants, 56,
102, 103, 151, 199, 225, 227,
315, 395, 408, 437, 447
Imperialism
Incest
See Rape; Sexuality
Independence and dependence, 2–3,
47, 144, 145, 205, 205, 237,

238, 239, 250, 275, 294–295,
303, 340, 358, 391, 399, 421
Industrialism
See Economics and economies
Inequality
See Equality and inequality
Initiation, 125
Instincts
See Biology; Psychoanalysis
Intelligence, 71, 110, 116
International League for Peace and
Freedom, 441
International Woman Suffrage
Alliance (IWSA), 445
Isolation, 132, 133, 271, 328

Jarrett v. *Jarrett* (1979), 334
Johnson v. *Transportation Agency,
Santa Clara County* (1987), 372
Journalism
See Mass media
Juries
See Courts
Justice, 32, 77, 79, 155, 216, 418,
446

Labor-saving devices
See Technology
Labor unions, 24, 28, 103, 106,
119, 136, 149, 178, 226, 368,
370, 372, 383–385, 433, 434,
436–437, 441, 442, 445
early attitudes toward women's
employment, 136
history, 384–385
Lactation
See Reproduction
Language and communication, 1, 3,
7, 22, 31, 35–36, 50, 62, 71, 72,
83, 96, 114, 150, 157–158, 164,
167, 181–182, 189, 218, 221,
237–269, 271, 274–275, 276,
299, 300, 375, 399, 400, 449
and feminism, 242, 449
and occupations, 244, 247, 250,
258

Pacifism
  See also Military; War and
    revolution
Parenthood and parenting, 20, 26,
    62, 77, 83–84, 86, 110, 115–116,
    119, 133, 152, 290, 308–343,
    351
  and socialization, 83
  different treatment of girls and
    boys, 83–84, 110
  gender differences, 152, 271, 308,
    311, 327, 328, 329, 333, 336
  impact on marriage, 290, 291, 327
  legitimacy, 62, 298, 337
  reasons for, 77, 311
  single, 20, 26, 133, 152, 341, 398
  parent-teacher organizations,
    115–116, 119
  See also Children; Family; Fathers
    and fatherhood; Mothers and
    motherhood
Parnham v. Hughes (1979), 337–338
Passivity
  See Activity and passivity
Patriarchy, 46–47, 78, 79, 158, 205,
    263, 299, 330, 332, 334
  definition, 46
Pay equity
  See Employment and occupations
Penis envy, 61, 76, 77, 78, 79, 80
  See also Phallus; Psychoanalysis
Perception, 31, 32, 35, 36, 54,
    71–72, 78, 88, 90, 110, 144,
    188, 267, 275, 441
  selective perception, 188
  self-perception, 32, 88, 110
  visual-spatial skills, 31, 36, 71–72
Personality, 2–3, 28–33, 60, 63, 66,
    74, 79, 87, 158, 239, 280, 284,
    287, 351
  gender differences, 28–33, 449
  See also Psychoanalysis; Psychology;
    specific characteristics
Phallus, 61, 80, 200
Philadelphia Female Anti-Slavery
    Society, 429
Philadelphia Women's Medical
    College, 99
Philanthropy, 170, 182

Phillips v. Martin Marietta (1971),
    210, 370
Philosophy, 1, 4, 22, 99, 148,
    238
  See also Theory
Planned Parenthood v. Danforth
    (1976), 320–321
Police
  See Crime and criminal justice
Politeness
  See Language and communication
Political activity, 37, 58, 102,
    150–151, 164, 193, 206, 208,
    209, 224–233, 282, 353, 384,
    431–445, 448
  community action, 225, 228
  impact of family roles on, 225,
    227, 228–229
  lobbying, 102, 193, 384, 439,
    442, 448
  mass participation, 224–227, 231,
    438, 440
  organizational activity, 353
  protest and demonstrations, 193,
    208, 226–227, 282, 353, 434,
    443–444, 448
  See also Elections and voting;
    Feminism, history of; Labor
    unions; Organizations; Social
    movements
Political leadership and politicians,
    28, 190, 206, 207, 209,
    227–233, 246, 253, 436, 447
  ambition, 228, 231
  discrimination, 228, 229, 231
  gender differences in behavior of
    public officials, 232
  women's roles, 28
  See also Courts; Crime and criminal
    justice; Elections and voting;
    Government
Political parties, 214, 220, 226, 227,
    229, 231, 410, 434, 438–439,
    440, 441
  See also Elections and voting;
    Political activity; Politics
Politics, 9, 48, 56, 62, 170, 173,
    178, 186, 189, 204–234,
    258–259, 264, 286, 321, 413,
    419, 422, 427–451

attitudes toward women in,
    229–230
  knowledge about, 258–259
  See also Courts; Crime and criminal
    justice; Elections and voting;
    Government; Law and policy;
    Political activity; Political
    leadership and politicians;
    Social movements
Pornography, 165, 201, 274,
    282–283, 315
  and violence against women, 201,
    283
Poverty and wealth, 9, 26, 39, 56,
    103, 105, 141, 142, 147, 209,
    250, 281, 303, 312–313, 315,
    352, 380–382, 393, 399,
    400–401, 407, 429
  female-headed households, 26
  feminization of poverty, 26, 381
Power, 20, 44, 46, 47, 51, 52, 54,
    59, 60–64, 79, 80, 81, 93, 99,
    147, 167, 173, 177, 194–195,
    205, 215, 233, 237, 240, 251,
    259, 264, 275–276, 294–295,
    297–298, 333, 362, 368, 386,
    390, 407, 418, 421
Pregnancy
  See Reproduction
Pregnancy Discrimination Act
    (1978), 138, 210, 288–289,
    370–371
Prejudice, 48, 83, 89, 90, 287
  gender differences, 90
  See also Stereotype
Primogeniture, 396
Printers, 178, 180
  See also Mass media
Prisons
  See Crime and criminal justice
Privacy
  See Abortion; Contraception;
    Rights; Space; U.S.
    Constitution
Privilege, 46, 62, 407, 418
  definition, 65
Progress, 48, 56, 58, 79, 191
Property, 46, 50, 51, 60, 161, 205,
    206, 209, 215, 216, 277, 289,
    301–302, 303–304, 305,

498

Name Index